1996

CONSTITUTIONAL GOVERNMENT
The American Experience

James A. Curry
Department of Political Science
Baylor University

Richard B. Riley
Department of Political Science
Baylor University

Richard M. Battistoni
Department of Political Science
Baylor University

©1989 West Publishing Company
St. Paul • New York • Los Angeles • San Francisco

Composition: Parkwood Composition
Copy editor: Judith Peacock
Design: Roslyn M. Stendahl, Dapper Design
Photographer: Betsy Ritz

COPYRIGHT ©1989   By WEST PUBLISHING COMPANY
50 W. Kellogg Boulevard
P.O. Box 64526
St. Paul, MN 55164-1003

Printed in the United States of America

96 95 94 93 92 91 90 89   8 7 6 5 4 3 2 1 0

Library of Congress Cataloging-in-Publication Data

Curry, James A.
  Constitutional government: the American experience/
James Curry, Richard Riley, Richard Battistoni.
  p.   cm.
Includes index.
ISBN 0-314-47010-7

Dedication

For our children,

Douglas   Mary
Jennifer   John
Alyssa and the soon-to-be-born twins

whose future rests on our nation's ability to reflect upon,
understand, and wisely interpret the Constitution of the United States
for their and future generations

Contents

Table of Cases

Preface

The study of American constitutional government traditionally has been addressed in a number of different ways, ranging from detailed historical analysis to the highly legalistic casebook approach. While these approaches provide certain advantages in accounting for the development of constitutionalism in America, each by itself leaves something of the story untold. Consequently, this book has been written to integrate the time-tested historical and legalistic approaches used in the study of constitutional government. We believe that a combined emphasis upon history, politics, and law offers a productive format for examining the growth and development of the United States Constitution.

This book is divided into three parts: Part I, titled "The Constitutional Text and Context," focuses upon the principles of constitutional government, the theory and practice of American constitutionalism, and the framers' efforts to construct an enduring document. Part II, titled "Structures and Processes of American Constitutional Government," analyzes several key principles of American constitutional thought and practice that have contributed to constitutional regimes around the world. The chapters in this section deal with judicial review, the separation of powers, and federalism. The final section of the book, "Constitutional Rights and Liberties," is by far the longest, largely as a result of the constantly expanding demand for and adjudication of individual freedoms in modern society. Topics covered in Part III include the due process of law and criminal procedures, equal protection of the law, the right of privacy, and the freedoms of speech, press, and religion. A concluding chapter addresses the prospects for constitutional revision and reform.

A few explanations to the reader about appendices are appropriate. First, to minimize having to document cases throughout the book, we have included a table which lists all cases discussed in the text. In most instances, the citation refers to *United States Reports,* the official publication of decisions of the United States Supreme Court. In a few instances, commercial reporting systems are used to refer to very recent Supreme Court cases or those at the lower federal court level (e.g., *Supreme Court Reporter* or the *Federal Supplement*).

Three other appendices provide the student with some useful reference material. One is a glossary of terms that includes short definitions for quick reference to those concepts or words that have been used at different points in the text. Additionally, a chronological appendix listing some basic statistical information about the various justices who have been appointed to the Supreme Court over the past 200 years is included. Finally, a general subject index appears in the back of the text.

In weaving together the strands of American constitutional development, we have sought to balance our concern with historical factors with an awareness of developments in today's world. While the book is organized in a topical fashion, material within each chapter generally follows an historical pattern, culminating in a discussion of current and up-to-date developments. Having each taught numerous courses dealing with the American Constitution and constitutional government, we are convinced that this approach is the most effective way to present the rich variety of themes, issues, and concepts that have pervaded the nation's development.

A project of this magnitude clearly would not be possible without the assistance and support of many people. We are grateful for the many helpful comments and suggestions provided by the numerous colleagues who read the manuscript at various stages: Wilbourn E. Benton, Texas A & M University; Donald C. Dahlin, University of South Dakota; Larry Elowitz, Georgia College; Tracey L. Gladstone, University of Wisconsin-River Falls; Adolph H. Grundman, Metropolitan State College; Donald W. Jackson, Texas Christian University; Fred R. Mabbutt, California State University, Long Beach; Priscilla H. Machado, University of Vermont; Charles R. Pastors, Northeastern Illinois University; Charles H. Sheldon, Washington State University; J. Malcolm Smith, California State University, Hayward; and Theodore M. Vestal, University of Tulsa. The professionalism and encouragement of the editorial staff of West Publishing Company helped us throughout the completion of this book. We are grateful to Tom LaMarre, who saw the potential of this project and provided support along the way. Other West editors who helped immeasurably in the preparation, editing, and production of this book deserve our thanks: Theresa O'Dell, for her editorial expertise; Stacy Lenzen, who guided us through the maze of production; and Ann V. H. Swift, who helped us realize the importance of promotion and marketing.

Closer to home, we owe a tremendous debt to Baylor University for its support of this research. Through Baylor's generosity, two of the authors received a Baylor University Sabbatical, while the third worked with the benefit of a Baylor University Summer Sabbatical. Completion of this project would have been delayed considerably without the sabbatical support provided by Baylor University. Our department chairman, Dr. Robert T. Miller, has supported this research in untold ways. His expertise as a constitutional scholar helped us to resolve many problems as they arose, and his careful reading of the final manuscript proved invaluable. We also wish to thank Pat Bibb and Nancy Stone for their skill at the word processor and for their tireless efforts on our behalf in producing the finished copy of the manuscript. Thanks also to Betsy Ritz who provided the excellent photographs used on the cover and to introduce each chapter. Finally, to the several graduate and undergraduate students who have both served as sounding boards for our ideas in the classroom and helped with various research steps in the project, we express our thanks. Particular credit goes to Andrew Hanson, who did historical research on the Ninth Amendment.

A project of this magnitude invariably requires sacrifices to be made, and large amounts of time must be spent away from home and family. This project was no exception, and, as a result, we are especially thankful to our wives, Kay, Judy, and Betsy, for their patience, understanding, and continued support. This book certainly would not have been possible without them.

J.A.C.   R.B.R.   R.M.B.

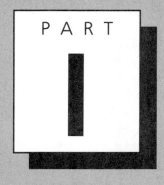

PART I

The Constitutional Text and Context

AMERICAN CONSTITUTIONALISM exists and flourishes within a rich historical and intellectual context. Constitutionalism in America first appeared in a rudimentary form in the seventeenth century and developed until the writing of the U.S. Constitution in 1787. The three chapters in Part I explore the texts and contexts of American constitutionalism. Chapter 1 introduces the subject by examining the underlying principles of constitutional government and by comparing the world's constitutions for insight into these basic principles. Chapter 2 delineates the two theoretical approaches to government at the heart of American constitutionalism—individualism and communitarianism—and discusses the various historical and intellectual influences on eighteenth-century American constitutionalists. Chapter 3 chronicles the history of the founding period in American constitutionalism. It begins by addressing the major constitutional concerns of the American revolutionaries in the 1760s and 1770s and concludes with an examination of the Constitutional Convention in Philadelphia in 1787 and the document drafted there. These three chapters detail the basic themes of American constitutionalism that form the basis of the specific discussions in Parts II and III.

1

The Principle of Constitutional Government

Syllabus

The United States, France, the Soviet Union, Mexico, the Republic of South Africa, Iran, and Cuba are all countries that possess written constitutions. However, these constitutions differ greatly from each other in the principles they espouse and in their conception of the role of government in people's lives. Great Britain does not have a written constitution but possesses many of the characteristics associated with constitutional government. This suggests that it may be more than the simple written form of a constitution that makes a government constitutional. Accordingly, the basic principles of constitutional government must be looked at from a comparative perspective in order to understand the difference between constitutions and constitutionalism.

This Chapter Examines the Following Matters

☐ The basic theory of constitutionalism includes a belief in limited government, in the rule of law, and in the fundamental worth of each individual citizen.

☐ The central features of the American Constitution and the central features of the constitutions of other countries show similarities in outward structure but great differences in purpose and content.

☐ Although the constitutions of most countries contain preambles, the Preamble to the U.S. Constitution differs dramatically from those of other nations. The American Preamble is a much shorter and simpler statement of purpose, whereas the preambles of other constitutions contain quite lengthy ideological messages.

☐ Constitutions have been referred to as "power maps," since each one lays out the blueprint for governmental rule making and power holding in that country. The American Constitution contains three distinctive features in its "power map": separation of powers, judicial review, and federalism.

☐ All successful governments must make arrangements for change within the constitutional structure. In comparison with the constitutions of other nations, the U.S. Constitution is difficult to formally amend, which makes the informal amending process more important.

☐ In comparison with the provisions of constitutional rights granted by different nations, the American Constitution places specific limits on government power in the interest of individual liberty. Other nations' constitutions grant a wide variety of substantive rights not found in the U.S. Constitution.

Photo: Two hundred years after Americans first put pen to paper in Philadelphia, constitution writing has become an international practice. While most governments in the world now have written constitutions to guide them, very few can be called constitutional governments. *(Photographed with the courtesy of the Philadelphia Convention and Visitors Bureau).*

The Basic Theory of Constitutionalism

In 1987, Americans began a three-year celebration of the 200th anniversary of the U.S. Constitution, the world's oldest surviving written national constitution. During this celebration, major events in the document's drafting, signing, and ratification were duly marked and recognized. The major provisions of the federal Constitution of 1787 and the Bill of Rights were explained to the public and even exalted. But, to truly appreciate the Constitution, Americans should take the time not only to celebrate the document but also to "cerebrate" it[1]—to reflect upon and analyze its principles, its content, and its contemporary meaning. The text that follows attempts to *cerebrate* the American constitutional experience.

A study of the American Constitution may be approached from many perspectives, ranging from an historical overview of American political, social, and economic changes to a legalistic analysis of the formal rules that have developed over two hundred years. In reality, American constitutionalism must take into account historical, legal, and political factors that have played pivotal roles in forming a long-standing relationship between the American government and its people. The central focus, of course, must be the federal Constitution of 1787 and that document's impact upon American political institutions and processes; however, an understanding of American constitutionalism is not possible by limiting inquiry solely to the written constitution. While it is difficult to overrate the significance of the 1787 Constitution, it is similarly difficult to ignore the changes the document has undergone since its drafting. Accordingly, the study of American constitutional development must consider the theory underlying the written constitution along with the practices of government that have evolved over time. In succeeding chapters, attention will be given to both the theory and the practice of American constitutional experience.

In the broadest sense, a constitution refers to a framework providing basic principles of organization and operation. In government, a constitution describes the arrangement of political and governmental institutions and the powers and functions assigned to them. The American Constitution, for example, is organized around creating and defining the powers of the major branches of government, beginning with the legislative branch in Article I, and moving to the executive and judiciary in the following articles. Yet, the American Constitution has come to be recognized as far more than just a descriptive treatment of American government; it has risen to the level of a powerful symbol to which generations of citizens defer and give allegiance. The manner in which the constitution accomplishes its roles as organizational framework and national symbol can be termed **constitutionalism.** The discussion now turns to that concept.

The distinction between a "constitution" and "constitutionalism" is more than a simple exercise in semantics. The twentieth-century world is full of countries with written constitutions, but very few possess constitutional governments. The reason for this is that constitutionalism requires a government limited in its power and accountable for its actions. In short, constitutionalism, in addition to providing the theory underlying a constitution, must include an effective limitation upon governmental power.

As constitutional scholars have noted, constitutionalism is tied to a suspicion and distrust of power in general and to the concentration of power in
particular. Writing in an earlier time, the Englishman Lord Acton noted that
"all power tends to corrupt, and absolute power corrupts absolutely." [2] Lord
Acton's observation would certainly find no shortage of adherents among
today's advocates of constitutionalism, although the agreement would begin
to fade if a search for an acceptable solution to the problem were begun. On
the one hand, it is easy to see how power in government can become concentrated and, perhaps, abused, but it is quite another thing to conclude that
power should never be handed over to leaders because of the dangers involved.
In fact, for proponents of constitutionalism, Lord Acton's statement lays the
basis for a real dilemma. How is it possible to avoid the pitfalls of an overly
powerful and potentially irresponsible government while at the same time
providing government leaders and institutions with the ability to solve society's
problems? James Madison, the "Father of the American Constitution," recognized the dilemma of modern constitutional government in *Federalist
No. 51:*

> In framing a government which is to be administered by men over men, the great
> difficulty lies in this: You must first enable the government to control the gov-
> erned; and in the next place, oblige it to control itself. [3]

Madison went on to note that while the primary method of controlling
and limiting government power was reliance upon the people, it was further
necessary to construct "auxiliary precautions." These, of course, would provide
for the division and separation of power among institutions of government,
along with various devices designed to "check and balance" the actions of
others (see Chapter 5 for further discussion). It should be noted, however,
that the solution presented by Madison did not favor the elimination of a
government's power, but merely its subordination to competing interests and
to the will of the people.

The preceding discussion indicates that constitutional government means
government limited in its powers and functions. Constitutionalism is also
premised on the **rule of law** as opposed to the rules of everyday men and
women. A constitution places a higher law above the policies and practices
of transient leaders or ruling majorities, and it requires that they abide by that
constitutional higher law. The general structures and principles found in a
constitution reflect the long-term interests of a people and should therefore
supersede the short-term wishes of even a popular leader or an overwhelming
majority. Of course, everyday women and men must hold rulers accountable
to these legal principles, to ensure the effectiveness of the rule of law. But
Americans in general possess a deep-seated belief in the rule of law, which
may contribute to the strength of American constitutionalism.

In addition to emphasizing limited government and the rule of law,
constitutionalism, in varying ways, recognizes the fundamental worth of each
individual and the rights and liberties that accompany each person. This is
not to say that individuals possess universally recognized freedoms in all constitutional governments of present times, but it is clear that a constitutional
government, by limiting the power of institutions and leaders, gives some value
to its citizens as individuals.

In summary, modern constitutionalism limits the power of sovereign rulers, makes leaders subject to the law, takes precautions against tyranny, and protects the rights and liberties of individuals. None of these factors developed quickly, as the following chapter will attest to, and none has reached its conclusion. In fact, constitutionalism is by no means a static concept, especially where limited government and individual rights are involved. The relationship between constitutionalism and government is constantly changing, with the constitution itself the most obvious proof of that development.

Comparative Constitutions and Constitutionalism

With more than 160 independent nations in the world today, constitution writing has become a legitimate growth industry! Moreover, given that well over half of these nations achieved independence after 1945, such constitution writing has occurred in recent times and under the pressures imposed by the modern world. In Africa, for example, nearly 90 percent of the nations have achieved independence since 1960, but relatively few of these have managed to maintain uninterrupted constitutional government. The military coup d'état seemingly has replaced the constitutional convention for making changes in government leadership and institutions in many countries. Robert Clark noted that, on average, "a coup or attempted coup occurred once every 4 months in Latin America (from 1945 to 1972), once every 7 months in Asia (1947 to 1972), once every 3 months in the Middle East (1949 to 1972), and once every 55 days in Africa (1960 to 1972)!"[4]

Not surprisingly, few of the newly independent countries have been overly concerned with limiting government power when the first order of business is to establish a workable and powerful central authority. Even though the practices of constitutional government have not been followed with great regularity throughout the newly independent states, the written constitution has continued to be adopted on a near-universal basis. Regardless of a country's commitment to constitutional government, most leaders view a written constitution as a badge of respectability and legitimacy. Consequently, the written constitution has attracted adherents from widely different backgrounds and geographical areas. A brief survey of constitutional patterns provides a basis for comparison.

Given the diversity in governmental organization among the world's nations, scholars might expect considerable difficulty in comparing the constitutions of different countries. While differences certainly exist, there are definite similarities in most constitutional arrangements, at least insofar as the structure of the constitution itself is concerned. Ivo Duchacek, a leading scholar of constitutional development, has identified four "core ingredients" in all national documents. These central features include a preamble or statement of purpose, an organizational chart of the government, amendatory articles that describe the manner in which the supreme law may be changed, and, finally, a bill of rights.[5] The American Constitution can be used as a guide to analyze each of these ingredients in more detail.

The Preamble: A Statement of Purpose and Goals

The Preamble to the Constitution of the United States provides a general statement of purpose and lays the foundation for a theory of governmental action. It is clear in the Preamble's first words that "We the People" are the force underlying the document's legitimacy. Government, in short, may be created by the consent of the governed, and individuals may form a compact with one another to achieve those ends considered desirable. As will be discussed in Chapter 2, this perspective was shared by a number of early American settlers, primarily those for whom religious factors were of paramount importance.

Having stated the premise that the people are authorized to ordain and establish a constitution, the Preamble offers a list of social and political goals: "to form a more perfect Union, establish Justice, insure domestic Tranquility, provide for the common defence, promote the general Welfare, and secure the Blessings of Liberty to ourselves and our Posterity." The degree to which these goals have been realized in the United States remains a major focus of this book.

When compared with other constitutions, the American Preamble is relatively free of ideological content and partisan rhetoric. Although it reflects the twin conceptual poles of individualism and communitarianism (to be outlined in the next chapter), the Preamble seems short and simple. By comparison, the preambles to the constitutions of other countries make strong political statements and are often used to promote a specific and detailed ideology. Some countries, particularly those with a history of revolution or warfare, go to elaborate lengths in their preambles to chronicle the events and accomplishments of past generations. In this category, the Cuban, Vietnamese, Soviet, and Chinese constitutions provide particularly good illustrations. Other countries use their constitution's preamble to identify the regime's leading ideological foundations—the Islam of Iran, Pakistan, Bangladesh, and others; the worker's socialism of Romania, Czechoslovakia, and the rest of Eastern Europe; "home-grown" ideologies such as the "Burmese Way to Socialism" and the "Pantja Sila" Democracy of Indonesia; and international orientations such as the neutrality of Switzerland and the Japanese renunciation of war. As Table 1.1 indicates, most countries combine history, ideology, and other aspects into one preamble, ranging in length from a paragraph to several pages. Accordingly, numerous preambles read as tributes to the glorious past accomplishments, military victories, and future greatness of a nation's people.

Organizational Chart

According to Duchacek, constitutions serve as "the official blueprint for the uses of public power" and may be referred to as "power maps."[6] That is to say, every constitution establishes the institutions of government, lays out procedures by which rules are made, and provides in some manner for the resolution of conflicts and disputes. The manner in which these steps are taken varies widely, even among "constitutional" governments. The American Constitution addresses the functions of rule making (legislative), rule implementation (executive), and adjudication (judiciary) in its first three articles. Article

Table 1.1   Some Dominant Themes in Preambles to Selected National Constitutions

The Victorious Struggle Through Revolution

Vietnam (1980)—"Throughout their four-thousand year history, the Vietnamese people have worked hard and fought heroically to defend their country . . . In the spring of 1975, the Vietnamese people won total victory."

People's Republic of China (1982)—"China is one of the countries with the longest histories in the world. The people of all nationalities in China have jointly created a splendid culture and have a glorious revolutionary tradition."

Kampuchea (1981)—"Meanwhile, U.S. imperialism—ringleader and policeman of world imperialism—employed all kinds of maneuvers, from interference to armed aggression . . . Once again, our people rose and struggled against the American aggressor."

Cuba (1976)—"We, Cuban Citizens . . . GUIDED by the victorious doctrine of Marxism-Leninism . . . AND HAVING DECIDED to carry forward the triumphant Revolution . . . under the leadership of Fidel Castro . . . AWARE . . . that only under socialism and communism . . . can full dignity of the human being be attained."

Ordained by God

Colombia (1886)—"In the name of God, Supreme Source of all authority."

Bangladesh (1972)—"In the name of Allah, the Beneficent, the Merciful . . . the high ideals of absolute trust and faith in the Almighty Allah . . . shall be the fundamental principles of the Constitution."

Iran (1979)—"The Constitution of the Islamic Republic of Iran . . . is based upon Islamic principles and standards."

Socialism of the Working Classes

Burma (1974)—"We, the working people . . . shall . . . build a socialist economic system by the Burmese Way to Socialism."

Czechoslovakia (1960)—"We, the working people of Czechoslovakia, solemnly declare . . . Socialism has triumphed in our country."

USSR (1977)—"In the USSR a developed socialist society has been built."

Source: Albert P. Blaustein and Gisbert H. Flanz, eds., *Constitutions of the Countries of the World* (Dobbs Ferry, N.Y.: Oceana Publishers 1988).

IV moves from the national level to the states, primarily addressing the matter of relationships between states. While each of these articles will be analyzed in detail in later chapters, it is important to note three key principles that provide for much of the American constitutional structure. These three principles—separation of powers, judicial review, and federalism—are not mentioned per se in the text of the document, although their presence is not difficult to infer. For many observers, these three principles perhaps more than any others truly distinguish the American style of limited government.

Separation of Powers

The threefold delineation of political functions presented in the first three articles is generally cited as proof of the **separation of powers** between the legislature, executive and judiciary. The separation was clearly intended by the framers of the Constitution to avoid the concentration of power in the hands of the executive. In *Federalist No. 51,* Madison expressed the logic underlying this principle with the statement that "ambition must be made to counteract ambition." [7] This counteracting of ambition was to be accomplished by a system of checks and balances, enabling one branch of the federal government to wield some power, although not too much, over the others. In actuality, however, these checks and balances have served to produce a series of overlapping relationships among the three branches of government. Each branch of government has some intrusive powers in the affairs of another, whether in the Congress's power to restrict the appellate jurisdiction of the Supreme Court, the Court's ability to "legislate" through its powers of judicial review, or the president's powers of appointment.

If the separation of powers divides governmental functions only nominally, it does separate the branches in one key area—personnel. Members of the legislative branch, for example, do not hold positions in the other branches of the federal government. The president may not hold a seat in Congress, presumably because such an arrangement might create a concentration of power in a single individual.

For many Americans, the separation of powers is essential to limited government, but is it a prerequisite? Strictly speaking, the answer would seem to be negative. In fact, of the two dozen or so truly constitutional governments today, only a few employ a formal separation-of-powers system. Most democracies of Western Europe—as well as those of Japan, Canada, and Australia—employ a **parliamentary system** of government. Under this arrangement, executive power is wielded by a prime minister and cabinet chosen from the members of the majority party in the legislature. Such a system is more properly described as a fusion of power rather than a separation of power. However, in keeping with the spirit of constitutionalism, even in parliamentary systems without a formal separation of powers, limits upon the abuses of governmental power do exist. In recent years, critics of the American separation of powers have called for a greater fusion of power to break what they see as a "deadlock of democracy." [8] More will be said about criticisms of the American organizational chart and suggestions for reform in the concluding chapter of this book.

Judicial Review

Somewhat like the separation of powers but more controversial, judicial review is not specifically mentioned in the Constitution. **Judicial review** refers to the power of the judicial branch to review and, if necessary, invalidate legislative and executive action when it is inconsistent with the Constitution. Chapter 4 will examine the origins, history, and contemporary controversy of judicial review, but a brief discussion of its constitutional basis is in order here. In one sense, judicial review can be seen as a powerful check on the abuse of power because it makes government ultimately responsible to the limits of the Constitution. On the other hand, it should be remembered that every time judicial review is employed, the limits of the Constitution are being defined by the judges currently serving on the federal courts. Nonetheless, judicial review has been considered an integral part of limited government in the United States for many years. But is it essential for other constitutional governments as well?

A survey of other constitutional systems quickly shows that, once again, the American pattern is not closely followed elsewhere. Japan and West Germany recognize the principle of judicial review in their national documents, but their constitutions, not surprisingly, were influenced heavily by Americans during the post-World War II period. The British, with their principle of parliamentary supremacy, logically deny the practice of judicial review. Even the French, who have sought to limit legislative power drastically in the Fifth Republic, have created only a limited type of judicial review. Once again, it becomes apparent that judicial review, a powerful constitutional force in America, is not a prerequisite for constitutional government.

Federalism

Power can also be divided and distributed along territorial lines. When a constitution recognizes the existence of subnational units such as states or provinces and leaves powers for them to exercise, the result is known as **federalism.** In a sense, federalism is a further check upon the consolidation of power in a few hands. As will be discussed later, the American colonies favored autonomy above unity, resulting first in a loosely structured confederation and then in a new constitutional system based upon federalism. While some early architects of the Constitution saw the system as essentially a national-dominated arrangement, many others believed that the states had retained ultimate sovereignty. This was to be a key basis for disagreement throughout the development of the Constitution, as Chapter 6 will explain.

Federalism as a specific form of government can be combined either with a separation-of-powers arrangement as in the United States or with any number of other systems. Clearly, however, federalism, much like separation of powers and judicial review, has been viewed as a fundamental principle of limited government in the United States. But, when constitutionalism outside the United States is examined, the results are mixed. Not all federal governments are constitutional, and not all constitutional governments are federal. Countries such as Britain, France, Sweden, and Japan—all constitutional governments— have chosen a **unitary system,** whereby all powers emanate from the central government (although local subdivisions exercise some functions in these countries). The Soviet Union, on the other hand, touts its federal system of fifteen republics as evidence of decentralized power and local autonomy, although the republics lack authority, and the system as a whole cannot claim to espouse constitutionalism. In summary, federal systems make constitutional governments when the constitution establishes effective restraints on *all* governmental power. When this is not done, federalism often becomes nothing more than a structural arrangement that serves a political purpose.

Amendatory Articles and a Supreme Law

By its own statement in Article VI, the American Constitution is the "supreme Law of the Land." A supreme law cannot remain supreme if it can be changed easily and informally. Therefore, some formal mechanism for amendment of the document must be established. The Constitution's framers, cognizant of their limitations in predicting the future, provided such a mechanism in Article V. But also aware of the need for stability in the rule of law, they made it difficult to change the supreme law. More will be said about the difficulties in amending the Constitution in the discussion of constitutional reform in the book's concluding chapter.

The framers arranged for amendments to pass through a two-stage process prior to incorporation into the Constitution. The first stage, *proposal,* requires either a two-thirds vote of both houses of Congress or a national constitutional convention. Of the twenty-six amendments added since 1789, all have been proposed by Congress. In fact, a constitutional convention has not even been called to consider a proposed amendment. While current support for a balanced budget amendment has increased calls for a convention, many experts are divided over the method of calling a convention, the matter of selecting representatives, and the setting of an agenda.

Once proposed, the next stage is *ratification.* This process, based upon the federal principle, lies with the states. Amendments must be ratified by three-fourths of the states, either in their legislatures or by special conventions called for this purpose (the manner is determined by Congress). Twenty-five of the twenty-six successful amendments to the Constitution have been ratified by legislatures. The states have refused to ratify amendments on such topics as prohibiting child labor and granting equal rights to women.

The twenty-six amendments added to the Constitution since 1789 can be grouped into several broad categories. First are those amendments that establish, confirm, or create a specific right. The first ten amendments naturally fall into this group, along with the post-Civil War Thirteenth, Fourteenth, and Fifteenth Amendments concerning the rights of ex-slaves. In addition, provision for the popular election of senators (Seventeenth), expansion of franchise to women (Nineteenth), participation in presidential elections for the District of Columbia (Twenty-third), removal of the poll tax as a barrier to voting in federal elections (Twenty-fourth), and right of eighteen-year-olds to vote (Twenty-sixth) constitute other guarantees relating to individual rights and liberties.

A second category of five amendments might be considered structural changes in the institutions and procedures of the national government. In nearly all instances, the appropriate amendment was not added until events produced an obvious need for change. For example, the Supreme Court's decision in *Chisholm* v. *Georgia* (1793) went against state interests and resulted in the Eleventh Amendment's restriction of the Court's original jurisdiction. The rise of political parties and a deadlocked electoral vote in the presidential election of 1800 showed the need for the Twelfth Amendment and the separate listing of presidential and vice-presidential candidates on the ballot. Next, due in large part to the Progressive reform movement and a desire to reduce the power of lame-duck (defeated in the election but not yet replaced) public officials, the Twentieth Amendment in 1933 shortened the time between national elections (November) and the taking of office (changed from March to January of the year following the election). The Twenty-second Amendment (1951) limited a president to two elected terms in office. Of course, the need for this amendment was not apparent until a president had exceeded the unwritten two-term limit. Franklin Roosevelt's four election victories provided the stimulus for change. Finally, the matters of presidential succession, disability, and presidential and vice-presidential resignation were the subjects of the Twenty-fifth Amendment in 1967. Interestingly, just six years after ratification, the amendment came into play twice in a short time period: first, with the resignation of Vice-President Spiro Agnew to avoid federal criminal charges and the appointment of Gerald Ford to fill the vacancy; and, second, with the resignation of President Richard Nixon in the aftermath of the Watergate affair. Also interesting is that four of the five structural amendments have dealt primarily with the presidency.

The third category contains two reforms not specifically related either to individual rights or to government structure. Of these two reforms, the approval of a national income tax in the Sixteenth Amendment (1913) has become well established, while national Prohibition under the Eighteenth Amendment (1919) was ultimately repealed by the Twenty-first Amendment in 1933. The Prohibition amendment shows the difficulties associated with the regulation of morality through constitutional amendment.

A formal amending process, of course, makes little difference when a constitution does not limit the government. Amendments may be added on top of other amendments, but the net effect remains unchanged. Compared with other nations and considering its age, the United States has formally amended its Constitution very sparingly. However, it should not be assumed that the American Constitution has changed little over the years. In fact, for every formal amendment added, perhaps a hundred or more changes have occurred through different procedures. These developments constitute the main subject matter of this book.

Before leaving the topic of constitutional change, it is helpful to place the American situation in comparative perspective. Discounting the unwritten British variety, the Constitution of the United States is by far the world's oldest. Perhaps many Americans take for granted that a constitution is an enduring document. The experiences of other countries, even those considered to have constitutional governments, suggest that constitutional change is far from rare, (see Table 1.2). Oftentimes the stimulus for scrapping an existing constitution is a crisis, defeat in war, or change in leadership. Of the major powers defeated in World War II, for example, all have new constitutions (West German Basic Law, 1949; Japanese Constitution, 1947; Italian Constitution, 1948). A costly Algerian crisis and possible military coup were responsible for the French decision in 1958 to replace the Fourth Republic with the Fifth Republic by means of a new constitution. Other constitutional governments such as Sweden have written new constitutions (1975) for reasons of efficiency and structural change.

Communist systems seemingly write new constitutions when the current leadership discredits the practices of a past regime. The 1977 "Brezhnev" constitution in the Soviet Union and the 1982 "post-Mao" constitution in the People's Republic of China are examples of this phenomenon. Many third-world nations are on their second or third constitution in only thirty years. Of course, as constitutions are normally not much more than organization charts in these countries, a new constitution becomes necessary when the organization changes. Given this overall perspective, the longevity of the Constitution of the United States is all the more remarkable, making the development of American constitutionalism one of the longest running stories in the modern world.

Bills of Rights: Limits on Government

Most constitutions include a section that purports to list the rights of the citizens. Whether called a **bill of rights** (by the way, no mention of this term

Table 1.2   Current National Constitutions: Ages and Origins

COUNTRY	MOST RECENT CONSTITUTION	REASON FOR CONSTITUTION
USA	1787	Failure of Articles of Confederation. Strengthen the national government.
Norway	1814	Desire for a Norwegian state. Attempt to avoid a forced union with Sweden.
Switzerland	1874	Consolidation and unification of confederation.
Colombia	1886	Compromise reached to end bloody war and military strife.
Mexico	1917	Institutionalize the 1910 revolution.
Japan	1947	Defeat in World War II. American occupation.
Italy	1948	Defeat in World War II. Referendum abolished monarchy and called for a republic.
West Germany	1949	Defeat in World War II. Allied occupation.
India	1949	Independence from Britain. Promote unity.
France	1958	Fourth Republic's failure to deal with Algerian war. Return of Charles de Gaulle to government.
Sweden	1975	Consolidate Social Democratic reforms. Removal of all power from king. Replaced 1809 constitution.
Greece	1975	Downfall of military junta in aftermath of Turkish invasion of Cyprus.
USSR	1977	"Brezhnev" constitution replaced the "Stalin" constitution.
Spain	1978	Death of Franco in 1975; King Juan Carlos opened way for a constitutional monarchy.
Iran	1979	Overthrow of the shah. Establishment of an Islamic republic.
China (PRC)	1982	Deng Xiaoping's constitution.
Canada	1982	Desire to "patriate" own Constitution. Amended the 1867 British North America Act.

appears in the U.S. Constitution) or something similar, the listing represents those freedoms, rights, and liberties that, at least theoretically, are beyond the government's power to abridge. In reality, the true measure of individual rights and civil liberties cannot be determined from merely reading the constitution itself, but also from observing the degree to which a government actually abides by the guarantees of individual rights found in its constitution.

One of the major undertakings of the First Congress of the United States (1789–91) was the addition of a bill of rights. A full listing of these rights is unnecessary at present, as each requires considerable attention. Suffice it to say that the liberties listed in the first ten amendments are among the best-known features of the American Constitution, and yet they have been subject to more interpretation and refinement than any other section of the document. Not all constitutional rights are found in the Bill of Rights. Americans have seen their freedoms and liberties grow with time, often, as noted previously, by means of constitutional amendment. Many other rights to be discussed in later chapters have been discovered by the Supreme Court from within the Constitution itself. Furthermore, certain guarantees that safeguard the individual from arbitrary government intrusion, such as provisions for *habeas corpus* and protection from *ex post facto* laws and bills of attainder, are found in Article I of the original Constitution of 1787.

The constitutions of most other countries also contain a chapter or section dealing with rights and liberties guaranteed to the people. Not surprisingly, the genuinely constitutional systems, such as the democracies of Western Europe, emphasize political rights and civil liberties. Socialist and communist regimes typically stress economic or social rights, such as the right to work, choose an occupation, and even enjoy leisure. Finally, a large number of constitutions, generally in the more autocratic states, identify the duties, as well as the rights, of citizens. Some routinely included duties are paying taxes, keeping state secrets, defending the nation against enemies, and serving in the armed forces. Some countries carry the list of duties much further, generally resulting in a loss of liberty for the individual citizen. Table 1.3 provides some examples of rights, liberties, and duties found among the constitutions of the world's nations.

Conclusion

The essence of constitutionalism lies in its distrust and restraint of power. As noted throughout this chapter, limitations upon government have taken many forms. In the American case, emphasis has been placed upon the separation of powers and corresponding checks and balances, judicial review, and federalism, combined with an effective Bill of Rights. Other countries have selected different structural devices to organize and restrain government power, although all constitutional systems have recognized and respected the rights of individuals to liberty, equality, and participation.

With this broad picture of constitutionalism, attention must now be directed to the forces underlying the American experience. The remainder of Part I focuses upon the ideas and events that influenced America's constitution writers. As will become apparent, these ideas were much less established in the eighteenth century than they are today. For some, such ideas were radical and dangerous, while others saw them as simply impractical. Despite these obstacles, the Constitution was written and, most importantly, constitutionalism took root. Part II examines in greater depth the three distinctive features of rooted American constitutionalism mentioned earlier in this chapter: judicial review, separation of powers, and federalism. Part III analyzes the historical struggle to secure greater liberty and equality for all Americans under the Constitution and the uprooting of traditions and experience this struggle has caused. Finally, a concluding chapter explores remaining issues surrounding the American Constitution as well as the prospects for constitutional reform.

Table 1.3   Rights and Liberties in Constitutions of Countries of the World

Rights Relating to Work/Labor

"Every person has the right to choose the profession he wishes, provided it is not contrary to the principles of Islam, to the public interest, or to the rights of others" **Iran** (Art. 28).

"The exploitation of man by man is proscribed" **Paraguay** (Art. 104).

"Work is the primary right, obligation, and privilege of citizens. Citizens have the right to work. People fit for work must work" **Vietnam** (Art. 58).

"The State guarantees the right to safety, security, and hygienic conditions at work" **Algeria** (Art. 63).

"Work in a socialist society is a right and duty and a source of pride for every citizen" **Cuba** (Art. 44). "All those who work have the right to rest" **Cuba** (Art. 45).

"All Germans shall have the right freely to choose their trade, occupation, or profession, their place of work, and their place of training" **Federal Republic of Germany** (Art. 12).

"Citizens of the USSR have the right to rest and leisure" **USSR** (Art. 41).

Education/Welfare

"Everyone has the right to physical education, sports and recreation" **Cuba** (Art. 51).

"Academic freedom is guaranteed" **Japan** (Art. 23).

"Paid maternity leave shall be guaranteed" **Romania** (Art. 20).

"All inhabitants have the right to education to develop their mental and physical capabilities" **Paraguay** (Art. 89).

"Citizens have the right to housing" **Vietnam** (Art. 62).

Freedoms of Expression

"Citizens enjoy freedom of speech, freedom of the press . . . No one may misuse democratic freedoms to violate the interests of the state and the people" **Vietnam** (Art. 67).

"Publications and the press may express ideas freely, except when they are contrary to Islamic principles" **Iran** (Art. 24).

"Journalism in any of its forms may be practiced freely. Press organs lacking responsible direction shall not be permitted, nor shall the publication of immoral subject matter be printed" **Paraguay** (Art. 73).

"Citizens . . . enjoy freedom of speech, of the press, of assembly, of association, of procession and of demonstration" **People's Republic of China** (Art. 35).

Two Sample Limitations

"The exercise by citizens of the People's Republic of China of their freedoms and rights may not infringe upon interests of the state, of society and of the collective, or upon the lawful freedoms and rights of other citizens" **People's Republic of China** (Art. 51).

"Enjoyment by citizens of their rights and freedoms must not be the detriment of the interests of society or the state, or infringe on the rights of other citizens" **USSR** (Art. 39).

Source: Albert P. Blaustein and Gisbert H. Flanz, eds., *Constitutions of the Countries of the World* (Dobbs Ferry, N.Y.: Oceana Publishers, 1988).

Questions

1. Americans tend to take separation of powers, judicial review, and federalism for granted as essential features of constitutionalism. But a look at other constitutional governments demonstrates that these are distinctively American features. Are these three features necessary conditions for constitutional rule? Which one of the three is most important?

2. The selections from various constitutional preambles in Table 1.1 reveal differences in constitutional philosophy around the globe. Comparatively speaking, is the Preamble to the U.S. Constitution too short and simple? How might the Preamble read if it were to take on the characteristics of more ideological documents?

3. Looking at Table 1.3 what comparisons can you make between the U.S. Constitution's provision for individual rights and liberties and the provisions of other nations? Are there any constitutional rights in these other documents that the U.S. Constitution could profit from adopting?

Endnotes

1. This term has been coined by James MacGregor Burns in a number of bicentennial lectures and articles.

2. Quoted in Carl J. Friedrich, *Limited Government: A Comparison* (Englewood Cliffs, N.J.: Prentice-Hall, 1974), 16.

3. Alexander Hamilton, John Jay, and James Madison, "Federalist No.51," *The Federalist Papers* (New York: Modern Library 1937), 337.

4. Robert P. Clark, *Power and Policy in the Third World,* 3d ed. (New York: Wiley, 1986), 109.

5. Ivo D. Duchacek, *Rights and Liberties in the World Today: Constitutional Promise and Reality* (Santa Barbara, Calif.: ABC–CLIO, Inc., 1973), 25.

6. Ivo D. Duchacek, *Power Maps: Comparative Politics of Constitutions* (Santa Barbara, Calif.: ABC–CLIO, Inc., 1973), 3.

7. Madison, "Federalist No. 51," 337.

8. See James MacGregor Burns, *The Deadlock of Democracy: Four-Party Politics in America* (New York: Harper & Row, 1963).

Suggested Readings

Duchacek, Ivo D. *Power Maps: Comparative Politics of Constitutions.* Santa Barbara, Calif.: ABC–CLIO, Inc., 1973.
_____. *Rights and Liberties in the World Today: Constitutional Promise and Reality.* Santa Barbara, Calif.: ABC–CLIO, Inc., 1973
Dworkin, Ronald. *Law's Empire.* Cambridge, Mass.: Harvard University Press, 1986.
Friedman, Lawrence M. *American Law.* New York: Norton, 1984.
Friedrich, Carl J. *Limited Government: A Comparison.* Englewood Cliffs, N.J.: Prentice-Hall, 1974.
Hart, H. L. A. *The Concept of Law.* London: Oxford University Press, 1961.

CHAPTER

2

American Constitutionalism: Theory and Practice

Syllabus

Contemporary American politics is often dominated by ideological battles between liberals and conservatives, between left and right. Americans are polarized over such issues as abortion, church-state relations, sex education, welfare, and foreign policy. For example, organizations like the National Abortion Rights Action League and the National Right to Life Committee find themselves constantly pitted against each other over the abortion issue. But what differentiates American politics from the politics of other countries is that these polarized debates take place within the parameters of the U.S. Constitution; that is, radically conflicting sides in the political arena draw their support from the same constitutional structure and value foundations. The theoretical and historical influences upon American constitutionalism may help to describe this unique element in American politics, and may explain why strident conflict is often contained short of violent revolt.

This Chapter Examines the Following Matters

☐ American constitutionalism was built upon the twin pillars of the individualist and communitarian approaches to government. Major contrasts exist between the two theories, but examples of each concept can be found in the American constitutional system.

☐ Religion and religious ideas have had a significant influence upon American political thought and practice, in large part because of the elements religion shares with the basic principles of constitutionalism.

☐ Constitutionalism in Greece and Rome influenced American political ideas in the eighteenth century, as did medieval constitutionalism. The Greeks and Romans emphasized the rule of law, while medieval thinkers stressed the importance of natural law and the value of the individual human being. These ideas formed a legacy for the framers of the U.S. Constitution.

☐ Perhaps the greatest historical impact upon American colonists came from English common law and parliamentary history. The principles of judicial review and legislative checks on executive authority originated in America's British heritage.

☐ Political and legal theorists like John Locke, Baron de Montesquieu, Jean-Jacques Rousseau, and Sir Edward Coke also had a great influence on the thinking of the founding generation. John Locke can be seen as one of the fathers of the individualist approach to constitutionalism, while Jean-Jacques Rousseau helped inform eighteenth-century communitarians.

☐ Different colonial structures contributed to the distinctness of American constitutionalism. Colonial experience dating back over 150 years set the stage for revolution and constitution writing in eighteenth-century America.

Photo: Thomas Jefferson was one of the few men at the time of the Constitution's drafting who brought together the various influences discussed in this chapter. Shaped by his religious heritage and learning, well-read in the Greek and Roman classics as well as in the modern political theories of Locke, Rousseau, and Coke, and informed by colonial practice in a revolutionary era, Jefferson helped found the new American nation and influenced its constitution.

The Twin Pillars of American Constitutionalism

The preceding chapter outlined the general principles and attributes of constitutionalism. As explained in Chapter 1, the United States is a government of laws and not of men. However, two points in particular require further explanation.

First of all, American history shows that laws, including the "higher law" of the Constitution, can only govern through particular men and women. This textbook is devoted to discussing the historical development of various constitutional principles and provisions by particular individuals and groups. The focus is especially upon the justices who have served on the U.S. Supreme Court. As Chief Justice Charles Evans Hughes once said, "We are under a constitution, but the constitution is what the judges say it is."[1] Therefore, students of the American constitutional system must look at more than the document of the Constitution itself; they must also examine its interpretation by the Supreme Court.

Countless examples prove that the American constitutional system can change without a change in the Constitution itself. A shift in the Supreme Court's understanding, a movement within Congress, even a mood swing among the American people can drastically alter the way the government works or the rights it protects. For instance, the Fourteenth Amendment to the Constitution (passed in 1868) provides that "no State shall . . . deny to any person . . . the equal protection of the laws." The Supreme Court at first interpreted this provision to allow states to segregate transportation, education, and other public facilities on the basis of race, and to pass laws denying equality to women. Finally, in 1954, the Supreme Court reversed its position, saying that racial segregation in education was a violation of the Fourteenth Amendment. And by the 1970s, the Court began to use the Fourteenth Amendment to strike down laws that discriminated on the basis of gender. With these two shifts in the Supreme Court's understanding of the Fourteenth Amendment came a revolution in American law and social life, without a single change in the wording of the Constitution itself. These and other constitutional developments caused by historic changes in judicial interpretation and legislative policy will be examined by topic throughout the book.

A second and more important point that requires explanation is that constitutions are never politically neutral documents. Americans tend to regard the U.S. Constitution as being "above politics," a neutral set of rules and procedures by which people play the political "game." People with individual biases and interests may use the provisions and mechanisms of the Constitution to achieve desired results, but the procedures themselves are presumed unbiased and disinterested. Such thinking ignores the fact that rules and procedures in every game make certain assumptions about the nature of the game and its players, assumptions that may bias the direction or outcome of the action. The rules of any competitive sport, for example, assume that the players will try to use the rules to beat their opponents. The rules of Monopoly® assume that the players will try to drive their opponents out of business. Anyone who tries to play a "friendly" game of Monopoly® will not get very far!

The American Constitution is no exception here. The Constitution contains certain assumptions about human beings, about their nature and goals, and about the type of political system appropriate to them. An inherent bias exists in the constitutional system toward a particular notion of government and politics. The Constitution describes and tries to establish a specific kind of politics and political life—one based upon certain theories of human nature and of the government's proper role in people's lives. In *The Federalist Papers,* James Madison asked:

> What is government itself but the greatest of all reflections on human nature? If men were angels, no government would be necessary. If angels were to govern men, neither external nor internal controls on government would be necessary.[2]

As Madison acknowledged, to understand the Constitution requires an understanding of the particular political theories and assumptions it embodies.

Actually, the American Constitution and American historical political practices embody not one but *two* different theories of politics. This text will refer to the two strands of political thought underlying the American Constitution as the **individualist** (or classical liberal) approach and the **communitarian** (or classical republican) approach to government. While existing alongside each other in the nation's constitutional history, these two competing philosophies of government contain different assumptions about human nature and politics. Historically, these divergent assumptions have produced conflict over which course the nation should pursue. Many of the constitutional clashes in the nation's history have erupted between those adhering to an individualist theory of government and those following a more communitarian approach.

The Individualist Theory of Politics

The individualist theory of politics appears more prominently as a foundation underlying the American constitutional system. The individualist approach assumes that individuals take precedence over government. They inherently possess certain natural rights that the government should preserve and promote. The individualist perspective assumes that human beings are capable of choice and development on their own, without governmental help. Government should merely provide institutions and mechanisms that will enable individuals to exercise their rights and pursue their private interests. Under this concept of politics, individuals are more important than the political community, and their rights and interests supersede those of the community.

Still, individualists see government as necessary, because people may have irreconcilable interests. The clash of individual interests creates conflict. Individuals whose private interests conflict require institutions that can mediate and accommodate these differences. Individualists seek to create a political order that can regulate the anarchy arising from egoistic human behavior. And yet, the individualist wants to allow people the greatest possible personal freedom. The ideal government as envisioned by individualists would be one in which general, impersonal laws and disinterested judges provide the peace and security under which each person can pursue private interests. Thus, the individualist has a notion of justice that is purely procedural in nature. A **procedural** view of **justice** sees the political system as legitimate as long as it applies fair rules and procedures equally to all persons. Persons using these procedures to obtain vastly different results are not seen as being unjust. For example, a college admissions system may be based upon merit. High school seniors will be admitted to college if they achieve a certain grade point average and adequate scores on college admissions tests. Those who do not meet the standards are not admitted. Though this system differentiates between people, it is procedurally just because it applies what are believed to be appropriate standards equally to all persons.

For individualists, however, beyond these minimal functions, the government must be strictly limited in its scope. People only call upon government to protect and secure their rights and interests. The individualist approach sees no intrinsic value fulfilled by the political order. Because the political order fills no intrinsic needs, people ought to be given the widest possible arena of unregulated activity. And because individuals only enter the public realm to secure their private interests, they have no reason to participate directly in all aspects of politics—especially as long as the leaders they choose satisfy their desires. Individuals enter the public realm as free and independent persons with particular desires, and the political system ought to allow—even guarantee—the continuation of their privacy and independence. In this sense, the individualist approach to politics corresponds to what political scientists call the concept of **negative freedom.**[3] Individualists are concerned with strictly limiting government interference with personal freedom. They do not evaluate the uses to which individuals put their freedom. The individualist contends that women and men are free if no government power is controlling their choices and beliefs; what individuals may do with their freedom is a private matter of little or no concern to government (as long as individuals do not, in their choices, harm or restrict the rights of others).

What has been described here as the individualist approach to politics has also been termed the liberal tradition in Western political thought. This classical theory of liberal individualism appears in the writings of such historical figures as John Locke in the seventeenth century and John Stuart Mill in the nineteenth century. In contemporary American society the individualist approach to politics is expressed in the writings of the economist Milton Friedman,[4] as well as in the actions of organizations like the American Civil Liberties Union.

The Communitarian Theory of Politics

The communitarian perspective emphasizes the positive role that government plays in the lives of its people. The communitarian approach asserts that individuals are not completely independent, but rather, have an inherent need for association with their fellows in the political community. Whereas the individualist approach assumes that people can choose and develop on their own, the communitarian approach contends that people need the community and its values to nurture their development and enable them to make proper choices.

Under this view, democratic government exists not only to recognize and protect individual rights and to satisfy personal interests, but also to bring individuals together into a participatory political community. People receive intrinsic satisfaction from political participation. Such participation educates and transforms their self-interest into a larger public interest, and better fulfills them as human beings. Communitarians see the political community in a positive light, as a place where individuals come together to share common interests and to do the public's business. Politics is not a necessary evil to be limited in scope and function. Thus, communitarians recognize that the "public interest" (as defined by the majority in a political community) may override the individual's rights. Whenever a conflict occurs between individual rights and government regulation in the public interest, the communitarian resolves the conflict on the side of the public interest. Because the public interest is seen as intrinsically valuable to individuals, the political majority may sometimes need to impose certain values upon individuals who find themselves in the minority.

In this sense, the communitarian theory of politics corresponds to what political scientists call the concept of **positive freedom** (as opposed to the negative freedom of the individualist). The communitarian views true liberty occurring not in private, but rather in political participation and in political action. Communitarians, concerned with civic as well as personal virtue, see the government playing a positive role in helping individuals define their choices and exercise their freedom. Communitarians want to assure that liberty is not merely devoted to the pursuit of personal ends but that individuals also pursue the common good.

Communitarians take a **substantive** view of **justice**. Whereas the individualist is satisfied with fair procedures as a measure of justice, the communitarian is more likely to look at the fairness of the results obtained. A substantive view of justice contends that vast inequalities among individuals are potentially damaging to society as a whole. Communitarians, adhering to their substantive notion of justice, are willing to use governmental power to achieve greater justice. For example, in college admissions systems, communitarian theory supports affirmative action by government on behalf of minorities to redress institutional inequalities that resulted from past discrimination. Under an affirmative action program, a college may give admissions preference to minority group members in order to increase their numbers in higher education and certain professions. Even though such action may discriminate against individuals who are not minority group members, communitarians see the importance of government's role in obtaining just results for all elements in society. The strict individualist, on the other hand, would be opposed to government affirmative action, arguing that affirmative action unfairly burdens individuals who had nothing to do with the past discrimination.

The communitarian theory of government has also been labeled the republican tradition in Western political thought. The earliest roots of this community-oriented republican theory appear in the writings of Aristotle and Cicero. More modern examples of republicanism appear in the eighteenth-century writings of Jean-Jacques Rousseau and Thomas Jefferson. In contemporary American society, communitarian beliefs are found in the writings of those who advocate participatory democracy.[5] The many citizens currently arguing for a universal citizen service program (both military and nonmilitary) also reflect the communitarian approach to politics.

Admittedly, the preceding discussion of the two theories of government underlying the U.S. Constitution draws each viewpoint starkly in black and white. The theories of individualism and communitarianism are set in high contrast for purposes of study and analysis (see Table 2.1). However, very few Americans actually adhere to either theory in its purest form. Indeed, the

Table 2.1   Individualists and Communitarians Contrasted

	INDIVIDUALIST	COMMUNITARIAN
Priority of social system	On the individual	On the community
Function of government	Protect property and other rights of individuals, especially those of minorities	Protect human rights of community, as defined by majority
Focus of system	Fulfill private interest	Fulfill public interest
Pursuit of justice	Procedural regularity; merit-based	Substantive change in objective conditions; results orientation
View of equality	Natural inequality exists in society and should be preserved	Devoted to creating more equality of condition through government effort
General view of government	Negative force; government must not interfere with personal freedoms	Positive force; government can realize communal development and public interest
View of political participation	Conditional; limited participation	Essential; maximal participation

Constitution fuses the classical liberal and republican traditions (see Brief 2.1). This fusion is evident in *Federalist No. 51*, where Madison talked about the importance in a constitutional democracy of balancing "the rights of individuals, or of the minority" against the regular "combinations of the majority."[6]

Both individualism and communitarianism are also evident in the views of the nation's most recent past president. Ronald Reagan has often been described as an individualist, as he advocated taking government out of people's daily lives. He supported limited government involvement in the economy and in spending for social services. But President Reagan also had his more communitarian side. On such issues as pornography, drug abuse, and school prayer, he proposed more government action to promote what he saw as the public interest. He supported the active teaching of civic values and patriotism in the schools. Furthermore, in the area of criminal law he argued that the courts excessively catered to the rights of accused suspects and not enough to the needs of the community. Thus, in the nation's highest office the conjunction of the individualist and communitarian approaches to politics can be found.

However, as the historical evidence will show, many constitutional conflicts in the United States have occurred between individualists and communitarians. Important clashes have occurred when the government has tried to restrict individual liberties, especially those of minorities, in the public interest. At the same time, individuals have claimed that their rights superseded the government's powers. Examples abound. In eighteenth-century New England, individual claims for religious freedom, a principle dear to many citizens, often conflicted with the community's attempt to infuse Puritan values and practices

❑ *Brief 2.1   Contemporary Liberals and Conservatives*

Students accustomed to thinking about politics in terms of the labels "liberal" and "conservative" may be confused by the terminology in this chapter. Individualist theory and classical liberalism as used here refer to the tradition of belief that distrusts government power and exalts individual freedom of choice in most matters. The label "liberal" in contemporary usage often refers to the opposite of individualism, that is, a belief in the use of government power to regulate the affairs of individuals, especially in the economy. Communitarian theory and classical republicanism as used in this chapter refer to the tradition of belief that, supports the promotion of the public interest and public virtue over individual rights, and that upholds at least some participation by citizens in self-government. This does not compare favorably with many contemporary "conservatives," who usually rule out any public involvement in economic affairs, and who tend to be suspicious of mass citizen participation in government.

In considering that the labels "liberal" and "conservative" are applied loosely to a wide range of belief systems, and that there is often wide variation within the "liberal" and "conservative" camps in contemporary American politics, students may become even more confused. Differences exist between traditional conservatives, "New Right" conservatives, and "neoconservatives"; and between traditional liberals, "New Left" liberals, and "neoliberals." Because of the dangers of using these contemporary labels, this text relies on the more generic concepts individualist and communitarian, and defines each starkly and simply. These two concepts of politics should be more useful in analyzing American constitutional development and the ongoing clash between majority rule and minority rights.

in all its people. In the nineteenth century, private enterprises seeking profit were confronted by state governments attempting to impose regulations for the general welfare. And today an issue such as pornography pits publishers and readers seeking the freedom to publish and view explicit materials against communities desiring to restrict such publication and thus uphold public morals and decency. Eventual resolution of many of these constitutional conflicts has involved a tension between individualist and communitarian concepts of politics.

While these two theories lie at the foundation of the American Constitution, describing them is not enough. Further examination of the heritage of these ideas about politics and constitutionalism is necessary. Where did Americans' ideas about constitutional government originate? How did the individualist and communitarian strands of political thought come to be expressed in the eighteenth-century American setting? Actually, the American constitutional heritage is a mixture of intellectual influences and practical political experiences in the colonies. Each will be discussed in turn.

Historical Influences on American Constitutionalism

Constitutional historian Edward S. Corwin once said that "the American Revolution replaced the sway of a king with that of a document."[7] The document to which Corwin referred, of course, is the U.S. Constitution. The preceding chapter emphasized that constitutional government is limited government. Constitutions place limits on the day-to-day powers and activities of government in the name of more immutable general principles. A people under a constitution believe in the rule of law—specifically the rule of a law superior to the will of transient human governors. This belief in a higher law that rules daily human endeavors was not born in eighteenth-century American political thought. It originated over two thousand years before in Greek political thought, was nurtured in the soil of Roman theory and practice, and reached fruition during medieval times, especially in England. The Protestant Reformation and the European Enlightenment both furthered the development of ideas and practices associated with modern constitutional government.

Religious Ideas and Practices

The impact of religion upon American constitutional development is unmistakable. For one reason, religion and constitutional theory share a belief in a higher law that orders human behavior. Both religion and constitutionalism are based upon the idea that unchanging universal principles ought to exist as standards by which to judge changing human authorities. The Constitution itself is the "sacred text" containing these principles of government. In his essay *Rights of Man*, Thomas Paine said that Americans treated their written Constitution like a bible:

> It was the political bible of the state. Scarcely a family was without it. Every member of the government had a copy; and nothing was more common, when any debate arose on the principle of a bill, or on the extent of any species of authority, than for the members to take the printed constitution out of their pocket, and read the chapter with which such matter in debate was connected . . . It is the body of elements, to which you can refer, and quote article by article; and which contains everything that relates to the complete organization of civil government, and the principles on which it shall act, and by which it shall be bound.[8]

In addition, the specific form and content of the American Constitution reflects an imperative, law-giving feature that parallels religious imperatives and laws. This parallel is no small coincidence, as many of the American colonies had strong religious foundations. The Mayflower Compact was an early colonial constitution based largely upon religious ideas of covenant and compact, which will be discussed in a later section of this chapter. Moreover, one of the greatest sources of American political thought at the time of the Revolution is found in preachers' sermons. These sermons, many of which advocated rebellion against English rule, were not only heard by congregations; they were published and read by people throughout the colonies. These sermons contained theories of human nature and government that are at the heart of the constitutional system.

Furthermore, the combination of individualism and communitarianism found in American political thought can also be found in the Judeo-Christian religious tradition. The Christian belief in the sanctity of the individual human being, a being whose capacity for free choice and free will sets him or her apart from other beings, is similar to the political individualist's belief in the sanctity of individual rights in the face of government power. On the other side, the Judaic tradition celebrates the community of the Jewish people, bound together both in the here and now and in the kingdom yet to come.[9] And, the glorification in Christian doctrine of a community of fellow believers who share values and interests, who work together and sacrifice for each other, parallels the communitarian political outlook described earlier. Thus, the religious ideals of the Judeo-Christian tradition have exerted an important influence upon America's constitutional development.

Ancient Constitutionalism

Western political thought—going all the way back to the fifth century B.C. in Athens—also has affected the American constitutional system. The ancient Greek origins of American constitutional theory find their clearest expression in Aristotle's writings. Though Plato also recognized that governments ought to operate according to the universal precepts of a higher law (found in his theory of ideas), Aristotle best articulated this outstanding feature of constitutionalism in *The Politics* (his foremost work on government). Aristotle argued that no matter what person or class is chosen to rule, the law ought to rule above all individuals in the well-ordered state. The law is general and thus embodies reason; human rulers are subject to passion and self-interest. Therefore, the rule of law is preferable to the rule of men. With Aristotle, then, can be found the first inklings of the belief in a higher law superior to human decrees—a belief fundamental to constitutional government.

This higher-law tradition developed further in Roman political thought four centuries later. Indeed, the Romans had a much greater and more direct intellectual impact upon American colonists than did the Greeks. American revolutionaries often referred to Roman history and Roman writers in justifying their cause against the Crown. They saw themselves extolling the virtues of the Roman Republic against the corruption of imperial power. They viewed the English as modern-day Caesars. Americans in the 1760s and 1770s avidly read *Cato's Letters,* an anti-establishment English publication, and Joseph Addison's play entitled *Cato.* Both works were obvious references to the semi-mythical figure of the Roman Republic and to the similarity between ancient Rome and modern colonial life.

The colonists also read and cited the works of Cicero, a politician and political theorist at the time of the Roman Republic. With his discussion of natural law, Cicero added to Aristotle's notion of a superior higher law that ought to rule men and women. Cicero felt that a universal justice and reason are found in the permanent elements of nature, including human nature. Human law, coming either from legislative bodies or from individual rulers, must embody this universal justice in order to claim allegiance from the people. Existing governments must be limited by natural law. Whenever they act contrary to the natural law and its reason, they are no longer legitimate. Cicero's writings not only contain a fuller expression of constitutional principles, but also the early roots of modern ideas about human nature and popular rule. And in Cicero's works can also be found rudimentary justification for the practice of judicial review, a fundamental feature of American constitutionalism. Cicero's impact appears clearly in the writings of important colonial thinkers in America. Men like John Winthrop, Roger Williams, Thomas Hooker, John Wise, and Thomas Jefferson all refer to Cicero and other natural-law theorists in making their political arguments.

Although ancient Greek and Roman thinking was important to the development of modern constitutionalism, one crucial element was missing: the idea of individual rights. As many scholars have noted, ancient constitutionalism, though committed to government limited by the rule of law, was not devoted to securing individual rights in the same way as is modern constitutional government. In this sense, Aristotle and Cicero could be called pure communitarians. For ancient thinkers, a law-abiding community where justice prevailed for all held highest importance. Individuals were expected to abide by the common good as reflected in the community's laws and rituals. The idea that individual rights might supersede the public good was alien to ancient thinkers.

Medieval Constitutionalism

Medieval thinkers were the first to combine (though not completely) limited government with individual rights to form the crux of modern constitutional theory. And in medieval England, citizens took the earliest steps toward achieving modern constitutionalism in practice.

Higher-law notions pervaded the Middle Ages. Medieval thinkers like Saint Thomas Aquinas and John of Salisbury spoke of the natural law as coming directly from God and existing as the ultimate standard of human law and conduct. Whereas ancient thinkers saw natural law as something that readily made its way into human laws and customs, medieval thinkers saw it as a higher standard outside of politics. Natural law *limited* human authority. By the medieval period governance had become more personalized, the rule of a monarch rather than a legislative body. This made government potentially more arbitrary and autocratic. Thus, natural-law reasoning existed to set external norms for proper kingship and to judge existing rulers. For example, both Aquinas and John made a distinction between kingship and tyranny. The legitimate king is one who rules in accordance with the natural law; the tyrant rules oppressively, based upon force, and is thereby an illegitimate ruler. This medieval idea that the higher natural law places inherent limits upon rulers directly contributed to American notions of higher law under constitutional government. The American colonists drew specific sustenance from medieval arguments about legitimate resistance to tyranny.

This shift from ancient to medieval notions of natural law and its applications to human law was evolutionary rather than revolutionary. For the first time during the medieval period a concept of natural right emerged to go along with that of natural law. The rise of Christianity and its emphasis upon the individual as the final value profoundly influenced Western European ideas about individual worth and dignity. A belief that individuals were invested by nature with certain rights that the state must, at least in theory, respect began to emerge in medieval Europe. With the Protestant Reformation, this natural-rights doctrine became a stronger root of both religious and political dissent.

The earliest practical (as opposed to theoretical) steps toward modern constitutionalism were taken in England. And for all the impact continental European thought and practice had, it was from England that the framers of the American Constitution took most of their cues. The Magna Carta, granted in 1215, is often cited as one of the first steps toward limiting the absolute power of the monarchy. In it, King John promised not to infringe upon the customary feudal rights of the nobility. By the fourteenth century, the range of classes protected by the Magna Carta had broadened; the interpretation of what limits were placed upon royal authority had also broadened. However, the concessions originally granted in the Magna Carta did not positively affect the lives of most Englishmen, and the king continued to make the key decisions for the realm. Still, the Magna Carta was the beginning of a gradual process of limiting governmental authority and is part of the first chapter in modern constitutional development. Moreover, references to the Magna Carta and to the "ancient constitution of England" (ninth- and tenth-century Anglo-Saxon principles of government and constitutionalism) that predates it can be found in much of the colonial resistance literature of the eighteenth century.

English Common Law and Parliamentary Practice

More important to the origins of American constitutional politics, however, was English common law and commentaries upon it by English jurists. English common law, which combined indigenous customs with judicial pronouncements and interpretations, came to be seen as a higher law, containing universal precepts that existed above human authorities. Because of the case-oriented (as opposed to code-oriented) nature of British law, the British constitution came to be an unwritten higher law. The common law was used first to limit the power of kings, and later, in seventeenth-century England, to limit Parliament's power. American constitutional theory and practice received two kinds of principles from English common law tradition. First, it inherited general concepts such as the judicial doctrines of precedent and reasonableness. Second, the common law tradition passed along to American constitutionalism specific guarantees such as the rights to due process of law and to a trial by jury. Both general and specific inheritances from English common law found their way into the U.S. Constitution and have been significant in shaping American historical practices over the past two hundred years.

In addition to English common law, the rise of the English Parliament as a challenger to the monarch's absolute sovereignty had an important influence on eighteenth-century American political thought. Parliament emerged as a significant political force during the seventeenth century. The dispute between king and Parliament contributed to the English civil war (1642–49). The war ended with Parliament's ordering the execution of King Charles I in 1649. Later, with the Glorious Revolution of 1688, Parliament's power culminated when it declared the royal throne vacant and selected William and Mary of Holland to occupy it. Moreover, in this period, Parliament passed laws of constitutional significance, most notably the Petition of Right, the Act of Habeus Corpus, and the Bill of Rights. The American colonists came to see Parliament, and by extension their own legislative assemblies, as the defender of people's rights and liberties against the Crown's incursions. Parliament's rise in power after its seventeenth-century battles with the English king taught the colonists important lessons about checking arbitrary royal authority and about the general need for a separation of governmental powers with built-in checks and balances. Ironically, the colonists would use their own concept of the constitutional rights of Englishmen to challenge what they considered to be oppressive parliamentary legislation in the 1760s.

Coke, Locke, and Rousseau

Finally, in addition to the general influence of religious notions, classical authors, and English common law and parliamentary traditions, specific political theorists in the seventeenth and eighteenth centuries directly affected the thinking of those who forged the American Revolution and the political institutions that followed. The colonists identified with a number of anti-establishment English writers of the eighteenth century whose names today are relatively unknown. These writers, some of them members of Parliament, argued for greater liberty both within Parliament and against the royal court. The colonists used the arguments of the English writers to build support for their identical cause in America. Of course, the French philosopher Baron de Montesquieu, whose *Spirit of the Laws* contained a strong argument for a strict separation of governmental powers, was also an important influence. So was Sir Edward Coke (see Brief 2.2). However, two other political theorists in particular deserve further mention here: John Locke and Jean-Jacques Rousseau. Locke, parts of whose *Second Treatise of Government* made their way almost word for word into the Declaration of Independence, was widely read by both colonial politicians and New England preachers. He represents the individualist strain in American political thought. Rousseau's political ideas, found in such works as *The Social Contract,* are closely akin to those of Thomas Jefferson. Having brought together a long tradition of continental republican thought, Rousseau reflects the communitarian concept of politics.

American revolutionaries extensively cited Locke in making their arguments against the British. In fact, after the Bible, Locke was the principal authority cited by American preachers to make their political claims. Locke's political teaching appealed to the colonists because it was based firmly upon

---

❑ *Brief 2.2   Sir Edward Coke's Legacy*

Seventeenth-century jurist Sir Edward Coke contributed significantly to American constitutionalism. First as a judge (rising to the rank of chief justice of the King's Bench) and later as a member of Parliament, Coke led the fight against the British monarchy in the early 1600s. Beginning with King James I, the Stuart kings tried to bolster their authority over an unruly Parliament by asserting that God had vested kings with absolute authority to rule. Coke rejected this divine-right-of-kings doctrine, offering instead a legal theory that placed both king and Parliament under a higher law. As a judge he argued that "the king hath no prerogative, but that which the law of the land allows," judges being the appropriate interpreters of this law. As a member of Parliament, he asserted Parliament's power as lawmaker over the King's power as ruler. Coke's contributions in this area of legislative supremacy and the proper separation-of-government powers was felt by American colonists struggling with royal authority in the eighteenth century.

But more important than this were Coke's judgments regarding the higher-law nature of the British constitution and the common law. His famous statement in Dr. Bonham's Case in 1610 was an inspiration to eighteenth-century American constitutional ideas. The London College of Physicians had punished Bonham under an act of Parliament for practicing medicine in the city without a license from the college. In invalidating the action against Bonham, Coke stated:

And it appears in our books, that in many cases, the common law will controul acts of Parliament, and sometimes adjudge them to be utterly void: for when an act of Parliament is against common right and reason, or repugnant, or impossible to be performed, the common law will controul it and adjudge such act to be void.[10]

Coke's argument that English common law was fundamental, and could be used to judge the validity of acts of Parliament, is the precursor to the American principle of judicial review. Moreover, American courts, in judging the constitutionality of governmental acts, often use a standard of "reasonableness," which is the natural outgrowth of Coke's "common right and reason" standard.

Sir Edward Coke's writings and actions, especially in the area of judicial review, contributed greatly to American constitutional theory and practice. Though he proposed a theory of parliamentary supremacy in the lawmaking area, Coke believed that both king and Parliament were answerable to the higher law of the British constitution. He felt that judges were the proper interpreters of the law of the land and could void governmental actions that violated the higher law. Coke's contribution of these two principles alone makes him a towering presence in American constitutional theory and practice.

individual rights, and it applied aptly to the colonial situation. Locke's *Second Treatise* begins with a discussion of the "state of nature," the condition human beings find themselves in prior to the existence of society or government. Locke asserted that nature invests persons with equal rights (the most fundamental of these being life, liberty, and property) and the liberty to pursue their private interests. Locke believed in natural law, but felt each person could know and interpret its commands. For Locke, then, government is not intrinsically necessary to human development. Government only becomes necessary to mediate conflicts between individuals attempting to protect their property and to pursue their private interests. However, because individuals ought to be able to fully exercise their rights so long as such exercise brings no injury to others, government must be limited in its scope and functions. Locke said that individuals contract with government to perform certain legislative, administrative, and judicial functions that they cannot provide for themselves. But the purpose of government is to secure individual rights and liberties, and it cannot exercise power beyond this purpose. Individuals entrust government with power. They consent to obey its rules. But when government abuses its power and goes against the people's interests or abuses their rights, the people have a right to resist. Ultimately, Locke granted citizens the right to overthrow an oppressive government and to establish a new one in its place.

It is no wonder that colonial Americans read Locke's writings. His ideas about individual rights, limited government based upon the consent of the governed, and the right to revolt against oppressive rule offered a perfect prescription for many of the American colonists' ills.

Americans relied upon Rousseau's writings as well. Rousseau captured the communitarian spirit among Americans of the revolutionary period. *The Social Contract* contributed significantly to American democratic theory. Rousseau also began with individuals in the "state of nature." Rousseau's individual in the state of nature, like Locke's, is endowed with freedom and equality. But unlike Locke, Rousseau believed that people have a natural dependence upon others. For Rousseau, people have an intrinsic need for communion with others in society. Because of this dependence, the political community is necessary to fulfill inherent human needs; it does not exist simply to adjudicate conflict and protect private interests. Rousseau's goal was to set up a legitimate government in the face of both the natural freedom and the social needs of individuals. He sought a method by which individuals would be brought together into political community without sacrificing their natural freedom and equality. How could these seemingly contradictory ends be accomplished? Rousseau's solution was the **social contract.** In Rousseau's social contract, individuals agree to obey a government, but one in which the people themselves make the laws governing them. Rousseau contended that the only legitimate government is a democracy, where the people directly decide the rules and procedures governing their lives. The community as a whole could dictate to the individual, but it would be a community where each individual has a direct say. In this way, each person could be part of a larger whole without losing his or her individual freedom. To accomplish the goals of the social contract, Rousseau realized that political communities would have to be small and relatively homogeneous in social and economic composition. But he did believe that both direct democracy and meaningful community are possible on a small scale.

In Rousseau, then, a more communitarian emphasis can be found. This emphasis also appealed to the eighteenth-century American character. Rousseau also justified greater citizen participation in government, an idea that would be echoed by Jefferson during the founding period.

Colonial Influences on American Constitutionalism

Religious ideas, ancient and medieval constitutionalism, English common law and practice, and the writings of political theorists constituted the basic intellectual heritage in eighteenth-century America. Combined with over 150 years of colonial political history, they built the foundation of the American republic. In looking at the contribution of colonial history and experience to American constitutional development, two features stand out. The first concerns governmental structure: the distribution of power among the branches of government, and the relationship between local and central authority. The second relates to colonists' ideas about human nature and the role government should play in people's lives. Both issues were shaped by the colonists' experiences in the New World and by the relationship with the imperial government in England. The following discussion will first examine the structural impact of each colony's origins, and then the historical record and its importance to colonial constitutional development.

Structure of Government: Types of Colonies Established

Three distinct methods were used to establish colonies in the New World: the corporate charter, the social compact or covenant, and the royal proprietary grant. Each type had an impact upon the structure of colonial government, especially in the seventeenth century.

Corporate Charter Colonies

Virginia and Massachusetts Bay were the two most prominent corporate charter colonies. Granted by the Crown, these charters gave commercial companies rights to establish colonies in particular regions and govern them according to specific guidelines. Both the Virginia and Massachusetts Bay charters provided for rule by a governor and an advisory council. Ordinary settlers at first had little say in governance in Virginia, and in Massachusetts only through attendance at the general courts each year (even here, however, only church members could attend).

Three things are worth noting about these two corporate charter colonies. First, although the original charters called for rule by an elite few, both Virginia and Massachusetts Bay were transformed into more democratic communities later in the seventeenth century. The political base was broadened to include more people in the day-to-day operations of the government. Moreover, legislative bodies were established. These became increasingly powerful, ultimately challenging the authority of both the colonial governors and the central imperial authority in London. Second, the charter colonies became somewhat more independent from English rule than the other types as a result of their origins. Though England would exert authority over both Virginia and Massachusetts Bay over the next 150 years, the original autonomy granted in their corporate charters served these communities well in exerting independence during the political crises of the 1760s and 1770s. Finally, the corporate charters granted to Virginia and Massachusetts Bay foreshadowed the establishment of constitutional government. By setting out the method and institutions of government in writing, these charters initiated the idea of government limited by a written higher law.

Social Compact Colonies

Government by social compact was the foundation of the colonial communities in Plymouth, Rhode Island, and Connecticut. Though these colonies were never as politically prominent as Massachusetts Bay—and would, in fact, borrow many of their political practices from Massachusetts Bay—they were still important influences. The idea of democratic self-governance based upon an original compact among the governed (discussed in conjunction with Rousseau's writings) was born with these New England communities.

The compact-based communities were founded largely for religious reasons. Seeking separation from the Church of England, a number of Calvinists began forming churches on the basis of a covenant between believers. Persecuted by James I at the beginning of the seventeenth century, these separatist Calvinist churches first sought refuge in Holland, which at the time was alone in offering religious toleration. But a number of people wanted to found a new community in America. The first and most famous was the group who traveled on the *Mayflower* to settle in Plymouth, Massachusetts, in 1620. Before landing, all the male members of this "body of believers" came together and applied their notions about religious covenants to politics. The Mayflower Compact, the basis for the Plymouth government, issued from this notable ship meeting. A part of it read:

> We whose names are underwritten . . . do by these presents solemnly and mutually in the presence of God, and one of another, covenant and combine ourselves togeather into a civill body politick, for our better ordering and preservation . . . and by vertue hearof enacte, constitute, and frame such just and equall laws, ordinances, acts, constitutions, and offices, from time to time, as shall be thought most meete and convenient for the general good of the colonie, unto which we promise all due submission and obedience.[11]

Later, settlers in Rhode Island and Connecticut would similarly establish themselves as self-governing communities. The significance of such voluntary associations through social compact in New England and the democratic ideals expressed therein will be discussed further in the next chapter.

Proprietary Grant Colonies

The last method of establishing colonies overseas was the royal proprietary grant. In Maryland, for example, King Charles I granted Lord Baltimore lands along with an almost absolute right to rule over them. Under this proprietary grant, Lord Baltimore enjoyed kingly status over his subjects in Maryland. Although a legislative assembly similar to Virginia's House of Burgesses was later established in Maryland, this proprietary charter colony offered an example of the direct transfer of English political structures to the New World. Carolina and New York were established as proprietary grant colonies under Charles II. In 1681, the famous Quaker William Penn obtained a proprietary grant to found a colony west of the Delaware River. The colony included a legislative assembly in its original design. Pennsylvania's assembly provided a countervailing source of power to the royal executive and would be the sole governmental authority after the American Revolution.

Structure of Government: Colonial Experience

The three types of colonies offered Americans different concrete structures for their political institutions. All three would play a role in making up the constitutional system that was put in place in the late 1700s. In addition to the original methods of colonization, Americans drew upon over a century and a half of political experience. Political conflicts between England and the colonies and within the colonies themselves shaped the way Americans looked at government and how it ought to be organized.

It would be a mistake to see American colonial history as the same throughout the colonies. Differences between colonies were significant. Differences existed between northern and southern colonies in the degree to which the colony's legal system adhered to the English model. The northern colonies deviated more from English legal traditions than did the southern colonies, which on the whole were more conservative.

In addition, a colony's religious principles often meant different laws and political institutions. For example, religion clearly influenced the government's character at Massachusetts Bay. Primarily middle-class Puritans seeking refuge from Anglican church domination, the people at Massachusetts Bay believed that God had covenanted with them to establish this distinct community. Religious belief formed the foundation for the polity and many of its laws. In addition, the colony's leaders, most notably Governor John Winthrop, saw themselves as commanded by God to rule the people in line with Calvinist principles. Winthrop's views about a people's religious calling and their covenant with God translated into more conservative, authoritarian political ideas. In the eighteenth century, however, John Wise would use the same Puritan foundations to argue for more democratic church and state governance.

The mode of church governance adopted was another aspect of religion affecting colonial politics. As a rule, colonies where the congregational form of church government was predominant tended toward greater decentralization and diffusion of power. Those colonies containing more churches governed upon the presbyterian model tended to be more hierarchical and centralized in their political decision making.

Of course, differences in colonial structure and experience would produce difficulties in bringing the former colonies together after the Revolution, as Chapter 3 will indicate. Still, despite these and other significant differences, a number of factors were felt across the American colonies. Two crucial developments—which ultimately ran at cross-purposes—uniformly molded colonial political theory and practice: the increased coordination of colonial affairs from England and the rise of the colonial assembly as a lawmaking body. By the late 1600s England began forcing its administrative will on all the colonies. By setting up new courts, passing navigation and tax laws, achieving greater central coordination through the royal governor, and increasing the colonies' commercial dependence, England brought the colonies more in line with the English legal system. At the same time, however, imperial England began to deny that the colonists had the same rights as Englishmen. Especially after the Glorious Revolution and the Parliament's passage of the Bill of Rights in 1689 (see Brief 2.3), many colonists began to press for recognition of the "constitutional rights of Englishmen." The right to be represented in elected assemblies, to initiate legislation on all matters (even fiscal matters), and to be free from arbitrary deprivation of liberty and property were continually invoked by colonists after 1688. English leaders denied these claims, viewing the colonies as royal dominions and their inhabitants as possessing no inalienable constitutional rights. The full "rights of Englishmen" aside, by the 1700s the colonies had adopted many of the practices and institutions of England.

However, the rise in prominence of the colonial assemblies counteracted this imperial thrust from London. Each colony's legislative assembly had by the 1700s become a formidable power, with Pennsylvania leading the way. The colonists became accustomed to self-rule through their local legislatures, using them to make their own laws as well as to challenge imperial authority. By waiting until later in the seventeenth century to assert imperial control, England may have begun too late. The ideals and practices of home rule were already in place, not to be dislodged without a fight.

From their experiences with England beginning in the late 1600s, the colonists learned that discretionary executive power was the greatest threat to their liberty and autonomy. Time and again the colonists had to defend themselves against arbitrary royal power, exercised by both king and royal governor alike. Of course, this lesson had been learned by the English themselves. The conflict between king and Parliament was clear in the colonists' minds. Having experienced the oppressiveness of royal authority, newly independent Americans wrote state constitutions designed to limit the authority of their chief

---

☐ *Brief 2.3   The English Bill of Rights*

Drafted by Parliament and accepted by William and Mary on February 13, 1689, the Bill of Rights stands as the cornerstone of the Glorious Revolution, which had deposed James II and returned Parliament to ultimate sovereignty. The Bill of Rights begins by documenting the crimes committed against the people and the Protestant religion by Catholic King James II. It concludes by declaring Parliament supreme, disallowing future kings from suspending any laws or their execution and from spending money without parliamentary consent.

But the Bill of Rights also contains specific guarantees that would become important in the revolutionary battles in the American colonies in the 1760s and 1770s and would be written into the U.S. Constitution. The 1689 act establishes the right of British subjects to petition the king, which the American colonists made use of on a number of occasions prior to 1776. It makes illegal the keeping of a standing army in time of peace without parliamentary consent, a principle the colonists fought for vociferously, as the next

chapter will indicate. Moreover, the English Bill of Rights exists as a precursor to the American Bill of Rights. Specific guarantees against "excessive bail [or] fines" and "cruel and unusual punishments" found in Parliament's 1689 law are contained word for word in the Eighth Amendment, while the general provisions about jury trials read much like the U.S. Constitution's wording in the Sixth and Seventh Amendments. In addition, the bill protects the free speech and debate rights of members of Parliament by preventing them from being questioned or impeached over statements made during parliamentary proceedings. An identical protection for members of Congress appears in Article I, Section 6, of the U.S. Constitution.

The English Bill of Rights signaled the culmination of a revolutionary century in Great Britain and was a watershed in the historical relationship between king and Parliament. But it also existed as a precedent for the revolutionary claims of American colonists in the next century and would serve as a landmark in their adoption of constitutional provisions in 1787 and 1791.

executive. In these state constitutions the former colonists also indicated a preference for legislative over executive power. (The specific problems the new republic experienced as a result of this preference will be examined in the following chapter.)

Americans would ultimately emerge from their eighteenth-century battles with a constitution based upon a separation-of-powers system, with a specific set of checks and balances to give each branch in the government the authority to enforce the separation of powers. Some people have mistakenly argued that the separation-of-powers doctrine was already present in the colonies prior to 1776. On the contrary, the colonies, again borrowing from classical Roman and contemporary English practices, had exhibited the principles of the **mixed constitution**. Under the mixed constitution, different components (governor, council, assembly, courts) representing different classes or interests *shared* government powers. The different branches of colonial government were not separated during the prerevolutionary era, but combined to exercise authority. It was only after 1787 that a separation of powers was put into place.

The other important question about government structure concerned the amount of power to give local authority. Colonial experience favored decentralized authority. The New England township, in conjunction with the congregational church, wielded considerable authority over many local policy matters. Similarly, in the mid-Atlantic and southern colonies, the county was the principal unit of local administration. Though often dominated by the upper classes, local governments thrived throughout the American colonies and provided a major impetus toward independence. By the mid-1700s many colonists had come to feel that the desired combination of liberty with meaningful political community could only flourish under a system favoring strong local government.

Conclusion

As this chapter indicates, American constitutionalism comprises a number of elements. The individualist theory of politics (or classical liberalism), as exemplified in the writings of John Locke, certainly underlies many constitutional principles and structures. The other theoretical pillar of American constitutionalism can be found in the communitarian theory of government (or classical republicanism), exhibited in writers like Jean-Jacques Rousseau. Additionally, a rich intellectual heritage of Western political and religious thought, beginning in ancient Greece, informs American constitutional theory and practice. Finally, over a century of historical experience in the colonies, involving political interaction within colonies as well as between the colonies and Great Britain, influenced the molding of American political institutions.

These basic elements of American constitutionalism were all in place by the 1760s. The colonists' ideas about human nature and the proper role of government in individual's lives had been formed by a rich intellectual and practical heritage. Specific conflicts in the 1760s and 1770s provided the final impetus toward independence. The specific actors and issues surrounding the making of the American Constitution are the subject of Chapter 3.

Questions

1.   Do you find the tension between the individualist and communitarian strands of political thought present in contemporary policy controversies such as abortion, AIDS, drug testing, pornography, and affirmative action? If so, given the severe conflict over these contemporary issues, is it fair to describe the two theories as co-existing in tension (which may be beneficial), or are they really locked in mortal conflict?

2.   What role does religion play in the history of American constitutionalism? If religion and religious ideas carry such an important weight in influencing American constitutionalism, why is it that judges interpret the Constitution as requiring a strict separation between church and state? Shouldn't the Constitution be more accommodating to religion, given its historic role in the foundation of American constitutionalism?

3.   As you will see in Chapter 4, difficult questions arise over the method and functions of judicial interpretation in a constitutional democracy. What role should judges interpreting and applying the U.S. Constitution give to the general theories and historical traditions discussed in this chapter? If you were a Supreme Court justice, how would you incorporate these factors into your judicial analysis and interpretation?

4.   What English legal and political practices contributed to American constitutionalism? What role did the different types of colonial settlements play in establishing constitutionalism? What were the significant differences between the colonies that made union more difficult?

5.   What writers in the history of Western political thought had an influence on America's constitution writers? What ideas did Americans borrow from the tradition of Western thought, and what ideas were homegrown?

Endnotes

1.   Charles Evans Hughes, speech at Elmira, N.Y., March 3, 1907, quoted by Sanford Levinson, "On Interpretation," *Southern California Law Review* 58 (1985): 724.

2.   Alexander Hamilton, John Jay, and James Madison, "Federalist No. 51," *The Federalist Papers* (New York: Modern Library, 1937), 337.

3.   Use of the concept negative freedom is most associated with Sir Isaiah Berlin, who fully explained it and distinguished it from positive freedom in his *Four Essays on Freedom* (London: Oxford University Press, 1969). A more recent attempt to refine the concept appears in Richard Flathman's *The Philosophy and Politics of Freedom* (Chicago: University of Chicago Press, 1987). In judicial circles the concept is embodied in Justice Louis D. Brandeis's famous defense of "the right to be let alone" by the government.

4.   The best example of Friedman's individualism can be found in his book *Capitalism and Freedom* (Chicago: University of Chicago Press, 1962), where he argues against such governmental intrusions into personal liberty as social security, public education, and civil rights legislation.

5.   See, e.g., Benjamin Barber, *Strong Democracy* (Berkeley, Calif.: University of California Press, 1984): Jane Mansbridge, *Beyond Adversary Democracy* (New York: Basic Books, 1980)

6.   Madison, "Federalist No. 51," 339.

7.   Edward S. Corwin, "The 'Higher Law' Background of American Constitutional Law," *Harvard Law Review* 42 (1928): 149.

8.   Thomas Paine, *Rights of Man* (New York: Penguin Books, 1969), 187.

9.   See Wilson Carey McWilliams, *The Idea of Fraternity in America*

(Berkeley, Calif.: University of California Press, 1973), 496–98.

10. Quoted in Corwin, "The 'Higher Law' Background," 368.

11. "The Mayflower Compact, November 11, 1620," in Henry Steele Commager, ed., *Documents of American History,* 8th ed. (New York: Meredith, 1963), 15–16.

Suggested Readings

Bellah, Robert N., et al. *Habits of the Heart: Individualism and Commitment in American Life.* New York: Harper & Row, 1985.

Berman, Harold. *Law and Revolution.* Cambridge, Mass: Harvard University Press, 1983.

Corwin, Edward S. "The 'Higher Law' Background of American Constitutional Law." *Harvard Law Review* 42 (1928): 149–85.

Kammen, Michael. *Deputyes and Libertyes: The Origins of Representative Government in Colonial America.* New York: Knopf, 1969.

Locke, John. *The Second Treatise on Government.* Ed. Peter Laslett. New York: Cambridge University Press, 1960.

McLaughlin, Andrew C. *The Foundations of American Constitutionalism.* New York: Appleton-Century, 1932.

Montesquieu, Baron de. *The Spirit of the Laws.* New York: Hafner Press, 1949.

Parrington, Vernon L. *Main Currents in American Thought.* Vol. 1. New York: Harcourt, Brace & World, 1927.

Pocock, J. G. A. *The Ancient Constitution and the Feudal Law: A Study of English Historical Thought in the Seventeenth Century.* New York: Cambridge University Press, 1957.

Rousseau, Jean-Jacques. *The Social Contract.* Ed. Roger D. Masters. New York: St. Martin's Press, 1978.

3

American Constitutionalism: The Founding Generation

Syllabus

A number of constitutional scholars as well as politicians believe that the only legitimate way to interpret the U.S. Constitution is by reference to the original intentions of its framers. These advocates of a "constitutional jurisprudence of original intention" contend that the original intentions of those who drafted the Constitution have been subverted by contemporary judges applying their own standards and values to constitutional interpretation. But even if this approach is adopted, it must be realized that the intentions of the framers can only be understood within the context of a revolutionary generation and the political events that shaped their understanding of constitutional government. It is impossible to understand, for example, the framers' compromise over slavery at the Constitutional Convention without taking note of the competing economic and political interests that clashed at Philadelphia. Accordingly, the entire range of political opinion and interests during late eighteenth-century America must be examined to fully appreciate the original intention of the Constitution's framers.

This Chapter Examines the Following Matters

☐ Colonial legal and political issues in the 1760s and 1770s moved Americans toward independence from Great Britain and raised *constitutional* concerns that would predominate throughout the founding period.

☐ By the time the colonists made their final break with the British Crown and Parliament in 1776, they had already formulated innovative constitutional ideas and practices. The Declaration of Independence exemplifies many of these revolutionary political ideas.

☐ Provisions for postrevolutionary governments in the states and at the federal level (issuing in the Articles of Confederation) created problems that impelled American leaders to propose a meeting in Philadelphia in 1787 to solve the constitutional crisis.

☐ Originally convened to amend the Articles of Confederation, the state representatives who met in Philadelphia during the summer of 1787 actually created a new constitutional document. The delegates' purposes are revealed in the issues they debated and placed in the U.S. Constitution.

☐ The ratification struggle between Federalists and Anti-Federalists was at times ferocious. A wealth of competing political theories exists in this debate over the effects and desirability of the new federal Constitution.

☐ The Constitution has continued to be characterized by some, beginning with the Anti-Federalists, as a betrayal of the revolutionary goals of the Declaration of Independence. Critics have charged that the Constitution is an antidemocratic document.

Photo: The meeting room in Independence Hall is arranged as it was when delegates congregated over the summer of 1787 to draft the U.S. Constitution. The document produced from this room represents the revolutionary experiment of an entire generation *(Photographed with the courtesy of the Philadelphia Convention and Visitors Bureau).*

Constitutionalism and the American Revolution

The American Constitution adopted in 1787 was actually the culmination of a revolution started in the early 1760s. A generation of rebellion against English rule and of American experiments in popular government preceded the writing of the U.S. Constitution. The revolutionary events that predated the Constitution must be examined in order to understand the structure and content of that document. The discussion turns first, then, to the events that caused the American Revolution.

In one respect, the American Revolution was not all that revolutionary. The revolution of 1776 differs from revolutions in the modern world. It did not involve the violent upheaval of social forces and institutions. And, unlike modern third-world anticolonial revolutions, the American revolutionaries were not out to create a system to guarantee political rights that were previously nonexistent. In fact, the colonists saw themselves as trying to preserve their ancient constitutions (which they traced all the way back to the tenth century) and the basic liberties that they had enjoyed for 150 years until English rule suddenly became oppressive.

Americans had already declared independence from their homeland by the very act of their emigration. They had, like their Saxon ancestors, uprooted themselves, leaving their previous communities to find a new life in the New World. Many had come to seek asylum from religious, political, and social oppression. Upon arriving, they set up institutions based upon popular consent. Emigrants sought control over those matters in which they had invested their lives and fortunes. The colonists accepted imperial rule from London, but only insofar as English governments did not trample on their basic liberties.

A look at colonial documents and writings during the 1760s and 1770s supports this perspective. References abound to the colonists' circumstances of emigrating to the New World. Resistance originally took the form of petitions to the king and Parliament to stop interfering with the colonists' fundamental rights. American revolutionaries saw America as destined to fill the role of preserving the ancient constitution going all the way back to Saxon times. England had grown corrupt and decadent, they argued, and it was up to America to purge the English constitution of its impurities in order to preserve ancient liberties enjoyed in earlier times. All the way up until the summer of 1776, American revolutionaries themselves insisted that their action was constitutional resistance to unconstitutional governance by the British Parliament. In their own minds, the colonists revolted not against the English constitution but on behalf of it. The essentially conservative nature of the American Revolution was grasped by the famous English conservative Edmund Burke, who took the colonists' side in the struggle and argued that it was the British who were suddenly revolting from decades of political history and practice.

The lasting power of the colonial heritage lends further credence to the fact that the American Revolution was basically conservative. After independence was won, Americans drew liberally upon their colonial charters and upon English law and customs in setting up their new institutions. In fact, two states, Rhode Island and Connecticut, basically kept their colonial charters as their state constitutions well into the 1800s.

In another important sense, however, the American Revolution and what it accomplished *was* truly revolutionary. The generation who made the revolution not only sought independence from Great Britain. In addition, they wanted to create, as the Great Seal of the United States reads, "a new order of the ages." They established political institutions in line with revolutionary beliefs about human equality, popular sovereignty, and natural rights. When the colonists broke with Great Britain, an experiment began to create institutions that would truly be based upon the consent of the governed. Furthermore, a revolution in constitutional thinking took place after 1776 as well.

Emerging American Constitutionalism (1760–1776)

Events in the 1760s brought the conflict between England and the American colonies to a head. The crisis created by British attempts to rule the colonies in this period structured the way Americans looked at politics and constitutionalism. Three constitutional issues emerged from this period that would lead Americans to revolution and would shape the constitutions they wrote following independence.

First, the colonists asserted that they had certain fundamental rights, found in nature as well as in the British constitution. Colonists argued that Parliament could not interfere with these rights. Any law attempting to deprive colonists of their rights was unconstitutional and could be resisted. As the conflict between Parliament and the colonies intensified, the colonists became more fervent in their defense of these natural rights. This defense culminated in the Declaration of Independence, which begins with the statement that natural rights are the foundation for all government. One of the first examples of the individualist strain in American political thought is seen in this assertion of inalienable natural rights.

The second issue related to the fact that American colonists began forming a different concept of law and legislative power. They began to distinguish between what was "constitutional" and what was "legal." The British never made this distinction, believing that the constitution, the common law, and acts of Parliament were all mixed together. The British believed that Parliament's actions were part of the constitutional heritage and could not be set against the British constitution. But as a result of laws passed by Parliament to which the colonists objected, Americans began to speak of basic principles in the constitution that stood above lawmaking authority. Americans came to believe that a constitution establishes general principles that could never be overridden by legislation, no matter how representative the legislature was of the people. Origins of American constitutionalism and the doctrine of judicial review can be seen in this distinction.

Finally, the crisis beginning in the 1760s raised the issue of local colonial autonomy. As was mentioned in the preceding chapter, Americans had been accustomed to regulating their affairs locally, through town and county meetings and through their colonial assemblies. Americans had adopted the classical republican view that popular rule and public virtue were best maintained at the local level. The attempt by Parliament to control matters from London led the colonists to assert a right to colonial self-rule within the empire. The belief in local self-government contributed to powerful states and localities in the early postrevolutionary years and to the peculiar brand of federalism found in the American constitutional system today.

In addition to these three constitutional issues, the colonists continually proclaimed their republican virtue over what they saw as British corruption. American revolutionaries saw the battle with England as one between power and liberty, between rigid social distinctions and equality, between corrupting luxury and independent republican virtue. The colonists' Protestant background made them suspicious of those in power; human nature made power a tool for domination and corruption. Many references appear in revolutionary era writings to the king's "licentious ministry," his corrupt use of power to "enslave the colonies." John Adams contended that England could not provide the proper environment for liberty because it was a place "where luxury, effeminacy and venality are arrived at such a shocking pitch [and where] both electors and elected become one mass of corruption." [1] By contrast, Americans, free from debilitating social distinctions and corrupting luxuries and refinements, were capable of constructing republican institutions that could preserve civic virtue and pious industriousness. The theme of corruption recurs after independence, and once again in the constitutional ratification fight in 1787.

The Stamp Act

As discussed earlier, Parliament's powers over the American colonies were first exercised in the navigation and trade acts beginning in 1651. But until the close of the Seven Years' War (also called the Great War for the Empire and the French and Indian Wars) in 1763, Americans did not feel the full force of parliamentary rule. After the Treaty of Paris which ended the war, however, England introduced changes in imperial policy designed to alleviate its huge war debt and make colonial administration more efficient. After closing the area west of the Alleghenies to further colonial settlement, Parliament passed two bills to help finance the large public debt: the Sugar Act of 1764 and the Stamp Act of 1765. The Sugar Act placed a small tax on a variety of goods imported into the colonies—including molasses, sugar, coffee, indigo, wines, and linens. The Stamp Act was an excise tax requiring revenue stamps for a variety of legal documents, newspapers, and even playing cards. The Stamp Act touched almost every area of economic life in the colonies. Both the Sugar Act and the Stamp Act were measures designed solely to raise revenue (as opposed to regulating colonial trade or commerce), to "defray the expenses of defending, protecting, and securing the colonies." [2]

Colonial resistance to these two attempts at direct taxation by Parliament was swift and strong. Some historians have claimed that the colonists' main objections to the laws were economic. But this is clearly not borne out by documentary evidence. After all, Britain had imposed taxes upon imports earlier in the 1700s in order to regulate colonial trade. In fact, the tax upon imported molasses during the 1730s was twice that imposed by the Sugar Act, with little colonial complaint. Opposition to the Stamp and Sugar acts was primarily constitutional. Colonists responded to these laws, especially the Stamp Act, with the famous slogan "No taxation without representation." Underneath that slogan lay all three constitutional issues mentioned earlier.

The first constitutional complaint was that these acts of Parliament interfered with the colonists' fundamental rights to liberty and property, rights derived both from nature and from their British heritage. The colonists, following Locke, conceived of property as a natural right, the very source of life and liberty. Not only do persons need material possessions to sustain their lives, but also they need a secure source of property to maintain their independence. Without property a person must depend upon the mercy of other people for food and clothing. Property and liberty were considered one and inseparable. As a result, colonists argued—and they had ample support from British history—property must not be taken from individuals without their consent, either directly or through their representatives: "No taxation without representation." This argument is reflected in a resolution proposed by Patrick Henry in the Virginia House of Burgesses, which declared that "the Taxation of the People by themselves, or by Persons chosen to represent them" was a "distinguishing Characteristick of *British* Freedom, without which the ancient Constitution cannot exist." [3] In addition, the method the British used to enforce the revenue-raising measures was felt to directly invade the colonists' rights. General warrants were used extensively to search and seize the merchandise in ships and warehouses. Colonists fought this invasion of their right to be secure in their property and effects, and would later enshrine the right against such general warrants in the Fourth Amendment (see Brief 8.3).

A second and related argument, offered most forcefully by James Otis in his *Rights of the British Colonies Asserted and Proved*, was that any law in violation of the constitution and "common reason" could be declared void and unenforceable. Otis claimed that, given the constitutional principle that property not be taken without consent, Parliament had violated this principle in passing the Sugar Act. Citing Coke, he argued that "acts of Parliament against natural equity [or] against the fundamental principles of the British constitution are void." [4]

Finally, colonists objected to the invasion of colonial home rule which these acts represented. Parliament's attempt at direct taxation interfered with the colonial assembly's right to rule over internal police and taxation matters. Patrick Henry proclaimed that Virginians had always enjoyed, through their legislative assembly, "the inestimable right of being governed by such Laws, respecting their internal Polity and Taxation, as are derived from their own consent." [5] Only the colonial legislature in its representative capacity could lay taxes on its own people, not Parliament.

All but two of the American colonies made official objections to the Stamp Act. The Stamp Act Congress, an intercolonial assembly representing nine colonies, was convened during October 1765. It issued a set of resolutions and petitions to the king and Parliament requesting repeal of the Stamp Act and denying Parliament's authority to tax them. The Stamp Act Congress agreed with Patrick Henry that "the only Representatives of the people of these colonies are people chosen therein by themselves, and that no taxes have been, or can be constitutionally imposed upon them, but by their respective legislatures." [6]

The British response to American opposition reflected a different conception of fundamental rights and constitutionalism. To the colonists' first complaint about taxation without representation, Parliament responded with the doctrine of virtual representation. Though not *actually* represented by members chosen from the colonies, all citizens within the empire were virtually represented by Parliament. Parliament similarly denied the distinction between its actions and the British constitution. Most members of Parliament thought it heresy to declare that the British constitution, which Parliament had helped establish, set boundaries on what Parliament could do. Finally, Parliament denied the colonists' assertion of a divided sovereignty within the empire. The colonists were contending that the functions and powers of imperial government could be split up, with Parliament issuing laws governing the empire as a whole but the colonial legislatures retaining power over their internal matters. If sovereignty were so divided, Parliament responded, government would lose its supreme authority. In parliamentary debates over proposed repeal of the Stamp Act, Lord Lyttleton stated that "in all states . . . the government must rest somewhere, and that must be fixed, or otherwise there is an end of all government . . . The only question before your lordships is, whether the American colonies are a part of the dominions or the crown of Great Britain? If not, Parliament has no jurisdiction, if they are, as many statutes have declared them to be, they must be proper subjects of our legislation." [7]

American protest against the Stamp Act, including nonimportation agreements against British products and popular demonstrations against those administering the tax in the colonies, did succeed in getting Parliament to repeal the act in 1766. But in repealing the Stamp Act, Parliament did not give in on the question of sovereignty. The Declaratory Act of 1766 stated that Parliament had full authority to make laws for the colonies "in all cases whatsoever." Most Americans celebrated the Stamp Act's repeal, but some were concerned about the extent of parliamentary authority claimed in the Declaratory Act. John Adams questioned "whether they will lay a tax in consequence of that resolution." The answer, he would soon see, was yes.

The Townshend Acts

In 1767, under prompting by Chancellor of the Exchequer Charles Townshend, England continued its efforts to tax the colonies to raise needed revenues. Townshend had devised a tax plan that he felt could not be objected to by Americans. When Benjamin Franklin had come to Parliament in 1766 to testify before the House of Commons on the Stamp Act, he had distinguished between internal taxes, which the colonists opposed, and external taxes, which presumably would be acceptable to them. Acting on Franklin's distinction, Townshend proposed a full series of external taxes. Parliament passed a revenue measure levying duties upon items imported into the colonies such as glass, lead, paints, paper, and tea. The duties were designed to pay for governing the colonies. Townshend also proposed a separate board of customs commissioners, located in Boston, to supervise the collection of American duties. At the same time, Parliament approved new admiralty courts to try violations of navigation and customs laws and authorized writs of assistance, which gave colonial officials open-ended search powers in customs cases.

The Townshend Acts brought immediate resistance from the colonies. Americans reestablished nonimportation associations, reconvened their Sons of Liberty associations to fight the hated measures, and called extralegal assemblies throughout the colonies to declare the acts invalid. John Dickinson in Pennsylvania and Sam Adams in Massachusetts led the opposition to the Townshend Acts and made powerful constitutional arguments against compliance (see Brief 3.1).

Americans objected to the Townshend Acts for a number of reasons. Not only were these measures a renewed attempt to tax the colonists oppres-

☐ *Brief 3.1   Early Revolutionary Leaders: Samuel Adams and John Dickinson*

In the early years of resistance to British rule, two men led the constitutional fight: Sam Adams and John Dickinson. Their writings and actions stirred colonists to desire independence. Moreover, the principles behind their arguments against the British Parliament formed the crux of emerging American constitutionalism, principles that would find their way into the Declaration of Independence and the U.S. Constitution.

Adams came from a prominent Massachusetts family, and, after graduating from Harvard in 1740, devoted himself to local and state politics. He was a founder of the Sons of Liberty association and later of the Committee of Correspondence, which fueled American independence. One of his most important writings in this early revolutionary period was a 1772 statement entitled "The Rights of the Colonists," in which he laid out the basis of colonial resistance to parliamentary actions. Adams stressed the natural rights of the colonists—as men, as Christians, and as British subjects—which he felt were fixed and immutable. Taking his cue from earlier thinkers like Locke, Adams believed that Parliament was empowered to guarantee these natural rights and could not abridge them. To do so was tantamount to political heresy and could be rightly resisted. The natural-rights basis of American constitutionalism is reflected in Adams's position.

Dickinson, a distinguished lawyer from Pennsylvania and Delaware, was a more conservative man than was Adams. But he consistently spoke out against British actions after 1763 and was a leader of the American Revolution and of the government that succeeded it. In his "Letters from a Farmer in Pennsylvania to the Inhabitants of the British Colonies," written in 1767 and 1768, he laid out his arguments against the Townshend Acts. Dickinson was generally supportive of parliamentary power to regulate trade and to act as superintendent over the colonial empire. But when it came to taxation, he believed that the colonial assemblies had sole authority to act. He argued that the colonists' political liberty depended upon their sovereignty over taxation. They must be allowed to make tax policy directly, or through their own chosen representatives. Dickinson was calling for a divided sovereignty between Parliament and the colonial assemblies. In his writings can be found the precursor to American federalism.

These two men were widely read and followed. Their respective positions on natural rights and divided sovereignty would also be followed in 1776, and later in establishing a new federal government in the late 1780s.

sively without their consent, but also they represented a new system of enforcement. Customs commissioners in the past had been guilty of greed and corruption. Now they would be more numerous, independent from any colonial control, financed by colonists' money, and potentially tyrannical in their rule. Moreover, this enlarged bureaucracy would be supported by a judicial system that was less independent. The new admiralty courts would systematically undermine the much-heralded colonial jury system, and judges would owe their allegiance to the Crown rather than to colonial assemblies, which in the past had paid their salaries. Furthermore, newly authorized writs of assistance would allow customs officers to search colonists' homes and properties at will, a clear violation of their natural property rights as Englishmen.

This time resistance was more adamant. In Boston, the Massachusetts Assembly sent a circular letter to the other colonies denying Parliament's right to tax the colonies and asking the other assemblies to pass declarations against the Townshend Acts. Lord Hillsborough, English secretary of state, ordered Massachusetts to rescind the letter and asked the other colonies to treat it "with the contempt it deserves." [8] Massachusetts refused, and the other colonial assemblies showed their solidarity by formally approving the letter. Meanwhile, in Massachusetts customs officials had requested help from England in enforcing the laws in the wake of the colonists' open defiance. Hillsborough sent British troops to Boston in September 1768 to enforce the Townshend Acts.

British troops stationed in the colonies raised a number of critical issues. Americans had long felt that a standing army was inconsistent with liberty. It was a long-held tenet of classical republican thought that professional armies, especially ones not composed of the local population, threatened a community's liberty. The threat lay, in Thomas Jefferson's words, in making "the civil subordinate to the military." [9] The republican solution was to arm citizen-soldiers for such time as was necessary to the community's defense. Not only was there a threat to liberty, however, but also maintaining a standing British army would eat into the colonists' pocketbooks. Under the Quartering Act of 1765 colonial assemblies were required to furnish food and shelter to soldiers stationed in their provinces. New York had incurred Britain's wrath by defying this command for a time.

To protect their liberty as well as their property, colonists fought the quartering of British troops. As the troops were to arrive, Bostonians called a town meeting. A declaration was passed that stated that the keeping of a standing army "without their consent in person or by representatives of their own free election, would be an infringement of their natural, constitutional and charter rights; and the employing such Army for the enforcing of laws made without the consent of the people in person or by their representatives would be a grievance." [10] The colonists would soon find that these were not mere abstract constitutional concerns. On March 5, 1770, British troops fired on an unruly Boston crowd, killing five and wounding six others. Memories of the abuses incurred by the forced quartering of British troops would remain through the founding period, and the colonists' initial concerns would make their way into the Third Amendment to the U.S. Constitution. It commands that "no Soldier shall, in time of peace, be quartered in any house, without the consent of the owner, nor in time of war, but in a manner to be prescribed by law."

The Tea Act

A colonial revolution was averted in 1770 when Parliament repealed all the new taxes except the duty on imported tea (a duty still existed on molasses as well). Colonial boycotts ended, and a period of relative peace and prosperity began that would last until 1773.

Colonists had not forgotten their constitutional complaints against England. Following Adams, they still asserted their natural and constitutional rights to liberty, to property, and to a jury trial. They believed that any law Parliament passed that abridged these basic liberties was illegitimate. And following Dickinson's arguments, they pressed for local autonomy and colonial self-government. Over internal police matters, the payment of judges and governors, and taxation, the colonists firmly held to a notion of colonial sovereignty. But at this point, most colonists were not willing to break with England. They deferred to Parliament's right to regulate matters concerning trade and the general welfare of the empire and wanted to remain British subjects. If Britain only would concede sovereignty to the colonial assemblies and refrain from trampling on their constitutional rights as Englishmen, the colonists could live in peace with their British brethren.

In 1773, the struggle between British power and colonial liberty continued. The people of Boston had created the Committee of Correspondence in late 1772. This committee drafted a statement of colonial rights (written by

Sam Adams) and encouraged other towns to form similar committees to do likewise. By March 1773 the Virginia House of Burgesses was calling for committees of correspondence on an intercolonial basis. These committees were important sources of the resistance movement and would later conduct local government and war preparations.

Meanwhile, the Massachusetts Assembly had become embroiled in a fight with the royal governor appointed by the British Crown, the hated Thomas Hutchinson. In response to a series of Hutchinson's letters published in Massachusetts newspapers defending king and Parliament and bemoaning the sedition carried on by the colony, the assembly replied with a fervent defense of colonial sovereignty. A look at what the legislature said provides a sample of colonial constitutional ideas. Members of the Massachusetts Assembly claimed that as English citizens, they had a fundamental right "to be governed by laws made by themselves and by officers chosen by themselves." They declared they had "never consented that the Parliament of England or Great Britain should make laws binding upon us in all cases." [11] The desire for republican self-rule was strong.

By the spring of 1773, then, the colonists were primed to react simultaneously to Parliament's next move. Parliament acted in May. It passed the Tea Act, giving the East India Company a direct line to sell in America, without paying duties and without going through American wholesalers. The company could undersell all competitors and would drive many American merchants out of business. Committees of correspondence throughout the colonies spread the word to resist attempts to deliver the company's tea. In Boston, Governor Hutchinson, still angry at the open defiance with which the assembly had addressed him, ordered the tea-carrying ships to unload their cargo. Of course, on December 16, 1773, the people of Boston unloaded the tea themselves— into the harbor.

The Boston Tea Party brought the wrath of the English Parliament down upon the colonists, particularly those in Massachusetts. In early 1774, Britain passed a series of coercive measures known as the Intolerable Acts. In March, Parliament closed the port of Boston to all commerce until restitution was made to the East India Company. In May, Parliament changed the charter of Massachusetts to bring it under more direct British control. The Governor's Council, formerly selected by the assembly, would now be appointed by the king of England. The royal governor was given sole power to appoint judges, and regular town meetings were declared illegal. In addition, Parliament passed a law providing that any officer of the British Crown indicted for a felony committed within the colony of Massachusetts could be brought to England for trial, where he would not have to face a colonial jury. And to add insult to injury, Parliament provided that troops be quartered in Boston, by force if necessary, and that authority be given to quarter troops in other towns throughout the colonies.

The English government obviously hoped that other colonies would learn a lesson of obedience from these harsh actions taken against Massachusetts. But instead colonists rallied to support Massachusetts in its defense of colonial rights. Committees of correspondence took up a proposal from Boston to boycott all trade with Great Britain. And in September 1774, at the call of several colonies, the first intercolonial congress met in Philadelphia.

The First Continental Congress

All the colonies except Georgia sent delegates to the First Continental Congress. The delegates who came to Philadelphia had been chosen largely by local committees of correspondence, and they acted more like ambassadors of twelve distinct nations. An extralegal assembly throughout its term, the Continental Congress did not represent the existing colonial governments, but rather those people dissatisfied with British rule. And yet, some of the most distinguished men in America attended, including Sam Adams and John Adams of Massachusetts; John Dickinson of Pennsylvania; Roger Sherman of Connecticut; George Washington, Richard Henry Lee, and Patrick Henry of Virginia; and John Jay of New York. Many of these men would also meet in Philadelphia in 1787 to draft a new constitution for the United States.

The congress was split between conservatives and radicals. Joseph Galloway of New York, representing the more conservative faction at the meetings, offered a conciliatory plan for union between England and the colonies. Under it, colonial policy would be made by a joint British and American legislature. Galloway's plan provided for a grand council, representing the people in all the colonies and presided over by a president-general appointed by the king. Either the grand council or the English Parliament could originate laws regulating the colonies, but both legislatures would have to agree to make a law official.

The more radical delegates were in no mood for conciliatory measures, however. They rejected Galloway's plan and proposed one of their own. Thomas Jefferson, too ill to attend the congress, sent resolutions announcing a more complete break with England and Parliament. Later published under the title "A Summary View of the Rights of British America," Jefferson's resolutions began by asserting that having "spilt their own blood" and "expended their own fortunes" in emigrating to America, the colonists were independent from parliamentary control. He made reference to the ancient Saxon constitution and the common law tradition as the source of colonial rights against the king and Parliament. Jefferson denied Parliament's authority to legislate for the colonies and declared that acts passed by Parliament "prove a deliberate and systematical plan of reducing us to slavery."

The delegates to the First Continental Congress adopted milder language than Jefferson's, thanks to revisions offered by John Dickinson and John Adams. The official Declaration and Resolves of the First Continental Congress asserted the colonists' rights to life, liberty, and property and to assemble peaceably in order to consider their grievances and petition the king. They stated that the colonists were entitled to the common law of England and all the "privileges and immunities of free and natural-born subjects within the realm of England." The resolutions denounced British actions meant to deny the colonists' rights, particularly the placement of standing armies and the interference with colonial justice and legislation.

The most important statement of the congress appears in Article IV of the declaration. Authored by John Adams, Article IV asserted the legislative independence of the colonies over all internal matters. It stated:

> The foundation of English liberty, and of all free government, is a right in the people to participate in their legislative council: and as the English colonists are not represented, and from their local and other circumstances cannot properly

be represented in the British Parliament, they are entitled to a free and exclusive power of legislation in their several provincial legislatures, where their rights of representation can alone be preserved, in all cases of taxation and internal polity, subject only to the negative of their sovereign, in such manner as has been heretofore used and accustomed. But, from the necessity of the case, and a regard to the mutual interest of both countries, we cheerfully consent to the operation of such Acts of the British Parliament, as are bona fide restrained to the regulation of our external commerce, for the purpose of securing the commercial advantages of the whole empire to the mother country, and the commercial benefits of its respective members; excluding every idea of taxation, internal or external, for raising a revenue on the subjects in America without their consent.[12]

Radicals also pressed for and won the creation of a continental association, which would coordinate a nonimportation and nonconsumption agreement against all British goods. If Parliament did not repeal the Intolerable Acts within a year, the association would begin prohibiting all exports to Britain as well. So with strong words and deeds, the First Continental Congress defied British authority in colonial affairs.

Despite the radicals' victory, there was still no general call for complete independence. Most delegates still saw themselves as part of the British Empire under the king, with the constitutional rights of Englishmen. As Article IV had noted, they had begrudgingly granted Parliament the authority to regulate external commerce and general imperial matters. They accepted royal prerogative to act for the common good of all English subjects. However, the Continental Congress had moved to a more extreme denial of parliamentary authority to legislate on any colonial matters, not just matters of taxation. Had the British accepted a federal structure of imperial governance, giving the colonists home rule, this may have met the most important colonial demands.

The Continental Congress represented an extralegal political organization at the intercolonial level. But the colonists were also busy forming revolutionary governments at the local level. Formal governments were dissolved, either by the king's governors or by the colonists themselves, and provincial congresses were elected to take their place. By the end of 1774, eight colonies had established provincial congresses. At the local level, committees of correspondence began assuming many governmental powers. These town committees led the resistance to British rule. They gave force to nonimportation agreements by publicly shaming and intimidating those who would not comply with the boycott. They later raised funds for local militia to fight the British. The committees of correspondence constituted a striking example of successful direct popular governance in American history.

Thus, two years prior to independence, the stage was set. Revolutionary governments were in place at every level in the American colonies. When Massachusetts militiamen and British troops engaged in battle at Concord and Lexington in April 1775, the political institutions necessary to independence and to carrying on the war to secure it were already functioning.

The Second Continental Congress and the Call to Independence
The Second Continental Congress met in May 1775. Delegates voted to raise a regular continental army to continue the war against Britain. They chose Washington to command the army. Even at this point, however, most members

of the congress wanted to remain within the British realm. They would fight Parliament's unconstitutional rule, but they thought it might be possible to remain under the king with their separate assemblies acting as Parliament's equals in the colonies. While they organized for war, the Second Continental Congress sent the so-called "Olive Branch Petition" to King George III, asking him to intervene and end Parliament's oppressive rule.

But King George instead issued the Proclamation of Rebellion in August, two days after the Olive Branch Petition arrived in London. And in December, Parliament passed the American Prohibitory Bill, cutting off all trade and commerce with the colonies and commanding seizure of American ships on the high seas. These two British actions impelled many colonists who had previously been opposed to independence in that direction. The king's declaration brought him directly into the struggle, where before the colonists' opposition had been to Parliament or to "king-in-Parliament." Richard Henry Lee confirmed the importance of the Prohibitory Bill and the anger of colonists toward it when he declared:

> Whilst people here are disputing and hesitating about independancy, the Court, by one bold Act of Parliament, and by a conduct the most extensively hostile, have already put the two countries asunder. The measure of British crimes is running over, and the barbarious spoilation of the East is crying to Heaven for vengeance against the Destroyers of the Human Race.[13]

Americans were ready for separation from England by the beginning of 1776, but the publication of Thomas Paine's *Common Sense* in January provided the catalyst for independence. Paine's pamphlet expressed brilliantly and in language easily understood what Americans were waiting to hear. In it, Paine argued that the king was as oppressive as Parliament, and that the colonists' rights were incompatible with the British monarchy. He called upon Americans to throw off the yoke of monarchy and aristocracy and to take up the mantle of republican government. Asserting that "of more worth is one honest man to society, in the sight of God, than all the crowned ruffians that ever lived," Paine urged the colonists to abolish both the monarchy and the nobility in devising new political institutions. *Common Sense* was widely read throughout the colonies (it sold 120,000 copies in three months), and it changed the basis of colonial demands from the constitutional rights of Englishmen to the natural rights of humanity in general. Paine told the colonists, "The cause of America is in great measure the cause of all mankind." Conservatives recoiled from many of Paine's more radical arguments, but by April 1776, the formal establishment of independence along Paine's recommendations appeared inevitable.

Beginning in April, the congress acted swiftly to make the final separation from Great Britain. On April 6, it opened all American ports to foreign trade, thereby nullifying British trade restrictions. On May 15, the congress transferred all government power from Great Britain to the people of the colonies, and it instructed each colony to end all vestiges of royal authority and create new governments. On the same day the Virginia House of Burgesses instructed its congressional delegates to propose independence. Richard Henry Lee acted upon these instructions on June 7, 1776, when he introduced the following resolution before the congress:

> *Resolved*, that these United Colonies are, and of right ought to be, free and independent States, and that they are absolved from all allegiance to the British Crown, and that all connection between them and the State of Great Britain is, and ought to be, totally dissolved.[14]

The Declaration of Independence

Lee's resolution was referred to a five-man committee (Thomas Jefferson, John Adams, Benjamin Franklin, Roger Sherman, and Robert Livingston) to draft a declaration of independence while the rest of the delegates consulted their constituents on the wisdom of declaring independence. At this point not all Americans favored independence. The middle colonies in particular (New York, Pennsylvania, and Delaware) were initially opposed to Lee's resolution. The ease with which the radicals proposed separation from England made conservatives worry about what the result of independence might be. They feared what they might lose if the revolt were unsuccessful, or even if it succeeded, given the possibility of anarchy or mob rule.

Jefferson's Declaration of Independence was presented to the congress on July 2, with all but three delegates voting for adoption (New York abstained from voting). It was read in Philadelphia after some revision on July 4, and signed by the members of the congress on August 2, 1776.

The Declaration of Independence has been aptly described as more of a propaganda device than a real declaration of independence. The Continental Congress had already declared independence, informally at least, and the colonists had been engaging in a war of independence for over two years. The Declaration stands as a formal announcement, and more importantly as a justification to Britain and to the world of the decision to separate from the British Empire.

But the Declaration of Independence is more than propaganda. It is also an important constitutional document. It contains ideas about human nature and the proper foundations and ends of government that would guide Americans in setting up their independent political institutions. In fact, seven of the eleven states that wrote new constitutions after 1776 attached the Declaration to their state constitutions. The Declaration reflects the bipolar elements of individualism and communitarianism discussed in Chapter 2. Although there are some dramatic differences between the Declaration of Independence and the Constitution of 1787, which have led some to call the Constitution a betrayal of the Declaration's ideals (see the critique of the Constitution at the end of this chapter), the delegates to the constitutional convention saw the Declaration as the foundation of the document they were drafting.

Furthermore, the Declaration has been used since the founding period by Americans calling for basic changes in the constitutional system. Abolitionists used the Declaration to support their cause throughout the nineteenth century; Southern secessionists referred to it in 1861; populists cited it in calling for greater social justice in the late 1800s. The Supreme Court has used the Declaration on a number of occasions to justify the expansion of civil and political rights. A brief examination of the Declaration of Independence will bear out its importance as a constitutional document.

Jefferson began by stating the general principles that "impel . . . [the] people to dissolve the political bands which have connected them with another, and to assume among the powers of the earth the separate and equal station which the laws of nature and nature's god entitle them." The Declaration continues with the famous statement of natural rights and the ends of government, which follows the argument found in John Locke's *Second Treatise of Government:*

> We hold these truths to be self-evident: that all men are created equal; that they are endowed by their creator with certain unalienable rights; that among these are life, liberty and the pursuit of happiness.

Nature invests people with certain *inalienable* rights, which it is government's purpose to protect. Government derives its power solely from the consent of the people constituting it. The Declaration goes on to say that "when a long train of abuses and usurpations" of the people's rights occurs, "it is their right, it is their duty to throw off such government, and to provide new guards for their future security."

A seemingly straightforward individualist statement of the natural-rights foundation of politics, Jefferson's document also contains elements of the communitarian theory of government. The commitment to popular rule evident from Jefferson's words reflects the republican ideal of citizens deliberating in communities and embodying the common good in law. The bulk of the Declaration is devoted to detailing the specific "history of injuries and usurpations" done to the colonies by the king, most of which have to do with interfering with the people's right to republican self-government.

Moreover, communitarian strands can be found in the statement of "natural rights" to life, liberty, and the pursuit of happiness just cited. "Liberty" as understood by Jefferson and his Whig colleagues was primarily public or political liberty, the people's liberty to make policy in line with their concept of public virtue. "Rights" had most to do with the rights of the people against the privileged interests of the few, not the rights of the individual against the community. In conducting their state's business after the Revolution, Americans found no contradiction between liberty and government restrictions on speech, private property rights, and other private interests. Similarly, the "pursuit of happiness" meant government's pursuit of "public happiness," the good of society as a whole, rather than the individual's hedonistic pursuit of private pleasure.

The Declaration of Independence ought to be read alongside the U.S. Constitution as a statement of American constitutionalism. It not only presents both the individualist and communitarian political theories that characterize American political history, but also it expresses the general principles later embodied in American political institutions. Many of these institutions cannot be understood without reference to the Declaration. The Declaration states the ends of government, while the Constitution contains the means of achieving those ends.

Postrevolutionary Constitutionalism

The American colonists had established their independence by the summer of 1776. Though a war would be fought with the British to maintain this independence, Americans were constitutionally separated by Jefferson's declaration. It became the task of the revolutionaries to draft new documents to "constitute" themselves as political communities and institutionalize new power relationships. At both the state and continental levels, Americans wrote constitutions and experimented with various governmental structures. The discussion now turns to the story of the successes and failures of postrevolutionary constitutionalism.

The Revolutionary State Constitutions

The Declaration of Independence was made on behalf of the "free and independent states." Several colonies had begun writing state constitutions before the Declaration was even approved. This might be expected since the overarching preoccupation of the American revolutionaries was the creation of healthy state governments. They were concerned that government be conducted on a small scale, close to the people. Sam Adams felt that once Americans "[had] governments set up by the people in every colony, the colonies [would] feel their independence." [15] The process of forming new governments at the state level occurred with remarkable speed. New Hampshire, South Carolina, Virginia, and New Jersey drafted new constitutions prior to the formal Declaration of Independence on July 4, and, by the end of that year, ten state governments were already in place. The war delayed the process in New York and Georgia until 1777. The people of Massachusetts put a provisional government in place in 1777, deciding to go through a different process before formally adopting a new constitution in 1780. Vermont framed a new constitution in 1777, three years before other states even recognized its independence. In addition to conducting the war against the British, then, Americans were busy engaging in state constitution writing.

Since Americans distinguished between "constitutional" and "legal" during colonial resistance it might be expected that these new state constitutions would reflect this principle. The constitution would exist as fundamental law, separated from and superior to statutes passed by a legislature. But how to make the higher-law nature of state constitutions *effective* was a problem. Initially, the state legislatures (or provincial congresses) wrote, interpreted, and easily amended their state constitutions, thus making the distinction between constitution and statutes meaningless. Massachusetts would be the first state to call a constitutional convention, with delegates especially selected to draft a constitution by the people. Once drafted, the Massachusetts Constitution was taken back to the people for ratification (requiring a two-thirds majority of all the towns to take effect). With adoption of the Massachusetts Constitution in 1780, a new method had been devised to give authority to the principle that government be founded upon the people and be answerable for its daily actions to a written, higher law.

A second problem lay in the vesting of sovereignty. Americans agreed that the states would establish a republican form of government, vesting power in the people rather than in the Crown or Parliament. But the question was, What kind of republic should be formed? How would revolutionary leaders provide both popular governments and effective, orderly rule? The English example of mixed government no longer offered a model Americans could emulate. The British form of mixed government was premised upon a power-sharing arrangement among three distinct classes: the monarchy, the aristocracy, and the propertied middle classes. Having deposed the monarch and having no real aristocracy in the European sense, Americans had no basis for mixed government. They relied upon the separation-of-powers principle to organize their new governments.

Separation-of-powers theory divides and balances government according to function rather than according to social class. Without a method of limiting government itself and keeping it running effectively and rationally, constitutionalism cannot survive (remember the Madisonian dilemma discussed in Chapter 1). By providing for separate legislative, executive, and judicial branches, each with its own distinct powers, the proper governmental balance could be struck. A separation of powers could stop plural office holding and prevent one branch from manipulating another—problems felt to be sources of corruption and tyranny during the colonial era.

This was how the separation-of-powers system was to work in theory. In practice, none of the new state constitutions effectively instituted a true separation of powers. Royal governors, the colonies' chief executives, had been the sources and symbols of tyranny. These governors had the power to stop colonial legislation. They could appoint their followers to government offices, including the judiciary, and so build webs of influence from which to dominate the people. Receiving their orders from the Crown, the governors often carried into execution coercive British measures. Americans like Jefferson vowed to "destroy the kingly office . . . to absolutely divest [it] of all its rights, powers and prerogatives." [16]

The new state constitutions created governments where the legislature reigned supreme and the governor was demoted to no more than an administrator of the law. Governors were stripped of all prerogative powers. Eleven states denied the governor veto power. The governor's appointment powers were either limited, shared with the state legislature, or taken over completely by the state legislature. In eight states the legislature elected the governor; ten states provided for annual elections and limited re-election in order to prevent the governor from gaining too much power. Pennsylvania's radically democratic constitution of 1776 eliminated the governor entirely, replacing him with a twelve-man executive council elected directly by the people.

At first people applauded the fact that governors would be completely dependent upon their legislatures, since that would tie them to the people's representatives. Only later would attempts be made to strengthen the governor against an unruly legislature. And the framers of the new state constitutions made sure the legislature would *be* representative by increasing the number of representatives and requiring them to stand for annual elections. John Adams, echoing the old Whig maxim, stated, "Where annual election ends, tyranny begins." Annual election to at least one house of the state legislature, a practice adopted in every state except South Carolina, was a radical departure from past colonial practices.

The states adopted one device to slow down legislative power: the bicameral legislature. Inspired by the British Parliament, the newly independent states created a lower and upper house in their legislatures (Pennsylvania was the only state to adopt a unicameral legislature). Requiring a bill to pass through a second house of the legislature would prevent impetuous actions on the part of thoughtless and transient majorities. The second house would thus serve as a double representative of the people, tempering well-intentioned but careless and harmful acts. In addition, some believed that the upper house of the legislature could furnish a place for the "natural aristocracy," those citizens with leadership skills or special wisdom without whose authority a government would suffer. John Adams had this natural aristoracy in mind when he proposed the idea of bicameralism to the states in 1776. However, in many states little difference existed between the requirements and qualifications in the lower and upper houses. Critics worried that bicameral legislatures were not providing in practice the wisdom and deliberative functions asked of them in theory.

In addition to the bicameral legislature, eight of the states attached bills of rights to their constitutions to check governmental power. These bills of rights, many of which read like rough drafts of the U.S. Constitution's Bill of Rights ratified in 1791, were intended to check the government's power to threaten individual liberty. However, these state bills of rights did not protect individuals against the state legislatures.

The state constitutions also created an independent judiciary. By the 1770s, colonists saw that an independent judiciary could provide the most important check on the executive's prerogative powers. Had an independent judiciary existed in the colonies, it could have ruled on the constitutionality of Parliament's actions. So the new constitutions moved to establish judicial independence. Governors were denied the intimidating power of exclusive judicial appointment, and legislators were denied the right to sit as judges. To further enhance independence, judges were allowed to serve during good behavior or for fixed-year terms; they were not on the bench at the pleasure of the chief magistrate.

But as with the separation-of-powers principle in general, judicial independence was present only in theory. In fact, state legislatures dominated the judiciary as they did the executive. Legislators elected judges, paid their salaries, overruled their decisions with new laws or constitutional amendments, and subjected them to impeachment if all else failed. True judicial independence would only come with the federal Constitution of 1787.

The legislature reigned supreme in the early American state governments. The other branches did not provide a check upon its actions. Neither did the state constitutions themselves. Republican theory placed its emphasis upon the community rather than upon the individual. The people, through their representatives, had the right to act for the common good. Constitutions were not thought to place limits on what a legislature could do in the public interest. Even the eight states that attached bills of rights to their constitutions allowed the legislature to interfere with individual rights. The irony is that having based their resistance to Parliament upon a differentiation between constitutional principles and legal actions, Americans immediately enshrined the kind of legislative supremacy exercised by Parliament in their new state governments. Problems caused by this state legislative supremacy will be discussed later in this chapter.

A frequent question asked about the newly created state governments is, How much of a change had occurred as a result of the Revolution? Americans had proclaimed the principle of democratic equality in their Declaration of Independence—and had demonstrated a commitment to new forms of republican rule—based upon the people themselves. They had separated not only from England, but also from the principles of government expressed by the

British system. The historian Merrill Jensen has said that the American Revolution was not only a dispute about home rule, but also about who should rule at home.[17] The revolutionary movement brought hope to those previously excluded from politics, especially westerners, tenant farmers, city laborers, and the propertyless. Did the American Revolution actually change things in accordance with the expressed commitment to republican rule based upon all the people?

Although there is some dispute among historians, the evidence suggests that changes in the composition of government actually did take place after 1776. State constitutions lowered requirements for participating in elections, expanding the number of people who could vote. Between 1776 and 1789, property requirements for voting were eased—and, in some cases, eliminated. The Pennsylvania constitution required only residency and the payment of public taxes to vote, which qualified 90 percent of its adult males. Vermont went even further, in effect instituting universal adult male suffrage. Only in the Massachusetts Constitution of 1780 was the property qualification increased. Where property qualifications for suffrage existed, they were justified on grounds that only people with property had an independent will and a sufficient stake in the community's affairs.

At the same time, states began to eliminate religious oaths as tests for voting or holding public office, thereby bringing people who had been previously disenfranchised into state politics. Polling places were increased and added to remote locations to enhance participation in sparsely populated areas. People who would have been excluded in colonial times now participated in government and even held seats in their state legislatures.

Moreover, most government still took place at the local level, in town meetings and county courthouses. Resistance and revolutionary activities in the towns offered more people the chance to participate in community politics. Committees of correspondence turned into committees of correspondence and safety and were important forms of direct political participation for citizens who previously had no say in government.

Still, it would be a mistake to overestimate the extent to which the Revolution democratized American politics. The circle of power holders did not change that much after 1776, and many people were still excluded from political participation altogether. Women, blacks, adherents to unpopular religions, and very poor white males all would have to wait for American democracy to reach into their ranks.

The state constitutions established beginning in 1776 were true to the Revolution that preceded them. They created republican governments where citizen majorities could have their will embodied in public policy. The ease with which Americans adopted new systems of government was remarkable, especially given the wartime conditions that existed. By the 1780s, however, major problems with these early state constitutions arose, which contributed to the calling of the federal Constitutional Convention in 1787.

The Articles of Confederation

While patriots in the states were busy drafting constitutions following the Declaration of Independence in 1776, the congress was debating proposals for a new continental union of the states. At the same time that Richard Henry

Lee placed a resolution for independence before the Continental Congress, he also proposed that "a plan of confederation be prepared and transmitted to the respective colonies for their consideration and approbation." [18] On June 12, 1776, a committee was appointed to draft what would later become the Articles of Confederation.

When the congress began to debate the first draft of a new federal constitution (written largely by John Dickinson) in the summer of 1776, problems with forming a more permanent national union arose. Quarrels that divided the colonies before 1763—sectional differences, philosophical arguments, territorial disputes—resurfaced. An inherent mistrust of distant central authority, even one created by Americans, added to the colonists' suspicions of each other. Communal consciousness existed at the state and local level, but not at the national level.

In spite of these inherent problems, enough common ground existed to proceed with a national organization. The common fight against England beginning in 1763 had contributed to a growing social and cultural interaction among the colonies. The colonists had experienced a multitiered united government under the British Empire and, experimentally, under the Continental Congress. And the short-term pressures of war and the need for united action further drove the colonists toward union. In November 1777, after a year and a half of sporadic debates on and revisions of the Dickinson report, the congress finally adopted the Articles of Confederation and sent the document to the states for approval.

The states, most of which had their own constitutions in place, were not that eager to ratify the document. Concern over the amount of power given to the confederation government caused many states to delay action. Maryland held out until 1781. Only after its worries about the western territories were assuaged did Maryland ratify the Articles. In March 1781 the confederation was finally operating.

Unlike the state constitutions, which at least paid lip service to the separation-of-powers principle, the Articles of Confederation lodged all governmental power in the congress, a unicameral legislative body. No separate, permanent executive branch or judiciary was created by the Articles. Being suspicious of executive power, the founders of the Articles established no clear executive authority. Provision was made for the congress to create committees to deal with matters of policy, and several departments—such as foreign affairs, war, and treasury—eventually became entrenched. Nonetheless, with no single individual responsible for executive authority, such power was extremely weak. Of course, it should be recalled that weak executives were commonplace during this period, as most states routinely subordinated their governors to legislative authority.

The Articles did not provide for a federal judicial system, although the congress was given some narrow authority to create ad hoc courts, and these courts did resolve several disputes between states and on the high seas. However, the lack of a national judiciary meant that states retained full sovereignty in their dealings with the confederation and with each other.

The Articles of Confederation reflected American distrust of central authority. Furthermore, the confederation established by the Articles was simply that: a confederation of the separate states. The congress represented the separate states rather than the people directly. There were no national elections.

The states sent delegates to the congress and paid their salaries, and each state had one vote in determining national questions. To further enforce state equality, the Articles provided that the vote of nine states be required to adopt all important measures, and all states had to agree before an amendment to the Articles was approved.

On paper, the Articles of Confederation granted the congress formidable powers. The congress had exclusive authority over foreign relations—including matters of war and peace, diplomacy, and trade and treaty-making powers. It had powers over coining money and establishing weights and measures, over postal communications, over disputes between states, and over admiralty cases. In addition, the Articles authorized the congress to borrow money and to requisition the states for money and soldiers.

In reality, however, the central government proved to be anything but formidable. Only expressly delegated powers could be exercised by the national government, and the Articles of Confederation gave no power whatsoever to the congress to tax or to regulate commerce. The dispute with Parliament had arisen primarily over these two powers, and to give them to the newly created central government would have caused immediate controversy and suspicion. The power over taxation was the most critical; without it, the federal government could not remain solvent, especially given the past war expenses. The congress could requisition the states for money, but if they refused, the Articles provided no means to enforce the request. The confederation government received only $1.5 million of the $10 million they had requested from the states from 1781 to 1787.

This lack of enforcement power over the states applied to all other areas as well. Article II, inserted into the Dickinson draft in 1777, provided the ultimate safeguard of states' rights and the final testimony to the confederation's weaknesses. It stated, "Each state retains its sovereignty, freedom, and independence, and every power, jurisdiction, and right, which is not by this confederation expressly delegated to the United States, in Congress assembled." The Articles of Confederation failed to grant sovereignty to the new federal government. It merely established, to use its own words, "a firm league of friendship" among the states. Without crucial taxing and commerce powers, and without mechanisms to enforce the powers it did have, the confederation foundered.

The nineteenth-century historian John Fiske called the years during which the United States was governed under the Articles of Confederation "the critical period." It is still commonplace for people to refer to the period from 1781 to 1789 as a dark time in American history. But the nation also achieved great things under the Articles of Confederation. The war for independence was successfully concluded and a favorable treaty was signed with Britain. Those Americans who had supported Britain during the war were reintegrated into American society. The crisis in the western territories was solved in terms that allowed further national development according to republican principles (see Brief 3.2). The country weathered a postwar depression and by the late 1780s was beginning to grow both economically and demographically. No matter how weak the central government was under its provisions, the Articles of Confederation kept alive the idea of national union and lodged formal powers with the congress. Important principles of interstate **comity** and relations (such as "full faith and credit"—see Chapter 6 for further explanation) contained

☐ Brief 3.2 The Northwest Ordinance: A Legacy of the Articles of Confederation

The year 1787 in American history is most remembered as the year in which the federal Constitution was drafted. But the year also marks the passage of the Northwest Ordinance, a law of lasting significance in its own right. The Northwest Ordinance was designed to provide for government in the lands north and west of the Ohio River (acquired in 1784 as part of the peace settlement with Great Britain). At the time, some congressional support existed for two basic options: making the territory a permanent colony, or granting immediate statehood. But the congress, which had been created by the Articles of Confederation, instead decided upon a compromise plan to gradually ease the territorial population into self-government.

Under the Northwest Ordinance, the entire territory would be run by a governor, secretary, and three judges—all appointed by the congress. Once the adult male population reached five thousand, an assembly could be elected to make laws for the territory, subject to the governor's veto. Eventually, from three to five states would be created out of the territory, to come into the Union on an equal basis with the original states once the population totaled sixty thousand each. The

congress made provisions to protect freedom of religion, due process of law, and contractual obligations from any legislative interference either before or after statehood. Slavery was permanently excluded from the Northwest Territory.

The Northwest Ordinance made important contributions beyond solving the sticky issue of the western lands. It provided a process of expansion and union that thirty-one of the fifty states eventually followed. By guaranteeing the equality of the new states, it offered a glimpse of American federalism. The protections of individual rights found in the Northwest Ordinance actually preceded those found in the Bill of Rights. And the answer the Northwest Ordinance gave to the question of slavery struck sectional chords that endured through the next century.

The Northwest Ordinance was truly a remarkable feat, accomplished by a government that would soon be replaced. It stands today as an important constitutional legacy to go along with the more famous founding period documents, the Declaration of Independence and the U.S. Constitution.

in the Articles would later be put into the Constitution of 1787. The first inklings of a national civil service corps came in these years. In many ways it was a remarkable eight-year record for a new nation.

But the national government's failures outweighed its successes. The confederation government's financial problems topped the list. The revolutionary war required constant expenditures for soldiers and materials. Unable to tax to raise revenues and impotent to force the states to pay what was asked to finance the war, the congress resorted to issuing paper money to support the war effort. This scheme worked well at first, but by 1780 the congress had printed so much paper money that it became worthless. By the end of the war, the financial crisis was severe. The government owed money to army veterans, to foreign governments (France and Holland had lent millions to the United States during the war), and to private citizens and supporters who had lent money. The congress could not even pay the interest that had accrued on all the loans. The states grew even less willing to fill congressional requisitions.

To solve the financial crisis, the confederation congress proposed an amendment to the Articles giving it the power to impose a 5 percent tariff on foreign imports. But Rhode Island alone was able to block this proposal, since unanimity was required to amend the Articles. A year later New York would defeat a similar revenue-power amendment. So from 1781 until 1787, when the sale of western lands brought in some revenue, the congress was completely dependent upon the states for money and, as a result, hovered near bankruptcy.

Moreover, the congress could not even enforce the powers it did have under the Articles of Confederation. Independent of the congress, the states waged war, provided armies of their own, and conducted negotiations with foreign nations. The states failed to carry out provisions of treaties between the United States and foreign governments, especially the peace treaty of 1783 with Great Britain. As a result, other European powers refused to enter into commercial treaties with the United States, and the British kept troops in the Northwest Territory. The congress could not regulate commerce or trade among the several states, and, in the absence of federal controls, the states were engaging in trade and tax wars with each other. Robert Morris, superintendent of finance during the early years of the confederation government, accurately described the situation:

> Imagine the situation of a man who is to direct the finances of a country almost without revenue surrounded by creditors whose distresses, while they increase in their clamors, render it more difficult to appease them; an army ready to disband or mutiny; a government whose sole authority consists in the power of framing recommendations.[19]

Neither resting nor operating directly upon the people of the United States, the confederation government lacked the power to act as a sovereign body.

To deal with the most pressing problem for the confederation—commercial regulation—Virginia proposed an interstate convention in the fall of 1786. Delegates from five states—New York, New Jersey, Delaware, Pennsylvania, and Virginia—met in Annapolis in September to make recommendations for changes that would enable the congress to conduct trade policy for the states. The delegates agreed that the reform of the Articles of Confederation needed to go beyond mere trade matters. They called for a general convention of all the states to meet at Philadelphia in May 1787. The convention's purpose would be "to render the constitution of the Federal government adequate to the exigencies of the Union."[20] The confederation congress later endorsed the Annapolis report and urged all states to attend the convention in Philadelphia.

"The Critical Period" and the State Governments

The states, whose authority did derive directly from the people themselves, *were* acting as sovereign bodies. Revolutionaries had been committed to the classical republican ideal of small, relatively homogeneous communities where people actively participated in the public's business. The Articles were designed to prevent the central government from infringing upon the rights of states and localities to exercise popular rule. In line with the republican ideal, the first state constitutions permitted majorities to abridge individual rights if the people deemed it to be in the public interest to do so.

The republican ideal soon turned sour, however. The state legislatures became oppressive. Legislatures began to assume the powers normally reserved to other branches of government and to take on matters normally considered beyond the scope of government. State legislatures were routinely confiscating property (especially from British loyalists), altering land titles, remitting fines, granting individual exemptions to standing laws, issuing pardons, modifying or suspending judges' decisions, and authorizing judicial appeals. They interfered with private financial transactions by printing paper money, suspending debts and collections, and canceling legal contracts. In some instances state legislatures even cancelled scheduled executions and dissolved marriages! The British complained that state legislatures were impeding enforcement of the peace treaty with the United States by interfering with British creditors and continuing to confiscate loyalist property.

Throughout the land, cries of "majority tyranny" and "democratic despotism" rang out. Madison argued that "wherever the true power in government lies, there also lies the source of oppression." In the state governments during the 1780s, the power and source of oppression lay with popular majorities. Madison worried that "the few will be unnecessarily sacrificed to the many." [21] The pendulum had swung from monarchs abusing their power to the people abusing their liberty.

In addition, factionalism and infighting grew within the states. Political parties formed. Towns and cities vied for favorable legislation. But most importantly, creditors clashed with small farmers and merchants who were in debt because of the burdens of the war and the postwar depression. Farmers and merchants were often able to gain a sympathetic majority in the state legislature, which would then pass laws authorizing the printing of paper money and the suspension or transferral of debts. Creditors made bankrupt by these debt-relief statutes were distressed by the abrogation of their property rights and of other liberties by state legislatures.

A call for reform of the state governments went out. Steps to reform state governments were taken in the 1780s. Beginning with the Massachusetts Constitution of 1780, revolutionary leaders put measures into effect to counter legislative domination of state governments. They strengthened the governor's office. Governors now would be elected directly by the people, given longer terms in office, and granted more extensive veto and appointment powers. Concerned leaders also tried to make the judiciary more independent of the legislature. The power of judicial review was discussed by some reformers as an important check on legislative power. The principle behind all of these reforms of the 1780s was to provide a system, as Jefferson put it, "in which the powers of government should be so divided and balanced among several bodies of magistracy, as that no one could transcend their legal limits, without being effectually checked and restrained by the others." [22]

But the reforms at the state level came too little, too late. The final straw for many property owners came in Massachusetts in the autumn of 1786. Farmers and artisans, especially in the western part of the state, angered over their economic situation and the government's inability and unwillingness to come to their aid, turned to armed rebellion. Under the leadership of Daniel Shays, they closed down court proceedings, thereby preventing creditors from suing to collect their debts. They attacked and almost took the U.S. arsenal at Springfield; only the state militia prevented them from throwing the government into complete chaos. And though the armed rebellion failed, candidates sympathetic to the rebel cause won victories at the polls that November. Shays's Rebellion and its aftermath convinced many Americans who had been wavering that a stronger central government was necessary to check the excessive power of state governments. Only three states had initially responded to the call to come to Philadelphia in 1787; the news from Massachusetts helped nudge most of the others to attend. By early 1787, it was clear that something drastic needed to be done to improve the workings of government at both the state and national level. The Philadelphia convention would be the perfect vehicle for constitutional reform.

The Constitutional Convention and Its Aftermath

Seventy-four delegates were selected by their respective states to attend the Philadelphia convention. Only fifty-five of those actually attended, but twelve of the thirteen states were eventually represented, with only Rhode Island failing to send delegates. The convention stayed in session from May 25, 1787, until September 17, 1787, when the new Constitution was signed and sent to the confederation congress for consideration. Although James Madison and four other delegates kept notes of the convention's proceedings, the delegates adopted a rule to keep the deliberations secret, which remained in effect until thirty years afterward. The secrecy rule was adopted both to encourage the delegates to speak freely and candidly and to prevent those skeptics outside Philadelphia from misconstruing the convention's purpose and sabotaging its deliberations.

The men who debated and drafted the nation's new Constitution were many of America's most respected statesmen. Thomas Jefferson, who was in Europe and unable to attend, referred to the convention as "an assembly of demigods." Some important names were missing, of course. In addition to Jefferson and John Adams (who was representing the United States in England), Sam Adams and John Hancock were absent. Patrick Henry, having been selected to go to Philadelphia, grew suspicious of the convention's purposes and chose not to attend. In fact, only eight of the fifty-six signers of the Declaration of Independence attended the convention.

On the whole, the delegates were relatively young men. Benjamin Franklin of Pennsylvania was the oldest delegate at eighty-one, but six of the delegates were under thirty-one. In addition, it was a group with considerable wealth and social position. Most were bankers, lawyers, planters, and merchants. Only one representative—William Few of Georgia—came from the yeoman farmer class (the largest social class in America at the time). No one represented back-country folk or the city mechanics (who were essentially wage-laborers). Still, some of the finest republican minds of the eighteenth century gathered at Philadelphia "to form a more perfect Union." Virginia and Pennsylvania sent six of the men who would be most influential at the convention. George Washington, James Madison, and Edmund Randolph came from Virginia. In addition to Franklin, Gouverneur Morris and James Wilson ably represented Pennsylvania. Other convention notables included John Dickinson of Delaware, Roger Sherman of Connecticut, Elbridge Gerry and Rufus King of Massachusetts, John Rutledge and Charles Pinckney of South Carolina, Alexander Hamilton of New York, and William Paterson of New Jersey. On the first day, Washington was chosen to preside over the meetings.

Initially, differences of opinion existed over the purpose of the Philadelphia meeting. Although the Annapolis resolution granted the delegates rather broad authority to revise the national government, the confederation congress had authorized that the delegates meet "for the sole and express purpose of revising the Articles of Confederation." [23] The majority of delegates wanted to end the anarchy resulting from the confederation's weaknesses. But they disagreed on how far to go in reforming the continental government. Roger Sherman argued that the needs of the Union were few: defense, commercial regulation, treaty making, revenue raising, and domestic good order. He felt that revising the Articles to meet these needs would suffice.

But James Madison wanted a complete overhaul of the national government. In April 1787 he had prepared a paper entitled "Vices of the Political System of the United States" in preparation for Philadelphia. In it, he outlined the defects in the Articles of Confederation and in the current state governments. Madison was particularly critical of the legislative excesses of the states. They had, in his mind, passed too many laws, invaded minority rights, and failed to prevent "internal violence" (an obvious reference to Shays's Rebellion). Madison sought to establish a "more extensive republic" with greater national power to solve the problem both of weak central government and of excessively strong state governments. For Madison, providing safeguards for private rights and providing adequate powers for the national government were two parts of the same problem. Madison's forces would ultimately win in Philadelphia.

The Virginia Plan and the Problem of Representation

The Virginia delegation came to the convention's first session armed with a new plan for governing the United States. Though written by Madison, the plan, which came to be known as the Virginia Plan, was introduced to the convention by fellow Virginian Edmund Randolph. The Virginia Plan proposed a completely different structure of government from the Articles of Confederation. In it, the central government's powers were to be separated into a bicameral legislature, an executive branch, and a judicial branch. The new national government would represent and operate directly upon the people rather than working through the sovereign states. The bicameral congress would be given greater powers than the congress had under the Articles of Confederation, plus the authority to veto any acts of the various state legislatures.

The Virginia Plan was a bold nationalist proposal. Randolph himself stated that his plan would establish a "strong consolidated union in which the idea of states should be nearly annihilated." Delegates from the less populous states, frightened by the prospect of diminished influence in a new national structure, put forth a proposal of their own. On June 14, William Paterson presented the New Jersey Plan, a proposal to modify the Articles of Confederation. The New Jersey Plan would give the congress taxing and commerce powers and would strengthen the federal government's enforcement powers over disobedient states. But apart from these specific powers, the New Jersey Plan contained little else significantly different from the Articles. It retained the principle of state equality in the federal legislature and created a federal executive that was directly subject to the state legislatures. Some of the New Jersey Plan's specific provisions were eventually incorporated into the Constitution, but it was rejected as a whole early in the convention's deliberations.

The only other plan presented was Alexander Hamilton's proposal for a constitutional monarchy on June 18, but this received no delegate support. The Virginia Plan and its nationalist principles were to be the basis for the new Constitution.

Representation in Congress under the new federal Constitution was the first and most important problem discussed by the Philadelphia delegates. The Articles of Confederation had established a union that was not representational, but rather, territorial, in that it gave the states in their corporate capacity equal representation in the congress. Republican ideals of popular government and majority rule had already led the states to tie representation to population rather than to territorial units. Now the Virginia Plan was calling for direct popular rule at the national level, through a system where the people would elect congressmen who represented districts in proportion to the population (at least in one house of the national legislature). Delegates to the Philadelphia convention would have to decide whether the new government would be based upon the states or upon the people; and whether the state legislatures, or the people, would elect members of the federal legislature.

Although the delegates agreed that the new government being created would have to operate directly upon the people in order to have the enhanced authority necessary to cure the ills of the confederation, delegates from the small states wanted to ensure the continued equality of the states. They also sought protection against large-state domination in the newly composed federal legislature. A deadlock existed on the question of representation, with the small states in favor of equal state representation and the large-state faction in favor of proportional representation. A committee was chosen to draft a compromise acceptable to a majority of the states.

The Connecticut Compromise, as it was known, recommended that representation be proportional in the lower house of Congress (each state would be allowed one member for every forty thousand inhabitants), and that each state have an equal vote in the upper house. The people would directly elect members to the House of Representatives; the state legislatures would choose members of the Senate. As an added concession to republican principles and to prerevolutionary disputes, a provision was made to initiate all bills for raising or spending money in the lower house, with no amendments by the upper house possible. On July 16 the convention narrowly approved the Connecticut Compromise by a 5-4 vote, with Massachusetts divided and New York not voting. Although the large-state faction was temporarily displeased, it basically received what it wanted. The dual provision for representation in Congress would reflect a constitutional system that was, to use one delegate's phrase, "partly national, partly federal." The composition of Congress decided, the delegates moved on to discuss how to enhance this new legislature's powers.

Powers of Congress Under the New Constitution

The convention delegates wanted to make the federal government more powerful, not only over certain matters like taxation and commerce, but also in relation to the state legislatures. But how to achieve this increased power created controversy. In addition to the powers the congress had under the Articles of Confederation, the Virginia Plan granted it the power "to legislate in all cases to which the separate states are incompetent, or in which the harmony of the United States may be interrupted by the exercise of individual legislation." [24] Several delegates objected to this additional power, claiming that the language (especially the word "incompetent") was too vague and needed more "exact enumeration." After approving a general grant of congressional power with more specific language, the committee of detail scrapped the entire resolution, in favor of a list of specific powers that Congress might need to exercise. The convention finally agreed upon seventeen specific grants of power, beginning with the powers to tax and to regulate commerce. Article I, Section 8, of the constitution concludes with a more general grant of authority to Congress "to make all Laws which shall be necessary and proper for carrying into Execution the foregoing Powers, and all other Powers vested, by this Constitution in the Government of the United States." The interpretation of this last provision, called the Necessary and Proper Clause, has raised a number of controversies in the nation's history and will be addressed in Chapter 6.

The granting of specific powers to Congress was the perfect solution to the problem of creating a government that would overcome the weaknesses of the confederation and yet not be too powerful (as a result of a vague, general grant of congressional power). But the delegates wanted to be sure that Congress did not overstep its legitimate bounds. Immediately following the grants of congressional power, they included provisions that would specifically *limit* congressional power. Many of the limitations resulted from conflicting sectional interests. Southern slave owners in particular feared that the new federal government would act to prohibit the slave trade or make it economically unfeasible. North Carolina, South Carolina, and Georgia all threatened to abandon the new Constitution if it prohibited the slave trade or allowed excessive duties upon "imported persons." Many delegates opposed the "infernal traffic" of slavery, but a compromise was reached in late August. Congress would not be allowed to prohibit the importation of slaves until 1808 and would only be allowed a minimal taxation power of $10 a person. Slave owners also worried that the new congressional taxing power would be used to levy a capitation, or head, tax that would specifically include slaves. Accordingly, Congress was prohibited from taxing directly, "unless in Proportion to the Census" (Art. I, Sec. 9). Questions about what constituted a direct tax would haunt Congress and the courts until the Sixteenth Amendment was passed in 1913 (see Chapter 7 for further discussion of taxation).

Finally, differences between the northern and southern economies led to a prohibition on export taxes. The southern states, whose economy was based heavily upon agricultural exports, did not want to bear the burden of a taxing program ordered by the northern majority whose trade was not as dependent upon commodity exports.

These questions of federal congressional power decided, there still remained the problem of how to assert federal power over the states and the question of federal versus state sovereignty. Theoretically, the new Constitution would solve the problem of sovereignty by basing sovereignty directly upon the people themselves. The new federal government would operate directly upon the people rather than working through the separate states. But practically, the states would still be exercising power over their internal affairs through their **police powers** (the power to legislate for the health, safety, welfare, and morals of the people—see Chapter 7 for further details). Even ardent nationalists understood that the states would retain the largest share of power. Given this fact, the delegates needed a way to allow the federal government to exert its supremacy over the states when necessary. The Virginia Plan called for a congressional veto, the power to "negative all laws passed by the several states contravening in the opinion of the National legislature the articles of Union." [25] Madison was adamant that Congress have this veto power as a way of exercising national supremacy over the often pernicious state legislatures.

Gouverneur Morris responded that to give Congress this veto power would "disgust all the states." He understood that given the state loyalties that existed at the time, the sovereignty of the states would have to be recognized to a significant degree. Moreover, he contended, "A law that ought to be negatived will be set aside in the Judiciary Department." So the veto was dropped and what is called the Supremacy Clause in Article VI of the Constitution was drafted to take its place as a statement of national supremacy over the states. It states that the Constitution and all federal laws made under its authority "shall be the supreme Law of the Land." Judges in state courts are bound by the Constitution and by federal law, regardless of what their state laws or constitutions say. The Supremacy Clause is an important assertion of national sovereignty because it makes the Constitution a law enforceable in all courts throughout the land. It has been the basis for numerous Supreme Court opinions about the locus of sovereignty, federal or state (see Chapters 6 and 7).

Of course, the Supremacy Clause only offered a general statement of national supremacy. Given the delegates' specific concerns about debt-relief and paper-money legislation being passed in the states, they wanted exact language in the Constitution to forbid certain kinds of state actions. The delegates agreed, among other things, to prohibit the states from coining or printing money, from making anything other than gold or silver acceptable in the payment of debts, and from passing any law that would interfere with the obligation of contracts. These provisions are found in Article I, Section 10.

Separation of Powers and the Presidency

The preceding sections have discussed the composition and the powers of Congress. Unlike the system under the Articles of Confederation, however, Congress was not to be the only branch of the federal government. Experience with both the federal and state governments in the "critical period" led the delegates to call for a true separation of governmental powers in the new Constitution. Madison complained that the states had not adequately separated the different functions of government. This had led, in his mind, to a situation where each state's legislature had become tyrannical, "absorbing all power into its vortex." [26] Madison and his colleagues had already provided for a bicameral legislature in which the Senate could deliberate and exercise restraint on an impetuous majority in the lower house. But this was not enough. Madison, Hamilton, and others also wanted to create a strong federal executive and judiciary to further divide governmental powers and provide necessary leadership.

The powers and composition of the new executive stirred controversy among the delegates. To the traditional republicans—which included Franklin, Randolph, and George Mason of Virginia—danger lurked in a too-powerful executive. These delegates wanted a chief executive who was elected by and dependent upon the legislature. Moreover, they wanted to disperse executive power by placing it in the hands of several men, who would sit as an executive council or cabinet. Experience with the British had proven to these Whiggish republicans that too much power in the hands of an independent executive leads to corruption and tyranny. For example, Randolph contended that a single executive was "the foetus [fetus] of monarchy." The Virginia Plan—with its call for a plural executive with limited powers, elected by the legislature—embodied these republican concerns.

But the old-line republicans were not the only voices at the convention, and they would eventually lose the battle over the presidential office. The younger group of men in Philadelphia (plus a few elder statesmen like Washington) had seen the dangers of legislative dominance and wanted to create a unified, energetic executive as a check upon legislative excesses. Led by Madison and Hamilton, as well as by Morris and Wilson of Pennsylvania (where a unicameral legislature virtually unchecked by an executive council had been in power), the "radicals" called for a single executive elected by the people (either directly or indirectly). Radicals like Wilson and Madison opposed an executive council that might dilute presidential leadership and "cover [rather] than prevent malpractice." They proposed that the executive have a full range of prerogative powers, including full appointing and veto powers, and those of commander in chief of the armed forces. For support, they drew upon the writings of Locke and Montesquieu.

A majority of the delegates agreed upon a single executive on June 4, but continued debating the issues of presidential selection and powers throughout the summer. Wilson later declared that the provisions for the executive were "the most difficult of all on which we have had to decide." Finally, the delegates sent the matter of presidential election to a committee of eleven men to work out a compromise proposal. In early September the committee reported back with a plan for election that would encompass the ideas of both sides. Presidential electors would be chosen in a manner prescribed by the state legislatures (which could include popular selection). These electors would then choose a president, with each state having a number of votes equal to its total representation in Congress. The choice of a majority of these electors would be president, with the runner-up becoming vice-president. If no one person received a majority of the votes, the Senate would choose a president from among the five highest vote-getters. The members of the Committee of Eleven were certain that both the people and the legislature would have a hand in the presidential selection process, since they felt it would be rare for one man to gain a majority of the votes. The compromise would make for a president independent of the legislature, yet usually selected by it. With one friendly amendment giving the House of Representatives the final say rather than the Senate, the committee's proposal was approved and the electoral college was born. Of course, the framers could not foresee the rise of political parties in the presidential selection process, which quickly made the two-stage election process obsolete. Only two presidential elections (1800 and 1824) have been decided by the House of Representatives.

Along with the selection proposal came a provision for a four-year term, with the possibility of reelection to additional terms. The delegates finally voted to give the president a limited veto power, in line with that given to many state governors, as well as the power to act as commander in chief. The president was also given authority to make treaties and appoint judges, ambassadors, and other government officers "with the Advice and Consent of the Senate" (Art. II, Sec. 2). The new president would not merely administer the laws made by Congress, but would energetically exercise restraint and control over the federal legislature. He would be truly independent, the guardian of the people as a whole against legislative tyranny and factional plots among the wealthy. The radicals had won on the matter of the presidency.

The Federal Judiciary and Individual Rights

All delegates agreed upon the need for a national judiciary as the third branch in the federal separation of powers. The judiciary's power to judge the constitutionality of federal and state laws was considered essential to check legislative and executive power (see Chapter 4 on judicial review). The absence of a permanent federal judiciary separate from the legislature was seen as a major weakness in the Articles of Confederation. Even the New Jersey Plan called for the creation of a federal supreme court. The delegates wanted to ensure that the judiciary would truly be an independent body. They understood that to make it so, judges would serve during good behavior rather than at the command of the president or Congress.

Two major points of disagreement did exist over this new national judiciary, however. The first concerned the extent of the federal judiciary. The New Jersey Plan had only called for a supreme court. The Virginia Plan provided for inferior courts as well as for a supreme court. Some delegates contended that the presence of inferior courts would dilute state judicial power. Others, including Madison, felt that a hierarchy of federal courts was essential to an effective judiciary that could check legislative majorities. Finally, the convention compromised by providing for a supreme court and leaving the establishment of inferior federal courts up to Congress.

The second dispute arose over the selection of federal judges. The Virginia Plan called for Congress to elect federal judges. The convention's delegates, however, fearing that judges might lose their independence if elected by the legislature, rejected this proposal. Conflict ensued over whether the president or the Senate should appoint federal judges. As with other matters, the convention ultimately accepted a compromise from the Committee of Eleven. The president would appoint Supreme Court justices "by and with the Advice and Consent of the Senate" (Art. II, Sec. 2).

To many delegates, the federal judiciary would not only restrain the other branches of the government, but also would defend the constitutional rights of individual citizens. The Constitution would contain a number of specific prohibitions on the federal government that the courts could enforce, most notably against Congress's passing **bills of attainder** and **ex post facto laws** (these the states were also forbidden to pass). Individuals would be guaranteed a jury trial on all federal criminal charges and could not have their right to petition for a **writ of habeas corpus** suspended except during rebellion or invasion. But no larger bill of rights was included at the Philadelphia convention. The majority of delegates concluded that a longer declaration of rights was unnecessary, given the existence of the bills of rights attached to the separate state constitutions. The absence of a bill of rights would be remedied quickly, however, as Congress would use the amending process specified in Article V to add a bill of rights (the first ten amendments to the Constitution) in 1789.

These major issues decided, the delegates appointed a committee of style to draft the final wording and arrange the articles agreed upon in an orderly fashion. Gouverneur Morris is credited with doing most of this committee's work and is therefore the man most responsible for the final wording of the Constitution. The final document was presented to the forty-two delegates still in attendance on September 17. Thirty-nine delegates signed, with Edmund Randolph, the man who was responsible for many of the document's initial provisions, among the nonsigners. The document then went to the states for ratification.

Ratification of the Constitution

The new Constitution would go into effect once nine states agreed to ratify it. The delegates removed the requirement of unanimity found in the Articles of Confederation for obvious practical reasons. Rhode Island had refused to send delegates to the Philadelphia convention, and it was felt that other states might refuse to ratify the Constitution. The delegates chose the number of states required to ratify based upon the fact that nine states had been required to pass major legislation under the Articles of Confederation. The nine-state requirement was one which, to use George Mason's words, was "familiar to the people."

In addition, delegates adopted a provision in the Virginia Plan that called for ratification by conventions specifically elected for that purpose rather than by the existing state legislatures. As a matter of principle, Madison felt that a new government founded and operating directly upon the people needed to be approved by the people. But, as a matter of practicality, those who favored the Constitution's adoption also saw that entrenched interests in the state legislatures might prevent ratification because of the Constitution's implications for their positions of power.

Under these new rules, the battle over ratification began. Victory came for the new Constitution's supporters (who called themselves Federalists) only after a hard struggle with its opponents (Anti-Federalists). In the end, persuasion, compromise, and a few less-than-ethical tricks were required to get the Constitution adopted by the nine required states. The fight between Federalists and Anti-Federalists partly involved a conflict between commercial and noncommercial elements in the population. In some states, the ratification battle reflected differences between urban and rural interests, between coastal and interior towns. But most importantly, the ratification debate was argued upon the battleground of political principles and ideals. Federalists and Anti-Federalists stood for competing concepts of politics and the role of government in people's lives. To understand the Constitution's purpose as well as many of the constitutional battles that have occurred since its adoption, these differences in principles between Federalists and Anti-Federalists must be understood.

The Anti-Federalist Argument Against Ratification

It is much more difficult to discuss Anti-Federalist political theory than to discuss that of the Federalists. In many states, the Constitution's opponents shared nothing beyond their contempt for this new, and—in many of their minds—radical document. The opposition was often disorganized, inarticulate, and generally unimpressive compared with the Constitution's supporters. Moreover, the Anti-Federalists had the disadvantage of having no viable alternative document to defend. Very few opponents to the Constitution wanted to keep the Articles of Confederation intact. Even the name "Anti-Federalists" is somewhat of a misnomer, since many of the Constitution's opponents saw themselves as "true" federalists, defenders of state sovereignty against national consolidation (which points to the political skills of the Federalists, who initially grabbed the high moral ground in their name selection).

Still, the Anti-Federalists agreed upon certain fundamental political ideas and were able to launch a coherent, principled attack on the Constitution. Most Anti-Federalists shared five constitutional concerns. The first concern was with the radical nature of this new document being debated. Many Anti-Federalists thought the Constitution granted the federal government powers too broad and too ill-defined. They wanted to move more cautiously, granting the new federal government limited powers above what it possessed under the Articles. The majority of Anti-Federalists favored a stronger union, but not at the expense of political liberty and state autonomy. For example, though most opponents to the Constitution admitted the need for an enhanced federal taxing power, they saw the Constitution as granting Congress an unlimited "power To lay and collect Taxes, Duties, Imposts and Excises" (Art. I, Sec. 8). They felt that this excessive taxing power would not only bleed the people but also would leave the states with little revenue-raising power of their own. The Anti-Federalists also complained about the radical changes in the rules for ratification (i.e., less than unanimity, popular ratifying conventions) made by the Federalists. Richard Henry Lee, one of the most outspoken opponents of the Constitution, believed that it was better to retain the principles of state sovereignty under the old confederation than to adopt the consolidation plan of the "hot-headed" Federalists. The consolidation plan could only bring political inequality and a loss of liberty. In response to Federalists' claims about the need for new governmental institutions, he stated, "To say that a bad government must be established for fear of anarchy is really saying that we should kill ourselves for fear of dying."[27]

A second concern had to do with the scale and size of the new federal government. The Anti-Federalists believed that republicanism could only flourish in small states, where the people would have greater control over and access to their governments. The "small republic" could preserve equality, homogeneity of character and custom, and civic virtue against the corruption and divisiveness that would come with large size. As one Anti-Federalist in New York put it, the federal government established by the new Constitution "would be composed of such heterogeneous and discordant principles, as would constantly be contending with each other." The Anti-Federalists were opposed to the "extended republic" the Constitution would establish, not only because it could lead to divisiveness and corruption, but also because it placed magisterial power in a distant president who could easily become "kingly." Accordingly, the Anti-Federalists wanted to leave as much power as possible in the states, where government could be most responsive to the people and most reflective of popular values and virtues.

A third concern among Anti-Federalists was with "civic virtue." Corruption—the deterioration of public spiritedness—appears as a strong motif running through many Anti-Federalist writings. They saw the Federalists as promoting a large, commercially oriented republic that would operate based upon the private interests of its citizens. The Federalist focus upon efficiency, commercial growth, and private interests would breed luxury and inequality and would lead to the downfall of republican values. Moreover, many Anti-

Federalists complained about Federalist disregard for religious principles as the foundation of republican government. Anti-Federalists worried that without an emphasis upon civic education and positive public and religious values, the political community would have no moral foundation and would degenerate into monarchy, tyranny, or anarchy. This concern with civic virtue is related to that of scale, since Anti-Federalists believed that only the states ("small republics") could provide proper schools of citizenship and civic virtue.

A fourth constitutional concern related to democratic representation. Most Anti-Federalists wanted a government that would be responsive to its citizens' needs. Lodging most power in the state governments would accomplish this, but the federal government also needed to be directly responsible to the people. The Anti-Federalists thought that the new Constitution limited popular responsibility: it removed the chief executive, the Senate, and the judiciary from direct popular control. Moreover, even members of the House of Representatives would be distant and unresponsive. The first federal House of Representatives would contain only fifty-five members, a body smaller than many of the state legislatures! By not providing for a representative federal government that would be directly responsible to the people, the Anti-Federalists felt the Constitution inclined toward aristocracy and monarchy. They thought popular government itself would be endangered by the new national government.

Finally, most Anti-Federalists opposed the Constitution's failure to contain a bill of rights. Anti-Federalist fear of a gargantuan, distant government that would be corrupt and tyrannical was only enhanced by this omission. To the Anti-Federalists, it was a basic premise of government—enshrined in most state constitutions of the time—that the people's liberties could only be maintained by a written declaration of rights that would limit what the government could do. Even Thomas Jefferson, who supported the Constitution's adoption, agreed with the Anti-Federalists on this point: "A bill of rights is what the people are entitled to against every government on earth, general or particular, and what no just government should refuse, or rest on inference." [28] As it turned out, this final concern was the only one the Anti-Federalists saw materialize in the U.S. Constitution. Nevertheless, these five concerns would remain prominent among large numbers of Americans throughout the early years of the republic.

The Federalist Response

Describing Federalist political theory is much easier than describing its counterpart. Not only were the Federalists united in support of the same document, but also they had articulate leaders in many states who could buttress their position with strong supporting ideas. For example, to persuade the people of New York to adopt the Constitution, James Madison, Alexander Hamilton, and John Jay wrote a series of essays entitled *The Federalist Papers*. These essays defend the basic principles and specific provisions of the Constitution of 1787. Though other sources of Federalist thought exist, the Federalist theory of politics can be gleaned largely from this series of essays. The essays contain specific responses to the Anti-Federalist concerns just detailed.

Most Federalists saw themselves as "progressives," inheritors of the liberal, enlightenment tradition in Europe. This tradition believed that new political institutions could be created and that major improvements in people's collective lives could be made. Federalists believed that the abstract principles of men like Montesquieu and Locke could be embodied in positive constitutions. As such, they were not afraid of radical, new proposals for government. After all, Americans had already overturned political traditions in 1776. Why not drastically revise the federal government to correct its major defects? Furthermore, in Federalist eyes, these major defects in the state and confederation governments were hampering the people's ability to progress toward their ultimate destiny.

The Federalists differed drastically from the Anti-Federalists in their views of the nature and purpose of government. To Federalists like Madison, people were motivated primarily by private interests, not by a desire to serve the public good. The role of government was to protect individuals from others who might harm them in the pursuit of private gain. Government existed to secure persons and property. It was at most a regulator of conduct, not a teacher of civic virtue or molder of character.

Moreover, people's private interests were diverse: if allowed to dominate the public arena, they could lead to a tyranny of the majority's interests over those of the rest of the population. This was the problem the Federalists saw happening in the state governments, where arbitrary and capricious majorities were trampling on individual liberties. The Federalist solution to majority tyranny and to the repression of the individual's right to satisfy his or her private interests was to provide for an "extended republic" (the federal government), where majority factions could not form, and where individual liberty would thereby be protected. Under the Constitution, the federal government would take the majority, with its capacity for excesses, out of the daily picture of government operations. This would protect the rights and interests of all citizens, provide security for economic investment and growth, and make government more stable and effective in its functions.

The Federalists responded to the Anti-Federalist concern that the new government was unrepresentative by offering their own republican theory of leadership. As mentioned in the discussion of the Constitutional Convention, the Federalists saw indirect representation as desirable. By removing the people from a direct and intimate say in who would represent them in government, responsible leaders from the right social background could emerge and run the country. Hamilton stated:

> All communities divide themselves into the few and the many. The first are the rich and well born, the other the mass of the people. The voice of the people has been said to be the voice of God; and however generally this maxim has been quoted and believed, it is not true in fact. The people are turbulent and changing; they seldom judge or determine right. Give therefore to the first class a distinct, permanent share in the government. They will check the unsteadiness of the second, and as they cannot receive any advantage by a change, they therefore will ever maintain good government. Can a democratic assembly, who annually revolve in the mass of the people, be supposed steadily to pursue the public good? Nothing but a permanent body can check the imprudence of democracy.[29]

This elite group would have the people's best interests at heart, protect private rights from majoritarian impulses, and be less susceptible to corruption. Indeed, government by an elite corps chosen by the methods found in the Constitution would be more "responsible" to republican values than one directly responsive to "the mob" of citizens.

Thus far the Federalists appear as classic supporters of what was described in Chapter 2 as the individualist perspective of government. They sought an efficient government, one that could secure private rights rather than public virtue, one where the natural leadership of a national elite would replace the more direct popular rule of local communities. The Anti-Federalists, by contrast, were more communitarian in their approach, believing that civic virtue must override private interests. So why weren't the Federalists the ones supporting a bill of rights? Federalists had been unconcerned with such libertarian provisions because they thought the federal government would be limited to solely those powers granted it in the Constitution. All powers not granted to the government would remain in the people's hands. In addition, the people would have some specific protections in the Constitution, as mentioned previously (bills of attainder, etc.), and the state bills of rights would still operate to protect individual citizens from state governments (which to Federalist minds were the more dangerous). Here the Federalists found themselves upon shaky ground, however, given the ambiguity surrounding the actual powers granted to the new federal government. The Anti-Federalists would finally convince the Federalists to change their minds about a bill of rights—in fact, it took a promise that an attached bill of rights would be the first order of business of the new government to gain approval of the Constitution in several states. Massachusetts, Virginia, New Hampshire, South Carolina, and New York all ratified the Constitution with the understanding that a list of recommended amendments be added immediately.

The Federalists won adoption of the Constitution, but not without difficulty (see Brief 3.3). After some delay, George Washington, who received one vote from every presidential elector, was finally inaugurated as the first president of the United States on April 30, 1789. For the revolutionary generation, Washington was a symbol of the republican values that had guided the nation's struggle for independence and self-preservation. As such he lent a legitimacy to the new government that it desperately needed in its early years. Congress's immediate work on the constitutional amendments that had been proposed at the various state ratifying conventions also won the government acceptance in many quarters. James Madison eventually pared the more than two hundred suggestions down to nineteen proposals that he wanted woven into the text of the Constitution. Congress approved twelve of these as the Bill of Rights, but only after the House insisted upon placing the amendments at the end of the Constitution and the Senate demanded that the amendments apply only to the national government—not the states.

Ten amendments received the necessary support of three-fourths of the states and became part of the Constitution on December 15, 1791. Actually, only the first eight amendments contain *specific* protections of individual rights against governmental interference. The Ninth and Tenth Amendments are more general in nature. The Ninth Amendment, though presently controversial (see Chapter 10), protects other rights not enumerated in the Constitution from government intrusion. The Tenth Amendment provides that "the powers not delegated" to the federal government "are reserved to the States respectively, or to the people." More will be said about the states' "reserved powers" stemming from this provision in Chapters 6 and 7. With approval of the Bill of Rights, the opening chapter in American constitutional history was complete. But the political conflict between Federalists and their opponents continued. Anti-Federalist principles remained salient, especially on the question of the nature of American federalism, for years to come.

☐ *Brief 3.3   The Difficult Struggle over Ratification*

The ratification battle began in October 1787, when several states issued their calls for ratification conventions and set the dates and rules governing the ratification procedure. It did not end until nine months later, when New Hampshire cast the clinching ninth vote required to put the Constitution into effect. By the end of July, Virginia and New York, without whose presence the union of states would have failed, had come into the fold by narrow margins and after long and bitter debates.

Although a few states, including Delaware (the first state to ratify on December 7, 1787), were unanimous in their approval, in many others the vote was close. In fact, not counting North Carolina and Rhode Island, where ratification did not initially succeed, in four other states (Massachusetts, New Hampshire, Virginia, and New York), a majority of the delegates were publicly *opposed* to the Constitution when they sat down to meet on the first day of their state ratifying conventions. New Hampshire and New York probably would have rejected the new document had they not felt pressured by the approval of the other states. Alexander Hamilton even threatened New York's delegates

with the secession of New York City from the state if they failed to approve the Constitution, by then already ratified by ten other states. In Massachusetts, Governor John Hancock had to be bribed with the promise of the presidency or vice-presidency to get his crucial support for the Federalist cause.

The states that approved the Constitution only on the condition that a list of proposed amendments be considered took that reservation seriously: the Virginia delegates attached a list of twenty-nine proposed constitutional amendments to their official convention report. As mentioned, North Carolina and Rhode Island did not approve the new document by the summer of 1788. North Carolina postponed ratification until a lengthy set of proposed constitutional amendments could be drafted, finally ratifying on November 21, 1788. Rhode Island remained obstinate, refusing even to call a state ratifying convention until 1790. In the face of threats emanating from the new United States government, Rhode Island begrudgingly voted their approval on May 29, 1790, by a vote of 34–32.

A breakdown of the original thirteen states, in order of their ratification, appears in Table 3.1

Table 3.1   Ratification of the U.S. Constitution

STATE	DATE OF RATIFICATION	VOTE	AMENDMENTS PROPOSED?
Delaware	December 7, 1787	30–0	No
Pennsylvania	December 12, 1787	46–23	Yes
New Jersey	December 18, 1787	38–0	No
Georgia	January 2, 1788	26–0	No
Connecticut	January 9, 1788	128–40	No
Massachusetts	February 6, 1788	187–168	Yes
Maryland	April 28, 1788	63–11	No
South Carolina	May 23, 1788	149–73	Yes
New Hampshire	June 21, 1788	57–47	Yes
Virginia	June 25, 1788	89–79	Yes
New York	July 26, 1788	30–27	Yes
North Carolina	November 21, 1788	194–77	Yes
Rhode Island	May 29, 1790	34–32	Yes

Source: Data taken from Murray Dry, ''The Case Against Ratification: Anti-Federalist Constitutional Thought,'' *The Framing and Ratification of the Constitution,* ed. Leonard W. Levy and Dennis J. Mahoney (New York: Macmillan, 1987); and Joseph T. Kennan, *The Constitution of the United States: An Unfolding Story* (Chicago: Dorsey Press, 1988).

Conclusion

It remains our task to characterize the Constitution generally. The American Constitution, like the revolution for independence which preceded it, reflects the tension between the communitarian and individualist strains of political thinking outlined in Chapter II. On the one hand, the Framers drafted a document which would theoretically place government on the foundation of the people, and would allow democratic majorities to rule in the interest of the nation as a whole (as opposed to the Articles of Confederation, where minorities of states could block actions favored by the majority). On the other hand, the men in Philadelphia placed roadblocks in the way of steamrolling majorities who would threaten individual rights (e.g., separation of powers, checks and balances, specific provisions guaranteeing individual rights against both federal and state governments). The tensions found in the original Constitution have been played out in conflicts throughout American history, as will be shown in the following chapters.

Nevertheless, one question remains: does the Constitution truly represent the democratic principles advanced by the American revolutionaries of 1776? Controversy rages among historians and constitutional scholars over whether the Constitution lives up to the ideals announced in the Declaration of Independence. From the beginning of this century, a few historians and other scholars have cast the Constitution and the Federalists who supported it in a bad light. Probably the most famous attack on the Constitution's framers occurred in 1913, when Charles Beard published *An Economic Interpretation of the Constitution of the United States*. Beard argued that the Constitutional Convention was actually an economic conspiracy by an elite to safeguard their own interests at the expense of the popular majority. The framers of the Constitution, whom Beard contended represented the economic interests of "personalty" (capital in manufacturing, trade and shipping, public securities, and other paper assets), imposed their vision of a stable and efficient national government that would protect their own economic interests against democratic majorities. Those who opposed the Constitution represented "realty" interests (landed property, the local agrarian and debtor classes). They placed greater stress upon local government and the protection of personal liberties. Beard contended that the Federalists, who represented an economic elite, outmaneuvered the Anti-Federalists, who represented a majority of the population. Through property restrictions and other devices used at the state ratifying conventions, the Federalists were able to win approval for a government reflective of their limited economic concerns.

While Beard's thesis has been successfully challenged by historians, his critique of the Constitution persists, although in a different form. A number of critics following Beard have continued to take the position that the Constitution was an undemocratic document, radically out of step with "the spirit of '76." For example, Merrill Jensen contended that the Articles of Confederation, which lodged power in the states, was actually the true expression of the democratic spirit found in the Declaration of Independence. The Federalists, on the other hand, did all they could to stifle popular majorities in the states, by framing a Constitution that would protect an economic and social elite from the masses. Jensen declared:

> The Articles of Confederation were designed to prevent the central government from infringing upon the rights of the states, whereas the Constitution of 1787 was designed as a check upon the power of the states and the democracy that found expression within their bounds.[30]

Other critics point to the evidence that only eight of the signers of the Declaration of Independence were present at Philadelphia to help make this case against the Constitution. They see the Constitution as failing to reflect the principles of equality and democratic self-government announced in the Declaration. Moreover, the Constitution contains no reference to the people's right to revolution in the event that government becomes oppressive or unresponsive to the people's will. In these critics' minds, the Anti-Federalists represent the concerns of virtuous agrarian democrats over conservative counter-revolutionaries.

The critique that the Constitution is undemocratic has much greater historical support, especially if the rhetoric of the Constitution's opponents is taken seriously. The Anti-Federalists constantly hammered away at the aristocratic tendencies they found in the Constitution. They saw the Constitution as establishing the rule of the wealthy over the people as a whole.

Rhetoric aside, however, the Anti-Federalist attack is not completely fair. The revolutionary generation could legitimately say that the Constitution generally embodied the principles of the American Revolution. It established a stronger Union, which almost all Americans, even those who opposed the Constitution, argued was necessary to maintain independence and to build a stable political order. It established a system of divided sovereignty between federal and state governments, a principle the colonists had fought for in their battle with Parliament and the king. Though constitutional interpretation in this century has done much to change matters, the federal government's power was initially limited, and most government activities and functions after 1787 would still take place at the state and local level, where more direct popular control existed. Moreover, the Constitution embodied the revolutionaries' concepts of constitutionalism and higher law by providing a written constitution, which limited what everyday rulers and representatives could do, and by attaching a bill of rights, which contained specific written protections of citizens' natural rights.

The Constitution was the result of action taken by a group of dedicated American nationalists, who feared the American Republic would not survive without strong federal institutions. At the Philadelphia convention, no economic or social faction was able to work its will on the rest. Constitutional provisions were the result of extended debate, deliberation, and political compromise. Though the Constitution did work to protect property rights, property was more widely dispersed and was possessed more equally than it is today. If the Constitution involved a conspiracy to subvert the ideals of the American Revolution, the leading revolutionaries were themselves duped, since a great majority of them supported the Constitution (thirty of the forty-three living signers of the Declaration of Independence supported ratification).

The Constitution was not undemocratic, for the eighteenth century. The procedures used to ratify it allowed more people to participate than had participated in approving the Articles of Confederation or a majority of the state constitutions. And by the time of Rhode Island's ratification in 1790, a majority of the people, as reflected in their representatives, supported the new Constitution. The Constitution of 1787 was truly the climax of a revolution begun in the 1760s, a revolution in political principles as well as in political practices. The text must now turn to a discussion of these principles and practices as they have worked themselves out in the course of American constitutional history.

1.   Eighteen constitutions were written between 1776 and 1789. How did the various state and federal constitutions written during this period differ in their political principles and structures?

2.   Given the three constitutional issues that emerged among the American colonists during the 1760s, was the American Revolution inevitable? How might the revolution have been averted and the colonies kept within the British Empire?

3.   Critics of the Constitution of 1787 have pointed to the Articles of Confederation as a more democratic document. In what ways is the government of the Articles more democratic? Even if a person preferred its structures, given its perceived weaknesses in the 1780s, would the Articles be adequate for governing the nation today?

4.   Much of the wording and many of the specific provisions of the Constitution of 1787 must be understood in light of their origins in the prerevolutionary struggle with Great Britain. What examples can you cite? Does this fact date the document, or are the concerns expressed perennial political questions?

5.   The Anti-Federalists lost the ratification debate, but many of their arguments resurfaced after 1788. During what periods have some of the Anti-Federalists' concerns been presented? Do any of their ideas still ring true today?

1.   Quoted in Bernard Bailyn, *The Ideological Origins of the American Revolution* (Cambridge, Mass.: Harvard University Press, 1967), 135.

2.   "The Stamp Act, March 22, 1765," in Henry Steele Commager, ed., *Documents of American History,* 8th ed. (New York: Meredith Publishing, 1963), 53.

3.   "Virginia Stamp Act Resolutions, May 30, 1765," in Commager, *Documents of American History, 56.*

4.   James Otis, "The Rights of the British Colonies Asserted and Proved," in Merrill Jensen, ed., *Tracts of the American Revolution, 1763–1776* (Indianapolis, Ind.: Bobbs-Merrill, 1967), 19–40.

5.   "Virginia Stamp Act Resolutions, in Commager, *Documents of American History, 56.*

6.   "Resolutions of the Stamp Act Congress, October 19, 1765," in Commager, *Documents of American History, 58.*

7.   Quoted in Alfred H. Kelly et al., eds., *The American Constitution: Its Origins and Development,* 6th ed. (New York: Norton, 1983), 51.

8.   Quoted in Edmund S. Morgan, *The Birth of the Republic, 1763–1789* (Chicago: University of Chicago Press, 1956), 42.

9.   "A Summary View of the Rights of British America," in Merrill Petersen, ed., *The Portable Thomas Jefferson* (New York: Viking Press, 1975), 20.

10.   Morgan, *Birth of the Republic,* 45.

11.   Quoted in Charles H. McIlwain, *The American Revolution: A Constitutional Interpretation* (New York: Macmillan, 1923), 137.

12.   "Declaration and Resolves of the First Continental Congress, October 14, 1774," in Commager, *Documents of American History,* 83.

13.   Quoted in Merrill Jensen, *The Articles of Confederation: An Interpretation of the Social-Constitutional History of the American Revolution, 1774–1781* (Madison, Wis.: University of Wisconsin Press, 1940), 90–91.

14.   "Resolution for Independence, June

7, 1776," in Commager, *Documents of American History,* 100.

15. Quoted in Gordon S. Wood, *The Creation of the American Republic, 1776–1787* (Chapel Hill, N.C.: University of North Carolina Press, 1969), 136.

16. "Jefferson's Third Draft of a Virginia Constitution," in Wood, *Creation of the American Republic,* 136.

17. Jensen, *Articles of Confederation.*

18. "Resolution for Independence, June 7, 1776," in Commager, *Documents of American History,* 100.

19. Quoted in Andrew C. McLaughlin, *A Constitutional History of the United States* (New York: Appleton-Century-Crofts, 1935), 139.

20. "The Annapolis Convention, September 14, 1786," in Commager, *Documents of American History,* 133.

21. James Madison, "Letter to Thomas Jefferson, October 17, 1788," in Julian Boyd, ed., *The Papers of Thomas Jefferson,* vol. 14 (Princeton, N.J.: Princeton University Press, 1950), 19–20.

22. Thomas Jefferson, *Notes on the State of Virginia,* ed. William Peden (Chapel Hill, N.C.: University of North Carolina Press, 1955), 120.

23. "Resolution of Congress, February 21, 1787," quoted in Herbert J. Storing, *What the Anti-Federalists Were For* (Chicago: University of Chicago Press, 1981), 7.

24. "The Virginia Plan," in Commager, *Documents of American History,* 134.

25. Ibid.

26. "Vices of the Political System of the U.S.," quoted in Wood, *Creation of the American Republic,* 410.

27. Storing, *What the Anti-Federalists Were For,* 17.

28. "Letter to James Madison, July 31, 1788," quoted in Wood, *Creation of the American Republic,* 537.

29. "Speech on a Plan of Government," in *The Papers of Alexander Hamilton,* vol. 4 (New York: Columbia University Press, 1961), 200.

30. Jensen, *Articles of Confederation,* 243.

Suggested Readings

Bailyn, Bernard. *The Ideological Origins of the American Revolution.* Cambridge, Mass.: Harvard University Press, 1967.

Corwin, Edward S. "The Progress of Constitutional Theory Between the Declaration of Independence and the Meeting of the Philadelphia Convention." *American Historical Review* 30(1925): 511–36.

Hamilton, Alexander, John Jay, and James Madison. *The Federalist Papers.* New York: Modern Library, 1937.

Jensen, Merrill. *The Articles of Confederation: An Interpretation of the Social-Constitutional History of the American Revolution, 1774–1781.* Madison, Wis.: University of Wisconsin Press, 1940.

Levy, Leonard W., and Dennis J. Mahoney. *The Framing and Ratification of the Constitution.* New York: Macmillan, 1987.

Lutz, Donald S. *Popular Consent and Popular Control: Whig Political Theory in the Early State Constitutions.* Baton Rouge, La.: Louisiana State University Press, 1980.

McIlwain, Charles H. *The American Revolution: A Constitutional Interpretation.* New York: Macmillan 1923.

Morgan, Edmund S. *The Birth of the Republic, 1763–1789.* Chicago: University of Chicago Press, 1956.

Storing, Herbert J. *What the Anti-Federalists Were For.* Chicago: University of Chicago Press, 1981.

Wood, Gordon S. *The Creation of the American Republic, 1776–1787.* Chapel Hill, N.C.: University of North Carolina Press, 1969.

PART II

Structures and Processes of American Constitutional Government

WHEREAS THE DECLARATION of Independence dealt more with liberty and equality, the American Constitution, as drafted in 1787, was most interested in the responsible exercise of political power. As the chapters in Part I indicate, the framers were deeply concerned with the capacity of their new system of government to resolve a perplexing dilemma—how to create a government that had sufficient power to maintain stability over time, but also one that would not arbitrarily violate individual rights.

The four chapters in Part II concentrate upon the political structures and processes of American constitutional government that both allocate power and ensure its responsible usage. Chapter 4 discusses the organizational structure of the federal judiciary, the selection process for federal judges and Supreme Court justices, and the policy-making role of those courts, with special emphasis upon the doctrine of judicial review. Chapter 5 concentrates upon the division of power among branches in the American system and the historical struggle that has persisted between Congress and the president. Chapter 6 discusses the theory of American federalism that divides power between levels of government in the American system. This chapter also examines some modern dimensions of American federalism and the changes in that structure brought about by demands of the late twentieth century. Finally, Chapter 7 discusses American federalism in the context of the historical struggle in American society over property rights and economic liberty, and the increasing tendency in recent decades to regulate for the larger public good. After reading this chapter, it should become apparent that the individualistic versus communitarian conflict has assumed new meaning in the twentieth century.

Together, these chapters in Part II and their emphasis upon the responsible exercise of political power by government will serve as an important foundation for a later consideration in Part III of freedom and equality in American society.

Judicial Power and Judicial Review

Syllabus

During the past two decades, the United States Supreme Court has played a major, if not dominant, role in deciding substantive policy issues. The Supreme Court has made far-reaching decisions concerning the death penalty, a woman's right to an abortion, affirmative action plans to benefit disadvantaged groups, mandatory minimum wage, job discrimination, court-ordered busing, community antipornography regulations, and public aid to parochial schools. In fact, in one decision in 1983 dealing with an otherwise routine immigration case, the Court struck down a legislative veto provision of a federal law and implied that a similar provision in some two hundred other existing federal laws was also suspect. All of this activity stems from a power known as "judicial review," a concept that has assumed some rather unique proportions in the American judicial system.

The Supreme Court has acted to sustain or strike down actions of the other coordinate branches of the federal government, as well as the activities of states and municipalities. As such, it has usually been at the center of a democratic system that has historically placed great power and authority in the hands of nonelected, lifetime-tenured justices. This chapter will attempt to convey some of the rich diversity reflected in American judicial power, with particular emphasis upon the Supreme Court's use of judicial review. Judicial review has been used as an instrument to reconcile the frequent experiments of a pluralistic federal system with the rule of law as embodied in the United States Constitution.

This Chapter Examines the Following Matters

☐ The Supreme Court rests at the pinnacle of a federal judicial hierarchy containing several hundred judges with differing views about how to interpret and apply the U.S. Constitution. Each of the three levels of federal courts in the United States possesses a different type of jurisdiction, which significantly influences both the type and duration of the controversy advanced through the federal judiciary.

☐ Federal judges have seen their dockets and workloads increase in recent years as a result of the growth in certain categories of cases and the relatively modest increase in number of judgeships in federal courts generally.

☐ Historically, federal judges and Supreme Court justices have devised several judicial "rules of the game" that serve to limit the power of courts to resolve legal disputes between contending parties. Most of these rules have enabled the courts to avoid those controversies that might result in increased tension between branches or levels of government. Additionally, a few limitations upon judicial power are available to Congress to impose in certain rare circumstances.

☐ The manner in which federal judges and Supreme Court justices are selected is a highly politicized process. This process reflects not only sound judicial temperament, high personal integrity, distinguished professional training, and demonstrated powers of communication, but also political partisanship and probable policy views.

☐ As an evolving instrument of judicial policy making, judicial review has been justified on several different grounds—including framers' intent, historical acceptance, and the need to check majority rule.

☐ The history of the Supreme Court has exhibited several different periods wherein the justices have acted to resolve contentious legal issues before them. These legal questions have frequently been a prologue to subsequent constitutional debates.

Photo: The Supreme Court building, erected in 1935, bears above its columns the inscription "Equal Justice Under Law." Once described by Alexander Hamilton as "the least dangerous branch" of government, the Supreme Court today wields formidable power in our constitutional system through its exercise of judicial review.

The Paradox of Judicial Review

On a typical spring day in May 1987, the U.S. Supreme Court handed down several decisions in which it:

- □ upheld the right of an Iraqi-American professor denied tenure at a small Pennsylvania college to file suit under an 1866 law claiming racial discrimination;

- □ upheld the right of state courts to compel disabled veterans to pay child support;

- □ supported the right of labor unions to discipline members working for firms that did not have contracts with the union; and

- □ left intact a lower federal court ruling freezing the transfer of funds from the sale of New York property purchased by deposed Philippine dictator Ferdinand Marcos and his wife Imelda with money allegedly stolen from the Philippine government.[1]

These four rulings were only a small portion of the thousands of cases appealed to the Supreme Court in its 1986 term by various parties claiming a violation of a constitutional right. They confirm what Alexis de Tocqueville noted more than 150 years ago, when he stated, "The power vested in the American courts of justice, of pronouncing a statute to be unconstitutional, forms one of the most powerful barriers which has ever been devised against the tyranny of political assemblies." [2]

As this chapter will reflect, the practice of judicial review suggests a profound paradox in the American political system: rather than deciding major legal issues themselves or through their elected representatives, American citizens have consistently turned to jurists appointed for life to resolve such issues. They have allowed the Supreme Court to overrule actions of the other two popularly elected institutions of a democratic system. Throughout its history, the Court has tried to resolve this paradox by maintaining a procedural and legal commitment to preserving the rule of law and the principle of limited government. The Court seeks to ensure that the legislative and executive branches act within the enumerated and implied powers of the Constitution. It has done this in an active manner by upholding the constitutionality of a challenged statute or, far more frequently, in a passive manner by refusing to hear a case. Occasionally, as the latter portion of this chapter will indicate, the Supreme Court has found an action by other branches or levels of government to have violated some tenet of the Constitution.

As stated in Chapter 1, constitutional government requires that governmental power be ultimately constrained by law. Any governmental action not grounded in law is null and void. This is one of the basic premises that guided John Marshall in *Marbury* v. *Madison* (1803). Ultimately, the power of the Supreme Court rests not upon any device crafted by justices in the early 1800s, but rather upon whether the Court exercises its power responsibly. This power flows from its ability to give authoritative meaning to a "living" Constitution. In large part, it rests upon the Court's ability to persuade through reasoned judgment, institutional prestige, the cooperation of other political institutions, and, finally, the climate of public opinion. Without these essential supports, a Supreme Court decision has little effect.

The Structure of Federal Judicial Power

Since the founding, both the American states and the federal government have maintained a dual court system. In the fifty states, separate trial, appellate, and specialized courts exist to handle a wide variety of civil and criminal cases. At the federal level, a judicial hierarchy exists that has several important implications for the process of judicial selection, jurisdiction, and workload of the federal courts. One first must distinguish between two types of federal courts within this federal judicial hierarchy.

Legislative and Constitutional Courts

The U.S. Constitution authorizes two types of federal courts—**legislative** and **constitutional**—which differ in authority, function, and degree of independence from other political institutions. **Legislative courts** are authorized by Article I, Section 8, Clause 9, which gives Congress the power to "constitute Tribunals inferior to the supreme Court." **Constitutional courts,** on the other hand, are established by Article III, Section 1, which states that "the judicial Power of the United States, shall be vested in one supreme Court, and in such inferior Courts as the Congress may from time to time ordain and establish."

Legislative courts perform certain quasi-judicial tasks, such as administering on a regular basis specific congressional statutes. Constitutional courts perform strictly judicial functions. Legislative courts frequently submit advisory opinions, which are rulings on the constitutionality of a hypothetical governmental action, even though an actual controversy may not yet exist. By custom, constitutional courts have not provided advisory opinions ever since Chief Justice John Jay refused to consider a hypothetical situation when asked to do so by President George Washington in 1793. A final difference between legislative and constitutional courts concerns tenure, salary, and autonomy from Congress. Article I, Section 8, simply says that Congress has the right to create courts inferior to the Supreme Court and omits any reference to tenure or salary. This means that Congress is free to determine the tenure and salaries of legislative court judges. It does not have this freedom with regard to judges of constitutional courts. Article III, Section 1, of the Constitution reads:

> The Judges, both of the supreme and inferior Courts, shall hold their Offices during good Behaviour, and shall, at stated Times, receive for their Services a Compensation, which shall not be diminished during their Continuance in Office.

Two matters are at issue here—removal from office and salary. The only way that Congress can remove constitutional court judges is by a bill of impeachment (approved by a majority vote in the House of Representatives) and subsequent conviction in the Senate (two-thirds vote of members present). This device has rarely been used against federal judges.[3] Article III, Section 1, compels Congress to not *reduce* the salaries of federal judges on constitutional courts while the latter are in office. The stipulations regarding tenure and salaries derive from the framers' effort in 1787 to establish a federal judiciary largely independent from the two elected branches of the government.

The two federal court categories comprise various courts. The formal structure of the U.S. federal judiciary is depicted in Figure 4.1. Before the discussion proceeds to a more detailed description of legislative and consti-

FIGURE 4.1
Hierarchy of the
Federal Court System

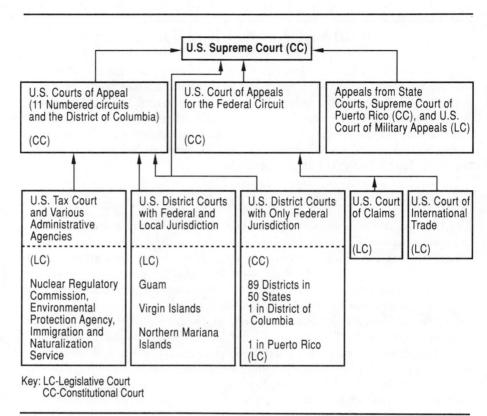

Key: LC-Legislative Court
CC-Constitutional Court

tutional courts, a general note about jurisdiction is warranted.

The **jurisdiction** of federal courts is their authority to hear a case or controversy when the proper parties are present and when the point to be decided is among the issues authorized to be handled by those courts. **Original jurisdiction** refers to courts of first resort, or courts holding trials, where the legal action begins. Within the federal judiciary, district courts are the primary trial courts. **Appellate jurisdiction** is the power of federal courts to review and, if necessary, correct errors of law that may have occurred in the trial court. If certain errors in interpreting or applying the law have occurred, the appellate court can order the lower court to retry the case under the prescribed new interpretation of the law. In the federal judicial system, the primary appellate courts are the U.S. Courts of Appeal and the U.S. Supreme Court.

Because the United States actually has fifty-one judicial systems—fifty state and one federal—the terms **exclusive jurisdiction** and **concurrent jurisdiction** also warrant brief comment. Exclusive federal jurisdiction means that only federal courts can hear the case or controversy that might arise in society. Concurrent jurisdiction means that, depending upon its nature, the case may be heard in either a federal or a state court. For instance, if a resident of Massachusetts files suit against a person living in Mississippi for damages resulting from an automobile accident, the person could go to a state court for recovery of damages or to a federal court, if the amount involved exceeded $10,000. Concurrent jurisdiction, thus, enables two different court systems to exercise jurisdiction over the same subject matter. State court systems have exclusive jurisdiction over all matters decided upon adequate and independent state grounds.

Legislative Courts: Jurisdiction, Personnel, and Workload

Currently, there are four legislative courts in the federal judicial system—the U.S. Tax Court, the U.S. Court of Military Appeals (USCMA), the U.S. Court of Claims, and the several territorial courts.

U.S. Tax Court.   The U.S. Tax Court used to be an administrative agency under the Internal Revenue Service (IRS), but in 1969 it was changed to a legislative court by an act of Congress. It is charged with reviewing various tax issues dealt with by the IRS, such as income tax, inheritance tax, and self-employment tax. Like other specialized courts, rulings by the U.S. Tax Court can be reviewed by the Supreme Court. The U.S. Tax Court consists of sixteen judges appointed by the president and confirmed by the Senate for fifteen years at an annual salary of $76,024 as of 1985. In recent years, this court has seen its workload increase from about 17,000 actions in 1979 to over 42,000 in 1985.

U.S. Court of Military Appeals.   The U.S. Court of Military Appeals was created by Congress in 1950, in response to criticisms that the system of military justice was biased in favor of the chain of command and against the defendant in court-martial proceedings. The USCMA is charged with applying and interpreting military law, which differs from civilian justice and judicial proceedings with respect to certain protections afforded the defendant. Since all military courts are legislative or Article I courts, other federal courts do not normally review their judgments. However, some decisions by the USCMA can be reviewed by constitutional courts, including the Supreme Court. Under a writ of *habeas corpus,* a person convicted under military law can appeal to a constitutional court for review of questions of jurisdiction or the alleged unconstitutionality of a military court action.

The USCMA is composed of three civilian judges who are nominated by the president and confirmed by the Senate. They are appointed for staggered fifteen-year terms and are paid an annual salary of $80,392 as of 1985. The USCMA can review at its discretion any decisions involving court-martials for bad conduct and any prison sentence exceeding one year. It must review all court-martial decisions that have been upheld by a lower court of military review in which the death penalty has been assessed. There have been very few such cases in recent decades. The USCMA accepts for review about two hundred of the approximately three thousand cases appealed to it annually.

Territorial Courts.   Territorial district courts are located in Guam, the Virgin Islands, Puerto Rico, and the Northern Mariana Islands. With the exception of the one in Puerto Rico, these courts exercise jurisdiction over local as well as federal cases. The territorial court in Puerto Rico has only federal jurisdiction, since there exists a separate state-local court system on that island. Territorial judges of the United States are, like other federal judges, nominated by the president and confirmed by the Senate. However, unlike the other legislative courts, judges of territorial courts (again, with the exception of Puerto Rico) have terms of office that vary from four to eight years, and their salaries can be reduced by Congress. Since 1966, territorial court judges in

Puerto Rico have been appointed for life under the normal federal guideline of "good behavior."

U.S. Court of Claims.   Prior to the 1980s, there were three additional legislative courts within the federal judiciary: the U.S. Court of Customs, the U.S. Court of Claims, and the U.S. Court of Customs and Patent Appeals. The former U.S. Court of Customs, since 1980 known as the U.S. Court of International Trade, has nine judges who receive an annual salary of $76,084 as of 1985. This court serves now as a constitutional trial court to hear disputes between private citizens, corporations, and the federal government involving matters relating to customs duties, the value of imported goods, and the exclusion of merchandise from the United States.

The U.S. Court of Claims, created by Congress in 1855 as a legislative court, was converted to a constitutional court in 1953. The primary function of this court for over a century was to hear claims brought by private citizens against the federal government in regard to public contracts. In 1982, Congress passed the Federal Courts Improvement Act which designated the Court of Claims as a legislative court again and increased the number of judges from seven to sixteen. These judges are also nominated by the President and confirmed by the Senate. They presently serve fifteen-year terms and are paid $76,024 each year (1985).

The 1982 law also gave to the U.S. Court of Claims only trial court functions, and its former appellate functions were transferred to a new federal judicial body, the U.S. Court of Appeals for the Federal Circuit. This new constitutional court also replaced the former U.S. Court of Customs and Patent Appeals, created originally in 1910 to hear appeals on custom, patent, and tariff matters. The new Court of Appeals for the Federal Circuit is charged with several review functions: decisions concerning all patent appeals from federal district courts; cases filed against the U.S. government for damages or refunds of federal taxes; appeals from the new U.S. Court of International Trade; and appeals from the Patents and Trademark Office. Decisions of the Court of Appeals for the Federal Circuit are subject to review by the Supreme Court.

Constitutional Courts: Jurisdiction, Personnel, and Workload

The three main constitutional courts in the United States are the U.S. Supreme Court, the eleven numbered U.S. Courts of Appeal, and ninety-four federal district courts. There is also a twelfth U.S. Court of Appeals for the District of Columbia, which is a more specialized constitutional court. As mentioned earlier, these are referred to as constitutional courts because they are authorized by Article III of the U.S. Constitution. The U.S. District Court for the District of Columbia is the only territorial court within the continental United States, and since 1970 (with passage of the District of Columbia Court Reorganization Act) the D.C. District Court has handled only *federal* cases, leaving local cases to the municipal lower courts in the District. Judges of both the D.C. District Court and U.S. Court of Appeals for the District of Columbia enjoy lifetime tenure and salaries that cannot be reduced by Congress. Administrative duties within the federal judiciary are distributed among several administrative bodies at both the numbered circuit and the national levels. These bodies include the Judicial Conference of the United States, the Administrative Office of the United States Courts, and the Federal Judicial Center.

U.S. District Courts.   The bottom tier of the federal judiciary is the *district court* level. With at least one district court in every state, these tribunals are the system's primary trial courts, exercising only original jurisdiction. At the beginning of 1984, there were eighty-nine district courts scattered throughout the United States, with a total of 515 district judgeships authorized by Congress. By mid-1984, Congress increased the number of federal district judgeships by sixty positions, bringing the total authorized number of judgeships to 575. Federal district judges are paid an annual salary of $89,500, as of 1987. Assisting these several hundred federal judges are law clerks, secretaries, court clerks, probation officers, bankruptcy judges, and U.S. magistrates.

In 1987, nearly 239,000 civil cases and over 43,000 criminal cases were filed in federal district courts, only a fraction of which (13,162 civil and 6,823 criminal) ever went to trial. The vast majority of federal cases are either settled out of court, plea-bargained, or dismissed. This is especially true with respect to civil cases. As some of the data in Table 4.1 indicate, since 1980, district courts and their judges have witnessed a major increase in their workload, on both their civil and criminal dockets. This was especially true before 1985, when two factors intervened to lessen the workload. First, Congress increased the number of authorized judgeships, as noted earlier, which served to decrease the number of cases per judgeship. Secondly, the decrease in civil filings by 6 percent in both 1986 and 1987 was greatly affected by a decline in filings for overpayments of veterans' benefits, defaulted student loans, and claims for Social Security benefits. Although recent changes in the total number of civil case filings account for the negative growth in filings, terminations and cases per judgeship in 1986–87, the data still indicate significant growth in civil case workload of federal district courts since 1980.

Table 4.1   U.S. District Courts Civil Cases Filed, Terminated, and Pending for years ending June 30; 1980–1987

YEAR	AUTHORIZED JUDGESHIPS	FILED NUMBER	FILED CASES PER JUDGESHIP	TERMINATED	PENDING
1980	516	168,789	327	160,481	186,113
1981	516	180,576	350	177,975	188,714
1982	515	206,193	400	189,473	205,434
1983	515	241,842	470	215,356	231,920
1984	515	261,485	508	243,113	250,292
1985	515	273,670	476	269,848	254,114
1986	575	254,828	443	266,765	242,177
1987	575	238,982	416	238,000	243,159
Percent Change, 1980–87	11.4	41.6	27.2	48.3	30.7
Percent Change, 1986–87	0.0	−6.2	−6.1	−10.8	0.4

Source: Director of the Administrative Office of the United States Courts, *Annual Report,* 1987, p. 6.

Data in Table 4.2 reflecting the criminal case workload for district courts likewise indicate considerable growth in case filings, terminations and pendings since 1980, as well as a one-third increase in the number of criminal cases per authorized judgeship. The overall increase in criminal cases in district courts in 1987 resulted mainly from increased prosecutions for fraud (especially mail fraud), drunk driving, other traffic violations, and drug violations. In spite of the increased judgeships authorized by Congress in 1984, the caseload per judgeship has grown steadily since 1980. In addition to increased prosecution of drunk driving, fraud, and drug violations, much of the growth of the criminal docket in the past fifteen years has resulted from changes in federal laws relating to civil rights, environmental protection, social welfare, and criminal procedure.

Although there is at least one federal district in every one of the 50 states—as well as Puerto Rico, the District of Columbia, Guam, the Virgin Islands, and the Northern Mariana Islands, some states (Texas, California, and New York) have as many as four district courts, and the number of federal judges in each district can vary from four to twenty-three. In exercising only original jurisdiction, these courts consider cases involving federal criminal and civil matters and **diversity cases** (controversies between citizens of different states) where the contested amount exceeds $10,000. However, when necessary, they can enforce and review actions and orders of federal agencies and departments, and some cases can be assigned to district courts from state courts under specific authorization by Congress. In addition to trying most federal cases in these areas, district courts also process various administrative matters, such as naturalization of aliens, passport applications, bankruptcy

Table 4.2   U.S. District Courts Criminal Cases Filed, Terminated, and Pending for years ending June 30; 1980–1987

YEAR	AUTHORIZED JUDGESHIPS	FILED[1] NUMBER	FILED[1] CASES PER JUDGESHIP	TERMINATED	PENDING
1980	516	28,932	56	29,297	14,759
1981	516	31,328	61	30,221	15,866
1982	515	32,682	63	31,889	16,659
1983	515	35,913	70	33,985	18,587
1984	515	36,845	72	35,494	19,938
1985	575	39,500	69	37,139	22,299
1986	575	41,490	72	39,328	24,453
1987	575	43,292	75	42,287	25,458
Percent Change, 1980–87	11.4	49.6	33.9	44.3	72.5
Percent Change, 1986–87	0.0	4.3	4.2	7.5	4.1

[1]Includes transfers

Source: Annual Report of the Director of the Administrative Office of the United States Courts, 1987, p. 13.

proceedings, and federal prisoner paroles. In the vast majority of cases, decisions by federal district courts are final.

Cases in the district courts are normally heard by one judge and a federally convened jury, although special three-judge panels without a jury can be convened for important cases requiring quicker resolution. Three-judge panels have dealt with such important issues as congressional or state legislative districting and matters relating to protection of individual voting rights. The party that loses in a district court can appeal the ruling, generally to the court of appeals in the circuit wherein the district court lies. Under some circumstances, an appeal can be made directly to the U.S. Supreme Court, such as when district court rulings are heard by a three-judge panel, when a federal law is declared unconstitutional, and when a case is of major public significance and requires immediate resolution. Examples of cases appealed directly to the Supreme Court include *Youngstown Sheet and Tube Company* v. *Sawyer* (1952) and *United States* v. *Nixon* (1974), both of which are discussed in Chapter 5, and *New York Times* v. *United States* (1971), which is covered in Chapter 12.

U.S. Courts of Appeal.   Directly above the eighty-nine district courts are the twelve U.S. Courts of Appeal, all of which exercise primarily appellate jurisdiction. In some rare instances, these courts may exercise original jurisdiction in cases involving behavior of district court judges. Appellate jurisdiction covers all cases tried by the district courts (except those that can be appealed directly to the Supreme Court). These intermediate courts of appeal were created in 1891 to reduce some of the workload of Supreme Court justices. During the past century, the federal courts of appeal have disposed of 85–90 percent of federal cases appealed beyond the trial court level. In 1986, there were 34,292 cases filed in the appeals courts, representing more than a 47 percent increase from 1980 (see Table 4.3 below). Included in this statistic were 29,425 appeals from the district courts, and 3,187 petitions to review or enforce administrative orders. Again, the major increases in federal litigation since 1980 have been at the civil level, with more than a 75 percent increase in the number of private civil cases being appealed, and over 93 percent of private civil cases since 1980 being terminated.

The twelve federal courts of appeal have from six to twenty-eight judges assigned to them by Congress, depending upon the workload. As of 1987, circuit appellate court judges were paid $95,000 per year. In disposing of their workload, appellate judges normally sit as three-judge panels, with the senior judge assigning opinions. In controversial cases, all the judges within the circuit may hear the case (referred to as an *en banc* proceeding). Another special procedure in cases considered urgent is a mixed three-judge panel composed of both district and appellate judges, with any appeal going directly to the Supreme Court.

Besides its regularly assigned appellate judges, each circuit has assigned to it a particular Supreme Court justice. The two most senior associate justices and the chief justice are each assigned to two circuits, and the other justices are each assigned to one numbered circuit. This tradition dates from the era when Supreme Court justices actually "rode the circuit" and sat as appellate judges. Their contemporary duties, however, are largely confined to acting on petitions within their respective circuit when the Supreme Court is not in

Table 4.3   *U.S. Courts of Appeal,* Civil and Criminal; 1980–86, for years ending June 30

CASE DISPOSITION	1980	1981	1982	1983	1984	1985	1986	% CHANGE '80–'86
Cases Commenced	23,200	26,362	27,946	29,630	31,490	33,360	34,292	+47.8
Criminal	4,405	4,377	4,767	4,790	4,881	4,989	5,134	+16.5
U.S. civil	4,654	4,940	5,517	5,820	6,259	6,744	6,415	+37.8
Private civil	10,200	12,074	13,267	14,429	15,466	16,827	17,876	+75.3
Admin. appeals	2,950	3,800	3,118	3,069	3,045	3,179	3,187	+8.0
Cases Terminated[1]	20,887	25,066	27,984	28,660	31,185	31,387	33,774	+61.7
Criminal	3,993	4,192	4,522	4,777	4,876	4,892	5,134	+28.6
U.S. civil	4,346	5,021	5,508	5,505	6,074	6,363	6,535	+50.4
Private civil	8,942	11,327	13,115	13,710	15,309	15,743	17,276	+93.2
Admin. appeals	2,643	3,303	3,549	3,260	3,212	2,760	3,235	+22.4
Cases Disposed of[2]	10,607	12,168	12,720	13,217	14,327	16,369	18,199	+71.6
Affirmed or granted	8,017	9,004	9,560	10,174	10,961	12,286	13,398	+67.1
Reversed or denied	1,845	2,246	2,138	2,173	2,382	2,770	3,249	+76.1
Other	745	918	1,022	870	984	1,313	1,552	+108.3

[1]Includes original proceedings and bankruptcy appeals not shown separately.
[2]Terminated on the merits after hearing or submission.

Source: Bureau of the Census, U.S. Dept. of Commerce, *Statistical Abstract of the United States,* 1988, p. 171.

session (e.g., on a request for a stay of execution in capital cases). The U.S. Court of Appeals for the District of Columbia is concerned exclusively with contested rulings of the several administrative agencies. As federal regulations and rulings have grown in recent years, so has the activity of this very specialized and important court. Before being nominated to the Supreme Court by President Reagan in 1986, Justice Antonin Scalia served on this court. The newest addition to the Supreme Court, Judge Anthony Kennedy, served on the U.S. Court of Appeals for the Ninth Circuit.

One final note should be made about the workload of both the district courts and courts of appeal. As Table 4.4 indicates, since 1984 there has been a modest increase in the number of authorized federal district and appellate judgeships (11 percent and 27 percent, respectively), which has two major implications. First, the increase has lessened somewhat the caseload per judge, as indicated earlier in Table 2.2. At least in the short term, that probably has some positive consequences for the administration of justice. Secondly, the increased authorizations on the federal bench beginning in 1985 gave President Ronald Reagan and future presidents more opportunities to influence the long-term complexion of the federal judiciary through the appointment of favored personnel.

Table 4.4 U.S. District Courts and Courts of Appeal—*Status of Federal Judgeships, on June 30, 1980–1985*

	1980	1981	1982	1983	1984	1985	% CHANGE '80–'85
U.S. Courts of Appeal (including Court of Appeal for Federal Circuit)							
Authorized	132	132	132	144	144	168	+27.3
Vacancies	6	9	7	4	2	22	+266.7
Senior Judges	45	45	54	55	52	59	+31.1
U.S. District Courts							
Authorized	516	516	515	515	515	575	+11.4
Vacancies	32	41	20	25	16	75	+134.4
Senior Judges	126	149	163	175	185	191	+51.6

Source: Director of the Administrative Office of the United States Courts, *Annual Report,* 1985, 8–9.

U.S. Supreme Court.   At the top of the federal judiciary is the United States Supreme Court. Although in many respects the most authoritative and controversial of the several federal courts, the Supreme Court is still only one of more than one hundred federal courts, and it includes only nine of more than seven hundred judgeships within the federal judiciary. The Supreme Court consists of a chief justice and eight associate justices who, like all constitutional court judges, are nominated by the president and confirmed by the Senate with lifetime tenure. As a result of legislation passed by Congress in late 1987, the chief justice earns $115,000 per annum, and associate justices earn $110,000 each year. Supreme Court justices can only be removed by impeachment in the U.S. House of Representatives and conviction in the U.S. Senate, in accordance with Article I, Sections 2 and 3, of the Constitution.

The Supreme Court exercises both original and appellate jurisdiction, only the latter of which can be regulated by Congress. Its original jurisdiction can be exercised in many instances—including cases between two or more states or between a state and the federal government; cases involving foreign ambassadors, ministers, consuls, and their staffs; and cases initiated by a state against citizens of another state or nation. In cases between two or more states and in cases against foreign diplomatic personnel, the Court has exclusive original jurisdiction. In all other instances, it has concurrent original jurisdiction with district courts. In reality, the Supreme Court rarely exercises its original jurisdiction (only one of 4,339 cases in the 1986 term ending in June 1987 involved original jurisdiction). The Supreme Court hands down full, written opinions in relatively few of the hundreds of cases that it disposes of

Table 4.5   U.S. Supreme Court—Final Disposition of Cases, October Terms, 1965; 1975; 1986

	1965		1975		1986		% CHANGE '65–'86 DISPOSED/REMAINING
	DISPOSED OF	REMAINING	DISPOSED OF	REMAINING	DISPOSED OF	REMAINING	
Original Docket	9	8	7	7	1	11	
Appellate Docket (petitions granted)	1,172 (134)	254	1,810 (154)	542	2,099 (242)	448	+79.0/+76.4 (+80.6)
Miscellaneous Docket (petitions granted)	1,502 (43)	329	1,989 (18)	406	2,239 (26)	325	+49.1/–1.2 (–39.5)
Total Appeals granted this term	(177)		(172)		(273)		(+54.2)
TOTAL	2,683	591	3,806	955	4,339	784	+61.7/+32.7
No. of Written Opinions	107		156		152		+42.1

Source: *Harvard Law Review,* "The Supreme Court Term, 1965," vol. 80, November 1966, pp. 143–44; "The Supreme Court Term, 1975," vol. 90, November 1976, p. 276; 279; "The Supreme Court Term, 1986," vol 101, November 1987, p. 362; 366.

annually. In its 1986 term, the high court provided written opinions in 152 of the 4,339 cases filed with the Court (3.5 percent), as depicted in Table 4.5. It is also apparent from these data that since 1965 there has been a major increase in several aspects of the Supreme Court's workload. The number of cases appearing on the appellate docket has grown substantially since 1965, as has the total number of petitions disposed of during the court term.

For the Supreme Court to hear a case, there must be a clear collision between contending interests in a concrete instance. Article III refers specifically to "Cases . . . Controversies." Furthermore, the parties involved in the case or controversy must have **standing** to sue in federal courts. Standing refers to a legal right to sue wherein the party must prove that he or she has suffered or will suffer direct personal injury as a result of the enforcement of some federal law or action. In the twentieth century, more and more parties have enjoyed "standing to sue" in federal courts, as an entire body of civil rights, environmental, and consumer legislation has emerged. As might be expected, this has extended the workload of federal courts.[4]

Self-Limitations on Federal Judicial Power

For decades, the most prominent body of judicial rules used by the justices to limit standing before the Supreme Court has been the *"Ashwander* rules," named for the guidelines compiled by Justice Louis D. Brandeis in *Ashwander* v. *Tennessee Valley Authority* (1936). As a long-time protector of civil liberties during his twenty-three years on the Court, Brandeis maintained that courts could best serve society by following carefully prescribed rules of judicial behavior. His guidelines for limiting Court authority have assumed an almost semiconstitutional status. Although the Supreme Court has often ignored these rules during the past half-century, justices frequently quote from them and thereby reaffirm their legitimacy. In deciding cases, the Court:

1. will not offer advisory opinions or pass upon the constitutionality of legislation in a nonadversary opinion;

2. will not anticipate a constitutional question prior to having to decide it;

3. will not formulate a rule of law broader than the facts of a case require;

4. will not pass on the validity of a statute or complaint by one failing to show direct injury to person or property;

5. will not pass upon the constitutionality of a statute if the plaintiff has accepted the benefits of it previously;

6. if possible, will dispose of a case on statutory, rather than constitutional, grounds; and finally,

7. whenever possible, will interpret a statute in order to avoid a constitutional issue.

After more than fifty years, these rules are still major "gatekeeping" devices that federal judges use with great discretion to resolve legal disputes in cases brought before them.

Three other self-limitations upon the exercise of judicial power concern **ripeness, mootness,** and **political questions. Ripeness** compels the plaintiff (the party filing suit in federal court) to establish that he or she has exhausted all other available administrative remedies before coming to federal court. If the plaintiff cannot prove this, he or she has no standing in federal court because the case is not "ripe" for federal adjudication. In other words, the plaintiff has come to court too early.

There have been several instances of this absence of ripeness. Two of the more prominent are *United Public Workers* v. *Mitchell* (1947) and *Poe* v. *Ullman* (1961). The first case involved federal civil service employees who were claiming that the Hatch Act prohibition against taking any active part in political management or in political campaigns violated their First Amendment rights. Only one of the plaintiffs in the case admitted to having actually violated the law, although the others insisted that they wanted to do so in the future. The Supreme Court ruled that the case did not present a "ripe," or "justiciable," issue capable of judicial remedy, and, therefore, it would offer no advisory opinion in a case involving only hypothetical constitutional issues.

In *Poe* v. *Ullman,* several married couples and their physician filed suit in federal court challenging the constitutionality of an 1879 Connecticut law prohibiting the use of contraceptive devices and the offering of medical advice about the use of such devices. After observing that the state had shown no desire to prosecute possible offenders of the law, the Supreme Court, with Justice Felix Frankfurter writing for the majority, noted that "the lack of immediacy of the threat described by these allegations might alone raise serious questions of nonjusticiability of appellants' claims." After referring to the *Ashwander* rules, standing, and ripeness, the Court dismissed the challenge to the state law. Four years later, of course, the same law would be challenged successfully in the case of *Griswold* v. *Connecticut* (1965) and handled quite differently by the Court (see Chapter 10).

Whereas ripeness involves a plaintiff's coming prematurely to the courts, **mootness** is when an individual arrives too late in federal court. Federal courts should not consider questions without a clear personal injury to the person bringing suit in federal court. For the person to have standing, there must be a truly adversial circumstance involving real personal or property damage. A good example of a case that was declared "moot" appears in Brief 4.1.

The final principle limiting federal courts in the exercise of their power is the political-questions doctrine, which dates from at least 1827 and John Marshall's decision in *Martin* v. *Mott,* as well as his earlier opinion in *Marbury* v. *Madison* in 1803. This concept maintains that courts should not intrude into disputes that can be more reasonably settled by the other two branches of the government. As elected public officials accountable to the majority will, legislators and presidents should resolve disputes that involve differing views of public policy. This concept does not actually address whether politics is involved in certain public policy issues and not in others, since politics is inherent in virtually all policy choices. Rather, it asks whether the separation-of-powers principle compels each branch to avoid intruding into the proper domain of the other coordinate branches of government.

In recent years, political questions have been most prominent in the policy areas of foreign affairs and national defense. In these areas, the Supreme Court has frequently refused to intervene in many matters considered to be within the chief executive's policy realm.[5] But in recent years, the doctrine has been invoked less frequently as the Supreme Court has intervened in an increasing number of areas earlier thought to be off-limits to federal courts. Examples include legislative apportionment (to be discussed later in this chapter) and,

🔲 *Brief 4.1   De Funis and the Court*

The case of *De Funis* v. *Odegaard* (1974) was a precursor to the important affirmative action cases of the 1970s and 1980s. The case dealt with an individual by the name of Marcus De Funis who had been denied admission to the University of Washington Law School. A state court had upheld his claim that the school had practiced reverse discrimination and violated the Equal Protection Clause when it had admitted minority students with lower qualifications. The university appealed the lower court ruling and won in Washington state superior court, but the ruling was delayed. By the time De Funis appealed the case to the U.S. Supreme Court, he had already reapplied and was enrolled in his final

term of law school. The Court then ruled 5-4 in a *per curiam* opinion that the case was "moot." According to the Court, "Mootness in the present case depends upon . . . the simple fact that De Funis is now in the final quarter of the final year of his course of study, and the settled and unchallenged policy of the Law School is to permit him to complete the term for which he is now enrolled." Ironically, Justice William O. Douglas dissented in the case, arguing that the case presented a live controversy. Douglas, one of the most liberal justices to ever sit on the Supreme Court, seemed very opposed to affirmative action, insisting that "there is no constitutional right for any race to be preferred."

---

to a lesser degree, several areas of prisoners' rights (to be discussed in Chapter 8), the seating of members of Congress (*Powell* v. *McCormack* [1969]), and the use of the legislative veto (to be discussed in Chapter 5, involving *Immigration and Naturalization Service* v. *Chadha* [1983]).

Congressional Restrictions on Federal Judicial Power

If the Supreme Court refuses to impose certain limitations upon its own ability to hear cases and issues brought before it, several external factors have historically worked to limit the degree to which the Court has been able to change the status quo. Obvious examples of political checks upon the Supreme Court include the following:

- ☐ the rare threat of judicial impeachment,
- ☐ the climate of public opinion,
- ☐ alterations in the size of the Court (e.g., the "court-packing" incident in the 1930s, which will be referred to later),
- ☐ action by Congress which changes laws that have been construed by the Court (e.g., passage of the Civil Rights Restoration Act in 1988, which will be discussed in Chapter 9),
- ☐ constitutional amendments,
- ☐ congressional control over the dates of judicial sessions, and
- ☐ professional criticism flowing from law reviews and other academic commentary.

In addition to these external devices for limiting the exercise of judicial power by the Supreme Court, Congress can also intervene to prevent the federal courts from exercising their appellate authority. This action by Congress involves an important distinction between original and appellate jurisdiction, especially as it affects the U.S. Supreme Court. Since *Marbury* v. *Madison* in 1803 (see discussion later in this chapter), one of the long-established principles in American constitutional law is that, in accordance with Article III, Section 2, Clause 2, Congress can revise the *appellate* jurisdiction of the Supreme Court. Although it has seldom voted to do so, on at least two occasions (both in wartime), the Congress limited the ability of the Supreme Court to act by regulating its appellate jurisdiction.

The first example arose in the post-Civil War case of *Ex Parte McCardle* (1869). On February 5, 1867, Congress voted to authorize federal courts to grant *habeas corpus* writs to persons detained illegally. Those persons claiming illegal detention could appeal any adverse ruling to the Supreme Court. William McCardle had been imprisoned for publishing allegedly libelous statements criticizing the reconstruction government in Mississippi. After losing in a lower court in Mississippi, McCardle appealed his conviction to the U.S. Supreme Court. Faced with a challenge to its reconstruction policy and the possibility that the Court might declare the 1867 statute unconstitutional, Congress repealed the statute in 1868, and thereby denied McCardle the right to appeal his conviction. The major constitutional question raised in *McCardle* was whether the Supreme Court had the right to hear the case after repeal of the statute. The Court ruled that, given the repeal of the law on which McCardle had relied, it had no authority to exercise its appellate jurisdiction and hear the case. In the words of Chief Justice Salmon P. Chase:

> Without jurisdiction the court cannot proceed at all in any cause. Jurisdiction is power to declare the law, and when it ceases to exist, the only function remaining to the court is that of announcing the fact and dismissing the cause.

The other case that found Congress voting to limit the Supreme Court's appellate jurisdiction is *Yakus* v. *United States* (1944). Soon after declaring war against Japan and Germany in 1941, Congress passed the Emergency Price Control Act of 1942, which instituted price controls on various priority items needed in wartime. It also created the Emergency Court of Appeals and gave to that appellate court "exclusive jurisdiction to determine the validity of any regulation or order of the Price Administrator." The act declared that "no Court, Federal, State or Territorial, shall have jurisdiction or power to restrain, enjoin, or set aside any provision of this Act." In *Yakus,* the defendant argued that the Price Control Act violated the Fifth Amendment by depriving him of his property without due process of law. Over a powerful dissenting opinion by Justice Wiley Rutledge who said that "even war does not suspend the protections which are inherently part and parcel of our criminal process," a 6-3 Court upheld the act. Chief Justice Harlan Stone argued for the majority that the act was a broad, but legal, delegation of legislative authority to the Office of Price Administration. Since Yakus could have appealed his conviction to the Emergency Court of Appeals, there was no Fifth Amendment violation.

In recent years, Congress has not been as successful in regulating the appellate jurisdiction of federal courts, especially the Supreme Court. Recent examples have involved bills introduced in Congress barring appellate review of contentious "social agenda" items of the Reagan administration. Although no such bills won majority support from Congress, given the Reagan administration's staunch support for oral school prayer and its opposition to busing and abortion, there is little doubt that if passed, the White House would have welcomed this limitation upon federal courts to make public policy.

How a Case Reaches the U.S. Supreme Court

There are three main routes by which cases from lower state or federal courts can be appealed to the Supreme Court—writs of *certiorari, appeal,* and *cer-*

tification. Only the first two are of any major significance in the modern era, since they comprise the overwhelming majority of cases decided annually by the Supreme Court.

A **writ of certiorari** involves an order by the Supreme Court to a lower court to "send up the record" of the case so that the Court can determine if the law was correctly interpreted and applied. Congress has given the Court complete discretion to grant a writ of certiorari. Because of a commitment made many decades ago to Congress by Chief Justice William Howard Taft, certiorari is granted whenever four or more justices consent to hear the case (referred to as the "Rule of Four"). If a full court is not sitting, three votes will suffice. If the Court chooses not to hear a case, certiorari is denied and no explanation from the justices is necessary. In recent years, as many as 85 percent of all cases appealed to the Supreme Court each year arrive on a petition for certiorari.

The second most typical form of appeal petition to the Supreme Court involves the **writ of appeal.** As provided for in the Judges' Bill of 1925, certain cases must be heard by the Supreme Court as a matter of right. However, since 1928 the Court has had great discretion here as well to refuse to hear appeal petitions. This technical right to an appeal exists in the following instances:

- □ when the highest court in a state has declared either a federal law or a treaty unconstitutional;
- □ when a state law or provision of a state constitution has been upheld against a challenge that it conflicts with a federal statute, treaty provision, or the U.S. Constitution;
- □ when the U.S. Court of Appeals has ruled as unconstitutional either a state law or a provision of a state constitution; or,
- □ when a district court or the U.S. Court of Appeals for the Federal Circuit rules a federal law unconstitutional in a case where either the federal government or federal employees are parties to the suit.

In practice, most cases "on appeal" come from state courts, and between 10 and 20 percent of the Supreme Court's cases arrive by this route annually. If the high court accepts such cases for review, it normally handles most of them without oral argument. Although litigants normally have the right to appeal, like the certiorari cases, the Rule of Four normally applies, and the court can simply dismiss the case for lack of a substantial federal question or for want of jurisdiction. In other words, recent practice suggests little meaningful difference between cases that have arrived on appeal or by certiorari. If the Court does not want to hear a case for any of several reasons, it can normally find grounds for effectively ignoring it. The final basis for Supreme Court action, called **writ of certification,** is a lower court's request for clarification on a particular point of law, although it is seldom granted by the Supreme Court.

The most frequently traveled paths to the Supreme Court are the certiorari and appeal writs, and, as stated previously, less than 4 percent of the cases handled by the Court each year are ever treated to full, written opinions. The remainder of the cases and those for which no oral argument is allowed are normally disposed of through a *per curiam* opinion, which is a short, unsigned opinion meaning "by the court." In some instances, a brief memorandum order indicates that the lower court decision is "dismissed," "affirmed," "vacated," or "reversed and remanded." (Reversed and remanded means that the lower court ruling is overruled and the case is sent back to the lower court for proper implementation.)

A major reason for much of the Court's increased workload in recent years has resulted from the large number of cases filed and disposed of in the so-called "miscellaneous docket" (see Table 4.5). Most of the petitions for review in this category are handwritten or typewritten and filed by indigents and prison inmates. These are referred to as *paupers'*, or IFP, *petitions (in forma pauperis)* and customarily lack the more essential material required in other petitions. From the 1965 to 1986 Court terms, as Table 4.5 indicates, the number of petitions in this category disposed of increased from about 1,500 to over 2,200, or an increase of 49 percent. However, the percentage of petitions on the miscellaneous docket actually granted by the Supreme Court decreased by 39 percent.

The Supreme Court needs six justices hearing a case in order to have a quorum. The Court meets from the first Monday in October until late June or early July, with some of the most important decisions generally coming in the final weeks of the Court's term. As the following section will reflect, many factors influence the recruitment process for this elite judicial body. The simple fact that since 1789, only 104 individuals (Justices Antonin Scalia and Anthony Kennedy being the newest additions) have served on the Supreme Court dramatizes the extent to which this is truly a position to which many aspire, but few are chosen.

The Appointment of Judges and Justices

Before considering how the U.S. Supreme Court has historically exercised its judicial authority, it is appropriate to mention those factors that influence selection to the federal bench. Key questions here are, What is the nature of the judicial selection process? What variables are most important in the nomination and selection of persons to fill vacancies within the federal judiciary? Although this text deals primarily with the Supreme Court, the selection process is basically the same for a federal district judge, an appellate judge, or a Supreme Court justice.

The Judicial Selection Process

A key point to remember about the judicial selection process is that it is inherently a *political* process with very few formal requirements. Unlike constitutional prerequisites for members of Congress or the president (e.g., age, citizenship, residence), Article III does not mention any formal requirements for Supreme Court justices or any members of the federal judiciary. In fact, there is not even any requirement that Supreme Court justices have a law degree, although in practice, only lawyers have served on the high court.

At first glance, the selection process for federal judges and justices is deceptively simple. To become a federal judge requires four elements: a vacancy, a presidential nomination, confirmation by a majority vote of the Senate, and a formal presidential signature and issuance of a commission. Although the delegates at the Constitutional Convention supported the creation of a national judiciary, there was some disagreement over how its members should be selected. Those who proposed the Virginia Plan (see Chapter 3) wanted the judiciary to be chosen by Congress. An alternative proposal envisioned by the New Jersey Plan was that judges would be chosen by the president. As happened so frequently at the Philadelphia convention, the delegates compromised by agreeing that members of the national judiciary should be nominated by the president and confirmed by the Senate. Article II, Section 2, reads that "the President . . . shall nominate, and by and with the Advice and Consent of the Senate, shall appoint . . . Judges of the Supreme Court."

This brief mention of the power of appointment disguises the uneasy partnership that has existed for two hundred years between the president and Congress concerning the selection of federal judges. Although the president can nominate individuals to fill those vacancies, the Senate has an important veto over those nominations, especially at the federal district court level. Even at the Supreme Court level, since 1793 over 20 percent of a president's nominations to the Supreme Court have failed to win confirmation by the Senate.[6]

In fact, the judicial selection process contains several potential pitfalls for a president bent upon leaving an imprint upon the federal judiciary. Many political actors are involved: the president; Department of Justice officials; the Federal Bureau of Investigation; U.S. senators; state and local party leaders; supporters of other potential nominees (including members of the Supreme Court!) who lobby for their candidates; personnel from the American Bar Association's Committee on the Federal Judiciary; and members of the powerful Senate Judiciary Committee. At any of these several levels, complications may arise for nominees desiring a seat on the federal bench.

The initial hurdle for potential nominees to the lower federal courts is the approval of senators from the president's party and the state in which a vacancy occurs. This important selection variable normally affects only nominees for lower federal judgeships and is referred to as **senatorial courtesy.** Senatorial courtesy dates from the original design of the federal judicial structure in 1789, which ensured that district courts reflected the localism and conservatism imposed by state political boundaries. The Department of Justice (DOJ) maintains files on potential appointments to fill vacancies within the federal judiciary, but normally considers candidates recommended by senators and other key party members. In practice, it means that presidents extend to senators of their party the courtesy of first passing upon the acceptability of prospective nominees. As soon as a lower court vacancy is announced, the senators from the state with the vacancy begin working with their staffs to compile their own list of favorite nominees. Once they have agreed upon a candidate, assuming that they are from the president's political party, the president then submits that name to the Senate for formal hearings and a confirmation vote. Senatorial courtesy usually does not significantly affect the selection process of a prospective nominee to the Supreme Court, although presidents are wise to at least check with home-state senators about their views of the nominee.

If approved by home-state senators, the prospective candidate is then screened by the Department of Justice, which conducts its own internal investigation and submits the list of potential nominees to the Committee on the Federal Judiciary of the American Bar Association (ABA). This professional committee has played a pivotal, though not decisive, role since the mid-1950s. When evaluating candidates for the lower federal courts, the ABA committee summarizes its judgment according to "Exceptionally Well qualified," "Well

Qualified," "Qualified," and "Not Qualified." When considering candidates for the Supreme court, the committee awards the ratings of "Highly Qualified," "Not Opposed," and "Not Qualified." A lower bench candidate supported by key U.S. senators and state party leaders within the president's party is normally assured nomination and confirmation if he or she also satisfactorily meets the informal standards of the Justice Department and the ABA. Depending upon the president, Justice Department officials have exercised varying degrees of influence in screening prospective candidates. In recent decades, Presidents Dwight Eisenhower, John Kennedy, and Jimmy Carter deferred more to key Justice Department officials. President Lyndon Johnson often played a more personal role in selecting the nominee, and Presidents Richard Nixon, Gerald Ford, and Ronald Reagan deferred more to their respective attorneys general for recommendations for the federal bench.

In recent years, but particularly during the Nixon and Reagan administrations, candidates for federal judgeships have been asked to complete a questionnaire providing extensive information about their personal and professional backgrounds and policy views. In addition to providing a nominating president with a more complete profile of the individual, especially the candidate's policy views, this information has also been helpful to the Federal Bureau of Investigation (FBI) for use in screening judicial candidates. During the Reagan administration, the most important screening body dealing with federal judicial appointments was the Committee on Federal Judicial Selection (see Brief 4.2).

If administration officials are encouraged by this internal investigation, the name of the nominee is formally announced by the president and sent to the U.S. Senate, which then assigns it to the Senate Judiciary Committee for scheduled confirmation hearings. Assuming that the home-state senators from

---

❑ Brief 4.2   The Reagan Years: Changes in the Judicial Selection Process

Throughout the Reagan presidency, the most important factors governing judicial selection were policy orientation relating to criminal procedure, family values, and conservative social issues. And the most important body within the administration for picking the "right" federal court nominee was the Committee on Federal Judicial Selection. The highest levels of White House staff and Department of Justice personnel have served on the committee, created in 1981. In 1986, the president's chief of staff, his special counsel on judicial selection, the attorney general, the deputy attorney general, the associate attorney general, and the assistant attorney general for legal policy were key participants in influencing judicial selection in the Reagan administration. The screening group developed its own list of judicial nominees and conducted independent investigations on those nominees, with ideology being the paramount consideration.

Throughout the Reagan years, the emphasis was upon judges who "interpret the law, not make it," to use the words of both Attorney General Edwin Meese and the president. The committee's screening procedure worked well in the nominations of Sandra Day O'Connor in 1981 and Antonin Scalia in 1986, both of whom won easy confirmation by the U.S. Senate. It led to disastrous consequences for Judges Robert H. Bork and Douglas H. Ginsburg, both of whom were nominated by the Reagan administration following the announced resignation of Justice Lewis Powell in June 1987 (see Brief 4.3). The Reagan White House finally settled upon Judge Anthony Kennedy, a federal appellate court judge from California, who won unanimous approval by the Senate in February 1988.

the president's party approve of the nominee, and the Judiciary Committee finds nothing during its investigation that might prove unacceptable to its members or to the full Senate, the committee normally votes to recommend confirmation of the nominee by the full Senate. Although opposition can develop in the Senate, normally that body confirms candidates who have made it this far in the selection process. Finally, the nomination receives the president's signature, and the commission is offered. This characterization applies to nominees to the lower federal courts only, since, as stated earlier, confirmation of nominees to the Supreme Court can be much more problematic. It must be remembered that presidents have seen their nominations to the high court disapproved over 20 percent of the time during the past two centuries.

Judicial Selection Variables

A few crucial factors dominate the judicial selection process. Throughout the twentieth century, three variables have been vital to winning eventual confirmation by the Senate: *professional* or judicial qualifications; *representational,* especially party, considerations; and *doctrinal* or policy views.

Professional Competence.   The most formal determinant of whether a candidate is *professionally* qualified for a seat on the federal bench is the ABA's stamp of approval. Ever since President Woodrow Wilson nominated Louis D. Brandeis to the Supreme Court in 1916, over the objection of the conservative American Bar Association, that group's approval has been somewhat controversial. Generally, criticisms have centered on what role a private occupational group, with an historically conservative Republican bias, should play in influencing who occupies high judicial office. ABA endorsement of a candidate—which normally is based upon that organization's assessment of the nominee's judicial temperament, personal integrity, and professional competence—does not guarantee confirmation. As any student of American constitutional law might recall, Brandeis did not have ABA approval. He was eventually confirmed by the Senate after a four-month delay and went on to become one of the most distinguished justices ever to serve on the Court. And in 1968, when the ABA supported Justice Abe Fortas's nomination by President Johnson to succeed Earl Warren as chief justice, that endorsement was insufficient to win Fortas's confirmation. Fortas resigned from the Court in 1969 amid public charges of ongoing conflict-of-interest involving a Florida financier and reports that he continued to advise President Johnson while serving on the Court.

Since the mid-1960s, the role of the ABA's Committee on the Federal Judiciary has changed for several reasons, at least with respect to nominees to the Supreme Court. First, the Senate's successive rejections in 1970 of Clement Haynsworth, Jr., and G. Harrold Carswell (both of whom had received ABA approval) to fill the Fortas seat greatly angered President Nixon. It also diminished the prestige of the ABA's stamp of approval, at least in Nixon's eyes. Secondly, since the Watergate scandal, the ABA may have shed some of its traditional conservative stance, as evidenced by its continued support for certain public policy issues, such as legal aid for the poor. A third reason for the diminished role of the ABA committee in recent years was the creation of the U.S. Circuit Judge Nominating Commission by President Carter in 1977. This panel was an attempt to increase the chances of merit selection to the federal judiciary and to reduce the excessively political nature of the process. Although this screening commission was eventually abolished by President Reagan in 1981, during its existence it reduced somewhat the role of both the U.S. Senate and the ABA Committee on the Federal Judiciary. When President Reagan nominated Sandra Day O'Connor to fill the Supreme Court seat vacated by retiring Justice Potter Stewart, the ABA was not even consulted.[7] Notwithstanding these recent developments regarding ABA screening of judicial nominees, serious contenders for federal judicial appointment can be expected to reflect high professional skill and integrity. But those criteria alone are certainly not sufficient for confirmation by the U.S. Senate.

Political Affiliation.   A second important selection variable is *political party affiliation* and political activity. Simply stated, Republican presidents nominate Republican candidates to the federal bench, and Democratic presidents nominate loyal Democrats. As Table 4.6 indicates, with the sole exception of President Ford, incumbent presidents in the twentieth century have nominated representatives of their own party at least 80 percent of the time, and most have nominated party loyalists over 90 percent of the time.

Some might argue that political patronage should play no role in filling vacancies on the federal bench. But by nominating party loyalists, presidents can indirectly increase their chances of having their programs prevail in legislative-judicial struggles over policy. Even President Carter, who created the U.S. Circuit Judge Nominating Commission, had one of the highest judicial patronage percentages of the twentieth century. In recent decades, political parties have declined in their ability to attract and retain party faithfuls. As campaign organizations have become tied more closely to candidates rather

Table 4.6   Percentage of Federal Judicial Appointments Belonging to the Same Political Party as the Nominating President, 1901–1985

PRESIDENT	PARTY	PERCENTAGE
T. Roosevelt	Republican	95.8
Taft	Republican	82.2
Wilson	Democrat	98.6
Harding	Republican	97.7
Coolidge	Republican	94.1
Hoover	Republican	85.7
F. D. Roosevelt	Democrat	96.4
Truman	Democrat	90.1
Eisenhower	Republican	94.1
Kennedy	Democrat	90.9
L. B. Johnson	Democrat	93.2
Nixon	Republican	93.7
Ford	Republican	79.0
Carter	Democrat	94.7
Reagan	Republican	97.0

Source: Howard Ball, *Courts and Politics: The Federal Judicial System*, 2d ed. ©1987, p. 176. Reprinted by permission of Prentice-Hall, Inc.

than party, judicial patronage has assumed increasing importance for presidents and party loyalists alike.

Policy Views of the Nominee.   The final major selection variable discussed here—*policy stances* of the nominee—is easy to understand but impossible to guarantee. As might be expected, presidents naturally want individuals on the federal bench who agree with them on issues they deem most important for implementing their policy agenda. Democratic presidents might be expected to nominate individuals to the judiciary who have been more liberatarian on personal-freedoms issues, but more communitarian on government intervention in the social and economic order. Conversely, Republican presidents might be expected to support a more individualistic approach to government that places a greater emphasis upon economic freedom and the free market. In spite of favorable references to Franklin Roosevelt and John Kennedy, President Reagan nominated few Democrats to the federal bench. And Democratic presidents in the future will most likely not nominate ideological conservatives. Because the prospective nominee may remain on the bench long after the retiring president has left the White House, any president normally nominates a person who supports the same ideas and programs.

Influence of Major Selection Variables.   Because this book is concerned primarily with the U.S. Supreme Court and its historical impact upon American constitutional development, some remarks about how the three variables of party representation, professional competence, and doctrinal views have historically influenced Supreme Court nominations are appropriate. With few exceptions, Supreme Court appointments since 1789 have gone to highly regarded individuals trained in the law from the president's party who have subscribed to the president's political and programmatic views. Notwithstanding the controversy in 1987 over the nominations of Judges Robert H. Bork and Douglas H. Ginsburg to fill a Supreme Court vacancy (see Brief 4.3) American presidents have always placed considerable emphasis upon the political and philosophical views of their nominees.

One profile of the individuals appointed to the Supreme Court indicates that they have been native born (only six exceptions); white (Thurgood Marshall, now on the Court, is the only black justice ever to serve); male (Sandra Day O'Connor the only female); Protestant (eight Roman Catholics and five Jews the only exceptions); in their mid-50s when appointed; Anglo-Saxon in background (except for six, including the recently appointed Antonin Scalia, the first Italian-American); upper-middle-to-high in social status; graduates of prestigious law schools; and politically active.[8] Furthermore, the overwhelming majority of the justices have occupied high political or judicial office just prior to being appointed to the Supreme Court. Another study reports that over 80 percent of the justices were either a federal officeholder in the executive branch, a judge of an inferior federal or state court, a member of Congress, or a governor.[9]

Ever since Presidents George Washington and John Adams first appointed staunch Federalists to the Court in the 1790s, political and philosophical traits have been major factors guiding the selection process. However, as stated earlier, there is no guarantee that nominees will conduct themselves as their benefactors expect. Departures from presidential expectations include Teddy

☐   *Brief 4.3   The Saga of Bork I and Bork II*

Following the retirement of Justice Lewis F. Powell, Jr., from the Supreme Court in June 1987, President Ronald Reagan nominated one of his long-time favorites— Judge Robert H. Bork of the D.C. Court of Appeals— to fill the vacancy. Given the extensive and controversial record established by Bork as legal scholar, law professor, former U.S. solicitor general (responsible for firing Special Prosecutor Archibald Cox during the Watergate investigation), and federal judge, the Senate confirmation hearings promised high drama during the fall of 1987.

Even before the formal hearings convened in mid-September, the lobbying began in earnest both for and against the Bork nomination, with some members of the Senate Judiciary Committee announcing their opposition to the Bork nomination. In addition to some predictable Republicans and Democrats arguing for and against the Bork nomination, respectively, such prominent Democrats as former White House counsel Lloyd Cutler and former Attorney General Griffin Bell testified in favor of Judge Bork. But arrayed against the nominee were several groups, including the National Organization for Women, the National Abortion Rights Action League, People for the American Way, and the Public Citizen Litigation Group. These groups and others insisted that throughout his career, Judge Bork had spoken and written extensively *against:* a broad constitutional right to privacy, a woman's right to an abortion, First Amendment protection for any form of speech other than political speech, federal regulation of campaign spending, legislative reapportionment, and most actions by Congress that restricted presidential power.

As the hearings progressed in September, it became clear that the nomination was in serious trouble. As the senators on the committee questioned both the nominee and numerous witnesses, the focus of the hearings seemed to change. What had begun in July as a debate over certain policy goals of the Reagan revolution, the meaning of the Constitution, and the Supreme Court's political role eventually shifted primarily to Bork's judicial philosophy and the public perception that it was profoundly different from that of the broad majority of American citizens. When the committee finally voted 9 to 5 against the Bork nomination in mid-October, it was clear that Senate approval was in doubt. On October 23, 1987, the full Senate voted 58 to 42 against him.

Deeply disappointed at the Senate's rejection of his favorite judicial conservative, Ronald Reagan announced on October 29, 1987, his choice of Judge Douglas H. Ginsburg, also of the D.C. Court of Appeals, to fill the Powell vacancy. Convinced that one of the main reasons Bork had failed to win Senate approval was because of his controversial judicial views, the administration saw in Judge Ginsburg a young, conservative intellectual without the controversial track record of Bork. Ginsburg, age forty-one, was a graduate of Cornell and the University of Chicago Law School, a former Harvard law professor, and a former official within the Justice Department and the Office of Management and Budget. Apart from his major expertise in regulatory, antitrust, and other technical aspects of federal law, not much was available for groups to use against him in the confirmation process.

But as fate would have it, the administration again miscalculated the likelihood of quick approval. In addition to selecting a person with little judicial experience (less than one-year's service on the D.C. Circuit Court), some issues relating to personal integrity and professional conduct soon emerged. Within days after his nomination, it was widely reported in the press that Ginsburg had owned $140,000 worth of stock in a cable television station while serving in the Justice Department and drafting the government's position on the cable TV industry. This raised some questions about a possible conflict of interest. But the event that ultimately led to Ginsburg's downfall in the eyes of his staunchest supporters in Congress and the private sector was the revelation that the nominee had regularly smoked marijuana as late as 1979 while teaching law at Harvard Law School. With Ginsburg's support dwindling by the hour, on November 7, 1987, the nominee asked the president to withdraw his name from nomination.

The issue in Bork's defeat by the Senate was undoubtedly judicial philosophy, and the belief that this individual, though brilliant and of high integrity, did not comport with the mainstream of American constitutional law. With Ginsburg, the withdrawal was compelled by the sense that the administration's enforcement of the criminal code and a well-publicized antidrug campaign had been marred by the past behavior of the nominee. To recover as quickly as possible from the fallout of the Bork-Ginsburg affair, the administration wasted no time in nominating in early November Judge Anthony M. Kennedy of the Ninth Circuit Court of Appeals to fill the Powell vacancy. A graduate of Stanford University and Harvard Law School, Kennedy had twelve years experience on the federal bench. He had written over four hundred opinions and had exhibited a sense of moderation and balance on prominent issues. On January 19, 1988, the Senate voted unanimously, 97-0, in favor of the Kennedy nomination.

Roosevelt's selection of Massachusetts Supreme Court Justice Oliver Wendell Holmes, Jr., in 1902; Franklin Roosevelt's nomination of the supposedly "activist" Felix Frankfurter in 1939; and Dwight D. Eisenhower's tapping of former California governor, Earl Warren, in 1953. President Harry Truman once remarked, "Packing the Supreme Court simply can't be done . . . I've tried and it won't work . . . Whenever you put a man on the Supreme Court he ceases to be your friend. I'm sure of that." [10] The four Nixon appointees to the Supreme Court (Warren Burger, Harry Blackmun, Lewis Powell, and William Rehnquist), in addition to being Republicans, were expected to be "strict constructionists," which generally means an interpretation of the Constitution that emphasizes a literal reading and the historical context of constitutional provisions. But during the Nixon era, the phrase meant a disavowal of the "liberal jurisprudence" of the Warren Court and more support for state-local prerogatives. In the years following their appointment to the Court, these four justices departed in many instances from what President Nixon might have preferred. No doubt the verdict in the Nixon Tapes Case in 1974 (*United States* v. *Nixon,* see Chapter 5) was not quite to the president's liking!

Other Selection Variables: Residence, Religion, Race, Sex, and Ethnic Origin. In addition to professional competence, party representation, and policy views, such considerations as geographical representation, religion, race, sex, and ethnic origin have some influence. The importance of *geographical distribution* on the Supreme Court has declined since the nineteenth century, when Supreme Court justices rode the circuit and assisted trial courts in handling cases. Additionally, if faced with opposition to a prospective nomination in the U.S. Senate, presidents might well consider the gains to be made by nominating an individual from a certain geographical area of the country. President Nixon clearly wanted to appoint a southern "strict constructionist" to the Court in 1969–70 to fill the vacancy created by Justice Abe Fortas's resignation. He finally succeeded in 1971, with the appointment of Lewis Powell of Virginia.

With respect to *religion,* the Supreme Court has always been, as stated earlier, dominated by Protestants. There have been eight Roman Catholics (Chief Justice Roger B. Taney being the first and current Associate Justices Antonin Scalia and Anthony Kennedy being the most recent) and five Jews (Louis D. Brandeis, Benjamin Cardozo, Felix Frankfurter, Arthur Goldberg, and Abe Fortas) on the Court.[11] With respect to *race* and *gender,* again the current Supreme Court serves as the exception. Thurgood Marshall and Sandra Day O'Connor are the only black and the only woman, respectively, to serve on the Supreme Court in its entire history, and there is little doubt that their selections (Marshall by Lyndon Johnson in 1967 and O'Connor by Ronald Reagan in 1981) were calculated political decisions. Finally, *ethnic origin* seems to be a largely secondary consideration. Antonin Scalia is the first Italian-American to serve on the Supreme Court, but he was undoubtedly chosen by President Reagan more for his judicial philosophy and policy views than for his Italian background.

One study of federal judges at the lower court levels indicates some interesting comparisons among recent administrations with regard to judicial appointments.[12] Given the previous discussion of party, competence, and policy determinants, some of the lesser selection variables have had different impacts under recent presidents. President Reagan's 129 appointees to federal district courts during his first term were overwhelmingly male (90.7 percent), white (93 percent), and moderately Protestant (61.2 percent). Contained within these summaries are some differences from previous administrations. During his first term, Reagan compiled the second highest percentage of female appointees to the district courts (Carter was first with 14.4 percent, compared with Reagan's 9.3 percent), whereas the Ford, Nixon, and Johnson administrations had a weak record of appointing women to district courts. Reagan also displayed the best record of the five most recent administrations in appointing Roman Catholics to the district courts (31.8 percent). This may well reflect an important change in party identification among Roman Catholics in recent years, and it most probably is influenced by the high percentage of Catholics that voted for Ronald Reagan in 1980 and 1984. However, Reagan was much less successful in finding black appointees to fill district court vacancies (he appointed one), probably because of the scarcity of black Republicans who agreed with the Reagan social agenda.

At the appellate level, the Reagan record is even more traditional, although some caution should be exercised here given the fact that only thirty-one vacancies were filled during the Reagan first term at the appellate level. On these lesser selection variables, the record can be summarized by stating that Reagan appointed only one woman, one black, and one Hispanic, compared with President Carter, who easily appointed the most minorities during his term of any of the last five administrations (nearly 20 percent females; over 16 percent blacks). Reagan and Carter appointed approximately the same proportion of Roman Catholics, whereas Carter appointed decidedly more Jews to the courts of appeals than did Nixon, Ford or Reagan.

The Policy-Making Function of the U.S. Supreme Court

Following the 1984 Supreme Court term, a debate was renewed at the highest levels of the federal government about the role of courts within the American constitutional system. In an address before the annual meeting of the American Bar Association in July 1985, Attorney General Edwin Meese criticized the Supreme Court for what he viewed as a "jurisprudence of idiosyncrasy." Meese placed special emphasis upon what he saw as the framers' desire for judges to "resist any political effort to depart from the literal provisions of the Constitution." In criticizing recent Supreme Court decisions concerning federalism, criminal procedure, and freedom-of-religion questions, Meese noted that "far too many of the Court's opinions were, on the whole, more policy choices than articulations of constitutional principle." He recommended that the Court adopt a "jurisprudence of original intention" and place more emphasis upon the historical context of constitutional provisions. Meese also criticized the "intellectually shaky foundation" of applying the Bill of Rights to the states through the Due Process Clause of Fourteenth Amendment.[13]

By the following October, Meese's comments had drawn a reaction from Justice William Brennan, perhaps the one member of the Burger Court with whom Meese disagreed the most. Without mentioning Meese by name, Brennan questioned "those who find legitimacy in fidelity to what they call 'the intentions of the Framers.' " He referred to this philosophy as "little more than arrogance cloaked as humility." Brennan argued that this view of judicial decision making is suspect for several reasons. He insisted that the historical record is incomplete and imprecise on the framers' intent, there is disagreement over particular constitutional provisions, and it is virtually impossible to determine whose intentions were most relevant—those who gathered in Philadelphia, the congressional debaters, or ratifiers in the states. Brennan said that the current justices on the Supreme Court must address contemporary issues with an eye on what the Constitution means today, not two hundred years ago. One week after Justice Brennan's remarks, Associate Justice John Paul Stevens specifically criticized Meese by name and the attorney general's displeasure with applying the First Amendment to the states. Stevens noted that no justice on the Court since 1925 had ever questioned the process of applying the guarantees of the Bill of Rights to the states.[14]

This exchange between two justices on the Supreme Court and the attorney general highlights a debate that has raged for a long time in American law. But it glosses over several complicated questions about constitutional interpretation. The questions focus on precisely *what* the Constitution says, *who* has the responsibility for interpreting that document, *how* that interpretative process should proceed, and *what techniques* are the most legitimate for authoritative interpretation. Time and space do not permit adequate treatment of these major analytical questions, but a brief outline of some issues prior to discussing a major aspect of the Meese-Brennan-Stevens debate is necessary.[15]

Some Thoughts on Constitutional Interpretation

One set of questions addresses what individuals see in the Constitution itself. Does interpretation deal exclusively with the actual wording and formal text of the document, or does it include certain other writings and practices that characterize the cumulative body of American political writing and practice? Should the Constitution be considered as a static, unchanging document that speaks with the same voice and specificity from age to age, or should it be seen as a changing, adaptable document that must be stretched and accommodated to a dynamic agenda of people dealing with contemporary problems? Should the Constitution be viewed as a body of strict rules for application to all public problems, or might it be seen also as an instrument that embodies more than simple procedures for resolving all conflicts, and articulates larger goals, aspirations, and values, such as pursuit of human dignity and self-fulfillment? This set of questions about the U.S. Constitution implies that at the first level of interpretive analysis, much is unsettled about what the "fundamental law" of American government actually says.

A second set of questions about the Constitution deals with the different approaches for interpreting the document. As might be expected, the approach to interpretation is intimately affected by whether the document is viewed as a static or dynamic statement of the law. Is more gained by concentrating upon a *verbal analysis* of the actual words, the *historic setting* of when the document and its amendments were drafted and ratified, or the *structural contradictions* that appear in the Constitution (i.e., the Establishment Clause and the Free Exercise Clause of the First Amendment; the collision between government authority and individual freedom)? Are the *doctrinal concepts* that have evolved over two centuries of constitutional practice (i.e., judicial review, executive privilege, "one person-one vote," "wall of separation," right to privacy, etc.) as important to defining the Constitution as the actual text itself? Finally, should those who are charged with interpreting the Constitution be intimately concerned with what has been referred to as *prudential* analysis, which compels the interpreter to ask what would be wise or good public policy? The Supreme Court's handling of racial discrimination cases beginning in the 1930s, and culminating with the *Brown* v. *Board of Education* decision in 1954, serves as an example of prudential analysis, as does the turnaround by the Court on economic management issues beginning with the *West Coast Hotel* v. *Parrish* case in 1937 (see Chapter 7).

A final set of questions deals with the different instruments or techniques used by judges to interpret the Constitution. Most of these techniques have certain limitations that inhibit a thorough and practical application of the technique. *Literalism* insists on a strict interpretation of the actual words in the document. This suggests that "establishment of religion," "equal protection of the laws," and "full faith and credit" presumably hold the same meaning for all people. But, in addition to differences over the meaning of these phrases, passages such as "necessary and proper," "general welfare," "unreasonable search and seizure," and countless others make literalism a baffling mode of analysis. The *intent of the framers* is another technique that has become popular in recent years for divining the meaning of the Constitution. As many have noted, however, recapturing the past and the actual intentions of those who drafted the Constitution and its twenty-six amendments assumes a perfect consensus among the framers. Furthermore, a complete record of what was intended is not available. Another device for interpreting the Constitution and resolving disputes is the *balancing of interests* that often emerges in many disputes. This, of course, directly involves the individualistic-communitarian continuum, since it implies that protection of individual rights sometimes finds the Court weighing countervailing societal rights. This approach became more prominent in the twentieth century as judges were urged to address not only the legal facets of a case, but also the economic, sociological, and ethical aspects as well. But balancing of interests has been criticized as both injecting the biases and predispositions of judges into judicial decision making and skewing the balance in favor of either governmental order and stability or individual freedom. Finally, the use of *stare decisis* (meaning that the previous decision stands) has been a favorite approach for resolving legal conflicts. A judge looks for past cases that resemble a current case, finds the rule of law used in those cases, and applies the same rule to the present case. Building on previous decisions not only develops a cumulative body of law but also ensures the development of incremental, rather than radical, change in the law. Applying this technique may present fewer problems than the other three just mentioned. However, given the tendency for modern science and technology to precede developments in the legal field, it is clear that few precise answers exist concerning the legal rules involved in surrogate motherhood, genetic engineering, euthanasia, and fetal-tissue transplanting—to name but a few.

The Restraint-Activism Dimension of Judicial Decision Making

The many approaches, orientations, and techniques available for interpreting the Constitution make judicial decision making a complex process. In recent years, much has been made of terms such as *strict constructionist, judicial activist,* and *social engineer*. As a result, citizens can get a rather simplistic view of judicial decision making and assume that all they have to know about a judge is his or her political orientation in order to predict how that individual will decide various types of cases. Although judicial-role analysis in recent years has yielded some impressive predictions of justices adopting a particular philosophical stance on selected policy issues, forecasting judicial behavior can sometimes prove inaccurate.

As mentioned earlier, the Meese-Brennan-Stevens exchange actually highlights a debate that has raged for a long time in American law; namely, What should be the role of courts and judges under the American Constitution? The debate involves two concepts that have contributed partially to the distortion in constitutional interpretation—**judicial restraint** and **judicial activism**.[16] Judicial restraint argues that judges should take every precaution to avoid overturning the actions of the political branches of government—Congress, the president, or the state legislatures. Judicial activists, on the other hand, are much more willing to intervene and countermand actions of popularly elected branches. Because these two concepts are not accurate reflections of "liberal" or "conservative" ideologies, which the Meese-Brennan-Stevens exchange might suggest, a more thorough discussion of each with reference to some prominent judicial figures is necessary.

Judicial Restraint and the Thayer-Frankfurter-Harlan Prescription

The concept of judicial restraint implies that judicial authority should be very limited. John Marshall was one of the first to articulate this limited court role in the famous case of *Marbury* v. *Madison* (to be discussed later in this chapter). In that case, Marshall emphasized that the Supreme Court should use its power only when there is a clear conflict between a statute and the Constitution. Because laws supposedly represent the voice of the popular majority, they should not be dismissed lightly by judges who are traditionally less accountable to the people. A serious problem with this reasoning, of course, is that not all laws reflect majoritarian preferences. Frequently, courts must review the impact of legislation in order to safeguard individual rights, the primacy of the Constitution, and, ultimately, popular sovereignty. But for much of the nineteenth century, the Supreme Court rarely overruled state or federal laws, due mainly to its limited workload and the infrequency of state-federal regulation of private activities. However, those self-imposed restraints upon judicial power subsided in the latter part of the nineteenth century. Courts began to play a much more prominent role in overseeing the conflicts of a more complex social, economic, and political order.

One of the clearest allusions to judicial restraint was made in the late nineteenth century by the noted Harvard law professor, James Bradley Thayer, in a classic essay entitled "The Origin and Scope of the American Doctrine of Constitutional Law." [17] Thayer argued that by the 1890s, courts were unwisely turning away from a century of deference to legislative bodies. Like Marshall, he insisted that laws should be declared invalid only when they were clearly irrational, unreasonable, and in direct opposition to the Constitution.

Justices Felix Frankfurter and the second John Marshall Harlan were two later proponents of judicial restraint. A one-time student of Thayer's at Harvard, Frankfurter became a primary spokesperson for restraint during his tenure on the Court (1939–62). In many notable opinions, and in sometimes verbose, lecture-like language addressed to his colleagues, Frankfurter extolled the virtues of judicial deference to legislative supremacy. Frankfurter's restraint philosophy can be seen in his dissenting opinions in *West Virginia State Board of Education* v. *Barnette* (1943) and *Baker* v. *Carr* (1962), his concurrence in *Dennis* v. *United States* (1951), and his opinion for the majority in *Rochin* v. *California* (1952). Like Frankfurter, John Harlan was a strong proponent of judicial restraint whose judicial philosophy was embodied in several careful and scholarly opinions while he was on the Supreme Court between 1955 and 1971. Of particular merit are his dissenting opinions in *Mapp* v. *Ohio* (1961), *Baker* v. *Carr* (1962), and *Flast* v. *Cohen* (1968), as well as his opinion for the Court majority in *Barenblatt* v. *United States* (1959).

Judicial Restraint and the Holmes-Brandeis-Stone Prescription

A somewhat different example of judicial restraint emerged in the twentieth century among some Supreme Court justices whose adherence to this judicial role depended upon what rights were at stake. Following World War I, Justices Oliver Wendell Holmes, Jr., Louis D. Brandeis, and Harlan Fiske Stone became most protective of First Amendment rights against many forms of state-federal regulation, but they also were quite willing to defer to legislative assemblies attempting to regulate aspects of the American economy. The first hint of this variant form of judicial restraint arose in two dissenting opinions of Holmes in the landmark decisions of *Lochner* v. *New York* (1905) and *Hammer* v. *Dagenhart* (1918). In both decisions, the Court majority struck down laws contrary either to the Fourteenth Amendment or to a literal reading of the Commerce Clause. Holmes disagreed with the Court in both instances, authoring what became two of his most famous dissenting opinions, both of which "disavowed the right [of the Court] to intrude its judgment upon questions of policy or morals." [18] Holmes's colleague on the Court in 1918, Louis Brandeis, joined in the dissenting opinion. During the next twenty years, Brandeis became another practitioner of judicial restraint toward various forms of economic regulation. So persuasive were these two that a third justice, Harlan Stone (1925–41), continued to advocate this philosophy with reference to economic regulation after both Holmes and Brandeis had left the Court. One of the best articulations of Stone's tolerance of economic regulation is his dissenting opinion in *United States* v. *Butler* (1936), in which the Supreme Court struck down the Agricultural Adjustment Act of 1933 as an illegal delegation of legislative authority and an unwarranted exercise of commerce authority by Congress. In arguing for the Court to uphold the statute, Stone noted in dissent that

> the only check upon our own exercise of power is our own sense of self-restraint. For the removal of unwise laws from the statute books appeal lies not to the courts but to the ballot and to the processes of democratic government.

According to Stone, the only question that courts should concern themselves with is whether a legislature has the power to deal with the subject. Whether the law is wise or unwise policy is not within the power of a court to determine. It is strictly a political matter best left to popularly elected representatives, not jurists appointed for life and largely unaccountable to the people.

The Holmes-Brandeis-Stone model of judicial restraint reflected growing public and professional disenchantment with a Supreme Court majority during the 1930s. This majority had invalidated several state and federal laws that

Brief 4.4   The Supreme Court Revolution of 1937

The early years of the New Deal saw much conflict among the three branches of government. Having captured over 57 percent of the popular vote, forty-two states, and 472 electoral votes in the 1932 presidential election, Franklin Roosevelt was eager to begin work on economic recovery, and the Democratic-controlled Congress was poised to assist him. The first one hundred days of the Roosevelt administration saw a flurry of legislation intended to restore public confidence and economic prosperity. In 1933, Congress passed some major federal statutes, such as the National Industrial Recovery Act, the Bituminous Coal Conservation Act, and the Agricultural Adjustment Act—all of which attempted to regulate several aspects of the depressed national economy. But by 1936, the Supreme Court had declared all three of these major acts unconstitutional, with its rulings in *Schechter Poultry Company* v. *United States* (1935), *Carter* v. *Carter Coal Company* (1936), and *United States* v. *Butler* (1936). Roosevelt's initial reactions to the Court's refusal to allow this intervention were cautious. After the *Schechter* decision, the president reportedly referred to the Court's actions as returning the country to the horse-and-buggy age.

The 1936 presidential election became a public referendum on the Roosevelt New Deal and on the Supreme Court's refusal to recognize these new tools for managing a recovering national economy. Roosevelt won 61 percent of the popular vote in 1936, which he immediately interpreted as a mandate for his policies and a substantial base from which to attack the conservative Supreme Court. His strategy for changing the judicial status quo had ironically been recommended originally by one of the conservatives, Justice James McReynolds, when he had served as attorney general under President Woodrow Wilson in 1913. Convinced

that the Court needed help from younger men with a more sympathetic view of the Constitution, Roosevelt sent to Congress a plan providing for voluntary retirement of all Supreme Court justices at the age of seventy. If the justice did not retire, the president could appoint an additional justice for each justice over seventy years, up to a maximum of fifteen. Roosevelt hoped this plan would provide a working majority that supported his programs. According to the president, the plan had two purposes:

> By bringing into the judicial system a steady and continuing stream of new and younger blood, I hope, first, to make the administration of all federal justice speedier and therefore less costly; secondly, to bring to the decision of social and economic problems younger men who have had personal experience and contact with modern facts and circumstances under which average men have to live and work. This plan will save our National Constitution from hardening of the judicial arteries.[10]

Congress never passed the "Court-packing" plan of Roosevelt, in part because it was not well received by the American public, which saw it as a thinly disguised plan to place on the high court ideological clones of the president. Ultimately, the plan was unnecessary. During the 168 days that Congress debated the suggested reorganization, the Supreme Court began to reverse its view of New Deal legislation. The so-called "switch in time that saved nine" occurred without a single new appointment to the Court. Instead, it occurred through a crucial change in voting patterns by Chief Justice Charles Evans Hughes and Justice Owen Roberts in the *West Coast Hotel* v. *Parrish* decision in May 1937, and *National Labor Relations Board* v. *Jones & Laughlin Steel Corporation* in June 1937 (see Chapter 7).

were enacted in an attempt to bring economic recovery from the Great Depression. With the "Court revolution" of 1937, referred to as the "switch in time that saved nine" (see Brief 4.4), the Supreme Court became more receptive to Congress's attempts to deal with the economic emergencies then plaguing the country.

Judicial Activism from John Marshall to Warren Burger

Ever since John Marshall stated in *Marbury* v. *Madison* that it is "emphatically the province and the duty of the courts to say what the law is," courts and judges in the federal judicial system have been asked to interpret federal law and the Constitution. Depending upon the extent to which federal judges have felt compelled to depart periodically from limitations on their authority, they often hear a broad range of social and political issues in American society. In many instances, the Supreme Court is called upon to perform a major policy-making function that departs greatly from judicial self-restraint. It does this, in many cases, because the other two branches, especially Congress, have been unable or unwilling to resolve important policy issues in accordance with the Constitution. In the latter half of the twentieth century, the Court has intervened in such contentious issues as desegregation, right to privacy, legislative apportionment, and rights of criminal defendants. The consequence has often found a Supreme Court effecting major policy changes in these volatile areas. Court intervention to change prevailing policy established by either of the other coordinate branches is referred to as judicial activism.

When the Supreme Court has overturned actions of one of the other two branches, the justices have often been criticized for injecting their own social, economic, or political views into the decision. The Meese-Brennan-Stevens exchange noted earlier is relevant in this respect. Attorney General Edwin Meese was the spokesperson for an administration (or at least a White House) that disagreed with the substance of many decisions made by the Supreme Court. He criticized the Court for limiting state-local prerogatives in favor of national standards (i.e., minimum wage, defendants' rights, and school prayer). This quarrel over the role of courts is, at base, a struggle over who should "legislate" public policy—the courts or the people's elected representatives. When there are questions dealing with fundamental personal rights and the legitimacy of governmental power, the proper question to ask is actually, *When* should the courts intervene? The debate is often complicated by stereotyped references to the justices as "liberal" and "conservative." But as the following discussion notes, these labels do not fully clarify why the justices make particular decisions.

Judicial restraint should not be correlated with "conservative" and activism with "liberal" decision making, as Figure 4.2 indicates (see also Brief 2.1). "Liberal" justices of the past three decades have often been described as the most protective of Bill of Rights guarantees and the Reconstruction amendments, especially the Fourteenth Amendment. They have also been most supportive of reformist legislation of the past fifty years considered essential to achieving economic prosperity, social justice, and equality in American society. Along the political ideology dimension, "liberal" justices might be described as activist in overturning most state-federal legislation considered a threat to fundamental constitutional rights. But on the judicial-role dimension, they

Political Ideology

Figure 4.2
The Politics of Judicial
Decision Making

Role Concept	Liberal	Conservative
Activist	Civil Rights and Civil Liberties	Economic Policy Management
Restraint	Economic Policy Management	Civil Rights and Civil Liberties
	Warren Court, 1953-69	Pre-New Deal Court, 1890-1937

would reflect more support for self-restraint as they defer to the president and Congress in their programs to maintain economic prosperity through extensive governmental regulation. Justices Oliver Wendell Holmes, Louis Brandeis, Harlan Stone, William O. Douglas, Hugo Black, Earl Warren, William Brennan, Thurgood Marshall, and perhaps John Paul Stevens might fit into this category of "liberal." The Supreme Court under Chief Justice Earl Warren (1953–69) would best reflect this form of decision making—activist on civil rights and liberties, but restrained on economic and social management questions.

The "conservative" label has often been used to describe those justices who have been less willing to intervene to protect civil rights and liberties. They believe that government must be given great latitude to maintain social order and stability. In this respect, they usually allow legislation regulating personal civil liberties to stand. On the other hand, the same individual might place greater emphasis upon economic liberty and a free market unencumbered by government regulations. If legislation restricts this economic liberty, it is ruled illegal on any of several constitutional grounds. Justices Willis Van Devanter, Pierce Butler, James McReynolds, and George Sutherland in particular reflected this orientation as the "Four Horsemen" of the pre-New Deal era. They were especially averse to any form of governmental interference— state or federal—that sought to regulate economic relations and private property rights. Justices Felix Frankfurter, John Harlan, and Potter Stewart and Chief Justices Warren Burger and William Rehnquist may best reflect this model of judicial decision maker in the more modern court eras. Their judicial behavior normally found them deferring to legislatures attempting to regulate *civil* liberties (restraint), and eagerly guarding against an intrusive government that violated *economic* liberties of the people (activism). With some notable exceptions, the Supreme Court from 1890 to 1937 reflected this preference for a judiciary committed to the free market. From the 1890s until World War I, the Due Process Clause of the Fourteenth Amendment was interpreted as banning any form of state regulation of property rights (see Chapter 7 on economic liberty and its discussion of substantive due process). During the 1930s, the Court disallowed several federal laws aimed at restoring the American economy from the depths of the Depression.

This discussion of liberal and conservative emphasizes that ideological labels do not adequately explain how judges interpret and apply the law in concrete situations. In some respects, there appears to be a two-tiered arrangement of constitutional protections afforded individuals, which is essentially what Justice Stone argued many years ago. According to Stone, economic and social policies should generally be determined by popularly elected majorities in an open, reasonably well-informed democracy. If questionable policies are enacted, a vigilant public and its representatives should act to repeal them. Good causes will be reflected in good policy enacted by responsive policymakers, and judicial interference is not normally necessary.

But majoritarian preferences are not infallible. As a consequence, courts must sometimes intervene, as Justice Stone argued in *Ashwander* (see Chapter 10). In protecting those constitutional guarantees dealing with the Bill of Rights, exercise of the vote, or equal protection for distinguishable minority groups, Stone noted that judges are not as likely to act as surrogates for private economic interests, given their specialized legal training and constitutional responsibilities. As such, they are better equipped to take the "long view" than are legislative or executive officials. By assuming this role, the judiciary could better protect socially or politically isolated groups in society from an abusive majority. This claim certainly describes the Warren Court, which throughout its existence saw its mission as protecting racial, religious, and political minorities; the criminally accused; the poor; and the mentally handicapped. A more cautious Burger Court in later years was also criticized for its judicial activism, although it tackled some issues not encountered by the Warren Court.

Thus, during the late twentieth century, there has been an enduring debate about what should be the role of federal courts, especially the Supreme Court. This perennial clash between some arguing for judical restraint and others advocating judicial activism will surely continue into the future.[20] As government has grown larger and more complex in order to handle the growing expectations of modern society, citizens have looked to the Supreme Court as the best safeguard against irresponsible government. Whether it has been activist or restrained in interpreting and applying the law, the Court has been accepted generally as educator and arbiter in American government. As Justice Robert H. Jackson once wrote:

> People have seemed to feel that the Supreme Court, whatever its defects, is still the most detached, dispassionate, and trustworthy custodian that our system affords for the translation of abstract into concrete constitutional commands.[21]

As the latter half of this chapter will indicate, the manner in which the Supreme Court has fulfilled this role of "constitutional custodian" is a distinct aspect of America's experience with constitutional government.

Roots of Judicial Review: Theory and Practice

It is generally acknowledged that the Supreme Court is the most powerful judicial body in the world, and there is little doubt that a main reason for this is its use of judicial review. **Judicial review** is the power of any court to hold unenforceable any law, any official action based upon a law, or any other action by a public official that it considers to be in conflict with the Constitution. This power has given the United States Supreme Court a significant instrument for fulfilling its role as the "constitutional custodian" mentioned earlier.

As Table 4.7 indicates, the Court's use of judicial review to invalidate legislation has varied over a long period, with the majority of nullifications occurring in the twentieth century. State actions have been overturned much more frequently than have federal laws, and state laws form nearly 80 percent of all laws declared unconstitutional since 1789. Another fact gleaned from this table is that the large majority of statutes declared unconstitutional since 1789 have been struck down since 1910. Seventy-four percent of federal laws and nearly 83 percent of state laws declared invalid have been struck down since the advent of the White Court in 1910. Finally, having previously mentioned the rise of judicial activism, especially since the early 1950s, special note should be made of the Court's increased tendency to nullify state and federal laws since 1953. As an indication of how political ideology cannot always predict whether justices will be activist, the Burger Court, which was supposed to be more "conservative" than its predecessor, overturned more federal and state statutes than did the Warren Court.

Why did the practice of judicial review evolve in the American constitutional system? Although Chapter 2 indicated that there were strong hints of it in early English practice, the American Constitution nowhere specifically

Table 4.7   Decisions of the U.S. Supreme Court Overruled and Acts of Congress Ruled Unconstitutional, 1789–1985; and State Laws and Municipal Ordinances Overturned, 1789–1980

SUPREME COURT ERA	SUPREME COURT DECISIONS OVERRULED	ACTS OF CONGRESS INVALIDATED	STATE LAWS OVERTURNED	LOCAL LAWS OVERTURNED
Pre-Marshall (1789–1800)				
Marshall Court (1801–35)	3	1	18	
Taney Court (1835–64)	6	1	21	
Chase Court (1864–73)	3	10	33	
Waite Court (1874–88)	11	9	7	
Fuller Court (1888–1910)	4	14	73	15
White Court (1910–21)	6	12	107	18
Taft Court (1921–30)	5	12	131	12
Hughes Court (1930–40)	14	14	78	5
Stone Court (1941–46)	24	2	25	7
Vinson Court (1946–53)	11	1	38	7
Warren Court (1953–69)	46	25	150	16
Burger Court (1969–86)	50	34	192	15
TOTAL	183	135	873	95

Source: Reproduced from *Storm Center, The Supreme Court in American Politics,* by David M. O'Brien, by permission of W. W. Norton and Company, Inc., p. 43, © 1986.

authorizes the Supreme Court or any inferior federal court to judge the constitutionality of actions taken by coordinate branches. And yet, it has evolved into the most significant instrument used by federal courts to reconcile the actions of governments with the Constitution. At least four reasons explain the development of judicial review in the American constitutional system: the framers' intent; historical acceptance; the desire for a counterweight to errant majority rule; and the continual quest for neutral "first principles" by which to resolve controversies and to effect widespread public compliance.

The Framers' Intentions and Judicial Review

Justifying judicial review by arguing that the framers *intended* it is difficult, since the actual record of the Constitutional Convention is incomplete. There was widespread agreement in 1787 that a national judiciary should be established, although explaining precisely what the framers thought its powers should be is more difficult. Approximately one-half of the regular delegates to the convention favored judicial review, and approximately three-fourths of the convention's leaders—including people like Gouverneur Morris (see Chapter 3)—publicly endorsed the idea.[22] Although *Marbury* v. *Madison* is often credited with beginning the practice of judicial review, there were many cases of this important power long before 1803.[23]

Special attention should be paid to Alexander Hamilton—the brilliant, ambitious, and arrogant citizen of New York who had a major impact upon a young United States. Although he had little influence at the convention itself, especially after advocating the adoption of a British form of centralized government, Hamilton played a vital role in pressing the ratification fight in New York, Virginia, and Massachusetts by co-authoring *The Federalist Papers* in 1787–88. In fact, in *Federalist No. 78,* Hamilton insisted that "the judiciary, from the nature of its functions, will always be the least dangerous to the political rights of the constitution."[24] He also argued that written constitutions must be obeyed and constitutional limits must be rigorously enforced by the courts:

> The interpretation of the laws is the proper and peculiar province of the courts. A constitution is, in fact, and must be regarded by the judges as, a fundamental law. It therefore belongs to them to ascertain its meaning, as well as the meaning of any particular part proceeding from the legislative body. *If there should happen to be an irreconcilable variance between the two, that which has the superior obligation and validity ought . . . to be preferred; or in other words, the Constitution ought to be preferred to the statute, the intention of the people to the intention of their agents.*[25] [Emphasis added]

This language eventually provided major support for John Marshall in *Marbury* v. *Madison,* for it says that a written constitution limits legislative power, that the unique function of the courts is to interpret the law, and that the Constitution compels the practice of judicial review. But this is somewhat of a leap of faith by Hamilton because, as stated earlier, the Constitution is silent on judicial review. Furthermore, other democratic systems that have been successful with limited government have trusted other political branches, not just the judiciary, to abide by the law. Whatever the case, Hamilton's reasoning in *Federalist No. 78* created an important precedent for this unique feature of American constitutional government.

Another claim supporting the argument that the framers endorsed judicial review concerns the Supremacy Clause in Article VI, Clause 2. This provision states:

> This Constitution, and the Laws of the United States which shall be made in Pursuance thereof; and all Treaties made, or which shall be made, under the Authority of the United States, shall be the supreme Law of the Land; and the Judges in every State shall be bound thereby, any Thing in the Constitution or Laws of any State to the Contrary notwithstanding.

The precise meaning of the words "in Pursuance thereof" is debatable. Marshall interpreted them to mean "consistent with"; therefore, state judges need not enforce illegal laws. But what about federal judges? Again, the ambiguity of the Constitution defies precise definition.

The final piece of "founders' intent" evidence that implies a desire for judicial review concerns the Judiciary Act of 1789, passed by the new Congress to create the federal judicial system. Section 25 of the act allowed the Supreme Court to review state court decisions when the constitutionality of a federal law was challenged. This crucial provision, passed by a Congress dominated by many of the framers, indicates that those who created the federal judiciary fully intended for the Supreme Court to oversee state court decisions affecting the new Constitution. Oliver Ellsworth, a primary drafter of Article III of the Constitution and the Judiciary Act of 1789, would most likely not have contradicted himself while formulating these important documents—both of which imply the practice of judicial review.

In summary, the evidence indicates that those who labored in Philadelphia in 1787 to construct a new national government anticipated that the Supreme Court might eventually have to rule on the constitutionality of actions of the other branches or levels of government. But why the framers never specifically inserted judicial review into the new document is still not clear. It may have been omitted because of the rush to conclude the business of the convention, the wisdom of dealing in generalities on certain subjects, or the framers' inability to anticipate how important the power of judicial review would become. However, this vital tool of American constitutional government eventually gained widespread acceptance, even when the Supreme Court handed down very unpopular decisions.

Judicial Review and Historical Acceptance

The charge is frequently made that activist judges should not defy the popular will by overruling legislation passed by majority rule. These charges often distort the extent to which judicial review has been generally accepted as an essential device of American constitutional government. As one observer of the Supreme Court has noted:

> The most encompassing argument to "democratize" the Court's power as ultimate constitutional arbiter has been that judicial review [has] been institutionally adopted by a continuing consensus of American society as an integral rule of the system; that, thus, judicial review operates by majority will, with the consent of the governed.[26]

Undoubtedly, experience during the first few decades of the Supreme Court's existence was crucial to the formation of this consensus. Reference to a few cases during this early era should establish this point.

Chisholm v. Georgia (1793)

One such case is *Chisholm* v. *Georgia* (1793), where the Supreme Court held in a very unpopular decision that the Constitution allowed a citizen of one state to sue another state in federal court. This case actually dealt more with the jurisdiction of the Court, rather than any specific instance of the Court reviewing the actions of another branch of government. But it also led in 1798 to the ratification of the Eleventh Amendment to the Constitution, which provides that citizens of one state may not sue another state against its will. Although this amendment is one of only four constitutional amendments that directly overrule a decision by the Supreme Court,[27] it is the only one that was directly aimed at curtailing federal *judicial* power.

Hylton v. United States (1796)

In the case of *Hylton* v. *United States* (1796) the Supreme Court exercised judicial review of a federal law. Had the Court found the statute in question unconstitutional, *Marbury* v. *Madison* would have been just another case. In any event, by 1800 and the advent of the Jeffersonian era, many had already assumed that the Supreme Court was the appropriate body to rule on the constitutionality of congressional legislation. The election of Thomas Jefferson as president in 1800 indicated that two prominent sons of Virginia were about to tangle in one of the most celebrated cases in American constitutional law.

Marbury v. Madison (1803)

Marbury v. *Madison* (1803) is a good example of how trivial facts of a case can occasionally give birth to very important rules of law. Before leaving office in 1800, the Federalists under John Adams passed the Judiciary Act of 1801. Among other things, the statute created several new judicial posts, to which Adams and the Federalist-dominated Congress were expected to appoint several loyal supporters of the party. Also, in January 1801, Adams named his outgoing secretary of state, John Marshall, to become the fourth chief justice of the Supreme Court. Another law passed just prior to the inauguration of the new president authorized forty-two new justice-of-the-peace positions in the District of Columbia.

Some of these minor appointments—including one for William Marbury, a loyal Federalist—were still in the office of the secretary of state and had not been delivered when Thomas Jefferson was inaugurated on March 4, 1801. Having just won the presidential election and eager to see the passing of the Federalist era, Jefferson was determined to stop any further entrenchment of Federalists in the federal judiciary. As a result, he ordered the incoming secretary of state, James Madison, not to deliver the commission to Marbury, even though it had been signed by Adams.[28]

William Marbury decided to press the issue of his appointment. Relying upon a rather obscure provision of the Judiciary Act of 1789, he asked the Supreme Court to issue a writ of *mandamus* (literally, "we command") under its original jurisdiction. (Such an order, in effect, means that a court directs a lower court or other authority to perform a particular act.) In accordance with Section 13 of the act, Congress had authorized such an action "in cases warranted by the principles and usages of law, to any courts appointed, or persons holding office, under authority of the United States."

Chief Justice John Marshall was confronted with a major dilemma. He knew that President Jefferson would most likely ignore any assertion of judicial authority, which would surely have a negative effect upon the Court. But he also thought that Marbury was legally entitled to his appointment. What was he to do? His strategy and reasoning were entirely adequate to the task before him.

In answering the three questions posed by *Marbury* to the Court, Marshall handled the first two with dispatch. First, did Marbury have a right to the commission? Marshall said yes, since the commission had been signed by the president and sealed (but not delivered!) by the secretary of state (at the time, Marshall himself). By refusing to give Marbury his appointment, Jefferson and Madison were denying Marbury a "vested legal right." Second, if Marbury had such a right, did the laws of the United States afford him a remedy? Marshall again said yes, since the United States was a "government of laws, and not of men." Finally, and this was the crucial question, had Marbury sought the proper remedy, namely, a writ of *mandamus* issued by the Supreme Court under its original jurisdiction? To this question the chief justice said no. Although the proper remedy was a writ of *mandamus*, it could not be issued by the Supreme Court under its original jurisdiction.

Marbury's attempt to obtain his appointment was defective because it relied upon a provision of a federal law that was unconstitutional. In writing his opinion, Marshall focused specifically upon Article III, Section 2, as it concerns both the Court's original and appellate jurisdiction:

> It has been insisted . . . that as the original grant of jurisdiction, to the supreme and inferior courts, is general, and the clause, assigning original jurisdiction to the supreme court, contains no negative or restrictive words, the power remains to the legislature, to assign original jurisdiction to that court in other cases than those specified in the article . . . If it had been intended to leave it in the discretion of the legislature to apportion the judicial power between the supreme and inferior courts according to the will of that body, it would certainly have been useless to have proceeded further . . . If congress remains at liberty to give this court appellate jurisdiction, where the constitution has declared their jurisdiction shall be original; and original jurisdiction where the constitution has declared it shall be appellate; the distribution of jurisdiction, made in the constitution, is form without substance.

Marshall's main argument here is that, under Article III, Congress had the right to regulate the appellate jurisdiction of the Supreme Court, but not its original jurisdiction. Since the latter is defined solely by the Constitution, it could only be changed by a formal amendment to the Constitution, not by any mere act of the legislature. Since Section 13 of the Judiciary Act attempted to alter this constitutional grant of original jurisdiction, Marshall said that the Supreme Court was left with no choice but to declare the provision null and void. His reasoning was deceptively straightforward. First, he argued that the Constitution is the supreme law of the land, and that ordinary acts of the legislature are subordinate to the Constitution. Furthermore, it is the unique duty of courts to interpret the meaning of the fundamental law. And finally, "A law repugnant to the constitution is void; and . . . courts, as well as other departments, are bound by that instrument." As stated previously, this reasoning is virtually identical to that cited earlier by Hamilton in *Federalist No. 78*.

One of the amazing aspects of this decision is how the chief justice had grasped judicial victory from the jaws of an apparent defeat for the Court. He gave Jefferson nothing to defy, since he avoided giving the newly elected president any ultimatum. Jefferson, who denied that Supreme Court decisions were binding upon the other branches of government, was left with nothing to do but silently regret this advancement of judicial power at the expense of Congress.

Marbury v. *Madison* is significant for several reasons. First, the decision firmly established the practice of judicial review in American government. Although it had been invoked in several cases earlier, both in England and the American colonies, judicial review had never been used to overturn a federal law on the grounds that it was subordinate to the Constitution. And never before had the role of the Supreme Court been as forcefully articulated as it was here in *Marbury*. There would later be, of course, much debate about precisely *how* judicial review should be exercised, as the earlier discussion about what the Constitution says and how judges should interpret it indicated. But *Marbury* firmly entrenched the practice of the Supreme Court's reviewing legislation in order to ensure that it conforms to the Constitution.

Secondly, the decision is important because it also firmly secured the original jurisdiction of the Supreme Court on constitutional, rather than mere legislative, grounds. This principle is very important, for if the Congress could amend *both* the original and appellate jurisdiction of the Court, it could conceivably remove all power of the Court to act. Although the vast majority of Supreme Court activity has stemmed from the exercise of its appellate, rather than original, jurisdiction, Marshall's powerful lecture on the legitimacy of courts and their obligation to uphold the Constitution was a critical test of the rule-of-law principle.

Finally, *Marbury* is important because it equipped Marshall and later Supreme Courts with a most effective instrument to monitor *state* legislation and actions. One of the major unanswered questions after the Constitutional Convention in 1787 was what precisely was the nature of the American union. More specifically, which level of government is supreme within this federal union that emerged from Philadelphia? To what extent are national and state powers equal? Given Marshall's broad reasoning in *Marbury* about the superiority of the Constitution and the courts' obligation to interpret it, Marshall's primary target in 1803 was probably *state*, rather than federal, legislation. Indirectly, the *Marbury* precedent diminished state authority as it advanced federal judicial power. Marshall seemed to sense the necessity for some instrument to monitor state legislatures prone to defying national authority and the new Constitution. This implication would soon become apparent a few years after *Marbury* was decided.

Fletcher v. Peck (1810)

As noted, *Marbury* is important because it found the Supreme Court declaring a *federal* act unconstitutional for the first time. Seven years later, in the case of *Fletcher* v. *Peck* (1810), the Court for the first time declared a *state* law to be unconstitutional. In this case, Marshall ruled that the repeal of a 1795 act by the Georgia legislature was an unconstitutional impairment of a contractual obligation. According to the Court, repealing the statute violated vested property rights (discussed in Chapter 7) of the repurchasing parties; and, therefore, the act was contrary to the Contract Clause in Article I, Section 10, of the Constitution. But more than a chance for Marshall to advance property rights of individuals, *Fletcher* v. *Peck* further advanced the Court's exercise of judicial power and its role as a necessary umpire between contending parties.

Martin v. Hunter's Lessee (1816)

The final case which supports judicial review being accepted as a "necessary evil" in the American constitutional system is *Martin* v. *Hunter's Lessee* (1816). This case presented the first important challenge to the Court's right to review state court decisions under its appellate jurisdiction. It grew out of a state law passed in Virginia that denied aliens the right to inherit property in the state. A wealthy Virginia landowner had willed his estate to a British relative and citizen by the name of Martin. Under a Virginia law, the state refused to allow foreign subjects to inherit property in the state, and it proceeded to sell the land to its own citizens. Martin sued in Virginia courts to regain title to the estate, arguing that the state law violated a 1794 treaty between the United States and Great Britain that guaranteed certain rights to British citizens living in the United States. A Virginia court upheld the state law, and Martin appealed to the Supreme Court, which found in favor of Martin and ordered the state court to return the land to Martin. The state court refused to do so, claiming state sovereignty, and the case then went back to the Supreme Court.

The primary question in this case was whether the U.S. Supreme Court had appellate jurisdiction to review state court decisions. In a unanimous opinion for the Court, Justice Joseph Story said that federal appellate power "does extend to cases pending in the state courts; and . . . the 25th section of the judiciary act [of 1789], which authorizes the exercise of jurisdiction is supported by the letter and spirit of the constitution." This decision was important because of its strong assertion of national sovereignty and federal judicial power. The Story opinion stressed that the Constitution was established not by the individual states, but by "the people of the United States":

> It is manifest, that the constitution has proceeded upon a theory of its own, and given or withheld powers according to the judgment of the *American people,* by whom it was adopted . . . The constitution has presumed . . . that state attachments . . . prejudices . . . jealousies . . . and interests, might sometimes obstruct, or control . . . the regular administration of justice. [Emphasis added]

Story also justified the monitoring of state court actions by the federal judiciary for another reason:

> Judges of equal learning and integrity, in different states, might differently interpret the statute, or a treaty of the United States, or even the constitution itself; if there were no revising authority to control these jarring and discordant judgments, and harmonize them into uniformity, the laws, the treaties and the constitution of the United States would be different, in different states, and might, perhaps, never have precisely the same construction, obligation or efficiency, in any two states. The public mischiefs that would attend such a state of things would be truly deplorable.

This line of reasoning was similar to that used by Marshall in *Marbury* v. *Madison.* The significance of the *Martin* case was that in upholding a federal treaty over a state law, and in reversing a state court decision, Justice Story strengthened national law and the practice of judicial review and stressed the need for some impartial institution to umpire controversies between levels of government.

All of these cases demonstrate how even in those instances where the states were temporarily disadvantaged by the decision, the eventual outcome was a stronger Union and the perception that some tribunal had to have the final word. Without a doubt, a major reason for these developments in early American law was the presence of John Marshall (see Brief 4.5). But there are still other explanations for why the practice of federal courts' reviewing the actions of other branches of government prevailed in the American system.

Judicial Review as a Check on Majority Rule

In light of the persistent clash of individualistic and communitarian political cultures in American society, judicial review can serve as a check upon the

---

☐ *Brief 4.5   John Marshall and Judicial Nationalism*

John Marshall's appointment to the Supreme Court by President John Adams in 1801 forever changed American constitutional law. His most famous decisions upheld congressional power and national authority, and his intellectual skill and persuasiveness were vital to building American constitutionalism.

Marshall's judicial philosophy embodied four main ideas that are sometimes referred to as **judicial nationalism.** First is the principle of *popular sovereignty,* which means that the American Constitution is derived from the American people in a communal sense. They ratified it in 1788, and it should always be interpreted so as to secure for them the fullest benefits of its several provisions. According to Marshall, the Necessary and Proper Clause (Art. I, Sec. 8) implies this need to legislate for the benefit of the sovereign American people.

A second principle of his judicial philosophy was his insistence upon a *supreme national government,* which is implicit in the Supremacy Clause (Art. VI). The national government is supreme in all spheres of its activities and should not be inhibited by the states. This idea is also reflected in many of his key decisions, especially *Marbury* v. *Madison* (1803), *McCulloch* v. *Maryland* (1819), *Cohens* v. *Virginia* (1821) and *Gibbons* v. *Ogden* (1824).

Third, in several decisions Marshall emphasized that it was the ultimate *role of the Supreme Court* to interpret authoritatively the Constitution and not the prerogative of Congress, the president, or the individual states. All decisions of the Court are binding upon the states and the other branches of government. As first articulated in *Marbury,* this idea periodically generated much debate and denial in the United States.

But eventually, Marshall's frequent claim that the Court is the premier interpreter of the Constitution and arbiter of legal conflicts in American society was accepted.

The last principle embodied in Marshall's legal thinking was the inherent *flexibility* of the Constitution. It is necessary for those interpreting and living under it to treat it as a "living" document that can be accommodated to the changing needs of the American people. Marshall insisted that this flexibility was essential in order to forestall massive overhaul of the fundamental law. The Constitution was not intended to be changed easily, as the rather cumbersome amending process embodied in Article V confirms. The primary instrument for updating the Constitution would be the frequent actions of the justices to breathe life into this formal document. As Marshall observed in *McCulloch* v. *Maryland* (1819), "We must never forget that it is a constitution that we are expounding."

Marshall's true genius as the architect of the American constitutional system was not fully appreciated until after his death in 1835. During his tenure, only a few of his opinions attracted much popular acclaim, and the principle of judicial review would require many more years of practice by the Supreme Court before the doctrine gained widespread public support as the one judicial instrument that could reconcile popular control of government with judicial elitism. Although generally remembered for establishing the practice of judicial review firmly in American law, the majority of Marshall's work on the bench dealt primarily with relatively mundane property disputes brought by private individuals.

legislative results of majority rule. To what extent is the legislature, the executive, or the judiciary the more proper guardian of individual rights? Which of these institutions is better equipped to define the larger public interest of a community? The sad truth is that American history is littered with many instances where popular majorities seemed all too eager to codify majority preferences in ways that denied rights to vulnerable minorities. And, occasionally, judges have had to intervene and curb these majoritarian tendencies that violate minority rights.

In one respect, this is the counterargument to the principle of judicial restraint—the point that popular majorities are the best judge of what is just and good in a democratic society. The framers believed in representative democracy, but one limited by the rule of law that safeguarded the rights of minorities. As noted in Chapter 3, Madison found the need for "auxiliary precautions" in order to control and limit government power. Examples of these checks upon the majority include the separation of powers, the equality of the states, the Senate filibuster, and the need for special majorities in Congress and the states to amend the Constitution.

Judicial review is one of these "auxiliary precautions." Compared with the other departures from simple majority rule, the practice of judicial review is normally seen as less arbitrary or political, although this usually depends upon how well the judges secure their decisions in rationally sound legal opinions. Granting special power to a minority in the political process—be it public or private—can obstruct majoritarian wishes. Whether it is a long-winded bigot in the U.S. Senate trying to block civil rights legislation, or five justices on the Supreme Court who overturn a popular law passed by Congress, the effect is the same. The one difference, of course, is that the Court's action is more likely grounded in logic and objectivity. The justices on the Supreme Court have legal training and precedents upon which to form a more philosophical and rational decision.

However, this does not mean that five or six countermajoritarian justices on the Supreme Court have the last word on all controversial issues facing the Republic. When Congress and the president have opposed the Court's actions, history has shown that legal compromise or outright capitulation by the Court often occurs. As one student of the judicial process has noted:

> Even in the U.S., where judicial review is most firmly entrenched, the Supreme Court has consistently come out second best in direct confrontations with a strong executive-legislative coalition.[29]

Therefore, it has been argued that even though judicial review may sometimes be necessary to check temporary majorities, it does not prevent enduring majorities from adapting to the changing needs of citizens. The Supreme Court crisis of the 1930s and the Court revolution of 1937 testify to this adaptability of the Court. The difficulty lies in determining whether the Court should follow the majoritarian crowd or assert its power against that majority.

Two good examples of how Supreme Court decisions can be a vital corrective to popular majorities concern the issues of racial segregation and legislative malapportionment, as confronted by the Court in the mid-twentieth century. The long battle against racial discrimination will be discussed in more depth in Chapter 9 dealing with the Equal Protection Clause. But the significance of how the American system has sometimes produced major policy change through the courts acting as national policymakers warrants comment in this context of majoritarian rule.

Before the Supreme Court acted in *Brown* v. *Board of Education* (1954) to overturn racial segregation, popular majorities in seventeen states required the segregation of blacks and whites in public schools. Segregation was also required in the District of Columbia, and four other states made the segregation of public schools optional. With the Court's unanimous decision on May 17, striking down the separate-but-equal doctrine, the United States began to emerge from more than three centuries of racial discrimination. Legislation passed by popular majorities reflects democratic procedures, but it may also deny basic constitutional rights to impotent minorities. The words engraved above the Supreme Court building in Washington announcing "equal justice under law" were an unfortunate overstatement until other decisions following *Brown* began to change the status quo in the United States.

Another issue that the Supreme Court finally moved to rectify—legislative malapportionment—for decades had resulted in state legislative and congressional districts' distorting the principle of equal representation. During the twentieth century, the American people had, in increasing numbers, continued to move from rural to urban and suburban areas. But several states refused to acknowledge this trend and failed to reapportion their legislative chambers or congressional districts to reflect the new population distribution within their borders. As a result, several state legislatures seriously underrepresented some portions of their population, while overrepresenting other less populated, more entrenched political and economic elites. In a series of decisions beginning with *Baker* v. *Carr* (1962), the Supreme Court finally accepted jurisdiction in legislative apportionment cases over the criticisms of many, including Justices Felix Frankfurter and the second John Harlan, who maintained that the Court was meddling in areas better left to elected representatives. As Justice William Brennan argued in the first of what would be momentous judicial orders to reapportion grossly distorted legislative districts:

> The question here is the consistency of state action with the Federal Constitution . . . Judicial standards under the Equal Protection Clause are well developed and familiar, and it has been open to courts since the enactment of the Fourteenth Amendment to determine . . . that a discrimination reflects no policy, but simply arbitrary and capricious action.

Baker v. *Carr* found the Court saying that malapportioned state legislative districts may violate the Equal Protection Clause of the Fourteenth Amendment, and that federal courts, after other decisions over several years to the contrary, could provide a remedy to this injustice. With this 6-2 decision in 1962, with only Justices Harlan and Frankfurter dissenting, the Supreme Court effected a major change in reviewing the apportionment actions of state legislatures. But Justice Thomas Clark used the very words from Justice Harlan's dissent in characterizing the grave situation presented in *Baker* v. *Carr*—a situation which found the franchise of entire groups of voters hopelessly devalued:

> The majority of the people of Tennessee have no "practical opportunities for exerting their political weight at the polls" to correct the "invidious discrimination." I have searched diligently for other "practical opportunities" present under the law. I find none other than the federal courts. The majority of the voters have

been caught up in a legislative strait-jacket. Tennessee has an "informed, civically militant electorate" and "an aroused popular conscience," but it does not sear "the conscience of the people's representatives."

Majoritarian preferences have their limits, and the reapportionment cases of the 1960s demonstrate the vital role that judicial intervention must play on occasion to right legislative wrongs.

Judicial Review and the Articulation of First Principles

A final justification for judicial review is that judicial decisions should reflect reasoned decision making that articulates general principles for use in resolving later conflicts. Courts are supposed to educate the public about democratic values, principles of fairness, and collective justice. By hearing and deciding cases, and advancing clear principles that compel compliance through logic and objectivity, courts can persuade the public to comply with rational principles of law and social behavior. According to this explanation, the Supreme Court is the great educator of the body politic as it interprets and applies the law and upholds the constitutional order. Legal decisions must be grounded in the law, rather than on the political biases of the justices.

One of the strongest reflections of this argument was posed many years ago by constitutional scholar Herbert Wechsler, who maintained that the essence of the law and the authority of the Supreme Court lie in the latter's ability to articulate "neutral general principles" of the law:

> The main constituent of the judicial process is precisely that it must be generally principled, resting with respect to every step that is involved in reaching judgment on analysis and reasons quite transcending the immediate result that is achieved.[30]

A **neutral principle** is one that transcends the immediate case at hand and is useful to courts in resolving future cases. If general principles of judicial neutrality are not available to use in different settings, the future resolution of conflict will be susceptible to subjective analysis and bias. As a result, the public will recognize this bias and disregard the law.

There is a temptation to find examples of Wechsler's neutral principles in various passages of the Constitution. The same First Amendment guarantees of free speech and assembly that the American masses have relied upon for decades—provided that they do not violate the law—also are available to neo-Nazis, Ku Klux Klansmen, or Rev. Louis Farrakhan of the Nation of Islam, all of whom have well-known anti-egalitarian philosophies. "Neutral principles" derived from interpreting and applying provisions of the Constitution do not discriminate between the content of the message or the bigotry of the messenger. First Amendment rights should be accorded to all, regardless of their political or racial philosophy. But a key point to remember is that individuals or groups wanting to enjoy their constitutional rights must also ensure that in so doing, they not violate the rights of others.

Another example in certain respects is the volatile topic of affirmative action. An argument in recent years by those supporting affirmative action programs is that granting preferential treatment to racial minorities is essential in order to compensate for decades, if not centuries, of invidious discrimination (see Chapter 10 for a discussion on this controversial topic). But opponents of such programs argue that such treatment is merely discrimination in reverse.

If discriminating against black people in housing, employment, or public schools denies them equal protection of the laws under the Fourteenth Amendment, then critics of these different compensatory programs argue that giving blacks and other minorities *preferential* treatment in these areas denies the majority the same equal protection. Wechsler's "neutral principles" compel complete neutrality or, to quote the first Justice John Harlan in *Plessy* v. *Ferguson* (1896), a Constitution that is "color-blind."

This "neutral principles" argument in support of judicial review is rather weak, in part because American constitutional law exhibits few decisions in which the Supreme Court has rendered timeless principles that compel a perfect consensus. As two noted constitutional scholars have observed, "Neutrality, save on a superficial and elementary level, is a futile quest." [31] If "neutral principles" means adherence to a value-free form of decision making, then the concept is unachievable. Furthermore, since most decisions of the Court are usually the result of collective decision making, achieving perfect neutrality among all participants in a decision is a distant ideal. Majority opinions are often carefully crafted to hold together a fragile coalition of justices who may have compromised on certain points in order to achieve a convincing majority. The result is frequently a negotiated narrative that lacks consistency. In many instances, it is the *dissenting* opinions of the justices where the reasoning is the most crisp and eloquent. History records several justices whose reputations were forged more for their dissenting opinions than for their majority, or concurring, opinions. The first John Harlan, Oliver Wendell Holmes, Jr., Louis D. Brandeis, and Harlan Fiske Stone come to mind. Likewise, the dissenting opinion of Justice Sandra Day O'Connor in *Akron* v. *Akron Center for Reproductive Health* (1983), where she disagreed with the Court's upholding of a woman's right to an abortion, reflects both the difficulty of achieving lasting neutral principles in constitutional law and the need to persist in formulating principles that will withstand the test of time. At the present time, Justice Harry Blackmun in *Bowers* v. *Hardwick* (1986) and Justice William Brennan in *McCleskey* v. *Kemp* (1987) are extremely powerful voices for the need to protect individual privacy and human dignity at all costs. Although these two cases deal with vastly different subjects (laws prohibiting sodomy and sanctioning the death penalty), they reflect an eloquence often absent in many Court opinions that require negotiation, multiple drafts, and, sometimes, forced unity.

A few of the Supreme Court's most historic decisions reflect how an American society, deeply divided over certain issues, has struggled with the Court's attempts to settle these controversies with neutral legal principles. The ill-fated *Dred Scott* v. *Sandford* decision (discussed more fully in Chapter 9) is a good example of the justices' inability to forge a consensus with enduring neutral principles when none existed in society. The slavery issue, which had been carefully avoided by the framers in 1787, intensified throughout the first half of the nineteenth century. Congress was unable to defuse it with the Missouri Compromise in 1820. When the *Dred Scott* case reached the Taney Court in 1857, the justices stumbled toward their first "self-inflicted wound," to use the words of later Chief Justice Charles Evans Hughes. Chief Justice Roger Taney argued that blacks were not citizens of the United States and therefore not able to sue in federal courts, but were instead a "subordinate and inferior class of beings."

The *Dred Scott* case and its tragic aftermath testify to the importance of the public perception of an issue and to how the Supreme Court must always strive to enlighten and ennoble the public spirit. The legitimacy of a judicial decision rests ultimately upon the public's willingness to accept the expertise and authority of the Court. This legitimacy is especially dependent upon the ability of the justices to persuade by careful reasoning and objective values. By appealing to shared beliefs, the existence of which may be only dimly apparent to the public at large, the Court tries to convince the public that a decision is "right" not because the Court is completely neutral in its choices, but because the decision is the proper and just thing to do. What doomed the *Dred Scott* decision was the fact that the Taney opinion for the Court majority attempted to make the alleged inferiority of blacks a principle of American constitutional law. What was so offensive to a large segment of the public after this decision was the Court's open justification of racial discrimination by the legal system. To insist, as Taney did, that blacks deserved unfair treatment, given the original wording of the Constitution, struck at the very core of a legal system supposedly grounded in respect for human dignity. Although it took a tragic civil war and eleven more years before blacks became citizens of the United States, it would take much longer to restore the reputation of both Taney and the Supreme Court, and more than a century for the country to begin to live up to many of its founding principles of equality and justice.

Roughly a century after *Dred Scott*, the *Brown* v. *Board of Education* decision in 1954 also shows how difficult it is for the Supreme Court to accomplish its tasks by articulating neutral principles of legal objectivity. This historic decision is generally regarded as a forceful statement of sociological opinions and conclusions about the cruel injustice of forced racial segregation. It is not a carefully constructed and logically developed body of legal principles and axioms compelling public support. The Constitution does not explicitly require racially mixed public schools; in fact, when the document was drafted in 1787, public schools did not even exist in the United States! Nor does an analysis of the debates preceding the adoption of the Fourteenth Amendment in 1868 yield conclusive evidence about historical intentions. In the Court's unanimous decision striking down the separate-but-equal doctrine in 1954, Chief Justice Earl Warren placed the major emphasis upon the psychological and sociological burden imposed by racially segregating public school children:

> To separate them from others of similar age and qualifications solely because of their race generates a feeling of inferiority as to their status in the community that may affect their hearts and minds in a way unlikely ever to be undone.

This is persuasive prose, but it is not justified by either the text of the Constitution or the letter of the law. It is relatively easy to evaluate *Brown* three decades after its development as a truly momentous decision. But the test for those arguing from "first principles" is to ask how accurately it reflected a public consensus on race relations in American society in the mid-1950s. The unfortunate reality, confirmed by more than a decade thereafter, is that *Brown* fell on a society that did *not* agree on the principle of racial equality. Consequently, the decision was vehemently and violently ignored in the 1950s and 1960s in many states. *Brown* prevailed because of the persistence of federal implementation and a slowly evolving public attitude that racial discrimination was wrong, regardless of what the framers had intended. It was not the sheer weight of neutral principles embodied in the *Brown* decision that immediately moved American public opinion to comply with the holding. It was the clout of federal troops and the Department of Justice that pressed compliance.

These, then, are several factors that help explain why judical review has been such a prominent feature of American constitutional experience. As the following chapters will indicate, the saga about how the American people and their representatives have tried to resolve the constitutional dilemma continues. The perennial struggles between individualism and communitarianism and between governmental authority and individual liberty have never been fully resolved to the complete satisfaction of all the diverse elements that make up this country. It has been a journey with many stops and starts, and the struggle continues into the third century of American constitutional government. This discussion of judicial power and judicial review now concludes with a brief look at the several constitutional periods that have composed this continuing experiment in self-government.

The Cyclical Nature of Supreme Court Decision Making

At the risk of generalizing about two centuries of American constitutional development, it might be helpful to summarize the past two hundred years by referring to several periods of Supreme Court activity. The following discussion will focus upon a few main characteristics of the several court periods that serve as chapters in the continuing saga of American constitutional government. As will become clear, the Court justices seldom wrote on a clean slate, but rather added to a continuing story of controversy and precedent. Their decisions reflected both themselves and the society in which they lived. During two centuries of constitutional government, there have been nine different Supreme Court eras, each of which has left its unique mark upon American government and practice. These eras include (1) the pre-Marshall era; (2) the Marshall Court; (3) the Taney Court; (4) the revival of judicial power; (5) the era of judicial self-confidence; (6) the New Deal Court; (7) the Warren Court; (8) the Burger Court; and (9) the Rehnquist Court. In examining these different periods, reference should be made to Table 4.8, which summarizes the major issues, political-economic ideology, key decisions, and locus of political power during these nine court eras.

The Pre-Marshall Era (1789–1801)

During the first era of the American Republic, Congress was regarded as the most important branch of the federal government. An important issue that dominated the decade of the 1790s was how best to consolidate power under this new form of government in order to protect against foreign enemies and preserve domestic order. Discounting the imposing presence of George Washington as the first president, if that is possible, the American people distrusted executive power and looked to Congress as best-suited to represent popular needs and interests. Initially, both the American people and public officials showed very little interest in the Supreme Court. During the 1790s, state courts

Table 4.8 The American Constitutional Experience

COURT ERA	DOMINANT ISSUES	LOCUS OF POLITICAL POWER	POLITICAL-ECONOMIC PHILOSOPHY	KEY COURT DECISIONS
Pre-Marshall 1789–1801	Consolidation and nation building	Congress and president	Federalist economic conservatism	*Chisholm v. Georgia; Hylton v. U.S.*
Marshall Court 1801–1835	Judicial nationalism; expanding democracy; states' rights	Congress and the states	Jeffersonian democracy	*Marbury v. Madison; McCulloch v. Maryland; Dartmouth College v. Woodward; Gibbons v. Ogden*
Taney Court 1835–1864	Slavery; states' rights; sectionalism	Congress and the states	Jacksonian democracy	*Charles River Bridge v. Warren Bridge; Dred Scott v. Sandford*
Judicial Revival 1864–1890	Reconstruction; economic development; territorial expansion	Congress; states; private power	Laissez-faire	*Munn v. Illinois;* Slaughterhouse Cases; Civil Rights Cases
Judicial Self-Confidence 1890–1937	Trust building; World War I; economic depression	Supreme Court in re. to business/economic development	Social Darwinism; progressivism	*Plessy v. Ferguson; Lochner v. New York; Schechter Poultry v. U.S.*
New Deal Court 1937–1953	Economic recovery; World War II; cold war	President and Congress	New Deal collectivism	*West Coast Hotel v. Parrish; Korematsu v. U.S.; Dennis v. U.S.*
Warren Court 1953–1969	Desegregation; political equality; minority rights	Congress in early years; president in later years	New Deal collectivism	*Brown v. Board of Education; Baker v. Carr; Gideon v. Wainwright*
Burger Court 1969–1986	Vietnam War; Watergate; economic deregulation	President	Collectivism; Goldwater-Reagan conservatism	*U.S. v. Nixon; Roe v. Wade; University of California v. Bakke*
Rehnquist Court 1986–Present	Economic recovery; national defense; budget deficits	Congress and the president		*McCleskey v. Kemp; California Federal Savings v. Guerra; Edwards v. Aguillard*

handled most legal matters, and during its first three years of operation, the Court did not hear a single case! It also suffered from a noticeable lack of prestige. Both Patrick Henry and Alexander Hamilton declined the chief justiceship, and John Jay, the first chief justice of the United States, eventually resigned in 1795 to serve as governor of New York. Other individuals either declined appointment or resigned in order to serve in state judicial posts, something that would probably not occur today. Unlike the other two branches, the Supreme Court met in basement apartments or in congressional committee rooms. In fact, the Supreme Court of the United States did not have its own building until 1935! To say the least, this first period of the Court was not an especially impressive time to serve on what would eventually become the most important court in the world.

The Marshall Court Era (1801–1835)

As depicted more specifically in Brief 4.5, the Marshall Court era was a very formative period for American constitutional law. Federalist economic conservatism dominated the Court during this period, but Jeffersonian democracy envisioned an expanding democratic order based upon more open political processes, party competition, and a much different society than that of Washington, Adams, and Hamilton. Congress and the several states eclipsed the executive during much of this period, although the imposing presence of John Marshall and other strong Federalists on the Supreme Court meant that judicial nationalism was a major force in molding the emerging nation.

The Taney Court Era (1835–1864)

Like Marshall, Roger B. Taney had great political experience and ability. Although once a Federalist, Taney became an avid supporter of Andrew Jackson, serving as secretary of the treasury under Jackson just prior to his appointment to the Court in 1835. The characteristics of Jacksonian democracy—such as states' rights, agrarian property, decentralized power, participatory democracy, and easy credit—all found their way into Supreme Court decision making under Taney. The Taney Court never completely broke with the Marshall era, although the focus and effect of many earlier decisions were revised in some respects. Taney's leadership was less bold than that of Marshall, and he interpreted the Commerce and Contract Clauses to the benefit of the states. He was more sympathetic to the economic rights of the masses, rather than to Marshall's economic elite. Unfortunately, more than any other event during his tenure on the Court, Chief Justice Roger B. Taney is remembered most for the *Dred Scott* decision in 1857. Ironically, the severe damage that attended the Taney Court as a consequence of that decision eventually became a victory for judicial control over national policy. By striking down the Missouri Compromise, the Court was saying that a mere legislative act could not change the letter of the Constitution. Only a formal amendment could do that, which is precisely what happened later with the ratification of the Reconstruction amendments following the Civil War.

Revival of Judicial Power (1864–1890)

From the low point of the Taney years, the Court made an impressive recovery, aided considerably by what was happening in the United States after the Civil

War. Congress and the presidency were pitted against each other over the shape and substance of Reconstruction. This allowed the Supreme Court, under Salmon P. Chase (1864–74) and Morrison R. Waite (1874–88), both Republicans who favored property rights and preservation of the status quo, to resurface as a constitutional referee in national conflicts. The problems of reintegrating the seceded states into the Union and the new forms of taxing and finance enacted during the Civil War created new problems for those explaining the purpose of government.

The 1870s and 1880s were years of considerable economic growth and territorial expansion in the United States. As the frontier pushed westward, economic enterprise reached new proportions. The railroads became a major instrument for settlement and service, although by the 1870s, they were exploiting farmers and ranchers dependent upon the rail for transporting their stock and commodities. Giant industrial corporations developed in the steel, tobacco, railroad, and mining industries and accelerated development in new urban centers in the Midwest and West. This was also the era of *laissez-faire*— which meant that business should be allowed to operate with a minimum of governmental restraints. But by the 1870s, farmers and laborers began to call for increased regulatory activity by government against these new masters of the marketplace. By 1890, the cries for regulatory reform had produced numerous state laws regulating business, and, at the federal level, the Interstate Commerce Act of 1887 and the Sherman Antitrust Act of 1890.

Amid these rapid social and economic changes, the Supreme Court became more active in exercising its judicial authority, especially as it concerned interpretation of the Reconstruction amendments (Thirteenth-Fifteenth). Important decisions in the Slaughterhouse Cases (1873) and the Civil Rights Cases (1883) found the Supreme court interpreting very narrowly the role of the federal government in protecting newly won freedoms of blacks. Between 1864 and 1874, the Court overturned ten acts of Congress and over thirty state laws, mostly on the grounds that the laws interfered with property rights of individuals and corporations. The Court under Chief Justice Morrison Waite continued to advance property rights, although *Munn* v. *Illinois* (1877) found the Court upholding a state regulation of business "affected with the public interest." This recognition of state "police power" had an important impact in the early twentieth century, with the advent of protective regulatory policy. By 1890, the Supreme Court began to interpret the Fourteenth Amendment as an instrument to protect property rights, rather than to safeguard the civil rights of black Americans (see discussions of substantive due process in Chapter 7 and equal protection in Chapter 9).

The Era of Judicial Self-Confidence (1890–1937)

For the next near half-century, the Court used its authority to protect property rights of individuals and corporations. Under a succession of rather conservative justices partial to private property, the Fuller Court (1889–1910), the White Court (1910–21), the Taft Court (1921–30), and the Hughes Court (1930–40) targeted state and federal laws designed to regulate various aspects of the economy. From 1889 to 1940, the Supreme Court declared fifty-two federal laws and 389 state statutes to be unconstitutional, usually on the grounds that they violated property rights under the Fifth Amendment and Fourteenth Amendment. Under the banner of progressivism, the states and the federal government passed several laws to regulate many aspects of a changing American economy, such as working hours, working conditions, minimum wages, child labor, antitrust matters, compulsory arbitration, employer liability, and economic production. With the justices' preferences for a market economy unburdened by intrusive government regulations, the usual outcome was the death of the statute.

Even with the arrival on the Court in the early twentieth century of Holmes, Brandeis, Stone, and Cardozo, who supported many government regulations, it remained very difficult for Congress to deal with the problems of economic growth. The battle raging on the Court over the fate of federal legislation reached its peak in the 1930s, as discussed in Brief 4.4.

The New Deal Era (1937–1953)

Beginning in 1937, Supreme Court decision making followed two prominent paths of constitutional concerns. One was that the Court became less concerned with personal property rights and laissez-faire capitalism. Extensive federal regulation became a fact of American life in the mid-twentieth century, and the Supreme Court participated in building the modern service state. As opposed to actively striking down state and federal legislation aimed at regulating the economy, the Court after 1937 became very supportive of national supremacy in a broad range of economic affairs. From 1936 to 1954, only three minor pieces of federal legislation were declared unconstitutional by the Court.[32]

The second major Court trend after 1937 was the increased protection afforded civil rights and civil liberties. In the 1935 Court term, of the 160 written opinions authored by the Court, only *two* dealt with either civil rights or civil liberties. By the mid-1940s, twenty times more cases dealing with these crucial areas of constitutional law occupied the Court's time.[33] Unfortunately, this new trend had a few exceptions, two of which were the Japanese Internment Cases—*Hirabayashi* v. *United States* (1943) and *Korematsu* v. *United States* (1944), as covered in Chapter 5—and the first of the Flag Salute Cases—*Minersville School District* v. *Gobitis* (1940), discussed in Chapter 13.

The Court under Chief Justice Charles Evans Hughes (1930–41) began to defend more earnestly the letter and spirit of the Bill of Rights, as did the Stone Court (1941–46). But the Vinson Court (1946–53) was more reluctant to intervene in important civil liberties cases when national security questions were raised, as some key cases in the late 1940s and early 1950s reflected. But it began to establish some important civil rights precedents that were very important for later decisions in the 1950s.

Warren Court Era (1953–1969)

Under the leadership of Earl Warren, the Supreme Court seemed more determined than ever to protect personal freedoms. Following the crucial *Brown* decision in 1954, the Warren Court plunged into the most aggressive stance toward individual rights in the history of the Supreme Court. Although this judicial posture had its roots in the stances of the first Justice Harlan and Justices Holmes, Brandeis, and Stone, it matured during two phases of the Warren Court era. The first phase lasted from 1953 to 1962, when the Court often found itself divided into two voting blocs. One coalition was comprised of civil libertarians—Justices Black and Douglas (both Roosevelt appointees),

Brennan, and Warren himself. This coalition undertook to safeguard civil rights and liberties, promote social welfare, and carefully scrutinize state legislation attempting to restrict Bill of Rights guarantees. Another bloc included Justices Frankfurter, Stewart, Clark, Stanley Reed (until 1957), Charles Whittaker (1957–62), and the second John Harlan. This group maintained that the primary responsibility for self-government rested with the people and their elected representatives, which meant a limited role for judicial policy making.

The retirement of Frankfurter and Whittaker in 1962, revealed a second phase of the Warren Court when more activist justices, such as Arthur Goldberg, Abe Fortas, and Thurgood Marshall, assumed their seats on the Court. This period, which lasted until Warren retired in 1969, brought judicial control over criminal law and defendants' rights, rights of the underprivileged under the Equal Protection Clause, and reapportionment issues and continued activity in the civil rights area. The Warren Court era was one of the most activist in American history (twenty-five federal and 150 state statutes declared unconstitutional between 1953 and 1969). By the late 1960s, with the United States in the midst of social and political upheaval, critics of the Warren Court argued that it had fueled social disintegration through its decisions concerning race relations, religion, and rights of criminal defendants. Little did these critics know that the next court would be just as activist as its predecessor.

The Burger Court (1969–1986)

By the mid-1980s, the Burger Court had certainly modified some major Warren Court rulings relating to criminal law, religion in public schools, and obscenity law, but much of the Warren Court legacy was still intact. Though deeply divided and lacking a sound and consistent legal rationale for its decision making, the Burger Court ventured into previously unchartered judicial waters and surprised many observers by its independence from Republican administrations in the 1970s and 1980s. In a series of decisions that included the Pentagon Papers Case (1971), *Roe* v. *Wade* (1973), *United States* v. *Nixon* (1974), and several affirmative action decisions, the Burger Court established an even more activist record than its predecessor. Through the 1984 term, the Burger Court had declared thirty-four federal and 192 state statutes unconstitutional, slightly more than had the Warren Court. The Burger Court also saw the appointment of the first woman to the Court, Sandra Day O'Connor. When Chief Justice Burger announced in 1986 that he intended to retire, it meant that the Reagan administration, which had bristled at many of the earlier Burger Court decisions, would have another opportunity to appoint someone more closely aligned with a conservative political agenda.

The Rehnquist Court (1986–present)

The retirement of Chief Justice Burger from the Court in 1986 provided the Reagan administration with an important opportunity to change the direction and content of several judicial precedents of the past two decades. The promotion of William Rehnquist to the chief justiceship, the addition of appellate judge Antonin Scalia in 1986, and the arrival of Judge Anthony M. Kennedy on the Court by early 1988 led many to predict a more conservative tilt to the Supreme Court. The rulings of the 1986–87 term of the Rehnquist Court were moderate-to-liberal on social policy banning racial and sexual discrimination, permitting abortion, protecting AIDS patients, and separating church and state. However, on issues relating to criminal law and some civil liberties, the Court proved to be more conservative and pragmatic in its basic policy instincts. Close votes by the justices during 1986–87 in decisions upholding racial quotas in state police forces and banning certain evidence in criminal trials indicated a closely divided Court and the importance of the pragmatist, Justice Powell, to the Court.

The 1987–88 term of the Rehnquist Court revealed a continuation of prevailing policy in many areas and a few surprises that went against the Reagan administration's preferred position on selected issues. Some key decisions of this most recent Court term established that black employees cannot be prevented from using statistics to prove that they have been discriminated against on account of their race; labor unions cannot require nonmembers to help finance union political lobbying for positions with which they disagree; federal laws that provide money to religious groups to counsel teenage girls to abstain from sexual relations and to avoid abortion do not violate the First Amendment separation of church and state; and states may not unconditionally execute people for capital crimes committed when they were less than sixteen years old.

Finally, one of the most significant Supreme Court decisions in recent decades found the Rehnquist Court overwhelmingly endorsing the federal law that provides for independent prosecutors to investigate suspected crimes by high-ranking executive branch officials (see Brief 5.5). The Court's decision in *Morrison* v. *Olson* (1988) was the first time in more than a decade that the high Court sided with Congress in a separation-of-powers dispute with the president.

After two terms of the Rehnquist Court and the distinct possibility of additional vacancies in the near future, there seems to be much uncertainty about the direction of the Court in the next decade.

Conclusion

This examination of judicial power and the practice of judicial review in American constitutional development has emphasized several points. Structurally, the federal judiciary is a multilayered bureaucracy that has expanded considerably since its creation in 1789. Although this book stresses the role of the Supreme Court within this bureaucracy, it is only one of over one hundred federal courts and includes only nine of over seven hundred federal judges who bear immense responsibility for interpreting federal laws, federal treaties, and the U.S. Constitution.

A second aspect is that the process used since the beginning of the American Republic to select federal judges and Supreme Court justices is a very *political* process. That should not detract from the impressive qualifications exhibited by those chosen to interpret and apply the law in a diverse society of 240 million people. But it does emphasize that judges and justices are never very far from the political arena, both before they are chosen and after they assume their judicial posts.

Third, because the selection process is inherently political, it should not surprise anyone to learn that historically the decision-making process has been

political in nature. As the discussion on Supreme Court decision making indicates, the justices have never been completely immune to the social, economic, and political forces surrounding them. Providing them with lifetime
tenure ensures that they will not be punished for making unpopular decisions.
However, it has certainly never insulated them from the political winds that
continuously blow through a dynamic society trying to cope with complex
problems while living under the rule of law.

Finally, the practice of judicial review by the U.S. Supreme Court has
seen the justices operating in one of the most unique judicial bodies in the
world. Few other societies give to nine judicial officers the power to resolve
ongoing social conflicts as occurs in the United States. Although sixty-five
other nations in 1985 had some form of judicial review, none of them have
operated in quite the same manner as the Supreme Court of the United States.
At times, that body has changed policy in a way rarely seen in organized
societies, as the Marshall, Warren, and Burger courts demonstrate. On other
occasions, the Court has been eclipsed by the other two branches of government
(e.g., during the pre- and post-Civil War eras). The Court has also been a
major economic and social innovator, as the New Deal Court and the Warren
Court reflect; and, at times, it has been the recipient of enormous public
criticism (the Taney Court after *Dred Scott* and the Hughes Court in the mid-
1930s).

But after two hundred years of interpreting the Constitution, the Supreme
Court still serves as the preeminent conscience of the country. As one student
of judicial review stated many years ago, the justices on the Supreme Court
are "inevitably teachers in a vital national seminar" that never ends.[33] They
are expected to perform this noble task with intelligence, integrity, reflection,
and impartiality, in a society that is still experimenting with the art of self-
government. The justices are certainly not infallible, nor are the people they
serve. But with patience and forebearance—and an abiding faith in a democratic people's ability to govern themselves—the Supreme Court can continue
to serve a nation embarking upon its third century.

Questions

1. A paradox of judicial review is that it has evolved within a representative democracy
that allows a presidentially appointed, life-tenured federal judiciary to monitor and
potentially overrule the actions of popular majorities. To what extent does this *reflect*
or *violate* the intentions of the framers and the spirit of the Constitution?

2. Article III gives Congress virtually unlimited authority to regulate the appellate
jurisdiction of the Supreme Court. Does the infrequency with which Congress has acted
to limit the Court's jurisdiction indicate the historical acceptance of unlimited appellate
power to review state and federal laws and actions of public officials, or does it merely
reflect one of the many myths that have surrounded the Supreme Court and the Constitution?

3. It is generally recognized that presidents have a right—some might even say an
obligation—to nominate personnel to the federal courts who hold similar views on
substantive policy areas. Recently, however, the Senate Judiciary Committee has been
criticized for the manner in which it has conducted confirmation hearings to delineate
more clearly how nominees feel about prevailing public policy. To what extent do you
think that this is a fair criticism of the committee and the Senate? Should policy views
of the nominee be beyond scrutiny by the senators? Does congressional interrogation

of these matters demean the role of courts and judges, or is it essential given the lasting role that these judges may play in determining public policy?

4.   Recent political debate has focused upon the role and function of federal judges and their tendency to "make law," rather than to interpret and apply it to existing controversies. To what extent do you think federal judges invariably find themselves compelled to move beyond the literal confines of the Constitution and federal statutes in resolving legal disputes between contending parties?

5.   Academicians have long made a practice of dividing the political and historical landscape into discernible eras or periods, ascribing certain broad political, economic, and sociological characteristics to those periods, and evaluating the relative strength or weakness of the different governmental institutions that existed in those periods. What factors do you think best explain the relative strength of the Supreme Court compared with Congress and the presidency? To what extent has it largely been determined by the personnel in these several branches at any one point in time? What structural or institutional factors of the Supreme Court, apart from the particular justices, may have the greatest impact upon the relative power and influence of the Court?

Endnotes

1.   Appropriate citations for these respective precedents are *St. Francis College* v. *Majid Ghaidan Al-Khazraji,* 107 S. Ct. 2022 (1987); *Rose* v. *Rose,* 107 S. Ct. 2029 (1987); *National Labor Relations Board* v. *International Brotherhood of Electrical Workers, Local 340,* 107 S. Ct. 2002 (1987); and *New York Land Company* v. *Republic of the Philippines,* 107 S.Ct. 1367 (1967).

2.   Alexis de Tocqueville, *Democracy in America,* Vol. 1 (New York: Vintage Books, 1945), 107.

3.   For a complete summary of the impeachment and conviction proceedings by Congress against federal judges since 1789, see Henry J. Abraham, *The Judicial Process: An Introductory Analysis of the Courts of the United States, England, and France,* 5th ed. (New York: Oxford University Press, 1986), 45–48. The most recent instance of Congress initiating impeachment proceedings against a sitting federal judge occurred in 1986. Judge Harry Claiborne from Nevada had just been convicted of federal income tax evasion and was serving a prison term in Louisiana. He had refused to resign his seat on the federal bench, and Congress decided to take action.

On July 22, 1986, the House of Representatives voted 406 to 0 on four separate articles of impeachment. On October 9, 1986, the Senate, acting as a jury in accordance with the Constitution, voted overwhelmingly (87-10; 90-7; 89-8) on three of the four articles, and Judge Claiborne became the first federal judge in over fifty years to be impeached and convicted while serving in a federal judicial post.

4.   During the 1970s, in part because of Chief Justice Warren Burger's continued pleas for judicial reform, several court watchers suggested the addition of a national court of appeals that would ease the increasing workload of the U.S. Supreme Court. Support for this new court level subsided when critics claimed that it might dramatically change the nature and potency of Supreme Court rulings. Increasingly in recent years, the Supreme Court has tried to manage its workload by limiting standing of certain parties to bring suit in federal courts. See the cases of *Laird* v. *Tatum,* 408 U.S. 1 (1972); *Schlesinger* v. *Reservists Committee to Stop the War,* 418 U.S. 208 (1974); *United States* v. *Richardson,* 418 U.S. 166 (1974); *Warth* v. *Seldin,* 422 U.S. 490 (1975); and *Simon* v. *Eastern*

Kentucky Welfare Rights Organization, 426 U.S. 26 (1976).

5. See *Massachusetts* v. *Laird*, 400 U.S. 886 (1970), where the Supreme Court ruled that the state of Massachusetts lacked standing to sue on behalf of its citizens questioning the constitutionality of the Vietnam War; and *Goldwater* v. *Carter*, 444 U.S. 996 (1979), where the Court said that the president could terminate a treaty without the approval of the U.S. Senate. The latter case is discussed more extensively in Chapter 5 in the context of the separation-of-powers principle.

6. Howard Ball, *Courts and Politics: The Federal Judicial System*, 2d ed. (Englewood Cliffs, N.J.: Prentice-Hall, 1987), 184.

7. Robert A. Carp and Ronald Stidham, *The Federal Courts* (Washington, D.C.: Congressional Quarterly Press, 1985), 108.

8. Ball, *Courts and Politics*, 209.

9. Henry J. Abraham, *Justices and Presidents: A Political History of Appointments to the Supreme Court*, 2d ed. (New York: Oxford University Press, 1985), 61.

10. Truman lecture at Columbia University, April 28, 1959; quoted in Abraham, ibid., 70.

11. Henry J. Abraham, *The Judiciary: The Supreme Court in the Governmental Process*, 7th ed. (Boston: Allyn and Bacon, 1987), 65.

12. Sheldon Goldman, "Reaganizing the Judiciary: The First Term Appointments," *Judicature* 68 (April-May 1985): 313–29; "Reagan's Second Term Judicial Appointments," *Judicature* 70 (April-May 1987): 324–39.

13. Quoted from Meese speech reprinted in *The Great Debate: Interpreting Our Written Constitution* (Washington, D.C.: Federalist Society, 1986), 1–10.

14. Ibid., 29.

15. This discussion of constitutional interpretation relies heavily upon the discussion in Walter F. Murphy, James E. Fleming, and William F. Harris II, *American Constitutional Interpretation* (Mineola, N.Y.: Foundation Press, 1986), 289–313.

16. One of the first constitutional scholars to use the terms *judicial restraint* and *judicial activism* was C. Herman Pritchett in his book *The Roosevelt Court* (New York: Macmillan, 1948).

17. Although this seminal article has appeared in numerous publications, it first was published in Volume 7 of the *Harvard Law Review* in 1893.

18. Holmes dissenting in *Hammer* v. *Dagenhart*, 247 U.S. 251 (1918), at 280.

19. From *Senate Reports*, 75th Congress, 1st session, Document #711.

20. The literature on this debate is extensive, but those interested in pursuing it have many sources from which to choose. On the restraint side, see Donald Horowitz, *The Courts and Social Policy* (Washington, D.C.: Brookings Institution, 1977); Nathan Glazar, "Toward an Imperial Judiciary," *Public Interest* 41 (1975): 104–23; Raoul Berger, *Government by Judiciary* (Cambridge, Mass.: Harvard University Press, 1977); Raoul Berger, "Lawyering vs. Philosophizing: Facts or Fancies?" *Dayton Law Review* 9 (Winter 1984): 171; and Robert Bork, "Commentary: The Impossibility of Finding Welfare Rights in the Constitution," *Washington University Law Quarterly* (1979): 695. For those advocating judicial activism, see Abram Chayes, "The Role of the Judge in Public Law Litigation," *Harvard Law Review* 89 (May 1976): 1281; Ralph Cavanaugh and Austin Sarat, "Thinking About Courts: Toward a Jurisprudence of Judicial Competence," *Law and Society Review* 14 (Winter 1980): 371; and Thomas C. Grey, "Do We Have an Unwritten Constitution?" *Stan-*

ford Law Review 27 (1975): 703. For a recent compilation and analysis of these differing views and a rather novel synthesis toward a new "aesthetic" prescription for courts to follow, see Leif Carter, *Contemporary Constitutional Lawmaking* (New York: Pergamon Press, 1985).

21. Robert H. Jackson, *The Supreme Court in the American System of Government* (Cambridge, Mass.: Harvard University Press, 1955), 23.

22. Abraham, *The Judiciary,* 71.

23. Robert K. Carr in *The Supreme Court and Judicial Review* (New York: Farrar and Rinehart, 1942) documents over 460 cases of the Privy Council in London overruling laws adopted by American colonial assemblies during the seventeenth and eighteenth centuries. Charles G. Haines in *The American Doctrine of Judicial Supremacy* (New York: Russell and Russell, 1959) discusses eight occasions in which American state courts between 1778 and 1788 had either claimed or used this power. In the 1790s, there were four instances of national laws being reviewed by the U.S. Supreme Court to determine their constitutionality (Hayburn's Case in 1792, *Chandler* v. *Secretary of War* and *United States* v. *Yale Todd* in 1794, and *Hylton* v. *United States* in 1796). Had any of these four found the Court overturning the federal statute, *Marbury* v. *Madison* in 1803 would clearly not have been the first instance of a federal law being declared unconstitutional.

24. Alexander Hamilton, John Jay, and James Madison, "Federalist No. 78," *The Federalist Papers* (New York: New American Library, 1961), 465.

25. Ibid., 467.

26. Jesse Choper, "The Supreme Court and the Political Branches: Democratic Theory and Practice," *University of Pennsylvania Law Review* 122 (1974): 848.

27. The other three are the Fourteenth Amendment, ratified in 1868, overruling *Dred Scott* v. *Sandford* and making blacks citizens of the United States; the Sixteenth Amendment, ratified in 1913, which overruled *Pollock* v. *Farmers' Loan & Trust* and authorized passage of a federal income tax; and the Twenty-sixth Amendment, adopted in 1971, which overruled *Oregon* v. *Mitchell* and guaranteed eighteen-year-olds the right to vote.

28. There was a serious conflict of interest brewing in this eventual landmark case before the Supreme Court. Outgoing Secretary of State John Marshall, for some unexplained reason, never delivered the commission to Marbury. Under present protocol, any justice sitting on the Supreme Court who had played as important a role as Marshall had in this case would have excused himself from participating in *Marbury* v. *Madison* in 1803. Undoubtedly, without Marshall's strong assertion of judicial power and persuasive reasoning, *Marbury* would not have been the significant precedent that it was. But Marshall never absented himself from either hearing the case or assigning the opinion to himself.

29. Joseph Tanenhaus, "Judicial Review," *International Encyclopedia of the Social Sciences* (New York: Macmillan, 1968).

30. Herbert Wechsler, "Toward Neutral Principles of Constitutional Law," *Harvard Law Review* 73 (1950): 15.

31. Arthur S. Miller and Ronald F. Howell, "The Myth of Neutrality in Constitutional Adjudication," *University of Chicago Law Review* 27 (Summer 1960): 661.

32. In *Tot* v. *United States* (1943), the Court struck down a section of the Federal Firearms Act as a violation of the Fifth Amendment Due Process Clause; in *United States* v. *Lovett* (1946), it invalidated a rider to an appropriations bill; and in *United*

States v. *Cardiff* (1952), it declared unconstitutional a provision of the Pure Food and Drug Act.

33. Cited in Abraham, *The Judicial Process,* 365.

34. Eugene V. Rostow, "The Democratic Character of Judicial Review," *Harvard Law Review* 66 (1952): 195.

Suggested Readings

Abraham, Henry J. *The Judiciary: The Supreme Court in the Governmental Process.* 7th ed. Allyn and Bacon, 1987.

Carp, Robert A., and Ronald Stidham. *The Federal Courts.* Washington, D.C.: Congressional Quarterly Press, 1985.

Choper, Jesse. *Judicial Review and the National Political Process.* Chicago: University of Chicago Press, 1980.

Ely, John Hart. *Democracy and Distrust: A Theory of Judicial Review.* Cambridge, Mass.: Harvard University Press, 1980.

Jackson, Robert H. *The Struggle for Judicial Supremacy: A Study of a Crisis in American Judicial Power.* New York: Knopf, 1941.

————. *The Supreme Court in the American System of Government.* Cambridge, Mass.: Harvard University Press, 1955.

O'Brien, David M. *Storm Center: The Supreme Court in American Politics.* New York: Norton, 1986.

Tribe, Laurence H. *God Save This Honorable Court: How the Choices of Supreme Court Justices Shape Our History.* New York: Random House, 1985.

5

Balancing Governmental Authority: The Evolving Pattern of Separation of Powers

Syllabus

During the summer of 1987, the American public witnessed a recurring image of American politics—conflict between the president and Congress. In more personal terms, the confrontation pitted Lt. Colonel Oliver North, former employee of the National Security Council, against Sen. Daniel Inouye (D-Hawaii) and Rep. Lee Hamilton (D-Ind.), cochairmen of a joint select committee investigating the Iran-contra affair. The White House was trying to limit the damage inflicted by disclosures of some ill-advised overtures to a foreign country and possible violations of federal law. The Democratic-controlled Congress was trying to regain control over what it considered its legitimate role in foreign policy. Reports of arms transfers to the terrorist state of Iran, the diversion of funds to rebel forces fighting in Nicaragua, and the White House's circumvention of Congress and the normal foreign policy establishment had seriously tarnished the public's perception of its president and his operatives. But in a larger sense, the Iran arms scandal and the funds diversion were merely the latest front page stories of a continuing problem in American politics—how to make governmental power more accountable to the people and their representatives.

This Chapter Examines the Following Matters

☐   To prevent a minority from exercising power arbitrarily and violating the rights of the citizens, the framers of the U.S. Constitution deliberately checked governmental power with "auxiliary precautions," one of which was the important principle of separation of powers. One of the most prominent divisions of governmental authority in the American political system has been that between the president and Congress.

☐   The growth of presidential power in the twentieth century has resulted from a tendency of American presidents to act independently to protect national interests in times of national crisis. In most instances, Congress was either unable or unwilling institutionally to deal with the demands of the moment. The relationship between the president and Congress has been affected by the delegation of authority to the executive branch, as well as by the migration of governmental power to the American presidency.

☐   The president's major responsibilities in domestic and foreign policy—and his roles as commander in chief, treaty negotiator, budget manager, economic planner, and chief of the executive branch—have often spawned conflict with Congress. Congressional efforts since the early 1970s to check presidential war power and to reform the annual budgetary process have found the president and Congress at frequent odds with one another.

☐   The sharing of powers between the executive and legislative branches in the United States requires a measure of trust. Public officials must consult one another while arriving at authoritative decisions for addressing public problems. Without an institutional ability to overcome constitutional constraints against unified rule, the system can become immobilized with petty partisanship and interbranch distrust.

Photo: Although the Constitution provides for a separation of powers among the branches of the federal government, the balance of power in this century between the executive and legislative branches has been skewed in the direction of the White House, given the domestic and foreign policy demands of the United States in the modern world.

Separated Powers

Throughout the twentieth century, federal authority has grown in response to an evolving national and international economy, the expanding role of the United States in foreign affairs, and the perceived need for greater federal involvement in several domestic policy arenas. But the growing list of responsibilities for the federal government to shoulder has also spawned public perceptions of an ineffective government. Frequently, public criticisms have been directed at the very institutions upon which it has come to rely for protection from life's many risks: at a Congress that increasingly seems overpaid, underworked, and motivated largely by the need to be reelected; at a Supreme Court that has usurped the powers of and seems unaccountable to the elected branches of government; at a president who is both impotent in the face of an opposition Congress and arrogant when circumventing the normal apparatus of policy-making; and, finally, at a bureaucracy that seems unaccountable to the voters, unresponsive to real citizen needs, and virtually impossible to reform.

These mounting criticisms strike directly at one of the primary tasks undertaken by the framers in 1787 and discussed in Chapter 3. Given the human tendency to pursue private interest rather than public virtue, how can power be made both capable of effective governance in a diverse community and yet protective of individual rights? In short, how can it prevent both majority and minority tyranny? In the judgment of many legal historians and scholars, the framers of the American constitutional system tried to manage this "constitutional dilemma" by separating institutional power and by equipping each unit of the new government with several tools to check the actions of the other.

Early Writings on Separated Powers

The U.S. Constitution reflects a heritage of liberal democracy that germinated long before the "assembly of demigods" in Philadelphia during the summer of 1787. As the British commentator James Bryce noted nearly a century ago, very little in the American Constitution is "absolutely new."[1] The political system created in 1787 was the product of a substantial consensus on the fundamentals of republican self-government. As stated in Chapter 3, popular commitment to fundamental rights, a distinction between constitutional rules and legal rules, and local autonomy all inspired the American colonists. If drafting a constitution means controlling and containing the excesses of the preceding order, the American Constitution was a direct reaction against two earlier conditions—the *abuse* of power by the British prior to 1776 and the *absence* of power under the Articles of Confederation. Given these antecedents, it is natural to expect that throughout their deliberations in Philadelphia, the framers of the Constitution were deeply concerned about how best to manage political power.

One of the primary ideas guiding the framers in their struggle to manage political power was the separation-of-powers principle, which several English and European writers of the seventeenth and eighteenth centuries had addressed earlier. Such commentators as James Harrington, John Locke, and

Baron de Montesquieu, as well as Thomas Hobbes and Jean-Jacques Rousseau, wrote extensively about two major themes—the growing power of the state and the assertion of individual freedoms. Both ideas were basic to the French Enlightenment and the English civil war (1642–49) and their aftermath. Although both Hobbes and Locke agreed that the source of ultimate authority should be the people, and that the purpose of the state should be to manage conflict and protect private property, they disagreed about the best arrangement for political authority. Whereas Hobbes favored giving political power to a single office, the monarchy, Locke divided that authority between a representative assembly and the monarchy. Although twentieth-century commentators have noted the expansion of executive or judicial authority to "imperial" proportions,[2] John Locke viewed one poltical power as paramount: "One Supreme Power, which is the Legislature, to which all the rest are and must be subordinate."[3]

Separated Powers in the Constitution

Like Locke's *Second Treatise,* Montesquieu's primary work, *Spirit of the Laws* (1748), was well known to the colonists who instigated the American Revolution and drafted the Constitution. Although James Madison and others periodically referred to Montesquieu when writing about political power, as constitutional scholar C. Herman Pritchett notes, *Spirit of the Laws* itself may not have been that important to the delegates in Philadelphia.[4] The eventual division of governmental power among Congress, the presidency, and the Supreme Court was probably motivated more by the practical problems of a dispersed and diverse people that distrusted any centralized authority. After all, memories of executive tyranny—whether by the English monarch or a succession of royal governors in the colonies—were fresh in the colonists' minds. To guard against the abuse of executive authority, the new state constitutions erred by investing too much authority in state legislatures. These legislatures increasingly dominated state executives and judicial bodies and frustrated the national congress under the inept Articles of Confederation.

This consuming distrust of executive power and a desire that government protect "ordered liberty" sustained the framers throughout the summer of 1787.[5] Though they were pessimistic about human nature, they remained optimistic about their own capacity to structure political power in order to preserve social *order* and individual *liberty.* As numerous commentators have observed, those who devised the American constitutional system never envisioned a complete separation of power. Rather, they saw "separate institutions sharing power."[6] Unlike virtually every other democratic system in the world today, the U.S. Constitution gives both Congress and the president the power and prerogative to determine policy and govern the nation. Article I gives to Congress "all legislative powers" but limits them to just those "herein granted." Legislative powers are detailed rather extensively in Section 8. Article II, dealing with the chief executive, omits any detailed list of policy-making powers and grants executive authority in only a very vague and general manner. This textual distinction in Articles I and II has led some authorities to assert that legislative powers are specifically limited in the Constitution, whereas executive powers are more extensive and unlimited. Many of the legal controversies covered in this chapter involve the historical debate about the proper scope of legislative and executive powers.

According to the new Constitution, each of the three branches was to share in the power exercised by the other two coordinate branches. For example, Congress (more specifically, the Senate) would share in the judicial power by confirming judicial appointments, determining the appellate jurisdiction of the courts, and creating federal courts and judgeships. The president would share in legislative power through the ability to veto legislation, address Congress annually on the state of the Union, propose legislation to Congress, and convene special legislative sessions. Finally, although the role of judicial power envisioned by the Constitution in Article III was the most vague, the judiciary would hear all controversies arising under the new Constitution, federal laws, and federal treaties. As discussed in Chapter 4, the evolving concept of judicial review gave the Supreme Court a powerful instrument for judging the constitutionality of both legislative and executive actions. Each branch of the government would thus share in the exercise of power by the others, and each would have to obtain the concurrence of the others, at least in the long term, in order to accomplish anything of a lasting policy nature.

In *The Federalist Papers*, James Madison spoke about the "separation of power" that concerned the framers of the Constitution. As discussed briefly in Chapter 3, these essays were written by Madison, Alexander Hamilton, and John Jay to win ratification of the new Constitution. They attempted to persuade critics that the new system would improve upon the Articles of Confederation without unduly infringing upon individual freedom. In *Federalist No. 37*, Madison noted that one of the crucial difficulties encountered at the Constitutional Convention dealt with "combining the requisite stability and energy in government, with the inviolable attention due to liberty and to the republican form." Madison cautioned:

> Experience has instructed us that no skill in the science of government has yet been able to discriminate and define, with sufficient certainty, [government's] three great provinces—the legislative, executive, and judiciary.

In *Federalist No. 47* and *No. 48*, Madison again emphasized the importance of Montesquieu's maxim that "there can be no liberty where the legislative and executive powers are united in the same person or body of magistrates." But Madison's major thrust in these three essays was that (1) the separation should not be complete, and (2) no branch should have an "overruling influence over the others in the administration of their respective powers."[7]

In *Federalist No. 51*, Madison argued that separated powers are "essential to the preservation of liberty," and he provided his most extensive prescription for avoiding tyranny. In talking about the "necessary partition of power among the several departments," Madison stated that the internal structure of government must be constructed so that "its several constituent parts may, by their mutual relations, be the means of keeping each other in their proper places." Although each department "should have a will of its own" and not be able to influence unduly such factors as appointment or compensation of members, the real device for ensuring responsible government goes much further than these safeguards:

> The great security against a gradual concentration of the several powers in the same department consists in giving to those who administer each department the necessary constitutional means and personal motives to resist encroachments of the others . . . *Ambition must be made to counteract ambition.* [Emphasis added]

And in the famous excerpt from *Federalist No. 51* emphasizing the dilemma of constitutional government (cited in Chapter 1), Madison noted the
need for government to control both the governed and the governors. His
pessimism about certain aspects of human nature was also evident when he
stated the necessity for "auxiliary precautions" to counter the tendencies of
concentrated power. The remainder of *Federalist No. 51* portrays the checks
and balances built into American government: republican government which
divides the legislature into two distinct houses elected by different means;
construction of a federal system that further divides power *between* levels of
government; and the establishment of several access points for special interests
to petition government for a redress of private grievances. In many respects,
these auxiliary precautions capture both elements of individualism and communitarianism, as discussed in Chapter 2.

Separated Powers in the Twentieth Century

These early reflections on how the new American system should operate under
a *balanced* arrangement among legislative, executive, and judicial powers have
not prevented independent action by any of the three branches on several
occasions, especially the executive branch. As will be noted later in this chapter,
one of the major developments in twentieth-century American constitutional
experience has been the gradual expansion of executive branch authority. This
would seem to contradict the historical democratic view that the legislature
should be the dominant federal institution. After all, Locke referred to legislative dominance in his *Second Treatise,* and Madison, in *Federalist No. 51,*
observed that "in republican government, the legislative authority necessarily
predominates." Throughout most of the nineteenth century, Congress was the
more prominent branch of government. As a recent account of presidential
power argues, "The role of the presidency in nineteenth-century American
political theory was essentially that of carrying out the will of Congress." [8]
The administrations of Andrew Jackson and Abraham Lincoln were important
exceptions to this rule.

But this situation of congressional influence eventually changed. With
the arrival of chief executives holding a more energetic vision of the presidential
office—and the advent of several national crises during the administrations
of Lincoln, Wilson, the two Roosevelts, Truman, Johnson, and Nixon—there
arose an increasing tendency for the public to see the American system as
personalized in presidential terms. As a result, the executive branch assumed
more initiative in the exercise of power, the resolution of conflict, and the
development of public policy. Additional factors facilitated this tendency to
augment the power of the American presidency. These included the increasing
tendency of Congress and the presidency to be controlled by different parties,
the need for more efficient policy management in times of crisis, electoral
"mandates," the power of electronic mass media, the decline of political parties,
the fragmentation of power in Congress, and the sheer force of presidential
personality. Whatever the relative influence of these several factors, the American public, as well as Congress and the courts, increasingly deferred to the
White House for speedy action on difficult problems. As a result, a tremendous
reservoir of extraconstitutional authority was created with which presidents
could achieve their policy goals.

As the following coverage of congressional-presidential relations indicates, rarely has the Supreme Court intervened to limit presidential authority. Although American presidents have vetoed hundreds of bills passed by Congress, and the Supreme Court has likewise declared unconstitutional scores of federal laws through the exercise of judicial review, the Court has seldom told an American president that his actions fall outside powers delegated in Article II of the Constitution. When the Supreme Court has denied the president authority to act, it has had the support of Congress. Although the principle of separated institutional power in theory might seem appropriate for protecting "ordered liberty," from a historical standpoint, it has seldom been strictly followed. In fact, the Constitution envisions the careful sharing of governmental power by the respective branches.

One other consequence of the careful separation of political power in the American system is important to note here. The American political system has always been biased in favor of moderate, incremental change in the status quo. The American system has never been kind to those wanting radical modification. Precisely because the system has so many access and veto points, the public must seek help from several political leaders to effect a change in prevailing policy. Legislative initiatives must run the gauntlet of separate institutional checks, and the result is often little or no change in the status quo. For example, the multitude of institutional rules and norms in Congress—including legislative committees and subcommittees, floor debate in both houses, conference committees, the requirements for a two-thirds majority in both houses to override a presidential veto—can frustrate major innovative change in existing policy. Constitutional amendments are even more problematic, as the discussion of the Equal Rights Amendment in Chapter 10 indicates, and as the examination of the formal amending process in Chapter 14 reflects. All this institutional bias in favor of checking political power with countervailing power makes for a system that rewards keeping things the way they are and discourages policy innovation at various levels.

In summary, the framers sought to allocate political power in a manner that provided both opportunities for and constraints upon the nation's political leaders, especially the president. They wanted to allow for ample authority when presidential actions were accompanied by a broad consensus on the best action to take, but also an important fail-safe mechanism that aborted the more questionable policy option. Perhaps this ideal constitutional blueprint for responsible power is impossible to achieve. Or maybe the original design needs to be modified in some way without doing irreparable harm to the perennial quest for "ordered liberty." Speculation on this point will be reserved for the concluding chapter on constitutional reform. For now, some of the major developments surrounding the evolving doctrine of separate institutions sharing power will be examined.

The Presidency: Emergence of a "Bully Pulpit"

As noted earlier, the framers of the new Constitution were greatly troubled by the question of executive power. When drafting the Constitution, they at first considered a plan that would have made the executive subordinate to the national legislature. Fortunately, the final draft of the Constitution opted for a more balanced system in which powers were to be shared by the president and Congress. Article I, which comprises nearly one-half of the words of the Constitution, states that "all legislative Powers herein granted shall be vested in a Congress" and then delegates several powers to that body in Section 8. Article II dealing with the executive describes very briefly the powers of the president, beginning with the rather vague phrase that "the executive Power shall be vested in a President of the United States of America."

A question arises over whether Article II powers of the president are a complete or a partial delineation of presidential power. Hamilton and Madison themselves had very different views about the scope of executive power. Hamilton, as might be expected of one favoring a constitutional monarchy, advocated a broader view of executive power "subject only to the exceptions and qualifications which are expressed in [the Constitution]." [9] But to Madison, presidential power as outlined in Article II was complete in itself and did not allow for any further expansion in time of crisis. [10]

These two views of presidential authority have evolved into what some have referred to as the "constitutional" and the "stewardship" theories of executive authority. According to the constitutional theory, based upon the Madisonian view, a president's power is carefully limited to those powers specifically delegated by the Constitution or by congressional statute. The stewardship theory allows the president, as Teddy Roosevelt once said, "to do anything that the needs of the nation [demand] unless such action [is] forbidden by the Constitution or by the laws." [11] According to the stewardship theory, a president functions as a steward or trustee of the people. This entitles presidents to do whatever they consider necessary for the public good unless it is *precisely* forbidden by the Constitution or by statutory law. In a sense, the Oval Office becomes a "bully pulpit," to use a concept usually applied to Teddy Roosevelt, from which the president uses his prestige and high visibility to inspire and moralize, with the entire nation as the attentive congregation. [12]

The stewardship view of presidential power has dominated American political experience, particularly in the area of foreign affairs, as will be apparent in the following discussion. As Harvard law professor Laurence Tribe noted recently, "It is only by an extraordinary triumph of constitutional imagination that the Commander in Chief is conceived as commanded by law." [13] Although the Constitution theoretically created three coequal branches, practical experience and constitutional fact have established the president as the strongest of the three in many respects. Whereas the Constitution allows Congress and the president to share concurrent power in matters of foreign affairs, constitutional experience has revealed that the separation-of-powers principle does not reflect reality. The Supreme Court has permitted Congress to delegate extensive legislative power in foreign affairs to the executive branch. A good example of this historical fact arose during the 1930s, amid a rather public struggle between judicial and legislative power.

The Recognition of Inherent Power:
United States v. *Curtiss-Wright Export Corp.* (1936)

One of the more prominent justifications for Congress's deferring to the executive in foreign affairs was provided by the Supreme Court in the case of *United States* v. *Curtiss-Wright Export Corp.* (1936). This case is generally credited with recognizing certain "inherent powers" of American presidents in foreign affairs. The case involved a congressional joint resolution that authorized President Franklin Roosevelt to forbid American arms sales to Paraguay and Bolivia if, in his opinion, the sale of such arms would likely prolong hostilities between the two nations. Curtiss-Wright Export Corporation tried to sell arms to Bolivia despite an embargo authorized by Roosevelt. The question before the Supreme Court in 1936 was whether the congressional resolution constituted an illegal delegation of legislative authority to the president.

A seven-member Court majority said that the president had acted within his constitutional authority when implementing the congressional resolution. Writing for the majority, Justice George Sutherland, a long-time critic of the congressional practice of delegating too much authority to the executive branch in *domestic* matters, distinguished between foreign and domestic affairs:

> The two classes of powers are different, both in respect of their origin and their nature. The broad statement that the federal government can exercise no powers except those specifically enumerated in the Constitution . . . is categorically true only in respect of our internal affairs.

Sutherland maintained that when the new Constitution in 1787 allocated power to the national and state governments, it only did so with respect to *domestic* affairs. With respect to *foreign* affairs, the national government retained all power and prerogatives inherited from the British Crown. He further argued that "the investment of the federal government with the powers of external sovereignty did not depend upon the affirmative grants of the Constitution." In other words, executive power in foreign affairs may extend beyond the letter of the Constitution. Sutherland reasoned that to avoid embarrassment and possible damage to American interests in foreign affairs, Congress "must accord to the President a degree of discretion and freedom from statutory restriction which would not be admissible were domestic affairs alone involved." National sovereignty implies that the power to formulate foreign policy must lie only with the national government, and practical necessities require that the president be the primary policymaker in this area. Sutherland went even further in distinguishing the considerable power of the president to act in foreign affairs:

> It is important to bear in mind that we are here dealing not alone with an authority vested in the President by an exertion of legislative power, but with such an authority plus the very delicate, plenary and exclusive power of the President as the sole organ of the federal government in . . . international relations.

This recognition of inherent executive authority in foreign affairs has prevailed throughout much of American constitutional experience. However, congressional-presidential developments in the 1960s and 1970s would eventually lead to some major disagreements within those two institutions about the limits of presidential power in foreign affairs.

Civilian Authority in Times of Crisis: The President as Commander in Chief

Although Article I gives Congress alone the power to declare war and regulate the armed forces (Sec. 8, Clauses 11–16), practical necessities for nearly two centuries have required American presidents to respond independently when vital national interests are threatened. The key question in most of these exercises of presidential power has been how to interpret "national interest" and "national security," and, if a consensus can be established on that point, which branch is best positioned to act responsibly. The president's power as commander in chief has expanded in response to at least three historical developments: the responsibility for protecting American life and property overseas; the difficulty of limiting undeclared wars; and the tendency for Washington and Moscow to define their interests historically as a global struggle between "capitalist" and "communist." Since World War II, these reasons for using national power in pursuit of national objectives have coexisted with the constant danger of a nuclear exchange between adversaries. Nuclear weaponry has, thus, made the pursuit of national goals much more risky.

Protecting American Citizens and Property Overseas

Ever since Thomas Jefferson ordered naval forces to protect American citizens in Tripoli in the early 1800s, American presidents have historically acted to protect American personnel and interests in foreign lands. A recent account indicates at least two hundred instances in which the United States has used armed force abroad to protect persons and property, and in only five of those cases did the action involve a *declared* war.[14] Some observers suggest that presidents have quite frequently cited citizens' safety or property protection as a cover for more immediate policy objectives. They point to the actions of President Lyndon Johnson in the Dominican Republic in 1965, President Richard Nixon's dispatching American troops into Cambodia in 1970 and Laos in 1971, and the invasion of Grenada by American troops in 1983. Whatever the judgment of history, many such actions by American presidents to achieve larger geographical objectives are partially justified by resorting to the life-and-property rationale.

Protecting National Interests

Secondly, the president's role as commander in chief has also expanded because of the need to protect larger national interests in the absence of a formal declaration of war. The need to react promptly when genuine national interests are threatened is a practical necessity, not a mere constitutional formality. As noted, in only five armed conflicts involving American military forces has Congress actually declared war: the War of 1812; the War with Mexico (1846–48); the Spanish-American War of 1898; and the two global wars of the twentieth century. Even the most costly war in American history, the Civil War, obviously never involved a declaration of war, since it was an internal conflict over different interpretations of what the Constitution implied about national and state sovereignty. Since 1789, American presidents have enjoyed great latitude to act, because of both constitutional ambiguity and practical necessity. Though bound by the written law in several cases, they acted under the mandate of a higher law, that of national self-preservation.

Presidential power in times of national crisis has been recognized by Congress and the courts on many occasions. One such instance involved executive actions at the outbreak of the Civil War. In 1861, President Lincoln acted independently while declaring the Confederate states to be in a condition of rebellion, ordering various military actions as commander in chief to protect federal forces and interests, and prescribing several punishments for illegal actions taken against federal law. Among other actions, Lincoln announced a military blockade of Southern ports and ordered the seizure of ships doing business with the Confederate states following the attack upon Fort Sumter in April 1861. Lincoln justified his actions on his inherent power as commander in chief and various federal laws of 1795, 1807, and 1861, which he felt delegated certain war powers to the president.

Writing for a very divided Supreme Court, Justice Robert Grier recognized in the Prize Cases (1863) an inherent executive power to repel an invasion or armed rebellion without first seeking congressional approval and the right to impose a naval blockade. Applying somewhat circular reasoning, Grier said that the blockade was itself "official and exclusive evidence that . . . a state of war existed which demanded and authorized a recourse to such a measure." Concerning whether the president was authorized to seize private property on the high seas, the Court reasoned that in doing business with any one of the belligerents in a recognized civil war, private parties run the risk of federal power being used to defeat the rebellious states. As Grier observed, "A civil war such as that now waged between the Northern and Southern states is properly conducted according to the humane regulations of public law as regards capture on the ocean." Four justices in dissent thought that Lincoln's actions were beyond his executive authority, that previous congressional acts did not authorize him to wage war against an individual state, and that confiscation of private property was clearly beyond his delegated power. Given the crisis of the moment, their views carried little force.

During World War II, congressional authorization of executive authority under quite different circumstances found another Supreme Court deferring to presidential power in a national crisis. Following the Japanese attack on Pearl Harbor on December 7, 1941, and Congress's subsequent declaration of war, the federal government took various actions against persons suspected of possible disloyalty to the United States. A series of executive orders issued by President Franklin Roosevelt in early 1942, and quickly endorsed by Congress, imposed a curfew on all persons of Japanese descent and excluded them from militarily sensitive areas. Congress went even further and authorized the forced relocation of Japanese-Americans to detention centers in the country.

In two cases decided in the midst of a declared war, the Supreme Court sanctioned, in effect, racial discrimination on grounds of national security. In Hirabayashi v. United States (1943), the Court upheld the constitutionality of the curfew order authorized by Roosevelt. Speaking through Chief Justice Harlan Stone, a unanimous Court said that the order was entirely within both executive and congressional powers because of the grave national emergency and the "critical military situation" that existed. One year after Hirabayashi, a divided Court upheld the military exclusion orders in the case of Korematsu v. United States (1944). Echoing the same rationale used in the previous decision, Justice Hugo Black recognized that Congress and the president did have the authority in wartime to segregate those who might pose "a menace to the national defense and safety." To those who argued that such action occasioned excessive sacrifice from a small, defenseless minority, Black wrote that "hardships are part of war, and war is an aggregation of hardships." When threatened by hostile forces, "the power to protect must be commensurate with the threatened danger," and, therefore, the actions were legitimate. In dissent, Justice Frank Murphy characterized the military exclusions as falling within the "ugly abyss of racism," and Justice Robert Jackson questioned the reasonableness of the military order and the credibility of the chief military officer imposing it.

Korematsu is significant for at least three reasons. First, in upholding the federal actions against the internees, the Court ironically referred to race as a "suspect" classification that demanded close scrutiny of a discriminatory law (see Chapter 10). But the majority insisted that its ruling should not be construed as an endorsement of racial discrimination, since the internment was seen as a necessary response to the crisis that existed following the Japanese attack on Pearl Harbor. The Court's reference to "suspect classification" would later become a very important consideration in the civil rights struggles of the 1950s and 1960s when state-federal laws denying social and political equality to racial minorities would be struck down as violating fundamental constitutional rights (see Chapter 9).

Secondly, despite its insistence to the contrary, the Court implicitly endorsed the idea that racial minorities could be denied basic rights on grounds of military necessity and protection of national security. As Justice Jackson noted in dissent, once courts rationalize the Constitution as allowing such action, racial discrimination is condoned and "the principle then lies about like a loaded weapon ready for the hand of any authority that can bring forward a plausible claim of urgent [need]."

Finally, it should be noted that the Supreme Court in *Hirabayashi* and *Korematsu* never reached the question of whether the relocation centers were themselves unconstitutional. It only dealt with the constitutionality of the curfews and the military exclusion orders. The Court's handling of issues in these two cases demonstrates how the justices have great latitude in setting the terms of legal debate. Rather than answering the far more delicate question of the constitutionality of these detention camps, the justices basically ignored the issue and ruled only on the lesser, more manageable question of whether the president was authorized to impose curfew and exclusion orders upon suspect American citizens. Some vindication of minority citizens' rights did occur decades later, when a federal appellate court in California overturned the conviction of Fred Korematsu. Furthermore, congressional hearings in the 1980s have been held to consider whether federal compensation is due those American citizens whose liberty and property were denied them without customary due process of law (see Brief 5.1).

Protecting the Non-Communist World

The third reason for increased executive authority under the role of commander in chief has been the greatly expanded responsibility of the United States since World War II to serve as the protector of the non-Communist world. Americans have been preoccupied since 1945 with international communism. They have tended to see most trouble in the world as emanating from Moscow, although this greatly oversimplifies the complex world in which the United States must coexist with others. This preoccupation with international communism has resulted in numerous collective security agreements, vaguely worded congressional statutes and resolutions, and successive annual defense appropriations. Additionally, the president has been allowed great discretion in using power to wage "defensive war" in order to protect American interests and fulfill treaty obligations. In the Korean War in the early 1950s and the Vietnam

☐ *Brief 5.1   A Nation Struggles with Its Conscience*

Following the Japanese attack on Pearl Harbor in 1941, President Franklin Roosevelt issued an executive order that affected 77,000 American citizens and 43,000 legal and illegal resident aliens of Japanese descent. These people were uprooted from their homes and businesses and forced into detention centers for the duration of the war. Many years after the last camp was closed in 1946, the United States slowly began to reexamine the actions of civilian and military officials at the time. In early 1988, an important event occurred in the U.S. Senate. Following a similar action taken in 1987 in the House of Representatives, the Senate debated and finally passed a bill to compensate survivors of the Japanese internment.

The compensation bill was cosponsored by several senators, including the two Democratic senators from Hawaii—Spark M. Matsunaga and Daniel K. Inouye, both of whom are of Japanese descent and had fought for the United States Army in the European theatre. Details of the bill differed slightly from the bill passed by the House of Representatives. The Senate version targeted an estimated 60,000 survivors of the detention camps, each of whom would receive about $20,000 beginning in October 1988. The bill would cost the federal government approximately $1.3 billion, with $500 million to be paid the first year, $400 million the next, $200 million the third year, and two final increments of $100 million each. The money, which would be tax free, would only go to surviving internees and not to estates of deceased internees.

In commenting upon the legislation, Senator Matsunaga stated in debate that "a stigma has haunted Japanese-Americans for the past 45 years. We are seeking Congressional action to remove that cloud over their heads." Senator Ted Stevens (R-Ala.), another cosponsor of the bill, said that the internees were "people who had done no wrong at all." Orrin Hatch, conservative Republican senator from Utah, indicated his support for the compensation order by echoing Stevens and saying, "It is clear that these citizens were denied their constitutional right of due process." [15]

The House and Senate worked during the spring and summer to reconcile slightly different versions of the legislation. The Reagan administration finally agreed to support the conference bill, after initially saying that it favored payments being made only to survivors of the internment. In a much-publicized ceremony held on August 10, 1988 (43 years and one day after the United States dropped the atomic bomb on Nagasaki, Japan), President Reagan signed the conference bill. Referring to the internment as a "mistake" and to the legislation as essential to "right a grave wrong," the president thus hopefully closed an unpleasant chapter in American history. Under the law, formal apologies will be extended to all survivors for all violations of civil liberties and constitutional rights. Additionally, the legislation sets up a $1.25 billion trust fund from which the U.S. Government will make a one-time award of $20,000 in tax-free payments to each eligible intern or designated beneficiary of the former internees. The president, however, stated at the signing ceremony that "no payment can make up for those lost years," for the purpose of the legislation and compensation "has less to do with property than with honor." [16]

conflict beginning in the 1960s, American presidents reacted to a perceived threat by invoking implied war powers. Both conflicts, though separated by a generation, extracted enormous costs in terms of human casualties and achieved only limited success in meeting national objectives. The Vietnam War also resulted in social protest and a loss of faith in national leaders and political institutions.

The Korean War was one of the first occasions for the American people to confront the moral dilemmas posed by rival ideologies locked in global struggle, nuclear weapons threatening mutual annihilation, and the questions raised by the burden of "collective security." When Communist North Korea invaded pro-Western South Korea in 1950, it ignited American fears of an imminent Communist takeover of an embattled ally in the Far East. Believing that the invasion confirmed the threat of Soviet imperialism, President Harry Truman sent American troops to South Korea under the auspices of the United Nations. Although Congress had not yet approved of the action, Truman relied upon various provisions of international law and the UN Charter that allowed

nations to defend themselves against armed aggression. The UN Security Council later passed two resolutions approving of the action, but the fact remains
that the United States acted *first* and then relied upon subsequent UN resolutions to legitimize the unilateral action. Whatever the political and strategic
merits of Truman's actions, they rested upon uncertain domestic and international legal grounds, since Congress never declared war in the conflict.

The Korean War also instigated a famous legal dispute between President
Truman and Congress over the scope of executive power. *Youngstown Sheet
& Tube Co.* v. *Sawyer* (1952) involved Truman's effort to prevent a prolonged
labor-management dispute and an imminent labor strike in the vital U.S. steel
industry. At issue specifically was the president's right as commander in chief
to invoke emergency powers in order to seize private property without congressional approval of the action beforehand. Through a series of laws passed by
Congress beginning in the 1930s, under a state of emergency, a president was
given extensive powers to seize private property, manage private means of
production in the United States, declare martial law, and control all transportation and communications in the country. The internment of Japanese-
Americans discussed earlier—as well as the bombing of Cambodia in the 1960s
and 1970s without the American people being told, and the surveillance of
private citizens by the federal government—are examples of such presidential
actions taken under alleged "national emergency." More on this subject of
delegated emergency powers will be discussed later in this chapter.

The outcome of the Steel Seizure Case found the Supreme Court taking
the unusual step of saying no to a president acting under his much-heralded
"inherent power" in foreign affairs. After federal efforts to resolve the dispute
between management and labor failed, and the union threatened to impose a
nationwide strike in early 1953, Truman issued an executive order instructing
his secretary of commerce to seize the steel mills and keep them operating.
The president argued that disruption of the steel industry would seriously
jeopardize the nation's defense preparedness and its ability to defend its interest
in the ongoing Korean conflict.

In *Youngstown Sheet & Tube Co.* v. *Sawyer,* the Supreme Court took
sharp issue with Truman, noting that the key issue in the case was whether
he had the authority to seize private property. Justice Black's majority opinion
concluded that his actions were not justified. For Truman's actions to prevail
in this instance, he had to be able to point to some provision of the Constitution
under his power as commander in chief or to some congressional delegation
of authority condoning the action. Just because presidents are responsible for
faithfully executing the laws does not mean that they are able to make the
laws themselves. As a participant in the lawmaking process, they are limited
to recommending laws they think wise and vetoing those they think unwise.
As Black and the Court majority saw it, "The Constitution is neither silent
nor equivocal about who shall make laws which the President is to execute."
That is purely a *legislative* function in which the president has an important
but limited role.

In a separate concurring opinion in the Steel Seizure Case, Justice Jackson
elaborated upon how the separation-of-powers system envisioned several levels
of presidential power. According to Jackson, presidential power relies upon
three sources of legitimacy: (1) if they act in response to an expressed or implied
authorization by Congress, their power is at its maximum; (2) if they act in

the absence of either congressional authorization or a denial of authority, there is a "zone of twilight" wherein both they and Congress may have concurrent authority; and, finally, (3) if they act against the expressed or implied will of Congress, "their power is at the lowest ebb." But even then, they may be able to rely upon some constitutional power they possess alone or with Congress. Jackson viewed Truman's actions as falling within the third category, and in this case to have been illegal because they were contrary to the expressed will of Congress as provided for in the Taft-Hartley Act of 1947. Jackson agreed with his majority colleagues that Truman's actions were an exercise of legislative authority by the executive without basis in law. As he noted in closing, "With all its defects, delays, and inconvenience, men have discovered no technique for long preserving free government except that the Executive be under the law." This principle was also crucial two decades later when the Court ordered a president deeply involved in an alleged cover-up of executive wrong doing to surrender privileged conversations needed in several criminal trials.

Executive Privilege: The Scope and Limitations of Presidential Secrets

Ever since 1798, when George Washington denied the House of Representatives access to executive correspondence regarding the Jay Treaty, American presidents have periodically invoked **executive privilege** and refused to divulge various types of political, military, or diplomatic information that they think should be protected from public disclosure. Although the concept is mentioned nowhere in either the constitutional debates or the document itself, executive privilege has been a common historical device used by several presidents to preserve secrecy in the Oval Office. The major rationale for presidents' invoking executive privilege is that in private discussions with advisors, presidents must gather a wide assortment of opinions and policy recommendations in order to ensure the greatest likelihood of success in achieving national policy goals. Accompanying this concept of privileged communication are two expectations that presidents have historically cultivated: the encouragement of candid intragovernmental deliberations; and the protection of that candor by ensuring that those discussions will not be disclosed. This, of course, raises the question of whether governmental secrecy is an acceptable or necessary precondition for candor. The historical record is probably very mixed on that question. Like any privilege, that of presidents shielding advisors and their counsel from public disclosure can be abused, as it was by President Richard Nixon during the Watergate era.

    It is not possible to analyze the complex events surrounding Watergate in this limited space. As Brief 5.2 indicates, the Watergate scandal in the early 1970s involved several questionable activities that ultimately tested the fabric of the Constitution and the power of the courts to force public officials to comply with the law.

    The Watergate affair suggests, at a minimum, a political scandal involving continual denials by the president that any of his advisors had either participated in or had prior knowledge of the break-in. It involved constant refusals by the White House to provide anything but the most grudging assistance to ongoing investigations. The inquiry also revealed that taped conversations existed that were essential to determining if this American president

❑ *Brief 5.2   What Was Watergate?*

Before June 17, 1972, the Watergate was just another rather plush apartment and office complex on the Potomac River in Washington, D.C. But after five employees of the Committee to Re-Elect the President (known by its critics as CREEP) were arrested inside the headquarters of the Democratic National Committee at the Watergate complex, it would eventually become a president's Waterloo. The burglars were carrying wiretapping equipment and several sequenced $100 bills, which immediately raised questions about both their purpose and their backing. Although White House Press Secretary Ron Ziegler immediately dismissed the break-in as nothing more than a third-rate burglary, the subsequent trial and conviction of the Watergate burglars resulted in stiff fines and prison sentences. A revealing confession by James McCord, one of the operatives, indicated that others were involved in the break-in, that certain individuals had perjured themselves at the earlier trial, and that the defendants had been pressured to plead guilty.

During the spring of 1973, due in part to increased coverage by the news media, events regarding the scandal accelerated. In April, White House Counsel John Dean was fired by the president. H. R. Haldeman and John Ehrlichman, Nixon's two closest personal advisors, resigned. In May 1973, the Senate Select Committee on Campaign Finance, chaired by Sen. Sam Ervin (D-N.C.), began televised hearings into the mounting Watergate scandal. In addition to some revealing testimony by Dean, the most startling revelations were those of a former communications employee at the White House, Alexander Butterfield. Butterfield testified that a White House taping system had for some time routinely recorded all conversations between President Nixon and his advisors. With this startling revelation, a protracted struggle began between the president and the special prosecutor (who had been appointed by the Justice Department in May to investigate the evolving Watergate affair) to obtain selected recordings of White House deliberations.

October 1973 was another busy month for the besieged Nixon White House. On October 10, Vice-President Spiro Agnew resigned from office after pleading "no contest" to charges of income tax evasion and reports that he had continued to accept payments from political supporters while serving as vice-president. Ten days later, in what came to be known as the "Saturday Night Massacre," President Nixon ordered Attorney General Elliot Richardson to fire Special Prosecutor Archibald Cox, who was apparently too persistent in pursuing the taped conversations needed in the Watergate investigation. When both Richardson and Deputy Attorney General William D. Ruckelshaus refused to fire Cox, Nixon finally found the next person in charge at Justice, Solicitor General Robert H. Bork, to terminate Cox. That incident occasioned a strong protest from American public opinion. It also led to the creation of the Rodino Committee in the House of Representatives, with instructions to investigate possible grounds for impeachment against the president.

By mid-January of 1974, technical experts in charge of examining some of the released White House tapes reported the existence of a curious eighteen-minute gap in a recorded conversation between Nixon and Chief of Staff Haldeman on June 20, 1972, three days after the break-in. They speculated that it was probably the result of five separate manual erasures. In March, a federal grand jury handed down seven indictments of former White House and Department of Justice employees and named President Nixon as an "unindicted co-conspirator." By early May, the Rodino Committee convened its hearings on possible impeachment articles against President Nixon.

In July 1974, the Supreme Court handed down the famous *United States* v. *Nixon* decision, ordering the president to turn over to the special prosecutor tapes needed in the ongoing federal trial. One week later the Rodino Committee voted overwhelmingly in favor of three articles of impeachment against the president. The White House was left with little recourse. On August 5, it finally released the tapes, one of which revealed a conversation on June 23, 1972—six days after the Watergate break-in—between Nixon and Haldeman. In the conversation the president was clearly orchestrating a cover-up of the investigation.

had broken the law. But the scandal also revealed illegal activities that seriously marred open elections in a representative democracy: the improper use of governmental agencies, especially the Central Intelligence Agency (CIA) and the Federal Bureau of Investigation (FBI); the misuse of funds by the president to refurbish his California White House; income tax evasion; the violation of constitutional rights of American citizens; and the refusal to comply with a congressional committee's request for relevant materials needed in an investigation.

The main relevance of Watergate that concerns this discussion of separation of powers is how the clash between a president's desire to protect a power base and the judiciary's need to determine guilt or innocence of criminal defendants was finally resolved. The case that reflects this clash between executive privilege and the judicial determination of guilt is *United States* v. *Nixon* (1974).

On March 1, 1974, a federal grand jury indicted seven former White House aides and campaign officials of conspiracy and obstruction of justice in connection with the 1972 break-in of the Democratic National Committee headquarters at the Watergate complex. To prepare for the trial of these individuals and pursuant to federal rules of criminal procedure, Special Watergate Prosecutor Leon Jaworski requested that President Nixon produce sixty-four White House tapes and documents relating to certain key conversations between the president and his aides. The president declined to turn over the requested information, insisting that this was an *internal* dispute between superior and subordinate offices within the executive branch and therefore not subject to judicial resolution and that the concept of executive privilege was *absolute* and enabled him to preserve the confidentiality of presidential communications under all circumstances.

A unanimous Supreme Court (8–0), with Justice William Rehnquist not participating (prior to being appointed to the Supreme Court in 1971, Rehnquist had served as deputy attorney general under John Mitchell, one of the indicted co-conspirators), disagreed with the president's claims and ruled on July 24, 1974, that the documented evidence had to be turned over to the special prosecutor. Regarding Nixon's first assertion that the dispute was internal and shielded by the separation-of-powers principle, Chief Justice Warren Burger observed that "the production or nonproduction of specific evidence deemed by the Special Prosecutor to be relevant and admissible in a pending criminal case" involved issues that "are traditionally justiciable." The fact that both the president and special prosecutor are part of the executive branch "cannot be viewed as a barrier to justiciability," since Congress in 1973 granted the special prosecutor the authority to proceed in the Watergate investigation. Unless that authority were rescinded, the special prosecutor had a special responsibility to produce the necessary evidence. Regarding the president's second claim of absolute executive privilege, the Court recognized the importance of maintaining the confidentiality of high-level discussions and the necessity to protect candor and objectivity so important to presidential decision making. But against this necessary confidentiality must be weighed the need for the judicial process to obtain information crucial to a criminal proceeding. To facilitate the administration of justice, judicial access to the requested tapes was essential. The Court concluded that Nixon's legitimate claim of privilege "cannot prevail over the fundamental demands of due process of law in the fair administration of justice."

The court's decision in July 1974 ordering the president to deliver the tapes signaled the end for the Nixon presidency. The tapes revealed that the president had subverted investigation into the Watergate break-in. Within a few days, the House Judiciary Committee overwhelmingly recommended three separate articles of impeachment against the president for obstruction of justice, violation of the constitutional rights of American citizens, and ignoring the subpoena power of the House Judiciary Committee. The three articles never went to the full House for a vote, where undoubtedly they would have resulted in a bill of impeachment, a subsequent trial in the Senate, and a probable conviction. Richard Nixon soon resigned as the thirty-seventh president of the United States on August 9, 1974, thus ending one of the most famous political scandals in American history.

Notwithstanding official and public sighs of relief in the fall of 1974 that the long nightmare was over and the constitutional system had prevailed, Nixon's undoing probably turned on the Supreme Court's order for the president to hand over the requested White House tapes. Without evidence from a "smoking gun" and the subsequent loss of support by even Nixon's most ardent defenders on Capitol Hill, he might well have been able to remain in office through his second term. Even the frequently asked question, "What did he know and when did he know it" became irrelevant when, by his own words, Nixon was heard on tape as participating in a cover-up of the Watergate investigation. Ironically, the White House Tapes Case reaffirmed the power of American presidents to use executive privilege, which, though not absolute, is essential to protect vital communications in policy-making, especially when it involves the sensitive area of foreign affairs. But at the same time, the entire episode contaminated congressional-presidential relations and led immediately in the post-Watergate era to some significant changes in both foreign and domestic policy-making powers of American presidents.

Treaties and Executive Agreements: A Twilight Zone of Executive Power

In addition to authority in times of crisis and executive privilege, the president has a few more obscure, but nonetheless important, executive powers. One is the treaty-making power of the federal government and, in recent years, the increasing practice by American presidents to substitute executive agreements for formal treaties.

The Constitution reflects the framers' preference for a careful partnership involving both Congress and the president performing unique roles in the making and implementing of American treaties with other nations. The president would be responsible for negotiating the treaties, which then had to be ratified by the Senate. Article II, Section 2, of the Constitution states that the president "shall have Power, by and with the Advice and Consent of the Senate, to make Treaties, provided two thirds of the Senators present concur." Article VI states that the Constitution, federal laws, and federal treaties "shall be the supreme Law of the Land." This means that a treaty overrides any *state* law. The Supreme Court also has held that even though federal laws and treaties are equivalent, when a conflict arises between them, the more recent expression of the "sovereign will" prevails. In other words, if an act of Congress conflicts with an earlier treaty, the federal law should be followed, although this does not allow a federal law to override treaty obligations. Likewise, a newly negotiated and ratified treaty prevails over a preexisting act of Congress.

The principle that federal laws supersede state laws was reflected in *Missouri* v. *Holland* (1920). Under the Migratory Bird Treaty of 1916 between the United States and Canada, Congress passed legislation to protect the migration of wild birds. Missouri tried to block this protective legislation, claiming that the law and the treaty upon which it was based interfered with the rights of the states. With only two justices dissenting, the Supreme Court upheld the supremacy of the federal treaty-making authority over state power. Writing for the majority, Justice Oliver Wendell Holmes implied that federal treaties were virtually synonymous with the Constitution itself and superior to federal laws: "Acts of Congress are the supreme law of the land only when made in pursuance of the Constitution, while treaties are declared to be so when under the authority of the United States."

But in recent decades, the dual partnership envisioned by the framers with respect to the making of agreements with foreign countries has become increasingly lopsided. Since World War II, a prominent instrument used by American presidents to achieve their international goals has been **executive agreements.** It is unclear precisely what latitude a president has in concluding such documents. Since the Constitution says nothing about executive agreements, presidents since George Washington have acted in many instances without the approval of two-thirds of the Senate. Since at least the mid-1800s, the importance of treaties as primary instruments by which presidents conduct foreign relations has declined greatly as executive agreements have increased in prominence. In fact, since the beginning of World War II, nearly 11,000 executive agreements have been used by successive presidents to accomplish what they do not want to subject to Senate ratification. The practice has become particularly attractive during the past two decades, as Table 5.1 indicates. Although most executive agreements involve relatively minor arrangements (e.g., postal relations, broadcasting rules, consulate protocols), in the modern era they have also been important in many substantive areas. What particularly irritated Congress in the post-World War II era was that the Senate was being asked to ratify treaties dealing with relatively trivial matters while the president, through executive agreements, was committing the United States to countless bilateral obligations with South Korea, Thailand, Persian Gulf countries, South Vietnam, and other strategic regions around the globe.

The practice of executive agreements was encouraged by the Supreme Court in two cases just prior to World War II. In 1933, Franklin Roosevelt recognized the Soviet government and entered into the so-called "Litvinov

Table 5.1 Treaties and Executive Agreements, 1789–1985

GOVERNING ERA	TREATIES	EXECUTIVE AGREEMENTS	TOTALS
1789–1839	60	27	87
1840–1889	215	238	453
1890–1939	524	917	1,441
1940–1973	364	6,395	6,759
1974–1979	102	2,233	2,335
1980–1985	101	1,940	2,041
Totals	1,366	11,750	13,116

Source: Congressional Research Service, Library of Congress.

Assignment." According to this agreement, the United States would help the Soviet Union recover assets of private Soviet companies from American nationals that had been seized by the Soviet government after the Russian Revolution. In order to transfer the assets to the Soviet Union, the United States filed suit against a New York banker in federal district court, August Belmont, who held the assets of a Soviet company. The court found that the confiscation of the assets violated state policy in New York, but the U.S. Supreme Court ruled in *United States* v. *Belmont* (1937) that the federal executive agreement upon which the action was based took precedence over state policy. The Court also held that "in the case of all international compacts and agreements . . . complete power over international affairs is in the national government and is not and cannot be subject to any curtailment or interference on the part of the several states." The Court thus established the principle that executive agreements have the same weight as formal treaties in their effect upon conflicting state laws.

Five years later, the same principle was upheld in a similar case, *United States* v. *Pink* (1942), involving assets of an insurance company that had been nationalized by the Soviet Union. Again, the Supreme Court in review found against the state law. According to Justice William O. Douglas speaking for the Court, "The powers of the President in the conduct of foreign relations included the power, without consent of the Senate, to determine the public policy of the United States with respect to the Russian nationalization." Executive agreements, like treaties, are considered the supreme law of the land, state laws are inferior to such federal authority, and "no State can rewrite our foreign policy to conform to its own domestic policies."

During the 1950s, conservative Republicans tried to check the extensive presidential authority to make executive agreements. In 1953, Sen. John Bricker (R-Ohio) introduced a constitutional amendment in Congress that would have required that body to approve such agreements. The action was vehemently opposed by many liberals and some prominent conservatives, including Secretary of State John Foster Dulles, who feared that, if ratified, the Bricker Amendment would augur a new era of isolationism with respect to American foreign policy. Ironically, the late 1960s and early 1970s brought renewed calls, now from liberals opposed to the Vietnam conflict, for limits on the power of the president to consummate agreements with foreign countries without seeking Senate ratification.

During the Carter and Reagan administrations, two other cases arose that again called into question the power of chief executives to act independently in foreign affairs through treaties and executive agreements. One incident during the Carter administration raised the question of whether a president can terminate a treaty ratified by the Senate without first getting the Senate's approval to do so. President Carter announced in December 1978 that he was extending full diplomatic recognition to the People's Republic of China and terminating a 1954 mutual defense treaty with Taiwan as of January 1, 1980, thereby ending formal recognition of the Republic of China (Taiwan). In support of this action, Congress soon thereafter passed legislation establishing "informal relations" with Taiwan. Sen. Barry Goldwater (R-Ariz.) and twenty-four other members of Congress filed a suit contesting the president's right to terminate the treaty. In October, a federal district judge ruled that Carter did not have the constitutional power to abrogate the treaty without first obtaining either two-thirds approval of the Senate or a majority vote of both houses of Congress. The District of Columbia Court of Appeals then ruled on November 30, 1979, that Carter did have the right to act alone in this instance, although it avoided the broader issue of whether Congress *ever* has a role in terminating treaties. On appeal, the Supreme Court ruled in *Goldwater* v. *Carter* (1979) that the matter involved a "political question" not susceptible to judicial resolution. Although there was no absolute majority that agreed with any one rationale for refusing to hear the case, four justices voted to dismiss the controversy for lack of a justiciable issue, meaning that the Court could not provide remedy in the controversy. Like the appellate court, the Supreme Court refused to rule on the constitutional issue of whether a president can independently terminate a Senate-ratified treaty. Absent a definitive ruling on this larger issue, there remains a "twilight zone" of respective presidential and congressional powers in this legal aspect of foreign affairs. Under such circumstances, presidential actions tend to prevail.

Another incident in the closing days of the Carter administration testifies to the Supreme Court's reluctance to overrule executive actions taken in the midst of a national crisis. In response to the seizure of the American embassy and the taking of American diplomatic hostages in Tehran in November 1979, President Carter, acting upon the authority of such laws as the International Emergency Economic Powers Act of 1977, froze all Iranian assets in the United States. A Los Angeles-based engineering firm, Dames and Moore, was one of several private creditors that tried to seize Iranian assets in the United States as settlement for outstanding debts owed by Iran. The company claimed that Iran owed it $3.7 million for services provided in the development of a nuclear power plant in Iran. As part of the eventual agreement ending the American hostage crisis, President Carter signed an executive order on January 19, 1981, which was later "ratified" by the Reagan administration in February 1981, revoking the conditional licenses gaining access to the Iranian assets and ordering that all assets be transferred to a bank in New York for return to Iran. Obviously, many disgruntled creditors in the United States, including Dames and Moore, did not think much of this arrangement!

Given the public outcry to end 444 days of national frustration and humiliation over the hostage crisis, the Supreme Court unanimously upheld President Carter's action over the claims dispute in *Dames & Moore* v. *Reagan* (1981). The Court held that the Hostage Act of 1868, the International Claims Settlement Act of 1949, and the International Emergency Economic Powers Act of 1977 all reflected "acceptance of a broad scope for executive action in circumstances such as those presented in this case."

The Iran Hostage Case in 1981 and the Steel Seizure Case thirty years earlier reveal a difference in the Supreme Court's reading of how Congress oriented itself toward presidential power. In the Steel Seizure Case, the Court read the *absence* of any explicit authorization to seize private property as an indication of congressional opposition to that action, whereas in the Iran Hostage Case, the absence of congressional authorization apparently condoned the right to transfer Iranian assets as a necessary precondition to release of the hostages. In both instances, a somewhat unpopular Democratic president, confronting a Democratically controlled Congress, met with a quite different response from both Congress and the Court. The difference may have been the public mood to get the hostages back in 1979 and 1980, even if the price were high for some American companies. Unlike Truman's attempt to seize the nation's steel mills in 1951, before the "age of television" would make most Americans more attuned to international affairs, the Iranian hostage crisis seemed to simultaneously anger, frustrate, and stimulate the larger American public in a manner seldom seen in recent years. If a settlement could be reached with Iran without doing any further damage to national prestige, the public, Congress, and apparently the Supreme Court were amenable to such a compromise.

Presidential Appointment and Removal Powers

Presidents can also greatly influence both domestic and foreign policy through their power to appoint and remove public officials. As presidential power has grown in recent decades in response to the realities mentioned earlier, so has the size and complexity of the vast federal bureaucracy. What began in the 1790s with three departments and a handful of officers performing state, treasury, and war department functions has grown to include in the 1980s, thirteen separate departments employing approximately 5 million civilian and military personnel. The federal bureaucracy literally employs professions from A to Z—agronomists to zoologists—and provides the many services to which the American people have grown accustomed. Even with a modern civil service system that theoretically shields the federal bureaucracy from partisan politics, American presidents still normally appoint about 2,500 to 3,000 top-level personnel during their term of office. This power of appointment derives from Article II, Section 2, wherein the president

> shall nominate, and by and with the Advice and Consent of the Senate, shall appoint Ambassadors, other public Ministers and Consuls, Judges of the supreme Court, and all other Officers of the United States.

In practice, this appointment procedure has meant that presidents can normally determine the selection of most top-level bureaucrats. However, because Congress creates the office, determines qualifications for holding that office, and funds the position through the normal appropriations process, it can also indirectly influence executive appointments. When Senate confirmation is required for offices created by statute, the president nominates and the Senate confirms by majority vote the nominee, who is then commissioned as an "officer of the United States."

Although Article II is fairly clear about the president's power to nominate qualified individuals to fill vacancies, a problem does occasionally arise, as the case of *Buckley* v. *Valeo* (1976) indicates. The 1974 amendments to the Federal Election Campaign Act of 1972 (FECA), passed in the wake of the Watergate affair, created the six-member Federal Election Commission to oversee the act's requirements for campaign spending. To ensure that the work of the commission would not be abused politically, Congress wanted to be able to influence the selection of the panel personnel. Therefore, it stipulated in the statute that the president, the president *pro tempore* of the Senate, and the Speaker of the House would each appoint two members of the commission. Furthermore, all six were to be confirmed by a majority vote of both houses of Congress.

But in *Buckley* v. *Valeo*, the Supreme Court held that since the commission officials were indeed "officers of the United States," they had to be selected in accordance with Article II, Section 2, that is, nominated by the president and confirmed by and with the advice and consent of the Senate. Therefore, the *Buckley* precedent held that Congress could not give to the president pro tem of the Senate and the Speaker of the House the power to appoint a majority of the members of the Federal Election Commission. The provisions of the FECA amendments of 1974 for selecting the commission did not conform to Article II and were thus unconstitutional.

Whereas Article II, Section 2, is fairly clear about the appointment process governing various public officials, it is quite vague about the *removal* of such personnel. As a result, this omission has had to be clarified by executive actions, legislative provisions, and judicial interpretation. An initial issue that had to be confronted was whether the removal of an executive official was purely an executive prerogative, or did the Senate, which must confirm these appointments, also have to be consulted? For several decades, Congress showed no interest in this matter, allowing presidents sole discretion to remove executive personnel. But in 1876, Congress passed amendments to the Tenure of Office Act prohibiting presidential removal of designated executive-level officials, including postmasters, unless approved by the Senate.

In *Myers* v. *United States* (1926), the Supreme Court finally decided to confront the issue of the removal of executive officials by the president and specifically dealt with the constitutionality of the 1876 amendments to the Tenure of Office Act. In 1920, President Woodrow Wilson fired a postmaster in Oregon, Frank Myers, before his four-year term had expired. The disgruntled former employee claimed that under the 1876 amendments, his removal was illegal unless approved by two-thirds of the Senate. Myers filed suit in the U.S. Court of Claims for back salary of his full four-year term, but the Supreme Court held in a 6–3 verdict that the 1876 provision requiring Senate approval was unconstitutional. In a very long majority opinion, Chief Justice William Howard Taft, himself a former president, argued that purely executive officials performing exclusively executive functions can be removed at the discretion of the president, without approval by the Senate. According to Taft, because presidents have the responsibility under the Constitution to execute faithfully the laws, they need faithful officers to assist them. Therefore, extensive appointment and removal powers are essential for performing constitutional duties. Presidents alone are best able to determine whether executive officers are properly assisting them in this duty, and power must reside with the office responsible for policy execution. For Taft, removal power was a necessary corollary to appointive power and could not be separated.

Taft's majority opinion in *Myers* v. *United States* serves as the modern source for removal power of executive officials. It seemed to settle the first major constitutional question of whether removal is solely an *executive* function. But it also left unsettled another issue: are there any *limitations* on that power, can it be regulated by legislation, and are there any distinctions between executive offices that affect removal authority? As would become apparent later when executive officials became more responsible for quasi-judicial and quasi-legislative functions (i.e., Internal Commerce Commission, Federal Trade Commission, Atomic Energy Commission), Taft's reasoning in *Myers* was little help in defining the question about the *limits* of the president's power to remove executive officials. That question was answered by the case of *Humphrey's Executor* v. *United States* (1935).

Soon after assuming the presidency in 1933, Franklin Roosevelt asked William Humphrey to resign from the Federal Trade Commission (FTC) on the grounds that administration policy could be better served by a commissioner of the president's own choosing. At the time, Humphrey had already been reconfirmed by the Senate to serve a second seven-year term that would not expire until 1938. Humphrey refused to resign, was fired, and, soon thereafter, died. A suit was filed by the executor of his estate for back wages during the period between his forced resignation and his death.

A unanimous Court in 1935 ruled that Roosevelt did not have unlimited power to remove commissioners on independent regulatory commissions. In striking down Roosevelt's attempt to fire Humphrey, the Court reasoned that when Congress created regulatory bodies like the FTC, it intended that the officers of such bodies should be independent of executive control. Congress also expected that the commissioners would serve a fixed term in office and that they could only be removed for cause. In denying Roosevelt's action, the majority interpreted very narrowly the *Myers* precedent by saying that public officials performing purely *executive* functions serve at the will of the president and can only be removed by the president. But the *Humphrey* case was different from *Myers* in that the former performed certain *nonexecutive* functions and therefore could only be removed for neglect of duty or malfeasance in office. Roosevelt's claim that he wanted an FTC that agreed with his policy directions was an unconvincing rationale to a Supreme Court that saw the necessity for preserving independence from executive manipulation or intimidation.

The *Myers* and *Humphrey* cases found the Court ruling that the particular *functions* performed by public officers appointed by presidents determine their power to remove them. If such officials take purely executive actions, they can be removed by the president. But officials performing quasi-legislative or quasi-judicial tasks can only be dismissed for cause, and not at mere presidential discretion. Executive agencies such as the Environmental Protection Agency, which has vast rule-making authority over environmental standards in the public and private sectors, and the Federal Communications Commission, which exercises extensive regulatory control in the broadcast industry, have been empowered by Congress to formulate rules and adjudicate disputes, respectively. These agencies, and several others that have been similarly constituted by Congress, are supposed to be independent of presidential interference. Finally, the sweeping rationale used by Chief Justice Taft in *Myers*— that presidents have virtually unlimited removal power in order to ensure faithful execution of the laws—also has an interesting corollary in the Watergate scandal. The "Saturday Night Massacre," which saw a president ultimately fire the official seeking the White House tapes, demonstrated how removal power can be abused by a president.

Delegated Emergency Powers

As noted earlier in this chapter, congressional delegation of legislative authority increased greatly in the twentieth century, especially during the 1930s with the onslaught of a worldwide economic depression and in the 1940s with the advent of World War II. This major development in American government in recent decades contributed to what political scientist Theodore Lowi has termed a "crisis of public authority" and the advent of "interest group liberalism." [17]

Private interests have been able to take advantage of the delegated power phenomenon devised by Congress to administer a wide range of governmental activities.

In 1933, President Franklin Roosevelt declared a state of emergency during the banking crisis, as did President Harry Truman during the Korean War. President Richard Nixon followed suit in 1970 and 1971, as American combat forces extended the fighting into Cambodia to interdict the Vietcong and the North Vietnamese from moving into South Vietnam.[18] Finally, the era of the "imperial presidency" in the 1970s prompted Congress to investigate these long-standing presidential declarations of national emergencies. By 1976, Congress passed the National Emergencies Act to curb the president's frequent use of emergency powers. The legislation requires the president to publicize any declared national emergencies in the *Federal Register*. Congress can terminate such a declared emergency by enacting a concurrent resolution. To ensure that declared emergencies do not last indefinitely, the statute mandates a six-month limit upon the president. Both houses of Congress must pass concurrent resolutions authorizing continuation of any declared state of emergency.

For many who insist upon extensive presidential powers in the face of major crises in American domestic and international affairs, the 1976 legislation improperly constrains presidents trying to deal with the demands of the crisis. Given their extensive policy responsibilities for maintaining economic growth and stability, administering a domestic entitlements budget exceeding $500 billion per year, overseeing a defense industry of more than 2 million uniformed and 1 million civilian personnel, and countless other public expectations of federal involvement that have become the norm in American government, strength and vitality in the presidential office are essential. It is very difficult to develop safeguards that will restrain presidents who would misuse their considerable powers without also inhibiting those who would use the same power and authority for legitimate democratic ends. As the discussion now turns to the other popularly elected branch in American government, it will become apparent that Congress has seen its legislative tasks grow much more complicated in recent decades, particularly with respect to its war-making power and the power over federal spending.

Congress: The People's Branch

Reflecting their own democratic impulses, the framers of the American Constitution made Congress the heart of the new nation and the recipient of most of the delegated power needed to govern effectively. To Congress, Article I gives "all legislative Powers," including the power to tax, to provide for the common defense and general welfare of the citizenry, to borrow money, to regulate commerce, to coin money, to establish lower federal courts, to declare war, and, finally, to make all laws considered "necessary and proper" for executing all the powers specifically enumerated in Section 8. Earlier chapters have elaborated upon some of the powers delegated or implied in Article I. This section will focus upon certain coordinate powers of American government over which the executive and legislative branches have periodically confronted each other. More specifically, it will examine several powers of Congress: the legislature's power of investigation; its infrequently used power of impeachment of public officials; its efforts in the 1970s and 1980s to limit presidential war-making authority; its attempt during the Nixon era to limit the impoundment authority of a president; its long-standing practice to limit bureaucratic rule-making through a "legislative veto;" and, finally, congressional attempts in the mid-1980s to deal more responsibly with the mounting problem of annual federal budget deficits. In all these legislative actions, which in most instances were *reactions* to the perceived expansion of executive authority, Congress has achieved only limited success in curtailing the growth of presidential power.

The Investigative Power of Congress

One of the more controversial powers of Congress has been its power to conduct investigations while fulfilling its legislative functions. Part of the controversy can be attributed to the fact that the U.S. Constitution nowhere specifically grants Congress the power to investigate as a corollary to its lawmaking authority. But over many decades, the authority to conduct investigations has been viewed as essential to its major purposes of passing legislation, administering that legislation, informing the people of various public affairs, and protecting the integrity of Congress. It is doubtful whether Congress could ever effectively execute any of its delegated powers in Article I, Section 8, without the authority to obtain factual information upon which to base its legislative decisions. The power to investigate and inform has long been recognized. In 1885, Woodrow Wilson concluded that "the informing function of Congress should be preferred even to its legislative function." [19] Just prior to his appointment to the Supreme Court in 1937, Sen. Hugo Black (D-Ala.) referred to congressional investigations as a useful and fruitful function of Congress. But others have disagreed with this assertion. National columnist Walter Lippmann once characterized the congressional investigation as "that legalized atrocity in which congressmen, starved of their legitimate food for thought, go on a wild and feverish manhunt and do not stop at cannibalism." [20]

Whatever the verdict on the importance of the congressional power to investigate, its legitimacy required more definition by the Supreme Court. In the 1880s, the Supreme Court in *Kilbourn* v. *Thompson* (1881) for the first time endorsed this investigative power as a necessary and legitimate part of lawmaking authority. This case arose from a congressional committee's probe of a defunct banking firm and its dealings with a real estate firm in Washington, D.C. Hallet Kilbourn had been summoned to testify before a House committee and to provide various documents to aid the committee in its investigation. When Kilbourn refused to testify or provide the requested documents, he was found in contempt of Congress and sentenced to forty-five days in jail. Upon his release, he sued the House sergeant at arms for false imprisonment. Speaking on behalf of the Court, Justice Samuel Miller supported the investigative power of Congress, but he also said that the power could only be used in pursuit of purely declared *legislative* ends. Congress could only investigate those areas in which it was allowed to legislate; it could not investigate matters over which the executive or judicial branches had authority. As to the merits of the case, the Court found that Kilbourn had been improperly investigated and compelled to testify, which the Court saw in this instance as a judicial, not a legislative, prerogative. Three limitations on the congressional power to investigate were established as a result of the *Kilbourn* decision: the right of inquiry is limited by the separation-of-powers principle; the inquiry must deal with a matter upon which Congress can legitimately legislate; and a congressional resolution authorizing an inquiry must specifically mention an intent to legislate on the matter under investigation.

In the twentieth century, several cases have dealt with how Congress can exercise its investigative power and whether it may invade certain rights of private individuals. One such incident arose in the 1920s amid the investigation of the famous Teapot Dome scandal of the Harding administration. In an attempt to investigate alleged profiteering in speculative public land ventures, a Senate committee began hearings into why Attorney General Harry Daugherty had failed to prosecute key figures in the scandal. The committee subpoenaed Mally Daugherty, brother of the attorney general, but he refused to testify on two occasions. He claimed that the committee had no power to inquire into a nonlegislative matter involving private citizens.

Although a district court ruled that the Senate committee had exceeded its legislative authority, a unanimous Supreme Court in *McGrain* v. *Daugherty* (1927) upheld the Senate committee action on the grounds that Congress had a right to investigate this matter and to recommend possible changes in law and policy governing the Department of Justice. The majority opinion drafted by Justice Willis Van Devanter noted that two general propositions should guide congressional investigations: (1) that Congress possesses both express and delegated lawmaking power, as well as "such auxiliary powers as are necessary and appropriate to make the express powers effective;" and (2) that although not entitled to a "general" power to inquire into private lives, Congress can compel private citizens to testify when its limited power of investigation is legitimately exercised and when it is able to establish the pertinency of the investigation to the legislative function.

The precedent established in *McGrain* v. *Daugherty*—that private citizens must testify in a trial or congressional hearings if the questions posed are pertinent to the legislative function—became a hotly contested principle in the post-World War II era. Given the expanding regulatory reach of the federal government since World War II, and the likelihood that virtually any congressional investigation falls within the ever-broadening legislative function, Congress could conceivably compel private citizens to answer many intrusive questions under the threat of fine or imprisonment. But several civil liberties considerations and the Supreme Court's recognition of these protections restricted this license to investigate. The Bill of Rights limits Congress with respect to laws passed and procedures used in making those laws. For example, a witness before a congressional committee can decline to answer questions by claiming Fifth Amendment protection against self-incrimination. As a general rule, Congress can neither pass laws that require people to incriminate themselves, nor require public testimony in a hearing that will lead to the same result. In this respect, Congress has recognized a witness's right to Fifth Amendment protection. But witnesses can rely on the Fifth Amendment only to avoid self-incrimination, not to protect others or to keep from providing *noncriminating* testimony.

In addition to self-incrimination protection, witnesses can also avoid answering questions from congressional committees on First Amendment grounds. Free speech and association guarantees under the First Amendment protect citizens' rights to dissent and to join groups, even unpopular groups, without fearing possible governmental punishment. Testifying before a congressional committee might lead to a person's being socially or professionally ostracized. It if does, being compelled to testify violates that person's First Amendment freedom *not* to speak. As Justice Hugo Black once observed in dissent, people should be allowed to "join organizations, advocate causes, and make political 'mistakes' without later being subjected to governmental penalties for having dared to think for themselves." [21] The problem is that these rights have never been interpreted as absolutes. As Chapter 11 argues, when the Supreme Court has been asked to balance the need for government to preserve order and the citizen's right to speak and act according to individual conscience, the balance has usually been struck in favor of government and social order.

The subject of the pertinency of questions posed in hearings in a congressional investigation arose in several prominent cases in the late 1950s, as the United States found itself preoccupied with alleged Communist subversion (see Brief 5.3). Congress seemed compelled to use its investigative power against individuals suspected of being Communist sympathizers or members of subversive front organizations. Whether or not the investigations were motivated

---

☐ *Brief 5.3   Limits on the Congressional Power to Investigate*

The power of Congress to hold investigations pursuant to its legislative function is important for allowing it to discharge properly its constitutional duties under Article I. Most congressional investigations occur without any great furor or threat to individual privacy. But like any power that can ultimately rely upon coercion, this investigative clout can be abused by Congress. Some congressional hearings held under that body's investigative powers have instigated great public controversy and seriously infringed upon the individual's right to be protected from the intrusive power of the state.

One of the most controversial of modern-day investigations by Congress occurred after World War II in a climate of growing concern about the spread of international communism. During the late 1940s and the 1950s, committees in both houses of Congress delved into a wide range of allegedly subversive activities and propaganda aimed at the overthrow of the federal government. The House Committee on Un-American Activities (HUAC) called over three thousand witnesses during this period and questioned many of them on their political beliefs, affiliations, and actions deemed potentially dangerous to the United States government. Many of the witnesses invoked the Fifth Amendment protection against self-incrimination and

refused to testify before the committee. Others insisted that the committee's interrogation exceeded Congress's legislative function and refused to appear. Nearly 150 of these uncooperative witnesses were cited for contempt of Congress. The two most famous cases pitting uncooperative witnesses against HUAC were *Watkins* v. *United States* (1957) and *Barenblatt* v. *United States* (1959).

In the Senate, the anti-Communist scare in the late 1940s and early 1950s was reflected in the activities of Sen. Joseph R. McCarthy (R-Wis.). McCarthy used a subcommittee of the Senate Foreign Relations Committee to make repeated, unsubstantiated charges against public officials and private individuals suspected of political dissent. His allegations, along with those of HUAC, resulted in a series of loyalty-security investigations into the backgrounds and activities of public employees, scientists, and academics, as well as imposed loyalty oaths and the passage of anti-Communist legislation. Even more damaging was the distrust of public officials, the practice of "guilt by association," and the climate of fear that permeated much of American society and perpetuated the cold war into the 1960s.

by a desire to score political points with an alarmed public, the hearings, in many instances, contributed directly to an atmosphere of public intolerance and political character assassination.

One such internal security case that arose in the 1950s involved John Watkins, a labor organizer and former union official, who had been subpoenaed by a subcommittee of the House Un-American Activities Committee (HUAC). Although he answered questions about his own relationship to the Communist party, he refused to answer anything about any personal acquaintances who supposedly had once been affiliated with the party. Watkins insisted that such information was irrelevant to the committee's power and purpose, and Congress consequently cited him for contempt.

On appeal of his contempt citation, Watkins found a Supreme Court more sympathetic to his position. Writing for a six-member majority (two justices did not participate) in *Watkins* v. *United States,* Chief Justice Earl Warren indicated that the witness could become informed of the subject matter of the investigations by examining such material as the authorizing resolution, the several remarks of the chairperson, the overall nature of the proceedings, and remarks by committee members. To the extent that these several sources provided necessary guidance and clarification about the relevance of the questioning, the witness could be expected to testify. But without such clarification and understanding, the witness could not be compelled to testify without violating due process of law. In *Watkins,* the Warren Court held that none of these conditions had been adequately met, and since "there is no congressional power to expose for the sake of exposure," Watkins was within his rights in refusing to testify. Soon after *Watkins,* the Court in *Sweezy* v. *New Hampshire* (1957) held that a *state* legislative investigation of a college professor's activities at a state university was not pertinent to any legislative purpose and therefore violated the professor's First Amendment rights.

Rather than quieting the public debate over Communist subversion and Congress's right to probe, these decisions instead merely fanned a smoldering issue. Congress threatened to limit the Supreme Court's appellate jurisdiction and criticized the Supreme Court whose members it claimed had "grown soft" on alleged subversive actions. Partly as a consequence of this public criticism, the Court seemed to abandon its strong civil libertarian stance over the next few years. One case in particular reflects this retreat by the Court.

Lloyd Barenblatt, a one-time graduate student and college instructor at the University of Michigan and Vassar College during the 1950s, had been called to testify before the same House Un-American Activities Committee that had extended its investigation of Communist subversion into the field of American higher education. Barenblatt refused to answer any questions regarding his past affiliation with the American Communist party. Unlike Watkins, who answered some of the committee's questions, Barenblatt claimed that the First Amendment protected his silence about past affiliation with the Communist party. For refusing to answer, he was fined and sentenced to six months in jail by the district court. After losing his appeal at the circuit level, the case went to the Supreme Court which upheld the conviction.

Divided by a 5–4 vote, the Supreme Court in *Barenblatt* v. *United States* reiterated that Congress's power to investigate is not unlimited. Congress may not inquire into matters that are the exclusive province of the judicial or executive branches. It must also exercise its rightful power within the limitations imposed by the Bill of Rights. In the case before it, the Court recognized the importance of preserving "academic teaching freedom and its corollary learning freedom." However, a college or university is not a "constitutional sanctuary," totally immune from inquiries into matters properly within the legislative domain. In the majority opinion, the second Justice John Harlan distinguished the *Watkins* case from *Barenblatt*. In *Watkins*, the petitioner had specifically objected to the committee's questions on the grounds of pertinency. In *Barenblatt*, the Court felt that the committee had properly informed the witness of the relevance and purpose of the questioning. Therefore, the witness was not free to refuse answering the questions posed to him. The majority also recognized the need of the courts to balance compelling public and private interests in this particular circumstance. In that respect, the Court said that Congress's power to investigate should not have been denied simply because it was investigating higher education.

Of the four justices dissenting in *Barenblatt*, the remarks of Justice Hugo Black, so reminiscent of his strong civil libertarian stance in earlier cases, reflected his view that *any* limitation upon vital First Amendment rights poses a dire threat to the liberty of all in a democratic order. For Black, the issue in *Barenblatt* was simple:

> whether we as a people will try fearfully and futilely to preserve democracy by adopting totalitarian methods, or whether in accordance with our traditions and our Constitution we will have the confidence and courage to be free.

Notwithstanding Black's forceful dissent, the *Barenblatt* decision is difficult to reconcile with *Watkins*. *Barenblatt* seemed to diminish Congress's fervent cry to revise the Court's appellate jurisdiction. The decision might also have been a reflection of the Court's partial intimidation by Congress and public opinion over early desegregation struggles following *Brown* v. *Board of Education* in 1954 and 1955. By the early 1960s, both Congress and the Court began to turn their attentions to other matters. The nation's preoccupation with Communist subversion and internal security subsided somewhat as the Supreme Court and Congress began to demonstrate more concern about civil rights, social policy, and foreign affairs.

The Impeachment Power of Congress

As stated, the investigative power of Congress must be related to its lawmaking authority. Without a distinct legislative purpose, Congress does not have the power, to quote Warren in *Watkins*, "to expose for the sake of exposure." But one of the more important nonlegislative powers that the framers considered an essential "auxiliary precaution" is the **impeachment power** of Congress. Article I, Sections 2 and 3, give Congress the important power to remove, under certain circumstances, various federal officials from office. Removal occurs following impeachment by a *majority vote* in the House of Representatives and conviction by a *two-thirds vote* of members present in the Senate. Stated more simply, the House serves as the grand jury to indict the suspected official, and the Senate operates as the judge of that indictment. Article II, Section 4, briefly defines who may be impeached and on what charges:

> The President, Vice President and all civil Officers of the United States, shall be removed from Office on Impeachment for, and Conviction of, Treason, Bribery, or other high Crimes and Misdemeanors.

Two important qualifications about the impeachment power of Congress should be noted. First, under the Constitution, impeachment by the House and conviction in the Senate are purely *political* penalties—removing from federal office and barring from holding office in the future. The impeachment process was not intended to require *legal* penalties, as is the case in Great Britain, although nothing in the Constitution prevents impeached and convicted federal officials from being tried, convicted, and punished according to civil and criminal law after being removed from federal office. Apparently, the framers wanted to encourage Congress to use impeachment against officials for gross misconduct in high office, but they also provided for due process subsequent to an official's removal from office.

The other important qualification that the framers placed upon the power of impeachment was limiting impeachable offenses to "Treason, Bribery, or other high Crimes and Misdemeanors." This brief definition of possible grounds for impeachment was most likely intended to create an important check upon executive power, as well as some limitation upon Congress abusing its impeachment power and intimidating high federal officials for political purposes. But, as with most constitutional provisions, these components defining the impeachment process have required elaboration through historical experience of the constitutional system.

Fortunately for the Republic, there have been relatively few occasions when the impeachment process has been used to remove high public officials, and only rarely against a sitting president. Through 1987, the House of Representatives had investigated only sixty-seven federal officials for possible impeachment and had impeached only fifteen of them. The Senate convicted only five of these persons (all federal judges), the most recent one being a judge serving a prison term who had refused to resign his judgeship (see Chapter 4 endnotes on Judge Harry Claiborne). The only sitting U.S. president to be impeached was Andrew Johnson in 1868, but the Senate failed to convict Johnson by one vote.

The other presidential impeachment episode involved Richard Nixon, the thirty-seventh president of the United States. As discussed earlier in this chapter, a formal bill of impeachment against Nixon for his role in the Watergate scandal was never voted on by the House, although the House Judiciary Committee's overwhelming approval of three articles of impeachment in July 1974 was instrumental in persuading Nixon to resign from office on August 9, 1974. For much of 1973–74, a controversy existed over precisely what was an impeachable offense under Article II. President Nixon maintained that he could only be impeached after a criminal indictment, but the House Judiciary Committee and several legal scholars generally agreed that the impeachment process inherently involved a political, not a strict legal, definition. In other words, "high Crimes and Misdemeanors" was susceptible to definition by Congress, and an impeachable offense was whatever a majority of the House said it was. Like so many aspects of the Constitution, this allusion in the Constitution to the grounds for impeachment is ambiguous, and divining the original intentions and possible consensus is impossible. Alexander Hamilton's reference in *Federalist No. 65* to an "abuse or violation of some public trust" would seem to fit the circumstances of the Watergate scandal.[22]

Bombs, Budgets, and Bureaucratic Discretion: Congress Reasserts Itself in the Late Twentieth Century

The 1960s began on an optimistic note, especially with respect to relations between Congress and the president. Although the 1950s were fairly passive, the decade did see divided government, with the Democrats in control of Congress most of the time and the White House under the care of a popular Republican president. In the 1960 presidential election a dashing young senator from Massachusetts, John Kennedy, captured the White House and inspired a new generation of Americans to strive for excellence in several fields. Although civil rights, public education, military preparedness, arms control, and collective security would soon demand greater attention, the dawn of the New Frontier promised more cooperation between Congress and the president and a renewed commitment to solving problems at home and abroad. But during the 1960s and 1970s, American society underwent great testing as its people learned that national resources and resolve were not unlimited. No sooner had the nation put the 1960s behind it, with its social upheaval and public questioning of government performance and policy, than a new crisis—the Watergate affair—added to the public's sense that their public leaders, and maybe their public institutions, had somehow failed them.

In the aftermath of the Vietnam War and the Watergate scandal people began to distrust their leaders. Congress and the White House found themselves deeply questioning the tactics and programs of each other. By the early 1970s, Congress saw itself with both a right and a responsibility to reassert its authority over several areas of public policy. Congress soon acted to limit the president's power to wage war unilaterally, and to impound appropriated funds. Congress also acted to increase its own power to review bureaucratic rule-making and to control federal spending. The instruments used by Congress to restore the proper balance of power consisted of the War Powers Act, the legislative veto, the Congressional Budget and Impoundment Control Act, and the Balanced Budget and Emergency Deficit Control Act. Most of these instances of a "resurgent Congress" were eventually checked by the Supreme Court in several decisions that limited congressional assertiveness. The result was a balance of power favoring presidential rather than legislative prerogative. This last section on congressional-executive relations will begin with Congress's attempt to rein in the war-making power of the president.

War: A State of Things or an Act of Legislative Will?

In a prophetic letter to Thomas Jefferson in 1798, James Madison observed:

> The Constitution supposes what the history of all governments demonstrates, that the Executive is the branch of power most interested in war, and most prone to it. It has accordingly with studied care vested the question of war in the legislature.[23]

Several American presidents in this century—including both Roosevelts, Wilson, Truman, Eisenhower, Kennedy, Johnson, Nixon, Ford, and Reagan—

independently committed American troops to combat overseas. Since 1950, executive action in Korea, Lebanon, Cuba, the Dominican Republic, Vietnam, Laos, Cambodia, Grenada, and the Persian Gulf, and a succession of covert operations, military assistance programs, top-secret high-altitude surveillance missions, and distant naval operations in global trouble spots have all increased the chances of the United States becoming involved, willingly or unwillingly, in foreign combat, with little or no opportunity for congressional consultation. The Vietnam War is a case in point and was, in fact, the event that occasioned a congressional attempt to limit executive war power in the absence of a formal declaration of war.

American involvement in the Indochina War grew as a consequence of four different American presidents acting under their powers as commander in chief. After the fall of the French at Dienbienphu in 1953, President Dwight Eisenhower and later President John Kennedy committed both American advisors and a small combat force on the premise that a geopolitical vacuum had been created by a divided Vietnam and the exodus of the French from Indochina. But the growing American presence in Southeast Asia and the eventual escalation of the conflict occurred primarily during the Johnson and Nixon administrations in the 1960s and 1970s.

A major turning point in America's involvement in a largely civil conflict in Vietnam came in August 1964. Following an alleged, provocative attack by North Vietnamese torpedo boats against two American warships in the Gulf of Tonkin, President Lyndon Johnson seized the opportunity and asked Congress for enlarged power to respond in defense of American forces and to protect national interests. With only two dissenting votes, the U.S. Senate passed the Tonkin Gulf Resolution on August 10, 1964, which stated that "the United States is . . . prepared, as the President determines, to take all necessary steps, including the use of armed force . . . to repel any armed attack against the forces of the United States and to prevent any further aggression." Throughout the remainder of his presidency, Johnson relied upon this single resolution as authorization for subsequent American operations in Vietnam, including the saturation bombing of North Vietnam and a massive build-up of American combat troops in the region. As that involvement increased and the chance of a clear military and political victory declined during 1967–68, members of Congress grew more critical of the war and claimed that they had been manipulated by the president in order to extract a congressional endorsement of executive actions. Public and congressional protest against the war eventually dissuaded Johnson from seeking the Democratic nomination by his party in 1968, which paved the way for another American president to ignore the emerging "multiple" or "decisive consensus" of Congress and the American people.[24]

Efforts by Congress to regain temporary control over executive war-making activities in Vietnam were greatly accelerated in 1970, when President Nixon, in the familiar claim of protecting American forces, extended military operations into Cambodia without first consulting Congress. The operation had only limited success and led to the Cooper-Church Amendment in 1970, which prohibited the use of funds for American combat forces in Laos, Thailand, and Cambodia. Convinced that it had been manipulated long enough, Congress voted in 1971 to repeal the Tonkin Gulf Resolution, although the resolution had more symbolic than substantive effect in constraining presidential intentions in Southeast Asia. President Nixon's embattled administration during the Watergate era had little resilience to defend the traditional war-making power of the American presidency.

While American involvement in the war in Southeast Asia was growing, the federal judiciary refused to support public and congressional criticism. As American casualties mounted in the late 1960s, without any formal declaration of war by Congress, the Supreme Court was frequently petitioned to rule on the constitutionality of the war. In *Mitchell* v. *United States* (1967), the Supreme Court refused to hear a case involving an individual who had been sentenced to a five-year prison term for failing to report for induction into the armed forces. In *Mora* v. *McNamara* (1967), the Court again refused to hear another case, this one involving three army privates who were protesting their reassignment to South Vietnam on the grounds that it was an illegal war. One year later, in *Holmes* v. *United States* (1968), the Court refused to rule on the constitutionality of the draft in the absence of a formal declaration of war by Congress. Finally, in November 1970, the Court declined another opportunity to rule on the constitutionality of the war in what was probably the most prominent Vietnam era case, *Massachusetts* v. *Laird* (1970). In all these instances, the Supreme Court followed the traditional pattern of not interfering when American presidents ostensibly act in times of suspected national crisis or to defend national interests and security at home and abroad.

The ultimate reflection of congressional resolve to control executive war power came in 1973, as Congress finally passed, over President Nixon's veto, the War Powers Act. The act provides that the president can commit American troops to overseas action under only three conditions: a formal declaration of war by Congress; congressional authorization of such deployment in the absence of declared war; an enemy attack upon the United States or its forces which creates a national emergency. The act compels the president to report the deployment of combat troops to Congress within forty-eight hours. Unless Congress declares war against the aggressor state, American forces must be withdrawn from hostilities within sixty days, although an additional thirty-day period can be granted to the president before the withdrawal of American troops. After ninety days, all troops must be withdrawn at the insistence of both houses of Congress, and the president cannot veto such a directive.

Congress was seeking to restore some balance to foreign policy decision making, and it viewed the War Powers Act as sending a forceful message to American presidents trying to ignore the legislative branch of government. Some critics of the act maintain that the legislation handicaps presidents in their capacity to deal responsibly with crisis situations. They also insist that Congress institutionally is poorly organized to deal with such situations and that most members individually have neither the interest, time, nor expertise to deal with such matters when they arise. These critics of the War Powers Act insist that having the *legal* power to restrain an activist president in foreign affairs is not the same as having the necessary *political* will to invoke provisions of the act and make the difficult decisions about war and peace around the world. Supporters of the War Powers Act say that American presidents for too long have made major decisions affecting the lives and fortunes of the American people without consulting Congress.

Has the War Powers Act worked as it was intended by Congress? Much evidence suggests that it is more form than substance. Although it was invoked in 1975, during the brief action to free the American merchant ship USS *Mayaguez* that had been captured by the Cambodians, and again in 1982, when American troops were sent to Lebanon, the act has largely been dismissed by the last four American presidents as both unconstitutional and impractical. Every president since Nixon has considered the act to be an encroachment upon his powers as commander in chief, and none has officially complied with it. They consider Section 5(b) of the act, which requires American troops to be withdrawn in sixty days unless Congress declares war or authorizes continuation of the commitment, to be both a tactical nightmare for presidents attempting to manage a crisis and an infringement upon the powers of the chief executive. During the 1980s, President Ronald Reagan ignored the act on numerous occasions: providing aid to the Nicaraguan contras; invading Grenada in 1983; retaliating against Libya on two occasions in 1986 for its support of terrorism; and, finally, stepping up U.S. military presence in the Persian Gulf when Kuwaiti oil tankers were reflagged. The War Powers Act was never invoked by Congress in any of these situations. Except for the reflagged tankers, Congress was informed *after* military action had been ordered.

For the most part, the War Powers Act has neither served as an effective restraint upon presidents determined to accomplish their agenda, nor weakened them in a foreign-policy crisis when both Congress and the American public have deferred to presidential initiatives. The legislation is vague about whether the regulatory provisions apply when presidents are acting within their unique constitutional authority as commander in chief as Congress interprets it, or only when they have exceeded that constitutional authority. The law would seem to require advance formal consultation with both the House and the Senate, and not merely congressional leaders. Such consultation is required "in every possible instance," but there is no clarification of what is meant by "possible." Finally, the resolution truly suffers from a lack of definition of "hostilities," which seriously impedes any consistent interpretation of the binding nature of the legislation from one episode to another and across administrations.

If the War Powers Act is ever to be more than a hollow directive to future presidents, Congress will have to redefine its scope as well as some of its regulations. It will also have to reform the mechanisms necessary to make it work. By early 1988, many in Congress voiced support for revising the act so that presidents will abide by its key provisions and take more seriously the consultative role of Congress in making foreign policy. But a few, including Rep. Dante B. Fascell (D-Fla.), one of the key architects of the War Powers Act, still argue that a continuing constitutional debate on the respective powers of Congress and the president in foreign affairs is a healthy situation, given the need for more openness and deliberation in committing American forces to conflicts overseas.[25]

The Legislative Veto Comes of Age

The War Powers Act is one of more than two hundred statutes passed by Congress in the last fifty years that contain a **legislative veto** provision whereby one or both houses of Congress (or one of its committees) can review and revoke the actions of a president or executive officers. Ever since passage of the Legislative Appropriations Act in the last days of the Hoover administration in 1932, the legislative veto has been aimed at a succession of bureaucratic rules dealing with such matters as federal campaign contributions, foreign trade, nuclear nonproliferation, defense appropriations, airline deregulation, farm credit, toxic waste dumps, aid to education, energy regulation, land management, and several other substantive policy issues. More directly, the legislative veto has sometimes, as in the War Powers Act, been aimed at limiting specifically *presidential* attempts to reorganize the executive branch, impound funds appropriated by Congress (see Brief 5.4), send troops to foreign conflicts, and transfer sophisticated weaponry and technology to foreign countries.

Basically, this legislative device offers legislators a chance to delegate the time-consuming task of rule making but at the same time to retain the power to counter selected executive actions. Since the 1930s, Congress has delegated vast amounts of legislative authority to the executive agencies of the federal government, while still retaining the capacity, through the legislative veto, to overrule particular agency decisions that the legislators dislike. The legislative veto has, as expected, attracted both proponents and opponents. Its advocates defend its use and constitutionality on several grounds. They maintain that the device is a noble one, namely, to keep administrators democratically accountable by making them more answerable to Congress. They insist that the veto ensures that promulgated rules of executive agencies conform to congressional intent. Not only does the legislative veto try to counteract the trend toward a broad delegation of legislative authority, but also it tries to reinvigorate Congress's responsibility for overseeing the administrative establishment. As for its constitutionality, proponents insist that the framers of the Constitution never envisioned a rigid legislative-administrative relationship and that the legislative veto actually facilitates a sharing of constitutional powers between the legislature and the executive, not a strict separation.

Critics of the legislative veto insist that the device is blatantly unconstitutional, especially when it is exercised by a single congressional committee (which is actually rare). They argue that the veto avoids the normal route for lawmaking established in Article I of the Constitution, namely, passage in identical form by both houses and signing by the president. They also argue that the device violates the separation-of-powers principle and checks-and-balances doctrine by allowing Congress to encroach upon the powers of presidents and the courts. Specifically, use of the legislative veto denies presidents the chance to sign legislation or exercise their own right to veto an act of Congress. And it also undermines the role of courts for reviewing the legality of rules formulated by executive agencies. Finally, opponents of the legislative veto insist that the technique is actually a very negative force against public policy-making by executive agencies and may even discourage bureaucratic officials from proposing necessary rules and regulations.

Congressional desires to contain presidential authority, review economic regulation, and maintain popular control of bureaucrats finally raised an important question about the constitutionality of the legislative veto in 1983. Ironically, the issue of the constitutionality of the legislative veto did not arise over a publicized exercise of executive war power or economic rule making, but rather in an insignificant debate over the deportation of an alien living in the United States. An Indian national, Jagdish Rai Chadha, born in Kenya and holding a British passport, had completed his graduate studies while living in

Ohio. After trying unsuccessfully to obtain a valid passport in 1972, to either Kenya or Great Britain, Chadha applied to the Immigration and Naturalization Service (INS) for permanent resident status under Section 244(a)(1) of the Immigration and Naturalization Act (INA), but was informed that he would soon be deported. He subsequently found a sympathetic immigration judge who suspended his deportation and granted him resident status. But eighteen months later, the House of Representatives voted to reverse this action and ordered his deportation from the United States. With the assistance of the Public Citizen Litigation Group, Chadha filed suit in federal court challenging the constitutionality of the legislative veto provision, Section 244(a)(1), of the INA. After the INS lost in the lower courts, it appealed to the Supreme Court. On June 23, 1983, a 7–2 Court majority in the case of *Immigration and Naturalization Service* v. *Chadha* (1983) struck down the legislative veto as an unconstitutional violation of the separation-of-powers principle.

The *Chadha* decision, which found Chief Justice Burger writing for the majority, stated that all action by Congress must be *legislative* in nature and must conform to the explicit procedures of Article I, Section 7, of the Constitution. These provisions require that all legislative action must pass by majority vote in both houses and be presented to the president for approval or veto. The Court insisted that the separation-of-powers principle is more than an "abstract generalization." Congress cannot make law by circumventing the procedural requirements of bicamerality and presentment of legislation to the president. Since the one-house veto of Chadha's permanent resident status was an exercise of legislative power, and since it was never approved by both houses or signed by the president, it was an unconstitutional exercise of legislative power and a violation of the separation-of-powers principle.

In a dissenting opinion, Justice Byron White reviewed the development of more than a half-century of Congress's delegating broad legislative authority to the executive branch, while still reserving its right to veto particular aspects of that delegated power with which it does not agree. White noted that the framers of the Constitution anticipated how "new problems of governance would require different solutions." Ironically, White argued, the Court's decision here meant that "the Executive Branch and the independent agencies may make rules with the effect of law, while Congress, in whom the framers confided the legislative power . . . may not exercise a veto which precludes such rules from having operative force." In expressing a final regret about the enormous judicial review implications of the *Chadha* ruling, White emphasized that the Court was "in one fell swoop" striking down more provisions of more laws passed by Congress than the Court had declared unconstitutional in nearly two centuries of constitutional interpretation.

Chadha is a broad and somewhat bewildering decision. The sweeping nature of the ruling derives from its questioning the constitutionality of scores of federal laws, as Justice White noted in his dissent. It is perplexing because it recognizes Congress's right to delegate rule-making authority to the bureaucracy, while at the same time denying Congress the right to delegate to itself the power to oversee that rule making. It both rightfully precludes quasi-judicial power to the Congress, but reaffirms the principle that executive agencies can exercise that same power when created by an act of Congress. Only Congress can fulfill the lawmaking function as intended by the framers, but it can also assign to administrative agencies a policy-making role largely immune from electoral accountability, which is itself a development, if not a perversion, that the framers could never have foreseen and probably would not have condoned. Finally, since *Chadha* only declared the veto provision of the Immigration and Naturalization Act unconstitutional, it seemed to imply that the many other legislative veto provisions of scores of other federal acts were "severable" from the respective laws. But that assumes that the veto provisions can be easily separated from the different laws, which is definitely not the case. In some instances, Congress only allowed administrators to exercise certain powers under the particular act as long as such powers could be checked through the legislative veto. This is particularly true of the War Powers Act. Since the severability issue is sometimes difficult to resolve, the courts will most likely hear additional legislative veto cases in the future.

In summary, *Chadha* testifies to the difficulty that Congress faces in trying to control the modern bureaucratic state and the painstaking task of cleansing numerous federal laws of the legislative veto provision. The first chore will be difficult enough, given the symbiotic relationship that exists within numerous policy triangles composed of members of Congress, bureaucrats, and special-interest lobbyists. And the second matter will probably be just as difficult, given the limited time that legislators have to attend to contemporary legislative demands, busy schedules, casework for voters back home, and endless fundraising and reelection commitments.

This chapter now turns to the final area of congressional-presidential conflict—the federal budget. The federal budget is the most politically significant policy statement that emerges each year from the federal government. It has been the source of considerable conflict between the two branches for many years, but not until the 1970s did the debate reach constitutional proportions.

To Spend or Not to Spend: An Emerging Controversy

For more than a century after creation of the American Republic, with few exceptions, both in theory and fact, Congress controlled the nation's purse strings in accordance with Article I, Sections 7 and 8. But as discussed in Chapter 7, through an evolving federal structure and expanded federal taxing authority, there have been many constitutional clashes over the federal government's use of its taxing power to regulate child labor, control agricultural production, and several other policy matters under federal police power. However, the increasing complexity of both the American economy and the governmental process in the twentieth century has led to fragmented congressional control over the budget and an expanded role for the executive branch. With the passage of the Budget and Accounting Act in 1921, Congress ceded its control over spending and revenue estimates to a new office within the executive branch, the Bureau of the Budget. During the next half-century, Congress found itself making only incremental changes in the yearly budget requests submitted to it by the president. Finally, in the early 1970s, an intense dispute arose between the Democratically controlled Congress and the Nixon administration over the latter's refusal to spend monies appropriated by Congress. As a result of this dispute, Congress tried to regain control over fiscal policy and spending priorities.

The process whereby a president either defers spending or refuses to spend money appropriated by Congress is known as **impoundment.** Article I,

Section 9, grants the power of appropriation only to Congress and allows a presidential role only through a veto of the legislation. But it is not the appropriation power alone that determines the success of policy goals. Whereas Congress provides the money for a program, how those monies are spent—indeed, if they are spent at all—is a crucial determinant of public policy. As a result, presidents can use impoundment as an important instrument for accomplishing their own policy goals (see Brief 5.4).

As noted in Brief 5.4, presidents have frequently impounded funds in order to achieve what they define as the national interest. But President Nixon extended the impoundment practice to new levels, impounding by some estimates as much as $25 billion that had been appointed by Congress for various purposes. Not only did Nixon shape domestic spending to conform to many of his policy preferences, as other chief executives had done, but also he tried to terminate several programs with which he philosophically disagreed. On both statutory and constitutional grounds, Nixon asserted his "constitutional right" to review levels of federal spending in the context of overall economic conditions, and then to reduce or terminate federal programs accordingly. This practice stimulated both legal disputes in the courts and legislation in Congress.

In one of the more important confrontations between President Nixon and Congress, the administrator of the Environmental Protection Agency, Russell Train, was ordered to withhold several billion dollars appropriated for sewage treatment plant construction under the Clean Water Act of 1972. Congress had earlier overridden Nixon's veto of the act, but the president seemed intent upon accomplishing his own policy goals. The city of New York filed a suit in federal court against the EPA administrator, in the hope of forcing him to release the monies. In the only impoundment decision ever handed down by the Supreme Court, the justices ruled in *Train* v. *City of New York* (1975) that the Clean Water Act did not allow the president discretionary

---

☐ *Brief 5.4   The Practice of Presidential Impoundment*

Presidential impoundment of monies appropriated by Congress is a practice almost as old as the Republic itself. In 1803, President Thomas Jefferson refused to spend $50,000 that Congress had appropriated to help defend the Mississippi River. Since the Louisiana Purchase had been completed between the time that Congress had approved of the funding and the actual expenditure of the money, Jefferson felt that fortifications along the river were no longer as important or the expenditures as necessary.

For the remainder of the nineteenth century, presidents rarely impounded appropriations, but additional problems arose early in the twentieth century. In 1905, Congress allowed the president more discretion to spend appropriated funds in order to reduce the chances of departmental deficits by the end of the year. And in 1921, when Congress created the Bureau of the Budget, it authorized the president to withhold funds in order to save money if excess funds had been

authorized by Congress. During the Harding, Coolidge, and Hoover administrations, monies appropriated for various domestic purposes were withheld, but no major confrontations between Congress and the president emerged.

That changed during the Roosevelt years, when FDR spend less money than Congress had appropriated for certain programs in order to deal with the problems of an economic depression and World War II. In the postwar era, Presidents Truman, Eisenhower, and Johnson periodically refused to spend full amounts authorized for several defense purposes and some domestic programs, and they justified their actions on the basis of their role as commander in chief. Although Congress criticized these practices at times, the several incidents never prompted widespread concern by the American public or a major constitutional question to be settled in the courts. Not until, that is, Richard Nixon arrived in the White House.

authority to refuse to spend the money. The Court read the legislation, passed by a two-thirds majority in both houses, as a firm commitment to resolve an urgent problem. As Justice White indicated in the majority opinion, "We cannot believe that Congress [scuttled] the entire effort by providing the Executive with the seemingly limitless power to withhold funds from allotment and obligation."

While this case was still pending in the courts, Congress acted on its own to resolve the impoundment question and reassert its constitutional power of the purse by passing the Budget and Impoundment Control Act of 1974. The legislation reformed many aspects of the budgetary process. One section of the law, dealing specifically with impoundment by the president, created two different procedures whereby Congress can check presidential impoundment actions. First, if presidents wish to *terminate* programs or *reduce* total spending, they must obtain from both houses of Congress within forty-five days specific approval to rescind the appropriations. Furthermore, if they merely want to *delay* the expenditures, they can do so independently, but Congress can later compel them to spend the money if either house passes a resolution to that effect. This particular provision is another example of the legislative veto, which was eventually found unconstitutional in *Chadha*. To prevent any misinterpretation of congressional intent, the Budget Impoundment and Control Act also contains language that specifically denies to the president impoundment authority. It also created new budget committees in both houses and the Congressional Budget Office with extensive new staff and information resources that were intended to equip Congress with more capacity to coordinate the annual budgetary process. Finally, the legislation made several changes that Congress hoped would encourage more timely and long-term budgetary planning and reduce the likelihood of delinquent and incremental budget decision making.

Many accounts of the Budget and Impoundment Control Act indicate that the legislation had only limited success in reforming the budgetary process and accomplishing many of the initial objectives of the legislation. It did have some success in equipping Congress with more staff resources for evaluating the annual budget and in bringing about a more long-term, better-coordinated schedule for assessing budgetary priorities. But it did little to control the overall level of federal spending or to initiate a national debate on spending priorities. And if the legislation were seen as forcing Congress to consider in one package all expenditure and taxing choices, and then making the difficult decisions about who benefits and who pays, then the 1974 legislation was not very effective. Congress found it virtually impossible to make the necessary intelligent cuts in the "untouchables" of entitlements and defense spending. In some respects, the new House and Senate Budget Committees merely provided new access points for members of Congress, along with special-interest groups, who could not win with the authorization and appropriations committee in both houses. In order to pass budget resolutions to set overall limits on expenditures and revenues, the budget committees had to accommodate these spending interests, and the outcome was higher spending in the 1970s and 1980s. Ironically, then, the new process probably encouraged the very thing that it was presumably designed to diminish—uncontrollable budgetary growth.[26] During the 1980s, Congress and the president disagreed continually over this very issue of taxing and spending. President Reagan insisted on no new taxes, much to the chagrin of many in Congress, which argued that new taxes, rather than spending cuts, were the way to restore fiscal sanity to government spending.

In many respects, this endless debate over the size and precise content of the federal budget may reflect a built-in conflict between the president and Congress, both of which have historically responded to different interests and incentives. Congress has always been a more locally focused political institution, the members of which respond to local constituents and pressures. The entire structure of Congress reflects decentralized power in terms of committees, the use of institutional rules and procedures, and incentives for reelection. Increasingly in the twentieth century, the presidency has been seen as a forum for national concerns and consensus-seeking politics. The American public has turned more and more to this one office in order to address national policy issues and avoid the entanglement of congressional debate and delay. The annual budgetary process in part reflects this disjuncture between the two elected branches of American government, some of which may well have been a consequence of the framers' intent in 1787. Unless Congress can restructure itself as a more centralized institution with a streamlined committee and subcommittee system and provide more authority in the leadership ranks of the institution, it will most likely have to continue deferring to the president on many budgetary matters. Given the members' distaste for making difficult decisions that might alienate them from their constituents and strip them of their individual power bases, the future will probably hold more instances of deadlock between the president and Congress on this critical area of national policy—the annual budget.

Whether the 1974 congressional Budget and Impoundment Control Act constituted the revolutionary piece of legislation that its advocates promised, it certainly was an attempt to recapture legislative authority over the budget and discipline a president who had disregarded congressional policy mandates. As one constitutional scholar has observed, both the 1974 Budget Act and the 1973 War Powers Act "constitute structural legislation . . . of great significance in the constitutional evolution of legislative-executive relations in both domestic and foreign policy." [27]

The Balanced Budget and Emergency Deficit Control Act: Symbolism or Substance?

The 1980s saw federal spending continue unabated. Throughout the Reagan years, both Congress and the president had very different views of what needed to be done to curtail runaway federal spending. As noted earlier, the Democratic Congress pushed for increased taxes to cover federal expenses, along with cuts in the defense budget. The president lobbied for cuts in domestic spending and against any new taxation. It probably makes little sense to criticize only one institution for the budgetary woes of the 1980s. They both contributed to political deadlock and failure. The public probably saw Congress as more guilty of fiscal irresponsibility, in part because the Reagan administration was able to convince the public that massive federal deficits were the fault primarily of an irresponsible, spendthrift Congress. The irony is that Ronald Reagan campaigned for the presidency in 1980, and for reelection in 1984, on a platform of curtailing the enormous appetite of the federal spending machine. Throughout his tenure in the White House, he advocated the need for a balanced budget amendment to the Constitution and executive authority to veto specific items in budget legislation that he considered unnecessary or irresponsible. And yet his administration saw the national debt double from $914 billion in FY80 to $1.84 trillion in FY85, and the federal budget deficit grow from $60 billion in FY80 to $220 billion in FY85. The primary factors contributing to this fiscal explosion have been the 1981 federal tax cut, the growth in defense spending, and the inability to reduce the rate of growth in domestic spending—particularly Social Security, Medicare, entitlements for a large percentage of American citizens, and pensions for civilian and military personnel. By the end of the first Reagan term, these mounting federal deficits and the limited success of the 1974 Budget Impoundment and Control Act occasioned an unusual display of consensus between Congress and the Reagan White House to finally move on the deficit problem.

In the fall of 1985, Congress passed by overwhelming margins the Balanced Budget and Emergency Deficit Control Act, otherwise known as the Gramm-Rudman-Hollings Act, in deference to the three primary authors of the bill in the Senate. As the title implies, the act was intended to eliminate the federal budget deficit. It required that the deficit be reduced by $36 billion in each of the five fiscal years up to FY91 (FY86-$171 billion; FY87-$144 billion; FY88-$108 billion; FY89-$72 billion; FY90-$36 billion; and FY91-zero).[28] If in any fiscal year, the estimated budget deficit exceeded the maximum allowable amount, the act required across-the-board cuts in federal spending to reach the targeted deficit levels, with one-half the reductions coming from domestic programs and one-half from the defense budget. The act also exempted several major programs (Social Security, Medicare, parts of the defense budget) from mandatory cuts.

These automatic reductions were to be accomplished each year through a rather complicated process. The directors of the Office of Management and Budget (OMB) and the Congressional Budget Office (CBO) would estimate the size of the federal deficit for the upcoming fiscal year. If that estimated deficit exceeded the targeted amount, then the OMB and the CBO were to determine the necessary reductions in each program in order to meet the maximum deficit amount. The directors of these two offices would then report the deficit estimates and the necessary cuts to the comptroller general. The comptroller general would report his conclusions and budget reductions to the president, who in turn was to issue an order requiring that the necessary budget cuts be executed. The Gramm-Rudman-Hollings Act also contained a "fall-back" provision for reducing the federal deficit in the event that the procedure just outlined was declared unconstitutional. This safety valve allowed for the estimated deficit forecasts and recommended cuts prepared by the OMB and the CBO to be submitted directly to a conference committee, which would report out a joint resolution to be voted on by Congress and submitted to the president for signing. This latter procedure would then become the mandated deficit reduction schedule to implement.

President Reagan signed Gramm-Rudman-Hollings into law on December 12, 1985, with much fanfare. But a few members of Congress, including Rep. Mike Synar (D-Okla.) and eleven others, took issue with the legislation and insisted that Congress had abdicated its power over federal spending and breached constitutional prescriptions. They filed suit in district court, claiming that the law violated the separation-of-powers principle embodied in the Constitution. The lower courts found the law unconstitutional and the case was appealed to the Supreme Court in the spring of 1986.

On July 7, 1986, the Supreme Court ruled by a 7–2 vote in *Bowsher* v. *Synar* (1986) that if the CBO and the OMB were unable to meet the deficit targets, the safety mechanism for reducing the budget deficit was unconstitutional because it encroached upon the president's authority to execute the law. The Court ruled that the provision giving the comptroller general executive power to estimate, allocate, and mandate the necessary budget cuts was illegal. As an officer of the Congress who is subject to removal by that body, the comptroller general could not carry out executive functions dealing with the annual budget. In tones reminiscent of *Chadha,* Chief Justice Burger wrote in the majority opinion that "to permit an officer controlled by Congress to execute the laws would be, in essence, to permit a congressional veto." Noting that the "dangers of congressional usurpation of Executive Branch functions have long been recognized," Burger said that Congress's intention to reduce the deficit could not be realized by resorting to an unconstitutional device. As the majority opinion noted:

> By placing the responsibility for execution of the Balanced Budget and Emergency Deficit Control Act in the hands of an officer who is subject to removal only by itself, Congress in effect has retained control over the execution of the act and has intruded into the executive function. The Constitution does not permit such intrusion.

As one of the two justices who dissented in *Bowsher,* Justice White, who had also dissented in *Chadha,* assailed the concurring members of the Court as "misguided" and chastised them for their "distressingly formalistic view of separation of powers." White was dismayed that the Court was here invalidating "one of the most novel and far-reaching responses to a national crisis since the New Deal." Several commentaries on the budgetary process since the *Bowsher* decision indicate that the ability of Congress and the president to avoid recurring crises over budgetary policy is still very questionable.[29]

One of the troubling questions that remains after the *Bowsher* decision is consistency in rationale. Ever since the *Schecter* decision in 1935, when the Supreme Court struck down the National Industrial Recovery Act, the Court has rather consistently upheld broad delegations of power to bureaucratic officials by Congress, even though that body retained ultimate authorizing and budgetary control over those officials. If the Court saw fit to strike down the Gramm-Rudman provision relying upon the comptroller general for deficit reduction as a separation-of-powers violation, then similar delegations of authority to all independent regulatory agencies would also seem to violate the same separate-powers doctrine.

In late 1986, Congress and the president were far apart on how best to meet the Gramm-Rudman-Hollings deficit reduction targets. With a president adamantly opposed to a tax increase and a Congress insisting that defense spending must be slowed, the chances of meeting the deficit targets seemed remote. Following the November election, which found the Democrats regaining control of the Senate for the first time in six years, the first session of the 100th Congress through 1987 indicated little improvement in congressional-presidential relations.

The Ayatollah and the Contras: The White House and the Congress Again at Odds

No sooner had the election returns been recorded when another political bombshell—the Iran-contra affair—began to dominate the news. Against established policy and without the approval of Congress, executive branch officials sold millions of dollars of arms to the Ayatollah Khomeini in order to persuade Iran to use its influence with terrorists holding American hostages in Beirut. To make matters worse, proceeds from these arms sales had apparently been diverted through secret Swiss bank accounts to the contras fighting the Sandinista regime in Nicaragua. Congress learned of these developments in November 1986, and televised hearings began in the summer of 1987. President Reagan vehemently claimed to have initiated the arms deal with "moderate" forces in Iran, but insisted that it was not an arms-for-hostages exchange. Throughout the summer, Reagan also insisted that he knew nothing about the diversion of monies from the arms sales to fund the contras in Nicaragua. Lt. Col. Oliver North, chief operative in the National Security Council (NSC) managing the arms sales and the diversion, claimed that he had always assumed that his orders to continue the operations came from the president. But Admiral John Poindexter, director of the NSC, stated that he had never informed the president of the diversion. The other key figure in the Iran-contra affair, William Casey, director of the Central Intelligence Agency, died of a brain tumor in 1987 before the hearings started and never divulged any incriminating evidence against presidential misbehavior. As a result, the proverbial search for a smoking gun directly implicating the president proved fruitless. As the hearings ended in late August, the president had suffered considerably in public opinion polls from the nagging question, paraphrased from the Watergate era, "What didn't he know, and why didn't he know it?" Federal prosecutions of individuals implicated in the Iran-contra affair, including Poindexter and North, brought to a climax judicial consideration by the Supreme Court of the special prosecutor law from post-Watergate days (see Brief 5.5).

Conclusion

A major idea contained in this chapter is that historically, and especially in the twentieth century, the gradual expansion in executive authority has had both positive and negative consequences for representative government. Since 1787, American presidents have acted independently in many instances to protect national interests in time of national crisis and when the Congress has been unable or unwilling institutionally to deal with the demands of the moment. The *Curtiss-Wright* case in 1936 found the Supreme Court recognizing certain "inherent powers" of the president as the chief foreign policy official of the United States. The Japanese Internment Cases in the 1940s also found the same president acting with the consent of Congress, although Roosevelt acted first and consulted with Congress later. When President Truman tried to act independently in the Steel Seizure Case of 1951, the Supreme Court intervened and denied him the inherent power to act without consulting Congress. But collectively, these several cases greatly legitimized emergency powers

❏ Brief 5.5   The Special Prosecutor Law: Who Will Guard the Guardians?

In the aftermath of the Watergate scandal (see Brief 5.2), Congress passed a so-called "special prosecutor law" as part of the Ethics in Government Act in 1978. The law was intended to shield investigations of high-level executive branch officials suspected of wrong-doing from presidential control. Amended in 1982 and 1987, the independent counsel provision, as it is now called, requires the attorney general to conduct a preliminary investigation of any allegations that certain high-ranking executive officials may have committed a crime. The attorney general may then request a special panel composed of three federal appellate judges to appoint an independent counsel to complete the investigation and prosecute the case if allegations prove substantial. The independent counsel can only be removed "for good cause."

On June 29, 1988, the Supreme Court, in a landmark separation-of-powers decision, upheld the constitutionality of the independent counsel law by a convincing 7–1 vote. The case of *Morrison* v. *Olson* dates from 1982 and a dispute then raging between Congress and the embattled Environmental Protection Agency (EPA). Members of Congress wanted the EPA to turn over documents concerning the clean-up of toxic waste dumps. Theodore Olson, an assistant attorney general at the Department of Justice, advised the EPA administrator, Anne Gorsuch Burford, on orders from the president, to withhold the documents from Congress on executive privilege grounds. The House Judiciary Committee began investigating the incident, and Olson testified before the committee in March 1983. In a 1985 report on the affair, the Judiciary Committee accused Olson of giving false and misleading testimony to the committee and requested that an independent counsel be appointed to investigate allegations of possible wrongdoing.

By May 1986, Alexia Morrison had been named as the independent counsel in the case. In 1987, a federal grand jury issued subpoenas ordering Olson to testify and to produce documents needed in the investigation. Olson refused to do so, filing a motion to quash the subpoenas and claiming that the independent counsel law was unconstitutional. In July 1987, a federal district court in Washington, D.C., upheld the constitutionality of the law, but in January 1988, another three-judge panel from the U.S. Court of Appeals of the District of Columbia ruled 2–1 (with two Reagan appointees in the majority) that the law was an unconstitutional transfer of executive authority to the courts by Congress.

In one of the most anxiously awaited judgments of its 1987–88 term, the Rehnquist Court somewhat surprisingly gave little importance to the administration's position that the law infringed upon executive power. In the majority opinion, the chief justice first focused upon Article II, Section 2, of the Constitution—the Appointments Clause—and noted that the initial question was whether the independent counsel is an "inferior" official who can be appointed by a congressionally devised procedure or a "principal" official who must be nominated by the president and confirmed by the Senate. Rehnquist concluded the former because the person (1) can be removed "for good cause" by the attorney general, (2) performs limited duties of investigation and prosecution, and (3) exercises only limited jurisdiction while investigating certain prescribed officials. The chief justice said that the act did not violate the separation-of-powers principle by unduly interfering with the executive branch. Unlike other cases involving the legislative veto and the Gramm-Rudman-Hollings Act, he said that the law "does not involve an attempt by Congress to increase its own powers at the expense of the executive branch." Nor does it try to usurp any "properly executive functions." Although it does give a federal court the power to review an attorney general's decision to remove an independent counsel, Rehnquist argued that this is a function well within the traditional power of the judiciary.

The lone dissenter in the *Morrison* case was Justice Antonin Scalia, who authored a scorching thirty-eight-page dissent insisting that the law seriously infringed upon executive authority and the separation-of-powers principle. Scalia's main objection was that the law gives investigative and prosecuting duties to the independent counsel, which he insists are purely *executive* duties accorded the president. According to Scalia, "We should say . . . that the President's constitutionally assigned duties include complete control over investigation and prosecution of violations of the law."

As the Watergate scandal of the early 1970s and possibly the Iran-contra affair of the 1980s may indicate, the question arises as to who will watch those charged with faithfully executing the law. Even in a constitutional democracy that applies the rule of law to official conduct, some procedures must exist to "guard the guardians," to paraphrase the ancient Roman satirist Juvenal. *Morrison* v. *Olson,* an important precedent, says that Congress can legislate to guard at least some of them.

deeded by Congress to the president for use in crisis management and diminished congressional control of presidential authority.

Executive power has also grown with the increased legitimacy of executive privilege and the use of executive agreements. Although *United States* v. *Nixon* established that even presidents do not have unlimited authority to abuse their public trust and tremendous power, they still have virtually unlimited opportunities to use their power and influence to achieve personal ends, and the system does not automatically take over to deny them that authority. Had there been no White House tapes, the Watergate scandal might well never have been uncovered. The increased use of executive agreements also reflects how modern American presidents have sought to avoid the "auxiliary precaution" of the ratification of treaties by the U.S. Senate. With the more extensive global responsibilities of the United States in foreign affairs in recent decades, the increasing fragmentation of power in Congress and the prevalence of divided government where one party controls Congress and another the White House, presidents have resorted to executive agreements to cement bilateral relations with foreign powers. The consequence has been for both branches to have quite different views of United States foreign policy, and the "advice and consent" of Article II has declined as an instrument for forging a bipartisan foreign policy.

In spite of the framers' efforts to make Congress the bedrock of representative government and a key check upon the executive branch, the twentieth century has seen the "people's branch" of American government cede more and more of its authority to the executive branch. Congressional war power and control of federal spending have been eclipsed by the actions of successive American presidents. Since 1945, the United States has found itself drawn into numerous foreign conflicts in defense of American interests around the world. On most occasions, this global defense of national interests has found the United States in direct opposition to various Communist regimes. The prolonged American involvement in Vietnam during the 1960s and 1970s was a good example of how the United States allowed itself to be drawn more and more deeply into a civil conflict between two different ideologies and models for development in postcolonial Indochina. The decade-long escalation of that involvement found three American presidents, with congressional authorization in most instances, attempting to prevent a Communist takeover of South Vietnam. The War Powers Act of 1973 reflected both congressional and public opposition to that war and the strategies of two presidents to prevail at all costs. The legislation found Congress acting to regain more control over the process by which the United States commits military personnel and materiel in pursuit of national interests.

Escalation in governmental spending also found Congress and several presidents in frequent conflict over national priorities. The result was a federal budgetary process that seemed unable to turn back endless requests for funding constituent demands. When the Budget Impoundment and Control Act of 1974 proved unable to curtail federal spending, Congress passed legislation in 1985 designed to force Congress and the president to make mandatory cuts in federal spending. A major message of the *Bowsher* v. *Synar* decision by the Supreme Court in 1986 is that neither institution can escape the normal lawmaking requirement of both houses of Congress agreeing to and the president signing the authorizing legislation.

Presidential consultation with Congress is essential to successful policy-making in American government. In recent years, a heightened and frustrating adversial relationship has developed between the two branches, which has seriously detracted from responsible policy-making at the federal level. The Vietnam War, the Watergate scandal, and, more recently, the Iran-contra debacle have all increased distrust between the two elected branches of the government. Both the White House and Congress represent the American people, admittedly in very different ways and with different incentives and rewards. But they both must act *together* to govern the nation in a wise and just manner.

A common ingredient in the escalation of the Vietnam War, the Watergate scandal, and the Iran-contra mishap was a president's refusal to recognize that he cannot go it alone, at least not for very long, without jeopardizing long-term policy objectives. Presidents may be able to prevail in the short term in order to achieve their immediate aims, but if they circumvent the democratic processes built into the system by the framers, which require consultation with Congress and communication with the American people, they are risking ultimate defeat for those policy goals. One reason that the framers two centuries ago checked power with power was because they realized that it was much better to have a president *limited* in the capacity to achieve only those goals acceptable to the people and their representatives, than it was to allow a president with *unlimited* power to achieve goals that were unacceptable to the people. If a president's power to persuade is inadequate to convince Congress and the electorate of the rightness of the cause, then that program is illegitimate in a purely democratic sense. Process counts for a great deal in the American constitutional system, which recent presidents seem to have forgotten. Unless the American people can be convinced of the virtue of a chosen policy, whether it deals with either domestic or foreign affairs, it has no place in a democratic system. Ultimately, if a representative government that is based upon a Jeffersonian faith in the people makes serious errors in selecting the right policy, then it is the people themselves who are to be blamed, as much as it is the leaders for insisting that they know what is "right" in all situations. Self-government compels a people to debate the major issues of the time, and to do so openly, honestly, and thoroughly. If they cannot act accordingly, if they cannot trust each other to arrive at proximate solutions to difficult issues, then a populace can never lay claim to democratic self-government.

Not only have relations between the two elected branches in American government reflected great tension and turmoil, but, as the next two chapters will indicate, relations between levels of government in the American federal system have not always been smooth either. But unlike the topics of judicial review and separated power, the theory and practice of federalism find the United States contributing a somewhat unique concept to modern-day government.

Questions   1. Those who drafted the Constitution envisioned a careful partnership between the president and Congress in both domestic and foreign policy, with each checking the other. But the modern era has drastically altered this original design, and the Constitution has been reinterpreted to accommodate these changes. To what extent does the modern presidency differ from the ideas of the framers?

2. How have executive privilege and the increasing use of executive agreements affected the spirit of openness and cooperation between Congress and the president? Has the Constitution been ignored by these recent practices, or do they logically flow from the framers' intent for an energetic chief executive?

3. Although the investigative powers of Congress are essential to the drafting of effective public policy in several areas, history indicates that this power to inquire and interrogate can be abused and result in both distrust in government and delay in addressing the public's problems. What parameters do you think should guide the exercise by Congress of its power to investigate?

4. During the 1970s, Congress finally sought to reassert itself as a co-equal branch of American government, with some success in budgetary and foreign policy development. But problems have continued to plague American government in these two areas in particular. What changes in congressional-presidential relations would ensure more responsible action with regard to budgetary policy? What changes would facilitate more cooperation between the two branches in foreign affairs?

5. A precedent flowing from the *Korematsu* decision is that an identifiable minority can be deprived of its liberty without due process and in times of national emergency. Given the mounting disease and death figures associated with the AIDS epidemic in the United States (54,000 diagnosed cases and over 30,000 deaths by February 1988), is there likely to be a similar quarantine and internment of AIDS patients through executive order? Has the American system of justice and protection for civil liberties advanced enough to prevent a similar forced relocation?

Endnotes

1. James Bryce, *The American Commonwealth* (London: Macmillan & Co., Ltd., 1896), 14.

2. See Arthur M. Schlesinger, Jr., *The Imperial Presidency* (Boston: Houghton Mifflin, 1973); Nathan Glazar, "Toward an Imperial Judiciary," *The Public Interest* 41 (1975): 104–23.

3. John Locke, *The Second Treatise of Government,* sec. 149, ed. Peter Laslett (New York: Cambridge University Press, 1960), 412–13.

4. See C. Herman Pritchett, *The Federal System in Constitutional Law* (Englewood Cliffs, N.J.: Prentice-Hall, 1978).

5. The phrase "ordered liberty" comes from Justice Benjamin Cardozo's majority opinion in *Palko* v. *Connecticut* (1937).

6. See Richard E. Neustadt, *Presidential Power: The Politics of Leadership* (New York: Wiley, 1960), 3; Michael D. Reagan, *The New Federalism* (New York: Oxford University Press, 1972), 3–28; Frank M. Coleman, *Politics, Policy, and the Constitution* (New York: St. Martin's Press, 1982), 25–30.

7. Quotations from James Madison appear in *The Federalist Papers* (New York: Modern Library, 1937).

8. Harry A. Bailey, Jr., and Jay M. Shafritz, eds., *The American Presidency: Historical and Contemporary Perspectives* (Chicago: Dorsey Press, 1988), vii.

9. John C. Hamilton, *Works of Alexander Hamilton* (New York: C.S. Francis and Co., 1851), 76.

10. Phillip R. Fondall, ed., *Letters and Other Writings of James Madison* (Philadelphia: J.P Lippincott, 1865), 621.

11. Theodore Roosevelt, *Autobiography* (New York: Macmillan, 1913), 389.

12. William Safire, *The New Language of Politics* (New York: Collier Books, 1972), 79–80.

13. Laurence H. Tribe, *American Constitutional Law* (Mineola, N.Y.: Foundation Press, 1978), 157.

14. William Safire, "Tug of War," *New York Times Magazine,* September 13, 1987, 66.

15. Quotations are from *New York Times,* April 21, 1988, sec. A, 1.

16. Julie Johnson, "President Signs Law to Redress Wartime Wrong," *The New York Times,* August 11, 1988, p. A1; 8.

17. Theodore J. Lowi, *The End of Liberalism,* 2d ed. (New York: Norton, 1979).

18. Louis Fisher, *Constitutional Conflicts Between Congress and the President* (Princeton, N.J.: Princeton University Press, 1985), 300.

19. Woodrow Wilson, *Congressional Government* (Boston: Houghton Mifflin, 1885), 303.

20. Walter Lippmann, *Public Opinion* (New York: Harcourt, Brace and Co., 1922), 289.

21. *Barenblatt* v. *United States,* 360 U.S. 109 (1959).

22. Alexander Hamilton, *The Federalist Papers,* 423.

23. Anthony Lewis, "An Ingenious Structure," *New York Times Magazine,* September 13, 1987, 41.

24. The author of these terms is V. O. Key, *Public Opinion and American Democracy* (New York: Knopf, 1961), 29–39. For an excellent chronicle of the prolonged war in Southeast Asia, from the defeat of the French to the eventual withdrawal of all American forces from Saigon in 1975, see Stanley Karnow, *Vietnam: A History* (New York: Penguin Books, 1984).

25. See Christopher Madison, "A Reflagged Policy," *National Journal* 19 (1987): 3026–30.

26. Allen Schick, *Congress and Money: Budgeting, Spending and Taxing* (Washington, D.C.: Urban Institute, 1980), 313, 330, 469–70, 475–81.

27. Tribe, *American Constitutional Law,* 198.

28. These targeted figures are noted in "Congress Enacts Far-Reaching Budget Measures," *Congressional Quarterly Weekly Report* 43 (1985): 2604–11.

29. See Donald Elliott, "Regulating the Deficit After Bowsher," *Yale Journal of Regulation* 4 (Spring 1987): 317–62; and Alfred C. Amar, Jr., et al., "Symposium: *Bowsher* v. *Synar,*" *Cornell Law Review* 72 (1987): 421–597.

Suggested Readings

Dodd, Lawrence C., and Bruce I. Oppenheimer, eds. *Congress Reconsidered.* 3d ed. Washington, D.C.: Congressional Quarterly Press, 1985.

Edwards, George C., III. *Presidential Influence in Congress.* San Francisco: Freeman, 1980.

Fisher, Louis. *The Politics of Shared Power: Congress and the Executive.* Washington, D.C.: Congressional Quarterly Press, 1981.

Henkin, Louis. "Foreign Affairs and the Constitution." *Foreign Affairs* 66 (Winter 1987–88): 284–310.

Margolis, Lawrence. *Executive Agreements and Presidential Power in Foreign Policy.* New York: Praeger, 1986.

Oleszek, Walter J. *Congressional Procedures and the Policy Process.* 2d ed. Washington, D.C.: Congressional Quarterly Press, 1983.

Pyle, Christopher H., and Richard M. Pious. *The President, Congress and the Constitution.* New York: Free Press, 1984.

Rockman, Bert A. *The Leadership Question: The Presidency and the American System.* New York: Praeger, 1984.

Schick, Allen, et al. *Crisis in the Budget Process.* Washington, D.C.: American Enterprise Institute, 1986.

Schlesinger, Arthur M., Jr. *The Imperial Presidency.* Boston: Houghton Mifflin, 1973.

6

Federalism: Theory and Development

Syllabus

Alexis de Tocqueville, the young Frenchman who traveled America in 1831 and 1832, found much that he admired in the United States. He saw particular promise for the American system of federalism. In his writings about the young country, Tocqueville proclaimed that Americans seemed to have a natural affinity for the federal system through their ability to easily separate national from state matters:

> I scarcely ever met with a plain American citizen who could not distinguish with surprising facility the obligations created by the laws of Congress from those created by the laws of his own state, and who . . . could not point out the exact limit of the separate jurisdictions of the Federal courts and the tribunals of the state.[1]

Identifying and separating federal and state matters have not been quite as easy as Tocqueville suggested. In fact, the history of American federalism is more one of disagreement than of agreement over the proper limits of federal and state jurisdictions. As recently as 1956, nineteen senators and seventy-seven representatives from southern states opposed to the Supreme Court's *Brown v. Board of Education* (1954) decision signed *The Southern Manifesto: A Declaration of Constitutional Principles,* in which they stated: "We decry the Supreme Court's encroachments on rights reserved to the States and to the people, contrary to established law, and to the Constitution."[2] Perhaps Tocqueville was correct in one sense. Most Americans can identify the limits of federal and state power—they simply cannot agree on them.

This Chapter Examines the Following Matters

☐ Federalism is a system of government practiced in a number of the world's nations. It offers both advantages and disadvantages.

☐ The origins of American federalism rest in the colonial experience, the Articles of Confederation, and a general suspicion of centralized power.

☐ The debate between advocates of national supremacy—such as Alexander Hamilton and Chief Justice John Marshall—and the supporters of states' rights—such as Thomas Jefferson and later John C. Calhoun—shaped the direction of federalism in the American experience.

☐ The Civil War solidified American federalism and gave rise to the Thirteenth, Fourteenth, and Fifteenth Amendments. The Fourteenth Amendment has been particularly significant for federalism.

☐ Later stages of federalism have witnessed the rapid growth of national power, especially in areas concerned with revenue raising and regulatory policies. The changes associated with the federal income tax (Sixteenth Amendment) and the New Deal policies of the 1930s and 1940s have been pivotal.

☐ Contemporary federalism involves a series of cross-cutting and overlapping intergovernmental relations (IGR), necessitating numerous grant and revenue programs at all levels of government. The quest for a "new federalism" by recent presidential administrations shows that the debate over federalism has not subsided.

Photo: The federal structure created by the Constitution has produced continuous debate between those advocates of states' rights and those of national supremacy. The view from state capitals like this one in Little Rock, Arkansas, is one of increasing erosion of power to the national government.

The Theory of Federalism

The two preceding chapters have emphasized judicial review and the separation of powers, two of the most significant concepts in American constitutional government. These principles have provided distinct limits upon the power of government, as well as ensured some degree of protection for individual rights. In this chapter and the next, a third key principle of constitutional practice is presented. This principle, termed **federalism,** lies at the root of the American experience.

The framers of the U.S. Constitution settled upon federalism as a means of creating the kind of strong national government not found in the Articles of Confederation. At the same time, federalism limited that same national government by vesting significant authority in the established state governments. As a result, American constitutional development often has revolved around competing views of government power. Nationalists of the founding era, exemplified by Alexander Hamilton, drew attention to the need for a strong central government. Hamilton saw this need as especially acute in matters of defense, commerce, and foreign relations. James Madison, another early nationalist whose views later shifted toward states' rights, emphasized the fact that a federal arrangement would enable state governments to protect the liberty of their citizens by virtue of their close proximity to the people.

Federalism has produced disagreement over the exact location of **sovereignty,** or ultimate authority, in the nation. Advocates of national supremacy, or a strong central government, have been challenged by supporters of states' rights and, on occasion, state sovereignty. Although these disagreements normally could be settled peacefully through court decisions, legislation, or political compromise, they occasionally led Americans into conflict. Indeed, the massive destruction of the Civil War stands as the most obvious monument to the divisive tendencies contained in federalism. And yet, the Civil War experience actually resulted in a much strengthened federal system by removing extreme state sovereignty as a valid constitutional position.

In this chapter, the historical and theoretical underpinnings of federalism will be examined, with special emphasis upon the contributions made by prominent Americans of several different eras. The early debates between nationalists such as Alexander Hamilton and Chief Justice John Marshall and states' righters such as Thomas Jefferson paved the way for variations on the federalism theme. This chapter will explore these variations, ranging from the state sovereignty of John C. Calhoun, through the dual federalism of Chief Justice Roger B. Taney, to twentieth-century developments that have added further to an understanding of this truly "made in America" phenomenon—the idea of federalism. However, before an analysis of American federalism is undertaken, it will prove helpful to examine the concept from a comparative perspective.

Federalism: A Comparative Perspective

Federalism is an arrangement in which a constitution formally establishes and divides powers between a national government and "subnational" (usually state or provincial) governments. Both governments are supreme within their proper sphere of authority, and both act directly on the same people. Therefore, the first characteristic of a federal system is that it guarantees at least two levels of governmental power. This can be contrasted to what is sometimes called a unitary system of government, in which one central government has complete sovereignty. Although local governments exist in a unitary system, they do so at the pleasure of the central government and possess only those powers granted to them by central authorities. In a federal system, on the other hand, states or provinces are constitutionally empowered to act in certain areas, free from national control.[3] Such an arrangement contains the likelihood of disagreement and conflict, as both national and state authorities may claim the same powers. This potential for disagreement and conflict may be considered a second characteristic of federal systems. Obviously, when two (or more) governments claim the same powers, the resulting conflict is likely to require a compromise of some sort. As long as compromise solutions are seen as possible and desirable by both national and state governments, the federal system can work through its problems. When compromise fails, as occurred in the United States as a prelude to the Civil War, the federal system may dissolve.

Since federalism was instituted in the United States nearly two hundred years ago, several other countries have adopted some version of the system (see Table 6.1). The gradual expansion of federal systems points up several related strengths and weaknesses of this division of governmental powers. In the first place, federalism appears to be quite popular among geographically large nations. Five of the world's six largest states—including the Soviet Union, India, Canada, Brazil, and the United States—have established some form of a federal system. Even though these countries place varying degrees of emphasis

Table 6.1   Federalism in Comparative Perspective

COUNTRY	FEDERAL UNITS*	MAJOR LANGUAGES	PRIMARY REASON FOR FEDERALISM	EXTENT OF STATES' POWER
USSR	15 Republics	Several	Nationalities/size	Weak
Brazil	27 States	One	Size/Colonial History	Weak
Canada	10 Provinces	Two	Size/Language	Moderate
India	22 States	Many	Language/Size	Moderate
USA	50 States	One	Colonial Heritage/Size	Moderate
Mexico	32 States	One	Colonial Administration/Size	Weak
Nigeria	19 States	Several	Tribalism/Size/Language/Colonialism	Weak-Moderate
Switzerland	26 Cantons	Several	History/Language	Strong
West Germany	10 States	One	Postwar Occupation/Regionalism	Strong
Yugoslavia	6 Republics	Several	Language/Ethnicity/Religion	Moderate

*For some countries, state totals may include federal districts and/or other types of subdivisions.

upon their federal systems (e.g., the Soviet system of republics is actually run by central party authorities), each has found federalism a useful way of governing a massive territory. The premise at work here suggests that federal systems are better than centralized systems for large areas, because the state (province, republic) governments can keep government closer to the people. Therefore, one perceived advantage of federalism seems to be in its ability to reduce the problems of distance in governing.

A second common pattern associated with the spread of federal systems in the twentieth century is the use of federalism to deal with various sources of diversity among a population. Factors such as ethnicity, language, and religion have plagued many newly independent states seeking to build themselves into nations. For example, the founders of India, facing an incredibly diverse linguistic pattern, discovered state governments to be the answer to such diversity. In Nigeria, the tribalism of the population seemed to suggest federalism as a natural solution, although the results have been less than spectacular. The Soviet Union might not even bother with a confusing federal system were it not for the maze of nationalities surrounding the Russian core. In short, federalism appears attractive to leaders seeking to deal with diversity while hoping for national unity.[4]

A third pattern of federalism can be traced to colonial practices of establishing territorial divisions to assist in administration. The Portuguese in Brazil and Spaniards in Mexico showed a tendency toward this type of arrangement. Among former British colonies, India and Nigeria stand out as examples of colonial administrative districts forming the basis for later federalism. In both India and Nigeria, the eventual states generally represented different language and ethnic groups. American federalism certainly owes a debt to British colonial practices, as the colonies eventually formed the original thirteen states. However, America differs from other former British colonies in that American colonies were settled much more individually, for varying reasons, and over a considerably longer time span.

Origins of American Federalism

Federalism falls somewhere between the centralization of a unitary system and the decentralization of a confederation. As discussed in Chapter 3, early settlers to America had experienced unitary government in England. In that arrangement, all power stemmed from the Crown and rested in the king and British Parliament. Laws regarding the entire British Empire were enacted in London, and the sovereignty of the Crown was indivisible. American colonies, despite attempts at some self-government, were clearly subject to the power of the Crown and Parliament. Naturally, since the unitary experience had culminated in revolution, there was little support among Americans for a unitary system of their own following independence.

In fact, early American leaders went first to the other extreme—a confederation—in their search for a workable governmental system. A **confederation** is a loose grouping of autonomous units with final authority, or sovereignty, resting in the individual units themselves. Central authority, to the degree that it exists, is subject to the overall sovereignty of the states which constitute it. For newly independent Americans in the late 1770s, such an arrangement was far superior to the centralized and, in their view, tyrannical British unitary system.

As Chapter 3 showed, the Articles of Confederation represented a clear departure from the centralization of a unitary system. National power was regarded as potentially dangerous, so the answer lay in creating as little of it as possible. The resulting arrangement, although often viewed as a failure by recent observers, was precisely what architects of the Articles had envisioned— a loosely bound confederation of sovereign and independent states. Despite their shortcomings, the Articles left a legacy to American federalism in the area of interstate relations (see Brief 6.1).

The major critics of the Articles of Confederation were those who disapproved of such a weak national government, both in its dealings with the states and in matters of foreign affairs, trade, and defense. The Constitutional Convention produced a compromise between the centralization of a unitary system (which almost nobody wanted) and the extreme decentralization of a confederation. Federalism, as the result is called, was untested as a governmental arrangement, having never been used by another nation. Naturally, then, Americans found a good amount of uncertainty surrounding federalism. Where was sovereignty located? Could the national government exercise powers not expressly granted by the Constitution? Could states restrict the activities of the national government within their borders? Who possessed the final word in resolving disputes between the national and state governments? While the formal divisions between Federalists and Anti-Federalists did not exist until after the Constitutional Convention, the Philadelphia delegates were at odds over the issue of governmental power, with some favoring a powerful national government and others pressing for continued state autonomy as practiced in

---

☐ *Brief 6.1   Horizontal Federalism: Legacy of the Articles of Confederation*

The Articles of Confederation established the importance of state-to-state relations and provided for specific areas of cooperation and "comity," or friendship. Drawn almost exactly as written in the Articles, these provisions were incorporated in the new Constitution as Article IV. This **horizontal federalism** among states contains three key elements:

1. *Full Faith and Credit Clause:* Each state must give "Full Faith and Credit" to the public acts, records, and judicial proceedings of the other states. This means, for example, that a marriage license or birth certificate obtained in one state is recognized as legal and authentic in another state. However, certain problems have been encountered in the area of divorce, especially in uncontested divorces obtained in other states. (See *Williams* v. *North Carolina* [1945].)

2. *Privileges and Immunities Clause:* This prohibits one state from abridging the "Privileges and Immunities" of citizens of the United States. Essentially, this means that a citizen of one state cannot

be discriminated against in another state, especially in areas such as legal protection, access to courts, property rights, and travel. However, it should be noted that privileges-and-immunities protections do not extend to certain political rights, such as voting, nor to some privileges reserved to a state's own citizens. The college student quickly will recognize out-of-state tuition at state universities as such an exception.

3. *Extradition:* **Extradition,** a term from international law, refers to the practice of returning escaped prisoners or persons wanted in another state. Although the Constitution places an obligation upon states to extradite wanted persons, federal courts will not order a state governor to do so. On rare occasions a governor has refused to comply with an extradition request, but the request generally is expected to be honored on moral grounds. (Also, of course, the next time it may be the other state that is making the request for extradition.)

the Articles of Confederation. From the two broad positions—one nationalist (Federalist), the other states' rights (Anti-Federalist)—was to come the basis for the federal system of the United States.

Nationalist Versus States' Rights Constitutional Perspectives

Prior to examining the Federalist and Anti-Federalist positions in detail, it may be helpful to review the constitutional basis for their differences. First, the national government holds those powers enumerated or delegated to it by the Constitution. These grants of authority center on Congress and are listed in Article I, Section 8. Although even enumerated powers are subject to considerable interpretation (see, for example, the discussion concerning commerce in the next chapter), their existence is conceded by even the most staunch opponent of national governmental power. Where nationalists and states' righters differ is in the manner of interpreting these powers. For the states' rights interpretation, the answer lies in the Tenth Amendment, added to the Constitution in 1791:

> The powers not delegated to the United States by the Constitution, nor prohibited by it to the States, are reserved to the States respectively, or to the people.

In other words, a states' rights vision of federalism shows a subordinate national government with only enumerated powers—all other powers being "reserved" to the states. Under this reasoning, the Constitution must be interpreted narrowly and strictly, making certain that the national government does not overstep its written authority and intrude upon the vast areas reserved to state control. The states' rights view complements the Anti-Federalist position that, if government is to be responsive to the popular will, government power ought to be lodged in units closest to the people. This early communitarian perspective—found among many Anti-Federalists—rested upon the belief that state governments were more likely to protect basic democratic values.

States' righters even hold a different idea of the nature of the Constitution itself. In their view, the Constitution is a compact among the original states that created the national government and gave it certain limited powers. Under this premise, the national government is an agent of the states, subject to their ultimate control and prohibited from interfering in their affairs. Any conflicts between national and state governments, of course, should be resolved in favor of the latter. As discussed in the next section, this "state compact" premise paved the way for several state attempts to resist national policies. Both views will now be examined in greater detail.

National Supremacy: The Federalist Position

For advocates of national supremacy, the Constitution is a supreme law stemming from "We the People of the United States," as stated in the Preamble, and not from sovereign states. As such, the nationalists, for their part, do not deny the existence of the states' reserved powers, but they differ substantially in their understanding of the powers delegated to the national government. Alexander Hamilton, an early nationalist spokesman, believed that the national government possessed powers implied from an interpretation of the Constitution. These "implied powers," as Hamilton argued, stem largely from the Necessary and Proper Clause in Article I, Section 8. Hamilton's assessment of government power angered and frightened his opponents, particularly when, as secretary of the treasury under President George Washington, he successfully pushed through a legislative program that rested heavily upon the **implied powers** of Congress. (See the discussion of implied powers in a later section of this chapter.)

The Federalists—supporters of national supremacy, broad constitutional construction, and implied powers—influenced the federal system in two stages. In the first, from 1789 to 1801, Federalists controlled the executive, legislative, and judicial branches of government. Predictably, attention was directed toward strengthening the national government, much of it under Hamilton's direction. The second phase, brought on by the failure of the Federalists to compete politically at the polls, might be considered to span from 1801 to 1835, precisely the years of John Marshall's chief justiceship on the Supreme Court. During this phase, the federalist perspective was essentially confined to the judicial branch while Congress and the president pursued different policies. As might be expected, the Supreme Court's decisions of this period were not always popular with the other branches.

Alexander Hamilton's view of federalism can be understood both from his writing before ratification and from his later actions as secretary of the treasury. In *Federalist No. 23*, Hamilton discussed four purposes served by the new Union: common defense, public peace, regulation of commerce, and foreign relations. To accomplish these ends, said Hamilton, it was necessary to establish a unified government. While Hamilton denied any intention to abolish the state governments, he did reject any attempt to divide national from state powers. To do so, he reasoned, would unnecessarily limit the freedom of action required by a supreme national government.

Federalists controlled the presidency until Jefferson's election in 1800, although their working majority in Congress had been lost somewhat earlier. Because the government was so new, however, the Federalists wielded the immense power of filling in the blanks in the Constitution at a time when few precedents existed. For this reason, it is important to examine some key developments of the Federalist era.

The Bill of Rights

To a number of Americans, the national government still posed a potential threat to certain freedoms and liberties. As mentioned in Chapter 3, the Anti-Federalists had pointed out the need for more specific limitations upon the national government, especially in its dealings with individuals. The eventual ratification of the Constitution ultimately rested upon a gentleman's agreement to add these protections to the Constitution.

However, on the matter of national supremacy and states' rights, the Bill of Rights had a negligible impact. The Tenth Amendment formally recognized what had been felt by most leaders all along, namely, that the powers not delegated to the national government were reserved to the states. Finally, since the Bill of Rights presumably did not limit the states (affirmed by the Supreme Court in *Barron* v. *Baltimore* [1833]; see Chapter 8), most Americans felt little effect from the changes, and states continued to deny many of the rights contained in the amendments. In short, the Bill of Rights seemed only marginally related to the issue of national supremacy and states' rights.[5]

The Judiciary Act of 1789

Beyond drafting the Bill of Rights, one of the chief tasks of the First Congress was to organize the federal judiciary. Since the constitutional basis of judicial power has been discussed previously, it is necessary at this point to focus only upon the issue directly related to federalism. The Judiciary Act of 1789, enacted by the First Congress, centered upon the establishment of federal courts, setting their size and number and spelling out jurisdiction when applicable.

The Judiciary Act also had a key impact upon the prevailing issue of national supremacy and states' rights. Certain states' rights advocates, fearful of federal power, had sought the use of state courts for hearing matters of national law. Since Article III of the Constitution requires only a Supreme Court, some individuals saw the possibility of limiting the federal judiciary to the Supreme Court alone. Under this arrangement, state courts would hear all cases involving federal law, excluding those over which the U.S. Supreme Court had original jurisdiction. However, supporters of national supremacy, predominantly Federalists, recognized the need for a federal judiciary separate from state influence.

The Judiciary Act of 1789 established this separate federal court system yet gave state courts concurrent jurisdiction in certain cases of federal law. The fundamental issue, however, involved the determination of final jurisdiction over federal law, a matter which the Constitutional Convention had left to a compromise of sorts. In Article VI, the Constitution, treaties, and national laws made in pursuance of the Constitution were declared to be the "supreme Law of the Land," but the "Judges in every State" were to be bound by this provision. Seemingly, it would be left to state courts to determine the supremacy of national law—a wholly unacceptable prospect for a Federalist. Now in control of the Congress, the Federalists saw less need to compromise over such an issue. Accordingly, Section 25 of the Judiciary Act reasserted the sovereignty of the national government by providing for the appeal of certain state court decisions to the Supreme Court. The act cited three instances in which appeal was possible:

1. When the state court ruled a federal treaty or law unconstitutional;
2. When a state court upheld a state law which had been alleged to conflict with the Constitution, treaties, or laws of the United States; or,
3. When a state court ruled against a right or privilege claimed under the Constitution or federal law.

As result of this provision, it could be inferred that final word on the constitutionality of federal law and the supremacy of the Constitution would henceforth come from the Supreme Court, not from the states themselves. The groundwork for national supremacy had been laid, although the debate would continue to rage until after the Civil War.

The Hamiltonian Economic Program

When the Federalists came to power in 1789, Alexander Hamilton was a logical choice for a key leadership position. Once Congress had created the executive departments of treasury, war, and state, President Washington chose Hamilton to be his secretary of the treasury. Since the secretary of the treasury was directed to furnish information to Congress, Hamilton in 1791 initiated a broad program of legislation upon which Congress subsequently took action. His proposals included refunding of the Articles of Confederation debt at face value, creation of a national bank by federal charter, and passage of a protective tariff for American industry. Of these, the latter two were to stir considerable controversy on constitutional grounds.

As a staunch Federalist, Hamilton was not troubled by the prospect of Congress creating a national bank, in spite of the fact that it possessed no enumerated power to do so. In fact, Hamilton argued that Congress possessed powers beyond those delegated to it by the Constitution. Of these, Hamilton placed his greatest emphasis upon the doctrine of implied powers, which, as he reasoned, stemmed from the clause in Article I, Section 8, giving Congress the authority to pass laws "necessary and proper" for carrying out its enumerated powers.

Chief opponents of the national bank, fearful of increasing national dominance of the economy, rallied behind James Madison (who had become disenchanted with Hamilton's program) and Hamilton's major ideological rival, Thomas Jefferson. As secretary of state until 1793, Jefferson was given an opportunity to express his views on the national bank, and his arguments became closely identified with a classic states' rights, Anti-Federalist position. These opposing views are expressed in Table 6.2.

Hamilton saw the bank as closely tied to several of Congress's enumerated powers relating to money and commerce, while Jefferson and Madison saw no such relationship. For Hamilton and the nationalists, the power to create a national bank could be implied as "necessary and proper" for carrying out congressional enumerated powers. The states' rights argument, on the other hand, by rejecting an enumerated power to create the bank, resorted to the Tenth Amendment's reservation of powers not delegated to the national government to the states. Hence, states legally might incorporate a bank, but not Congress. Finally, the two positions differed greatly on the issue of constitutional construction. At issue was the definition of "necessary," a term

Table 6.2   Federalists Versus Anti-Federalists: The National Bank

ISSUES	NATIONALISTS	STATES' RIGHTS
Leadership	Hamilton/Marshall	Jefferson/Madison
Enumerated powers related to bank	Taxation, coin money and regulate value thereof; regulation of commerce, etc.	No specific power
Constitutional authority	Necessary and Proper Clause	Tenth Amendment
Type of power	Implied	Reserved
Constitutional interpretation	Broad	Strict
Meaning of "necessary"	Convenient; useful; needful; incidental	Absolutely indispensable and essential

which Jefferson considered, when read strictly, to mean absolutely essential or indispensable. Whatever the relative merits of the proposed bank, not even Hamilton argued that it was absolutely essential to the enumerated powers of Congress. Rather, Hamilton pointed out that "necessary" did not have to mean indispensable, but merely useful or convenient. It was a classic case of broad versus strict construction of the Constitution. President Washington signed the law establishing the national bank in 1791. Apparently, Hamilton's views had prevailed.

While the first national bank's charter expired in 1811, a growing number of younger Republican political leaders—among them Henry Clay and John C. Calhoun—considered a national bank crucial to a strong national government. Accordingly, a law to create a second national bank was signed in 1816 by President Madison, ironically, one of the first bank's most vocal opponents. The bank's reemergence also coincided with a resurgence of states' rights in many state governments, based upon a growing resentment of federal intrusion into state affairs. For many states' righters the Second Bank of the United States epitomized national government interference, speculation, and mismanagement, and it quickly became a target of their anger.

John Marshall's Federalism: *McCulloch* v. *Maryland* (1819)

The unpopularity of the second U.S. bank had spread into a number of states by 1818. While some states had sought to limit the bank's operation, others like Maryland used their taxing powers to bring the bank under state control. Maryland's legislature levied a tax on all banks not chartered by the state, an obvious action against the U.S. bank's Baltimore branch. According to the law, the bank was directed to pay a $15,000 annual fee or place state tax stamps on all bank notes issued. James McCulloch, an employee of the Baltimore branch, refused to comply and was convicted in a Maryland court of violating the act. The Maryland Court of Appeals upheld the conviction, and McCulloch appealed to the U.S. Supreme Court. Counsel for the state of Maryland argued on two fronts: first, that the incorporation of a national bank was not provided for by the Constitution, thereby making the act of Congress unconstitutional; second, that Maryland, as a sovereign state, possessed the absolute power of taxation over all operations within its jurisdiction.

The Constitutionality of the Bank

Maryland's objections to the bank drew heavily from the states' rights interpretation that the Constitution is a compact entered into by sovereign and independent states, with only delegated powers given to the national government. As such, all national actions must be exercised in subordination to the states. Chief Justice Marshall, in his opinion, rejected the contention that states ratified the Constitution as sovereign entities, emphasizing rather that "the government proceeds directly from the people; is 'ordained and established' in the name of the people." The government of the nation, created by the Constitution, therefore, did not derive from state sovereignty but from the people themselves.

Far more pertinent to the case, Maryland argued for **strict construction** of the Constitution, a position long associated with states' rights. According to this argument, no enumerated power expressly authorizes the incorporation of a bank, and Congress may not legislate beyond its enumerated powers.

Marshall acknowledged the government to be one of enumerated and, hence, limited powers, but "supreme within its sphere of action." Under this analysis, incorporation of a national bank, if shown to be within the powers of Congress, would pass the test of constitutionality. Marshall directed his attention to the "great powers" (as he called them) to lay and collect taxes, borrow money, regulate commerce, declare and conduct war, and raise and support armies and navies, concluding that logic requires giving Congress the ability to execute its powers.

Having concluded that the national government's powers required execution, Marshall focused on the Necessary and Proper Clause to justify the bank's incorporation. It was not necessary that the power to incorporate a bank be specifically delegated, provided that it served as a "necessary and proper" means to achieve the enumerated powers that Congress clearly possessed. What followed was the now classic definition of Congress's implied powers: "Let the end be legitimate, let it be within the scope of the Constitution; and all means which are appropriate, which are plainly adapted to that end, which are not prohibited, but consist with the letter and spirit of the Constitution, are constitutional." Thus, the Second Bank of the United States was constitutional because it served as an appropriate means to the attainment of a legitimate end.

Maryland's Power of Taxation

The state power of taxation had been well established prior to the Constitution's ratification and was recognized as one of the chief attributes of state sovereignty. States were prohibited by the Constitution from taxing imports and exports, but no mention was made of other limitations. Accordingly, Maryland's argument centered upon the state's absolute power of taxation of all instruments within its jurisdiction. In this part of the opinion, Marshall leaned heavily upon the principle of national supremacy and its logical implications. Using the Supremacy Clause in Article VI of the Constitution, Marshall constructed the following argument:

> This great principle is, that the constitution and the laws made in pursuance thereof are supreme; that they control the constitution and laws of the respective states, and cannot be controlled by them. From this, which may be almost termed an axiom, other propositions are deduced as corollaries... These are, 1st. That a power to create implies a power to preserve. 2d. That a power to destroy if wielded by a different hand is hostile to, and incompatible with these powers to create and preserve. 3d. That where this repugnancy exists, that authority which is supreme must control, not yield to that over which it is supreme.

Marshall began from a major premise (national supremacy) and proceeded to demonstrate its logical consequences.[6] Since "the power to tax involves the power to destroy," it is illogical to suppose that Congress may create a national bank only to have it taxed and destroyed in the process by the state of Maryland, even though Maryland may use its taxing power over everything that exists by its own authority or is introduced by its permission. (Marshall even conceded that the bank's real estate could be taxed as long as the tax was consistent with other realty in the state.)

From a current perspective, *McCulloch* v. *Maryland* stands as one of Marshall's most important opinions, but it was far from popular with a majority of Americans of that era. Former Presidents Madison and Jefferson criticized the *McCulloch* decision, and several states went so far as to petition Congress for a constitutional amendment allowing states to exclude the national bank from their territory. The movement for an amendment was unsuccessful. Nevertheless, the principle of intergovernmental tax immunity became well established (see Brief 6.2).

Five years later, in *Osborn* v. *Bank of the United States* (1824) Justice Marshall was confronted with the open defiance of his *McCulloch* v. *Maryland* ruling. Ralph Osborn, the Ohio state auditor, had ignored a federal circuit court injunction forbidding him to collect Ohio's $50,000 tax on each branch of the bank. After the bank's refusal to pay, Osborn and his associates seized the bank's assets and notes for the state treasury. When the bank sued for damages, it was banned entirely by the state legislature. In the *Osborn* case, Marshall and his colleagues held that the Ohio acts were invalid due to their inconsistency with the *McCulloch* decision. Moreover, Ohio's contention that the Supreme Court lacked jurisdiction in a suit against a state (the Eleventh Amendment) was rejected because Osborn, and not the state of Ohio, was determined to be the party of record. Most significantly, the Court held that a state's agent, when acting under an unconstitutional law, can be held personally liable for damages inflicted by his actions. Osborn could be sued, found liable, and forced to make restitution. This ruling strengthened the Court's authority in dealing with state officials.

Marshall and Other Federalism Issues

For Marshall, the constant danger to federalism lay in state encroachment of national power. He considered the national and state governments to occupy a superior-subordinate relationship in which national law always took precedence over state challenges to the contrary. This relationship was challenged directly over the issue of the Supreme Court's appellate jurisdiction. As previously noted, the Constitution had originally compromised on the issue of federal judicial power, with state courts in possession of jurisdiction to hear numerous cases involving national law. Largely because of the Court's ruling

---

❑ *Brief 6.2   Intergovernmental Tax Immunity*

McCulloch v. *Maryland* established the idea that states may not tax the national government or its agents. This concept of intergovernmental tax immunity has remained an integral part of the overall federal system, although it has moved through several distinct stages. The doctrine was extended to prohibit national taxation of state agents and functions, and for a time even the salaries of governmental employees were tax exempt, but no more. The case of *Graves* v. *New York ex rel. O'Keefe* (1939) held that a state may tax the income of a federal employee and that the tax does not impose an unconstitutional burden upon the national government. (Federal taxation of state employees' salaries was upheld the previous year.)

Today, the doctrine is largely intact and protects the essential character of the federal system, despite some concessions to practical considerations. For example, in states with a large amount of national property, the tax-exempt land may prove a hardship for the state. Because of this problem, Congress may authorize certain payments to a state to ease the state's financial burden.[7] On the other hand, courts have held that state or local functions may be subject to federal taxation if they are nongovernmental in nature. The exact meaning of "nongovernmental" is difficult to determine, but state-owned liquor stores, for example, have been held subject to federal taxation. (See *South Carolina* v. *United States* [1905].)

in *Chisholm* v. *Georgia* (1793), the Eleventh Amendment was ratified in 1798. The Eleventh Amendment removed from the jurisdiction of federal courts all cases in which a citizen of one state brings suit against another state, as well as suits brought by citizens of foreign countries against states. If sued, states would require the suits to be heard in their own courts. When the Federalist-dominated First Congress enacted the Judiciary Act of 1789, the original compromise was undermined, much to the concern of states' righters. It will be recalled that, in addition to creating inferior federal courts, Section 25 of the act also provided for the appeal of cases from the highest state court to the U.S. Supreme Court, when the state court ruled against a federal law or denied a right or privilege claimed under the Constitution. The Supreme Court would serve as the final arbiter of the Constitution and national law.

Primary opposition to Section 25 came from the Virginia judiciary and Judge Spencer Roane, a longtime supporter of state sovereignty. Judge Roane and his colleagues repeatedly declared Section 25 of the Judiciary Act to be unconstitutional and denied the Supreme Court's right to review state court decisions on the grounds that the Constitution had not made the Supreme Court the final arbiter of national power. After several inconclusive cases (see *Martin* v. *Hunter's Lessee* in Chapter 4), Chief Justice Marshall and his colleagues responded forcefully to the Virginia judges in the case of *Cohens* v. *Virginia* (1821). In that case, the Cohen brothers were charged with violating a Virginia law forbidding the sale of lottery tickets. They claimed immunity from prosecution because they were selling tickets for a Washington, D.C., lottery that had been authorized by the U.S. Congress. Marshall's opinion rejected the Cohens' claim of immunity on the grounds that the federal law applied only within the District of Columbia. The Virginia law, in short, was a proper use of state power. With respect to federal-state relations, however, *Cohens* v. *Virginia* gave immense support to the sovereignty and supremacy of national power. Speaking to the Virginia judiciary, Marshall noted that the states were no longer totally sovereign, having surrendered part of their sovereignty to the new national government. National supremacy could not be maintained if each state were able to pass final judgment upon national laws, an effect that Marshall said "would prostrate . . . the government and its laws at the feet of every state in the Union." In fact, he concluded, "The constitution and the laws of a state, so far as they are repugnant to the constitution and laws of the United States, are absolutely void." Although the decision on the case's merits actually favored Virginia, the effect of Marshall's opinion was to soundly contradict the state sovereignty views of the Virginia judiciary and uphold the cornerstone of his constitutional philosophy of national supremacy.

Marshall confronted yet another "clash of sovereignties" issue in *Gibbons* v. *Ogden* (1824), the first case heard by the Supreme Court under the Commerce Clause. At issue was the dispute between one steamboat operator (Thomas Gibbons), who operated under a federal license as required by the Federal Coasting Act of 1793, and another (Aaron Ogden), who claimed that the state of New York had granted him the exclusive right to operate a steamboat in New York waters. While the commerce-related issues are discussed in the following chapter, the case also provided Marshall with an opportunity to further expand his views on national and state power, and the case brought into focus a conflict between national and state law. Gibbons was operating legally with respect to the national law, while Ogden had exclusive legal rights to the same area as granted by the state. Deciding that steamboat traffic was a subject of interstate commerce and, as such, within congressional regulation, Marshall upheld Gibbons' right to operate and declared the state law invalid, stating that "when state and national laws conflict, the latter must prevail." Marshall's powerful statement of national supremacy in *Gibbons* v. *Ogden* illustrates his commitment to the idea that the Constitution, and not the states, determines the proper balance of federalism in the nation.

States' Rights: The Anti-Federalist Position

In spite of setbacks such as those in *McCulloch* v. *Maryland* and *Gibbons* v. *Ogden,* supporters of states' rights continued to seek alternatives to the Hamilton-Marshall concepts of national supremacy and broad constitutional construction. What remedy was available to an individual or a state when faced with an unacceptable (and allegedly unconstitutional) national law? The options available to states' righters ranged from outright violent disobedience to more subtle forms of action. Several examples are presented in this section.

Whiskey Rebellion (1794)

Unlike the Articles of Confederation, the Constitution provided means by which the national government could enforce its will directly upon individuals. Congress was given the power "to provide for calling forth the Militia to execute the Laws of the Union, suppress Insurrections and repel Invasions" (Art. I, Sec. 8). For staunch nationalists, such a power of coercion was essential to national supremacy. When Congress in 1790, as part of its revenue program, levied a direct excise tax on whiskey, the stage was set for a test of federal power.

The whiskey tax was especially odious to small farmers and frontiersmen because it threatened a primary source of their livelihood and a major outlet for their surplus grain. When opposition to the tax began to intensify, Congress in 1792 authorized President Washington, largely at Hamilton's urging, to send the militia to restore order. In all, some thirteen thousand troops were dispatched to western Pennsylvania by 1794, and the insurrection was crushed. This episode was of great importance to the fledgling national government, for it demonstrated that national laws could be enforced, even against the threat of violent opposition.

Virginia and Kentucky Resolutions (1798)

By far the best-organized opposition to Federalist policies came from followers of Thomas Jefferson. Primarily small farmers and artisans, these Jeffersonian Republicans found the states' rights views of their leader quite compatible with their own. The Jeffersonian philosophy, built upon the principle that the government should provide for the happiness of the greatest number (small farmers and artisans), saw little need for the extensive legislative policies of the Federalists. Particularly with respect to Hamiltonian programs, Jeffersonians were more than a little suspicious of national favoritism for financial and commercial interests. When Jefferson resigned his post as secretary of state in

1793 and openly opposed Federalist policies, he found a ready-made constituency of supporters.

Probably the most significant Jeffersonian-inspired opposition to Federalist policies occurred in 1798 and 1799 over the issue of the Alien and Sedition Acts. Jeffersonians were aghast at the passage of the acts, which apparently had been inspired by the Federalists' fears of possible anarchy and revolution. The specific catalyst had been the 1789 French Revolution and bloody rejection of traditional authority in that country. As many Jeffersonian supporters saw considerable merit in such a "democratic revolution," they came to be regarded as a threat to order and stability in this country, at least by key Federalists. It was true that Jefferson's personal sympathies were with the French revolutionaries, but he had become critical of their violence and bloodletting. Many persons of French descent and pro-French views understandably flocked to the Jeffersonian cause, prompting concerned Federalists to enact the Alien and Sedition Acts in 1798.

The Alien Act authorized the president to order the deportation of any alien he considered dangerous to the United States, while the Alien Enemies Act authorized the president similar control over aliens from an enemy country. Because no one was deported under either act (President John Adams apparently did not favor such action), attention was focused upon the Sedition Act, which in effect made it illegal for any person to criticize the government of the United States. Specifically, it was illegal to "defame" the government, the president, or either house of Congress through writing, speaking, or publishing. Jefferson's supporters quickly challenged the Sedition Act as a clear violation of the First Amendment. Nevertheless, ten newspaper publishers were eventually convicted under the act. When the Sedition Act was challenged as unconstitutional in the federal courts, Federalist-appointed judges refused to invalidate the law. Convinced of the act's illegality but unable to gain relief from the courts, Jeffersonian supporters sought out states' rights as an answer.

In secret, James Madison and Thomas Jefferson each drafted a series of resolutions and had them introduced into the legislatures of Virginia and Kentucky respectively. Known as the Virginia and Kentucky Resolutions, they were adopted by the respective legislatures and sent to other states for concurrence in rejecting the Alien and Sedition Acts. Although the Virginia and Kentucky Resolutions ultimately failed to gain the approval of other states, they did provide an important theoretical basis for challenging the supremacy of the national government—the doctrine of **interposition.**

In truth, disagreement exists over the precise view of the Union presented in the resolutions. This is largely due to the fact that the resolutions did not provide a clear-cut framework for settling constitutional disputes. On the nature of the Union, both resolutions drew attention to the compact nature of the Constitution to which the states had agreed. This agreement, however, had not been made at the expense of each state's essential sovereignty. According to Virginia's resolution, the powers of the federal government resulted from "the compact to which the states are parties" and were "limited by the plain sense and intention of the instrument [constitution] constituting that compact." [8] The Virginia Resolution spoke of the state's duty to "interpose" itself between an invalid national law and the people. The theory of interposition was not spelled out further, but the implication could be drawn that state governments might exercise some duty to interpret the Constitution for themselves and their citizens. In a second declaration in 1799, Kentucky inserted the contention that states, "being sovereign and independent, have the unquestionable right to judge" an infraction of the Constitution, even pointing to a "nullification of those sovereignties" as a possible remedy.[9] Neither Kentucky nor Virginia took action against the Alien and Sedition Acts, so a constitutional crisis was avoided. Since other states refused to pass similar resolutions, the threat posed to the national government did not materialize. Nevertheless, some thirty years later, a serious challenge would be mounted against national authority, using many of the ideas first proposed in the Virginia and Kentucky Resolutions.

As for the clearly unconstitutional Alien and Sedition Acts, the defeat of President Adams and the Federalists in 1800 sealed their fate. The Sedition Act was repealed by the new Jeffersonian-controlled Congress, although it appears that the act actually expired "according to its original terms" with the close of the Adams administration.[10] President Jefferson exercised his power of pardon to free all those convicted under the Sedition Act. Thus, a constitutional debate was ended and a crisis avoided by a political solution.

Roles Reversed: Jeffersonians as Supporters of National Power

While the Federalists governed, states' rights and strict construction were primarily Jeffersonian Republican principles. Virtually all northern state legislatures had rejected the positions put forward in the Virginia and Kentucky Resolutions and had urged acceptance of federal authority. Thomas Jefferson's presidential victory in 1800 and the control of Congress by his Republican supporters, however, brought about a significant shift in the states' rights position.

Thomas Jefferson's view on states' rights and strict construction of the Constitution showed some flexibility, depending upon the requirements of the situation. While serving as president, Jefferson was called upon to exercise his authority in ways that contradicted his constitutional principles, and he generally seemed willing to sacrifice principle to the demands of the office. Two situations stand out: the purchase of the Louisiana Territory from France in 1803, and the decision to embargo all foreign trade in 1807.

The Louisiana Purchase (1803)

When President Jefferson received information that Napoleon would sell French-owned Louisiana for $15 million, he recognized the nature of the opportunity. The new territory would provide vast new areas for expansion and a plentiful supply of land—two developments strongly favored by most Jeffersonians. Moreover, the purchase would remove the direct threat of the French from American shores.

Jefferson's Federalist opponents feared such a purchase because of its possible economic and political impact upon their already declining fortunes, so they resorted to constitutional arguments in support of their position. Specifically, they stated that the purchase directly contradicted Jeffersonian strict construction and compact theory arguments. First, as the Constitution contains no provision authorizing the national government to acquire territory, such a purchase is unsupported by the enumerated powers granted to Congress. Sensitive to this criticism, President Jefferson sought to obtain a proposed constitutional amendment authorizing such a move, but time constraints were too pressing, and he abandoned the attempt. Second, the purchase of such a large area capable of being further divided into additional states seemingly challenged the fundamental assumptions of the compact theory, a long-standing Jeffersonian position. If the Constitution had been made by a compact of the original states, as the theory posited, what effect would possible new states have upon the arrangement? As one constitutional historian has concluded, the Louisiana Purchase "contradicted the compact theory, with which Jefferson had been identified and which underlay the doctrine of states' rights." [11] Nonetheless, Jefferson's eventual decision to purchase Louisiana proved to be one of the single most important developments in his presidency and for the nation in general, even though it had required some reshaping of constitutional principles.

The Embargo Act (1807)

The predominantly Federalist and commercial-minded New England states increasingly found themselves in opposition to national authority during the administrations of Jefferson and Madison. In 1807, Congress enacted the Embargo Act whereby all foreign trade, including exports and imports, was banned. This law had been motivated by the repugnant practices of Britain and France, locked in a bitter war against each other, against American shipping. While the United States had declared its neutrality in the conflict, neither the British nor French were reluctant to employ blockades and even attacks upon neutral shipping headed for their enemy. Most distasteful for Jefferson and his supporters was the British practice of impressment—the seizure of American sailors on merchant ships as alleged deserters from the Royal Navy.

The Embargo Act had a devastating impact upon the commercial interests of the New England states. One report holds that the value of American exports dropped from $128 million to $22 million as a result of the act. [12] Accordingly, the act's opponents challenged it as an unconstitutional violation of the Commerce Clause. Ironically, the Federalist opposition rested upon a strict construction argument, namely, that the congressional power to regulate foreign commerce does not allow for outright prohibition. Congressional power, they reasoned, must be used only to protect commerce, not to ban its existence. For their part, the normally strict construction Republicans embraced the broad view that prohibition was but one means of regulation. The only consistency in this dispute was the position of the judiciary which, in a federal district court opinion, upheld the constitutionality of the act by citing the broad discretion of Congress over commerce and the power of Congress to take measures in preparation for war.

From a states' rights perspective, the situation was very similar to the one that had surrounded the Alien and Sedition Acts ten years earlier. Not surprisingly, several New England state legislatures, including Massachusetts and Connecticut, adopted resolutions reminiscent of the Virginia and Kentucky Resolutions, and Connecticut then dusted off the idea of interposition. Despite the Embargo Act's repeal in 1809, the situation grew even worse with the decision to declare war on Britain in 1812. Much anti-British feeling existed in the southern and western regions, but the war was extremely unpopular in the predominantly Federalist northeast, and nearly all of the New England states took steps to deny federal power over their militias and the conscription of their young men. At the Hartford Convention, convened in 1814, the states proposed seven amendments to the Constitution that would protect New England's interests. Several of the proposed amendments were hardly subtle: No president could serve two terms; no two successive presidents could come from the same state (Jefferson and Madison, of course, were Virginians); embargoes could not extend beyond sixty days; and a two-thirds vote of Congress would be required to admit a new state, ban foreign trade, or declare war except when an actual invasion had occurred. Had the war not ended about this same time, a constitutional crisis might well have occurred.[13]

State Sovereignty: The Extension of States' Rights

By 1820, certain developments had begun to push opposition to federal policies further south. For one, the northern states' population advantage was becoming obvious, producing the fear among southerners that they would become a perpetual minority in the House of Representatives. The consequences of such a situation, according to southern interests, were potentially devastating. They were frightened by a growing, but by no means yet widespread, abolitionist movement in the northern states, threatening their ownership of slaves and, ultimately, their economic well-being. Secondly, Congress seemed determined to protect American manufacturing and industry through a series of increasingly high protective tariffs on imported goods. Since most manufacturing was located in northern states, the tariff forced southern agrarian interests, as they saw it, to subsidize northern manufacturers by paying higher prices for finished goods. Finally, the country was in the process of expansion. Purchase of the Louisiana Territory in 1803 had opened up a vast new frontier, and new states had begun to join the Union as a result. These four factors—population shifts, slavery, northern protectionism, and territorial expansion—helped to produce extreme opposition to federal authority.

The Missouri Compromise (1820–1821)

Because of northern domination of the House, control or at least parity in the Senate was seen as essential by slave interests. When the Missouri Territory, part of the Louisiana Purchase with a history of slavery, petitioned for statehood in 1818, it threatened to unbalance the current eleven free and eleven slave states. At issue was the constitutional procedure for admitting new states to the Union and the question of whether Congress could place restrictions upon a prospective state as a condition of its admittance.

The constitutional language states that "new States may be admitted by the Congress into this Union" (Art. IV, Sec. 3), and Congress previously had admitted states under this provision (see Brief 6.3). However, in the previous instances, the state's geographic location and history had largely determined its status as slave state or free state, and Congress had not been concerned with the issue. Anti-slave interests opposed to the expansion of slavery argued that the Constitution's use of the words "may admit" provided Congress with discretion to impose conditions upon a prospective state—in this case, no slavery. Slave interests, on the other hand, favored the unconditional admission of Missouri as had been done for the nine states added to the Union since 1789. Other constitutional issues such as the status of free Negroes added to the rather confusing set of arguments.

☐ *Brief 6.3 States, Territories, and Federalism*

The Constitution in Article IV, Section 3, dictates the rules concerning prospective states:

> New States may be admitted by the Congress into this Union; but no new State shall be formed or erected within the Jurisdiction of any other State; nor any State be formed by the Junction of two or more States, or Parts of States, without the Consent of the Legislatures of the States concerned as well as of the Congress.

Beyond the thirteen original colonies, most new states (thirty) have advanced to statehood from territorial status (generally involving the four steps of petition for statehood, an enabling act by Congress, a state constitution, and a final act of admission). Five states (Kentucky, Maine, Tennessee, Vermont, West Virginia) were taken from other states, while two states—Texas, an independent republic, and California, acquired from Mexico—entered by other means.

New states have been admitted on a fairly regular basis in the nation's history. Counting the original thirteen states, the Union had grown to sixteen states by 1800. Another fifteen joined by 1850, and fourteen more were admitted by 1900, bringing the total to forty-five at the beginning of the twentieth century. Since then, the pace has slowed: three new admissions by 1950, followed by Alaska and Hawaii in 1959. Currently, of the territories that could be considered prospective states, only Puerto Rico has been mentioned seriously in that regard.

Article IV, Section 3, also authorizes Congress to make rules for territories of the United States. Territorial possessions currently include Guam, Puerto Rico, Samoa, the Virgin Islands, and the Territory of the Pacific Islands. Residents of Guam, Puerto Rico, and the Virgin Islands are citizens of the United States. The District of Columbia, although neither a state nor part of any state, is not considered a territory.

Ultimately, compromise was made possible by the admission of Maine, formerly a part of Massachusetts, as a free state and, after considerable debate, the admission of Missouri as a slave state. In addition, slavery was to be prohibited on the remaining Louisiana Purchase north of 36°30′ latitude. Congress hoped that it had finally put the issue to rest.

The Missouri Compromise is significant in the development of American federalism, for it marked the clear delineation of northern from southern states over the issue of slavery and virtually ensured a states' rights position for the latter. Since the 36°30′ agreement allowed for more potential states north than south of the line, slave states were cast into the minority position they had long feared. Even though the prohibition of slavery in the territories was repealed by the Kansas-Nebraska Act of 1854 and declared unconstitutional by the Supreme Court in *Dred Scott* v. *Sandford* (1857), it stood for nearly thirty-five years as evidence of the sectional and regional problems facing the Union.

John C. Calhoun: State Sovereignty and Nullification

The extreme states' rights position as developed in the South prior to the Civil War was primarily the work of John C. Calhoun. As a young politician, Calhoun had been an active supporter of the expansion of national power, favoring among other things the Second Bank of the United States and a protective tariff as ways of bringing unity to the nation. Apparently, during his tenure as vice-president of the United States from 1825 to 1832, Calhoun's thinking began to change. Much of this change was due to the factors of northern population dominance, slavery, and economic stagnation in Calhoun's native South Carolina, but the specific cause was the increasingly unpopular protective tariff (see Brief 6.4).

☐ *Brief 6.4   The Webster-Hayne Debate*

For nearly two weeks in 1830, the United States Senate galleries were crowded with onlookers as two of the nation's most skillful orators engaged in a running debate. Senator Robert Y. Hayne represented the anger and frustration of his fellow South Carolinians over the dominance of northern interests. His specific target was the 1828 "Tariff of Abominations." Hayne traced the South Carolina doctrine of nullification back through Jeffersonianism, the Virginia and Kentucky Resolutions, and even the Hartford Convention recommendations of 1814. His statement of the problem still stands as the classic states' rights view:

> If the federal government in all or any of its departments is to prescribe the limits of its own authority, and the states are bound to submit to the decision and are not allowed to examine and decide for themselves when the barriers of the Constitution shall be overleaped, this is practically "a government without limitation of powers." The states are at once reduced to mere petty corporations and the people are entirely at your mercy.[14]

Massachusetts Senator Daniel Webster defended the Union with the claim (long advanced by other nationalists) that the people and not the states had formed the Constitution of 1787. Accordingly, Webster saw the solution to unpopular and unacceptable laws to rest with the people and their power to amend the Constitution "at their sovereign pleasure." But, he added, as long as the people "are satisfied with it, and refuse to change it . . . who can give to the state legislatures a right to alter it, either by interference, constriction, or otherwise?"

While it is unlikely that the Webster-Hayne debate changed the minds of many Americans, it is clear that the competing views of federalism were never more eloquently debated. Unfortunately, in the final resolution of the conflict between nationalists and states' righters, guns replaced oratory, and bloodshed replaced eloquence.

Drawing upon earlier states' rights theory, Calhoun constructed the most convincing and extreme rejection of national sovereignty the nation had yet encountered. According to Calhoun, sovereignty was expressed as the highest will of the community and, as such, could not be divided. The old notion that sovereignty was vested in both national and state governments was incorrect; sovereignty existed in only one political community. Since the states had existed as sovereign entities before the Union, particularly in the Confederation, they were the logical respondents of sovereignty in the Union itself. The Constitution had not deprived states of their sovereignty, because the states had not surrendered it. Rather, the Constitution was a compact that had been entered into by sovereign states to create a central government to act as an agent of the state. As an agent, the national government had been delegated certain powers by the states, but it had not displaced the states as sovereign.

It is easy to see how **nullification,** Calhoun's most famous concept, derived from this analysis. Because states had retained their sovereignty, they alone could render the final interpretation of the Constitution. Should a state find a violation of the Constitution, it possessed the ultimate sovereignty to "nullify" the unconstitutional act.

While reasonably understandable in theory, nullification in its practical aspects was dealt with less successfully in Calhoun's thinking. Calhoun recognized the possibility that one state's nullification might be overruled by a convention of states, but this would be possible only after at least a three-fourths vote of the states. Here was Calhoun's other key concept, that of the concurrent majority.

As defined by Calhoun, a concurrent majority is a series of separate majorities of the "dominant interests" (states). It is achieved by "dividing and distributing the powers of government" and giving "each division or interest, through its appropriate organ, either a concurrent voice in making and executing the laws or a veto on their execution." [15] Under this idea, no decision could be made unless it commanded a majority of support in a majority of the states. Calhoun argued that this arrangement allowed for different interests to be represented and resulted in a far more democratic procedure than the standard principle of numerical majority (50 percent plus one) used in Congress. In fact, Calhoun saw the principle as an integral part of constitutional government "by making it impossible for any one interest or combination of interests, or class, or order, or portion of the community to obtain exclusive control." Although vague on certain points, particularly those relating to implementation of a concurrent majority system, Calhoun seemingly held the principle of a simple numerical majority (which, of course, South Carolina and other southern states could not command) to be incompatible with democratic government. As such, Calhoun's views supported the position of the minority against a dominant majority.

South Carolina's Nullification

In 1832, South Carolina's States' Rights party, in control of the state legislature, called a state convention to consider action against the national protective tariff acts passed in 1828 and 1832. By an overwhelming vote, the convention adopted an ordinance of nullification, declaring the 1828 and 1832 tariff acts to be "null, void, and no law, nor binding upon this state, its officers or citizens." [16] The ordinance directed the legislature to give the ordinance legal effect and prohibited the nullification from being challenged in state courts. Neither was appeal to the Supreme Court possible. Finally, should the national government seek to enforce the tariff acts, coerce the state, or interfere with the state's ports and commerce, South Carolina would secede from the Union.

The implementation of Calhoun's doctrine of nullification was indeed a bold step, for it was done without knowledge of the reaction it would provoke. President Andrew Jackson, cognizant of the threat to the Union, publicly warned South Carolinians that nullification was illegal and secession was tantamount to revolution. Both would be met with force if necessary. In support, Congress enacted legislation (Force Bill) authorizing President Jackson to dispatch troops to South Carolina if necessary. Faced with strong national opposition (no other states had taken South Carolina's side) and given the promise of future tariff reductions, South Carolina formally withdrew its ordinance of nullification in early 1833. The ordinance's leaders claimed victory, but it was clear that nullification had failed as a state weapon against national supremacy. Although Calhoun's chief concept continued to command respect in parts of the South, it seemingly would not work when implemented by a single state. Of course, for extremists, nullification's failure simply made secession a more viable alternative.

Secession: The Nature of the Union

For proponents of extreme state sovereignty the failure of nullification seemingly left only one course of action in the event of unjust national legislation. The right of secession, or leaving the Union, had been admitted by Calhoun in his writings, but it was left to his followers to carry secession to its conclusion. With the 1860 presidential election victory of Abraham Lincoln, an anti-slavery Republican, Southern states quickly began a rapid secession from the United States. Citing the compact nature of the Constitution and undivided state sovereignty as arguments, all seven states of the Deep South had seceded by January 1861, several months before Lincoln's inauguration. In early March, a Confederate Constitution based upon state sovereignty was adopted, and the Confederacy was born (see Brief 6.5). The stage was set for a titanic struggle.

In his inauguration address, Lincoln carefully rejected secession as a constitutional possibility, arguing that the Union was perpetual and that secession, as such, was illegal. Lincoln refrained from waging war on the Confederacy, and he took the position that the Southern states were still part of the Union, even though some state leaders were guilty of fomenting rebellion and insurrection. In short, Lincoln's position was based upon national sovereignty, a perpetual Union, and a supreme Constitution. However, when Confederate forces attacked Fort Sumter in Charleston, South Carolina, in 1861, the constitutional arguments were pushed aside. Four more states then seceded, and the Civil War had begun.

It is unnecessary to debate the legal nature of the Civil War at this point. Suffice it to say that Unionists, denying the legal right of secession, claimed the conflict was an insurrection in which, at least in theory, seceding states could not be recognized as belligerents (to recognize as belligerents would imply recognition of the South as an independent nation). For their part, Confederate spokesmen argued that the conflict was a true international war between the United States and the Confederate States of America. Of course, legal niceties aside, even without a formal declaration of war against the Confederacy, the conflict certainly resembled a war in its military aspects.

While the Confederacy's surrender in 1865 gave a *de facto* answer to the question of secession, the constitutional position did not emerge until the Supreme Court decided *Texas* v. *White* (1869). By this time, of course, the conquered states were in the throes of Reconstruction, a policy undertaken by Congress to both punish and "rebuild" the insurrectionists. At issue in *Texas* v. *White* was the legal right of Texas to bring suit in federal courts to recover

☐ *Brief 6.5   The Constitution of the Confederate States of America*

A side-by-side comparison of the United States Constitution and the Constitution of the Confederate States of America yields numerous insights into the thinking of Southern advocates of state sovereignty. Woodrow Wilson's classic text *A History of the American People* provides such a comparison.[17] Several highlights from the Confederate Constitution follow:

The Issue of Sovereignty
"We, the people of the Confederate States, each state acting in its sovereign and independent character, in order to form a permanent federal government . . ." (Preamble).

Taxation, especially the protective tariff
"The Congress shall have power—To lay and collect taxes, duties, imposts, and excises, for revenue necessary to pay the debts, provide for the common defense, and carry on the government . . . but no bounties shall be granted from the Treasury; nor shall any duties or taxes on importations from foreign nations be laid to promote or foster any branch of industry" (Art, I, Sec. 8).

Slaves and Property Rights—*Dred Scott* **upheld**
"No . . . law denying or impairing the right of property in negro slaves shall be passed" (Art. I, Sec. 9).
"The citizens of each state shall . . . have the right of transit and sojourn in any State of this Confederacy, with their slaves and other property; and the right of property in said slaves shall not be thereby impaired" (Art. IV).
Executive Power
"[The President] and the Vice-President shall hold their offices for the term of six years; but the President shall not be re-eligible" (Art. II).

Other interesting provisions in the Confederate Constitution included the **line-item veto,** which allows the executive to veto selective portions of proposed legislation. The practice is followed in several states today (see Chapter 14). With respect to the six-year presidential term with no reelection, a proposal favored in some circles today, the Confederacy simply did not last long enough to test the idea.

bonds issued by the Confederate government of that state in 1862. Underlying the issue, however, was the question of whether secession had stripped Texas of the legal and constitutional remedies afforded states in the Union.

In its decision, the Supreme Court held that "the Constitution, in all of its provisions, looks to an indestructible Union, composed of indestructible states." Following this reasoning, "Texas continued to be a state, and a state of the Union," during the Civil War. Although admitting that relations between Texas and the Union had changed, the Supreme Court rejected any permanent alteration in the Union as a result of secession. The right of Texas to bring suit in federal courts was affirmed, and secession was, for all practical purposes, a constitutional impossibility.

Chief Justice Taney and Dual Federalism

Roger B. Taney was appointed chief justice by President Jackson upon the death of John Marshall in 1835. Taney presided over the federal judiciary for twenty-eight years during a time when the Union experienced the greatest single threat to its existence. Through this period, Chief Justice Taney sought to balance his strong attachment for states' rights (especially state control over slavery) with a recognition that national supremacy was a fundamental pillar of the federal system. The resulting philosophy has been characterized as **dual federalism,** or "dual sovereignty."

Taney believed that both national and state governments were sovereign in their respective constitutional spheres of authority. In those areas within the states' Tenth Amendment reserved powers, the state exercised sovereignty, although Taney recognized the power of the federal courts to uphold the supremacy of the Constitution and national authority. While Taney's significant decisions are discussed elsewhere, several examples of dual federalism are evident in his opinions. His defense of "dual citizenship" in the *Dred Scott* case, for example, held that national and state citizenship stemmed from different sources and therefore could be granted only by the government possessing sovereignty over that particular citizenship. A person might be a state citizen but not a U.S. citizen under the theory of dual citizenship. Taney's dual federalism also led him to uphold the states' power to legislate in matters pertaining to slavery. By holding unconstitutional provisions of the Missouri Compromise prohibiting slavery in the territories, Taney upheld the reserved powers of state governments to regulate slave matters. It was classic dual federalism: using the Tenth Amendment's reserved powers to enable states to resist encroachments by the federal government into purely state concerns.

In regulatory matters, Taney saw the states as possessing powers in areas such as interstate commerce, provided that Congress had not taken steps to regulate the matter in question (see, e.g., *Cooley* v. *Board of Wardens* in Chapter 7). In sum, Taney's concept of dual federalism offered states greater flexibility and police power than they had experienced under Marshall's nationalist view. When extreme states' rights, nullification, and secession had been finally discredited by the Civil War, dual federalism offered a formula whereby state governments could defend their interests from federal interference. In fact, the defense of dual federalism served state property interests well into the twentieth century as a bulwark against increasing national economic regulation. This will be discussed further in the following chapter.

Federalism in the Post-Civil War Era

Radical Republican politicians held the upper hand in Congress for nearly ten years following the Civil War, and they undertook what they regarded as the "reconstruction" of the Southern states. A significant amount of their program was of dubious constitutionality, particularly the provisions found in several Reconstruction acts placing the defeated states under military authority and control. While it is beyond the scope of this chapter to analyze the full range of Reconstruction policies, several crucial developments pertaining to the national-state relationship require mention.

The addition of the Thirteenth (1865), Fourteenth (1868), and Fifteenth (1870) Amendments to the Constitution produced significant developments for the American federal system. The Thirteenth Amendment, by prohibiting slavery in the states and territories of the United States, denied state governments control over an institution that had been in their hands for years. While the amendment also limits the national government, it is more properly considered a constitutional restriction of the long-standing states' rights position. For nearly one hundred years following its ratification, the Thirteenth Amendment was regarded as a narrow limitation upon the institution of black slavery and not as the basis for extensive congressional action against various forms of discrimination. A sweeping Supreme Court ruling in *Jones* v. *Mayer* (1968) changed this long-standing view and provided for a significant change in the nation's concept of "slavery." The case is discussed fully in Chapter 9.

The Fourteenth Amendment unquestionably stands as the most important development for the federal system since the writing of the Constitution. Coming as it did following the massive defeat of such ideas as state sovereignty, nullification, and secession, the Fourteenth Amendment redefined the relationship existing between state governments and the national Constitution. Its primary importance can be seen in its treatment of subjects such as citizenship, due process of law, and equal protection guarantees. With respect to citizenship, the amendment begins with a rather clear definition: "All persons born or naturalized in the United States, and subject to the jurisdiction thereof, are citizens of the United States and of the State wherein they reside." This definition effectively repudiated Chief Justice Taney's opinion in *Dred Scott* v. *Sandford,* discussed in Chapter 9, and eliminated the possibility that state governments could withhold either state or federal citizenship from blacks.[18]

Two additional clauses of the Fourteenth Amendment have altered the federal-state relationship. The Due Process Clause, perhaps more than any other provision, has brought state governments into near uniformity on matters of constitutional rights and liberties. As a result, almost the entire Bill of Rights extends today over national and state governments alike, leaving states considerably less free to pursue policies they once followed. The other significant component of the Fourteenth Amendment—the Equal Protection Clause— came as a purposeful limitation by Northern Republicans on state policies aimed at black Americans. In the aftermath of the Civil War, with slavery formally abolished, the fate of the free Negro became a matter of great concern. The Equal Protection Clause presumably would keep states (particularly those in the South) from returning to the old days of white supremacy. Of course, no single constitutional clause by itself could have accomplished such a task quickly and completely. Nevertheless, the Fourteenth Amendment paved the way for an extensive overhaul of federalism, particularly in matters of state power. The Due Process Clause is discussed extensively in the following chapter as it pertains to issues of property and economic liberty. Its role in the nationalization of the Bill of Rights may be found in Chapter 8. The Equal Protection Clause and its ever-widening base occupy the subject matter of Chapters 9 and 10.

The last of the post-Civil War amendments was ratified in 1870 as the Fifteenth Amendment to the Constitution. Because voting rights are more fully discussed in Chapter 9, they need not be dealt with here. However, it should be noted that the Fifteenth Amendment addressed an issue—voting—which nearly all observers had long regarded as among the reserved powers of state governments. While the new amendment did not formally change that pattern, it did establish a foundation upon which congressional legislation such as the Voting Rights Act of 1965 could be based. State powers to limit voting opportunities eventually would be greatly reduced, despite the protections of the Tenth Amendment.

Federalism in the Twentieth Century

Early in the twentieth century, several developments combined to change the existing balance of federal-state relations. Passage of the Sixteenth Amendment in 1913 opened the door to a tremendous revenue imbalance between national and state governments. By allowing the federal government to tax capital, the amendment promised an ever-expanding revenue base—as national income rises, tax revenues follow suit. While it should be noted that states also may tax incomes (and nearly all do so), they are relegated to a distant second place behind the federal government in income tax revenues.

A second critical development that contributed to changing patterns of federalism involved the major economic crisis of the Great Depression. State and local leaders who had viewed earlier federal grants-in-aid as intrusions were now forced to care for a growing number of indigent and needy Americans, and these governments were woefully short of money. As a result, the federal government's entry into welfare programs met with relatively little opposition. In the first several years of President Franklin Roosevelt's New Deal administration, new national legislation was passed to deal with matters such as unemployment compensation, child labor, public housing, wages, and even old-age benefits.

World War II and its aftermath further shifted the balance toward the federal government, as more grant programs were undertaken. The 1957 Russian launch of Sputnik sent such shockwaves through American society that only the national government was regarded as strong enough to meet the challenge. Federal grants suddenly were viewed as essential for national defense and meeting the challenge mounted by Sputnik. As an example, the National Defense Education Act of 1957 provided federal grants and loans for students in higher education.

State Sovereignty and Nullification in the Twentieth Century

Despite the growing tendency toward national power in the twentieth century, several developments during the early 1950s showed that the extreme states' rights positions of interposition and nullification continued to attract some support. The catalyst for this development was the Supreme Court's decision in *Brown* v. *Board of Education* (1954), invalidating the long-standing separate-but-equal doctrine and threatening the segregated school systems of many states, including all of those in the Deep South. Equal protection and civil rights issues associated with this era are discussed in Chapter 9 and do not require mention here. However, it should be noted that in the aftermath of *Brown,* advocates of extreme state sovereignty began to appear in several states, arguing for a reversal of the decision and a continuation of segregated schooling. Interestingly enough, these groups reverted to the presumably discredited tactics associated with states' righters before the Civil War.

Following the *Brown* decision, the legislatures of eight states—Alabama, Georgia, Mississippi, Louisiana, Florida, Arkansas, Virginia, and South Carolina—passed resolutions condemning the Supreme Court's decision as an unconstitutional usurpation of state sovereignty and announcing their intention to nullify the effects of the decision. The following excerpts from Alabama's 1956 resolution—which was the first such resolution—are typical:

> WHEREAS the Constitution of the United States was formed by the sanction of the several states given by each in its sovereign capacity; and WHEREAS the states, being the parties to the constitutional compact . . .
> RESOLVED *By the Legislature of Alabama, Both Houses Thereto Concurring* . . .
>   That until the issue between the State of Alabama and the General Government is decided . . . the Legislature of Alabama declares the decisions and orders of the Supreme Court of the United States relating to separation of races in the public schools are, as a matter of right, null, void, and of no effect . . . we declare, further, our firm intention to take all appropriate measures honorably and constitutionally available to us, to avoid this illegal encroachment upon our rights, and to urge upon our sister states their prompt and deliberate efforts to check further encroachment by the General Government, through judicial legislation, upon the reserved powers to the states.[19]

All these nullification resolutions rested on the works of states' rights extremists such as John C. Calhoun. Although these states were able to postpone the effects of *Brown* for several years, nullification did not prove to be the reason for their success. It was ironic that the doctrine of nullification, which failed in South Carolina in the 1830s for want of support by other states, should garner the wholehearted support of eight governments more than one hundred years later. What might have been the future of state sovereignty and nullification had several states come to the aid of South Carolina in 1833? Would a united front, something which Calhoun considered essential, have made a difference then? Whatever the answer, the fact in 1956 was that nullification would not work as a device for settling disputes in the federal system of government. It offered the eight states in question a comforting theoretical position upon which they could rest, but in reality nullification was as much a lost cause as the legalized segregation that these same states were so desperately trying to maintain.

Creative Federalism and the Great Society

In spite of the highly emotional nature of desegregation and states' rights, the primary issues facing federalism in the twentieth century have been financial. As discussed previously, the national government has dominated the states in financial matters. President Lyndon Johnson presided over a rapid escalation of federal grants-in-aid programs, a large percentage of which were focused on health and welfare programs. President Johnson's Great Society program called for the national government to assume an even more direct role in providing for the needs of the poor, needy, and disadvantaged. In addition, growing minority awareness and activism increased the demand upon resources and planning.

President Johnson used the term **creative federalism** to describe his Great Society plan. Under creative federalism, the national government identified the problem, decided how it should be solved, and created a grant program to meet it. Despite its stated goal of expanding the federal-state partnership, creative federalism primarily expanded the role of the national government. More than ever before, federal grants were designed to flow directly to local governments, especially cities, bypassing states in the process. Categorical grants criss-crossed the federal-state partnership, creating numerous overlapping and burdensome requirements upon grant recipients.[20] Table 6.3 helps to identify several basic types of federal grants-in-aid.

The "New Federalism" of the 1970s

Reacting to the growing complexity, expanded federal requirements, and inadequacies of the categorical grant system, President Richard Nixon in 1972 announced his plan for a "new federalism." Acting upon Nixon's proposals, Congress passed the State and Local Fiscal Assistance Act of 1972, which

---

Table 6.3   Types of Grants-in-Aid

Categorical or Project Grants—States and localities must apply for these grants, and the money must be used for specific purposes or problem areas. Examples include waste disposal, housing, and law enforcement. Categorical grants provide the least amount of flexibility for states and localities.

Formula Grants—This specific type of categorical grant involves the establishment of a formula to govern the criteria under which federal monies are to be disbursed. Although the precise factors vary by program, typical measures include population and poverty level statistics. The school lunch program is an example of the formula grant principle.

General Revenue Sharing (GRS)—Associated with the Nixon administration's "New Federalism," GRS provided funds to state and local governments based upon a predetermined formula but without any real restrictions attached. Revenue sharing ended in late 1987.

Block Grants—These are broad grants within which several functional areas are combined. Block grants have enjoyed a period of popularity within the Reagan administration's "New Federalism." They offer considerable freedom and flexibility to state and local governments in deciding how the funds should be spent.

authorized general revenue sharing (GRS) with a budget of $30 billion spread over a five-year period. The money—two-thirds of which was to go directly to local governments such as cities, towns, and counties—was promised with very few restrictions attached. GRS funds were authorized for all recognized state-local functions—including public safety, pollution control, recreation, and transportation. Most recipient governments simply lumped their GRS funds with other monies and spent them for the normal range of items and services.

General revenue sharing was hailed by its supporters as a program to end bureaucratic red tape and federal domination. The concept of GRS held that the national government should emphasize revenue collection and allow states and localities to spend the money. Nevertheless, many existing grants-in-aid programs continued to function alongside revenue sharing. In 1976, Congress renewed GRS for forty-five months with a budget of $26.5 billion. GRS continued to be renewed until 1987, when Congress, acting upon the recommendation of the Reagan administration, allowed it to end.

The new federalism of the 1970s also proposed the use of block grants as an alternative to existing categorical grants. Block grants offered local leaders the advantage of determining specific allocations at the local level, provided that the money was spent within a broad category or functional area such as "community development" or "law enforcement." Congress passed the Housing and Community Development Act of 1974 based upon the block grant approach. The act consolidated several categorical grant urban programs—urban renewal, model cities, neighborhood facilities, open-space land, public facility loans, water and sewer facilities, and code enforcement—into a block grant based upon a three-part formula (population, poverty, and crowded housing conditions). Subject to certain restrictions, local governments are free to select the projects to be funded through the block grant. Although not as free of restrictions as revenue sharing, block grants do provide state and local leaders with increased decision-making authority.

The "New Federalism" of the 1980s

While the 1970s new federalism increased the role of state and local governments, large numbers of categorical grants continued to operate as before. Moreover, power and responsibility for most spending remained in Washington. In his 1982 State of the Union Address, President Reagan pointed to the "overpowering growth of federal grants-in-aid programs during the past few decades." This, he stated, had contributed to a system in which citizens felt lost and bewildered by "a maze of interlocking jurisdictions and levels of government." President Reagan then outlined a series of proposals—the "new federalism" of the 1980s—designed to remedy the situation.

Phase 1 of the plan, which actually had been proposed the previous year, called for substantial budget cuts and greater use of block grants. Reagan proposed cutting grant outlays to state and local governments by $13.4 billion, a cut of 13.5 percent, to be followed by subsequent cuts of $5 billion. Most of the cuts were to be located in areas that the president considered state and local responsibilities—housing, employment, education, transportation, and sewage treatment.

Phase 1 also called for the replacement of eighty-four categorical grants with seven block grants. Congress finally approved nine block grants and cut

$1.2 billion from these programs. The nine block grants created by Congress in 1982 were Preventive Health and Health Services; Alcohol, Drug Abuse and Mental Health Services; Social Services; Maternal and Child Health; Home Energy Assistance; Community Services; Community Development; Primary Health Care; and Education. In reality, many categorical grants were consolidated, but many others were retained, and Congress kept some restrictions attached to block grants. The overall reaction to the consolidation was more positive at the state than at the local level, owing primarily to the fact that the block grants went directly to the states where local allocations were then made.

Phase 2 of Reagan's program involved the so-called "swap," "turnback," and "trust fund" proposals. The president called for a "financially equal swap" in which the federal government would release control of the Food Stamp and Aid to Families with Dependent Children (AFDC) programs to the states but assume control of the states' responsibility for Medicare. Reagan later agreed to keep food stamps at the national level. Still, the swap appeared to be in serious trouble, and neither Congress nor the state governors endorsed the plan.

The "turnback" plan called for a number of federal grant programs to be given back to states. These areas were to include programs in child nutrition, sewer and water treatment, community development, community services, vocational rehabilitation, vocational and adult education, urban mass transit, airports, highways, alcohol and drug abuse, and mental health. Several years after the turnback proposals, these programs remain largely federal responsibilities. Congress has shown little inclination to implement the turnback proposals.

Anticipating opposition to his proposals, President Reagan urged creation of a federal trust fund to help states pay for their new responsibilities. The trust fund would be financed by federal exercise taxes on alcohol, gas, tobacco, and telephones, as well as the oil windfall profits tax. States would be given access to the trust fund starting in 1984, and it would be phased out between 1987 and 1991. After that, states would be allowed to impose excise taxes on their own and decide which programs to support.

The future of the 1980s new federalism is difficult to predict, although it would appear that the federal-state balance has shifted somewhat more toward the states in recent years. The federal government remains the dominant partner in the relationship, but states have seen their responsibilities increase. Federal aid to states in 1986 exceeded $100 billion, or approximately 11 percent of federal spending. However, with their new-found responsibilities, the states will also be called upon to find new revenue sources. Estimates for 1986 held that total federal aid would constitute only about 18 percent of total local and state expenditures, down from a 1977 high of 26 percent and a 1983 figure of 21.5 percent.[21] The loss of general revenue sharing funds also will impact upon the states' fiscal positions. Some observers have pointed to the problem of fiscal inequalities among the states, prompting concerns that poorer states will be unable to provide an adequate level of service without continued federal funding. Connecticut and Mississippi, for example, had approximately equal populations in 1984, but the value of total taxable resources in Connecticut was nearly 75 percent greater than in Mississippi.[22] The results are predictable. The maximum monthly AFDC grant was $546 in Connecticut and $96 in Mississippi as of 1985.[23] Declining federal expenditures to states may make the situation even worse. Whether the changes begun in the 1980s are temporary in nature or the beginning of a trend, new challenges will continue to arise. The federal system of government has faced numerous problems since its inception, and it would be naive to expect otherwise in the years ahead.

Conclusion

The acceptance of federalism as a method of dividing powers between the national and state governments ranks as one of America's foremost achievements in the field of constitutional government. In retrospect, federalism appears to have been a natural choice for the United States. After all, the Articles of Confederation had proven fatally weak in matters of finance and commerce, and almost nobody favored placing centralized power in the hands of a unitary government. However, before concluding that the framers of the Constitution were following an obvious path toward federalism, it should be recalled that such a system did not exist among the world's nations in 1787, and political thinkers had given the subject very little consideration. The compromise reached in Philadelphia seems all the more remarkable when placed in this perspective.

The development of American federalism has progressed through several identifiable periods. The early clashes between the Federalists—including such advocates as Alexander Hamilton and Chief Justice John Marshall—and the Anti-Federalists—following such leaders as Thomas Jefferson and James Madison—focused upon the very nature of the Union and the critical issue of sovereignty. The competing positions of national supremacy and states' rights occupied the attention of Americans during the nation's early stages. Advocates of each position clashed over such matters as the national bank, protective tariffs, the admission of new states, and, finally, slavery. As a result of the latter issue, American federalism quickly became associated with regional interests. States' rights became more extreme in its demands under such regional spokesmen as John C. Calhoun, and the Constitution simply could not resolve the elusive problem of sovereign power. That issue was settled by the Civil War, a crucial turning point in the development of American federalism.

The Civil War's primary effect upon federalism was to demonstrate the supremacy of the national government and to settle the long-standing dispute over ultimate sovereignty. Nevertheless, the rivalry between national and state governments did not end with the Civil War. In fact, Justice Taney's legacy of dual federalism offered a constitutional alternative to the proponents of states' rights in their efforts to resist intrusions by the national government into state matters. The tone of federalism remained one of suspicion and distrust well into the twentieth century, as states often sought refuge from national interference in the comfort of dual federalism—a safe haven created by the Tenth Amendment into which Washington bureaucrats could not intrude.

Only recently has the tone of federal-state relations begun to show some signs of mellowing, although the relationship is far from an equal partnership. The national government's massive advantage over the states in financial resources has finally produced something approximating the relationship desired by ardent national supremacists, perhaps an outcome of which even Alexander Hamilton would approve. States today often must go along with the "feds" if they wish to continue the flow of much-needed financial support from Washington. The various forms of "new" federalism have promised greater state input and participation, and some small changes have indeed occurred. However, the two hundred years of American federalism have produced an arrangement in which the national government is dominant and states are subordinate, particularly in economic terms.

Nowhere has this arrangement been more visible than in the realm of government regulation of the economy. In the following chapter, federalism will be analyzed with particular emphasis upon the issue related to property, economic liberty, and government regulation. Indeed, as the United States has been transformed from an agrarian, sparsely populated country into a highly urbanized nation and leading industrial power, the strains upon federalism have proven to be immense. The manner in which the Constitution has adapted to meet these changing conditions and the effect upon the federal system of government provide the primary focus in the following chapter.

Questions

1.   Federalism has been adopted by nations around the world. When viewed comparatively, what advantages appear to be associated with federalism as a way of organization? What disadvantages? In what settings or countries might federalism not be appropriate?

2.   What are "implied powers," how did they originate, and where are they found in the Constitution? What is their relationship to the so-called "enumerated" and "reserved" powers? Cite examples of how implied powers have been used in the years since the nation's beginning.

3.   How did the divergent positions of national supremacy and states' rights, along with regional rivalries, contribute to the Civil War? Could the conflict have been prevented? If so, what constitutional theories might have played the largest role?

4.   Which of the constitutional amendments discussed in this chapter have had the most significant impact upon the system of federalism? On balance, have these amendments generally strengthened the national government or the state governments?

5.   Is there anything essentially new about the "new federalism" of recent years, or have most of these ideas been around for some time? How might a genuinely "new" federalism actually look? How might it work, or could it?

Endnotes

1.   Alexis de Tocqueville, *Democracy in America,* Vol. 1 (New York: Vintage Books, 1945), 173.

2.   Walter F. Murphy, James E. Fleming, and William F. Harris, *American Constitutional Interpretation* (Mineola, N.Y.: Foundation Press, 1986), 279.

3.   The comparison of federal and unitary systems requires some awareness of the difference between formal and actual distribution of power. See Gabriel A. Almond and G. Bingham Powell, eds., *Comparative Politics Today: A World View,* 3d ed. (Boston: Little, Brown, 1984), 88–89.

4.   For a discussion of the Indian pattern, see Robert L. Hardgrave, *India: Government and Politics in a Developing Nation,* 3d ed. (New York: Harcourt Brace Jovanovich, 1980).

5. For a discussion of the debate concerning applicability of the Bill of Rights and state governments, see Forrest McDonald, *A Constitutional History of the United States* (New York: Franklin Watts, 1982), 36–38.

6. The "logical" approach to constitutional interpretation is discussed in Harold J. Spaeth, *An Introduction to Supreme Court Decision-Making,* rev. ed. (New York: Chandler, 1972), 49–52.

7. Jack C. Plano and Milton Greenberg, *The American Political Dictionary,* 5th ed. (New York: Holt, Rinehart & Winston, 1979), 38.

8. "The Alien and Sedition Hysteria," in Thomas A. Bailey, ed., *The American Spirit: United States History as Seen by Contemporaries* (Boston: Heath, 1963), 171.

9. Alfred H. Kelly, Winfred A. Harbison, and Herman Belz, *The American Constitution: Its Origins and Development,* 6th ed. (New York: Norton, 1983), 139.

10. Ibid., 140.

11. McDonald, *Constitutional History,* 97.

12. Allen Johnson, "Jefferson and His Colleagues," in Allen Johnson, ed., *The Chronicles of America,* vol. 9 (New Haven, Conn.: Yale University Press, 1921), 168.

13. "The Hartford Convention," in Bailey, *American Spirit,* 203–4.

14. "The Webster-Hayne Debate," ibid., 246–7.

15. John C. Calhoun, *A Disquisition on Government and Selections from the Discourse* (New York: Liberal Arts Press, 1953), 20. (First published in 1853.)

16. "South Carolina Threatens Secession," in Bailey, *American Spirit,* 257.

17. Woodrow Wilson, *A History of the American People,* vol. 4 (New York: Harper and Brothers, 1902), 313–43.

18. The Constitution confers citizenship on all persons born or naturalized in the United States, using the principle of *jus soli*—by reason of place of birth. The only exceptions to the *jus soli* principle are children born of foreign diplomatic parents stationed in the United States, because these persons are not subject to the jurisdiction of the United States. American Indians, obviously native born but long considered an exception, were not conferred citizenship through the Fourteenth Amendment but rather by congressional statute some years later. The principle of *jus soli* has received support from the Supreme Court as the basic rule of American citizenship. The landmark case of *United States* v. *Wong Kim Ark* (1898) established that even if the parents are aliens who are ineligible for citizenship themselves, children born to these parents in the United States are indeed citizens. Today, as illegal immigrants stream to the United States in search of a better life, it is not surprising to realize that many do so in order to have a child born on American soil. Congress has declared that American soil is found in Puerto Rico, Guam, the Virgin Islands, and the Northern Mariana Islands.

19. Richard Bardolph, *The Civil Rights Record: Black Americans and the Law,* 1849–1970 (New York: Crowell, 1970), 379–80.

20. For an excellent treatment of the changing federal-state relationship, see Deil S. Wright, *Understanding Intergovernmental Relations* (North Scituate, Mass.: Duxbury Press, 1978).

21. Charlotte Saikowski, ed., "The States Make a Comeback," *200 Years of the U.S. Constitution: Can America Govern Itself?* (Boston: Christian Science Publishing, 1987), 10, 11, 14.

22. Charles A. Bowsher, "Federal Cutbacks Strengthen State Role," *State*

Government News 29 (February 1986): 18–21.

23. Harold W. Stanley and Richard G. Niemi, *Vital Statistics on American* *Politics* (Washington, D.C.: Congressional Quarterly Press, 1988), 284–5.

Suggested Readings

Elazar, Daniel J. *Exploring Federalism.* Tuscaloosa, Ala.: University of Alabama Press, 1987.

Gunther, Gerald, ed. *John Marshall's Defense of McCulloch v. Maryland.* Stanford, Calif.: Stanford University Press, 1969.

Hale, George E., and Marian Lief Palley. *The Politics of Federal Grants.* Washington, D.C.: Congressional Quarterly Press, 1981.

Hyman, Harold M. *A More Perfect Union: The Impact of the Civil War and Reconstruction on the Constitution.* New York: Knopf, 1973.

McDonald, Forrest. *Alexander Hamilton: A Biography.* New York: Norton, 1979.

Schlesinger, Arthur M., Jr. *The Age of Jackson.* 2d ed. Boston: Little, Brown, 1953.

Spain, August O. *The Political Theory of John C. Calhoun.* New York: Bookman Associates, 1951.

White, Leonard D. *The Federalists: A Study in Administrative History.* Westport, Conn.: Greenwood Press, 1978.

Wright, Deil S. *Understanding Intergovernmental Relations: Public Policy and Participants' Perspectives in Local, State, and National Governments.* North Scituate, Mass.: Duxbury Press, 1978.

7

Federalism: Property Rights, Economic Liberty, and Government Regulation

Syllabus

"The central issue of federalism, of course, is whether any realm *is* left open to the States by the Constitution—whether any area remains in which a State may act free of federal interference." Writing these words in a dissent to *Garcia v. San Antonio Metropolitan Transit Authority* (1985), Justice Sandra Day O'Connor was echoing the concerns of other critics of federal power as it has evolved over the years. Has expanding federal regulation left even the slightest room for independent state action? What of the traditional power of state governments to deal with internal matters? The *Garcia* case, discussed later in this chapter, stands as one of the recent attempts to define what has been termed the "essence" of federalism—namely, the proper balance between federal regulation and state authority.

This Chapter Examines the Following Matters

☐ Although it does not identify a specific economic point of view, the Constitution reflects the concerns of the framers in protecting certain economic and property rights.

☐ Many early state attempts at economic regulation were at odds with the Contract Clause. In the twentieth century, however, the Contract Clause has lost most of its significance as a limitation upon state regulatory power.

☐ The rise of substantive due process of law safeguarded economic liberty and property rights well into the twentieth century, providing the constitutional justification for laissez-faire economic theory in the process. At the height of substantive due process, the Supreme Court exerted almost complete control over social and economic policy in the United States.

☐ The regulation of commerce has expanded federal power to unprecedented levels. Still, the process has been uneven and sporadic. The nationalist view of Chief Justice John Marshall, which gave way to the more balanced dual federalism of Chief Justice Roger Taney and his successors, laid the foundation for the present interpretation of the Commerce Clause.

☐ Through the regulation of interstate commerce, along with taxation policy, the federal government has reached out to control matters relating to the health, safety, morals, and welfare of its citizens. As a result, this so-called "police-power" legislation occupies such diverse areas as civil rights, gambling, and food and drug control, and a whole range of workplace issues—safety, working conditions, hours, and wages.

☐ The congressional powers to tax and spend "to provide for the common Defence and general Welfare" have brought about new legislation and federal programs in areas ranging from Social Security to the speed limit on the nation's highways. Critics contend the effect has been a tragedy for the traditional authority of state governments.

Photo: The railroads were one of the first areas to be brought under federal Commerce Clause regulation, beginning in the 1880s.

The Economic Tug-of-War

As discussed in the preceding chapter, national power has expanded gradually but impressively in the two hundred years since the Constitution's inception. Throughout, numerous issues have arisen concerning the proper role of any government in relation to its citizens' property and economic freedoms. These issues have ranged from disputed land claims to such employment-related matters as minimum wages, working conditions, and job discrimination. By no means has the federal government been alone in its growing attention to regulation of economic matters. State governments themselves have often sought to dictate rules and regulations on a wide range of issues. Further, as a result of the nation's federal system of government, governments at national and state levels have waged an ongoing struggle for regulatory control over numerous areas that touch the citizen directly. The result has been a three-sided tug-of-war, pitting the national government, state governments, and private individuals and groups against and sometimes in coalition with one another. Of course, the intensity of the competition has fluctuated markedly throughout American history, and today's tug-of-war offers much less drama than the contests of earlier years, owing primarily to the national government's huge advantage in resources.

This chapter will focus upon the evolution of the United States from a largely agrarian country to the world's leading industrial nation, and the economic, social, and political strains resulting from that process. It should be noted that the Constitution lacks reference to any specific economic theory or perspective, presumably leaving the direction of economic activity to private interests and government bodies acting in several clearly defined areas. As a result, the individualist and communitarian philosophies discussed in Chapter 2 have exerted heavy influence upon this transition, although they often have given way to compromise and gradual change. The upcoming sections will examine individualist and communitarian influences that have shaped national and state policies concerning property rights and government regulation. The struggle between an individualist concern for property rights and the communitarian demand for some regulation has been a constant theme of American constitutional development.

The Contract Clause

Numerous economic critiques have been advanced to account for the actions of the framers of the Constitution.[1] While no single economic explanation can be judged acceptable, it certainly must be conceded that the framers considered economic matters in formulating the powers and limitations of government. The American preference for **vested rights** of property is clearly evident in the finished document, particularly in the safeguarding of certain matters from state control. It appears certain that some early leaders feared radical state policies that might threaten the areas of currency, credit, and commerce. State governments were regarded as vulnerable to takeover by radical farm groups and others who might advocate such unthinkable measures as paper money and interest-rate ceilings. In this respect, the Constitution's writers sought to insulate currency, credit, and commerce from state government control. Article I, Section 10, states:

> No State shall enter into any Treaty, Alliance, or Confederation; grant Letters of Marque and Reprisal; coin Money; emit Bills of Credit; make any Thing but gold and silver Coin a Tender in Payment of Debts; pass any Bill of Attainder, ex post facto Law, or Law *impairing the obligation of contracts,* or grant any Title of Nobility. [Emphasis added]

> No State shall, without the Consent of the Congress, lay any Imposts or Duties on Imports or Exports, except what may be absolutely necessary for executing its inspection Laws.

Thus, Article, I, Section 10, seeks to place considerable economic limitations upon state governments. Not surprisingly, these matters quickly became controversial as state governments ventured into new public policy areas (see Brief 7.1). The italicized portion of Section 10 generally is referred to as the Contract Clause, and its prohibition upon state interference in the obligations of contracts serves as an early example of the American concern with government meddling in economic matters. Although probably written specifically to refer to private business-related contracts, the Contract Clause eventually was expanded to encompass agreements entered into by states themselves, thereby protecting some individual property rights from state interference. These changes took place largely under the Federalist-inspired leadership of Chief Justice John Marshall.

Expansion of the Contract Clause

Chief Justice John Marshall's court shaped the meaning of the Contract Clause in several ways. First, the Federalist-dominated Marshall Court consistently resisted changes in the creditor-debtor relationship, despite the fact that several states had begun in the early nineteenth century to legislate in the areas of bankruptcy and other forms of debtor relief. While the Constitution grants

---

☐ *Brief 7.1 The* Ex Post Facto *Law*

One early line of defense to prevent state legislation from interfering with property rights was the Article I, Section 10, prohibition against state-passed *ex post facto* laws. This issue surfaced in the case of *Calder* v. *Bull* (1798) involving the disputed will of Normand Morrison and the decision of a probate court to invalidate that will. The probate court's decision resulted in Morrison's property being given to Mrs. Calder. Connecticut law barred appeals in such cases. Two years later, however, the legislature passed a resolution calling for a new hearing and the right to appeal. This second time around, the probate court approved the will, allowing ownership of the property to pass to Mrs. Caleb Bull. The plaintiff (Mrs. Calder)) appealed unsuccessfully to the state superior court and the Connecticut Supreme Court of Errors before bringing the case before the U.S. Su-

preme Court. The decision of the Court upheld the Connecticut legislature's grant of a new hearing and appeal by defining an *ex post facto* law in rather narrow terms. Justice Samuel Chase, in his opinion, considered *ex post facto* laws to be "only those that create, or aggravate, the crime; or increase the punishment, or change the rules of evidence, for the purpose of conviction." In short, *ex post facto* laws applied only to changes in a state's penal codes of punishment and not to matters of economic liberty. Such laws were indeed "retrospective," said Justice Chase, "but every retrospective law is not an *ex post facto* law." For opponents of state interference in matters of economic liberty and property rights, it became clear that the *ex post facto* prohibition would offer no protection.

Congress the power to pass bankruptcy legislation, no federal statutes had been forthcoming, and state governments reacted to growing financial panic and disorder, particularly in the aftermath of the War of 1812. Creditor interests, however, regarded state bankruptcy statutes as unconstitutional violations of the Contract Clause, given that they offered a debtor an escape from a properly executed promissory note.

In *Sturges* v. *Crowninshield* (1819), the Marshall Court invalidated a New York bankruptcy law that applied to debts entered into before the passage of the act itself. Marshall's opinion recognized the power of states to regulate matters such as bankruptcy in the absence of specific federal prohibitions, although it deemed the New York law to be a violation of the Contract Clause by allowing debtors to escape previously incurred financial obligations. The chief justice's animosity toward state bankruptcy laws brought him into the Court's minority on a constitutional issue only one time in his thirty-five-year tenure. This was in the case of *Ogden* v. *Saunders* (1827). At issue here was the legality of a bankruptcy statute already in effect before contractual obligations were created. Marshall, joined by two fellow dissenters, argued that a bankruptcy law already in effect should be declared unconstitutional as applied to future contracts. The majority position, however, as stated by Justice Bushrod Washington, held that

> it is, then, the municipal law of the State, whether that be written or unwritten, which is emphatically the law of the contract made within the State. . . . It forms . . . a part of the contract, and travels with it wherever the parties to it may be found.

Bankruptcy laws, thus, are part of the body of law within which contractual obligations are made and form a "part of the contract." This has continued to be a consistent aspect of bankruptcy laws through the years since *Ogden*.

A second influence of the Marshall Court was its expansion of the meaning of the Contract Clause. In *Fletcher* v. *Peck* (1810), Marshall's majority opinion expanded the meaning of the clause to include public as well as private contracts. Under this ruling, states themselves might be subject to the Contract Clause in matters in which they had become involved directly. The case stemmed from the action of the Georgia legislature in 1795 to grant public lands to several groups of purchasers known as Yazoo Land Companies. Unfortunately, the entire transaction was riddled with bribery and corruption, prompting the Georgia voters to defeat most of the corrupt legislators and pressure the legislature to rescind the original grant. In the meantime, however, some of the lands had been purchased by presumably innocent third parties around the country. These buyers naturally challenged the Georgia rescinding act on Contract Clause grounds. In reasoning consistent with his broad constructionist approach to the Constitution, Marshall first defined a contract as "a compact between two or more parties," stated that a contract had been executed between Georgia and the purchasers in the grant of land, and reasoned that a "contract executed . . . contains obligations binding on the parties." As the Constitution makes no mention of who might be parties to contracts, Marshall concluded that states were bound by the very same obligations as were private parties to contracts. The Georgia rescinding legislation became the first state law to be declared void because it violated the Constitution. Of course, for states' rights supporters, it was unthinkable that a state legislature could not repeal its own acts, especially when it was seeking to undo the effects of illegal and unethical behavior.

The Marshall Court expanded the Contract Clause to its broadest point in *Dartmouth College* v. *Woodward* (1819), further protecting private property from state interference. New Hampshire's Republican-dominated legislature was exhibiting a growing disdain for the exclusive, Federalist-run Dartmouth College. In 1816, it passed legislation establishing a new board of overseers for the college. The legislature also took steps to make Dartmouth a public institution by amending its charter. The charter, granted in 1769 by King George III, gave trustees the right to govern the institution forever. Was such a charter equivalent to a contract? Did New Hampshire's actions amount to interference in contractual obligations?

Chief Justice Marshall's characteristically broad interpretation of the Contract Clause focused upon the elements of a charter that established contractual obligations and duties. He found that the charter was a "contract within the letter of the constitution, and within its spirit also." It would have been possible, although "an extraordinary and unprecedented act of power," for New Hampshire to repeal the charter prior to ratifying the Constitution and accepting the limitations of the Contract Clause. The New Hampshire statute was inconsistent with the Contract Clause and declared null and void. In a broader sense, the Dartmouth College decision had a tremendous impact upon a newly emerging form of economic enterprise—the corporation. Corporate charters, granted by state governments, henceforth would be protected from political interference, elevating private property rights to an all-time level of immunity from state control.

Challenges to the Contract Clause

With the death of John Marshall and the appointment of Chief Justice Roger B. Taney, however, the expansion of the Contract Clause came to a halt. As many scholars have noted, Taney did not repudiate the major Marshall Court rulings on the Contract Clause, although he clearly brought his greater tolerance for some types of state regulation into play. At issue in *Charles River Bridge Co.* v. *Warren Bridge Co.* (1837) was whether a charter granted by a state could be implied as exclusive of all other competing charters. In 1785, the Massachusetts legislature had incorporated the "Proprietors of the Charles River Bridge" and authorized it to build a bridge across the Charles River. Under the charter, the proprietors were allowed to collect tolls, but they also were obligated to provide for certain construction and maintenance requirements and to pay Harvard College an annual fee as compensation for not operating a ferry, which the state had authorized by charter previously. The Charles River Bridge Company completed these requirements, and in 1792 the Massachusetts legislature extended the charter for seventy years.

By the 1820s, public opposition to monopolies and exclusive privileges was on the increase, prompting some legislatures to begin seeking ways to better serve the interests of a greater number of citizens. In 1828, the Massachusetts legislature passed a statute incorporating the Warren Bridge Company and authorizing it to build a new bridge less than three hundred yards from the existing structure. After the Warren Bridge Company had been compensated for construction and operating expenses, the bridge would revert to the state for the free use of its citizens. Faced with the prospect of competing against a public bridge, the Charles River Bridge Company challenged the 1828 legislation as destructive of the obligations of the exclusive ferry right granted to Harvard College and the subsequent charters of 1785 and 1792 which, the company argued, replaced the earlier grant.

In delivering the opinion of the Court, Chief Justice Taney focused upon the relationship between the grants to Harvard College and the Proprietors of the Charles River Bridge:

> The fact that such a right was granted to the college, cannot by any sound rule of construction, be used to extend the privileges of the Bridge company beyond what the words of the charter naturally legally import. . . There is no rule of legal interpretation which would authorize the Court to associate these grants together, and to infer that any privilege was intended to be given to the Bridge company, merely because it had been conferred on the ferry. The charter to the bridge is a written instrument which must speak for itself, and be interpreted by its own terms.

Justice Taney continued by stating that any ambiguities or uncertainties in a contract must always be resolved in favor of the state, because "the object and end of all government is to promote the happiness and prosperity of the community by which it is established." Taney's communitarian perspective clearly emerges in the following passage dealing with the public interest and community rights:

> No one will question that the interests of the great body of the people of the State, would, in this instance, be affected by the surrender of this great line of travel to a single corporation. . . While the rights of private property are sacredly guarded, we must not forget that the community also have rights, and that the happiness and well being of every citizen depends on their faithful preservation.

Charters must be construed narrowly and specifically, limited only to clearly stated aims and carrying no implied rights. While the Proprietors of the Charles River Bridge might have presumed an exclusive privilege over the Charles River, the charter was silent on such rights, and such rights, he added, "cannot be inferred from the words by which the grant is made." Accordingly, the state of Massachusetts had not impaired the obligations of any earlier contracts.

It should be noted that Chief Justice Taney's decision accepted almost every aspect of earlier Marshall Court rulings on the Contract Clause. Although Taney dealt a blow to vested property rights, he upheld the ideas that a state is bound by its own obligations and that a charter constitutes a contract within the framework of the Constitution. In reality, Taney's ruling amounted to a practical decision more closely in tune with the communitarian feelings of the times. According to constitutional scholar Benjamin Wright, Taney left the Contract Clause "a more secure and broader base for the defense of property rights in 1864 than it had been in 1835."[2]

Decline of the Contract Clause

By the late-nineteenth century, the Contract Clause had begun a decline that would run until the present time. While reasons for the decline are varied, they include an increase in police-power usage by state governments, the careful drafting of charters, and the emergence of the Due Process Clause. Before 1889, the Court had considered the Contract Clause in almost 40 percent of all cases involving the validity of state legislation, and nearly half of all state laws struck down were a result of that provision. By contrast, from 1888 to 1910, less than 25 percent of all cases involving state law arose under the Contract Clause.[3] The number has declined steadily since.

The Supreme Court began to yield to state police power in the matter of charters and legislative-drawn contracts. The decision in *Stone* v. *Mississippi* (1880) upheld an 1870 statute that made lotteries illegal in the state of Mississippi. This was in spite of the fact that the legislature in 1867 had granted a twenty-five-year franchise to several individuals, including John Stone, to sell tickets for the lottery. The Court's ruling rested upon the state's power to protect its people, stating that "no legislature can bargain away the public health or the public morals." Accordingly, a franchise to sell lottery tickets is no more than the privilege to hold a license for that purpose—a privilege subject to the police powers of the state.

In *Home Building & Loan Association* v. *Blaisdell* (1934) the Supreme Court let stand the Minnesota Moratorium Law. Passed during the Depression, the Minnesota law prevented massive foreclosures on the mortgages of homeowners and farmers by postponing mortgage payments until conditions improved. Citing the emergency and an urgent public need for relief, the Court said that the states have the power to protect their citizens when addressing a "legitimate end" without violating the Contract Clause. Chief Justice Charles Evans Hughes, in the *Blaisdell* opinion, said that the clause's prohibition "is not an absolute one and is not to be read with literal exactness like a mathematical formula." In short, the state retains authority to safeguard the vital interests of its people. Most observers concede that the *Blaisdell* case effectively limited the significance of the Contract Clause, rendering it largely irrelevant in the process. Indeed, the ruling in *City of El Paso* v. *Simmons* (1965), which permitted Texas to change the time allowed for redeeming previously forfeited land, supports this view.

In *Allied Structural Steel Company* v. *Spannaus* (1978), the Court showed some tendencies toward reviving the Contract Clause. In *Spannaus,* the Court held that Minnesota's Private Pension Benefits Protection Act violated the Contract Clause. The law was designed to protect the pension benefits for employees whose employers either terminated pension plans or closed their in-state offices. It provided for a "pension-funding charge" if pension funds were insufficient to cover full pensions for all employees who had worked at least ten years. When Allied Structural Steel Company closed its office in Minnesota, a decision that had preceded passage of the law, the state held that the company owed a charge of $185,000. Justice Potter Stewart's majority opinion recognized the long-standing precedent that state police powers may involve some impairment of contractual obligations, but he added:

> If the Contract Clause is to retain any meaning at all, however, it must be understood to impose some limits upon the power of a State to abridge existing contractual relationships, even in the exercise of its otherwise legitimate police power.

In Stewart's judgment, the law differed from previous state laws that had survived Contract Clause challenges in several ways: it was not enacted to deal with emergency economic conditions as existed in *Blaisdell*; it was not enacted to deal with a broad, generalized economic or social problem; and it invaded an area that had not been subject to state regulation when the company had undertaken its contractual obligations. Accordingly, the law was unconstitutional. Despite its apparent erosion in earlier cases, the Contract Clause still must be recognized as a relevant but narrow limitation upon arbitrary state legislation.

Substantive Due Process of Law

As the Contract Clause declined in its protection of vested property rights, another constitutional provision was emerging to fill the void. The addition of the Fourteenth Amendment in 1868 brought due process of law considerations to bear upon property rights, despite the fact that the Fifth Amendment's Due Process Clause had existed for many years. An extended discussion of due process of law guarantees will be presented in Chapter 8, but it is important to provide a brief explanation of the concept at this point.

First, the Due Process Clauses of the Fifth and Fourteenth Amendments are identical, except that the former limits the national government and the latter specifically applies to states. For all practical purposes, both clauses have been interpreted in identical fashion by the courts. Secondly, due process is commonly thought of as either procedural or substantive. **Procedural due process** refers to the manner in which the law is enforced and the procedures to be followed in providing fair treatment to individuals. It is a central component of the individualist view discussed in Chapter 2. **Substantive due process,** on the other hand, refers to the existence of specific rights or liberties within the concept of due process itself. Constitutional expert Henry J. Abraham has defined substantive due process as "referring to the content or subject matter of a law or an ordinance, whereas procedural due process . . . refers to the manner in which a law, an ordinance, an administrative practice, or a judicial task is carried out."[4] For example, slave owners argued that their slaves were property that could not be taken away without violating the Due Process Clause. By holding slaves to be protected property under due process guarantees, slave owners were embracing a substantive view. While this chapter will concern itself with claims of economic substantive due process, that is, business-related liberty, subsequent chapters will examine the application of substantive due process to other matters.

Coming in the immediate post-Civil War era, the Fourteenth Amendment was intended to address the problems of newly freed Negroes in dealing with their state governments. Three clauses in the amendment—privileges and immunities, due process of law, and equal protection—restrict state governments from violating specific guarantees of individual liberty. The notion that these clauses might protect vested economic rights seemed unlikely and farfetched to early observers, but events were to prove otherwise. To clarify the path of substantive due process of law, three time periods will be examined:

1. The Dormant Period (Pre-1897);
2. The Triumph of Economic Substantive Due Process (1897–1937); and,
3. The Demise of Economic Substantive Due Process (Post-1937).

The Dormant Period (Pre–1897)

The association between due process and private property rights had been made prior to the Civil War, although without much significance. Chief Justice Taney's opinion in the *Dred Scott* case cited the Fifth Amendment's due process guarantees as the basis for protecting private property in slaves from congressional restriction. Largely on the basis of the Due Process Clause, Taney invalidated Congress's attempt in the Missouri Compromise to interfere with slave owners' property rights. However, most early attempts to invalidate *state* regulation on due process grounds were unsuccessful. The Slaughterhouse Cases (1873) provided the Court an opportunity to address the issue for the first time since the ratification of the Fourteenth Amendment.

An 1869 Louisiana act regulated slaughterhouses in New Orleans, in effect giving a monopoly to one company and requiring all other slaughterhouse operators to use its facilities on a fee basis. Although the law ostensibly had been passed to prevent further contamination of the city's water supply and to improve general health conditions, it was viewed by some critics as the result of corruption in the legislature. A group of small-slaughterhouse operators and butchers, the Butcher's Benevolent Association, who had been deprived of their businesses, challenged the law in state courts and lost. They contended that the statute violated the Thirteenth Amendment, as well as the Privileges and Immunities, Due Process, and Equal Protection Clauses of the Fourteenth Amendment. The Supreme Court brought forward three separate cases that it heard collectively as the Slaughterhouse Cases.

Writing for the majority, Justice Samuel Miller provided a strong defense of traditional state powers of regulation and found virtually no merit in the claims of the plaintiffs. The Thirteenth Amendment, he stated, was "a declaration designed to establish the freedom of four millions of slaves" and did not refer to private property in "certain localities." As for the clauses of the Fourteenth Amendment, the Court's reasoning was somewhat more involved.

First, the amendment's definition of citizenship identified both federal and state citizenship. As a result, the "privileges or immunities of citizens of the United States" noted in the amendment were not identical to whatever "privileges or immunities" might be associated with state citizenship. According to the Court, federal privileges and immunities might include such things as the right to peaceably assemble and petition for redress of grievances, the privilege of the writ of *habeas corpus,* and the right to use the navigable waters of the United States; but the privilege of doing business in a particular locality stemmed from state, not federal, citizenship. By holding that most privileges and immunities stem from state citizenship, the Court effectively barred use of the Fourteenth Amendment's Privileges and Immunities Clause to oppose state regulatory legislation. Even today, the clause is largely without significance.

As for the argument that Louisiana had deprived the plaintiffs of their property without due process of law, the Court stated:

> It is sufficient to say that under no construction of that provision that we have ever seen, or any that we deem admissible, can the restraint imposed by the State of Louisiana upon the exercise of their trade by the butchers of New Orleans be held to be a deprivation of property within the meaning of that provision.

Due process of law, rather than a substantive protection of private property rights, was a guarantee of procedural protections before the law. As for the Equal Protection Clause, the Court simply held that it applied only to matters of race. Louisiana's legislation had denied no rights guaranteed by the federal Constitution. In sum, the majority opinion in the Slaughterhouse Cases denied that the Fourteenth Amendment had changed the fundamental nature of individual rights. This view "taken as a whole, does seem to narrow considerably the scope of the first section [of the amendment] as conceived by its principal authors." [5]

The dissenting opinions of Justices Stephen Field and Joseph Bradley are important for the ideas they contain, particularly given the direction of later rulings. Bradley's words illustrate this direction, later to be incorporated in the Court's recognition of a "freedom of contract":

> The individual citizen, as a necessity, must be left free to adopt such calling, profession, or trade as may seem to him most conducive to that end . . . This right to choose one's calling is an essential part of that liberty which it is the object of government to protect; and a calling, when chosen, is a man's property and right.

Justice Bradley joined the majority in *Munn* v. *Illinois* (1877), leaving Justice Field and Justice William Strong in dissent. In this case, the majority upheld an Illinois law that fixed maximum charges for grain storage by grain elevators. The legislation was typical of the powerful Granger Movement in the midwestern United States. This movement, which began shortly after the Civil War, signified the growing unrest among the nation's farmers. This unrest resulted from increasing farmer indebtedness, discriminatory rail freight rates, and declining farm prices, to name but a few causes. In several states, these factors led Granger members to become actively involved in politics and work for the passage of favorable legislation. *Munn* v. *Illinois* was one of several Granger Cases ruled upon by the Supreme Court during this time. The Court, finding that the grain storage business had been long devoted to open use by the public, held that "when private property is devoted to a public use, it is subject to public regulation." Ira Munn, who had been fined for violating the maximum rate provisions of the act, claimed that he had been deprived of his liberty and property. Munn's claim, however, was not supported by long-standing interpretation of the Due Process Clauses of the Constitution.

The majority and minority positions of the Court in these cases represent a distinct disagreement over the appropriate role of courts in assessing legislative actions. Chief Justice Morrison Waite's majority opinion in *Munn* recognized potential abuses by legislatures, but stated that "for protection against abuses by legislatures the people must resort to the polls, not to the courts." Justice Field, on the other hand, drew attention to what he termed the "bold assertion of absolute power by the State" and the need to protect the rights of private property against legislative interference. Moreover, both positions are identifiable in the individualist and communitarian framework, as well as in their relationship to the judicial activism and self-restraint issues discussed in Chapter 4. Waite's concern with popular control at the polls reflects a communitarian fondness for the public interest, while Justice Field's yearning for the protection of property from government interference reflects an individualist perspective. Pressures were building upon the justices to begin evaluating the reasonableness and rationality of state regulation.[6]

The Triumph of Economic Substantive Due Process (1897–1937)

Substantive due process of law gradually expanded its hold on state courts during the latter decades of the nineteenth century. However, it was not until 1897 that the Supreme Court invalidated state legislation on substantive due process grounds. In other words, the Court slowly came around to accepting the idea that the Fourteenth Amendment protected property rights from state regulation. The case of *Allgeyer* v. *Louisiana* (1897) shows this change. The case emerged from a Louisiana law that required all insurance companies issuing insurance in the state to meet certain state standards. Allgeyer & Company, a Louisiana firm, paid premiums by mail to a New York insurance firm to insure cargo being shipped out of the state. Since the New York firm did not operate under Louisiana law, Allgeyer was charged with violating the law and ordered to pay a penalty as required by the statute. The owner of the company challenged the constitutionality of the law as violative of due process guarantees of the Fourteenth Amendment.

In striking down the state law in question, the Court showed its willingness to accept the substantive due process protections in the Fourteenth Amendment, going so far as to identify a new freedom in the Constitution— a **freedom of contract.** It was described in Justice Rufus Peckham's majority opinion:

> The "liberty" mentioned in that amendment means, not only the right of the citizen to be free from the mere physical restraint of his person, as by incarceration, but the term is deemed to embrace the right of the citizen to be free in the enjoyment of all his faculties; to be free to use them in all lawful ways; to live and work where he will; to earn his livelihood by any lawful calling; to pursue any livelihood or avocation; and for that purpose to enter into all contracts which may be proper, necessary, and essential to his carrying out to a successful conclusion the purposes above mentioned.

Under this reasoning, the Louisiana statute deprived Allgeyer of due process of law, because the law "prohibits an act which under the federal constitution the defendants had a right to perform." Economic substantive due process of law and its offspring, freedom of contract, had come to be recognized as the law of the land.

Most early freedom-of-contract cases involved employer-employee matters, such as hours of labor and working conditions, and some decisions clearly worked against labor unions. In *Adair* v. *United States* (1908) the Court struck down a provision in a federal labor-management law that outlawed the signing of "yellow-dog" contracts—agreements by which workers pledged not to join unions—and also prohibited employers from firing employees for having joined a union. This provision, said the Court, arbitrarily interfered with negotiations between labor and management. This case marked the first instance in which the Court found the "freedom of contract" in the Fifth Amendment's due process guarantees, holding that Congress could no more than state legislatures interfere "with the liberty of contract which no government can legally justify in a free land." A similar result was reached in *Coppage* v. *Kansas* (1915), where the Court struck down a state law outlawing yellow-dog contracts.

The Court elevated freedom of contract to perhaps its highest level in *Lochner* v. *New York* (1905). Acting upon concern over health and welfare considerations, the New York legislature passed legislation that prohibited employees from working more than ten hours a day or sixty hours a week in a bakery. Joseph Lochner, the owner of a bakery, was fined $50 for violating the act. When his conviction was upheld by state courts, Lochner brought his case to the Supreme Court on a writ of error.

Justice Peckham's opinion focused upon which of two powers or rights should prevail: "the power of the state to legislate or the right of the individual to liberty of person and freedom of contract." Finding that the limit of police power had been surpassed and that no solid basis existed to justify the measure as a health law, the Court reversed Lochner's conviction by 5-4 and upheld "the freedom of master and employee to contract with each other in relation to their employment."

The dissenting opinions of Justices Oliver W. Holmes and John Harlan took aim from different directions. Holmes, as was his practice, criticized his colleagues for their adherence to an economic theory (laissez-faire) "which a large part of the country does not entertain," pointing out that the "Constitution is not intended to embody a particular economic theory." Of course, Justice Holmes typically favored a position of self-restraint, so his criticism of the majority's activism was hardly surprising. Harlan's opinion, joined by the other dissenters, focused upon the problem of questioning the New York legislature's motives and substituting the judgment of the Court for that of the legislature. More importantly, Harlan filled his opinion with factual evidence relating to studies of the bakery industry and health consequences faced by bakers. The use of nonlegal evidence drawn from various sources was quickly to become an important part of the legal system.

Reformers and women's groups—citing health, safety, and welfare concerns—had pushed through legislation in Oregon limiting work by women in certain heavy mechanical establishments and laundries to ten hours per day. Having been retained as counsel for the state, Louis Brandeis (later an associate justice of the Supreme Court) introduced a new form of legal brief. The "Brandeis Brief," first submitted in *Muller* v. *Oregon* (1908), contained only about two pages of legal arguments but over one hundred pages of statistical, medical, sociological, and psychological data designed to show the injurious effects of prolonged labor on females.

Apparently the tactic paid off, as the Court sustained the Oregon law. But the Court carefully carved out an exception to the freedom of contract, citing the physical differences between the sexes and the need to protect the physical well-being of women "in order to preserve the strength and vigor of the race." In short, while convinced by the Brandeis Brief, the Court would not abandon the *Lochner* precedent upholding freedom of contract. The Brandeis Brief became a standard feature of the American legal system.

When the Court upheld an even more ambitious Oregon law in *Bunting* v. *Oregon* (1917), fixing maximum hours for men and women as well as provisions for overtime pay, it seemingly placed the *Lochner* precedent on hold. In *Adkins* v. *Children's Hospital* (1923), however, the Court resurrected *Lochner* to strike down a congressional minimum wage law for women and minors in Washington, D.C. The majority justices were vehemently opposed to the concept of a minimum wage, as evidenced by Justice George Sutherland's opinion:

The feature of this statute which, perhaps more than any other, puts upon it the stamp of invalidity is that it exacts from the employer an arbitrary payment for a purpose and upon a basis having no causal connection with his business, or the contract or the work the employee engages to do. . . A statute requiring an employer to pay in money, to pay at prescribed and regular intervals, to pay the value of the services rendered, even to pay with fair relation to the extent of the benefit obtained from the service, would be understandable. But a statute which prescribes payment without regard to any of these things . . . is so clearly the product of a naked, arbitrary exercise of power that it cannot be allowed to stand under the Constitution of the United States.

The Court's rather surprising settlement upon *Lochner* as the prevailing case in its opinion primarily resulted from economic and not constitutional consistency. Chief Justice William Howard Taft, in dissent, argued that the Court could not logically keep both *Lochner* and *Bunting* precedents alive, although Sutherland's majority opinion made no mention of overruling *Bunting*. Moreover, the chief justice wondered why *Muller* v. *Oregon*, a case involving working hours for women, did not control the *Adkins* decision. By striking down the minimum wage law, the Court had again arrived at the pinnacle of substantive due process and freedom of contract.

In reviewing the pattern of cases arising from the Fourteenth Amendment, several trends are evident. In the first place, the Supreme Court's *Santa Clara County* v. *Southern Pacific Railroad* (1886) ruling that corporations are "persons" for purposes of the Fourteenth Amendment escalated the number of corporation-related cases. From 1872 until 1910, for example, the Court heard 313 cases involving corporations under the amendment but only 28 based upon the claims of blacks for protection of their rights. A second trend is evident in the overwhelming dominance of property-related cases—property claims were litigated in 423 cases, with only 24 and 128 cases dealing with deprivations of life and liberty, respectively. The third trend shows the Court's tendency to invalidate state legislation on due process grounds, doing so ninety times between 1899 and 1921.[7]

At its height, substantive due process of law wielded a significant impact upon the pattern of judicial review. Specifically, it opened the way for the justices on the Supreme Court to rely exclusively upon their own personal policy preferences. Decisions often turned on the likes and dislikes of individual justices toward specific legislation. While the economic aspect of substantive due process did not survive much past 1937, it can be argued that the practice of judicial interpretation based upon the justices' individual preferences has become commonplace.

The Demise of Economic Substantive Due Process (Post–1937)

The Court gave the first sign that its commitment to freedom of contract was weakening in *Nebbia* v. *New York* (1934) when, by a 5-4 vote, it upheld a state law fixing maximum and minimum prices for milk. In reality, the *Nebbia* decision did not send shock waves through supporters of freedom of contract, primarily because the Court did not expressly repudiate its own right to pass judgment on the reasonableness of state laws. That step was taken in *West Coast Hotel* v. *Parrish* (1937).

In that case, a 1913 Washington state minimum wage law for minors and women was challenged when Elsie Parrish, a chambermaid, brought suit against her employer to recover the difference between the wages paid her and the state minimum wage. Writing for the 5-4 Court, Chief Justice Charles Evans Hughes reviewed the history of the freedom of contract up to the *Adkins* decision, concluding that "the decision in the *Adkins* case was a departure from the true application of the principles governing the regulation by the state of the relation of employer and employed." By overruling the vitality of *Adkins* as a precedent, the Court was doing more than simply accepting minimum wage legislation as constitutional. The Supreme Court seemingly had come full circle, recognizing that freedom-of-contract considerations were not absolute and beyond restriction by the state legislatures. Speaking of the rights of legislatures, Hughes added:

> The legislature had the right to consider that its minimum wage requirements would be an important aid in carrying out its policy of protection. The adoption of similar requirements by many States evidences a deepseated conviction both as to the presence of the evil and as to the means adapted to check it. Legislative response to that conviction cannot be regarded as arbitrary or capricious, and that is all we have to decide. *Even if the wisdom of the policy be regarded as debatable and its effects uncertain, still the legislature is entitled to its judgment.* [Emphasis added]

The *West Coast Hotel* v. *Parrish* decision opened the floodgates allowing numerous federal and state laws to pass through the Court's new-found acceptance of economic regulation. Since 1937, the Court has consistently refused to allow challenges to federal or state regulation of business on substantive due process grounds. A concluding example of this trend is presented in *Ferguson* v. *Skrupa* (1963), concerning a Kansas law prohibiting any person other than a lawyer from engaging in the business of debt adjustment. Justice Hugo Black's opinion upholding the law reviewed the long history of substantive due process by which Courts struck down laws they considered to be unwise or foolish. Those days, according to Black, were over:

> Under the system of government created by our Constitution, it is up to legislatures, not courts, to decide on the wisdom and utility of legislation. There was a time when the Due Process Clause was used by this Court to strike down laws which were thought unreasonable, that is, unwise or incompatible with some particular economic or social philosophy. . . The doctrine . . . that due process authorizes courts to hold laws unconstitutional when they believe the legislature has acted unwisely—has long since been discarded. We have returned to the original constitutional proposition that courts do not substitute their social and economic beliefs for the judgment of legislative bodies, who are elected to pass laws.

It should be noted that property rights continue to occupy much of the Court's attention, although not in substantive due process terms. Recent years have witnessed an increase in the number of cases coming to the Court under the following Fifth Amendment proviso: "nor shall private property be taken for public use, without just compensation." The concepts contained within that clause—"taking," "public use," and "just compensation"—refer to the government's power of **eminent domain**—the power to take property for public use. Recent Supreme Court rulings have held that a state may take property if it constitutes a public use and serves a public purpose. This line of reasoning was used in *Hawaii Housing Authority* v. *Midkiff* (1984), in which the Court upheld the power of a state to break up large landholdings and provide for private ownership of the smaller tracts. Despite the fact that the state itself did not intend to use the lands involved, the "taking" fell within the exercise of the state's powers and constituted a "public use," according to the Court.

The matter of "takings" will continue to occupy the Court's attention, as governments implement land-use planning, zoning, and other forms of regulatory control over private property. While it is generally true that government ordinances do not constitute a taking (and, thus, do not require just compensation), the Court's recent ruling in *First English Evangelical Lutheran Church of Glendale* v. *County of Los Angeles, California* (1987) suggests that exceptions may exist. In that case, the Court held that a land-use regulation (flood-control ordinance)) that prohibited the church from constructing buildings on its own property, although only on a temporary basis, was a taking within the meaning of the Constitution. While the Court limited its ruling to the case at hand, the decision is likely to increase the number of land-use zoning ordinances challenged as takings by property owners. As a result, the long-standing individualist and communitarian debate over property rights and government regulation is certain to continue.

In reality, the demise of substantive due process of law in economic matters has opened up vast new areas of authority for state and federal governments (see Chapter 10 for a discussion of substantive due process in non-economic areas). Legislation dealing with a variety of health, safety, and welfare considerations has become commonplace since 1937, with the result that the powers of government have expanded immensely. At the national level, this expansion has been tied most closely to the phenomenal growth of congressional powers in the areas of commerce, taxation, and spending. The resulting expansion of national power is the topic of the following section.

The Regulation of Commerce

Perhaps no single grant of power in the Constitution has exerted such impact upon the federal system as the power "to regulate Commerce with foreign Nations, and among the several States, and with the Indian Tribes" (Art. I, Sec. 8). While regulation of foreign commerce (including the Indian tribes) has been relatively free of controversy, the regulation of interstate commerce has been another matter entirely. The controversy over such regulation can be attributed to several factors. First, the constitution provides no definition of "commerce" that might more clearly describe the proper scope of congressional power. As a result, a good deal of attention has been devoted over the years to settling upon a commonly accepted view of those activities that constitute commerce. Secondly, changes in economic relations and technology, to name but two areas, have demanded the regulation of certain types of commerce that did not even exist when the framers did their work. Thirdly, in the face of ever-broadening federal control of commerce-related matters, state governments and their supporters have fought to retain their place in the federal system. It is difficult to argue with Felix Frankfurter's assessment that the Commerce Clause has "throughout the Court's history been the chief source of its adjudications regarding federalism."[8]

As the following discussion will show, the Constitution's grant of a commerce power to Congress must also be understood as a clear limitation upon the powers of state governments to regulate in the same areas. However, as states' rights supporters have argued, states should possess some concurrent jurisdiction over matters of commerce that affect their interests directly, particularly in areas in which Congress has remained silent. In order to trace the direction of the commerce power since its inception, the discussion begins with the very crucial contributions of two early constitutional experts—Chief Justices Marshall and Taney.

Chief Justice John Marshall and the Commerce Power

The first case to reach the Supreme Court resulting from a dispute over the regulation of commerce was *Gibbons* v. *Ogden* (1824), and it remains one of the classic expositions of the federal commerce power ever handed down by the Court. The controversy stemmed indirectly from the invention of the steamboat and its subsequent entry into the coastal trade of the early nineteenth century. Robert Fulton and Robert Livingston, pioneers in the steamboat's development, obtained an exclusive right to use steam vessels in New York's waters under a grant from the state legislature in 1808. Subsequently, Aaron Ogden leased the right to navigate the waters between New York and New Jersey under this exclusive privilege. He soon faced competition in the person of Thomas Gibbons, a former partner of Ogden's, who had begun to run his two steamboats on much the same New York-New Jersey route. Gibbons had obtained a license to operate his vessel from the federal government as required by the 1793 Federal Coasting Act, a measure designed primarily to license carriers engaged in the coastal trade. Ogden, having paid for what he considered to be a monopoly, obtained an injunction from the state courts prohibiting Gibbons from engaging in direct competition on Ogden's exclusive routes. Gibbons appealed to the Supreme Court—assisted by his well-known counsel, Daniel Webster of Massachusetts.

Ogden's attorney had argued for a definition of commerce limited to "traffic, to buying and selling, or the interchange of commodities," but not including navigation. This limited definition ran counter to Marshall's expansive view of national power, as he stated:

> This would restrict a general term, applicable to many objects, to one of its significations. Commerce, undoubtedly, is traffic, but it is something more: it is intercourse. It describes the commercial intercourse between nations, and parts of nations, in all its branches, and is regulated by prescribing rules for carrying on that intercourse.

In Marshall's mind, commerce included both the commodities of trade and the means of transportation employed, simply because, as he stated, "All America understands, and has uniformly understood, the word 'commerce' to comprehend navigation. It was so understood, and must have been so understood, when the constitution was framed." Marshall's description of commerce as intercourse, which he prefaced with the term "commercial," seemed to suggest that the power to regulate commerce could expand to meet even unforeseen activities of an economic or commercial nature. This view, with some exceptions, has generally prevailed throughout the Constitution's development, enabling Congress to regulate commerce carried on as the result of technological advances unknown to the framers. Examples of such court-approved regulation include telegraphs (*Pensacola Telegraph Company* v. *Western Union Telegraph Company* [1878]), railroads (*Wabash, St. Louis & Pacific Ry. Co.* v. *Illinois* [1886]), as well as radio, airplanes, and television.

Having rejected the argument that steamboat navigation was outside commerce, Marshall addressed the scope of congressional power to regulate commerce, a power which he termed "plenary" or exclusive. Congress had been granted the power to regulate commerce by the Constitution, and the power was unqualified by limitations or restrictions, according to Marshall. Under this analysis, the Federal Coasting Act of 1793 fell unquestionably under the plenary power of Congress to regulate commerce.

As Marshall concluded, the controversy really involved two competing laws—the New York grant of monopoly versus the Federal Coasting Act. Given Marshall's well-known national supremacy preferences, the national law was to be preferred over the state law. As a result, Gibbons—and anyone else with a federal coasting license—could engage in the steamboat business in New York waters. Importantly, the congressional commerce power might be used effectively against state monopolies that intruded into matters of interstate commerce.

As for the question of whether, in regulating commerce among the states, Congress might reasonably intrude into the internal affairs of states in the process, Marshall seemed to offer a strong affirmative answer. Marshall stopped short of ruling out all possible state involvement in matters of interstate commerce, but he seemingly implied that congressional powers of regulation were exclusive, assuming that Congress exercised its prerogative. Marshall recognized that this view could bring federal regulation of certain internal state matters:

> The word "among" means intermingled with. A thing which is among others, is intermingled with them. Commerce among the states, cannot stop at the external boundary line of each State, but may be introduced into the interior. . . Comprehensive as the word "among" is, it may very properly be restricted to that commerce which concerns more States than one.

That commerce "which is completely internal," he pointed out, would remain under the control of the states themselves. Of course, the practical application of these principles has sometimes been difficult to achieve (see Brief 7.2).

John Marshall's legacy with respect to the Commerce Clause supports broad and exclusive congressional regulation of all matters associated with "commercial intercourse" which "concerns more States than one." That definition provided the commerce power with the flexibility to expand with technological and social innovations, even moving into previously state-controlled intrastate concerns. An even more sweeping assessment of Marshall's legacy is provided by a twentieth-century Supreme Court justice:

> Marshall's use of the commerce clause greatly furthered the idea that though we are a federation of states we are also a nation, and gave momentum to the doctrine that state authority must be subject to such limitations as the Court finds it necessary to apply for the protection of the national community. It was an audacious doctrine.[9]

Chief Justice Roger Taney's Dual Federalism

Although Marshall's opinion in *Gibbons* had implied exclusivity for Congress in regulating interstate commerce, his ruling in *Willson* v. *Black Bird Creek*

☐ Brief 7.2   The Shreveport Rate Cases: Offspring of the Marshall Legacy

Under pressure from reformers, radical farm groups such as the Grangers, and even some railroads seeking protection from state legislatures, Congress in 1887 created the Interstate Commerce Commission (ICC), the nation's first independent regulatory commission. Despite some initial hostility from the Supreme Court over its rate-fixing powers, the ICC gradually came to regulate most aspects of the interstate railroad network in the country. This power occasionally brought the ICC into conflict with state commissions or boards that claimed regulatory control over railroad travel within their state boundaries.

Actually cited as *Houston, East & West Texas Railway Co.* v. *United States* (1914), the Shreveport Rate Cases involved a conflict between ICC-mandated interstate rail rates and intrastate Texas rail rates set by the Texas Railroad Commission. The facts of the case are as follows: Three railroads, including the Houston Railway Company, were charged by the Louisiana Railroad Commission with discriminating against interstate commerce between Louisiana and Texas. As such, they were charging much lower rates between Texas cities than for routes of approximately similar distance across the state line. The lower intrastate rates were the result of the Texas Railroad Commission's rate structure, presumably to encourage trade among Texas cities at the expense of Shreveport, Louisiana. After hearings, the

ICC set rates for both interstate and intrastate routes, and the railroads raised their intrastate rates, placing them in conflict with the maximum rates set by the Texas Railroad Commission. The Houston Railway Company brought suit to have the ICC order overturned.

Justice Charles Evans Hughes, writing for the majority, reiterated Marshall's view pertaining to the dominance of Congress in regulating interstate commerce and expanded it logically to apply to certain intrastate activities:

> Congress is empowered to regulate—that is, to provide the law for the government of interstate commerce. . . Wherever the interstate and intrastate transactions of carriers are so related that the government of the one involves the control of the other, it is Congress, and not the State, that is entitled to prescribe the final and dominant rule. . . This is not to say that Congress possesses the authority to regulate the internal commerce of a State, as such, but that it does possess the power to foster and protect interstate commerce, and to take all measures necessary or appropriate to that end, although intrastate transactions of interstate carriers may thereby be controlled.

The ruling in the Shreveport Rate Cases, upholding the ICC's authority to set reasonable intrastate rail rates to bring them into line with interstate rates, stands as an offspring of Marshall's view of interstate commerce. The resulting effect has been the whittling away of state regulation powers over even intrastate matters.

Marsh Co. (1829), which upheld the building of a dam across a navigable creek that might arguably have involved the interests of the United States, showed that states were still able to police their internal affairs. Indeed, Marshall's treatment of the controversy as a police-power matter seemed to open the way for future rulings. Marshall's successor, Roger B. Taney, was a strong supporter of certain state powers of regulation, particularly in matters not involving national concerns. His approach, discussed in the preceding chapter, became known as "dual federalism," reflecting the idea that the national and state governments are actually co-equal sovereign entities, each supreme in its own area of authority. Taney's dual federalism, as expressed in several rulings, was to become an effective counterpoint to Marshall's broader, more nationalistic approach to commerce matters until well into the twentieth century.

The Taney Court gave an indication of its willingness to allow some state interference in commerce matters in the case of *New York* v. *Miln* (1837). The ruling upheld a New York law requiring all ship captains entering port in New York to provide detailed reports on immigrant passengers and, in some instances, to post bonds for immigrants who later required public support. The law obviously was intended to limit immigration through New York City and, as such, could be regarded as an interference with foreign commerce.

The majority, however, ignored the commerce questions and settled instead upon the law as a valid regulation of police power.

In *Cooley* v. *The Board of Wardens of the Port of Philadelphia* (1851), the Taney Court handed down perhaps its most important contribution to the issue of interstate commerce and the concurrent authority of states. The case originated with an 1803 Pennsylvania law requiring ships entering or leaving Philadelphia to employ a locally-licensed pilot for navigation purposes. Certain exemptions were provided, but they did not apply to Aaron Cooley's two ships which had not used pilots. As such, Cooley was subject to the required penalty. Cooley lost his case at the state level and appealed to the Supreme Court on the grounds that the Pennsylvania law was an unconstitutional regulation of commerce by the states.

Speaking for the majority, Justice Benjamin Curtis noted that Congress had not legislated on the matter of pilots, citing a 1789 law that allowed existing state pilotage laws to continue in effect. Since no federal law covering pilots had existed to conflict with Pennsylvania's statute, the question before the Court concerned whether the Constitution's delegation of interstate commerce powers to Congress excluded states from exercising any authority of their own. The resulting doctrine, known as **selective exclusiveness,** held that

> the mere grant to Congress of the power to regulate commerce, did not deprive the States of power to regulate pilots, and that although Congress has legislated on this subject, its legislation manifests an intention, with a single exception, not to regulate this subject, but to leave its regulation to the several States. . . this opinion . . . does not extend to the question what other subjects, under the commercial power, are within the exclusive control of Congress, or may be regulated by the States in the absence of all congressional legislation.

In effect, the *Cooley* opinion held that Congress had not selected pilots as subjects of regulation, opting against exclusiveness in the matter. On the other hand, the Court recognized that some subjects "are in their nature national, or admit only of one uniform system, or plan of regulation." In these, Congress would have exclusive power. Importantly, these could be dealt with on a case-by-case basis, looking at the specific issues in each instance. However, in the absence of federal legislation, states could indeed regulate certain aspects of interstate commerce. The Pennsylvania law was upheld.

Justice Felix Frankfurter later summed up Taney's legacy in the following manner:

> Taney's chief difference with Marshall was in his challenge of the latter's central doctrine, that the "dormant" commerce clause operated to impose restrictions on state authority which it was the duty of the Court to define and enforce. . . He flatly denied that the mere grant of the commerce power operated to limit state power.[10]

Proponents of Taney's dual federalism in the years following *Cooley* sought to restrict federal regulation of commerce and thereby protect the states from federal intervention in their affairs. The subject of railroads, as noted in the Shreveport Rate Cases, was an exception,[11] but other activities such as production and manufacturing gradually were held by dual-federalist courts as falling outside the meaning of the Commerce Clause or not constituting one of the proper subjects for national regulation. In the sections that follow, attention will be given to several areas in which competing views of the commerce power have been most significant.

The Production and Commerce Dichotomy

In 1890, Congress passed the Sherman Antitrust Act, prohibiting contracts, combinations, and trusts that were "in restraint of trade" in interstate commerce. In *United States* v. *E. C. Knight Co.* (1895), the government brought suit against the American Sugar Refining Company, a large combination that included the Knight Company and controlled nearly 98 percent of sugar refining in the country. As this case represented the initial test of the Sherman Act, its outcome was crucial in establishing the Court's position.

Chief Justice Melville Fuller, writing for the 8-1 Court, held that the Sherman Act did not apply to monopolies such as the American Sugar Refining Company, because Congress was not authorized to regulate manufacturing or production. By defining commerce so narrowly as to exclude manufacturing and production activities, the Court was protecting state power from federal encroachment and promoting a laissez-faire approach to the economy. Fuller's attempt to establish the relationship between commerce and manufacturing is set out in part:

> That which belongs to commerce is within the jurisdiction of the United States, but that which does not belong to commerce is within the jurisdiction of the police power of the State. . . Doubtless the power to control the manufacture of a given thing involves in a certain sense the control of its disposition, but this is a secondary and not the primary sense; and although the exercise of that power may result in bringing the operation of commerce into play, it does not control it and affects it only incidentally and indirectly. *Commerce succeeds to manufacture, and is not a part of it.* [Emphasis added]

The Court's new standard for determining whether an activity was subject to congressional control revolved around the idea of "direct" and "indirect" effects upon commerce. If an activity affected commerce "directly," it was subject to federal regulation, but activities with "indirect" effects were beyond federal control. Production and manufacturing, said the Court, were of only secondary importance to interstate commerce and, as such, exerted only an indirect effect. The artificial distinction between manufacturing and commerce resulting from the **direct-indirect-effects doctrine** removed several important economic activities from federal control, most notably, mining, agriculture, and oil production.

The Court largely sought to maintain the distinction between direct and indirect effects until after 1937, even though the interpretation became extremely vague and inconsistent in later years. The cases of *Schechter Poultry Co.* v. *United States* (1935) and *Carter* v. *Carter Coal Company* (1936) illustrate the problems associated with the doctrine. In *Schechter,* the Supreme Court unanimously struck down the New Deal's National Industrial Recovery Act (NIRA). Although the law was overturned primarily on the grounds that legislative power had been illegally delegated, the commerce provisions of the act were also found invalid. (See a discussion of the delegation issue in Chapter 5.)

Briefly, the NIRA had sought to stabilize conditions within basic industries by creating "codes of competition" governing these industries. These codes were to govern virtually all aspects of an industry—including wages, prices, working conditions, production, and marketing. In reality, the NIRA had become something of an embarrassment to the Roosevelt New Deal, and it is quite probable that some members of the administration were hoping for the Supreme Court to invalidate the entire law. Even Franklin Roosevelt may have been in that group, although he reportedly favored keeping the act's "wages, hours, and child labor provisions." [12]

The Schechters ran a poultry business in New York City and were charged with failure to abide by the poultry code in the New York area. Because of the extraordinarily detailed and overlapping nature of the codes, however, the Schechters were charged with, among other things, selling an unfit chicken. As a result, the controversy has become known as the "Sick Chicken" Case. The case is important, though, for the Court's treatment of the poultry codes' direct and indirect effects upon commerce. Chief Justice Hughes stated:

> In determining how far the federal government may go in controlling intrastate transactions upon the ground that they "affect" interstate commerce, there is a necessary and well-established definition between direct and indirect effects. The precise line can be drawn only as individual cases arise, but the distinction is clear in principle. Direct effects are illustrated by the railroad cases we have cited. . . But where the effect of intrastate transactions upon interstate commerce is merely indirect, such transactions remain within the domain of state power. If the commerce clause were construed to reach all enterprises and transactions which could be said to have an indirect effect upon interstate commerce, the federal authority would embrace practically all the activities of the people.

The Hughes opinion clearly distinguished between matters of production and the earlier railroad cases. As noted, the Shreveport Rate Cases recognized federal power to regulate certain aspects of intrastate commerce that affected interstate commerce. But railroad regulation presumably was as far as the Court was willing to go. Production, as such, remained beyond federal authority.

In *Carter* v. *Carter Coal Company* (1936), the Court struck down a federal law regulating labor relations throughout the mining industry. The Bituminous Coal Conservation Act of 1935 regulated both prices and wages in the coal industry, and Congress had required that these provisions be considered as separate constitutional issues should the act be challenged in court. In *Carter*, the majority ignored the congressional directive.

Justice Sutherland's majority opinion showed how confusing and inconsistent the matter of direct and indirect effects had become, citing "the manner in which the effect has been brought about" as the key element in the process. Presumably, since the regulation of wages and hours for miners affects, in the Court's words, "the extraction of coal from the mine," such regulations affect production and not commerce:

> Commerce in the coal mined is not brought into being by force of these activities, but by negotiations, agreements, and circumstances entirely apart from production. Mining brings the subject matter of commerce into existence. Commerce disposes of it.

According to the Court, the "magnitude of the effect" was unimportant, so statistics concerning workers, production, and shipping were beyond consideration. In reality, whether an effect was direct or indirect seemed to turn on its timing with relationship to commerce. Since mining brought coal into existence before commerce began, it constituted only an indirect effect, much the same as had the wage, hour, and production requirements imposed upon the Schechter Poultry Company. Accordingly, the Court held the Bituminous Coal Act to be an unconstitutional use of the federal commerce power and an invasion of the reserved powers of the states.

The Court's refusal to consider production and manufacturing as proper subjects for congressional regulation stemmed both from a desire to protect limited state powers of control and from a general aversion to government interference in the economy. In support of the first objective, the Court consistently fell back upon the dual federalism of earlier years to oppose federal regulation, and the Tenth Amendment's "reserved" powers served as the primary constitutional barrier. As for the laissez-faire preferences of the Court, it need only be remembered that the justices responsible for the *Knight* ruling also constructed the freedom-of-contract doctrine discussed earlier. Professor Edward S. Corwin has noted that the Court's acceptance of laissez-faire as a constitutional doctrine after 1890 created a no-man's land in which business interests often escaped all regulation. He described the process in the following way:

> When a State in professed exercise of its reserved powers passed a law regulative of business and the Court found it to impinge directly on interstate business, the law was pronounced void on the ground of interfering with Congress's power over commerce among the States. Conversely, when Congress in professed exercise of its power to regulate commerce among the States, passed legislation which impinged directly upon certain processes of business which the Court held to be local, the act was pronounced void as an interference with the reserved powers of the States.[13]

It would take several years, numerous judicial decisions, and considerable economic strife before national and state governments would be able to escape the no-man's land of economic regulation.

The "Current" or "Stream of Commerce"

The formal, legalistic definition of commerce in the *Knight* case ignored the realities of business and trade, and the artificial distinction between direct and indirect effects was partly to blame. While *Knight* specifically held production/manufacturing to be only indirectly related to commerce, it said nothing about the effects of numerous other activities. Particularly troublesome were those local transactions that occurred in a fixed location as a part of the larger interstate transportation of goods. In the case of *Swift and Company* v. *United States* (1905), the Court addressed one type of local transaction, and Justice Holmes's majority opinion showed a willingness to consider commerce from a more practical standpoint than had past decisions.[14]

The government charged numerous meat packers, including Swift and Company, with a conspiracy to fix livestock prices at the stockyards—a violation of the Sherman Antitrust Act. Livestock producers who shipped their animals to another state for sale found that no price competition existed at the stockyards. The appellants claimed that the buying and selling of the livestock was a local transaction, occurring while the cattle were "at rest." As such, the transaction should be considered outside the normal movement of interstate commerce. According to Justice Holmes, the issues were very different from those in *Knight,* citing the fact that the earlier case had involved manufacturing while *Swift* concerned sales. Nonetheless, Holmes conceded that "the two cases are near to each other . . . but the line between them is distinct."

Having safely insulated the livestock transactions from production, the Court constructed a doctrine that allowed local transactions (other than production, of course) to be regulated as part of the flow of commerce. This doctrine, called the **current of commerce,** was described by Holmes as follows:

> Commerce among the States is not a technical legal conception, but a practical one, drawn from the course of business. When cattle are sent for sale from a place in one State, with the expectation that they will end their transit, after purchase, in another, and when in effect they do so, with only the interruption necessary to find a purchaser at the stock yards, and when this is a typical, constantly recurring course, the current thus existing is a current of commerce among the States, and the purchase of the cattle is a part and incident of such commerce.

The majority held that the local buying and selling of cattle was part of a larger interstate commerce in livestock and that the stockyard conspiracy to fix prices was "in restraint of trade" in interstate commerce. Seemingly, the *Swift* doctrine offered increased latitude to Congress in its efforts to regulate local activities related to interstate commerce. If commerce is to be viewed as a "current," surely it must flow through states, touching most business transactions in the process, perhaps even production. However, the *Swift* decision did not have an immediate impact upon the meaning of the Commerce Clause.

The Court did uphold the Packers and Stockyards Act of 1921 by relying heavily upon the same current-of-commerce or stream-of-commerce analogy in the case of *Stafford* v. *Wallace* (1922). The act authorized the secretary of agriculture to employ numerous methods to regulate prices and other business practices in stockyards, primarily as a reaction to well-publicized reports of illegal activity and corruption. Speaking for the Court, Chief Justice Taft likened stockyards to "a throat through which the current flows" in upholding the act.

Before 1937, however, the stream-of-commerce doctrine enjoyed very little success in broadening congressional power except perhaps in the nation's stockyards. The Court refused to extend the doctrine to the previously noted *Schechter* and *Carter* cases, although it did go to considerable lengths in *Schechter* to explain why the doctrine was invalid. According to Justice Hughes:

> The mere fact that there may be a constant flow of commodities into a State does not mean that the flow continues after the property has arrived and has become commingled with the mass of property within the State and is there held solely for the local disposition and use. So far as the poultry here in question is concerned, the flow in interstate commerce had ceased. . . Hence, decisions which deal with a stream of interstate commerce—where goods come to rest within a State temporarily and are later to go forward in interstate commerce—and with the regulations of transactions involved in that practical continuity of movement, are not applicable here.

As the Court's position in *Schechter* demonstrates, dual federalism continued to exert a powerful impact upon the federal commerce power. Even the stream of commerce had its limits, being unable to penetrate the local matters of production and manufacturing. However, when the support for dual federalism began to dwindle after 1937, it was to be the stream of commerce that helped lead the way toward an expanded federal commerce power.

Commerce as a Federal Police Power

The previous sections have focused upon the uses of the federal commerce power to regulate, promote, and protect economic activity. However, a broad interpretation of the Commerce Clause has allowed the federal government to become involved in a variety of noneconomic matters. There is no federal police power to be found in the Constitution, and earlier discussions have emphasized the reserved powers of states to protect matters of health, safety, morals, and welfare. How, then, does Congress exercise a police power when none exists? As will be discussed, Congress has often responded to popular demands and technological changes to enforce a kind of police power upon Americans. Primarily, it has used the two prominent powers of commerce and taxation (discussed in a later section of this chapter) to accomplish its purposes.

The first wave of commerce-based police-power legislation began in the late nineteenth century and continued through the first decade of the twentieth century. During this time, concern increased over matters which some considered to be societal problems and "evils" requiring a national solution. For example, responding to the demands of a powerful anti-gambling lobby, Congress passed a law in 1895 prohibiting the transportation of lottery tickets in interstate commerce. In reality, the law's central aim was the abolition of gambling through lotteries, rather than the regulation of commerce.

The law was tested in *Champion* v. *Ames* (1903) and upheld in a narrow 5-4 decision. Justice Harlan, who spoke for the majority, emphasized two important matters. First, by drawing heavily from Marshall's earlier *Gibbons* v. *Ogden* opinion, Harlan emphasized the plenary nature of congressional power over commerce, even extending it to include the lottery tickets in question. In the process, Harlan dismissed the appellant's claim that lottery tickets had no value in themselves and as such could not be considered "subjects of commerce." Secondly, Harlan's opinion dealt with the relationship between the regulation of commerce and Congress's prohibition of lottery tickets. Did the regulatory power authorize such prohibitions? Harlan answered the question in the affirmative using the following rationale:

> If lottery traffic, *carried on through interstate commerce,* is a matter of which Congress may take cognizance and over which its power may be exerted, can it be possible that it must tolerate the traffic, and simply regulate the manner in which it may be carried on? Or may not Congress, for the protection of the people of all the States, and under the power to regulate interstate commerce, devise such means, within the scope of the Constitution, and not prohibited by it, as will drive that traffic out of commerce among the States?

As for the possibility that this decision might open up the power of Congress to arbitrarily exclude any commodity or thing from commerce which it chose, Harlan did not seem overly alarmed, indicating that the Court could "consider the constitutionality of such legislation when we must do so." At any rate, the growth of a federal police power had begun.

In the early years of the twentieth century, the public became increasingly aware of numerous problems, often through the work of enterprising journalists and writers bent upon exposing society's ills and evils. Termed "muckrakers" by President Theodore Roosevelt, these writers aroused the public to demand some federal protective legislation. Their efforts can be seen in a number of laws: the Pure Food and Drug Act (1906); the Meat Inspection Act (1906); the White Slave Traffic Act of 1910 (Mann Act); and the Child Labor Act of 1916. Each of these laws used congressional power to prohibit certain materials from interstate commerce, as supported by the Court's *Champion v. Ames* decision.

The Pure Food and Drug Act was upheld by the Court in *Hipolite Egg Co. v. United States* (1911), which concerned the validity of a federal order seizing several cases of preserved eggs. In *Hoke v. United States* (1913), the Court ruled in favor of the Mann Act's constitutionality in prohibiting the transportation of women for immoral purposes in interstate or foreign commerce. This, the majority stated, did not invade the police powers of the states. But the Court's support for such a broadened federal police power had its limits, and these became evident in the controversy over child labor.

Spurred on by the efforts of reformers, Congress passed the Child Labor Act of 1916 to deal with the widespread use and exploitation of child labor in American industry and manufacturing. Given the well-established distinction between manufacturing and commerce, however, Congress carefully refrained from imposing any direct regulations upon the manufacturing process, choosing instead to use its powers to prohibit shipments of certain articles in interstate commerce. The act barred from interstate commerce the products of establishments that employed children under the age of fourteen. It also banned factory shipments when children between fourteen and sixteen were employed more than eight hours a day or more than six days a week. Roland Dagenhart, the father of two minor sons who worked in a cotton mill, filed suit against U.S. Attorney W. C. Hammer to stop the act's enforcement. Hammer appealed to the Supreme Court following a district court ruling against the act.

Writing for a 5-4 majority in *Hammer v. Dagenhart* (1918), Justice William Day found the Child Labor Act of 1916 to be an unconstitutional use of the commerce power. His opinion sought to distinguish the case from those earlier and quite acceptable police-power cases involving lotteries, impure food and drugs, meat inspection, and prostitution. According to Day, the prohibition of products made in factories employing children differed significantly from the earlier congressional prohibitions in which the commodities being barred from commerce were "harmful." The products in the present case "are of themselves harmless" and do not justify the congressional prohibition on their shipment. Congress may use its powers to prohibit the movement of interstate commerce only with regard to "harmful" products. Justice Day considered the alternative:

> If it were otherwise, all manufacture intended for interstate shipment would be brought under federal control to the practical exclusion of the authority of the States, a result certainly not contemplated by the framers of the Constitution when they vested in Congress the authority to regulate commerce among the States.

In striking down the act, the Court returned to the principles of dual federalism in protecting state interests from federal encroachment, even though it meant constructing a rather novel interpretation of the commerce power. The opinion reiterated the traditional arguments distinguishing production from commerce and made absolutely no mention of the current-of-commerce analogy. Justice Day and his colleagues concluded with what could be considered an unabashed acceptance of dual federalism:

> In our view the necessary effect of this act is, by means of a prohibition against the movement in interstate commerce of ordinary commercial commodities, to regulate the hours of labor of children in factories and mines within the States, a purely state authority. Thus the act in a two-fold sense is repugnant to the Constitution. It not only transcends the authority delegated to Congress over commerce but also exerts a power as to a purely local matter to which the federal authority does not extend.

The ruling in *Hammer* v. *Dagenhart* demonstrated the continued vitality of dual federalism and the production/commerce dichotomy. Insofar as its effect upon a federal police power, the results were less clear. Child labor legislation was unacceptable to the Supreme Court despite growing popular support for such policies. In fact, the entire child labor odyssey represented an ongoing conflict between what one author has termed "popular sovereignty and judicial supervision." [15] In the framework of this study, child labor pitted the communitarian and individualist theories of government against each other. For communitarians, society's interests in matters of health and welfare were paramount; individualists held tightly to the concept of individual liberty in the workplace and laissez-faire economic theory. The judiciary would uphold the individualist concept for more than twenty years following *Hammer* v. *Dagenhart*.

While federal attempts to police working conditions, hours, and wages, for example, were likely to be unsuccessful, "harmful" articles presumably still could be reached. Along this line, the Court upheld a federal law prohibiting the interstate transportation of stolen cars (*Brooks* v. *United States* [1925]) and one, popularly known as the "Lindberg Act," prohibiting the movement of kidnapped persons (*Gooch* v. *United States* [1936]). In summary, the Court's acceptance of federal police power during this era generally was limited to regulating such "sinful" or criminal activities as gambling, prostitution, and alcohol consumption. It did not extend to regulation or reform of the economy.

The Doctrines Resolved: Federal Power over Commerce

As previously noted with regard to substantive due process of law, 1937 marked a turning point in judicial attitudes toward economic regulation. In that same year, the Court embarked upon a path that would ultimately eliminate the inconsistency and uncertainty contained in the production/commerce dichotomy, the stream-of-commerce doctrine, and the police-power question.

The turning point in commerce cases came in *National Labor Relations Board* v. *Jones & Laughlin Steel Corporation* (1937). In that case, the Court took a significant step toward changing its long-standing opposition to government control over production, and it did so in part through reliance on the stream-of-commerce doctrine. The facts leading to the case are these: In 1935,

Congress passed the National Labor Relations Act (NLRA), which guaranteed labor the right to organize and bargain collectively. (Collective bargaining provisions in the NIRA had been struck down in *Schechter*.) The act authorized the National Labor Relations Board (NLRB) to investigate and prevent unfair practices against labor. When Jones & Laughlin Steel fired ten employees for engaging in union activities, the NLRB obtained a court order compelling the reinstatement of the fired workers. The company refused to comply with the order, claiming that the NLRA was an unconstitutional regulation of all production, invading the reserved powers of the states.

Writing for a 5-4 majority, Chief Justice Hughes upheld the unfair labor practice provisions of the NLRA on the grounds that labor-management unrest posed the type of threat to interstate commerce that Congress was empowered to prevent. While his opinion technically ignored the stream-of-commerce test, Hughes clearly considered the doctrine to be part of the government's broad interest in protecting interstate commerce. He stated:

> The fundamental principle is that the power to regulate commerce is the power to enact "all appropriate legislation" for "its protection and advancement" . . . to adopt measures "to promote its growth and insure its safety" . . . "to foster, protect, control and restrain". . . . That power is plenary and may be exerted to protect interstate commerce "no matter what the source of the dangers which threaten it."

Rather than directly overruling the earlier *Schechter* and *Carter* decisions, the opinion went to considerable lengths to distinguish those cases from the one at hand, declaring only that they "were not controlling." By upholding congressional authority to regulate labor-management relations, the Court dealt a crippling blow to the old "production is not commerce" doctrine and the confusing direct-indirect effects controversy.

An even broader step was taken by the Court in an accompanying case, *National Labor Relations Board* v. *Friedman-Harry Marks Clothing Co.* (1937). In this case, the respondent was a small manufacturer of clothing with certainly only a very modest effect upon interstate commerce. Nonetheless, Chief Justice Hughes noted the interstate nature of the clothing industry in general and essentially ignored the actual effect of the company's production upon commerce.

Interestingly, the stream-of-commerce doctrine actually began to play a smaller role in matters relating to the regulation of commerce, as the Court moved more strongly into a broadened view of the commerce power. A series of labor relations cases in 1938 and 1939 resulted in the Court's willingness to consider "potential" effects upon commerce as sufficient to justify regulation, it no longer being necessary to show a stream of commerce or a significant volume of business. In these cases, the Court upheld NLRB orders governing a fruit-packing business moving only 37 percent of its products in interstate commerce (*Santa Cruz Fruit Packing Co.* v. *National Labor Relations Board*), a power company that sold power only within a single state (*Consolidated Edison Co.* v. *National Labor Relations Board*), and a garment maker who sold his entire output within the state (*National Labor Relations Board* v. *Fainblatt*). Quite clearly, while the stream-of-commerce doctrine had laid the foundation for these changes, the commerce power had moved beyond it.

Whereas the *Jones & Laughlin* decision initiated a new judicial approach to commerce, later cases completed the transformation. In *United States* v. *Darby Lumber Co.* (1941), the Court upheld the constitutionality of the Fair Labor Standards Act (FLSA) of 1938. This law was applicable to all employees engaged in interstate commerce or in the production of goods for interstate commerce. For those workers, a national minimum wage of twenty-five cents per hour was established, along with a forty-four-hour standard work week and provisions for overtime pay. The act also prohibited the shipment in interstate commerce of any commodities produced in violation of the minimum wage provisions. Moreover, the statute also virtually restated the Child Labor Act of 1916, making it unlawful to ship goods in interstate commerce that had been produced in factories employing child labor within the previous thirty days.

The government prosecuted the Georgia-based Darby Lumber Company for failure to abide by the wage and hour provisions of the FLSA. In its defense, the Darby Company contended that the FLSA regulated wages and hours of persons engaged in manufacturing, an area reserved to the states for control. In writing for a unanimous Court, Justice Harlan Stone appropriately answered the manufacturing argument with John Marshall's well-known words from *Gibbons* v. *Ogden* that the power of Congress over interstate commerce "is complete in itself, may be exercised to its utmost extent, and acknowledges no limitations other than are prescribed in the Constitution."

Stone noted that the law did not invade state power "merely because either its motive or its consequence is to restrict the use of articles of commerce within the states of destination; and is not prohibited unless by other Constitutional provisions." The opinion placed responsibility for assessing the motive and purpose of legislation with the legislature and not the courts, noting that

> whatever their motive and purpose, regulations of commerce which do not infringe some constitutional prohibition are within the plenary power conferred on Congress by the Commerce Clause. . . Subject only to that limitation . . we conclude that the prohibition of the shipment interstate of goods produced under the forbidden substandard labor conditions is within the constitutional authority of Congress.

By upholding congressional power to regulate wages and hours of employees engaged in production or manufacturing, the Court was at odds with its previous decisions in several cases, particularly *Hammer* v. *Dagenhart* and the *Schechter* and *Carter* cases. The *Hammer* precedent was simply dismissed as "a distinction which was novel when made and unsupported by any provision of the Constitution. . . It should be and now is overruled." Hence, the word "harmful" was again removed from interpretations of the Commerce Clause. Finally, the significance of the *Carter* decision was limited as well.

The demise of dual federalism as a barrier to federal regulation of commerce was nearly completed in *Darby*. Historically, proponents of dual federalism had relied upon the Tenth Amendment's reserved powers as their shield against federal encroachment of state powers. Justice Stone's *Darby* opinion found that the Tenth Amendment "states but a truism that all is retained which has not been surrendered." Thus, the Tenth Amendment would offer no protection against the federal regulation of interstate commerce (see Brief 7.3).

☐ *Brief 7.3   The Federal Minimum Wage*

Since passage of the Fair Labor Standards Act (FLSA), the federal minimum wage has been raised numerous times, reaching a level of $3.35 per hour in mid-1988. Just as significantly, Court decisions since *Darby* have broadened the definition of the FLSA phrase "production of goods for commerce." As a result, millions of workers gradually have been encompassed by minimum wage legislation, including employees involved in the maintenance of a building in which others produce and sell clothing in interstate commerce (*A. B. Kirschbaum* v. *Walling* [1942]), a night watchman (*Walton* v. *Southern Package Corporation* [1944]), and elevator operators in an office building (*Borden Co.* v. *Borella* [1945]).

Amendments to the FLSA in 1974, however, posed a quite different problem. Under these amendments, the minimum wage was made applicable to almost all public employees at the state and local levels. In *National League of Cities* v. *Usery* (1976), the Supreme Court ruled 5-4 that the FLSA amendments were unconstitutional. Writing for the majority, Justice William Rehnquist invoked the Tenth Amendment and state sovereignty in a manner reminiscent of past dual-federalist courts:

> We have repeatedly recognized that there are attributes of sovereignty attaching to every state government which may not be impaired by Congress, not because Congress may lack an affirmative grant of legislative authority to reach the matter, but because the Constitution prohibits it from exercising the authority in that manner. . . One undoubted attribute of state sovereignty is the States' power to determine the wages which shall be paid to those whom they employ in order to carry out their governmental functions, what hours those persons will work, and what compensation will be provided where these employees may be called upon to work overtime.

In the following years, uncertainty over what these state "governmental functions" might include caused some erosion of the *Usery* doctrine. (See, e.g.,, the Court's upholding of the Surface Mining Control and Reclamation Act in *Hodel* v. *Virginia Surface Mining and Reclamation Association* [1981] and *Hodel* v. *Indiana* [1981].)

Finally, in the case of *Garcia* v. *San Antonio Metropolitan Transit Authority* (1985), the Court, in yet another 5-4 ruling, overturned the *Usery* precedent. The dispute in the case concerned the San Antonio Metropolitan Transit Authority (SAMTA) and several of its employees, including Joe Garcia, who had filed suit to recover overtime pay to which they were entitled under the FLSA. Relying upon the *Usery* precedent, SAMTA claimed immunity from the overtime provisions of the act.

Justice Harry Blackmun, who switched from his position in *Usery*, wrote the majority opinion in *Garcia*. He began by noting the heavy federal subsidization of urban mass transit in the United States, with particular reference toward SAMTA. Next, Blackmun stressed the relationship between state sovereignty and the federal commerce power, noting that the Commerce Clause was limited with respect to "States as States" only by the procedural safeguards found in the federal system itself. Courts, he added, should not insert their own limitations upon the federal commerce power. Nothing in the FLSA's overtime-pay or minimum-wage regulations could be perceived as "destructive of state sovereignty or violative of any constitutional provision." As a result, SAMTA would face the same FLSA provisions with respect to overtime pay as any other employer, public or private.

Justice Lewis Powell's dissenting opinion painted a dismal picture of the decision's effect upon the federal system: "Today's decision effectively reduces the Tenth Amendment to meaningless rhetoric when Congress acts pursuant to the Commerce Clause." Overstatement? Perhaps. Nevertheless, the closeness of the decision and the tone of both majority and dissenting positions indicated that the *Garcia* case had touched a nerve, and the federal system, as usual, was the cause.

If the *Jones & Laughlin* and *Darby* precedents had left any doubts as to the demise of dual federalism and the production/commerce dichotomy, these doubts were removed by the ruling in *Wickard* v. *Filburn* (1942). At issue was the Agricultural Adjustment Act of 1938, by which Congress established a marketing quota for wheat and authorized the secretary of agriculture to set acreage quotas for participating farmers. Producers agreeing to participate in the AAA plan accepted an allotment for wheat that they could market at a subsidized price approximately three times greater than the prevailing world market price. Penalties were to be imposed for excess production.

Roscoe C. Filburn, an Ohio farmer, exceeded his acreage allotment and produced several hundred bushels of wheat over his quota. He refused to pay the penalty due on the excess wheat, claiming that his excess production was intended for consumption on his own farm and, as such, was beyond the reach of the federal commerce power. The law stipulated that excess wheat could avoid the penalty only by being placed in storage.

In a strong, unanimous opinion, Justice Robert Jackson repudiated the long-standing production/commerce dichotomy and the issue of "direct" versus "indirect" effects, stating:

> Whether the subject of the regulation in question was "production," "consumption," or "marketing" is, therefore, not material for purposes of deciding the question of federal power before us. That an activity is of local character may help in a doubtful case to determine whether Congress intended to reach it. . . But even if appellee's activity be local and though it may not be regarded as commerce, it may still, whatever its nature, be reached by Congress if it exerts a *substantial economic effect on interstate commerce,* and this irrespective of whether such effect is what might at some earlier time have been defined as "direct" or "indirect." [Emphasis added]

In short, the determination of whether a local activity can be regulated by Congress under its commerce power rests upon practical considerations of cumulative economic effect. Using this premise, the majority opinion analyzed the effect of consumption of home-grown wheat on interstate commerce and found it to be "the most variable factor in the disappearance of the wheat crop," adding that "home-grown wheat in this sense competes with wheat in commerce." The distinction between production and commerce, long a standard dual-federalist doctrine, was gone. The proper regulation of interstate commerce would henceforth be determined by analyzing the practical economic effects of an activity, and such determinations would generally be left to legislative and not judicial consideration.

Two Applications of the Commerce Power

The expansion of national power through the regulation of interstate commerce has affected a number of policy areas. Two of the most important developments stemming from commercial regulation have involved antitrust prosecutions and increased federal protection of civil rights and liberties. This section will discuss each area briefly.

Antitrust Law

As noted earlier, the Sherman Antitrust Act of 1890 marked the national government's initial entry into the prosecution of monopolies and trusts for the purpose of preserving competition in the economy.[16] In part, the Sherman Act provided that "every contract, combination in the form of trust or otherwise, or conspiracy, in restraint of trade or commerce among the several states, or with foreign nations, is hereby declared to be illegal." The *Knight* case, discussed earlier, cast significant doubts upon the Sherman Act's future by excluding monopolies in manufacturing from the scope of the law. Gradually, however, the government's "trustbusters" under Presidents Theodore Roosevelt and William Howard Taft enjoyed some successes.

The government's celebrated first victory occurred in *Northern Securities Company* v. *United States* (1904), a case involving powerful railroad barons

James J. Hill and E. H. Harriman, as well as financier J. P. Morgan. The highly publicized case resulted in a 5-4 victory for the government, with the Court deciding that the Northern Securities Company, a New Jersey holding company organized by Hill and Harriman to merge their competing railroads, was in restraint of trade and an illegal combination in interstate commerce. Significantly, Justice Harlan's majority opinion suggested that a holding company, which was itself not directly part of interstate commerce, could nonetheless still operate "in restraint of trade." The following year, the Court's current-of-commerce holding in the *Swift* case (discussed previously) further opened illegal combinations to federal antitrust prosecution.

In the famous *Standard Oil* v. *United States* (1911) case, the Supreme Court announced the **rule of reason** for dealing with monopolies. According to this view, held by Theodore Roosevelt among others, the Sherman Act had not been intended to apply to "reasonable" monopolies. Although the decision upheld Standard Oil's conviction for violating the act, it opened the door for "reasonable" monopolies to avoid prosecution. In the same term, the Court ruled that the American Tobacco Company had violated the Sherman Act, but the majority favored a moderate reorganization rather than dissolution of the company. As a result, the Supreme Court's "rule of reason" allowed America's corporate structure to continue its "reasonable" monopolistic practices.

Did Congress intend the Sherman Act to apply to combinations of labor? As early as 1892 the government sought to apply the law to labor unions, in spite of their not having been mentioned in the act. For opponents of labor unions, of course, the prospect of using antitrust laws to break up labor unions was almost too good to be true. In the following years, the inconsistency of applying the Sherman Act to labor but not to manufacturing did not seem to bother business leaders or federal judges a great deal.

The case that opened the way for Sherman Act prosecutions of labor was *In re Debs* (1895). The case resulted from a strike against the Pullman Company in Chicago in which members of the American Railway Union blocked trains carrying Pullman cars. Eugene V. Debs, an avowed Socialist and president of the union, ignored a sweeping federal injunction against his strike and was subsequently arrested. The injunction had been based upon the government's contention that Debs's strike violated the Interstate Commerce and Sherman acts. The circuit court held Debs in contempt for violating the injunction on antitrust grounds. On a writ of *habeas corpus*, the Supreme Court upheld the Debs conviction on the broader grounds of national supremacy, stating: "The strong arm of the national government may be put forth to brush away all obstructions to the freedom of interstate commerce or the transportation of the mails." However, by refusing to examine the circuit court's reliance upon the Sherman Act, the Supreme Court through its silence opened the doors for future use of the antitrust injunction against labor combinations.

President Woodrow Wilson's administration saw passage of two significant laws: the Clayton Antitrust Act (1914) and the Federal Trade Commission Act of 1914. These laws added to the federal government's antitrust arsenal. The Clayton Act was important in dealing with such matters as price discrimination, but it also stipulated that the antitrust laws did not forbid the existence of labor unions or activities. The Federal Trade Commission—created to deal with unfair trade practices as an independent regulatory commission—had the authority to establish rules, obtain court injunctions, and bring action against violators.

In recent years, the Justice Department has continued to prosecute violations of antitrust law, with noteworthy cases such as the divestiture of American Telephone and Telegraph (ATT). However, the government's zeal for antitrust prosecutions has varied over the years, depending in part upon the commitment of certain key actors, including the president, attorney general and Justice Department, and even Congress (see Brief 7.4).

Observers have pointed to the high number of mergers and acquisitions in the 1980s as evidence of the Reagan administration's lack of strong commitment to antitrust prosecutions. Tied to a growing trend toward industry deregulation (trucking and airlines are two prominent examples), the recent lessening of antitrust emphasis is not surprising.

Civil Rights and Liberties

The commerce power also has been employed to better safeguard the civil rights and liberties of many Americans. While detailed treatment of civil rights is found in Chapter 9, this section will touch upon its commerce-related aspects. With passage of the Civil Rights Act of 1964, Congress sought to sweep away years of segregation and discrimination in American life. The crucial section of the act was Title II, which stated in part:

> All persons shall be entitled to the full and equal enjoyment of the goods, services, facilities, privileges, advantages, and accommodations of any place of public accommodation, as defined in this section without discrimination or segregation on the ground of race, color, religion, or national origin. (Section 201 [a])

❏   *Brief 7.4   Flood v. Kuhn (1972)—Baseball and Antitrust Law*

In October 1969, St. Louis Cardinal center fielder Curt Flood was traded to the Philadelphia Phillies without his consent. Flood went to Baseball Commissioner Bowie Kuhn and asked that he be made a "free agent" so that he could reach an agreement with a team of his choosing. When refused, Flood sued Kuhn under the Clayton Act for triple damages and costs. The specific target of the suit was baseball's so-called "reserve clause," an arrangement which Flood argued to be a monopolistic practice. Under the reserve clause, which the Supreme Court traced back to baseball contracts in 1887, a player was confined to the club which had him under contract. The club could assign his contract to another club, and the club also had unilateral rights to renew the player's contract annually.

While the Supreme Court agreed that professional baseball is a business engaged in interstate commerce, it recognized the existence of several precedents (one in 1922, another in 1953) that give baseball a special status as "the national pastime." Justice Harry Blackmun's opinion drew attention to decades of congressional inability and apparent unwillingness to change the reserve system of professional baseball, in spite of the fact that other professional sports did not enjoy antitrust exemption. As Blackmun added, "If there is any inconsistency or illogic in all this, it is an inconsistency and illogic of long standing that is to be remedied by the Congress and not by this Court."

In the years since *Flood* v. *Kuhn*, the concept of free agency has come to professional baseball, although representatives of the players' association argue that owners continue to conspire to limit true competition. The antitrust battles in professional sports appear to be moving into the football stadium and basketball arena. Players' associations in both the National Basketball Association and the National Football League have initiated litigation against their respective owners for alleged antitrust violations, with the latter group having waged a bitter strike during part of the 1987 season. With multimillion-dollar television and advertising contracts at stake, labor-management conflicts in professional sports undoubtedly will continue to escalate.

The act identified four classes of business establishments as "public accommodations." Each establishment was covered by the law "if its operations affect commerce, or if discrimination or segregation by it is supported by State action." The covered establishments included inns, hotels, and motels; restaurants and cafeterias; motion picture houses; and any establishment located within one of the others listed. Symbolically, the act went into effect on July 4, 1964.

The Supreme Court ruled on the constitutionality of the Civil Rights Act of 1964 in the case of *Heart of Atlanta Motel, Inc.* v. *United States* (1964). The case was tailor-made for the government prosecutors, given that the motel was located on a busy interstate highway, solicited convention business in magazine advertisements, and rented the bulk of its rooms to out-of-state or transient guests. In a unanimous opinion, Justice Thomas Clark reviewed more than one hundred years of Commerce Clause cases in which the power of Congress had been used for noncommercial purposes. He found racial discrimination to fall within the category of disruptive effects upon commerce over which Congress has regulatory power. Upholding the act, Justice Clark gave the following, and now virtually unanimous, view of interstate commerce:

> We, therefore, conclude that the action of the Congress in the adoption of the Act, as applied here to a motel which concededly serves interstate travelers is within the power granted it by the Commerce Clause of the Constitution, as interpreted by this Court for 140 years. It may be argued that Congress could have pursued other methods to eliminate the obstructions it found in interstate commerce caused by racial discrimination. But this is a matter of policy that rests entirely with the Congress not with the Courts. How obstructions in commerce may be removed—what means are to be employed—is within the sound and exclusive direction of the Congress.

The same day, in *Katzenbach* v. *McClung* (1964), the Court upheld the act in even more sweeping terms by applying it to Ollie's Barbecue, a small, family-owned restaurant located far from a major highway and not frequented by out-of-state travelers. Nonetheless, the Court agreed with the government's finding that the restaurant's annual purchase of more than $70,0000 worth of food that had moved in interstate commerce was sufficient to place the establishment under the terms of the act. According to Justice Clark's opinion, "The power of Congress in this field is broad and sweeping."

Finally, in *Daniel* v. *Paul* (1969), the Court upheld the application of the Civil Rights Act to a rural amusement park in the Arkansas hills. In solitary dissent, Justice Hugo Black argued that applying the commerce power to "this country people's recreation center" risked giving "the Federal Government complete control over every little remote country place of recreation in every nook and cranny of each precinct and county in every one of the 50 states." Without question, the ruling showed that Congress could use its plenary power over commerce to reach broad social objectives.

The Congressional Power to Tax and Spend

In Article I, Section 8, the Constitution provides that "Congress shall have Power To lay and collect Taxes, Duties, Imposts and Excises, to pay the Debts and provide for the common Defence and general Welfare of the United States; but all Duties, Imposts and Excises shall be uniform throughout the United States." This grant of power to Congress contains both taxing and spending authority. The taxing power is conditioned by the requirement that "Duties, Imposts and Excises shall be uniform" across the nation. By this qualification, Congress is prohibited from setting different rates for, say, excise taxes on tires or duties on imported cars in different states. The Constitution establishes two additional limitations upon taxation in Article I, Section 9:

> No Capitation, or other direct, Tax shall be laid, unless in Proportion to the Census or Enumeration herein before directed to be taken. No Tax or Duty shall be laid on Articles exported from any State.

To summarize, the congressional power to tax may not be applied to exports and must be uniform throughout the nation; furthermore, direct taxes must be based upon population. Despite these seemingly simple limitations, the taxing power has stirred considerable controversy over two hundred years.

The issue of direct taxes has arisen several times, although the Constitution offers little guidance in the matter apart from the linkage of "capitation" (head tax) with "direct" taxes. In *Hylton* v. *United States* (1796) the Supreme Court held that a congressional tax upon carriages was an "indirect" tax, with capitation (head tax) and land taxes being the only direct taxes. In part, however, it was clear that the Court recognized the difficulty of apportioning a tax upon carriages by population. In *Springer* v. *United States* (1881), the Court ruled that the income tax enacted during the Civil War was not a direct tax.

The most significant decision concerning direct taxes came in *Pollock* v. *Farmers' Loan and Trust Company* (1895), in which the Court voided the Wilson-Gorman Tariff Act of 1894. Under the act, individuals and corporations were taxed on all income above a $4,000 exemption. Charles Pollock, a shareholder in Farmers' Loan and Trust, sought to prevent the company's payment of the tax on several grounds. The primary argument against the law's constitutionality, however, was that a tax on income derived from land was in reality a direct tax, just as a tax on land itself. Accordingly, it should be apportioned among the states on the basis of population.

In a narrow 5-4 decision, the Court accepted the contention that a tax on income from land was a direct tax and declared the income tax law to be unconstitutional. As noted earlier, the Court in the mid-1890s had shown a strong protective instinct for private property rights and a disdain for much government regulation. In this light, the *Pollock* decision is hardly surprising. However, as Congress could find no realistic fashion in which to apportion an income tax by population, it was unable to tax incomes until the passage of the Sixteenth Amendment in 1913:

> The Congress shall have power to lay and collect taxes on incomes, from whatever source derived, without apportionment among the several States, and without regard to any census or enumeration.

Quite clearly, the amendment removed the "direct tax" issue from future consideration. More importantly, it opened up vast untapped sources of revenue for the federal government.

Most constitutional disagreements over the taxing power have concerned its use as a regulating device. Quite simply, while a tax raises revenue for government, it also imposes restrictions that allow government to shape public policies, consumer behavior, and production decisions. A study of regulatory taxation identified three schools of interpretation associated with the federal taxing power. The conservative interpretation, associated with persons such as John C. Calhoun, holds that taxation may be imposed only for revenue-raising purposes. A middle view accepts taxation for purposes other than raising revenue but rejects an "all-purpose grant of power." The liberal, or loose-constructionist, position recognizes taxation as a sweeping power, including the power to regulate or even destroy.[17] The central point of contention among these perspectives is the use of taxation as a police power enabling government to regulate matters of health, safety, and welfare. This issue was presented to the Supreme Court early in the twentieth century.

The case of *McCray* v. *United States* (1904) established the congressional police power in taxation. The case stemmed from a congressional tax on margarine, which had been enacted largely to assist the dairy industry. Specifically, the law provided for a tax of one-fourth cent per pound on uncolored margarine and a tax of ten cents per pound on colored margarine. When Leo McCray, a licensed retail dealer in oleomargarine, was fined for having failed to pay the proper tax, he challenged the tax as a transparent attempt by Congress to regulate the manufacture and sale of margarine, powers which rest with the states (see Brief 7.5).

According to the majority opinion of Justice Edward White, the power to tax is conditioned only by the Constitution's limitations, and the judicial branch should not undermine that power by investigating congressional motives. In upholding the constitutionality of the tax, he stated:

> The right of Congress to tax within its delegated power being unrestrained, except as limited by the Constitution, it was within the authority conferred on Congress to select the objects upon which an excise should be laid. . . . The judicial power may not usurp the functions of the legislative in order to control that branch of the government in the performance of its lawful duties.

The *McCray* ruling quickly ran into difficulty with the strengthening dual-federalist majority of the Supreme Court. In *Bailey* v. *Drexel Furniture Co.* (1922), the Court struck down the Child Labor Tax Law, which had been enacted by Congress following *Hammer* v. *Dagenhart*. The act imposed a 10 percent tax on the net profits of any firm that employed children under the age of fourteen. In classic dual-federalist reasoning, Chief Justice William

☐ *Brief 7.5   The Color of Margarine*

When members of the dairy lobby convinced Congress to levy a discriminatory tax on colored margarine, they opened a debate that raged for more than a half-century. In the early stages, uncolored margarine was sold along with coloring pellets that enabled the purchaser to do the coloring at home. By 1945, margarine's popularity had increased dramatically, especially since butter had been rationed so heavily during World War II. Groups began to call for repeal of the discriminatory tax on colored margarine, prompting the 1948 Democratic party platform to endorse the repeal.

In 1950, following a lengthy struggle, Congress repealed the tax, but the new law "required truthful labeling and margarine could be packaged only in one pound containers or less. If margarine was served in a public establishment the proprietor must notify the customer of such by a sign and serve it in a triangular shape or have its true name stamped on it."[18] In 1967, Wisconsin became the last state to permit the manufacture and sale of colored margarine, although it was still subject to a heavy tax.

Howard Taft, speaking for a 8-1 Court, held the regulation to be a "so-called tax" really designed to stop child labor. As such, he argued, it was not a tax but a penalty that Congress has imposed to indirectly regulate an area (child labor) it had no authority to reach.

Using essentially the same type of analysis, the Court in *United States v. Butler* (1936) struck down the Agricultural Adjustment Act of 1933. This New Deal legislation had been designed to counteract falling commodity prices by paying farmers for limiting their production. The money was to be obtained by levying a tax on certain agricultural commodities. William Butler, who worked for a cotton-processing company, refused to pay the tax, challenging both the spending and taxing provisions of the act. Writing for a 6-3 Court, Justice Owen Roberts sought to demonstrate why both taxing and spending powers had been abused by Congress. The result generally has been considered one of the most inconsistent and confusing opinions ever written.

The opinion entered into lengthy consideration of the "general welfare" provisions of the Taxing and Spending Clause, seeking to determine its proper interpretation. At issue was the long-standing debate between the position of Alexander Hamilton—taxing and spending for the general welfare is an independent power of Congress—and that of James Madison—taxing and spending powers must be related to a specific power in Article I, Section 8. After determining that the Hamiltonian view had prevailed over the years, Roberts concluded that it really did not matter anyway since the act "invades the reserved rights of states." The taxing and spending provisions were "but means to an unconstitutional end." Nonetheless, the opinion did indicate that congressional powers to tax and spend are separate and independent.

The erosion of dual federalism after 1937 produced changes in the congressional taxing power much as it had done in commerce matters. In *Mulford* v. *Smith* (1939), the Court upheld the second Agricultural Adjustment Act, which was quite similar to the one struck down in *Butler*. The new act imposed a penalty for tobacco production beyond a quota established by Congress's control over interstate commerce. The Court's decision in *Steward Machine Co.* v. *Davis* (1937) upheld a portion of the Social Security Act of 1935 that required employers of eight or more workers to pay a federal excise tax based upon their employees' wages. If employers contributed to a state unemployment program that had been approved by the federal government, however, they were permitted to credit those payments against up to 90 percent of the federal tax. Obviously, the law was designed to encourage states to create acceptable unemployment programs. Justice Benjamin Cardozo's majority opinion rejected the contention that the act coerced the states and invaded their powers. In *Helvering* v. *Davis* (1937), a companion case, a 5-4 Court upheld a Social Security tax for paying old-age benefits. Congress would henceforth be able to determine the proper subjects for which it could tax and spend to promote the general welfare. In the years since World War II, the congressional spending power has expanded dramatically into numerous areas. Congress has relied upon its spending powers to achieve results in matters ranging from civil rights to morality. Recent Supreme Court decisions in *Fullilove* v. *Klutznick* (1980) and *South Dakota* v. *Dole* (1987) serve as examples of the trend and merit brief discussion.

In 1977, Congress enacted the Public Works Employment Act of 1977, amending a previous act dealing with federal expenditures for local public works projects. The amendment contained the "minority business enterprise" (MBE) provision. This provision required that state governments use at least 10 percent of their allotted federal funds to purchase goods and services from businesses owned by minority group members—defined by the act as "citizens of the United States who are Negroes, Spanish-speaking, Orientals, Indians, Eskimos, and Aleuts."

The act was challenged by various contractors and businesses who contended that they were being denied equal protection of the law in violation of the Fifth and Fourteenth Amendments. Although the case of *Fullilove* v. *Klutznick* (1980) is primarily concerned with the affirmative action issues discussed in Chapter 10, it is instructive also as a strong view of the federal spending power. Chief Justice Warren Burger stated:

> The Public Works Employment Act of 1977, by its very nature, is primarily an exercise of the Spending Power. . . Congress has frequently employed the Spending Power to further broad policy objectives by conditioning receipt of federal moneys upon compliance by the recipient with federal statutory and administrative directives. This Court has repeatedly upheld against constitutional challenge the use of this technique.

The majority agreed that the act was also justified under congressional enforcement of the Fourteenth Amendment, but concluded that "the objectives of the MBE provision are within the scope of the Spending Power." Accordingly, the problems facing minority businesses were determined to be national in scope, thereby justifying the congressional power to spend to promote the general welfare.

The recent case of *South Dakota* v. *Dole, Secretary, U.S. Department of Transportation* (1987) provided even more direct evidence of an expanding federal spending power. The case resulted from a highway spending bill. Under this legislation, states not wishing to conform to a minimum drinking age of twenty-one simply forfeited 5 percent of their federal highway funds. South Dakota, with a policy of allowing nineteen-year-olds to purchase beer with no more than 3.2 percent alcohol content, challenged the federal legislation as an attempt by Congress to create a national drinking age—an unconstitutional law, according to South Dakota, because Congress lacks constitutional authority to do so.

Speaking for the Court, Chief Justice William Rehnquist upheld the federal law under the Taxing and Spending Clause. He indicated that Congress may attach conditions to federal funds that allow it to attain objectives which are "not thought of as within enumerated legislative fields." Even if Congress lacks power to establish a national minimum drinking age, Rehnquist added, it may use its power to spend money as an "encouragement to state action."

Despite broadened federal taxing and spending powers, certain limitations continue to be placed upon their use. In *Marchetti* v. *United States* (1968), the Court declared a federal occupational tax on gamblers to be an unconstitutional violation of the self-incrimination protections in the Fifth Amendment. In making the decision, the Court specifically noted that only constitutional prohibitions such as the protection against self-incrimination would justify the striking down of tax statutes. Federal tax laws that do not violate specific provisions of the Constitution are essentially beyond judicial scrutiny.

As for limitations upon spending, the Constitution requires that all spending provide for the common defense and general welfare. However, since the decisions in *Steward* and *Helvering,* the determination of what constitutes the common defense and general welfare rests with Congress. In recent years, the Court has slightly opened up the possibility of taxpayer suits against specific uses of federal spending (*Flast* v. *Cohen* [1968]), but subsequent decisions do not offer much hope to the taxpayer who hopes to challenge federal expenditures.

Conclusion

The debate between economic liberty and property rights, on the one hand, and governmental powers of regulation, on the other, has waxed and waned throughout the two hundred years since the nation's founding. These two positions, generally associated with individualist and communitarian perspectives on government, have each held the upper hand at various stages of American constitutional development. As a result, the nation has embraced elements of both positions—a strong individualistic belief in rights of property ownership blended with a communitarian concern with safeguarding society's interests in matters of health, safety, morals, and welfare. Four distinct constitutional clauses have played pivotal roles in the developmental process.

The Contract Clause provided the earliest constitutional conflict over property rights. Written primarily to prevent state government interference in financial and commercial matters, the Contract Clause became a source of bitter dispute between the Federalist-dominated judiciary led by Chief Justice John Marshall and the more communitarian-minded state governments. Decisions in *Fletcher* v. *Peck* and *Dartmouth College* v. *Woodward* demonstrated the Federalist preference for property rights and the expansion of the Contract Clause. As a limitation upon government interference with property rights, the Contract Clause entered a period of decline with the onset of Chief Justice Roger Taney's tenure, as state powers over issues such as bankruptcy and usury became more clearly defined. Despite some recent signs of a revival, the Contract Clause has not fulfilled the expectations of those early American individualists who envisioned it as a bastion against state control and regulation of contractual and property law.

The Due Process Clause of the Fourteenth (and Fifth) Amendment replaced the Contract Clause as the foremost constitutional protection against government interference. Coupled with the growing popularity of a laissez-faire economic theory, the Due Process Clause effectively throttled both federal and state attempts to legislate wages, hours, working conditions, and production. The high point of this substantive due process was reached in the freedom of contract of such cases as *Lochner* v. *New York* and *Adkins* v. *Children's Hospital.* Economic theory and constitutional interpretation both agreed that economic liberty and property rights could not be invaded by governments. The catastrophic effects of the Great Depression greatly weakened the sanctity of freedom of contract and other laissez-faire doctrines. When *West Coast Hotel* v. *Parrish* was decided in 1937, the Supreme Court had signaled a clear change in direction—the Due Process Clause no longer would serve as a shield against all forms of economic policy-making by governments.

The Commerce Clause, perhaps more so than any other constitutional vehicle, has extended the power of the national government over virtually every economically related activity in the nation. By no means, however, has such development been smooth and uninterrupted. The rise of dual federalism thwarted national commerce regulation, especially in matters of monopolies, manufacturing, labor relations, and agriculture. States and the national government operated in their respective spheres, and each sought to safeguard its authority from the other's intrusions. Beginning with early decisions such as the Shreveport Rate Cases, dual federalism was weakened in the face of growing economic interdependence and complexity. Ultimately, decisions such as *United States* v. *Darby* and *Wickard* v. *Filburn,* coupled with the national government's massive advantage in resources, relegated dual federalism to near obsolescence. The full impact of the congressional commerce power has become evident in recent commerce-based legislation dealing with civil rights, especially in the Civil Rights Act of 1964. Today, largely as a result of the commerce power, nearly all working Americans are covered by federal wage and hour legislation, with significant national regulation of such areas as labor relations, job discrimination, and employee safety. While arguments continue to be raised against some uses of the congressional commerce power, these generally tend to be political rather than constitutional in nature. In summary, the Commerce Clause has played a major role in bringing the Constitution of 1787 into the modern industrial era.

Finally, the Taxing and Spending Clause has opened vast new areas to federal government regulation. Through taxation policies, Congress has combined the raising of revenue with a police-power orientation. Accordingly, taxation has become one of the primary methods used to shape new domestic policies. Proposals to levy tariffs on items such as imported oil serve as illustrations of the role of taxation in policy formulation. The power to spend also has resulted in considerable legislation—including, of course, Social Security and a large number of entitlement programs. In promoting the general welfare through taxing and spending, Congress has enacted programs that affect most Americans on a regular basis.

Today, more than two hundred years since its inception, the United States Constitution has handled the nation's transition to the rank of world power in an effective manner. Nevertheless, it seems certain that new, perhaps unanticipated, challenges will continue to arise. State governments likely will continue in their efforts to exert greater autonomy from federal control, yet they may be unable to operate with the desired amount of freedom because of a less than adequate financial base. The national government, facing an ever-worsening national debt and trade imbalance, certainly will feel pressures to cut expenditures in many programs that have become heavily entrenched. If states are called upon to pick up the slack, will they have the human and material resources essential to do the job? Meanwhile, for a sizable number of Americans, the problem will continue to be government encroachment upon basic property rights and economic liberties. In some respects, in spite of the passage of two hundred years, some things are really not much different from the way they were in Philadelphia in 1787. Individualist and communitarian perspectives on the role of government, coupled with a contest between states and the federal government, are still important forces in American society.

1.   What were some of the most significant limitations that the framers of the Constitution placed upon state interference with economic and property matters? Do these

Questions

limitations help to place the framers in a clearer perspective as individuals? What were their primary concerns and motivations?

2.   What is substantive due process of law? What accounts for the expansion of substantive due process through its era of greatest influence? What accounts for its decline in economic matters? Do you see evidence of substantive due process in non-economic areas today?

3.   The power to regulate commerce has expanded greatly over the years. How would you assess the long-term significance of Chief Justice John Marshall's contributions in the interpretation of the Commerce Clause? What place would you give the contributions of Chief Justice Roger Taney? Of the more recent Supreme Court rulings on commerce, which do you regard as most significant? Why?

4.   What are several reasons for the growth of a federal police power to protect the health, safety, morals, and welfare of the American people? Can you identify specific uses of the police power which you oppose? In which areas might more police-power regulation be appropriate?

5.   Would you agree that the growth of federal commerce, taxing, and spending powers has rendered state governments powerless to resist national authority? What are areas in which states may still operate without fear of federal interference? Is it realistic to talk about a difference between interstate and intrastate commerce?

Endnotes

1.   See, e.g., the comments of Charles Beard in Chapter 3.

2.   Benjamin F. Wright, Jr., *The Contract Clause and the Constitution* (Westport, Conn.: Greenwood Press, 1938), 62.

3.   Ibid., 94–95.

4.   Henry J. Abraham, *Freedom and the Court: Civil Rights and Liberties in the United States,* 4th ed. (New York: Oxford University Press, 1982), 95.

5.   Joseph B. James, *The Framing of the Fourteenth Amendment* (Urbana, Ill.: University of Illinois Press, 1956), 197.

6.   Felix Frankfurter, *The Commerce Clause Under Marshall, Taney and Waite* (Chapel Hill, N.C.: University of North Carolina Press, 1937). Frankfurter considers the *Munn* case to have "laid the foundation for Congressional entry into fields of comprehensive regulation of economic enterprise," 83.

7.   James, *Framing of the Fourteenth Amendment,* 199.

8.   Frankfurter, *Commerce Clause,* 66–67.

9.   Ibid., 19.

10.   Ibid., 50.

11.   See *Southern Pacific Company* v. *Arizona,* 325 U.S. 761 (1945). In that case, the Court struck down an Arizona law limiting the length of a single train passing through the state to fourteen passenger or seventy freight cars. Despite noting that Congress had taken no action on the matter, the Court held that "the state interest is outweighed by the interest of the nation in an adequate, economical and efficient railway transportation service, which must prevail."

12.   Nelson Lloyd Dawson, *Louis D. Brandeis, Felix Frankfurter, and the New Deal* (Hamden, Conn.: Archer Books, 1980), 68–69.

13.   Edward S. Corwin, *The Commerce Power Versus States Rights* (Gloucester, Mass.: Peter Smith, 1962), 152–3.

14.   Earl W. Kintner, *An Antitrust Primer,* 2d ed. (New York: Macmillan, 1973), 18. Kintner considers the current-of-commerce ruling in *Swift* to be the

first significant change in the narrow, late-nineteenth-century view of commerce.

15. Stephen B. Wood, *Constitutional Politics in the Progressive Era: Child Labor and the Law* (Chicago: University of Chicago Press, 1968), 3.

16. Kintner, *Antitrust Primer,* 11. Antimonopoly feelings ran so deeply in

Congress that the Sherman Act passed with only one dissenting vote.

17. R. Alton Lee, *A History of Regulatory Taxation* (Lexington, Ky.: University Press of Kentucky, 1973), 5.

18. Ibid., 57–59.

Suggested Readings

Anderson, James E., David W. Brady, and Charles S. Bullock, III. *Public Policy and Politics in America.* 2d ed. Monterey, Calif.: Brooks/Cole, 1984.

Burns, James MacGregor. *Roosevelt, The Lion and the Fox.* New York: Harcourt, Brace, 1956.

Frankfurter, Felix. *The Commerce Clause Under Marshall, Taney and Waite.* Chapel Hill, N.C.: University of North Carolina Press, 1937.

Hoogenboom, Ari, and Olive Hoogenboom. *A History of the ICC: From Panacea to Palliative.* New York: Norton, 1976.

Lee, R. Alton. *A History of Regulatory Taxation.* Lexington, Ky.: University Press of Kentucky, 1973.

Miller, George H. *Railroads and the Granger Cases.* Madison, Wis.: University of Wisconsin Press, 1971.

Sinclair, Upton. *The Jungle.* New York: New American Library, 1906.

Wright, Benjamin F., Jr. *The Contract Clause and the Constitution.* Westport, Conn.: Greenwood Press, 1938.

PART

III

Constitutional Rights and Liberties

CONSTITUTIONALISM REQUIRES that individual rights and liberties be protected from encroachment by government. At the same time, however, the broader interests of society often must be balanced against individual concerns. As a result, the preservation of individual rights and liberties along with the protection of societal interests stands as one of the major tasks facing American constitutional government. The seven chapters in Part III address this relationship from several perspectives. Chapter 8 introduces the subject by focusing upon the nationalization of the Bill of Rights, followed by an analysis of the Fourth, Fifth, Sixth, and Eighth Amendments. Chapters 9 and 10 examine the fundamental issue of equality through the Constitution's equal protection guarantees. Racial equality issues are discussed in Chapter 9, while the "new" equal protection and the right of privacy are covered in Chapter 10. The next three chapters address different aspects of the First Amendment: Chapter 11 examines freedom of speech issues; Chapter 12 addresses free press, libel, and obscenity concerns; and Chapter 13 analyzes the rights and liberties protected in the amendment's religion clauses. In these chapters, attention is directed toward the individualistic and communitarian perspectives that help to define the most fundamental rights and liberties of Americans. Chapter 14 concludes the book by presenting an overview of American constitutional government and examining several proposals for constitutional reform.

8 The Bill of Rights and Due Process of Law

Syllabus

Ernesto Miranda's name came to the public's attention in 1966 as a result of the Supreme Court's ruling in *Miranda* v. *Arizona*. According to this case, a suspect in custody is entitled to explicit warnings and guarantees prior to any questioning. As such, the name "Miranda" became synonymous with protecting the rights of persons accused of crimes. Ernesto Miranda as a person, however, was not concerned with other people's rights. Although Miranda's first conviction for kidnapping and rape was overturned in the famous decision in 1966, he was convicted in a second trial in 1967 and spent the years until 1972 in jail. He was paroled in 1972, served additional time for other charges in 1974, was paroled again that year, and eventually was sent back to prison in 1975 for parole violations. The end came in a Phoenix, Arizona, bar in early 1976, when Miranda was shot and killed in an apparent dispute over a card game. As he was being arrested, Miranda's suspected assailant was read his rights from a so-called "Miranda card."[1] Here, of course, is the tragic irony of Miranda—a man who revolutionized American criminal justice could not change his own life.

Miranda's story seems to highlight the ongoing tension between individual rights and society's needs for security and protection. The American system of criminal justice—by seeking to serve both individual and societal interests—invariably produces an unevenness that supporters of each perspective find troublesome. Civil liberties or law and order—can the two sides coexist? The task of American constitutional government is to ensure that they do.

This Chapter Examines the Following Matters

☐ The protection of individual rights from government interference was a key concern for many of the Constitution's framers. The resulting Bill of Rights offers the constitutional protections upon which American society has come to depend.

☐ While the Bill of Rights was intended to protect individual rights from the federal government, the Supreme Court's use of selective incorporation through the Due Process Clause of the Fourteenth Amendment has extended most of these protections to the state governments as well.

☐ The American concern with privacy in personal matters has been evident in the Fourth Amendment's limitations upon "unreasonable searches and seizures." Nevertheless, the needs of society to protect the citizenry through effective law enforcement have produced disagreement over the amendment's interpretation.

☐ The Supreme Court's use of the exclusionary rule has limited the use of improperly obtained evidence, but observers debate the rule's overall rationale. Recent Supreme Court decisions suggest that cracks have begun to appear in the exclusionary rule.

☐ The U.S. Constitution, especially in the Fifth and Sixth Amendments, offers numerous procedural guarantees to individuals faced with a potential loss of liberty. These guarantees include protections against self-incrimination and double jeopardy, as well as the more positive guarantees of a speedy, public, and impartial trial by a jury of one's peers and the assistance of counsel.

☐ The Eighth Amendment forbids "cruel and unusual punishments," but it does not specify what those punishments might include. While certain forms of torture and physical punishment have been outlawed, most debate has surrounded the use of the death penalty and its continued role in American society.

Photo: Accused suspects in criminal proceedings as well as state and federal prisoners increasingly look to the Constitution to protect their right to "due process of law." Five of the ten amendments and thirteen of the twenty-three provisions that make up the Bill of Rights set down the procedural guarantees of citizens in the area of criminal justice.

Toward a National Bill of Rights

One of the central dilemmas in a constitutional political order is the balancing of individual civil liberties with the need to protect society and keep it safe. It is an issue with which the framers of the Constitution were familiar, prompting many leaders of that era to support the addition of a "bill of rights." For nearly two hundred years since that addition, Americans have debated, argued, and occasionally fought over the proper balance of individual rights and community rights. Civil libertarians who place their emphasis upon the rights of the individual clash repeatedly with those for whom the interests of society are paramount. The controversy has taken varying forms from generation to generation, but the underlying positions have remained remarkably stable. The following statement from Fred E. Inbau, an influential and rather controversial proponent of society's interests at the expense of individual liberties, illustrates one view of the problem:

> We cannot have "domestic tranquility" and "promote the general welfare" as prescribed in the Preamble to the Constitution when all the concern is upon "individual civil liberties." Our civil liberties cannot exist in a vacuum. Alongside of them we must have a stable society, a safe society; otherwise there will be no medium in which to exercise such rights and liberties. To have these liberties without safety of life, limb, and property is a meaningless thing. Individual civil liberties, considered apart from their relationship to public safety and security, are like labels on empty bottles.[2]

Supporters of Professor Inbau often like to consider themselves "tough on crime" and advocates of "law and order." In this view, excessive concern with liberties results in severe costs for the society as a whole. On the other hand, supporters of individual civil liberties disagree with the premise of Inbau's remarks, noting that the loss of individual liberties ultimately results in a loss for the overall society. If persons are not protected as individuals, they note, then the constitutional system of limited government becomes uncontrollable and potentially tyrannical.

Throughout this chapter, the controversy between these points of view surfaces on numerous occasions in a variety of areas. Perhaps the most controversial area is how to deal with the problem of crime in America. The United States does have a problem with crime, particularly so-called "violent" crimes. For example, the National Commission on the Causes and Prevention of Violence ranked fourteen nations on measures of violent crime. The United States was first by a wide margin—5.8 criminal homicides per 100,000 population during the 1960s. Britain, France, and Germany, by comparison, had rates of 0.7, 0.08, and 1.6 respectively.[3] Although crime statistics are unclear, they do show evidence of a decline in some areas. But 1985 figures still showed 7.9 murders, 36.6 forcible rapes, 209 robberies, and 303 aggravated assaults per 100,000 population.[4]

The evolution of individual rights and liberties in the United States has been a slow, often piecemeal, process. Experience has demonstrated that the existence of the Bill of Rights, while critical to the protection of individual rights and liberties, does not ensure an end to injustice. If anything, the protection of individual rights requires constant vigilance on the part of all citizens.

This chapter will begin with an examination of the Bill of Rights (particularly the first eight amendments, which contain protections for the individual), and then analyze the process by which these guarantees gradually were expanded to apply to all levels of government in the United States. Finally, the chapter will discuss the development of individual rights and liberties on an amendment-by-amendment basis, giving primary attention to the areas of criminal procedure, the rights of the accused, and the overall requirements of due process of law. As might be expected, the Supreme Court has played a prominent role in both the nationalization and interpretation of the Bill of Rights.

The Bill of Rights

When the state of Virginia on December 15, 1791, ratified the first ten amendments to the new United States Constitution, it became the eleventh state to do so. As a result, the necessary three-fourths requirement was satisfied, and the Bill of Rights became part of the Constitution.[5] The Bill of Rights, as noted in Chapter 3, owed much of its existence to the ratification struggles between Federalists and Anti-Federalists. According to author Robert Rutland, "A broad base of public opinion forced the adoption of the Bill of Rights upon those political leaders who knew the value of compromise."[6] Actually, the states had been called upon to ratify twelve, not ten, amendments. Two proposals—one dealing with a fixed apportionment of seats in the House of Representatives and the other with congressional salaries—were defeated. Nevertheless, the resulting first ten amendments opened a new dimension in the development of the American Constitution.

Some dispute occurred in the First Congress during the debates over the proposed Bill of Rights and its applicability to the state governments. James Madison, the chief architect of the proposals, actually favored an amendment protecting the rights of conscience, free speech, press, and trial by jury against state action. According to author Edward Dumbauld, "Madison thought this provision important, since some states did not have bills of rights."[7] The Senate, however, refused to include any provision that would apply the rights to the states, so the proposed amendments clearly limited only the new national government.

The Senate view of the Bill of Rights received overwhelming Supreme Court confirmation in the case of *Barron* v. *Baltimore* (1833). The case resulted from a dispute concerning the Just Compensation Clause of the Fifth Amendment. The final lines of the Fifth Amendment state, "Nor shall private property be taken for public use, without just compensation." For John Barron, the co-owner of a wharf located in Baltimore, Maryland, that specific guarantee had been violated by the city's efforts to change the direction of several streams and waterways. In the process of diverting the streams, vast amounts of sediment collected around Barron's wharf, making it inaccessible to ships and, therefore, worthless. After winning a judgment at the county level, Barron lost when the city appealed the decision. He subsequently asked the Supreme Court to uphold his award of damages.

Writing for a unanimous Court, Chief Justice John Marshall refused to hold the provisions of the Bill of Rights applicable to the states. In his view, the question was "not of much difficulty," given what he considered to be clear and convincing historical evidence. First, Marshall emphasized the national character of the Constitution itself:

> The constitution was ordained and established by the people of the United States for themselves, for their own government and not for the government of the individual States. Each State established a constitution for itself, and, in that constitution, provided such limitations and restrictions on the powers of its particular government as its judgment dictated.

Secondly, Marshall's opinion focused upon the process by which the first ten amendments were added to the Constitution. He rejected Barron's claim that these had been intended to apply additional limitations upon state governments, adding the following point:

> Had the framers of these amendments intended them to be limitations on the powers of the state governments, they would have imitated the framers of the original constitution, and have expressed that intention. . . These amendments contain no expression indicating an intention to apply them to the state governments. This court cannot so apply them.

In holding that the Bill of Rights could not be applied directly to the states, Marshall's Court established a legal precedent that has not been rejected even though, as a practical matter, most of the amendments do apply to the states today. Technically, the Bill of Rights was written to apply directly to the national government, and that has not changed. As a result of decisions such as *Barron* v. *Baltimore,* the Bill of Rights did not play a significant role in early American life. According to political scientist Richard Cortner:

> The Bill of Rights was thus confined to being a limitation only upon the power of the federal government and played a very limited role in American constitutional adjudication prior to the Civil War. For the protection of their most basic political and civil liberties from invasion by the states, Americans were required to look to their state constitutions and state bills of rights and not to the federal Bill of Rights.[8]

The Fourteenth Amendment and Due Process of Law

Some discussion of the impact of the post-Civil War amendments has been provided in Chapters 6 and 7. As a result, it is unnecessary to examine the entire range of issues underlying these amendments. However, the Fourteenth Amendment in particular raised numerous questions concerning the rights and liberties of individuals that related directly to the guarantees in the Bill of Rights. To better understand the issues, it will be helpful to examine the purposes for which the Fourteenth Amendment was proposed.

The historical evidence is not entirely clear with respect to the intentions of the framers of the Fourteenth Amendment. Did they intend for the Privileges and Immunities Clause and the Due Process Clause to change the long-standing relationship between the Bill of Rights and state governments? In other words, did they believe that the amendment would make the individual protections of the first eight amendments binding upon the states in the same manner as against the national government? Much historical analysis has taken place, and the results are inconclusive.

These analyses generally have focused upon the important role played by Representative John Bingham in the formation of the post-Civil War amendments, particularly the Fourteenth. Representative Bingham led the fight for proposal of the Fourteenth Amendment in the House of Representatives, and he seemingly favored the idea that the amendment should guarantee fundamental rights on a nationwide basis. According to Henry J. Abraham, sifting through the various points of view regarding the historical evidence, "There seems little doubt that the Amendment's principal framers and managers, Representative Bingham and Senator Howard, if not every member of the majority in the two houses of Congress, did believe the Bill of Rights to be made generally applicable to the several states via Section 1." [9]

Of course, whether the intention of persons such as Bingham, assuming they can be known, should be binding upon future generations presents another question. In a turn-of-the-century opinion, Justice Rufus Peckham of the Supreme Court expressed what generally has been the prevailing view of most justices concerning the origins of the Fourteenth Amendment:

> What individual Senators or Representatives may have urged in debate in regard to the meaning to be given to a proposed constitutional amendment . . . does not offer firm ground for its proper construction. [10]

Despite Justice Peckham's views, later Supreme Court justices kept the issue very much alive.

The years since the ratification have produced considerable disagreement concerning the proper relationship between the protections in the Bill of Rights and the meaning of the Fourteenth Amendment. Table 8.1 provides a chronological overview of several key developments in the nationalization of the Bill of Rights—from the situation prior to ratification of the Fourteenth Amendment until the Supreme Court's acceptance of the doctrine of selective incorporation. These events will provide the basis for the following discussion.

As discussed in Chapter 7, the Supreme Court's ruling in the Slaughterhouse Cases (1873) effectively rejected the contention that the Fourteenth Amendment had brought constitutional privileges and immunities under federal control. Similarly, the court held that the due process guarantees of the Fourteenth Amendment were applicable only to the procedural rights of Negroes. While the Due Process Clause gradually limited state economic regulation, it was not broadly regarded as a protector of federal constitutional rights. Several cases serve as examples.

In *Hurtado* v. *California* (1884), the Court held that California's practice of using a prosecutor's "information" in lieu of a grand jury indictment did not deprive a person of due process of law. At issue was a provision of the California Constitution that allowed a person to be tried without the use of a grand jury indictment to initiate a prosecution, despite the Fifth Amendment's guarantee of such a practice in all federal cases. Joseph Hurtado appealed his conviction and death sentence on the grounds that they violated the Due Process Clause of the Fourteenth Amendment.

In the majority opinion, Justice Stanley Matthews traced the idea of due process through its English and common law heritage but found no specific list of guarantees to be linked to a due process of law, stating that "it would be incongruous to measure and restrict them by the ancient customary English law." Because due process of law "was made for an undefined and expanding future," Justice Matthews held that it certainly would not be proper to impose past requirements of due process on state governments. States should be free to shape their own due process guarantees.

Table 8.1   Steps in the Nationalization of the Bill of Rights

DATE	EVENT	SIGNIFICANCE
1791	Bill of Rights Becomes Part of Constitution	The national government guarantees rights and liberties.
1833	*Barron* v. *Baltimore*	The Bill of Rights applies only to the national government.
1868	Fourteenth Amendment	The rights of ex-slaves are presumably safeguarded against state government interference.
1873	Slaughterhouse Cases	The Fourteenth Amendment did not apply the Privileges and Immunities of national citizenship to state governments. Due Process in the Fourteenth Amendment protects the procedural rights of Negroes.
1884	*Hurtado* v. *California*	The Grand Jury Clause does not apply in states through the Fourteenth Amendment. The Due Process Clauses of the Fifth and Fourteenth Amendments are identical.
1886	*Santa Clara County* v. *Southern Pacific Railroad*	Corporations are "persons" for purposes of the Due Process Clause of the Fourteenth Amendment. Corporate property rights can be protected from state interference.
1897	*Chicago, Burlington & Quincy Railroad Co.* v. *Chicago*	The Due Process Clause of the Fourteenth Amendment requires states to give just compensation for property taken.
1908	*Twining* v. *New Jersey*	Fifth Amendment self-incrimination protections are not applicable to the due process of the Fourteenth Amendment. But, the Due Process Clause might guarantee certain "fundamental" rights "similar" to those in the Bill of Rights.
1925	*Gitlow* v. *New York*	"For present purposes" the freedoms of speech and press are found in the liberties guaranteed by the Fourteenth Amendment.
1931	*Near* v. *Minnesota*	Freedom of press is applicable to the state governments.
1932	*Powell* v. *Alabama*	The right to counsel for indigents in capital cases is fundamental. The *Hurtado* rule contains some exceptions.
1937	*De Jonge* v. *Oregon*	The right of peaceable assembly is a fundamental liberty and applies to states through the Fourteenth Amendment.
1937	*Palko* v. *Connecticut*	Under the principle of selective incorporation those rights "implicit in the concept of ordered liberty" are binding upon the states.

Next, Justice Matthews drew attention to the identical wording used in the Due Process Clauses of the Fifth and Fourteenth Amendments. With respect to the Fifth Amendment, he noted, "That article also makes specific and express provision for perpetuating the institution of the grand jury." As a result, if the Fourteenth Amendment had intended states to require grand jury indictments in all cases, it would have stated that requirement clearly. This reasoning has produced what Richard Cortner terms the "doctrine of nonsuperfluousness." [11] The doctrine is based upon the Court's holding that the due process guarantees in the Fifth and Fourteenth Amendments are identical. According to the Court in *Hurtado*:

> According to a recognized canon of interpretation, especially applicable to formal and solemn instruments of constitutional law, we are forbidden to assume, without clear reason to the contrary, that any part of this most important Amendment is superfluous.

The existence of a Grand Jury Clause in the Fifth Amendment meant that grand jury provisions were not included in the Due Process Clause; to assume otherwise would violate the "nonsuperfluousness" doctrine. Accordingly, if not in the Due Process Clause of the Fifth Amendment, grand jury requirements could not be in the Fourteenth Amendment either. Then, with very little explanation, the majority's *Hurtado* opinion stated that the Due Process Clause protected the "fundamental principles of liberty and justice which lie at the base of all our civil and political institutions." Could it be that some of these "fundamental principles of liberty and justice" were among the provisions of the Bill of Rights? Only time would tell.

Two late nineteenth-century Supreme Court rulings added new significance to the due process controversy. First, in 1886, the Court held that corporations were "persons" within the meaning of the Due Process Clause. This ruling effectively brought corporate property rights under due process protection, thereby making government regulation especially difficult.[12] A review of the section on substantive due process of law in Chapter 7 will provide several examples of this development. Secondly, in the case of *Chicago, Burlington & Quincy Railroad Co.* v. *Chicago* (1897), the Supreme Court held the Fifth Amendment's Just Compensation Clause to be contained in the Fourteenth Amendment's Due Process Clause. Ironically, this first instance of applying a provision of the Bill of Rights to the due process guarantees of the Fourteenth Amendment involved the very provision unsuccessfully claimed by John Barron against the city of Baltimore. The Court's ruling seemed to be in direct conflict with the *Hurtado* precedent, especially the aspect of "nonsuperfluousness." After all, both the Grand Jury Clause and Just Compensation Clause are part of the same Fifth Amendment. How is it possible that the Grand Jury Clause cannot be contained in due process guarantees while the opposite is true for just compensation? The Supreme Court did not say.

The Court suggested a slightly broader test for determining matters of due process in *Twining* v. *New Jersey* (1908). In that case, Albert C. Twining and his associate had refused to take the witness stand in their own defense. The trial judge, in his instructions to the jury, made note of this fact. Following his conviction, Twining claimed on appeal that his silence had served as a form of self-incrimination. In rejecting Twining's claim that the Fifth Amendment's self-incrimination protections constitute "due process" in Fourteenth Amendment terms, the Court sought to

> inquire whether the exemption from self-incrimination is of such a nature that it must be included in the conception of due process. Is it a fundamental principle

of liberty and justice which inheres in the very idea of free government and is the inalienable right of a citizen of such a government?

The *Twining* interest in "fundamental" liberties suggested a possible opening for those hoping to expand the protections of the Bill of Rights into the states. If it could be determined that a particular liberty was indeed fundamental, would it not be logical to hold this liberty as binding against all governments, including the states? The court investigated the origins of the right against self-incrimination. Justice William Moody's conclusions showed the right to be "a privilege of great value," but not one that had been regarded "as a part of the law of the land of Magna Charta or the due process of law." Importantly, Justice Moody's opinion recognized that fundamental rights, if they should eventually be protected from state action (as was just compensation), would be protected not because they were found in the Bill of Rights— but rather because they fall into the accepted notion of due process of law.

A major step was taken in *Gitlow* v. *New York* (1925) with respect to the freedoms of speech and press. The *Gitlow* opinion (discussed further in Chapter 11) almost casually announced the following:

> For present purposes we may and do assume that freedom of speech and of the press—which are protected by the First Amendment from abridgement by Congress—are among the fundamental personal rights and "liberties" protected by the due process clause of the Fourteenth Amendment from impairment by the States.

Although the Court upheld the New York law under which Benjamin Gitlow had been convicted, it forged the link between freedoms found in the Bill of Rights and the "liberties" protected by the Fourteenth Amendment. Yet, the Court mentioned no freedoms beyond speech and press. Perhaps speech and press were more "fundamental" than other freedoms, but the *Gitlow* ruling opened the way for new questions concerning the fundamental nature of other rights and liberties.[13]

The Court's ruling in *Powell* v. *Alabama* (1932) held the Due Process Clause of the Fourteenth Amendment to require that counsel be appointed for indigent defendants in state criminal proceedings involving capital crimes. Accused of raping two white girls, the black defendants, characterized by the Court as "young, ignorant, illiterate," were convicted by a jury and given the death penalty all in a single day. Having lost in the state courts, the defendants appealed to the United States Supreme Court, alleging that due process and equal protection guarantees had been denied them. Specifically, they contended that they had not received a fair and impartial trial, that they had been denied the right to counsel, and that, since blacks had been systematically excluded from their juries, they had not received a proper trial by a "jury of their peers."

Justice George Sutherland, speaking for the majority, held that "the necessity of counsel was so vital and imperative that the failure of the trial court to make an effective appointment of counsel was likewise a denial of due process within the meaning of the Fourteenth Amendment." While the *Powell* ruling did not formally incorporate the Sixth Amendment in all cases, it recognized that "there are certain immutable principles of justice which inhere in the very idea of free government which no member of the Union may disregard." In the case at hand, at least, the Supreme Court felt that the right to counsel was one of those principles. Increasingly, the Court was being called upon to consider new due process questions arising from the guarantees in the Bill of Rights. When the Court held the First Amendment's freedom of assembly to be protected from state action by the Due Process Clause of the Fourteenth Amendment in 1937, it had moved a long way from the decisions in the Slaughterhouse Cases and *Hurtado* in the nineteenth century. The Bill of Rights was coming ever closer to a resolution with the Fourteenth Amendment.

The Doctrine of Selective Incorporation

In *Palko* v. *Connecticut* (1937), the Court accepted on appeal a case from the Connecticut Supreme Court of Errors involving the first-degree murder conviction of Frank Palko. Palko had actually been twice convicted of murder. The first trial ended in Palko's conviction for second-degree murder. Subsequently, the state filed notice of appeal, and the Supreme Court of Errors ordered a new trial. In the second trial, the state was allowed to introduce previously excluded testimony, with the result being a conviction for first-degree murder and a sentence of death. Palko contended that Connecticut's actions violated the Fifth Amendment's guarantee that no person shall "be subject for the same offence to be twice put in jeopardy of life or limb."

Writing for an 8-1 majority, Justice Benjamin Cardozo distinguished between types of rights and liberties found in the Constitution. Those such as freedom of speech, press, and religion, stated Cardozo, "have been found to be implicit in the concept of ordered liberty, and thus, through the Fourteenth Amendment, become valid as against the states." Elsewhere, he described these rights as being "of the very essence of a scheme of ordered liberty." Those rights that qualify as "fundamental" would therefore be as binding upon the states as they were upon the federal government. The process by which such rights were applied to the states has been termed **selective incorporation,** although Cardozo spoke of "absorption":

> We reach a different plane of social and moral values when we pass to the privileges and immunities that have been taken over from the earlier articles of the Federal Bill of Rights and brought within the Fourteenth Amendment by a process of absorption. These in their origin were effective against the federal government alone. If the Fourteenth Amendment has absorbed them, the process of absorption has had its source in the belief that neither liberty nor justice would exist if they were sacrificed.

Using this new standard, Cardozo ruled that double jeopardy protections were not fundamental to due process or liberty and that Palko's first-degree conviction was proper. The Fourteenth Amendment's due process guarantees definitely contained those rights "implicit in the concept of ordered liberty." It would be up to future courts to determine just which privileges and immunities should be absorbed or incorporated (see Brief 8.1). In the short term, and certainly from Palko's perspective, the decision was a blow to the expansion of the Bill of Rights, but the long-term effects of selective incorporation, as presented in Table 8.2, tell an entirely different story.

Table 8.2 presents the history of selective incorporation and the Supreme Court decisions that brought portions of the Bill of Rights into the liberties

❏ Brief 8.1   The Case for Total Incorporation

The Court's lone dissenter in the *Hurtado* and *Twining* decisions was Justice John Harlan, who argued that the Fourteenth Amendment's Due Process Clause had nationalized the entire Bill of Rights. The idea of **total incorporation** was given its strongest voice by Justice Hugo Black, in his dissenting opinion in *Adamson* v. *California* (1947). In that case, a majority of the Court refused to incorporate the Fifth Amendment's protection against self-incrimination, largely on the strength of the *Twining* precedent. Black criticized what he called the "natural-law theory" of his colleagues, which gave too much discretion to the whims of individual justices. He even attached an appendix to his opinion supporting his claim that the founders of the Fourteenth Amendment had specifically intended to make the first eight amendments applicable to the states and to overturn the *Barron* v. *Baltimore* precedent. According to Black:

> My study of the historical events that culminated in the Fourteenth Amendment, and the expressions of those who opposed its submission and passage, persuades me that one of the chief objects that the provisions of the Amendment's first section, separately, and as a whole, were intended to accomplish was to make the Bill of Rights applicable to the states.

Justice Black's opinion drew almost instant response from the legal community. Harvard Law School professor Charles Fairman, a leading scholar of the time, wrote a law review article highly critical of Justice Black's contentions. Fairman argued that the Fourteenth Amendment's framers had never intended to incorporate the entire Bill of Rights.[14] The community of American constitutional law scholars was, and to some extent remains, divided over the issue.[15] Among Justice Black's colleagues on the Court, the debate was no less real. Justice Felix Frankfurter took the consistent position opposing Black's total-incorporation view, choosing instead to decide due process claims on a case-by-case approach. Significantly, Frankfurter believed that each due process claim should be upheld if the claimant was denied a "fair trial," but he did not accept the concept of either selective or total incorporation.

Finally, recent developments have shown evidence of an even broader view of incorporation, termed by some **total incorporation plus.** Actually, the foundation for total incorporation plus was laid by Justice Frank Murphy. In his *Adamson* dissent, Murphy was not willing to hold the Fourteenth Amendment's due process guarantees to be "entirely and necessarily limited by the Bill of Rights." It was conceivable, according to Justice Murphy, that

> occasions may arise where a proceeding falls so short of conforming to fundamental standards or procedures as to warrant constitutional condemnation in terms of lack of due process despite the absence of a specific provision in the Bill of Rights.

This view generally is associated with the later opinions of Justice William O. Douglas and Justice Arthur Goldberg, especially visible in the case of *Griswold* v. *Connecticut* (1965) concerning the right of privacy. (See the discussion of this case in Chapter 10.) For present purposes, it is sufficient to note that the "plus" added to total incorporation suggests that the Court should not limit its concept of due process just to those guarantees found in the first eight amendments. Justices Goldberg and Douglas, for example, held that the provisions of the previously ignored Ninth Amendment could also contain due process protections related to privacy.

of the Fourteenth Amendment. Actually, only five of the ten amendments contain rights and privileges that lend themselves to possible incorporation. For example, the Second (right to bear arms), Third (quartering of soldiers during peacetime), Seventh (civil trials), Ninth (other rights), and Tenth (reserved powers) Amendments do not appear likely to be incorporated, primarily because of their subject matter.

The remainder of this chapter will examine the First, Fourth, Fifth, Sixth, and Eighth Amendments and the role of each in the selective incorporation controversy. Throughout this analysis, emphasis will be placed upon some problems that have arisen in the application of these rights and liberties to the states. Often, a single Supreme Court ruling did not spell the end of the incorporation debate in a specific matter, and a later controversy required the Court to reexamine its earlier position. As a result, the incorporation process has occurred on a case-by-case basis, spanning several decades and different Supreme Courts.

Table 8.2   Selective Incorporation of the Bill of Rights

AMENDMENT/RIGHTS	SUPREME COURT CASE/YEAR
First Amendment	
• Speech	*Gitlow* v. *New York* (1925)
• Press	*Near* v. *Minnesota* (1931)
• Free exercise of religion	*Cantwell* v. *Connecticut* (1940)
• Establishment of religion	*Everson* v. *Board of Education* (1947)
• Assembly	*De Jonge* v. *Oregon* (1937)
Second Amendment	Not incorporated
Third Amendment	Not incorporated
Fourth Amendment	
• Search and seizure	*Wolf* v. *Colorado* (1949)
• Exclusionary rule	*Mapp* v. *Ohio* (1961)
Fifth Amendment	
• Grand jury	Not incorporated
• Double jeopardy	*Benton* v. *Maryland* (1969)
• Self-incrimination	*Malloy* v. *Hogan* (1964)
• Just compensation	*Chicago, Burlington & Quincy Railroad Co.* v. *Chicago* (1897)
Sixth Amendment	
• Speedy trial	*Klopfer* v. *North Carolina* (1967)
• Public trial	*In re Oliver* (1948)
• Impartial jury	*Parker* v. *Gladden* (1966)
• Jury trial	*Duncan* v. *Louisiana* (1968)
• Notice	*Cole* v. *Arkansas* (1948)
• Confrontation	*Pointer* v. *Texas* (1965)
• Compulsory process	*Washington* v. *Texas* (1967)
• Assistance of counsel	*Gideon* v. *Wainwright* (1963)
	Argersinger v. *Hamlin* (1972)
Seventh Amendment	Not incorporated
Eighth Amendment	
• Excessive bail and fines	Not incorporated
• Cruel and unusual punishments	*Robinson* v. *California* (1962)
Ninth Amendment	Not incorporated**
Tenth Amendment	Not incorporated**

**The Ninth and Tenth Amendments, while ratified along with the first eight, generally are not considered to contain specific rights that could be incorporated. Many observers do not include them in the Bill of Rights.

First Amendment

Since several later chapters will be devoted to First Amendment issues of speech, press, and religion, it will not be necessary to examine them here. However, it should be noted that the First Amendment freedoms were among the earliest to be incorporated in the Fourteenth Amendment, prompting many observers to recognize what they saw as the amendment's "preferred freedoms." Justice Wiley Rutledge, writing for the majority in *Thomas* v. *Collins* (1945), expressed the typical **preferred-position doctrine:**

> The case confronts us again with the duty our system places on this Court to say where the individual's freedom ends and the State's power begins. Choice on that border, now as always delicate, is perhaps more so where the usual presumption supporting legislation is balanced by the preferred place given in our scheme to the great, the indispensable democratic freedoms secured by the First Amendment. . . Only the gravest abuses, endangering paramount interests, give occasion for permissible limitation. It is therefore in our tradition to allow the widest room for discussion, the narrowest range for its restriction, particularly when this right is exercised in conjunction with peaceable assembly.

The idea of a preferred position for First Amendment freedoms generally remained a minority view on the Court, with Justices Rutledge and Murphy standing as the doctrine's staunchest supporters. They received occasional support from Justices Black and Douglas, who often went much farther in suggesting that any attempts to limit rights guaranteed under the First Amendment were unconstitutional. (See the discussions on libel and obscenity in Chapter 12.)

With incorporation of the religion clauses in the 1940s, the Court made virtually the entire First Amendment applicable to the states. While controversy has continued to surround government efforts to legislate in various First Amendment-related areas, there has been no serious dispute of the First Amendment's applicability to the states in all its individual rights and liberties.

Fourth Amendment

The Fourth Amendment protects "the right of the people to be secure in their persons, houses, papers, and effects, against unreasonable searches and seizures." It goes on to require that search warrants be issued by a magistrate (judge) on the demonstration of "probable cause" by authorities. Quite clearly, the Fourth Amendment expresses the framers' reaction to the dreaded writs of assistance and general warrants used by British authorities in colonial times to search and seize colonist possessions (see Brief 8.2). The matter of warrants and what constitutes a "reasonable" search will be examined following a discussion of the Fourth Amendment's application to the states.

Incorporation of the Fourth Amendment

Incorporation of the Fourth Amendment into the Fourteenth Amendment's Due Process Clause actually has occurred in two stages. The first stage involved the amendment's enforcement, a matter having first arisen early in the twentieth century. In *Weeks* v. *United States* (1914), the Supreme Court ruled that evidence seized in violation of the provisions of the Fourth Amendment was inadmissible in a federal court. Known ever since as the **exclusionary rule,** this prohibition operated only at the federal level for many years, creating what amounted to a double standard for law enforcement. In fact, the double standard was responsible for what has been called the "silver-platter doctrine." Under this doctrine, state officials—for whom the Fourth Amendment was

☐ *Brief 8.2   Writs of Assistance and General Warrants*

A Boston town meeting in 1772 produced "A List of Infringements and Violations of Rights" that named numerous rights violated by British agents of the Crown. The list included complaints against the so-called "writs of assistance" employed by British officials in their search for contraband. Bostonians complained that "our houses and even our bed chambers are exposed to be ransacked, our boxes, chests, and trunks broke open, ravaged and plundered by wretches, whom no prudent man would venture to employ even as menial servants." [16]

The writs of assistance were a type of general warrant authorizing British agents to undertake indiscriminate searches of ships and houses to stop smuggling. While ordinary search warrants describe the object and the specific premises of the search, general warrants offer authorities complete discretion in their search and seizure decisions. Largely as a result of the abuses associated with general warrants, five states in their post-Revolution constitutions prohibited general warrants that did not specify the person, place, or purpose of a search. [17] Other states relied upon different methods to eliminate such abuses. As a result, the proposed Fourth Amendment to the new Constitution caused relatively little debate either in Congress or among the states during ratification. In the minds of most Americans of that period, general warrants were synonymous with "unreasonable searches and seizures."

---

inapplicable—could seize evidence illegally and then turn it over to federal officers "on a silver platter" for use in federal courts. This doctrine survived until 1960.

In the second stage, the Court held in *Wolf* v. *Colorado* (1949) that the Fourth Amendment's protections against unreasonable searches and seizures were applicable to the states. Since the Fourth Amendment contains no provisions for securing the compliance of law enforcement authorities, however, the *Wolf* decision had little practical effect. Moreover, the Court specifically resisted incorporating the exclusionary rule along with the Fourth Amendment, stating that "in a prosecution in a State court for a State crime, the Fourteenth Amendment does not forbid the admission of evidence obtained by unreasonable search and seizure." Accordingly, should state authorities engage in an unlawful search and seizure, the tainted evidence could still be used in the courtroom to obtain a conviction. While several justices believed that *Wolf* "undermined" the silver-platter doctrine, the practice continued.

Since the *Twining* decision in 1908, the Supreme Court had maintained that the guarantees in the Bill of Rights and the protections of due process applicable to states were not necessarily identical. This, of course, provided the justification for the seeming *Weeks/Wolf* paradox. Although the protections of the Fourth Amendment were binding upon states as a result of *Wolf*, they were not the exact, identical provisions that applied to the national government and did not contain the same enforcement mechanism. The Court's refusal to incorporate the exclusionary rule in *Wolf* largely rested upon the fact that only seventeen states at that time used the exclusionary rule, a fact noted in Justice Frankfurter's opinion. According to Justice Frankfurter, "It is not for this Court to condemn as falling below the minimal standards assured by the due process clause a state's reliance upon other methods which, if consistently enforced, would be equally effective." In short, the exclusionary rule was but one of several different methods available to state governments.

In 1961, the increasingly activist Warren Supreme Court accepted a case on appeal that was destined to extend the protection of the Fourth Amendment—including the exclusionary-rule method of enforcement—to the states by way of the Due Process Clause of the Fourteenth Amendment. *Mapp* v. *Ohio* (1961) also served as a landmark in selective-incorporation terms, standing as the case which began a decade of wholesale nationalization of nearly all the remaining guarantees in the first eight amendments.

Dolree (Dolly) Mapp, a Cleveland woman with known ties to the boxing world and a questionable reputation, was at her house one day in 1957. Police, acting upon a tip that Mapp was hiding a bombing suspect at her house, arrived at her residence and asked to enter. Mapp called her attorney, who advised her to refuse entry unless a search warrant was produced. About 4:00 P.M., some three hours after their arrival, the police forced their way into Mapp's house. During an ensuing scuffle Mapp grabbed what police said was a warrant and stuffed it into her blouse. Mapp was then handcuffed, and the paper was retrieved. At the same time, the police uncovered several pieces of "obscene materials." Mapp was charged with possession of obscene materials and subsequently convicted—even though no search warrant was produced at her trial.

Writing for the Court, Justice Thomas Clark brought the exclusionary rule into the Due Process Clause of the Fourteenth Amendment. He explained that the "same sanction of exclusion as is used against the Federal Government" was necessarily applicable to the states, stating:

> Were it otherwise, then just as without the *Weeks* rule the assurance against unreasonable federal searches and seizures would be "a form of words," valueless and undeserving of mention in a perpetual charter of inestimable human liberties, so too, without that rule the freedom from state invasions of privacy would be so ephemeral and so neatly severed from its conceptual nexus with the freedom from all brutish means of coercing evidence as not to merit this Court's high regard as a freedom "implicit in the concept of ordered liberty."

Justice Clark was mindful of the inconsistency that the previous, long-standing relationship between federal and state authorities had produced. He characterized the Court's decision to incorporate the exclusionary rule:

> There is no war between the Constitution and common sense. Presently, a federal prosecutor may make no use of evidence illegally seized, but a State's attorney across the street may, although he supposedly is operating under the enforceable provisions of the same Amendment. Thus the State, by admitting evidence unlawfully seized, serves to encourage disobedience to the Federal Constitution which it is bound to uphold.

The *Mapp* ruling completed the incorporation of the Fourth Amendment by providing for its enforcement in state courts. Today, both state and federal authorities must operate under the same constitutional standards governing searches and seizures. Still, opposition to the restrictions of the exclusionary rule has been on the increase in recent years. These matters will be explored in a later section.

The Fourth Amendment prohibits unreasonable searches and seizures without specifying the elements of unreasonableness, although it offers several hints. One such requirement is that no warrants may be issued "but upon probable cause, supported by oath or affirmation, and particularly describing the place to be searched, and the persons or things to be seized." As noted earlier, the framers' deep concern with the British general warrant makes the limitations concerning probable cause, oath or affirmation, and specificity rather unsurprising. In fact, it is quite certain that the early concerns surrounding searches and seizures were directed more at the use of general warrants than at the issue of searches without any warrant whatsoever.

In more recent times, the greater issue has been warrantless searches and seizures. The Fourth Amendment does not say that warrants are required for all searches and seizures, but it does appear that proper warrants will provide the necessary reasonableness required by the amendment's provisions. A preliminary conclusion can be stated thusly: a search or seizure undertaken under a specifically worded warrant, based upon probable cause, and sworn before an impartial judge will not be considered "unreasonable." However, few situations lend themselves to such a neat, well-ordered sequence of events. A case study involving the matter of "probable cause" in obtaining a warrant is presented in the following section.

Probable Cause: A Case Study

The Fourth Amendment's requirement of probable cause for obtaining a warrant has been subject to considerable interpretation. In *Henry* v. *United States* (1959), for example, the issue was whether the police had shown the necessary probable cause to arrest John Patrick Henry and then produce stolen radios in their search of his car. Justice Douglas began with an overview of the problem:

> The requirement of probable cause has roots that are deep in our history. The general warrant, in which the name of the person to be arrested was left blank, and the writs of assistance, against which James Otis inveighed, both perpetuated the oppressive practice of allowing the police to arrest and search on suspicion . . . since no showing of "probable cause" before a magistrate was required.

With the coming of the Fourth Amendment, however, Douglas noted a distinctly different situation concerning probable cause:

> And as the early American decisions both before and immediately after its adoption show, common rumor or report, suspicion, or even "strong reason to suspect" was not adequate to support a warrant for arrest. . . Probable cause exists if the facts and circumstances known to the officer warrant a prudent man in believing that the offense has been committed.

Justice Douglas added that "good faith on the part of the arresting officers is not enough." (Notice the "good-faith" discussion later in this chapter.) In determining if the arresting officers in the *Henry* case had acted under probable-cause standards, the Court considered the following facts:

> An interstate shipment of whiskey was stolen at a terminal in Chicago. The next day, FBI agents investigating the theft in the neighborhood saw Henry and a companion, Pierotti, get into a car outside a tavern. Pierotti's employer earlier had given the agents undisclosed information "concerning the implication of the defendant Pierotti with interstate shipments." No record showed that the employer had said he suspected Pierotti of the thefts. Agents followed the car to an alley and watched from about 300 feet away, as Henry got out of the car and went into "residential premises." He came out with some cartons and drove away. Agents could not follow the car but later found it back at the tavern. They later watched Henry and Pierotti repeat their earlier actions with the cartons. Officers could not determine the size, number, or contents of the cartons, but this time

they stopped the suspects. They then searched the car and found three cartons of stolen radios. Both suspects were convicted using the stolen radios as evidence.

If police had acted upon probable cause in stopping Henry, their subsequent search producing the radios would be valid. Was such the case? Justice Douglas, writing for the majority, ruled the arrest (seizure) to have taken place when agents stopped the car. At that time, he noted, the agents knew only that whiskey had been stolen earlier and that Pierotti had been named in some unspecified implication in some unknown interstate shipments. Accordingly, Douglas concluded that there was "far from enough evidence" to justify a magistrate in issuing a warrant. Several reasons were listed:

1. The petitioner had no record of criminal activity.
2. Riding in a car, picking up packages, and driving away are "outwardly innocent" acts.
3. Their movements were not those of men fleeing from a crime.
4. Packages were picked up in a residential section, not from a warehouse or terminal.
5. Nothing (weight, shape, etc.) indicated the packages contained liquor.

Reversing the convictions, Justice Douglas concluded with the following:

> To repeat, an arrest is not justified by what the subsequent search discloses. Under our system suspicion is not enough for an officer to lay hands on a citizen. It is better, so the Fourth Amendment teaches, that the guilty sometimes go free than that citizens be subject to easy arrest.

The dissenters argued that an earlier decision concerning automobile searches and seizures should apply, and that issue will be examined later. In leaving *Henry,* however, it is important to recognize the numerous elements involved in the case that would likely never be duplicated in another situation. What if the suspects had picked up the cartons from the loading dock of a truck terminal, for example, or perhaps acted suspiciously in some other way? Would the requirements of probable cause have been met then? The reasonableness of a search subsequent to a valid arrest will be examined further in the following section.

Exceptions to the Fourth Amendment's Warrant Requirements

It often is impractical to secure an arrest warrant, particularly since many persons in jeopardy of arrest will take the opportunity to flee the scene to avoid being apprehended. As a result, many arrests occur today without a sworn warrant, although, as the *Henry* example shows, even these warrantless arrests must be based upon probable cause. In *Draper* v. *United States* (1959), the Court ruled that it is impractical to obtain an arrest warrant in an emergency or "exigency." These emergencies might include believing the suspect will escape if an arrest is not made immediately or believing evidence is in danger of being destroyed by the suspect. In short, the realities of law enforcement often demand officers to act quickly and without the guidance of a magistrate. The resulting exceptions offer clear evidence of the problem's complexity.

The "Automobile" Exception

Stated first in *Carroll* v. *United States* (1925), the automobile exception permits authorities to stop and search a moving vehicle on probable cause without a warrant. This exception is necessary, according to the Court, because of the ease with which an automobile can be moved away from law enforcement authorities and the jurisdiction of the court issuing the warrant. The authorities should have probable cause to believe that the car is being used to commit a crime or contains evidence of a previously committed crime.

The rationale justifying a warrantless search of an automobile arguably applies to any movable container believed to contain contraband. That argument, however, was squarely rejected by the Supreme Court in *United States* v. *Chadwick* (1977). The *Chadwick* case concerned the legality of a warrantless search of a footlocker weighing two hundred pounds and secured with two padlocks. Federal railroad officials in San Diego grew suspicious of the heavier-than-normal footlocker with talcum powder leaking from its side. Since talcum powder was known to be used as a masking agent for marijuana, officials suspected that the footlocker contained contraband. Agents waited until Joseph Chadwick arrived, claimed the footlocker, and placed it in the trunk of a car. Officers then arrested Chadwick, seized the footlocker, and transported it to a federal building where it was opened without a warrant. Marijuana was found.

The Supreme Court ruled that the warrantless search was improper, specifically refusing to apply the *Carroll* exception to the case. According to the Court, "A person's expectations of privacy in personal luggage are substantially greater than in the automobile." Moreover, the rationale for a warrantless search is much less valid for luggage than for automobiles. The Court explained that there were fewer practical problems in the temporary detention of luggage to obtain a warrant than in the detention of an automobile.

The Supreme Court elaborated on the *Chadwick* rule in *Arkansas* v. *Sanders* (1979). The case involved an informant's tip that an incoming airline passenger was carrying a green suitcase containing marijuana. Authorities watched the arriving passenger take his green suitcase to a taxicab and place it in the trunk. They later stopped the cab just blocks away, opened the trunk, and seized the suitcase. Marijuana was found. Upholding the lower courts, the Supreme Court ruled the automobile exception inapplicable to the present case. It was the luggage being transported and not the moving automobile that was the "suspected locus" of the contraband. The relationship between the automobile and contraband was "purely coincidental," thereby making the warrantless search unreasonable and the contraband inadmissible as evidence.

Then, in *Robbins* v. *California* (1981), the Supreme Court encountered a slightly different question from that presented in the *Chadwick* and *Sanders* cases. What if police encountered closed packages and containers while conducting a search in which the automobile itself was the "suspected locus" of the contraband. Although the Supreme Court did not consider *Robbins* v. *California* to raise that precise issue, it did indicate growing signs of division. The facts of *Robbins* suggest a different scenario. Police stopped J. R. Robbins's station wagon after observing the suspect "driving erratically." When stopped, Robbins got out of the car to talk to the authorities but then had to go back to the car to get his registration papers. When the door was opened, the smell of marijuana smoke became apparent to the officers. They then searched Robbins and found a small vial of a liquid. Continuing, they searched the interior of the car for signs of marijuana, eventually opening the tailgate and looking inside the recessed luggage compartment. Inside, police found two packages wrapped in dark-colored plastic, unwrapped them, and found marijuana. The California court upheld the search, but the Supreme Court reversed. Justice Potter Stewart's plurality opinion rejected the argument that police could tell from the "outward appearance" of the packages that they probably contained contraband. In fact, the plurality's ruling extended the same protections to closed luggage in a car as would be given to closed luggage anywhere else. Critics complained that the effect upon law enforcement efforts would be catastrophic.

The Court clarified the moving vehicle exception in *United States* v. *Ross* (1982). In that case, the police received information from an informant that Albert Ross, alias "Bandit," was selling narcotics kept in the trunk of a car that was parked at a specified location. The informant, who had been reliable in other matters, also stated that he had just witnessed the sale of narcotics from the car. Police drove to the area and found the car but waited until later when they witnessed the suspect driving away. They stopped the car, told Ross to step outside, and searched both Ross and the vehicle. A pistol was found in the glove compartment, and Ross was arrested and handcuffed. A detective took the keys and opened the trunk, finding a closed brown paper bag which he opened. Inside, he discovered a number of glassine bags containing a white powder later determined to be heroin. He replaced the bag, closed the trunk, and drove the car to headquarters, where the car was searched thoroughly. This time, a zippered pouch was found containing $3,200 in cash. Ross was tried and convicted of possession with intent to distribute heroin. The court of appeals reversed his conviction, and the Supreme Court granted certiorari.

Justice John Paul Stevens delivered the majority opinion, which began with a thorough review of previous Supreme Court decisions on the warrantless search of automobiles from *Carroll* through *Robbins*. Several areas of uncertainty seemingly were resolved through the opinion. First, with respect to the fact that contraband placed inside containers is hidden from the plain view of authorities, Justice Stevens stated that this was neither surprising nor particularly troublesome for the Court:

> Contraband goods rarely are strewn across the trunk or floor of a car; since by their very nature such goods must be withheld from public view, they rarely can be placed in an automobile unless they are enclosed within some type of container.

Secondly, Justice Stevens dealt with the possible problems associated with opening a container inside an automobile when the container had not been the primary focus of the search at the start. This, he noted, was not much different from the lawful search of any "fixed premises." Such a search "generally extends to the entire area in which the object of the search may be found and is not limited by the possibility that separate acts of entry or opening may be required to complete the search." Under this reasoning, authorities with probable cause to search a house for a weapon logically would be allowed to open drawers and cabinets as part of the search; similarly, the search of a footlocker would justify the opening of packages found inside.

Significantly, the majority in *Ross* held that the search of an automobile based upon probable cause authorizes a search which is "no broader and no narrower than a magistrate could legitimately authorize by warrant." The concluding words of Justice Stevens indicate a major change in the long-standing doctrine concerning the opening of containers found in automobiles:

> The scope of a warrantless search of an automobile thus is not defined by the nature of the container in which the contraband is secreted. Rather, it is defined by the object of the search and the places in which there is probable cause to believe that it may be found. . . If probable cause justifies the search of a lawfully stopped vehicle, it justifies the search of every part of the vehicle and its contents that may conceal the object of the search.

The Court reversed the judgment of the court of appeals and remanded the case for further proceedings. The justifications for the automobile exception continued to be valid—the possibility of quick mobility and the reduced expectation of privacy in vehicles.

California v. *Carney* (1985) raised the interesting problem of placing motor homes within the Fourth Amendment's exceptions. Acting upon an informant's tip, agents of the Drug Enforcement Administration placed Charles Carney under surveillance on suspicion of exchanging marijuana for sex. Agents watched as Carney approached a youth in downtown San Diego and took him to his mini motor home parked in a nearby public parking lot. The youth remained inside for over an hour, and, confronted by agents upon his departure, he confirmed their suspicions. The agents returned to the motor home, knocked on the door and identified themselves, entered the motor home, and observed marijuana and other related items. They did not obtain a search warrant. Although the lower courts upheld the use of the marijuana as evidence, the California Supreme Court reversed the decision.

Writing for the 6-3 majority, Chief Justice Warren Burger reversed the California Supreme Court and held that the automobile exception clearly applies to motor homes. Carney's motor home, like an automobile, was a licensed motor vehicle subject to extensive governmental regulation. Moreover, according to the majority, the motor home could achieve immediate mobility on the highways simply by turning on the ignition key. The chief justice expressly refused to determine whether the automobile exception might apply to a motor home that was more clearly being used strictly as a residence. Justices William Brennan, Thurgood Marshall, and John Paul Stevens dissented, arguing that motor homes have a greater expectation of privacy than automobiles, particularly when they are not on public highways. Finally, it should be noted that the exception has been broadened in recent years to apply to other forms of transportation associated with suspected criminal activity. Boats and airplanes, for example, have begun to figure prominently in smuggling and other illegal activities. The exception will certainly continue to be tested.

The "Border" Exception

Given the ongoing controversy surrounding the movement of illegal aliens into the United States, the U.S. Border Patrol has been involved in numerous search and seizure cases. On this issue, the Supreme Court gradually has brought border searches into the coverage of the Fourth Amendment, while maintaining the long-standing practice of not requiring search warrants for searches at border crossings. However, in *Almeida-Sanchez* v. *United States* (1973), a 5-4 majority held that a roving search of an automobile by border patrol agents approximately twenty miles from the border without a warrant and lacking probable cause was unconstitutional. Two years later, in *United States* v. *Ortiz* (1975), the Court extended the probable cause requirement to vehicle searches at checkpoints away from the border.

In *United States* v. *Martinez-Fuerte* (1976), however, a 7-2 majority offered a slight readjustment of the Court's previously held views. The majority ruled that a permanent checkpoint situated at San Clemente, California, was properly within the border patrol's authority to administer and that the location of checkpoints was a matter properly left to the border patrol's discretion. As for the practice of referring some persons for secondary inspections at the checkpoint, the Court found no Fourth Amendment violation present in such actions, even if the reasons used to select some persons for secondary inspection would not justify a stop by a roving patrol. According to the Court, even if these referrals are made largely on the basis of "apparent Mexican ancestry," they are not improper.

The "Hot-Pursuit" Exception

Police authorities often must react to the fleeing suspect who seeks to avoid capture by any number of methods. The issue of "hot pursuit" arose in *Warden* v. *Hayden* (1967), a case involving an armed robbery of a cab company. The suspect, fleeing on foot with a reported $363, was described by the company dispatcher over the radio and followed by two cab drivers to a residence. Police received the information and arrived at the scene within minutes. They knocked on the door, announced their presence, and indicated to Mrs. Hayden that they wished to search for a suspected robber who had been seen entering the house. She did not object. Officers found Bennie Joe Hayden "feigning sleep" upstairs and no other man in the house. In the process of searching for the man and money, police discovered a shotgun and pistol in a running flush tank and assorted ammunition. In the washing machine, they found a jacket and trousers which matched the dispatcher's description. Hayden was arrested, the items of evidence were introduced at his trial, and he was convicted.

Speaking for the Court, Justice Brennan upheld the validity of the entry and search without a warrant. Critical to the permissibility of the search, said Brennan, was the fact that "speed here was essential" and that the authorities were required to make a thorough search of the house for persons and weapons. Police officers, he stated, are not required "to delay in the course of an investigation if to do so would gravely endanger their lives or the lives of others." Clearly, the exception remains confined to what the Court considers emergencies.

Such was the feeling in *United States* v. *Santana* (1976), in which a 7-2 majority upheld the arrest of Moms Santana, a felony suspect. Acting upon a tip that Santana had been involved in a narcotics deal, police drove to her home. When they arrived, Santana was on her front porch. She ran inside the house. The authorities followed her inside without a warrant and placed her under arrest—in "hot pursuit." According to Justice William Rehnquist, for the Court, "A suspect may not defeat an arrest which has been set in motion in a public place . . . by the expedient of escaping to a private place."

The "Stop-and-Frisk" Exception

Police officers on patrol may encounter what they regard as a suspicious person or situation. There is no time to obtain a warrant; indeed, the officers may be operating on something considerably less than probable cause. Detective Martin McFadden was on afternoon patrol in downtown Cleveland. While observing John W. Terry and a companion, McFadden noticed that something about the men "didn't look right," so he decided to watch them from a distance of a few hundred yards. He watched as one of the men walked down the street, stopped to look in a store window, walked past, looked back into the window, and eventually returned to his starting place. These actions were repeated several times and, when a third man arrived, McFadden decided to investigate further, believing that the men might be planning to rob the store. Approaching the men, he identified himself, asked the men their names, and received only a mumbled reply. At that point, McFadden grabbed Terry, turned him around, and patted down the outside of his clothing. Detecting what felt like a pistol, McFadden moved the men inside the store, ordered Terry to remove his coat, and confiscated the pistol. A pat-down search of the other men produced another gun. Terry and his companion were booked and subsequently convicted for carrying concealed weapons.

In *Terry* v. *Ohio* (1968), the Court heard Terry's claim that Officer McFadden had conducted an unreasonable search and seizure. Writing for an 8-1 majority, Chief Justice Earl Warren upheld Terry's conviction and clarified the "difficult and troublesome issues regarding a sensitive area of police activity." Noting that each case of this type will "have to be decided on its own facts," the chief justice gave strong support to stop-and-frisk:

> We merely hold today that where a police officer observes unusual conduct which leads him reasonably to conclude in light of his experience that criminal activity may be afoot and that the persons with whom he is dealing may be armed and presently dangerous, where in the course of investigating this behavior he identifies himself as a policeman and makes reasonable inquiries, and where nothing in the initial stages of the encounter serves to dispel his reasonable fear for his own or others' safety, he is entitled for the protection of himself and others in the area to conduct a carefully limited search of the outer clothing of such persons in an attempt to discover weapons which might be used to assault him.

In two companion cases to *Terry*, the Court showed the importance of specific facts in each stop-and-frisk encounter. A policeman who stuck his hand into a suspect's pocket to obtain narcotics he suspected to be there conducted an unreasonable search, according to the decision in *Sibron* v. *New York*. However, in *Peters* v. *New York*, a police officer who observed two unfamiliar men tiptoeing past his apartment door was justified in apprehending the suspects and patting them down. When he felt a hard object which "might have been a knife" in one suspect's pocket, the officer reached into the pocket and removed a small set of burglary tools. According to the Court, the burglary tools were discovered in a valid search and as such were properly admissible as evidence in court.

The "Search-Incident-to-Arrest" Exception

As far back as the exclusionary-rule case of *Weeks* v. *United States* (1914), the Supreme Court has recognized the need to allow a warrantless search following a lawful arrest. Today, in the United States, probably a majority of all searches occur "incident-to-arrest." The long-recognized reasons for such searches include the need to protect the officer from being harmed by weapons held by the suspect, as well as the need to prevent evidence from being destroyed. In *United States* v. *Rabinowitz* (1950), these reasons were stated as grounds for upholding a warrantless 1½-hour search of a one-room office following a valid arrest there. Following *Rabinowitz,* the Court seemed to broaden the exception of a search following a lawful arrest to the point that a person legally arrested at home might then be subject to a house-wide search.

Chimel v. *California* (1969) marked a distinct change in the Court's treatment of the valid arrest exception. Ted Chimel, the appellant, had been arrested at home on burglary charges. Despite his objections, the police undertook a complete search of the house, including the attic and garage. Certain items obtained in the search were introduced as evidence in Chimel's trial, in which he was convicted.

Justice Stewart's majority opinion reversed Chimel's conviction and enunciated new standards governing the scope of searches that follow a lawful arrest, significantly narrowing their permissibility in the process. According to Stewart, a lawful arrest provides "ample justification" for a search of the person arrested and the area "within his immediate control." Search of such an area would be justified to prevent the suspect from obtaining a weapon or destroying evidence. He continued:

> There is no comparable justification, however, for routinely searching any room other than that in which an arrest occurs—or, for that matter, for searching through all the desk drawers or other closed or concealed areas in that room itself. Such searches, in the absence of well-recognized exception, may be made only under the authority of a search warrant.

Under the *Chimel* ruling, police may no longer use a lawful arrest as a pretext for a broad-based search of the premises. The search must be confined to the narrow area within the arrested person's control. While *Chimel* has not been overturned by the Court, considerable attention has been directed at the issue of searches conducted following a valid arrest. Both the *Terry* stop-and-frisk and *Chimel* holdings were involved in a series of Court rulings in the early 1970s stemming from searches conducted after routine stops for traffic violations.

The 1973 decisions in *United States* v. *Robinson* and *Gustafson* v. *Florida* upheld police pat-down searches that produced heroin and marijuana respectively. Majority opinions by Justice Rehnquist in both cases held that "it is the fact of custodial arrest which gives rise to the authority to search." Rehnquist distinguished these searches made subject to lawful custodial arrests from the *Terry*-based "protective searches conducted in an investigatory stop situation based on less than probable cause." It did not matter that the officers in *Robinson* and *Gustafson* had no fear that the defendant was armed or that evidence might be destroyed. The lawful arrest provides all necessary justification for such a search.

The "Consent" Exception

Under long-standing doctrine, any search to which a suspect has consented voluntarily and freely is legal. In short, a person may waive the requirement for a warrant, but such waiver should be completely voluntary. *Schneckloth* v. *Bustamonte* (1973) raised the issue of whether such a waiver is ever truly voluntary if the person being searched is not aware that he or she has the right to refuse permission to authorities. In that ruling, Justice Stewart held for the majority that explicit notice of the right to refuse a warrantless search is not required to establish proof of voluntary consent. As a result, a prosecutor is not required to demonstrate that defendants know of their right to withhold permission to search. A quite different majority view of voluntariness in the matter of confessions will be discussed later in this chapter.

The "Plain-View" Exception

In *Harris* v. *United States* (1968), the Court issued the following announcement: "It has long been settled that objects falling in the plain view of an officer who has a right to be in the position to have that view are subject to seizure and may be introduced into evidence." This "plain-view" exception was given further elaboration in *Coolidge* v. *New Hampshire* (1971). In that instance, the police arrested Edward Coolidge at his home and towed his car from its spot in the driveway to the police station. The Court found the search warrants issued by the state attorney general, acting in his capacity as justice of the peace, to be defective for violating the Fourth Amendment requirement for a "neutral and detached magistrate." The attorney general also helped prosecute the *Coolidge* case.

Because the warrants were invalid, the state sought to have its search and seizure of the automobile (some incriminating evidence was found in the car) approved on other grounds—including the valid arrest, automobile, and plain-view exceptions. Justice Stewart's plurality opinion rejected all three exceptions and reversed the conviction, emphasizing three requirements for the plain-view search or seizure: first, the police must enter lawfully; second, the evidence must be discovered "inadvertently"; and third, it should be "immediately apparent" to police that the items in question are contraband or evidence of a crime. In the *Coolidge* case, police had not stumbled inadvertently over the car; rather, they had come with the express purpose of seizing it.

These three elements were central issues in *Arizona* v. *Hicks* (1987), one of the Court's recent attempts to clarify the plain-view exception. The facts of the case are summarized as follows:

> Police entered the apartment of James Thomas Hicks to search for the person who had fired a shot through the floor and into the apartment below. The bullet had struck and injured a person in the downstairs apartment. Inside the apartment, three weapons and a stocking-cap mask were discovered. One of the police officers, Officer Nelson, noticed two sets of expensive-looking stereo components. As he suspected the stereos might be stolen, he recorded their serial numbers, an action which required that he move some of the components. He called in these numbers to headquarters. Shortly afterward, headquarters reported back that a turntable had been stolen in an armed robbery. Since one of the turntables in the apartment matched the description of the stolen turntable, Officer Nelson seized it immediately and took it to the station. It was later determined that some

of the other equipment had been taken in the same armed robbery, and a warrant was executed to seize that equipment as well. Hicks was subsequently indicted for the robbery.

In writing for a 6-3 Court, Justice Antonin Scalia held that probable cause is required to invoke the plain-view doctrine, and that the "reasonable suspicion" (less than probable cause) that the stereo equipment was stolen was not enough to justify the seizure. As a result, the plain-view doctrine did not make the search "reasonable" under the Fourth Amendment.

Interestingly, the Court clarified several other matters. First, while the policeman's actions were covered by the Fourth Amendment, the mere recording of serial numbers was not a "seizure" under the amendment's meaning. This action did not "meaningfully interfere" with Hicks's "possessory interest" in the items. Second, moving the equipment was a search unrelated to the "exigency" (the shooting) that justified the entry. It was not important that the search uncovered nothing of any great personal value. According to Justice Scalia, "A search is a search, even if it happens to disclose nothing but the bottom of a turntable." Finally, Justice Scalia addressed the lack of a relationship between the reasons for entering the premises initially and for seizing the stolen stereo equipment. That problem "always exists," he stated, because the plain-view doctrine is "superfluous" where action is taken for the purpose that justified the entry. As a result, even though probable cause was not present in *Hicks,* the plain-view doctrine remains one of the established exceptions to the Fourth Amendment's warrant requirement.

Finally, the plain-view exception has been applied to certain uses of aerial surveillance, especially those uses designed to detect the cultivation of marijuana. For example, a majority of the Court upheld an aerial search of a fenced backyard in *California* v. *Ciraolo* (1986). In that instance, police, acting upon an informant's tip, flew over the defendant's property, saw the marijuana, and then obtained a search warrant. The majority's ruling emphasized the use of public air space to observe the property in question, holding that the Fourth Amendment was not violated by such activity. The Court has upheld similar uses of aerial surveillance by environmental enforcement agents to detect violations. Before leaving this discussion, it should be noted that at least two additional exceptions to the warrant requirement can be identified. These concern certain administrative searches and the emerging "good-faith" exception. Each is discussed in an upcoming section of this chapter. Finally, Brief 8.3 discusses yet another significant constitutional issue.

Wiretapping and Electronic Surveillance

Perhaps no issue contributes to the view of government as a prying "big brother" more than the use of wiretapping and other forms of eavesdropping by authorities. As technology has grown increasingly sophisticated, the potential for electronic abuse by authorities has grown to previously undreamed of levels. Not surprisingly, the Supreme Court's interpretation of the Fourth Amendment to include electronic evidence-gathering has also changed over the years.

In the first such case, *Olmstead* v. *United States* (1928), a 5-4 majority failed to see wiretapping as a Fourth Amendment issue. Chief Justice William

☐ *Brief 8.3   Bodily Intrusions*

The practice of entering the body of a suspect to obtain evidence raises both Fourth and Fifth Amendment (self-incrimination) issues, and the Supreme Court has ruled several times that such intrusions must be reasonable. But what guidelines help to distinguish reasonable from unreasonable intrusions? According to the Court, an individual's privacy and security interests must be weighed against society's need for evidence on a case-by-case basis. The case law offers some help in understanding which types of intrusions may be upheld as permissible.

In *Rochin* v. *California* (1952), the Court overturned a conviction based upon the forced pumping of the suspect's stomach after authorities reportedly saw him swallow two capsules. When the officers "jumped upon him" and were still unable to extract the capsules, they took him to the hospital and forced him to have his stomach pumped. The capsules were used as evidence to obtain the conviction. Justice Felix Frankfurter's opinion called the actions "conduct that shocks the conscience" and "too close to the rack and screw" to be allowable under the Due Process Clause.

However, in *Breithaupt* v. *Abram* (1957), the Court upheld the taking of a blood sample from an unconscious person who had been involved in a fatal traffic accident, primarily on the grounds that a blood test conducted under the authority of a physician was safe and inoffensive. In *Schmerber* v. *California* (1966), a compulsory blood test was upheld as reasonable even though the suspect was awake and opposed the test on advice of his lawyer.

The Court applied the *Schmerber* guidelines to the case of *Winston* v. *Lee* (1985) and ruled that a person cannot be compelled to submit to a surgical procedure requiring use of a general anesthetic to obtain evidence of a crime. At issue was a bullet lodged beneath the suspect's collarbone that presumably would have confirmed that he had been involved in a shooting with a shopkeeper. Writing for the Court, Justice William Brennan noted that factors such as the difficulty of the surgery and its likely effect upon the health or safety of the suspect must be considered along with the community's interest in obtaining the evidence. Characterizing the intrusion as "severe," Justice Brennan held the surgery to be a violation of the Fourth Amendment right to be secure in one's person. It should be noted that the Court recognized the significant amount of other evidence already available to the state, including the shopkeeper's identification, the area where the suspect was found, and the location of the bullet. As such, the state could not justify such an intrusive search.

Proposals for mandatory drug and AIDS testing have become much more prevalent, and it is likely that such tests will be subject to numerous court challenges. The constitutional issues in these areas are still unclear, but it is likely that the Court's precedents governing bodily intrusions will help to shape the direction of the law.

Howard Taft gave the following, rather traditional, interpretation of the amendment:

> The amendment itself shows that the search is to be of material things—the person, the house, his papers, or his effects. . . The amendment does not forbid what was done here. There was no searching. There was no seizure. The evidence was secured by the use of the sense of hearing and that only. There was no entry of the houses or offices of the defendants. . . The language of the amendment cannot be extended and expanded to include telephone wires, reaching to the whole world from the defendant's house or office. The intervening wires are not part of his house or office, any more than are the highways along which they are stretched.

A famous dissenting opinion by Justice Louis Brandeis focused upon the dangers inherent in the majority's position. The framers, he argued, "sought to protect Americans in their beliefs, their thoughts, their emotions and their sensations." Any unjustifiable government invasion of an individual's privacy, "whatever the means employed," would be unconstitutional. Justice Brandeis termed it "immaterial where the physical connection with the telephone wires leading into the defendants' premises was made."

The dissenting view came to be accepted by a majority in *Katz* v. *United States* (1967), in which the Federal Bureau of Investigation had "bugged" several public telephone booths in Los Angeles to obtain evidence of interstate gambling against Charles Katz. The listening device was attached to the outside of the phone booths, a distinction relied upon by the government in defense of its actions. Katz was convicted largely upon the basis of the recordings made of his telephone conversations.

The *Katz* opinion, written by Justice Potter Stewart, was significant for two reasons. First, it enunciated a notion that has come to be associated with the workings of the Fourth Amendment—namely, the idea of a "reasonable expectation of privacy." According to Justice Stewart, Katz had entered the telephone booth and closed the door so as to avoid being heard. It did not matter, as the government contended, that Katz could be seen through the glass-enclosed telephone booth:

> What he sought to exclude when he entered the booth was not the intruding eye—it was the uninvited ear. He did not shed his right to do so simply because he made his calls from a place where he might be seen. No less than an individual in a business office, in a friend's apartment, or in a taxicab, a person in a telephone booth may rely upon the protection of the Fourth Amendment. One who occupies it, shuts the door behind him, and pays the toll that permits him to place a call is surely entitled to assume that the words he utters into the mouthpiece will not be broadcast to the world.

In short, Katz had an expectation of privacy in his telephone conversation, and such an expectation should be respected. The expectation of privacy has become quite significant in Fourth Amendment matters in recent years, and the Court generally has held such expectations to be valid. Of course, as noted in the earlier section concerning warrantless searches of automobiles, the expectation of privacy may be less in some areas than in others. As Brief 8.4 describes, one area that is generating controversy is trash.

The Court's ruling in *Katz* was significant also for its effect upon the long-standing "trespass rule," which can be traced to the much earlier *Olmstead* case. Under the trespass rule, an unreasonable search and seizure could only occur when authorities invaded or physically intruded into some enclosure. Justice Stewart's statement that the Fourth Amendment "protects" people, not places" set the tone for a sweeping change in the Court's thinking. Despite the government's objections, the Court held that it was of "no constitutional significance" that the electronic device used to eavesdrop on Katz was placed outside the telephone booth. Hence, the electronic eavesdropping constituted a "search and seizure" within the meaning of the Fourth Amendment, and it did not matter that there had been no trespass or physical intrusion. As a protection of the "person," *Katz* also contributed to the growing "right of privacy" decisions (see *Griswold* v. *Connecticut* [1965] in Chapter 10).

Congress addressed wiretapping and electronic eavesdropping in the Omnibus Crime Control and Safe Streets Act of 1968. Title III of the act, titled "Wiretapping and Electronic Surveillance," authorized the attorney general to request court-approved interceptions by both federal and state officials investigating specific crimes. According to Henry J. Abraham, there were 302 such

☐ *Brief 8.4   Can We Expect Privacy in Our Trash?*

In early 1984, Laguna Beach authorities received information indicating that Billy Greenwood might be a narcotics trafficker. An informant had told federal drug enforcement officials that a large shipment of drugs would be delivered to Greenwood's address. Also, a neighbor had complained about heavy late-night traffic in the area. Following a period of surveillance, the police investigator asked the neighborhood's regular trash collector to pick up the plastic garbage bags that Greenwood had left on his curb and to turn them over to her without mixing their contents with other trash bags. The trash collector did so; the officer searched the rubbish and found items associated with narcotics use. Using the information from the trash, the officer obtained a search warrant. The search produced narcotics, and Greenwood was arrested, although he quickly posted bail. Less than a month later, another investigator repeated the trash search, found evidence of narcotics, and secured another search warrant. Greenwood was again arrested.

The California courts dismissed charges against Greenwood because of the illegality of warrantless trash searches. The state appealed, and the U.S. Supreme Court granted certiorari. The central issue of the case

rested upon Greenwood's argument that his "expectation of privacy" in his trash came under Fourth Amendment protections.

Writing for a 6-2 majority, Justice Byron White reversed the California courts. His opinion held that the expectation of privacy claims of Greenwood would have Fourth Amendment protection only if "society is prepared to accept that expectation as objectively reasonable." According to White, by exposing his garbage to the public, Greenwood had defeated any Fourth Amendment claims he might otherwise have. It was quite clear, said White, that society does not recognize an expectation of privacy in another person's garbage. According to the opinion in *California* v. *Greenwood* (1988):

It is common knowledge that plastic garbage bags left on or at the side of a public street are readily accessible to animals, children, scavengers, snoops, and other members of the public. . . Moreover, respondents placed their refuse at the curb for the express purpose of conveying it to a third party, the trash collector, who might himself have sorted through respondents' trash or permitted others, such as the police, to do so.

In short, individuals who place their trash bags at the curb in full public view can hardly expect a great deal of privacy.

court-authorized orders in 1969, rising to 873 in 1974 and declining to 626 in 1977. Of these, nearly 75 percent involved gambling offenses, with drug-related crimes following next.[18]

Two decisions in the 1970s showed that the 1968 act had not resolved the controversy over electronic surveillance. First, in *United States* v. *United States District Court for Eastern District of Michigan* (1972), the Supreme Court rejected the government's contention that domestic aspects of national security were exempt from the act's provisions. At issue were numerous, non-court-approved wiretaps undertaken to gather information concerning the bombing of a Central Intelligence Agency office. Speaking for the Court, Justice Lewis Powell swept aside the government's claims that prior judicial approval was not required for national security investigations. However, Powell's opinion specifically limited itself to domestic aspects of national security, leaving open the matter of surveillance against foreign powers or their agents.

A second ruling resulted in a different outcome. In *United States* v. *New York Telephone Company* (1977), the Court ruled that the 1968 act did not apply to "pen registers"—devices which record the phone numbers of outgoing calls. Justice Byron White's opinion distinguished between the act's concern with the "interception" of the "contents" of a conversation and a pen register's disclosure only of numbers dialed. In this case, the Supreme Court held that a district court had the authority to approve the use of pen registers outside any other requirements of the 1968 act. More importantly, the district court lawfully could compel the telephone company to assist federal officers by providing facilities and other help as needed. Four justices dissented.

The use of sophisticated electronic devices has begun to produce court rulings in entirely new areas. For example, in *United States* v. *Knotts* (1983), the Court upheld the use of an electronic beeper—a sort of "homing device"— without a warrant. That case involved a beeper placed in a drum of chloroform purchased by one of the suspects. The drum was placed in the suspect's car, and the electronic signals led authorities to a secluded cabin being used to manufacture illegal drugs. After visual surveillance of the cabin, the authorities obtained a search warrant and obtained evidence of the illegal activity. The Supreme Court unanimously rejected the contention that the suspects' expectation of privacy had been violated, although the *Knotts* opinion did not specifically address the question of whether a beeper could be *installed* without a warrant. As a result, the Court will likely deal with these matters on a case-by-case basis.

It should be noted that the *Katz* requirement has not been applied to conversations between suspects and third parties, even if one of the parties is an informant and/or is wearing a listening device. In *Hoffa* v. *United States* (1966), the government successfully had obtained a conviction of labor leader James Hoffa for attempting to bribe jurors in an earlier trial. Damaging testimony against Hoffa was provided by one Edward Partin, a paid government informant, who had been present during several conversations between Hoffa and other defendants. Hoffa contended that Partin's presence at those conversations amounted to an "illegal search," and evidence obtained should be excluded. Justice Stewart's opinion simply held that the Fourth Amendment does not forbid the use of government informers and that Partin's presence at Hoffa's hotel suite was by invitation. No legitimate Fourth Amendment right had been violated.

The Fourth Amendment and Administrative Searches

Government at all levels is empowered to carry out administrative rules and requirements, many of which involve periodic inspections and visits. The social worker, health inspector, revenue agent, and safety engineer are but a few examples of government employees whose jobs involve entering and inspecting both commercial and private premises on occasion. As government regulation has increased, the matter of the administrative inspection has grown ever more controversial.

Generally speaking, the Fourth Amendment warrant requirements apply to administrative searches with certain exceptions and limitations. For one thing, an administrative search warrant is considerably easier to obtain than one in a criminal matter. Rather than showing probable cause, an administrator simply is required to prove to a magistrate that an inspection is authorized by law and that it is part of a reasonable enforcement policy.

In *Camara* v. *Municipal Court* (1967), the Court addressed a section of the San Francisco Housing Code that provided for warrantless inspections of buildings by authorized employees of city departments. Roland Camara refused to allow a city building inspector to enter his apartment to conduct an annual inspection and was convicted for violation of the ordinance. Justice White's majority opinion noted that an earlier precedent, which allowed administrative inspection requirements without warrants, had become outmoded.[19] He stated that governments were making "increasing use of such inspection techniques," running the risk that Fourth Amendment rights might be jeopardized. In *Camara,* the majority found the existence of no emergency that would have required immediate entry into the building, and it saw as particularly interesting the fact that inspectors made three trips to the building to obtain consent to enter—"Yet no warrant was obtained and thus appellant was unable to verify either the need for or the appropriate limits of the inspection." Camara could not be convicted for refusing to allow a warrantless administrative search. In a companion case, *See* v. *Seattle,* the Court broadened the requirement of a warrant to inspect business and commercial properties.

Several decisions upholding warrantless inspections followed shortly after the *Camara* and *See* rulings. In *Colonnade Catering Corp.* v. *United States* (1970), the Court held that an establishment that had a liquor license could be searched by an inspector without a warrant. The Court's ruling was based heavily upon the long history of government regulation of the liquor industry. Two years later, in *United States* v. *Biswell* (1972), the Court upheld a treasury agent's warrantless search of a licensed gun dealer's premises. Such inspections, said the Court, are necessary to support governmental efforts at preventing violent crime and regulating firearms traffic. To this point, only the liquor and firearms industries appear to be clear exceptions to the search warrant requirement, although several courts have upheld the 1977 Mine Safety and Health Act's warrantless inspection provisions, citing the "enforcement needs in the mining industry." (See *Marshall* v. *Nolichuckey Sand Company,* United States Court of Appeals, Sixth Circuit, 1979.)

The Court addressed another administrative intrusion in *Wyman* v. *James* (1971). That case grew out of the practice followed by the New York Department of Social Services to have a caseworker visit the homes of recipients of Aid to Families with Dependent Children (AFDC). The purpose of such visits was to determine eligibility and the possible need for other services. When Barbara James was notified by mail of a scheduled visit to her home by a caseworker, she told the department that she would provide information but would not allow anyone inside her home. James and her attorney appeared at a pretermination hearing, but a notice of termination was later issued. James then brought suit to continue her AFDC eligibility on the grounds that a home visit was equivalent to a search without a warrant and, as such, was illegal. Her argument was upheld in the lower courts.

Justice Harry Blackmun, writing for the majority, reversed the lower court rulings and upheld the validity of the home visit system. His opinion listed numerous reasons for upholding the home visit—including the fact that James was in no danger of criminal prosecution for refusing entry by authorities (as contrasted with the *Camara* and *See* cases). Other significant reasons were the public's interest in protecting dependent children; the need for home visits for proper administration of the welfare system; and the use of proper notice and procedures by welfare officials. According to Justice Blackmun, James had the right to refuse the caseworker's visit knowing that she would probably suffer the loss of benefits—"The choice is entirely hers, and nothing of constitutional magnitude is involved."

The issue of searches by public authorities has extended into the nation's schools, most recently in *New Jersey* v. *T.L.O.* (1985). That case involved a fourteen-year-old girl, T.L.O., who was caught smoking in a restroom and brought to the principal's office. When she denied having been smoking, the assistant vice-principal demanded to see her purse, which he then opened to look for cigarettes. He found the cigarettes, but he also noticed cigarette papers normally used with marijuana. Searching further, he found a small amount of marijuana, money, a list of students who owed her money, and some letters implicating her in the dealing of marijuana. The state sought to have T.L.O. declared a delinquent on the basis of the seized evidence. The juvenile court allowed the evidence to be used and determined T.L.O. to be delinquent. Later, the New Jersey Supreme Court reversed the lower courts and held that the evidence should be suppressed as the result of an unreasonable search.

, Justice White's majority opinion began by holding that the Fourth Amendment applies to searches conducted by school authorities, and such searches must be reasonable. However, he noted also that it is necessary to balance schoolchildren's privacy interests with the school's "need to maintain an environment in which learning can take place." As a result, the standards required of a reasonable search may be quite different. First, on the issue of warrants, Justice White stated:

> The warrant requirement, in particular, is unsuited to the school environment: requiring a teacher to obtain a warrant before searching a child suspected of an infraction of school rules (or of the criminal law) would unduly interfere with the maintenance of the swift and informal disciplinary procedures needed in the schools. Just as we have in other cases dispensed with the warrant requirement when "the burden of obtaining a warrant is likely to frustrate the governmental purpose behind the search" . . . we hold today that school officials need not obtain a warrant before searching a student who is under their authority.

As for the requirement of probable cause, the Court held that the school setting "does not require strict adherence to the requirement that searches be based on probable cause to believe that the subject of the search has violated or is violating the law." Continuing, the Court stated more clearly just what kind of justification must exist for a reasonable search:

> Under ordinary circumstances, a search of a student by a teacher or other school official will be "justified at its inception" when there are reasonable grounds for suspecting that the search will turn up evidence that the student has violated or is violating either the law or the rules of the school. Such a search will be permissible in its scope when the measures adopted are reasonably related to the objectives of the search and not excessively intrusive in light of the age and sex of the student and the nature of the infraction.

Using these standards, the Court found the search of the purse to be reasonable. Even the decision by the vice-principal to read the list of people who owed money to T.L.O. and the letters—both of which were found in a separate, zippered compartment—were within the standards of a reasonable search. While searches by school officials fall under the Fourth Amendment, they clearly are not subject to the strict guidelines applied to other areas of the law.

Trends in the Exclusionary Rule and the Fourth Amendment

Controversy has long been associated with the exclusionary rule. The most famous expression of this controversy, in all likelihood, was phrased by Judge (later Justice) Benjamin Cardozo in *People* v. *DeFore* (1926): "Is the criminal to go free because the Constable has blundered?" Such a question suggests the problems posed by the exclusionary rule in reconciling individual and societal interests. In recent years, arguments over the exclusionary rule have become more intense. Supporters of the rule, including Justice Brennan, have argued for its continuation as a means of ensuring that protections of the Fourth Amendment are upheld. Under this view, the exclusionary rule is required by the Constitution to protect specific rights from being violated.[20]

With the onset of the Burger Court, the new chief justice, often joined by Justice White, frequently expressed his opposition to the restrictions of the exclusionary rule. Since the *Mapp* decision, no more than a plurality of the Court had held the exclusionary rule to be a constitutional requirement. Instead, most justices chose to emphasize the rule's deterrent effect upon illegal police conduct. As a judicial remedy and not a constitutionally guaranteed right, the exclusionary rule could be changed by legislation. The Burger Court repeatedly emphasized that the exclusionary rule was "judicially created."

Chief Justice Burger stated perhaps his most ambitious critique of the exclusionary rule while dissenting in the case of *Bivens* v. *Six Unknown Named Agents of the Federal Bureau of Narcotics* (1971). The six agents unlawfully and without a warrant broke into Webster Biven's apartment, arrested and shackled him, searched the apartment, and took him to their headquarters for questioning. Bivens sought $15,000 in damages from each agent, as compensation for the violation of his Fourth Amendment rights, and the Court majority held that he was entitled to the damages. In dissent, the chief justice used the opportunity to go far beyond the issue at hand into the failure of the exclusionary rule as a device for eliminating police misconduct. He noted that the *Bivens* case illustrated the difficulty and then proposed a system that would compensate victims of police wrongdoing without necessarily excluding the evidence obtained in the process of an illegal search and seizure.

An important first step in limiting the exclusionary rule was taken in *United States* v. *Calandra* (1974). In that case, the Court upheld the use of improperly obtained evidence for a grand jury investigation, noting that the exclusionary rule's deterrent effect upon police misconduct must be balanced against society's need to gather and obtain crucial evidence. The Court thought it unlikely that police would seize evidence illegally merely to obtain an indictment, knowing that the evidence could not be used in a trial. Following similar reasoning in the case of *United States* v. *Janis* (1976), the Court allowed evidence obtained by state officials through a defective search warrant to be used by the Internal Revenue Service in a civil case. The evidence could not be permitted in the state criminal matter for which it had been obtained originally.

Stone v. *Powell* (1976) stemmed from an incident involving Lloyd Powell and three friends, all of whom entered a liquor store and became involved in a fight with the manager over a bottle of wine. Powell shot and killed the manager's wife. Later, and some miles away, Powell was arrested for violating a local town vagrancy ordinance. In a search incident-to-arrest, a .38 caliber revolver with six spent cartridges in the cylinder was found. Expert testimony at Powell's trial contended that the .38 in Powell's possession had killed the liquor store manager's wife, and Powell was convicted of second-degree murder. Powell's conviction was upheld on appeal all the way through the California Supreme Court.

Later, while in prison, Powell initiated an action for federal *habeas corpus* relief on the grounds that the local vagrancy ordinance was unconstitutionally vague, thereby making the revolver inadmissible as evidence since it had been found as the result of an unlawful search. Powell lost at the federal district court level, but a federal appeals court reversed, and the government appealed to the Supreme Court.

Writing for a 6-3 Court, Justice Powell reversed the court of appeals and effectively held the exclusionary rule's purpose to be the deterrence of unlawful conduct on the part of police. He addressed the problems associated with applying the exclusionary rule:

> Application of the rule thus deflects the truthfinding process and often frees the guilty. The disparity in particular cases between the error committed by the police officer and the windfall afforded a guilty defendant by application of the rule is contrary to the idea of proportionality that is essential to the concept of justice . . . Thus, although the rule is thought to deter unlawful police activity in part through the nurturing of respect for Fourth Amendment values, if applied indiscriminately it may well have the opposite effect of generating disrespect for the law and administration of justice.

In summary, Justice Powell called for the application of the exclusionary rule to be balanced against the "acknowledged costs to other values vital to a rational system of criminal justice." Additionally, in a somewhat more technical holding, the majority rejected the practice of state prisoners, having been afforded the opportunity for a full and fair hearing on the exclusionary rule by the state courts at trial, to claim federal *habeas corpus* review of the conviction on the ground that illegally seized evidence was introduced at their trials. Since Powell's conviction at the state level had afforded him a fair opportunity to make his exclusionary-rule claims, it was unnecessary and counterproductive to require federal courts to reopen the matter.

Probably the most significant change made to the exclusionary rule by the Court is the "good-faith" exception first noted in *United States* v. *Peltier* (1975) and raised several times since. The argument can be summarized thusly: the deterrent effect of the exclusionary rule upon illegal police conduct is irrelevant if police do not knowingly engage in such conduct. Why should evidence obtained in good faith, even though later determined unlawful, be suppressed from the trial? After all, if authorities have taken all possible steps to safeguard the rights of the accused, why should evidence obtained in the process be ruled inadmissible? As Justice Rehnquist stated in his *Peltier* majority opinion, "If the purpose of the exclusionary rule is to deter unlawful police conduct, then evidence obtained from a search should be suppressed only if it can be said that the law enforcement officer had knowledge, or may properly be charged with knowledge, that the search was unconstitutional under the Fourth Amendment."

An interesting illustration of the good-faith argument is found in the Court's ruling in *Michigan* v. *Defillippo* (1979). The case stemmed from an incident in which Detroit police stopped Gary Defillippo in an alley under suspicious circumstances. Asked to identify himself, Defillippo refused and was arrested under an ordinance that made it unlawful to refuse such a request.

In a search incident-to-arrest, marijuana was found, and Defillippo was charged with possession. The Michigan court, however, held that the mandatory identification ordinance was unconstitutionally vague, making the arrest invalid. The Supreme Court reversed, holding that police officers have the obligation to enforce laws, even if they later turn out to be void. Since police arrested Defillippo for committing a crime, the subsequent search had been conducted in good faith and was thus valid.

A major development in the good-faith exception to the exclusionary rule occurred in *United States* v. *Leon* (1984). That case resulted from actions taken by the Burbank, California, Police Department following a tip by a confidential informant. The informant told police that he had knowledge of a large-scale drug-selling operation in the city, having witnessed a transaction and seen a shoe-box full of money. Acting upon the information, police initiated an extensive investigation and surveillance operation at several residences. Based upon numerous observations, including the identification of persons known to have drug-related convictions, an experienced narcotics investigator with the department prepared an application for a search warrant. The application was reviewed by several deputy district attorneys, and a facially valid search warrant (a warrant that seems correct but contains unseen errors or omissions) was issued by a state superior court judge. The searches produced large quantities of drugs and other evidence. Alberto Leon and other defendants were indicted by a grand jury and charged with a variety of drug-related crimes.

The U.S. district court held that the affidavit was insufficient to establish probable cause because it relied heavily upon the unproven reliability and credibility of the confidential informant. The district court did indicate that the officers had acted in good faith, but it rejected the contention that the exclusionary rule should not apply simply because the police did not know they were acting under a defective search warrant. The court of appeals affirmed the lower judgment, and the government sought certiorari from the Supreme Court.

Writing for the 6-3 Court, Justice White reversed the court of appeals and held that "the exclusionary rule can be modified somewhat without jeopardizing its ability to perform its intended functions." In recognizing the validity of a good-faith exception to the exclusionary rule, Justice White noted that "the substantial social costs exacted by the exclusionary rule for the vindication of Fourth Amendment rights have long been a source of concern." The majority opinion stressed the fact that the officers had acted reasonably in obtaining a warrant from a "neutral and detached magistrate." Because the affidavit reflected the officers' good faith, their reliance upon the magistrate's determination of probable cause was reasonable. The seized evidence should not have been suppressed.

In a concurring opinion written to show what he regarded as the "unavoidably provisional nature" of the decision, Justice Blackmun drew attention to the likelihood of continued change in the exclusionary rule:

> If a single principle may be drawn from this Court's exclusionary rule decisions, from *Weeks* through *Mapp* v. *Ohio* . . . to the decisions handed down today, it is that the scope of the exclusionary rule is subject to change in light of changing judicial understanding about the effects of the rule outside the confines of the

courtroom. It is incumbent on the Nation's law enforcement officers, who must continue to observe the Fourth Amendment in the wake of today's decisions, to recognize the double-edged nature of that principle.

Joined by Justice Marshall (Justice Stevens dissented separately), Justice Brennan's dissent was blunt in its concern for what the majority had done, stating that "the majority ignores the fundamental constitutional importance of what is at stake here." According to Brennan, the framers recognized that "the task of combatting crime and convicting the guilty" and "the temptations of expediency" would lure each generation "into forsaking our commitment to protecting individual liberty and privacy." For that reason, he continued, "The Framers of the Bill of Rights insisted that law enforcement efforts be permanently and unambiguously restricted in order to preserve personal freedoms." The courts were given the "sometimes unpopular task" of enforcing these protections.

With reference to the majority's reliance upon the "deterrence rationale" alone as the basis for the exclusionary rule, Justice Brennan countered that his colleagues had missed the true meaning of the Fourth Amendment:

> If nothing else, the Amendment plainly operates to disable the government from gathering information and securing evidence in certain ways. In practical terms, of course, this restriction of official power means that some incriminating evidence inevitably will go undetected if the government obeys these constitutional restraints. It is the loss of that evidence that is the "price" our society pays for enjoying the freedom and privacy safeguarded by the Fourth Amendment. . . Understood in this way, the Amendment directly contemplates that some reliable and incriminating evidence will be lost to the government; therefore, it is not the exclusionary rule, but the amendment itself that has imposed this cost.

Justice Brennan concluded by expressing a concern for the future of Fourth Amendment rights. He worried about the tendencies of the majority to see exclusionary-rule cases in "cost-benefit" terms, without consideration of the rights involved. Pessimistically, he concluded that he would not be surprised if, in the future, "my colleagues decide once again that we simply cannot afford to protect Fourth Amendment rights."

Of course, it may not be easy to ascertain the true "costs and benefits" associated with the rule. Political scientists Joel B. Grossman and Richard S. Wells have pointed out how difficult it has become to judge the exclusionary rule's effectiveness. They note that a 1982 National Institute of Justice report based upon California statistics showed that about 7 to 8 percent of all drug arrests and only 0.3 percent of nondrug arrests were rejected on exclusionary-rule grounds. Concluding, the authors state:

> An informed debate about the exclusionary rule must therefore consider whether the small number of criminals who are freed because of it is worth the protections that it affords. Conversely, it does not appear that adoption of a good faith exception, or some other modifications to the exclusionary rule will in fact result in the conviction and punishment of a substantially greater number of probably guilty persons.[21]

In concluding this treatment of the Fourth Amendment, it is important to recognize that no area of the law is more likely to undergo revision or change than the matter of searches and seizures. Because no two situations involving police and suspects are ever likely to be identical, it is difficult to foresee the Court's ability to reduce the workload produced by the Fourth Amendment. Balancing the interests of individual privacy with society's concern with protection and security will remain one of the difficult tasks facing the Court in coming years. In the words of Justice Blackmun's concurring *Leon* opinion, the exclusionary rule and its effect upon enforcement of the Fourth Amendment remains "subject to change."

Fifth Amendment

Of the five provisions in the Fifth Amendment, one—the Due Process Clause—was duplicated in the Fourteenth Amendment, while three others—Double Jeopardy, Self-Incrimination, and Just Compensation—have been incorporated as fundamental liberties. The lone unincorporated provision is the Grand Jury Clause, which states that "no person shall be held to answer for a capital, or otherwise infamous crime, unless on a presentment or indictment of a Grand Jury." Not all states require grand jury indictments, and many have chosen to allow a prosecutor's **information** in place of the **indictment**. An information affidavit stipulates that the prosecuting attorney possesses evidence to justify a trial. Of course, all criminal defendants in federal courts must be indicted by a federal grand jury prior to trial. Given the well-established use of the prosecutor's information, as well as some criticisms of the grand jury system, it is unlikely that the Grand Jury Clause will be incorporated in the Fourteenth Amendment and applied to the states.

Double Jeopardy

The matter of **double jeopardy,** of course, was raised by Palko in his unsuccessful 1937 attempt at incorporation of the privilege. In *Benton* v. *Maryland* (1969), the Court addressed the issue again, arriving at quite different results from those in *Palko*. John Benton had been charged with burglary and larceny in a single indictment. The trial resulted in his acquittal for larceny but conviction for burglary. Upon Benton's appeal, the indictment was found faulty because of a defect in the grand jury process. The state reindicted him, and this time he was convicted on both counts.

Charging that his double-jeopardy right had been violated, Benton appealed his larceny conviction to the Supreme Court. Writing for the Court, Justice Thurgood Marshall held that Benton's conviction for larceny could not be judged "by the watered-down standard enunciated in *Palko*, but under this Court's interpretations of the Fifth Amendment double jeopardy provision." Marshall's opinion clearly applied "federal double jeopardy standards" to the case and held that the larceny conviction could not stand. The majority had applied the double jeopardy standards of the Fifth Amendment to the states.

In dissent, John Harlan, joined by Potter Stewart, criticized the majority's "eagerness" to incorporate the provision and called for the use of the **concurrent-sentence doctrine,** in which a defendant receives concurrent sentences for multiple offenses. Justice Byron White, in a concurring opinion, described the doctrine as follows:

> Where a man has been convicted on several counts and sentenced concurrently upon each, and where judicial review of one count sustains its validity, the need for review of the other counts is not a pressing one since, regardless of the outcome, the prisoner will remain in jail for the same length of time under the count upheld. . . . This is not a rule of convenience to the judge, but rather of fairness to other litigants.

In spite of double jeopardy's incorporation in 1969, the subject has remained both controversial and uncertain. As a result of several Supreme Court rulings, the double jeopardy privileges are generally established, but considerable room for disagreement remains (see Table 8.3). A major development occurred in 1971 when Congress authorized government appeals in all criminal cases except when prohibited by the Double Jeopardy Clause.

It should be noted that the Double Jeopardy Clause does not prevent different governments (national and state) from trying a person for the same criminal activities. If a person commits an offense that violates both state and federal laws, he or she may be tried by both jurisdictions. Should a trial in one jurisdiction end in acquittal, the person may still be tried in the other. However, the Court held in *Waller* v. *Florida* (1970) that the defendant's conviction by the city of St. Petersburg for destruction of city property and disorderly breach of the peace prevented his subsequent conviction by the state of Florida for grand larceny. The relationship between a state and its subdivisions is not analogous to the relationship that exists between a state and the federal government. Because local subdivisions owe their existence to the state, they are considered to be part of a single government.

One final area of controversy relating to double jeopardy concerns the theory of **collateral estoppel,** or the so-called "single frolic" argument found in *Ashe* v. *Swenson* (1970). Bob Fred Ashe had been acquitted of robbing one of six poker players, primarily because of problems in identification. Authorities later tried Ashe for robbing another one of the same six players, and this time he was convicted. The Court set aside Ashe's conviction by considering the robbery of the poker players to be a single transaction, and since he had already been acquitted of robbing one of the victims, he could not be prosecuted again. In all likelihood, the problem of multiple offenses will continue to raise double jeopardy questions.

Self-Incrimination

The privilege against self-incrimination, though acquired from British law and part of the Fifth Amendment, probably "became widely known by many Americans during the 1950s, when legislative committees were conducting hearings in two major areas—political belief and activity, and organized crime." [22] Senator Joseph McCarthy's questionable tactics during committee hearings forced many persons to invoke their Fifth Amendment protections, prompting McCarthy to call them "Fifth Amendment Communists." [23]

Actually, the Fifth Amendment does not forbid all self-incrimination, only that which is considered compulsory. In other words, people are free to confess or provide otherwise incriminating evidence if they choose, as long as they are not forced to do so. However, as Table 8.4 illustrates, the protections against self-incrimination are limited. It is fairly clear that a man yelling out his guilt while being stretched on the rack is being compelled to incriminate

Table 8.3   Can a Defendant Be Retried If . . . ?

A. A trial ends in acquittal . . . . No
B. A trial ends with a guilty verdict . . . . No
   unless
   1. Defendant requests judge to set aside the verdict, OR
   2. Defendant appeals to a higher court.
C. A trial is halted before a final verdict . . . . It depends
   1. If indictment is dismissed due to insufficient evidence . . . . No
   2. If the interruption occurs for another reason . . . . Yes
   3. If the jury cannot agree on a verdict . . . . Yes
   4. If the defendant requests a stop to the trial for reasons which do not relate
      to guilt or innocence . . . . Yes
   5. If the prosecutor asks for a mistrial to prevent the defeat of "the ends of
      public justice." . . . . Yes

Note: These outcomes are the result of several Court decisions, the most significant being *North Carolina* v. *Pearce* (1969); *United States* v. *Scott* (1975); *United States* v. *Martin Linen Supply Co.* (1977); *Arizona* v. *Washington* (1978).

himself—but what, say, of the woman who offers a confession after a lengthy police interrogation? What if she asks for a lawyer to be present but is refused? As will be shown, the matter of compulsory self-incrimination is not always clear-cut.

The protection against compulsory self-incrimination was incorporated in *Malloy* v. *Hogan* (1964), overturning both the *Twining* and *Adamson* precedents discussed in an earlier section of this chapter. The Court summed up its ruling:

> The Fourteenth Amendment secures against state invasion the same privilege that the Fifth Amendment guarantees against federal infringement—the right of a person to remain silent unless he chooses to speak in the unfettered exercise of his own will, and to suffer no penalty . . . for such silence.

Self-Incrimination and Confessions

While *Malloy* brought federal standards to the states, it was not the first time that limits had been placed upon police methods of obtaining confessions. In *Brown* v. *Mississippi* (1936), the Court outlawed physical torture as a means of extracting confessions from three defendants. These tactics, according to the Court, violated the Due Process Clause of the Fourteenth Amendment. Using the same standards in 1940, the Court overturned a confession obtained as a result of isolation from friends and attorneys and long interrogations by rotating teams of police officers.[24] Over the next several decades, the Court was called upon to rule on various "coerced" confessions. One such case was *Spano* v. *New York* (1959). The facts are summarized in the following paragraph:

> Vincent Joseph Spano shot and killed a man who had beaten him earlier that same day. There was one eyewitness to the shooting. Spano fled the scene and remained hidden for several days. More than a week later, a grand jury indicted Spano for murder. Two days later, Spano called Gaspar Bruno, a childhood friend who was a "fledgling police officer" and said he would get a lawyer and turn

Table 8.4   When Do Self-Incrimination Protections *Not* Apply
and Why?

WHEN	WHY
Immunity from prosecution is granted.	If punishment cannot result from incriminating testimony, the threat of self-incrimination is removed. Still, a narrower "use" immunity common today means that only evidence obtained directly or indirectly from the testimony itself cannot be used. Prosecution is still possible using evidence obtained by other means.
"Nontestimonial" evidence is involved.	Evidence other than direct testimony (fingerprints, blood samples, handwriting, etc.) is "nontestimonial" and not protected by the Self-Incrimination Clause. Refusal to submit, say, to a breath test may be introduced as incriminating evidence (Brief 8.3).
Nonpersonal evidence is involved.	Self-incrimination protections apply only to the individual. They do not extend to corporate, partnership, or other records that are not the "private" papers of the individual.
The evidence is held by someone other than the person claiming protection.	Records and papers in the possession of another person are not protected, and the other person (e.g., accountant) holding the papers (e.g., tax records) may not claim self-incrimination protection on behalf of someone else.

himself in to authorities. The next day Spano and his lawyer went to headquarters. His lawyer warned him to answer no questions and left him in the custody of police. Starting about 7:15 P.M., police started questioning, but Spano persisted in his refusal to answer and asked for his lawyer. The request was denied. Several hours later Bruno was called in to assist in the interrogation. He was supposed to falsely say that Spano had gotten him "in a lot of trouble" with the earlier phone call and then to gain Spano's sympathy for Bruno's pregnant wife and three children. In all, Bruno was sent in four different times to play on Spano's sympathies and to obtain a confession. In the fourth visit, lasting over an hour, Spano finally gave in and agreed to make a statement. The time was 3:25 A.M., and the statement was completed at 4:05 A.M. Then, at 4:30 A.M., Spano was taken by detectives to look for the bridge from which he said he had thrown the murder weapon. He made some other incriminating statements to police before returning to the station after 6:00 A.M.

Was this a coerced confession? According to Chief Justice Earl Warren's majority opinion, the answer was yes—a clear violation of the Fourteenth Amendment. Looking at the "totality of the situation," the chief justice concluded that the police had gone well beyond acceptable limits, stating that "the petitioner's will was overborne by official pressure, fatigue and sympathy falsely aroused after considering all the facts in their post-indictment setting." Spano's conviction was reversed.

The totality-of-circumstances approach expressed in *Spano* and other cases called upon the Court to consider numerous elements separately in each situation (see Brief 8.5). Circumstances such as the age, educational level, and maturity of the defendant, as well as the length of interrogation and nature of the charges, were to be considered. While providing case-by-case fairness, the approach gave police and prosecutors little guidance in formulating acceptable procedures. Finally, in the landmark *Miranda* v. *Arizona* (1966) ruling, the Court largely abandoned the case-by-case approach in favor of a firm rule governing the admissibility of confessions. The forces leading up to *Miranda* will be examined before addressing the case itself.

☐ *Brief 8.5   Can God Coerce a Confession?: Colorado v. Connelly (1986)*

Francis Connelly approached a uniformed Denver police officer on the street and stated that he had murdered someone and wanted to talk about it. The policeman, who was not on duty at the time, advised Connelly of his *Miranda* rights, and Connelly said he understood and wanted to talk. A detective arrived and new *Miranda* warnings were given. Connelly then told of a murder he had committed in 1982. Later, he took officers to the location of the crime. While being interviewed the next morning, however, Connelly became "visibly disoriented" and began giving confused answers to questions. He stated that "voices" had told him to confess. A psychiatrist later testified that Connelly was following the "voice of God," and he believed that Connelly's psychosis had motivated his confession.

The trial court, although finding the police to have done nothing wrong or coercive, held that the confession was inadmissible because it was not completely voluntary—not a product of Connelly's free will. The Colorado Supreme Court affirmed the ruling.

The Supreme Court reversed, with Chief Justice Rehnquist writing for the majority. He stated that before a confession can be held involuntary, it must be shown to result from police coercion. Only coercive behavior on the part of authorities can make a confession "involuntary." Rehnquist added that the Fifth Amendment privilege against self-incrimination is not concerned with "moral and psychological pressures" to confess—even if the "voice of God" is the source of those pressures.

Justice Brennan, joined by Justice Marshall, dissented, holding the use of a mentally ill person's involuntary confession "antithetical to the notion of fundamental fairness embodied in the Due Process Clause." Noting that due process recognizes "the right to make vital choices voluntarily," Justice Brennan challenged the majority's equating of voluntariness with the absence of police coercion by stating:

> The absence of police wrongdoing should not, by itself, determine the voluntariness of a confession by a mentally ill person. The requirement that a confession be voluntary reflects a recognition of the importance of free will and of reliability in determining the admissibility of a confession and thus demands an inquiry into the totality of the circumstances surrounding the confession.

Despite the strong dissent, the law of the land, as a result of the *Connelly* decision, holds that voluntariness in confessions is tied to the coercive behavior of authorities. Apparently, all confessions made without official coercion are deemed to be voluntary.

In *Gideon* v. *Wainwright* (1963), discussed in the Sixth Amendment section, the Court incorporated the right to counsel at trial. As a result, one of the essential elements of proper interrogation procedure was created. This element materialized in *Escobedo* v. *Illinois* (1964), where the Court reversed a conviction based upon a confession obtained without a lawyer present, in spite of the defendant's repeated requests for counsel. Summing up for the 5-4 Court, Justice Goldberg sounded the clear note of things to come:

> We hold, therefore, that where, as here, the investigation is no longer a general inquiry into an unsolved crime but has begun to focus on a particular suspect, the suspect has been taken into police custody, the police carry out a process of interrogations that lends itself to eliciting incriminating statements, the suspect has requested and been denied an opportunity to consult with his lawyer, and the police have not effectively warned him of his absolute constitutional right to remain silent, the accused has been denied "the Assistance of Counsel" in violation of the Sixth Amendment to the Constitution . . . and that no statement elicited by the police during the interrogation may be used against him at a criminal trial.

Miranda v. *Arizona* (1966) was heard along with three other cases, all of which involved the admissibility of statements obtained by authorities during custodial interrogation. In all instances, the suspect provided a confession following police interrogation, and the confession was then introduced as evidence in the trial. Ernesto Miranda, age twenty-three, was arrested for kidnapping and rape. An indigent, Miranda had been educated through half of the ninth grade and suffered what one doctor termed "an emotional illness." After being picked out of a lineup, he was interrogated by two police officers. In less than two hours, apparently without any warnings of his rights to silence or counsel, Miranda "gave a detailed oral confession and then wrote out in his own hand and signed a brief statement admitting and describing the crime."

Chief Justice Warren's opinion for the 5-4 majority focused upon the nature of the custodial setting, calling it "incommunicado interrogation of individuals in a police-dominated atmosphere." In such a setting, individual liberties are jeopardized and subjected to great pressure, he stated, adding that "without proper safeguards the process of in-custody interrogation of persons suspected or accused of crime contains inherently compelling pressures which undermine the individual's will to resist and to compel him to speak where he would not otherwise do so freely."

The opinion called for procedural safeguards that would serve to protect the privilege against self-incrimination. These safeguards were spelled out in this now-familiar passage:

> Prior to any questioning, the person must be warned that he has a right to remain silent, that any statement he does make may be used as evidence against him, and that he has a right to the presence of an attorney, either retained or appointed. The defendant may waive effectuation of these rights, provided the waiver is made voluntarily, knowingly and intelligently.

Miranda's conviction, based upon the improperly obtained confession, was thereby reversed. Perhaps anticipating to some degree the storm of protest by critics of the decision, the chief justice stated that the ruling would not be "an undue interference" with law enforcement and noted that it would "not in any way preclude police from carrying out their traditional investigatory functions." Despite these words, the *Miranda* ruling produced a strong reaction in some circles.

Post-*Miranda* Developments

Following Earl Warren's retirement in 1969, Warren Burger was appointed to fill the chief justice position. Burger's appointment was followed by three additional appointments within two years. Many observers presumed that President Richard Nixon's avowed "law-and-order" appointments would change the Court's direction concerning criminal rights, perhaps even overturn the *Miranda* precedent. That has not yet occurred. However, the Court has limited the effect of *Miranda* in several cases, beginning with *Harris* v. *New York* (1971). Viven Harris was arrested by undercover police for selling heroin, and he then made certain incriminating statements without having been properly informed of his full *Miranda* rights. As such, his statements could not be used as evidence at his trial. In his own defense, Harris took the witness stand and told how he had tried to sell the police baking powder—not heroin. According to Harris, the undercover police were simply fabricating their testimony. Under cross-examination, the prosecutor confronted Harris with his previous, inadmissible statements. The judge informed the jury that the statements could not be considered by them in determining the defendant's guilt or innocence—only his credibility as a witness. The statements were then read aloud in the courtroom. Harris was found guilty.

By a 5-4 vote, the Court held that use of the improperly obtained evidence to impeach the credibility of the defendant was valid. Harris, said the Court, was under an obligation to speak truthfully once on the witness stand. The *Miranda* precedent "cannot be perverted into a license to use perjury by way of a defense, free from the risk of confrontation with prior inconsistent utterances." A slight crack had developed in the exclusionary rule, at least insofar as it pertained to the *Miranda* warnings.

The crack widened slightly in *Oregon* v. *Hass* (1975), a case somewhat similar to *Harris* except that the defendant had been given his full *Miranda* warnings and then asked to phone a lawyer. He was told that he could not do so until they arrived back at the station; before his arrival, he confessed. Later, when he told a different story on the witness stand, his confession was used as an impeachment device. The Supreme Court ruled that such use of the confession was proper.

Several other exceptions to the *Miranda* requirements have been recognized by the Court in recent years. The good-faith exception discussed with respect to the Fourth Amendment also has made its way into the area of confessions. The case of *Rhode Island* v. *Innis* (1980) is instructive. Thomas Innis, a murder suspect, was being taken by three police officers to the station for questioning having been given full *Miranda* warnings. Two of the policemen began discussing the danger posed by the missing murder weapon, a gun, particularly given the proximity to a school for handicapped children. One officer reportedly worried aloud about what might happen if one of the children found the gun. The suspect interrupted the conversation and asked to be taken back to the scene of the crime, where he produced the gun. The Supreme Court upheld the use of the gun, as well as the suspect's statements, as evidence at the trial. According to the Court, the officers had acted in good faith and had not undertaken to interrogate Innis. His sensitivity to their conversation was voluntary on his part.

Evidence obtained in violation of *Miranda* requirements also may be used against a defendant if the evidence "would inevitably have been found by lawful activity." This so-called "inevitable-discovery" exception to the exclusionary rule was recognized in *Nix* v. *Williams* (1984). Although extremely complex, the case generally came down to the fact that Robert Anthony Williams took police to the victim's body without the protection of his counsel. The body was located in an area about 2½ miles from a nearby search party and "essentially within the area to be searched." In other words, even though Williams had not received the full protection of his *Miranda* rights, the evidence which he provided would have been discovered anyway by lawful means. Evidence obtained in this fashion need not be suppressed. Although technically a Sixth Amendment assistance-of-counsel matter, this case also has direct application to the *Miranda*-related rules for interrogations and confessions.

In *New York* v. *Quarles* (1984), the Court carved out a "public-safety" exception to the requirement that *Miranda* warnings be given before any statements by a suspect may be admitted into evidence. The facts follow:

> A young woman told two New York City police officers that she had just been raped by an armed man who then entered a nearby supermarket. One of the officers entered the store and identified Benjamin Quarles as the man described by the young woman. Quarles ran toward the back of the store and the officer lost sight of him momentarily. Finally, the officer apprehended Quarles, frisked him, and found an empty shoulder holster. Three other officers then arrived, and Quarles was handcuffed. Before giving Quarles his *Miranda* warnings, the officer asked him where the gun was located. Quarles pointed to a pile of cartons and answered, "The gun is over there." The pistol was retrieved and Quarles was placed under arrest, followed by a reading of his *Miranda* rights. Quarles later responded to questions about the gun's ownership, stating that it belonged to him. At the trial, the judge excluded the gun and Quarles's statement as to the gun's location. Quarles, the lower courts held, should have been given his *Miranda* rights when taken into custody.

In the majority opinion, Justice Rehnquist reversed the lower courts and held that the evidence was improperly excluded. The key issue in the case was whether the police officer was justified in failing to give the *Miranda* warnings to Quarles. Justice Rehnquist's opinion found room for a public-safety exception to the *Miranda* warnings, particularly as a result of the fact that the gun was concealed somewhere in the supermarket. According to the majority, the "narrow exception to the *Miranda* rule" in *Quarles* will free officers "to follow their legitimate instincts when confronting situations presenting a danger to public safety."

Justice Sandra Day O'Connor, who concurred in part and dissented in part, was opposed to the majority's claim that the *Miranda* rule does not apply when the public safety is threatened. However, she believed that the gun, as nontestimonial evidence, should have been admitted into evidence. The dissenters—Justices Marshall, Brennan, and Stevens—drew attention to the lack of danger existing at the time of Quarles's arrest, and they openly feared that the effect upon established *Miranda*-based law would be devastating.

Finally, in *Oregon* v. *Elstad* (1985), Justice O'Connor wrote for a 6-3 Court in upholding the admissibility into evidence of oral and written statements obtained following a valid *Miranda* warning and waiver of rights, even though police had obtained an earlier voluntary but unwarned admission from the suspect. According to the suspect, nothing obtained by police should be admitted into evidence because the first, albeit voluntary, statements he made were given without benefit of *Miranda* warnings. As such, the later properly obtained confession was "fruit of the poisonous tree." Justice O'Connor's opinion rejected the Oregon court's conclusion that Elstad's initial statements had a "coercive effect" upon his later confession. While the initial statement was indeed inadmissible under *Miranda,* the admissibility of later statements should be determined by focusing upon whether they were made knowingly and voluntarily. Justices Brennan, Marshall, and Stevens again dissented.

Despite the Burger Court's series of limitations, the central elements of *Miranda* remain largely intact. Still, the *Miranda* guidelines are surrounded by considerably more uncertainty today than at any time in recent years. The Burger Court's attempts to weaken, if not eliminate, the guidelines have been relatively successful, as demonstrated in the cases discussed in this section. It will be interesting to see whether the newly formed Rehnquist Court continues to show the same tendencies as its predecessor toward the *Miranda* requirements.

Sixth Amendment

The provisions of the Sixth Amendment relate directly to the procedural rights of criminal defendants, with primary emphasis upon courtroom practices. At least eight separate privileges are stated in the amendment, and these can be grouped into three broad categories: those guarantees relating to the nature of the trial; jury considerations; and the defendant's right to mount a defense. Each of these areas will be examined in greater detail.

The Nature of a Fair Trial—Speed and Openness

The first two clauses in the Sixth Amendment guarantee a person's rights to a speedy and public trial. Table 8.2 shows that both provisions were incorporated into the due process guarantees of the Fourteenth Amendment and applied to the states at quite different times: speedy trial by *Klopfer* v. *North Carolina* (1967) and public trial by *In re Oliver* (1948). Both issues have arisen numerous times since their incorporation.

One reason that the right to a speedy trial has proven such a difficult area is the vague nature of the concept itself. Through several decisions, the Supreme Court has refused to apply a specific time frame to "speedy" trials, although the justices have helped to define its parameters. In *Smith* v. *Hooey* (1969), for example, the Court held that the state of Texas had denied due process to the defendant by failing to bring him to trial for six years, during which time he had been in a federal penitentiary. Accordingly, Texas authorities were required to drop the charge against him.

In other decisions, the Court has clarified other aspects of the speedy trial. On several occasions the Court has held that the speedy trial requirement applies only from the time of a person's indictment (see *United States* v. *Lovasco* [1977]). Of course, considerable delays in a trial are acceptable when they are requested by the counsel for the accused, and the many procedural safeguards built into the criminal justice system virtually guarantee that delays are inevitable.

In recent years, legislatures have begun to address the issue through passage of so-called "speedy trial acts." In 1974, Congress passed the Speedy Trial Act providing for a maximum of one hundred days between arrest and trial, although the law remains cumbersome and confusing. Under the statute, if the one-hundred-day limitation is not met, the judge is to dismiss the charges, either with or without prejudice. Charges dismissed with prejudice prohibit the defendant's being prosecuted again, but those without prejudice allow the prosecution to begin anew. A number of states have enacted their own statutes dealing with acceptable standards for speedy trials.

Overloaded court dockets are likely to continue causing significant problems for prosecutors in meeting speedy trial requirements both at the state and federal levels. Such delays, however, are part of the price which must be paid for a system that provides the accused with numerous procedural safeguards and guarantees. In fact, since delay often works to the advantage of the accused, it should not be surprising to know that the prosecution often may be ready for trial long before the defense.

The right to a public trial has also proven troublesome, particularly as it pertains to open courtrooms and the press. Because this issue is thoroughly covered in Chapter 12, it will not be considered here. It should be noted, however, that the right to a public trial belongs to the defendant alone, not to the public, members of the press, or other groups. A judge may indeed clear the courtroom in certain situations, but a defendant's right to a public trial must be protected.

Jury Trials

In *Duncan* v. *Louisiana* (1968), a 7-2 majority of the Court held that "trial by jury in criminal cases is fundamental to the American scheme of justice." As such, the majority held that "the Fourteenth Amendment guarantees a right of jury trial in all criminal cases which—were they to be tried in a federal court—would come within the Sixth Amendment's guarantee." In their incorporation of the Sixth Amendment's jury trial provisions, the Court reversed a Louisiana court's conviction of Gary Duncan, a black, for simple battery. Duncan, charged with slapping a white person on the elbow, had asked for a jury trial, but the judge had denied his request on the grounds that Louisiana law provided for jury trials only in cases in which hard labor or capital punishment might be imposed. While state law provided for as much as two years imprisonment and a $300 fine for battery, Duncan had been sentenced only to sixty days in jail and a fine of $150.

Justice White's majority opinion addressed the question of what constitutes a "petty offense" for purposes of a jury trial. The state of Louisiana had contended that Duncan's sixty-day sentence made the case a minor matter, but White's opinion focused upon the "penalty authorized for a particular crime." White noted the existence of "a category of petty crimes or offenses which is not subject to the Sixth Amendment jury trial provision and should not be subject to the Fourteenth Amendment jury trial requirement here applied to the States." Nevertheless, the fact that Louisiana had authorized up to two years' imprisonment for a simple battery conviction served, in White's view, to make it far from a petty offense. He noted that the federal system defined petty offenses "as those punishable by no more than six months in prison and a $500 fine," although his opinion stopped short of precisely defining the "exact location of the line between petty offenses and serious crimes." No matter where the line might fall, the Court was convinced that a crime punishable by two years in prison qualifies as a serious offense. In 1970, the Court defined a "serious crime" as one that involved imprisonment for six months or more.[25]

Not long after *Duncan,* the Court strongly indicated that not all of the traditional requirements associated with a jury trial were necessarily binding upon the states. One of these issues concerned the size of juries and the traditional requirement for twelve persons to determine guilt or innocence. The case of *Williams* v. *Florida* (1970) concerned a robbery conviction handed down by a six-person jury allowed under Florida law for all noncapital cases. Justice White's opinion sought to ascertain the basis for the twelve-person jury, but it ultimately concluded the requirement to be nothing more than a "historical accident, unnecessary to effect the purposes of the jury system and wholly without significance." Florida's use of a six-person jury did not violate the defendant's due process rights, because the twelve-person requirement "cannot be regarded as an indispensable component of the Sixth Amendment." Since the *Williams* decision, thirty-three states have authorized juries of fewer than twelve members in at least some types of cases.[26]

In *Colgrove* v. *Battin* (1973), the Court ruled that a six-person jury did not violate the Seventh Amendment right to a jury trial in a civil case, a decision seemingly consistent with the *Williams* ruling. However, in *Ballew* v. *Georgia* (1978), the Court was required to address the question of less than six-person juries. The state of Georgia had implemented a five-person jury for misdemeanor cases, in part to save both time and money. Not surprisingly, with overcrowded court dockets and costs increasing, states sought ways to streamline the criminal justice system, and jury size appeared to be an area of potential savings.

Writing for a fragmented plurality, Justice Blackmun stated that a jury should be large enough "to promote group deliberation, to insulate members from outside intimidation, and to provide a representative cross-section of the community." Using these criteria, along with several empirical studies conducted on jury size and noted by the Court, Justice Blackmun concluded that "the purpose and functioning of the jury in a criminal trial is seriously impaired, and to a constitutional degree, by a reduction in size to below six members." Apparently, while the Court can find no "bright line" to identify a minimum jury size, it will accept a jury of six but not five persons as consistent with the demands of due process.

The second important issue related to the jury trial requirement is unanimity. In *Apodaca* v. *Oregon* (1972), the Court upheld the jury convictions of Robert Apodaca and two codefendants on votes of 11-1, 11-1, and 10-2. Under Oregon law, the 10-2 split was the minimum verdict allowable for conviction. Apodaca and the others appealed their convictions on the ground that the Sixth and Fourteenth Amendments required convictions by a unanimous jury vote.

Once again, the Court showed real signs of division. Justice White, joined only by three others, delivered the judgment of the Court which upheld the non-unanimous verdicts as long as the jury "consists of a group of laymen representative of a cross section of the community who have the duty and the opportunity to deliberate, free from outside attempts at intimidation, on the question of a defendant's guilt." Four justices (Stewart, Douglas, Brennan, and Marshall) dissented, leaving Justice Powell squarely in the middle. According to Justice Powell, the requirement for unanimity is not applicable to juries in state courts, but it should be maintained in federal courts. He indicated that not "all of the elements of jury trial within the meaning of the Sixth Amendment are necessarily embodied in or incorporated into the Due Process Clause of the Fourteenth Amendment." Justice Powell could not accept what he considered to be the Court's primary assumption—namely, that the Sixth Amendment's trial by jury provisions "must be identical in every detail" in both federal and state courts. Such an assumption, according to Powell, was inconsistent with the federal form of government:

> In holding that the Fourteenth Amendment has incorporated "jot-for-jot and case-for-case" every element of the Sixth Amendment, the Court derogates principles of federalism that are basic to our system . . . the Court has embarked upon a course of constitutional interpretation that deprives the states of freedom to experiment with adjudicatory processes different from the federal model.

As a result, state juries need not convict only upon unanimous vote. Using the same reasoning, the Court in *Johnson* v. *Louisiana* (1972) upheld a 9-3 jury vote for conviction. On the other hand, in *Burch* v. *Louisiana* (1979), a state law which allowed conviction by a 5-1 vote for a petty offense was struck down. Obviously, due process is not simply a matter of percentages. Today, only five states (Oklahoma, Texas, Louisiana, Oregon, and Montana) allow conviction with non-unanimous jury verdicts in criminal cases.[27]

Notice, Confrontation, and Securing of Witnesses

The Sixth Amendment's concern with procedural guarantees is further evident in the Notice, Confrontation, and Compulsory Process Clauses. These clauses, all of which have been incorporated as fundamental rights, state:

> In all criminal prosecutions, the accused shall enjoy the right . . . to be informed of the nature and cause of the accusation; to be confronted with the witnesses against him; to have compulsory process for obtaining witnesses in his favor.

The right to be informed of the nature and cause of the accusation is commonly referred to as **notice.** In effect, the clause requires that laws be specific with respect to what constitutes a criminal act, thereby eliminating the use of overly vague laws to prosecute suspected violators. From a practical standpoint, the Notice Clause requires that a person be presented with a copy of all charges against him or her, including a copy of the indictment.

The right to confront witnesses stems from a long-standing tradition which recognizes that a defendant must be given the opportunity to see his or her accusers publicly and to cross-examine them. Under this rule, all testimony is to be given in open court, subject to intense cross-examination by the other party, although some very rare situations such as deathbed confessions may allow testimony by an absent witness to be introduced. The Supreme Court incorporated the right to confront witnesses in the case of *Pointer* v. *Texas* (1965). In that case, Robert Pointer had been charged with robbery. The victim, Kenneth Phillips, had testified against him at a preliminary hearing. Since Pointer had no attorney at the hearing, no one had cross-examined Phillips, who subsequently moved out of the state. At Pointer's trial, the prosecution introduced a transcript of Phillips's testimony, and Pointer was convicted. On appeal, Pointer claimed that the state of Texas had denied him the Sixth Amendment right to confront witnesses, and the Supreme Court agreed.

Since *Pointer,* the court has refined the Confrontation Clause in several instances: It reversed a conviction resulting from the state's refusal to allow its chief witness, a juvenile delinquent on probation for burglary, to be cross-examined (*Davis* v. *Alaska* [1974]); it refused to allow the use of a codefendant's confession as evidence when the codefendant refused to take the stand (*Bruton* v. *United States* [1968]); yet, the Court ruled that the right to confront witnesses may be lost if the defendant engages in disruptive behavior that will not allow the trial to continue without interruption (*Illinois* v. *Allen* [1970]) or if the defendant is voluntarily absent from the proceedings (*Taylor* v. *United States* [1973]).

The Sixth Amendment's right of compulsory process to secure witnesses allows the accused to call witnesses on his or her behalf, just as the state has the power to subpoena its witnesses. The Supreme Court incorporated this right in *Washington* v. *Texas* (1967), striking down a Texas statute that prohibited a codefendant from testifying on behalf of the accused. Texas held that this restriction was intended to reduce the likelihood of perjury in such situations, but the Court found the effect upon due process to be too severe. As a result, if a defendant calls an individual to be a witness, that witness may not refuse to testify by citing the accused's self-incrimination rights. Nonetheless, some communications have continued to remain privileged and, hence, not subject to testimonial requirements. Most notable among these are the husband-wife and certain lawyer-client privileges.

Right to Counsel

The final procedural guarantee in the Sixth Amendment has been perhaps the most controversial and certainly one of the most heavily litigated. A person's right to be assisted by counsel generally has been available to those able to afford such assistance for some time. In recent years, however, the right to appointed counsel has emerged in instances when the accused is unable to pay. The earliest recognition by the Supreme Court that the Due Process Clause of the Fourteenth Amendment requires the appointment of counsel in some circumstances occurred in *Powell* v. *Alabama* (1932). Although discussed previously in this chapter, the *Powell* case deserves some additional explanation. The nine young, uneducated black men accused of raping two white women were denied counsel and subsequently convicted. Justice Sutherland's majority opinion cited several critical facts of the case:

> the ignorance and illiteracy of the defendants, their youth, the circumstances of public hostility, the imprisonment and the close surveillance of the defendants by the military forces, the fact that their friends and families were all in other states and communication with them necessarily difficult, and above all that they stood in deadly peril of their lives—we think the failure of the trial court to give them reasonable time and opportunity to secure counsel was a clear denial of due process.

Further, Sutherland found the trial court's failure to appoint counsel a denial of due process, establishing the rule that

> in a capital case, where the defendant is unable to employ counsel, and is incapable adequately of making his own defense because of ignorance, feeble-mindedness, illiteracy, or the like, it is the duty of the court, whether requested or not, to assign counsel for him as a necessary requisite of due process of law.

Although the circumstances in the *Powell* case were clearly unusual, the movement for appointed counsel was well underway by the early 1960s, despite the Supreme Court's refusal in *Betts* v. *Brady* (1942) to incorporate the right to counsel as a part of the Fourteenth Amendment's guarantees. That major step occurred in *Gideon* v. *Wainwright* (1963), as a unanimous Court reversed its earlier *Betts* ruling and held the right to counsel to be a fundamental right. In that case, only two states sided with Florida in asking that *Betts* be upheld, while twenty-two states argued for its reversal.

The celebrated case of Clarence Gideon's conviction for breaking and entering a poolroom with intent to commit a misdemeanor (a felony under Florida law) has been the subject of a well-known book and movie, undoubtedly in large part because it highlighted such an obvious inequality in the criminal justice system. On the one hand, the state of Florida, which provided appointed counsel only in capital cases, showed the importance of legal help by relying heavily upon its own lawyers to prosecute defendants. Gideon, on the other hand, was penniless and thus could not afford to hire a lawyer to defend him. But when he requested counsel, the Florida trial court dismissed his request. Gideon—who was not skilled in the workings of the legal system—was forced to conduct his own defense "about as well as could be expected for a layman." In spite of his opening statement, cross-examination of witnesses, calling of his own witnesses, and a final argument, Gideon was convicted by a jury and sentenced to five years in prison. Following an unsuccessful appeal to the Florida Supreme Court, Gideon asked the U.S. Supreme Court, in a handwritten request, to reverse his conviction. Because of Gideon's lack of funds, the Court accepted his petition *in forma pauperis* and appointed legal counsel.

Justice Hugo Black's opinion strongly tied a defendant's prospects for a fair trial to the right to counsel, calling *Betts* "an abrupt break" with the Supreme Court's precedents upholding due process guarantees. He noted that "in our adversary system of criminal justice, any person, haled into court, who is too poor to hire a lawyer, cannot be assured a fair trial unless counsel is provided for him." The right to a lawyer, according to Justice Black, had become essential to the American system of justice:

> That government hires lawyers to prosecute and defendants who have the money hire lawyers to defend are the strongest indications of the widespread belief that lawyers in criminal courts are necessities, not luxuries. The right of one charged with crime to counsel may not be deemed fundamental and essential to fair trials in some countries, but it is in ours.

While the *Gideon* ruling incorporated the right to counsel in felony cases, it certainly did not settle the issue. In *Argersinger* v. *Hamlin* (1972), the Court extended the right to all cases, including misdemeanors involving imprisonment. While some observers believed the *Argersinger* holding was applicable to all cases involving the possibility of imprisonment, the Court in *Scott* v. *Illinois* (1979) stated otherwise. In that case, a defendant was given only a fine, although imprisonment had been a possibility. The Court held that under such conditions, a conviction would not be reversed simply because no counsel had been provided. Finally, the right to counsel has been extended into both pre- and posttrial areas, as presented in Table 8.5.

Political scientist Andrea Bonnicksen has examined the Court's recent decisions concerning appointed counsel, particularly those rulings listed in Table 8.5. She argues that the Court has insisted upon counsel at "critical" stages of the accusatory process, including custodial interrogation, postindictment lineup, and preliminary hearing:

> A lawyer's presence at these stages warns the police not to load the dice against the defendant and permits the lawyer to observe what is going on in order to prepare a better defense, see what evidence the state has against the defendant, raise procedural questions at the trial, and caution the suspect not to incriminate himself or herself.[28]

Just how the Court decides what constitutes a "critical" state of the process is not entirely clear. For example, the Court has held counsel to be required at a postindictment but not a preindictment lineup. A partial explanation, according to Bonnicksen, may lie "in the Court's changing composition."[29] Whereas the Warren Court initiated the pretrial right to counsel, the Burger Court was reluctant to extend the right. Given the maze of rulings upon the subject of the right to counsel, it is not too farfetched to say that an accused person may require a lawyer just to determine whether he or she is really entitled to have counsel appointed in the first place.

Eighth Amendment

Drawn directly from the English Bill of Rights (see Brief 2.3), the Eighth Amendment's protections concerning bail, fines, and punishments have provoked controversy and increased litigation in recent years. The protection

---

Table 8.5   Recent Supreme Court Rulings on the Assistance of Counsel

STAGES AT WHICH ASSISTANCE OF COUNSEL IS REQUIRED	CASE
First appeal after felony conviction	*Douglas* v. *California* (1963)
Arraignment	*Massiah* v. *United States* (1964)
"Accusatory" setting; preindictment	*Escobedo* v. *Illinois* (1964)
Custodial setting	*Miranda* v. *Arizona* (1966)
Postindictment lineup	*United States* v. *Wade* (1967)
Preliminary hearing	*Coleman* v. *Alabama* (1970)
Probation and parole revocation	*Gagnon* v. *Scarpelli* (1973)

STAGES AT WHICH ASSISTANCE OF COUNSEL IS NOT REQUIRED	CASE
Fingerprinting	*Davis* v. *Mississippi* (1969)
Preindictment lineup	*Kirby* v. *Illinois* (1972)
Mugshot session	*United States* v. *Ash* (1973)
Second appeal after felony	*Ross* v. *Moffitt* (1974)

against excessive bail and fines has not been nationalized, although the Supreme Court has addressed the matter of bail as "excessive." In *Stack* v. *Boyle* (1951), the Court held "excessive" to mean "set at a figure higher than an amount reasonably calculated" to ensure that the defendant will be present at his or her trial. Of course, whether bail is viewed as excessive depends upon various factors such as the nature of the offense, any potential threat to society, the defendant's own safety, and the likelihood of flight from the jurisdiction. In some states, bail may be denied for certain felonies.

The Bail Reform Act of 1984 was intended to reduce the number of crimes committed by defendants awaiting trial. The law allows federal courts to keep in jail defendants who are determined to be threats to the community. These may include defendants charged with offenses for which the sentence is life imprisonment or death, or certain drug offenses, or repeat offenders whose release would jeopardize the safety of others or the community. The act requires that specific factors be considered in each instance, supported by written findings and reasons, and subject to review. The length of detention may not exceed the limits of the Speedy Trial Act.

This practice, known as "preventive" or **pretrial detention,** was tested in *United States* v. *Salerno* (1987). That case concerned Anthony Salerno and Vincent Cafaro, charged in a twenty-nine-count indictment for numerous offenses such as fraud, extortion, gambling, and conspiracy to commit murder. The government argued that Salerno was a "boss" in the Genovese Crime Family of La Cosa Nostra and that Cafaro also was a participant. The defendants sought their release on due process grounds as well as on Eighth Amendment excessive-bail arguments.

Writing for a 6-3 majority, Chief Justice Rehnquist upheld the Bail Reform Act as part of the government's legitimate interest in preventing crime. His assessment of the balance between governmental regulation and individual rights touched upon the key issues of individualism and communitarianism:

> While the government's general interest in preventing crime is compelling, even this interest is heightened when the government musters convincing proof that the arrestee, already indicted or held to answer for a serious crime, presents a demonstrable danger to the community. Under these narrow circumstances, society's interest in crime prevention is at its greatest.

> On the other side of the scale, of course, is the individual's strong interest in liberty. We do not minimize the importance and fundamental nature of this right. But, as our cases hold, this right may, in circumstances where the government's interest is sufficiently weighty, be subordinated to the greater needs of society.

Justices Marshall and Brennan joined in a dissenting opinion attacking the majority's reasoning on several fronts, but most forcefully on the matter of a defendant's presumed innocence. According to Marshall's opinion:

> The statute now before us declares that persons who have been indicted may be detained if a judicial officer finds clear and convincing evidence that they pose a danger to individuals or to the community. But our fundamental principles of justice declare that the defendant is as innocent on the day before his trial as he is on the morning after his acquittal.

In a separate dissent, Justice Stevens also held the pretrial detention of persons based upon their "future dangerousness" to be unconstitutional.

Whereas the bail and fines provision of the Eighth Amendment has produced relatively little constitutional debate, the amendment's ban on "cruel and unusual punishments" has been a different matter entirely. Historically, the amendment has been regarded as banning such barbaric practices as drawing and quartering, crucifixion, burning at the stake, and use of the rack. The case of *Weems* v. *United States* (1910)) brought the twentieth-century Court into the controversy of cruel and unusual punishments. Paul Weems, an officer of the U.S. government stationed in the Philippines, was convicted of falsifying a public document. Under Philippine law, he was sentenced to fifteen years of "cadena temporal," a punishment of Spanish origin which required the prisoner to spend the entire sentence at hard labor and bound by heavy chains around the wrists and ankles. All civil rights were forfeited during the sentence, and the prisoner was subject to continual surveillance once the sentence was completed.[30] The Supreme Court ruled the punishment to violate the Eighth Amendment, emphasizing that the meaning of "cruel and unusual punishments" was not confined to the definition used by past generations. Rather, the Court suggested that changing standards of decency in a society would tend to change the meaning of cruel and unusual punishments.

The Supreme Court addressed the issue of punishment in *Robinson* v. *California* (1962), involving a California statute which made it a misdemeanor to be "addicted to the use of narcotics." The appellant, Lawrence Robinson, had been arrested by a police officer who observed scars and needle marks on Robinson's arms, although he was not under the influence of drugs at that time. Speaking for himself and four other justices, Justice Stewart found that narcotics addiction was an illness and not a criminal offense. Under the illness reasoning, he suggested that no state would consider making it a criminal offense to be "mentally ill, or a leper, or to be afflicted with a venereal disease." Punishment of an affliction such as drug addiction "inflicts a cruel and unusual punishment in violation of the Fourteenth Amendment." By this ruling, the Eighth Amendment's ban on cruel and unusual punishments was incorporated into the Due Process Clause of the Fourteenth Amendment. In dissent, Justice White criticized what he called the "novel" application of cruel and unusual punishment in this case.

The issue of punishment for an illness or an ongoing condition split the Court in *Powell* v. *Texas* (1968). In a narrow 5-4 vote, the Court upheld Leroy Powell's conviction and $50 fine for being drunk in a public place. Powell's appeal had contended that his drunkenness was beyond his own control, as he suffered from "the disease of chronic alcoholism." Justice Marshall's plurality opinion treated the Texas law as a "criminal sanction for public behavior which may create substantial health and safety standards," and not punishment of a "a mere status" as in *Robinson*. The four dissenters, recognizing alcoholism to be a disease which the defendant "had no capacity to change or avoid," saw no reason for distinguishing this case from *Robinson*. The implications for law and society were immense.

Most of the attention given cruel and unusual punishments in recent years has involved the punishment of death for certain crimes. Not until the case of *Furman* v. *Georgia* (1972) did the Supreme Court address the death penalty issue, although executions had been part of American justice for years. Critics of the practice, however, sought to draw attention to the arbitrary and discriminatory way in which the death penalty had been administered. In

Furman, the Court ruled 5-4 to strike down the use of the death penalty as then practiced, but no single majority opinion was written. Justices Brennan and Marshall held the death penalty per se to be violative of the Eighth Amendment, while three others—Douglas, Stewart, and White—found fault with the manner in which the death penalty had been administered. While Douglas noted the impact upon minorities, all were concerned with the system of arbitrariness and unguided discretion available to judges and juries. To summarize: of the five separate opinions, three justices opposed the absence of clear standards and the resulting arbitrariness of death penalty use but stopped short of deciding upon the legality of the death penalty itself; two justices opposed the death penalty in all circumstances; and four justices dissented.

The four dissenters, all Nixon appointees, found that legislatures, more so than courts, should decide upon the appropriateness of the death penalty. Chief Justice Burger's opinion was fairly typical of this view:

> Rather than providing a final and unambiguous answer on the basic constitutional question, the collective impact of the majority's ruling is to demand an undetermined measure of change from the various state legislatures and the Congress. While I cannot endorse the process of decisionmaking that has yielded today's result and the restraints which that result imposes on legislative action, I am not altogether displeased that legislative bodies have been given the opportunity, and indeed unavoidable responsibility, to make a thorough re-evaluation of the entire subject of capital punishment.

Chief Justice Burger's call for legislative activity took little time to show results. Many states undertook revisions of their death penalty statutes, spurred on by public opinion polls that showed a majority of Americans in favor of such laws. In 1976, the Court addressed the new laws in five separate cases. Four justices (Burger, White, Rehnquist, and Blackmun) found all five state laws acceptable, while two (Brennan and Marshall) held all five to be invalid. The crucial "swing" votes were held by Justices Stewart, Powell, and Stevens, all of whom delivered a joint opinion in each of the five cases—upholding three laws (Georgia, Texas, and Florida) and striking down two (North Carolina and Louisiana).

In *Gregg* v. *Georgia* (1976), a 7-2 majority upheld Georgia's new death penalty statute. Justice Stewart's plurality opinion held that the death penalty "does not invariably violate the Constitution," adding that it "is not a form of punishment that may never be imposed." The new Georgia law provided for several important factors to be considered before the death penalty could be imposed. First, Georgia specified ten "aggravating circumstances, one of which must be found by the jury to exist beyond a reasonable doubt before a death sentence can ever be imposed." (Examples include, Was the crime committed upon a peace officer or judicial officer? Was it committed in the course of another capital crime? Was it committed for money?) Second, the jury must consider "mitigating circumstances" as well, including each items as the defendant's youth, emotional state, and extent of cooperation with authorities. The statute provides that

> the jury is not required to find any mitigating circumstance in order to make a recommendation of mercy that is binding on the trial court . . . but it must find a statutory aggravating circumstance before recommending a sentence of death.

Third, all death sentences carry automatic appeal to the Georgia Supreme Court, which reviews each sentence of death to determine if it is disproportionate compared with other cases. The Court upheld similar laws in *Proffitt* v. *Florida* (1976) and *Jurek* v. *Texas* (1976). Both laws provided statutory guidance to judges and juries, as well as automatic judicial review of the death sentence.

The Court then addressed the matter of mandatory death sentences for certain types of offenses. Both North Carolina and Louisiana, although in different ways, had responded to the earlier *Furman* ruling by making mandatory the death penalty for first-degree murder convictions. In *Woodson* v. *North Carolina* (1976) and *Roberts* v. *Louisiana* (1976), the three-justice plurality was joined by the consistent opposition of Justices Brennan and Marshall to all death penalty statutes to produce a 5-4 result. Justice Stewart in *Woodson* found the North Carolina law to fall short of the objective standards required by *Furman* and held that the Eighth Amendment "requires consideration of the character and record of the individual offender and the circumstances of the particular offense as a constitutionally indispensable part of the process of inflicting the penalty of death." As a result, the legally acceptable death sentence is required to fall somewhere between the arbitrariness found in *Furman* and the mandatory requirements of *Woodson* and *Roberts*.

While the 1976 rulings seemingly resolved, for the time, the major constitutional issues in death penalty sentencing, several cases continued to raise slightly different problems. In *Roberts* v. *Louisiana* (1977), a totally different case from the previously mentioned *Roberts*, a narrow 5-4 vote struck down Louisiana's mandatory death penalty for the murder of a police officer or a firefighter. The same year, in *Coker* v. *Georgia* (1977), the Court overturned the petitioner's scheduled execution on grounds that the death sentence for the crime of rape is disproportionate. Particularly troublesome to the justices was the fact that Coker had committed the rape, along with an armed robbery, after having escaped from prison where he was serving life sentences for murder, rape, and kidnapping. Nevertheless, the plurality could not accept the death sentence as acceptable punishment for a crime that did not involve the taking of a human life.

In the years since *Gregg*, *Woodson*, and *Coker*, the Supreme Court has been called upon to review a number of death sentences, and the constitutionality of the death penalty has faced new challenges (see Brief 8.6). Beginning with the 1977 execution of Gary Mark Gilmore at the Utah State Prison, executions have resumed at a fairly steady rate into the 1980s. Still, death-row populations continue to rise, currently standing at over two thousand across the country. Perhaps this fact reflects the nation's uncertainty about the death penalty. Some states have begun searching for new, arguably more "humane" and "efficient," methods of execution. The current use of a lethal injection in Texas is a case in point.

In the recent case of *Thompson* v. *Oklahoma* (1988), a 5-3 Court reversed the death sentence of William Wayne Thompson, who had committed a murder when he was only fifteen years old. Four members of the Court agreed with an opinion written by Justice Stevens, which held that "evolving standards of decency" would make it unconstitutional under any circumstances to execute a person for a crime committed while under the age of sixteen. Justice O'Con-

☐ *Brief 8.6   The Death Penalty and Racial Discrimination*

A 5-4 majority in *McCleskey* v. *Kemp* (1987) ruled that Georgia's capital punishment system was constitutional, despite the existence of empirical data that showed killers of white people are far more likely to be sentenced to die than killers of blacks. Warren McCleskey, a black, had been convicted of murdering a white policeman in a 1978 robbery.

Writing for the majority, Justice Powell referred to a statistical study by Professor David C. Baldus of the University of Iowa which showed that killers of whites were more than four times as likely to get the death sentence than killers of blacks. These figures were adjusted to account for a number of factors and circumstances. Justice Powell assumed the validity of the study, but he described it as "clearly insufficient to support an inference that any of the decision makers in McCleskey's case acted with discriminatory purpose." Justice Powell acknowledged the discretion inherent in the criminal justice system, even recognizing that it may lead to certain disparities. Nevertheless, he added that a defendant "must prove that the decision makers in his case acted with a discriminatory purpose." Although the Court has accepted general statistics to prove discrimination in certain specific cases, Justice

Powell indicated that those instances were "not comparable" to applying them to a specific decision in a single trial.

> In light of the safeguards designed to minimize racial bias in the process, the fundamental value of jury trial in our criminal justice system, and the benefits that discretion provides to criminal defendants, we hold that the Baldus study does not demonstrate a constitutionally significant risk of racial bias affecting the Georgia capital-sentencing process.

The four dissenting justices—Brennan, Marshall, Blackmun, and Stevens—found the majority's position disturbing. Justice Brennan's opinion stands in sharp contrast to the majority view:

> It is important to emphasize at the outset that the Court's observation that McCleskey cannot prove the influence of race on any particular sentencing decision is irrelevant in evaluating his Eighth Amendment claim. Since *Furman* v. *Georgia* (1972), the Court has been concerned with the risk of the imposition of an arbitrary sentence, rather than the proven fact of one. . . [McCleskey's] message is a disturbing one to a society that has formally repudiated racism, and a frustrating one to a nation accustomed to regarding its destiny as the product of its own will. Nonetheless, we ignore him at our peril, for we remain imprisoned by the past as long as we deny its influence in the present.

nor, the fifth member of the majority, refused to go as far as Justice Stevens, but she indicated that states could not execute persons for crimes committed under the age of sixteen unless the state's capital punishment statute specified a minimum age. Because of the plurality and concurring opinions, however, the effect of the ruling upon a minimum age for executions is far from clear.

Before concluding the issue of cruel and unusual punishments, it should be noted that several new issues have been addressed in this regard. In *Ingraham* v. *Wright* (1977), a 5-4 majority held that the use of corporal punishment (paddling of students) does not constitute cruel and unusual punishment in Eighth Amendment terms. Speaking for the Court, Justice Powell stated that the Eighth Amendment was "designed to protect those convicted of crimes." Schoolchildren, he said, are free to leave the school, which is "an open institution," unlike criminals confined in prison. Of course, Powell stated, the use of excessive force may result in both civil and criminal liability. The dissenters, led by Justice White, drew attention to the severity of the beatings administered in the case, noting "that if they were inflicted on a hardened criminal for the commission of a serious crime, they might not pass constitutional muster."

Finally, some courts have found substandard prison conditions to constitute cruel and unusual punishment. In these rulings, such issues as the size of cells, provisions for prison safety, and the availability of library and recreational facilities have been addressed.

Other Developments in the Due Process of Law

Judge Henry J. Friendly, in a widely cited 1975 law review article, suggested that the due process "explosion" had produced a situation in which Americans felt entitled to "some kind of hearing" before facing any government action.[31] Judge Friendly's thesis drew heavily upon two influential Supreme Court decisions of the early 1970s. In *Goldberg* v. *Kelly* (1970), a majority held that the Due Process Clause requires that a welfare recipient be given an evidentiary hearing before benefits are terminated, even though welfare procedures provided for a "constitutionally fair proceeding" following termination. (See Chapter 10 for the equal protection implications of *Goldberg*.) The right to "some kind of hearing" was expanded in *Goss* v. *Lopez* (1975). Justice White's 5-4 majority opinion held that school suspensions of ten days or less "may not be imposed in complete disregard of the Due Process Clause." Students facing such suspensions are entitled to "effective notice and informal hearing permitting the student to give his version of the events." In both the *Goldberg* and *Goss* decisions, the majority stopped short of requiring formal trial-type hearings complete with appointed counsel, but hearings were required nonetheless.

Beginning in 1976, however, the Court seemingly shifted toward a "balancing test" in ascertaining the necessity of a hearing. In *Mathews* v. *Eldridge* (1976), Justice Powell's majority opinion denied a hearing for George Eldridge prior to the termination of his Social Security disability benefit payments. The majority went to considerable effort to distinguish this case from *Goldberg*, ultimately concluding that "the disabled worker's need is likely to be less than that of a welfare recipient." Further, the Court drew attention to the "fairness and reliability of the existing pretermination procedures" and the fact that Eldridge was entitled to a posttermination hearing with full retroactive benefits if he prevailed. Finally, an important step was taken in *Dixon* v. *Love* (1977). That case upheld an Illinois statute that authorized revoking of a driver's license for repeated traffic offenses without a hearing prior to revocation, although a posthearing was provided.

As the two sets of cases suggest, the Supreme Court's approach to demand for "some kind of hearing" increasingly has tended to balance due process considerations with broader societal and governmental concerns. The individualist right to be heard, while an integral principle of American justice, must be viewed alongside broader communitarian interests in safety, government efficiency in administration, and school discipline.

The protections of due process of law have been the subject of considerable activity in numerous other areas. While an exhaustive treatment of these areas is beyond the scope of this book, an attempt will be made to indicate a few of the more significant developments.

Due Process for Juveniles

A young person who breaks the law usually is brought before a juvenile court, as opposed to a regular trial court. These juvenile courts were developed late in the nineteenth century "by reformers who were appalled that children were being treated like adult criminals."[32] This reform movement basically held that youthful offenders were in need of guidance rather than punishment, correction rather than imprisonment. As a result, each of the states established a system of juvenile courts to treat the problems of young people. Seemingly, such a system would provide help for troubled young people without turning them into hardened criminals.

In the case of *In re Gault* (1967), the Warren Court addressed the issue of juvenile defendants and guarantees of due process. Gerald Gault, age fifteen, and a friend were picked up by an Arizona county sheriff after receipt of a complaint from a neighbor that the boys had called her on the phone and made lewd or indecent remarks. The boys were taken to a detention home and kept overnight, pending a hearing in juvenile court the next day. No record of the hearing was made and no decision was reached. Gerald Gault was then taken back to the detention home. He was released several days later, along with a note setting the date and time for another hearing. This time, following some questions and answers (again, no record of the testimony was kept), the judge committed Gault to Fort Grant, the state industrial school, for delinquency. Under the terms of the ruling, Gault would remain in detention until the age of majority (twenty-one), "unless sooner discharged by due process of law." In practical terms, Gerald Gault was probably looking at a six-year detention.

After unfavorable rulings through the Arizona courts, the Gaults and their attorney appealed to the U.S. Supreme Court. The appeal contended that the Arizona Juvenile Code was unconstitutional because it did not provide juveniles with due process of law under the Fourteenth Amendment. Writing for an 8-1 Court, Justice Abe Fortas noted that the juvenile justice system, although based upon "the highest motives and most enlightened impulses," had produced results not entirely satisfactory. The Court took note of the fact that, had Gault been eighteen instead of fifteen, he would have come under the jurisdiction of the criminal court, been subject to a small fine or two months in jail, and, most importantly, been entitled to all the rights and privileges of the U.S. Constitution. "Neither the Fourteenth Amendment nor the Bill of Rights is for adults alone," stated the Fortas opinion.

In the ruling, the majority laid down several specific requirements for juvenile courts. First, juveniles and their parents have the right to notice of the specific charges and of each scheduled court proceeding. Secondly, self-incrimination protections must be provided to a juvenile in Gault's situation, despite the fact that juvenile proceedings technically are not "criminal" in nature. When proceedings may lead to imprisonment, the Court said, the privilege against self-incrimination must be respected. Third, when commitment to an institution is possible, "the child and his parents must be notified of the child's right to be represented by counsel retained by them, or if they are unable to afford counsel, that counsel will be appointed to represent the child." Finally, the Court held that the rights to confront and cross-examine witnesses were essential in such a proceeding, ruling that reliance upon hearsay evidence was improper. In summary, the *Gault* decision brought certain guarantees of the Due Process Clause of the Fourteenth Amendment to bear on juvenile proceedings.

Due Process for Mental Patients

In the case of *O'Connor* v. *Donaldson* (1975), the Supreme Court addressed a situation in which a state mental hospital's superintendent, an agent of the state, knowingly confined a mental patient who was not dangerous and who was capable of surviving safely in freedom by himself or with the help of willing family members or friends. Looking at the virtual absence of due process protections for such a confined person, a majority of the Court held that the superintendent had indeed violated the patient's constitutional right to liberty as guaranteed in the Fourteenth Amendment. The Court did not allege a constitutional right to treatment, but it did hold that patients, harmless to others and capable of surviving safely on their own or with the willing help of others, may not be confined arbitrarily. Such confinement violates that patient's constitutional right to liberty.

Due Process for Probationers, Parolees, and Prisoners

As noted earlier, demands for "some kind of hearing" have swelled in recent years, to the point that practices traditionally considered to be purely administrative in nature are now embodied with a wide range of due process guarantees. Demands for such guarantees have been asserted by persons faced with the possibility of the revocation of their probation or parole, as well as those persons inside prison who find themselves the subject of disciplinary proceedings. In the case of *Morrissey* v. *Brewer* (1972), the Supreme Court ruled that a person on probation or parole may only be returned to prison after notice and a hearing. At the hearing, the probationer or parolee must be given "a written statement by the factfinders as to the evidence relied on," as well as the reasons for the hearing. Other due process requirements include the disclosure of evidence; the opportunity to be heard; the right to present evidence and witnesses; the right to confront and cross-examine witnesses (although subject to limitation if a good cause is presented); and a neutral hearing body. The following year, in *Gagnon* v. *Scarpelli* (1973), the Court extended a limited right to counsel in such revocation hearings. While the probationer or parolee is entitled to be represented by counsel, the state is not required to appoint counsel for indigents unless the hearing would not be fair otherwise. For example, the Court indicated that appointed counsel might be required when the issues were particularly complex or when parolees or probationers could not represent themselves effectively. Further, the Court required that anytime a request for counsel is denied, the reasons for refusal must be stated in the record.

Finally, the due process of law moved inside prison gates in the case of *Wolff* v. *McDonnell* (1974). At issue was the legality of a Nebraska prison's system of disciplinary proceedings for determining whether a prisoner could be deprived of "good time credits" or placed in confinement for serious misconduct. These proceedings also were used to deprive prisoners of certain privileges in the case of less serious misconduct. Under the Nebraska system, these proceedings included: a preliminary conference at which the prisoner, the chief corrections supervisor, and the charging party were present; oral notice of the complaint; a hearing before the adjustment committee; and the right of the inmate to ask questions of the charging party.

The Court held that proceedings inside prison must be governed by a mutual accommodation between institutional needs and generally applicable constitutional requirements. In short, certain minimal due process guarantees were required, but not the full range noted in the *Morrissey* and *Scarpelli* rulings. Specifically, the due process requirements for prison disciplinary hearings, the Court stated, should include advanced written notice of the charges no less than twenty-four hours before the adjustment committee meets; a written statement of the evidence relied upon and the reasons for the disciplinary action; and the inmates' right to call witnesses and present documentary evidence in their defense if this will not jeopardize "institutional safety or correctional goals." Significantly, the Court held that inmates have no constitutional right to confrontation or cross-examination of witnesses in prison disciplinary hearings; further, there is no right to retained or appointed counsel in such hearings, although counsel substitutes should be provided in certain instances.

As a result, the Due Process Clause has its place in the prison setting, although the Court indicated that its ruling was not "graven in stone" and that different requirements might be necessary in the future. Based upon prison statistics, it is likely that the Supreme Court will be called upon to hear more due process claims. According to Professor Harry Stumpf, the United States has the highest rate of imprisonment of any "nontotalitarian" state:

> By mid-1983, some 430,000 persons were in United States prisons and jails, roughly 177 prisoners per 100,000 population. This represents a 70 percent increase over 1974, when there were only some 230,000 imprisoned citizens. In 1985, the number of prisoners per 100,000 population leaped to 201, an increase of 45 percent over 1980.[33]

These figures, while perhaps indicating a conscious effort to put more criminals behind bars, also suggest the strong likelihood that the constitutional guarantees of due process will face future challenges from inside the nation's prisons.

Conclusion

When the first ten amendments became part of the new United States Constitution in 1791, it is unlikely that many of the leaders of that era could have visualized their profound impact upon future generations of Americans. The Bill of Rights, after all, had originated largely as the result of a compromise between Federalist and Anti-Federalist groups during the struggle for constitutional ratification. Moreover, because the new amendments specifically were limited in their effect to the national government and not the states, they would not have much significance in the everyday affairs of most Americans. The long-standing precedent established by Chief Justice Marshall's ruling in *Barron* v. *Baltimore* (1833) added further support to this view.

The ratification of the Fourteenth Amendment in 1868 laid the foundation that ultimately would change the relationship between the Bill of Rights and the states. After many years, the Court held in *Palko* v. *Connecticut* (1937) that the "liberties" of the Due Process Clause of the Fourteenth Amendment contained portions of the first eight amendments which were "implicit in the concept of ordered liberty." Under this doctrine, known as selective incorporation, future Supreme Courts gradually nationalized nearly all the provisions of the Bill of Rights, thereby making them binding against the states. As a result, the rights originally protected from the national government alone had become truly nationwide in scope.

Several of the first eight amendments apply to the rights of persons suspected, accused, or convicted of crimes against society. The Fourth Amendment, protecting against "unreasonable searches and seizures" and requiring the issuance of warrants based upon probable cause, has provoked much debate between the individualist interest in privacy and the communitarian interest in law, order, and society. Other provisions such as the Fifth Amendment's protection against self-incrimination and the Sixth Amendment's right to counsel have come together to establish a solid core of protection for the person accused of a crime.

The foregoing discussion suggests that the United States has witnessed an explosion in the demand for individual rights and liberties while simultaneously reacting to societal demands for peace, order, and protection. Ideas of constitutional government have changed a great deal since the nation's founding, as have understandings of individual rights, liberties, and the due process of law. Just as society has evolved in its efforts to balance individual with communitarian concerns, so, too, have the institutions of government shown signs of change. In recent times, the Supreme Court has moved with (and often led) society in searching out new rights and liberties. The activism of the Warren Court during the 1950s and 1960s nationalized the Bill of Rights, reaching into such sensitive areas as searches and seizures, custodial interrogations, the rights to counsel and trial by jury, and cruel and unusual punishments. Protection of the individual from arbitrary government action was given the highest priority.

America's constitutional development often moves in cycles, with the actions of one generation leading to reaction by the next. Such would appear to be the case with respect to the Supreme Court. The Warren Court's activism gave way to a more restrained judicial role under Warren Burger, particularly in matters concerning search and seizure, the exclusionary rule, custodial rights, and death penalty legislation. The current Rehnquist Court consistently has leaned toward judicial restraint, deferring to legislatures in matters of civil liberties and due process of law. While civil libertarians may find cause for alarm in some rulings of the Burger and Rehnquist Courts, proponents of "law and order" and "domestic tranquility" probably would applaud the change in direction. The strength of American constitutionalism is that individualists, communitarians, judicial activists, and judicial restrainers all look to the same sources for their inspiration and guidance. These sources, of course, are the Constitution and the Bill of Rights.

But these sources address numerous rights and liberties beyond those discussed in this chapter. The concern with equality, for example, has led Americans to question long-standing patterns of segregation and discrimination, although the quest for "equal protection of the laws" has been anything but easy. In fact, it has been in matters relating to equality that the United States Constitution perhaps has been most severely tested. These issues provide the subject matter of the following two chapters.

Questions

1. What were the major events leading to the incorporation of the Bill of Rights? Which cases do you consider especially significant in the process? Of the theories concerning incorporation, which do you find most persuasive?

2. What are the central elements of the Fourth Amendment? What are the major exceptions to the requirements of the amendment? Which exceptions do you find most and least compelling? Can you imagine any new exceptions that might emerge?

3. The exclusionary rule has generated a great deal of controversy. What do you see as the primary reasons for the exclusionary rule? What arguments can you give against the rule? Which Supreme Court decisions have been most and least supportive of the exclusionary rule? On the basis of recent developments, how do you assess the future of the exclusionary rule?

4. How does the Constitution protect persons taken into custody by the authorities? How may the authorities ensure that a confession will be admissible as evidence? At what points in the criminal justice process does the right to an attorney become critical?

5. According to the Court, what requirements must be met before the death penalty can be imposed upon a convicted person? What arguments can you give in support of the death penalty, and how might an opponent of that view respond? What other possible meanings of "cruel and unusual punishments" can you suggest?

Endnotes

1. Henry J. Abraham, *Freedom and the Court: Civil Rights and Liberties in the United States,* 4th ed. (New York: Oxford University Press, 1982), 127.

2. Fred E. Inbau, "Law Enforcement, the Courts, and Individual Civil Liberties," in Yale Kamisar, Fred E. Inbau, and Thurman Arnold, *Criminal Justice in Our Time* (Charlottesville, Va.: University Press of Virginia, 1965), 134.

3. Joel B. Grossman and Richard S. Wells, *Constitutional Law and Judicial Policy Making,* 3d ed. (New York: Longman, 1988), 438.

4. Harold W. Stanley and Richard G. Niemi, *Vital Statistics on American Politics* (Washington, D.C.: Congressional Quarterly Press, 1988), 337.

5. Robert Allen Rutland, *The Birth of the Bill of Rights* (New York: Collier Books, 1962), 217.

6. Ibid., 218.

7. Edward Dumbauld, *The Bill of Rights and What It Means Today* (Norman, Okla.: University of Oklahoma Press, 1957), 41.

8. Richard C. Cortner, *The Supreme Court and the Second Bill of Rights: The Fourteenth Amendment and the Nationalization of Civil Liberties* (Madison, Wis.: University of Wisconsin Press, 1981), 5.

9. Abraham, *Freedom and the Court,* 41.

10. *Maxwell* v. *Dow,* 176 U.S. 581, 601 (1900).

11. Cortner, *Supreme Court,* 20–21.

12. *Santa Clara County* v. *Southern Pacific Railroad,* 118 U.S. 394 (1886).

13. In *Grosjean* v. *American Press Co.,* 297 U.S. 233, 244 (1936), Justice Sutherland stated that the freedoms of speech and press had been held to be guarantees of the Due Process Clause in "a series of decisions of this court, beginning with *Gitlow* v. *New York* . . . and ending with *Near* v. *Minnesota.*"

14. Charles Fairman, " 'Legislative History,' and the Constitutional Limits

on State Authority," *University of Chicago Law Review* 1 (1954): 1.

15. Several influential sources include J. B. James, *The Framing of the Fourteenth Amendment* (Urbana, Ill.: University of Illinois Press, 1956); Horace Flack, *The Adoption of the Fourteenth Amendment* (Baltimore: Johns Hopkins University Press, 1908); and Raoul Berger, *Government by Judiciary: The Transformation of the Fourteenth Amendment* (Cambridge, Mass.: Harvard University Press, 1977).

16. Quoted in Rutland, *Birth of the Bill of Rights*, 25.

17. Glenn A. Phelps and Robert A. Poirier, eds., *Contemporary Debates on Civil Liberties: Enduring Constitutional Questions* (Lexington, Mass.: Heath, 1985), 123.

18. Abraham, *Freedom and the Court*, 144.

19. *Frank* v. *Maryland*, 359 U.S. 360 (1959).

20. For an interesting review of the case law and an argument for holding the exclusionary rule to be required by due process considerations, see Lane V. Sunderland, "The Exclusionary Rule: A Requirement of Constitutional Principle," in Gary L. McDowell, ed., *Taking the Constitution Seriously: Essays on the Constitution and Constitutional Law*

(Dubuque, Iowa: Kendall Hunt, 1981), 343–70.

21. Grossman and Wells, *Constitutional Law*, 493.

22. Ann Fagan Ginger, *The Law, the Supreme Court and the People's Rights* (Woodbury, N.Y.: Barron's, 1977), 283.

23. Ibid., 284.

24. *Chambers* v. *Florida*, 309 U.S. 227 (1940).

25. *Baldwin* v. *New York*, 399 U.S. 66 (1970).

26. Harry P. Stumpf, *American Judicial Politics* (San Diego, Calif.: Harcourt Brace Jovanovich, 1988), 348.

27. Ibid.

28. Andrea L. Bonnicksen, *Civil Rights and Liberties: Principles of Interpretation* (Palo Alto, Calif.: Mayfield Publishing Company, 1982), 248.

29. Ibid.

30. Phelps and Poirier, *Contemporary Debates on Civil Liberties*, 141.

31. Henry J. Friendly, "Some Kind of Hearing," *University of Pennsylvania Law Review* 123 (1975): 1267.

32. Ginger, *The Law*, 367.

33. Stumpf, *American Judicial Politics*, 351.

Suggested Readings

Abraham, Henry J. *Freedom and the Court: Civil Rights and Liberties in the United States*, 4th ed. New York: Oxford University Press, 1982.

Cortner, Richard C. *The Supreme Court and the Second Bill of Rights: The Fourteenth Amendment and the Nationalization of Civil Liberties*. Madison, Wis.: University of Wisconsin Press, 1981.

Kamisar, Yale, Fred E. Inbau, and Thurman Arnold. *Criminal Justice in Our Time*. Charlottesville, Va.: University Press of Virginia, 1965.

Lewis, Anthony. *Gideon's Trumpet*. New York: Random House, 1964.

Mashaw, Jerry L. *Due Process in the Administrative State*. New Haven, Conn.: Yale University Press, 1965.

Mendelson, Wallace. *The American Constitution and Civil Liberties*. Homewood, Ill.: Dorsey Press, 1981.

Phelps, Glenn A., and Robert A. Poirier, eds. *Contemporary Debates on Civil Liberties: Enduring Constitutional Questions.* Lexington, Mass.: Heath, 1985.

Rutland, Robert Allen. *The Birth of the Bill of Rights.* New York: Collier Books, 1962.

Skolnick, Jerome H. *Justice Without Trial: Law Enforcement in Democratic Society.* New York: Wiley, 1966.

Racial Equality
Under the Constitution

Syllabus

Recent events demonstrate that race continues to be what Swedish observer Gunnar Myrdal once called "an American dilemma." The trial of Bernhard Goetz, the racial incidents in Howard Beach, New York, in Cumming, Georgia, and on many college campuses, the studies connecting race and death penalty sentencing discussed at the end of Chapter 8, as well as the presidential candidacy of Jesse Jackson in 1988, to name but a few, have all raised renewed charges of racism and racial inequality in the American constitutional system. Of course, the U.S. Constitution requires that citizens be treated equally. But in a nation as racially and ethnically diverse as the United States, this ideal of equality has not often been satisfied. How does the Constitution reconcile the vast racial diversity and prejudice within American society with the demands for equal justice under law?

This Chapter Examines the Following Matters

☐   The ideal of equality undergirds the American Constitution, even though the framers compromised this ideal in dealing with slavery. The federal government, especially the Supreme Court, further compromised constitutional equality in the pre-Civil War years.

☐   The post-Civil War amendments (Thirteen–Fifteen) had a dramatic effect upon racial equality under the Constitution and gave Congress the authority to enforce their egalitarian dictates.

☐   In its early postbellum interpretation of the Equal Protection Clause, the Supreme Court applied three criteria to trigger judicial scrutiny under the Fourteenth Amendment: state action, rationality scrutiny, and purposeful discrimination. These criteria severely narrowed the vision of racial equality held by the Congress that drafted the Fourteenth Amendment.

☐   The struggle for racial equality in the United States over the past century has been arduous. After a period of narrowing equality's demands, the Supreme Court—beginning in the 1930s—has increasingly prohibited racial discrimination in such areas as housing, education, and voting rights.

☐   Congressional legislation, exemplified by the Civil Rights Act of 1964 and the Voting Rights Act of 1965, has also protected racial minorities from discrimination in employment, in public accommodations, and at the ballot box.

☐   The Supreme Court has significantly changed one aspect of its equal protection interpretation, that of rationality scrutiny, over the past fifty years. However, in its view of state action and purposeful discrimination, less has changed.

Photo: In *Brown* v. *Board of Education* (1954), the Supreme Court declared racial segregation in public education to be unconstitutional. The continued busing of schoolchildren to achieve racial desegregation is a constant reminder of the Supreme Court's role in insuring racial equality.

Racial Equality: An American Dilemma

Along with liberty, the ideal of equality buttresses the American constitutional system. The banner of equality is raised by both the individualist and communitarian traditions in American political thought. The individualist sees equality of opportunity as essential to individuals seeking to maximize their goods. Equality under the law is also valued because it guarantees the kind of procedural justice individualists support. For the communitarian, political equality is a prerequisite for the values mentioned in Chapter 2 of majority rule and maximum citizen participation. In addition, communitarian concerns over substantive justice dictate that society's institutions be judged by whether they achieve relative equality for all citizens.

But the ideal of equality is capable of a wide range of meanings. Throughout the nation's history, citizens have interpreted the demands of constitutional equality differently. One view, which has been termed the "antidiscrimination principle," [1] holds that equality's command is a negative one: equality merely means that the government and law should not discriminate against individuals in an arbitrary fashion. The problem this definition solves is that the government and the law must always distinguish between individuals, their characteristics, and their behavior. For example, a law that sets the speed limit at twenty-five miles per hour will draw a line between people who drive twenty-five miles per hour and those who drive forty-five miles per hour, and law enforcement officials will discriminate against the latter. This poses no obvious problem for equality. The antidiscrimination principle, then, merely forbids governmental discrimination against individuals upon irrational grounds unrelated to any legitimate state purpose. Discrimination based upon race, gender, and ethnic origin best exemplify the kind of impermissible distinctions covered by the antidiscrimination principle.

However, this first definition of equality leaves a wide range of distinctions between individuals acceptable. The antidiscrimination principle is perfectly compatible with vast inequalities between individuals in the society. For example, economic inequalities resulting from a history of race- or sex-segregated employment cannot be remedied simply by an end to government discrimination. That has led some citizens to argue for a more positive, substantive, results-oriented approach to constitutional equality. Under this approach, which constitutional scholar Owen Fiss has termed the "group-disadvantaging principle," [2] the government would have the positive duty to address inequalities between people and could operate from a group-based as opposed to an individual-based perspective. The law could take account of groups or classes of people who had been historically frozen out of the advantages and opportunities society has to offer.

An additional question about equality relates to the area its commands cover. Is equality under the Constitution limited to governmental and legal actions, or does it extend to other areas of public life? Is discrimination carried out by individuals in the private sector subject to constitutional prohibitions in the same way that state-based discrimination is? If so, how can private individuals be monitored to determine whether the ideal of equality has been subverted?

Many of these questions have been present from the beginning of the nation's history. Documents of the founding period abound with mention of equality. Of course, Thomas Jefferson proclaimed in the Declaration of Independence that "all men are created equal." A great debate exists over what Jefferson meant by equality. Most political theorists and historians would agree that he did not intend the statement to endorse a sameness of condition upon the American people. But they disagree over whether the Declaration of Independence promotes the ideal of equality of opportunity (a more individualist notion most compatible with the antidiscrimination principle just mentioned), or promotes the principle that all citizens be effectively granted equal legal and political status (a more communitarian understanding of equality). Some have even noted that Jefferson's phrase reflects the classical republican concern that vast economic and social inequalities among people can skew political decisions and thus damage the pursuit of the common good.

In addition to Jefferson's controversial statement, Chapter 3 pointed out that many of the early state constitutions granted greater political equality than did their colonial counterparts. And the Constitution itself is permeated with the ideal of equality, though it is not always explicitly stated. For example, the Preamble announces that one of the new Constitution's foremost purposes is to "establish Justice," which is given meaning by the motto inscribed on the Supreme Court building: "Equal Justice Under Law." The writers of the Preamble understood that justice cannot be brought about unless all are treated equally.

However, no one can honestly say that this underlying ideal of equality has been consistently applied to all people. At the time of the founding, all women, native Americans, black men, and the propertyless were excluded from the promises of equal justice. Over the past two hundred years these groups and others have struggled to secure equality. This chapter examines the struggle for racial equality under the American Constitution, while the following chapter looks at various contemporary issues relating to equality. It will be important to keep in mind the controversy surrounding equality and its meaning, how equality's meaning has changed over time, and the role of the federal government, especially the Supreme Court, in directing those changes.

Slavery, Race, and the Constitution

The legal treatment of blacks in particular has contradicted the principle of equality found in the Declaration of Independence. With the initial arrival of African slaves at Jamestown in 1619, the principle of universal equality found in the Declaration was compromised. In fact, at the time of independence in 1776, slavery was legally established in all thirteen colonies and was indeed an essential institution in the southern colonies (by historians' accounts, blacks constituted about 40 percent of the southern colonial population in 1776). There is no denying the unequal treatment accorded to African slaves during the founding period. Under law, slaves were treated not as persons, but as property. They could be bought and sold, compelled to work for their owner, and even physically abused to be brought into line. Laws prohibited slaves from being taught to read or write. Moreover, the institution was hereditary: the slave's offspring also belonged absolutely to the master.

The Constitution, while not specifically authorizing slavery, at least condoned its continued practice and the gross inequality for blacks that resulted from slavery. Although never mentioning slavery by name, three clauses in the original Constitution deal with slavery. The first, the so-called "Three-fifths Compromise," provided that slaves (actually designated as "other Persons" in Article I, Section 2) would count as three-fifths of a person for the purposes of determining representatives and direct taxation. This provision is called a "compromise" because, on the question of taxation, northerners wanted slaves to count fully while southerners wanted them to be excluded completely on the grounds that they were mere property. But for the purpose of determining representation, the stakes were reversed and southerners wanted slaves to count equally with freemen while northerners wanted to exclude them from the total census count. The Three-fifths Compromise resolved the conflict on both issues and had the effect of augmenting southern representation in the new House of Representatives by one-third.

The second slavery provision, the 1808 Compromise, as mentioned briefly in Chapter 3, concerned the future of the slave trade itself. The delegates at Philadelphia decided to prevent Congress from prohibiting the slave trade until 1808 (Art. I, Sec. 9). This clause has been interpreted two ways. Chief Justice Roger B. Taney, in his famous decision in *Dred Scott* v. *Sandford* (1857), said it meant that "the right to purchase and hold this property is directly sanctioned and authorized for twenty years." But historian Don Fehrenbacher has argued that the clause actually "authorized the future abolition of the slave trade and thus amounted . . . to a delayed repudiation of the slave system." [3]

The last clause dealing with slavery was the Fugitive-Slave Clause, found in Article IV, Section 2. It commands: "No Person held to Service or Labour in one State, under the Laws thereof, escaping into another, shall, in Consequence of any Law or Regulation therein, be discharged from such Service or Labour, but shall be delivered up on Claim of the Party to whom such Service or Labour may be due." This clause actually nationalized slave property, obliging the free states to assist in enforcing the slave system. It would later provide the basis for federal intervention on behalf of the institution of slavery, through the two fugitive slave laws passed by Congress.

The Constitution's remarks about slavery can be read in two ways. From one perspective, those who framed the Constitution justified slavery. The abolitionist William Lloyd Garrison called the sectional compromise over slavery "a covenant with death and an agreement with hell." [4] From this perspective, the Constitution allowed slaves to be treated as property, thus compromising the concept that all men are created equal.

But from another perspective, the ambiguous wording and limited acceptance of the institution lent itself to the eventual abolition of slavery. After all, the founders did purposely avoid using the words "slave" or "slavery." Two New Jersey delegates, William Paterson and Jonathan Dayton, claimed that the convention "had been ashamed to use the term 'Slaves' and had therefore substituted a description" in order to avoid a "stain" on the new government. [5] Madison indicated in *Federalist No. 54* that the ambiguous treatment of slavery in the Constitution reflects a sectional compromise necessary to keep all interests together in 1787. And the fact that Congress acted immediately in 1808 to prohibit any future slave trade indicates that the Philadelphia delegates foresaw slavery's ultimate demise, although they were willing to compromise with slave interests to secure the Union in 1787. Political scientist Herbert Storing argued that, overall, the founders saw slavery as "an evil to be tolerated, allowed to enter the Constitution only by the back door, grudgingly, unacknowledged, on the presumption that the house would be truly fit to live in only when it was gone, and that it would ultimately be gone." [6]

Slavery Under the Constitution: The Pre-Civil War Years

The Constitution may have been ambiguous on the question of slavery. But the federal government's actions under this new document prior to the Civil War are much clearer. In many ways, the new federal government implicated itself in the protection of slavery as an institution. The mere location of the nation's capital in a slaveholding community, governed by slavery-influenced local laws, contributed to federal support of slavery. So, too, did Congress, through both territorial management and its passage of laws designed to give authority to the Fugitive-Slave Clause in Article IV. Finally, the Supreme Court's rulings during this era also enhanced slavery's position.

Two cases in particular, *Prigg* v. *Pennsylvania* (1842) and *Dred Scott* v. *Sandford* (1857), deserve brief mention. Edward Prigg, a lawyer acting on behalf of a Maryland slave owner, had forceably returned a fugitive slave who had escaped to Pennsylvania. Prigg was convicted on kidnapping charges in Pennsylvania, since he had removed the slave without proper state judicial authority. The Supreme Court unanimously reversed his conviction and, in so doing, made significant concessions to slave owners (although the overall ruling itself is somewhat ambiguous). Justice Joseph Story announced for the Court that the Constitution "contains a positive and unqualified recognition of the right of the owner in the slave, unaffected by any state law or legislation whatsoever." Justice Smith Thompson concurred, stating that the Fugitive-Slave Clause "affirms, in the most unequivocal manner, the right of the master to the service of his slave . . . it prohibits the states from discharging the slave from such service by any law or regulation therein."

The *Dred Scott* case involved a number of issues, including the power of judicial review (see Chapter 4), the fundamental property rights of slave owners, and the nature of the federal system (see Chapters 6 and 7). But in terms of racial equality, the questions about slavery and the extent of the black man's constitutional rights are paramount. Dred Scott, a black slave born of slave parents, had sued for his freedom based upon his five-year residence on free soil. As a result of the Missouri Compromise of 1820, Congress had banned slavery in Wisconsin Territory. Scott maintained that Congress's conferral of nonslave status upon the Wisconsin Territory gave him a title to freedom based upon his residence there. The Supreme Court would ultimately rule that the Missouri Compromise had been unconstitutional, because Congress did not have the authority to restrict slavery in the territories, thereby depriving slave owners of their constitutional right to property under the Due Process Clause of the Fifth Amendment.

But the Supreme Court also dealt with Dred Scott's very right to bring suit in the federal courts. The first question Scott's suit raised was whether a black man of slave origins was a citizen and had the constitutional right to bring a suit against a citizen of another state in the federal courts. The Court answered this question with a resounding no. Chief Justice Taney proclaimed that neither Dred Scott nor any other black man (let alone woman) could be considered a citizen under the U.S. Constitution. Looking back to the founding period, Taney wrote that black men had for more than a century before been regarded as beings of an inferior order, and altogether unfit to associate with the white race, either in social or political relations; and so far inferior, that they had no rights which the white man was bound to respect; and that the negro might justly and lawfully be reduced to slavery for his benefit. He was bought and sold, and treated as an ordinary article of merchandise and traffic, whenever a profit could be made by it. This opinion was at that time fixed and universal in the civilized race.

Justice Taney's denial to blacks of any citizenship rights was the culmination of the Supreme Court's pre-Civil War rulings regarding slavery and the Constitution. The decision also figured in the tension-creating events that brought the nation to civil war four years later. But in terms of jurisprudence, the Court's interpretation of the Constitution would not last very long after these two cases.

The Post-Civil War Amendments and Racial Equality

The Civil War put an end to slavery and to the Constitution's acceptance of it. In December 1865, the Thirteenth Amendment to the Constitution was ratified, declaring that "neither slavery nor involuntary servitude . . . shall exist within the United States." As Chapter 6 discussed, the Reconstruction Congress acted quickly over the next decade to ensure that newly freed blacks were granted the full equality that the abolition of slavery promised. Richard Kluger believes that "viewed as a unit, the decade of legislation beginning with the adoption of the Thirteenth Amendment in 1865 and culminating in passage of the Civil Rights Act of 1875, may reasonably be said to have closed the gap between the promise of the Declaration and the tactful tacit racism of the Constitution." [7]

The newly reconstituted southern states did not participate in this push for racial equality, however. White southerners enacted what were called "Black Codes" beginning late in 1865. These codes restricted blacks from carrying arms or using the courts, compelled them to work, and segregated them in all public facilities. In response to the Black Codes and other prejudicial action, Congress used its legislative authority under the Thirteenth Amendment to pass the Civil Rights Act of 1866. In it, Congress conferred upon

the inhabitants of every race . . . the same right to make and enforce contracts, to sue, be parties, and give evidence, to inherit, purchase, lease, sell, hold and carry real and personal property, and to the full and equal benefit of all laws and proceedings for the security of person and property, and shall be subject to like punishment, pains, and penalties, and to none other, any law, statute, ordinance, regulation, or custom to the contrary notwithstanding.

At the same time, Representative John Bingham of New York introduced in Congress what would come to be the Fourteenth Amendment to the Constitution. This amendment would be the crowning achievement in these post-Civil War years. Ratified in 1868, the Fourteenth Amendment contains three specific provisions aimed at guaranteeing the freedman's rights. As mentioned in Chapter 6, it forbids the states from making laws that either (1) "abridge the privileges or immunities of citizens of the United States"; (2) "deprive any person of life, liberty, or property, without due process of law"; or (3) "deny to any person within its jurisdiction the equal protection of the laws." Moreover, the amendment gives Congress the power to pass laws enforcing these provisions. Chapter 7 contained a discussion of the Supreme Court's early weakening of the Privileges and Immunities Clause in its ruling in the Slaughterhouse Cases (1873). Full coverage of the Due Process Clause as it pertains to issues of economic liberty and to the nationalization of the Bill of Rights appeared in Chapters 7 and 8. The focus in this chapter will be upon the Equal Protection Clause.

Race and Constitutional Equality: The Court's Original Understanding

What did the Equal Protection Clause mean? The intentions of those who framed it are not completely clear. The Fourteenth Amendment's sponsors saw it as a 'necessary federal protection of the black man's civil rights against those in the states who might deny him these newly won rights. The framers of the amendment clearly had in mind the Black Codes and other examples of racially biased state laws. "Equal protection," then, was designed for newly freed blacks, to provide "that no discrimination shall be made against them by law because of their color." [8]

The Supreme Court announced this primary purpose of the Fourteenth Amendment in the Slaughterhouse Cases (1873). Justice Samuel Miller announced that "the one pervading purpose" of all the post-Civil War amendments was to protect the newly freed black man "from the oppression of those who had formerly exercised unlimited dominion over him . . . We doubt very much whether any action of a state not directed by way of discrimination against the negroes as a class, or on account of their race, will ever be held to come within the purview of this provision."

But what specific "rights" did the Equal Protection Clause protect? Section 2 of the Fourteenth Amendment and later the Fifteenth Amendment, ratified in 1870, were designed to guarantee *political* equality to blacks, specifically the right to vote. And it seems clear, given the backdrop of the Civil Rights Act of 1866, that Congress intended the Fourteenth Amendment to guarantee blacks equality in their *civil* rights. It would eliminate the Black Codes and any other laws that specified criminal offenses for blacks only or limited their right to hold property, make contracts, or seek legal justice in the courts.

Beyond these political and civil rights, the original purpose of the Equal Protection Clause remains somewhat uncertain. Was it meant to end discrimination against other racial groups besides blacks? This question was raised by the amendment's language, which protects "any person" rather than black men specifically. Was the amendment meant to guarantee blacks "social" as opposed to "civil" equality? Did it apply to racial segregation or discrimination in education, in transportation facilities, and in privately owned places of public accommodation (i.e., hotels, restaurants, theaters)?

The Supreme Court was left with the task of tackling these difficult issues of constitutional interpretation. At first, its decisions seemed to offer an expansive vision of the ideal of equality protected under the Fourteenth Amendment. In *Strauder* v. *West Virginia* (1880), the Court ruled that state laws that excluded blacks from serving on juries violated the Equal Protection Clause. Justice William Strong wrote:

> The very fact that colored people are singled out and expressly denied by a statute all rights to participate in the administration of the law, as jurors, because of their color, though they are citizens, and may be in other respects fully qualified, is practically a brand upon them, affixed by the law; an assertion of their inferiority, and a stimulant to that race prejudice which is an impediment to securing to individuals of the race that equal justice which the law aims to secure to all others.

Strong further argued that the Fourteenth Amendment itself "speaks in general terms, and those are as comprehensive as possible."

In *Yick Wo* v. *Hopkins* (1886), the Court continued this expansive vision, striking down a law which had been applied in a discriminatory fashion against Orientals. A San Francisco municipal ordinance required special permission to operate a laundry in a building constructed of wood. Of the approximately three hundred laundries made of wood, the municipality granted all but one application for such special permission filed by whites, but had denied all two hundred made by Chinese. Though the law itself did not discriminate, its unequal administration based solely upon racial prejudice violated the Equal Protection Clause. Justice Stanley Matthews, delivering the Court's opinion, wrote:

> Though the law itself be fair on its face and impartial in appearance, yet, if it is applied and administered by public authority with an evil eye and an unequal hand, so as practically to make unjust and illegal discriminations between persons in similar circumstances, material to their rights, the denial of equal justice is still within the prohibition of the Constitution.

So in *Yick Wo* the Court not only applied the dictates of equal protection to Orientals, but also it ruled against the discriminatory implementation of a facially neutral law.

Unfortunately, *Strauder* and *Yick Wo* were, as one author put it, "islands in a sea of judicial indifference to the rights of persons who were not white males." [9] Most of the Court's nineteenth-century equal protection rulings interpreted the demands of equality quite narrowly. The cases that stand out in this early period are the Civil Rights Cases (1883) and *Plessy* v. *Ferguson* (1896).

In the Civil Rights Act of 1875, Congress had asserted its authority to legislate positively on behalf of racial minorities whom the states might not protect from racial discrimination conducted by private individuals. Congress had made it illegal to deny any persons "full and equal enjoyment of the accommodations, advantages, facilities, and privileges of inns, public conveyances on land or water, theaters, and other places of public amusement." Acting under its perceived authority in Section 5 of the Fourteenth Amendment, Congress had moved to prohibit discriminatory actions by private individuals operating services subject to public regulation. In the five companion cases decided together as the Civil Rights Cases, the Supreme Court held the Civil Rights Act of 1875 to be unconstitutional.

Justice Joseph Bradley's opinion focused narrowly upon the exact wording of the Fourteenth Amendment. In response to the amendment's wording that "no State" shall deny equal protection, Justice Bradley wrote, "It is State action of a particular character that is prohibited. Individual invasion of individual rights is not the subject matter of the amendment." Congress was limited under the Fourteenth Amendment to correcting state laws or actions that denied equal protection or discriminated against persons based upon their race. The attempt by Congress to correct private racial discrimination was based upon a misconstruction of the Fourteenth Amendment, Bradley said, and was therefore an invalid exercise of federal power. In rather telling comments near the end of his opinion, Justice Bradley admitted that Congress had authority under the Thirteenth Amendment to abolish "all badges and incidents of slavery," but he denied that the individual discrimination prohibited by the Civil Rights Act constituted a "badge of slavery." Bradley went on to say that legislative aid to newly freed blacks had its limits. There has to be some point, he stated, at which the black man "ceases to be the special favorite of the laws" and takes on "the rank of a mere citizen."

In a lone dissenting opinion, Justice John Harlan, an ex-slave owner from Kentucky, stressed the breadth of congressional authority under the Thirteenth and Fourteenth Amendments. He contended that the subjects legislated by Congress in the Civil Rights Act of 1875 certainly "constitute badges of slavery and servitude" and fell legitimately under federal authority to prohibit. Harlan also felt, unlike the majority, that the racial discrimination legislated against in the act involved private "corporations and individuals in the exercise of *their public or quasi-public functions* [Emphasis added]," and thus could be reached by Congress. Furthermore, he disputed Bradley's contention that the black man was being "favored" by such legislation: "The statute of 1875 . . . is for the benefit of citizens of every race and color." Harlan bitterly concluded that "the substance and spirit of the recent amendments of the Constitution have been sacrificed by a subtle and ingenious verbal criticism."

The historian C. Vann Woodward argued that the Civil Rights Cases were the judicial ratification of the Compromise of 1877, which ended Reconstruction and transferred authority to protect civil rights from federal to state officials.[10] But regardless of how the Court's complicity in the matter of sectional politics is regarded, its decision in the Civil Rights Cases narrowly construed the Fourteenth Amendment. It also removed congressional authority to directly protect the black man's right to equal treatment, as Justice Bradley's opinion left the protection against private discrimination up to the states. This created a vacuum that a resurgent white southern elite would fill, capitalizing upon hostility toward Reconstruction and the newly freed black man to catapult themselves back into power. Once in power, southern legislatures began passing a bevy of "Jim Crow" laws, requiring racial segregation in a number of areas. The Supreme Court was asked to rule on the constitutionality of these Jim Crow laws in *Plessy* v. *Ferguson*.

In 1890, the Louisiana legislature passed a law entitled "An Act to Promote the Comfort of Passengers." It required railroads to "provide equal but separate accommodations for the white and colored races" and made it a criminal offense for any passenger to occupy "a coach or compartment to which by race he does not belong." A group of black citizens in New Orleans organized a committee to test the constitutionality of this Jim Crow law. They arranged for Homer Plessy, a light-complexioned mulatto, to get arrested for refusing to relinquish his seat in the white section of a train leaving New

Orleans. Plessy challenged the law on the grounds that it violated the Fourteenth Amendment. Here the state was enforcing a law that discriminated upon the basis of race.

The Supreme Court upheld Louisiana's separate train-car statute. Justice Henry Brown, speaking for a 7–1 majority, ruled that the Fourteenth Amendment had not been offended by this "Jim Crow" law. He wrote:

> The object of the amendment was undoubtedly to enforce the absolute equality of the two races before the law, but in the nature of things it could not have been intended to abolish distinctions based upon color, or to enforce social, as distinguished from political equality, or a commingling of the two races upon terms unsatisfactory to either.

"Social" inequalities such as those represented in this Jim Crow law were beyond the purview of the Fourteenth Amendment. Justice Brown declared, "If one race be inferior to the other socially, the Constitution of the United States cannot put them upon the same plane." Given this interpretation of the Fourteenth Amendment, the only question the Court had to address was whether the law was a "reasonable regulation." In determining reasonableness, Justice Brown said, the Court must grant legislatures "a large discretion." The legislature must be

> at liberty to act with reference to the established usages, customs, and traditions of the people, and with a view to the promotion of their comfort, and the preservation of the public peace and good order.

"Gauged by this standard," Brown concluded, "we cannot say that a law which authorizes or even requires the separation of the two races in public conveyances is unreasonable." The Court discounted as "fallacy" Plessy's claim that "the enforced separation of the two races stamps the colored race with a badge of inferiority. If this be so, it is not by reason of anything found in the act, but solely because the colored race chooses to put that construction upon it."

Again a lone dissenter, Justice Harlan wrote an opinion that did not convince his peers but would later be referred to by justices in this century. After attacking the notion that racial segregation did not imply any inferiority of blacks, Harlan launched into a ringing defense of racial equality:

> The white race deems itself to be the dominant race in this country. And so it is, in prestige, in achievements, in education, in wealth and in power . . . But in view of the Constitution, in the eye of the law, there is in this country no superior, dominant, ruling class of citizens. There is no caste here. Our Constitution is color-blind, and neither knows nor tolerates classes among citizens. In respect of civil rights, all citizens are equal before the law. The humblest is the peer of the most powerful. The law regards man as man, and takes no account of his surroundings or of his color when his civil rights as guaranteed by the supreme law of the land are involved. It is, therefore, to be regretted that this high tribunal, the final expositor of the fundamental law of the land, has reached the conclusion that it is competent for a State to regulate the enjoyment by citizens of their civil rights solely upon the basis of race.

The Court's decision in *Plessy* rendered state-imposed racial segregation compatible with the demands of equality under the Constitution. With *Plessy* the Court legitimized and encouraged the spread of Jim Crow laws. And what would come to be known as the **separate-but-equal doctrine** was to be the formula the Court used to reconcile a system of state-enforced segregation with the demands of equal protection under the Fourteenth Amendment. It would take fifty-eight years for the Court as a whole to agree with Justice Harlan about the incompatibility of racial segregation and equality under the laws.

Narrowing the Intention of the Framers

What can be said about this early history of Supreme Court interpretation, exemplified by the Civil Rights Cases and *Plessy?* The Court had moved rather quickly to narrowly construe the meaning of the post-Civil War amendments— and the requisite demands of racial equality that they imposed—in three important ways. First of all, the Court distinguished between public and private discrimination. The Court decided that these amendments would only apply to "state action." Only those discriminatory actions "done under state authority" or "sanctioned in some way by the state" could be attacked by the Constitution. The idea that state action was required to trigger the Court's constitutional scrutiny had a negative impact. The states had no positive duty to prevent racial discrimination; they only had to avoid being the direct agents of such discrimination itself.

A second way in which the Court initially limited the scope of the Fourteenth Amendment lay in the criteria it applied to examine legislative classification schemes. The problem, as mentioned in the beginning of this chapter, is that the Equal Protection Clause demands equality under the laws, but all laws classify persons and things, allowing for differential treatment. With the passage of the Fourteenth Amendment, then, the Court had to resolve the demands of equality with the legislative need to classify. In its early rulings, the Court did this by applying **rationality scrutiny** to all state laws. The state would only have to show that the classification drawn in a statute was "reasonable" in light of some legitimate public purpose. "Reasonableness" has usually required that "all persons similarly circumstanced shall be treated alike" (see Brief 9.1). This rationality scrutiny gives the states broad discretion in passing laws that may discriminate or differentiate between people and requires the individual challenging legal classifications to show that they are *unreasonable.* The separate-but-equal doctrine arises out of such rationality scrutiny, with the Court ruling that it was not unreasonable for Louisiana to segregate its train passengers "with a view to the promotion of their comfort." Similarly, the Court in 1883 ruled that an Alabama law prohibiting blacks and whites from marrying was reasonable, especially since it applied evenly to both blacks and whites (thus treating similarly situated people similarly).[11]

The third way in which the Court narrowly interpreted the Fourteenth Amendment was by requiring a showing of "purposeful discrimination" in order to act. In these early rulings, the Court would only invoke the Equal Protection Clause if there was proof of a racially discriminatory purpose on the part of the state. This discrimination could appear either on the face of the law itself, as in the *Strauder* case, or in the administration of the law, as in *Yick Wo.* Nevertheless, a finding of purposeful discrimination was necessary, as the Court's ruling in *Virginia* v. *Rives* (1880) shows. Decided at the same time as *Strauder,* the Court sanctioned Virginia's exclusion of blacks from

---

☐ Brief 9.1   Rationality Scrutiny Defined

Two early-twentieth-century cases set out the standards of rationality review used by the Supreme Court in Fourteenth Amendment cases. The general formulation of rationality scrutiny is found in *F.S. Royster Guano Co.* v. *Virginia* (1920): "[The government's] classification must be reasonable, not arbitrary, and must rest upon some ground of difference having a fair and substantial relation to the object of the legislation, so that all persons similarly circumstanced shall be treated alike." A more specific rendering of this standard occurs in *Lindsley* v. *Natural Carbonic Gas Co.* (1911):

1. The equal protection clause of the Fourteenth Amendment does not take from the State the power to classify in the adoption of police laws, but admits of the exercise of a wide scope of discretion in that regard, and avoids what is done only when it is without any reasonable basis and therefore is purely arbitrary.
2. A classification having some reasonable basis does not offend against that clause merely because it is not made with mathematical nicety or because in practice it results in some inequality.
3. When the classification in such a law is called into question, if any state of facts reasonably can be conceived that would sustain it, the existence of that state of facts at the time the law was enacted must be assumed.
4. One who assails the classification in such a law must carry the burden of showing that it does not rest upon any reasonable basis, but is essentially arbitrary.

---

juries because blacks could not prove a purposeful or systematic racial exclusion by the state of Virginia. The importance of this requirement will also be seen in more recent rulings discussed later in this chapter.

Toward Color Blindness: The Struggle for Racial Equality

By the turn of the century, then, the justices of the Supreme Court had abandoned the intention of the post-Civil War amendments' framers. They had denied congressional authority to legislate positively on behalf of blacks facing racial discrimination. They had refused to apply the ideal of equality to a number of areas, including racial segregation in public facilities and in education.[12] The majority of the justices had rejected the expansive view of the Fourteenth Amendment proclaimed by the Reconstruction Congress and by one of their colleagues. But Justice Harlan's vision would eventually triumph. In 1910, the National Association for the Advancement of Colored People, (NAACP), a civil rights organization dedicated to achieving equal justice for blacks was formed. Fueled by the NAACP's legal and political action, the courts slowly began to bring the promise of racial equality to fruition. The chapter now looks at the gradual process of achieving desegregation and racial justice in this century. The coverage will be organized by area, beginning with racial discrimination in housing.

Racial Discrimination in Housing

As mentioned earlier in this chapter, the Equal Protection Clause was clearly meant to cover equal rights in the buying and selling of property. Congressional intent was made manifest by the Civil Rights Act of 1866, which granted racial minorities "the same right in every state and territory as is enjoyed by white citizens thereof to inherit, purchase, lease, sell, hold and convey real and personal property." However, bolstered by the separate-but-equal ruling in *Plessy*, some cities began passing ordinances requiring geographic segregation of the races. Baltimore apparently began this process in 1910, followed by more than a dozen other cities. In Louisville, the city council passed a municipal ordinance in 1914 that provided for "separate blocks for residence, places of abode, and places of assembly by white and colored people respectively." The ordinance prohibited blacks from moving into neighborhoods where whites constituted the majority, and vice versa. Louisville's leaders believed the statute met the demands of the Fourteenth Amendment, since it imposed the same restrictions equally upon both races. But in 1917 the Supreme Court, in *Buchanan* v. *Warley,* invalidated the ordinance as an unconstitutional interference with property owners' rights to dispose of real estate as they saw fit. Later rulings confirmed this opinion, so that by 1930 the Court had firmly established the illegitimacy of municipal segregation laws.

Restrictive Covenants

This did not stop segregation in housing, however. Property owners wishing to prevent blacks from buying property in their neighborhoods used the device known as the **restrictive covenant** to continue racial segregation. Restrictive covenants are agreements entered into by property owners binding themselves not to sell or lease their property to blacks and other racial or ethnic minorities. Because these covenants resulted from actions by private individuals as opposed to state action, this method of residential segregation at first succeeded in meeting equal protection challenges.[13] The Federal Housing Administration even drew up a "model" racially restrictive covenant of the type approved by the Supreme Court for use in housing projects the federal government underwrote.

In 1948, the Supreme Court reconsidered its position regarding restrictive convenants in the case of *Shelley* v. *Kraemer*. The J. D. Shelleys, a black family, purchased a house from Josephine Fitzgerald in a St. Louis neighborhood covered by a racially restrictive covenant. The agreement, in force since 1911, bound property owners in the area from selling their property to "people of the Negro or Mongolian race" for fifty years. Louis Kraemer, a resident of the neighborhood with a similar racial restriction in his deed, sued to stop the Shelleys from taking possession of the property. The Missouri State Supreme Court eventually granted Kraemer's request and the Shelleys were ordered to vacate their newly purchased home. J. D. Shelley appealed to the U.S. Supreme Court, who heard his case along with a similar one coming from Michigan.

In a unanimous decision, the Court began by reiterating its earlier position that "restrictive agreements standing alone cannot be regarded as violative of any rights guaranteed . . . by the Fourteenth Amendment." But the case involved more than just a racially restrictive covenant "standing alone." The state courts had aided private discrimination by enforcing "the restrictive terms of the agreements." The Court decided that such judicial enforcement amounted to state action in violation of the Equal Protection Clause:

> We have no doubt that there has been state action in these cases in the full and complete sense of the phrase. The undisputed facts disclose that petitioners were willing purchasers of properties upon which they desired to establish homes. The owners of the properties were willing sellers; and contracts of sale were accordingly consummated. It is clear that but for the active intervention of the state courts, supported by the full panoply of state power, petitioners would have been free to occupy the properties in question without restraint.

The fact that the state courts were enforcing a purely private agreement did not matter: "It is still the judicial branch of the state government carrying out the discrimination . . . [and] state action, as that phrase is understood for the purposes of the Fourteenth Amendment, refers to exertions of the state power in all forms."

The Supreme Court's decision in *Shelley* v. *Kraemer* left restrictive covenants constitutional, but unenforceable. Five years later, in *Barrows* v. *Jackson* (1953), the Court extended its position to include civil suits brought by property owners in a restricted neighborhood to gain damages from another owner who sold his property to a black in violation of the restrictive covenant. The Supreme Court said that a California court's order to a property owner to pay damages for failing to observe a racially restrictive covenant was also a form of state action violative of the Constitution.

The *Shelley* decision not only opened up residential neighborhoods to blacks and other minorities, but also it signaled a shift in the Court's interpretation of the state-action requirement. In *Shelley* (as well as in *Smith* v. *Allright* decided four years before—to be discussed in a later section of this chapter), the Court indicated that it would take a more expansive view of the kind of state action it would consider violative of the Equal Protection Clause. As will be shown later, however, the Court has moved in recent years to read *Shelley* more narrowly.

Open-Housing Legislation

The *Shelley* decision may have aided blacks in their quest for fairness in buying and selling property, but the housing problem continued. As black populations in the cities increased, whites fled to the suburbs to make their homes. There, through private agreements and "understandings" (often tacitly involving realtors and local officials), these suburban residents sought to keep their communities white. Nevertheless, blacks fought for and won open-housing legislation prohibiting racial discrimination in the sale or rental of housing in numerous states and cities.

In California, white homeowners revolted against state laws prohibiting such discrimination. Exercising their initiative power, California voters passed a state constitutional amendment in 1964 providing that the state could not deny the right of any person "to sell, lease or rent any part or all of his real property to such persons as he, in his absolute discretion, chooses." Known as Proposition 14, this amendment in effect repealed state laws providing for fair housing. In *Reitman* v. *Mulkey* (1967), the Supreme Court ruled Proposition 14 to be a form of state action violating the Fourteenth Amendment. Justice Byron White wrote for the majority that in adopting the amendment approved by the voters, California had made the right to discriminate "one of the basic policies of the state." Passage of the amendment "embodied [racial discrimination] in the state's basic charter, immune from legislative, executive, or judicial regulation at any level of the state government." The state was thus involved in *encouraging* "private discriminations," something the Court could not allow under the Fourteenth Amendment. Here the concept of state action was extended to include potential state "encouragement" or "authorization" of racial discrimination.

A year later Congress for the first time passed a federal act containing wide-ranging open-housing provisions. The Civil Rights Act of 1968, passed following the assassination of Martin Luther King, Jr., prohibited all racial and religious discrimination in the sale or rental of housing. And a few weeks later the Supreme Court, in *Jones* v. *Alfred H. Mayer Co.* (1968), ruled that private discrimination in the sale or rental of housing was also prohibited by the Civil Rights Act of 1866 (see Brief 9.2). Open housing may not be fully realized today, but much progress has been made as a result of federal and state legislation beginning in the 1960s.

Racial Discrimination in Education

Educational segregation presented a much more difficult problem. A judicial precedent supporting racially segregated schools in Massachusetts was set almost twenty years before the passage of the Fourteenth Amendment. In the District of Columbia, separate schools were established for blacks as they were freed during the Civil War, and Congress beginning in 1864 gave legal authorization for racially segregated public education in the nation's capital. By the time the Court announced the separate-but-equal doctrine in the *Plessy* decision in 1896, thirty states had some type of separate-but-equal public-school law in force. In fact, the existence of racially segregated schools in Boston as well as the southern states made up an important part of the Court's rationale in the *Plessy* decision.

In the years following *Plessy*, the Court consolidated its position favoring segregated schools. In *Cumming* v. *Richmond County Board of Education* (1899), the Court allowed the school board to close down the only public high school for blacks while still maintaining the white high schools. Black

---

☐ *Brief 9.2 Congressional Authority Under the Thirteenth Amendment: The Jones Case and Beyond*

Jones v. *Alfred H. Mayer Co.* (1968) was a landmark Supreme Court decision. As mentioned earlier in this chapter, Congress passed the Civil Rights Act of 1866, under its Thirteenth Amendment authority to eliminate the "badges of servitude." In this act, Congress prohibited racial discrimination in a number of areas, including buying, selling, or renting property. But the Supreme Court, in the Civil Rights Cases (1883), seemed to narrow the applicability of Congress's legislative authority over *private* discriminatory action.

The *Jones* case involved the Mayer Company's refusal to sell Joseph Lee Jones, a black man, a home near St. Louis. Jones filed suit under the 1866 law, and the question was whether congressional authority extended to this kind of private, as opposed to public, racial discrimination. Justice Potter Stewart, for the majority, ruled that the Thirteenth Amendment conferred broad authority upon Congress "to eliminate all racial barriers to the acquisition of real and personal property." Thus, the Court had in effect overruled the decision in the Civil Rights Cases and reopened the possibility of litigation under the somewhat dormant 1866 statute. Moreover, the Court's decision opened the door for future Congresses to deal broadly with private acts of racial discrimination under Section 2 of the Thirteenth Amendment. Since *Jones,* the Court has allowed a number of legal actions to be taken to prevent private racial discrimination under the Civil Rights Act of 1866. For example, in *Runyon* v. *McCrary* (1976), a seven-justice majority decided that blacks could use the 1866 Civil Rights Act to sue privately owned, nonsectarian schools that discriminated against them. Most recently, the Court has even held that Jews, Arabs, and other ethnic groups racially regarded as Caucasians could sue under the provisions of the 1866 law.[14] The *Jones* legacy demonstrates two things: (1) that congressional authority under the Constitution is often broader than that of the Court's; and (2) that constitutional interpretation sometimes involves the Court's going far back into history to retrieve a previously dormant law or precedent.

taxpayers went to court to get an injunction against operating the white high schools until their black children were provided with equal facilities, a position they thought followed from *Plessy*. But writing for a unanimous Court, Justice Harlan avoided the question of segregation, merely stating that public education was "a matter belonging to the respective states" and that closing the white schools would not help the black children.

In 1908, the Court went even farther, allowing the state of Kentucky to outlaw racially integrated instruction in private colleges operating under state charters of incorporation. With the Court's ruling in *Berea College* v. *Kentucky,* a private college that had been integrated since its founding in 1859 was brought under a state law requiring it to separate the races for purposes of instruction.

Finally, in *Gong Lum* v. *Rice* (1927), the Supreme Court indirectly upheld educational segregation. The case involved a Chinese girl who was required to attend a black school under Mississippi school segregation provisions. While the Court was not directly asked to rule on the legality of segregated public schools, Chief Justice William Howard Taft nevertheless took the opportunity to offer his opinion on past Court "precedents" regarding school segregation:

> Were this a new question, it would call for very full argument and consideration, but we think it is the same question which has been many times decided to be within the constitutional power of the state legislature to settle without "intervention of the federal courts under the Federal Constitution" . . . The right and power of the state to regulate the method of providing for the education of its youth at public expense is clear.

So, without directly ruling on the issue of racial segregation in education, the Court had nonetheless sanctioned this widespread practice on three separate occasions. The problem for the Supreme Court was that even the *Plessy* doctrine required *equality* within a segregated system. By the 1920s, the southern states were spending between five and ten times as much money on the education of white children as they were spending on blacks. The actual condition of separate-but-equal schools was not lost on the NAACP.

School Desegregation Under the Separate-But-Equal Doctrine: *Sweatt* v. *Painter* (1950)

By the 1930s, the NAACP had risen to a place of prominence in the eyes of blacks and sympathetic whites. Armed with the Margold Report, a study it had commissioned in 1931 detailing the actual inequalities in segregated school systems, the NAACP established the Legal Defense and Education Fund, out of which it would bring legal actions to end educational segregation. With Thurgood Marshall at the helm, the Legal Defense Fund started its efforts by working to desegregate education at the graduate and professional school level. At the time, blacks were denied any access to public graduate schools in many southern states. The NAACP determined that faced with a court order, segregationist states would not be able to afford separate-but-equal graduate facilities. They would be forced to break down and admit qualified blacks to previously all-white state university law and graduate schools. This early litigation strategy focused upon the *equality* of separate-but-equal education. The NAACP was not yet ready to attack segregated education head on.

The strategy worked. After some early victories primarily involving state university professional schools,[15] the NAACP won perhaps the most important of these early decisions from the Supreme Court in *Sweatt* v. *Painter* (1950).

Herman Marian Sweatt, a black mailman from Houston, applied to the University of Texas Law School in 1946. He was rejected on racial grounds, the university being restricted by the state legislature to whites only. Sweatt sued for admission, and the district court ordered the state either to establish a black law school within six months or admit Sweatt to the white law school in Austin. Almost overnight, the state set up a Negro law school in a downtown office building. Sporting three basement rooms, three part-time faculty members, and a 10,000-volume library, the new law school invited Sweatt to attend. Instead, he went back to the district court. This time the court ruled against Sweatt, saying that the new Negro law school offered him "privileges, advantages, and opportunities for the study of law substantially equivalent to those offered by the State to white students at the University of Texas." He appealed to the U.S. Supreme Court, backed by the NAACP and Thurgood Marshall.

The Supreme Court unanimously ordered Sweatt's admission to the University of Texas as a requirement of the Equal Protection Clause. Chief Justice Fred M. Vinson, writing for the Court, declared, "We cannot find substantial equality in the educational opportunities offered white and Negro law students by the state." Vinson compared the two schools' faculty, administration, alumni, library, reputation, traditions, and prestige. "It is difficult to believe," he said, "that one who had a free choice between these law schools would consider the question close." Vinson went on to argue that to separate Sweatt from educational contact with whites, who made up 85 percent of the state's population and almost all of its lawyers, judges, and other legal officials, was to deny him equality in his legal education.

Sweatt v. *Painter* was a tremendous victory for blacks, as it was the first time the Court had ordered a black student admitted to a previously all-white school even though a separate black school was in place. But though seeming to suggest that segregation in education was inherently unequal, the Supreme Court refused to reexamine the *Plessy* doctrine. The Court's decision in *Sweatt* stuck to the standards of the separate-but-equal doctrine, focusing upon the inequalities between the separate law school facilities in Texas as the basis for its decision.

Nevertheless, *Sweatt* was a landmark case. The Court had begun to reinterpret the separate-but-equal doctrine by looking at the inequality of segregated educational facilities and, in so doing, had considered intangible factors (e.g., the future importance of Sweatt's educational contact with whites in law school) as well as physical resources. The implications of the decision were clear. In fact, many segregated school systems began pumping money into their black primary and secondary schools to head off a future challenge like the one in *Sweatt*. Meanwhile, buoyed by victories in *Sweatt* and other Supreme Court cases, the NAACP decided to press school desegregation to the limits. Suits were brought in five public school districts across the country to gain admission for black children into the white primary and secondary schools. The NAACP was challenging the constitutionality of segregation itself, asking the courts to overturn the long-standing separate-but-equal doctrine.

Brown v. *Board of Education* (1954) and the End of Segregation in Education

The five school segregation cases that made their way to the Supreme Court in 1952 originated in Clarendon County, South Carolina; Topeka, Kansas; Prince Edward County, Virginia; Claymont, Delaware; and Washington, D.C. The NAACP filed suits in the name of local black children demanding their admission to the white public schools. Their claim was not only that the black schools were inferior to the white schools (the *Sweatt* argument), but also that educational segregation itself violated the Equal Protection Clause of the Fourteenth Amendment (or, in the Washington, D.C., case, the Due Process Clause of the Fifth Amendment). To support their claims, the NAACP presented current psychological and sociological findings about the negative impact of segregated schools upon black children. In their defense, the segregated school districts invoked *Plessy* and either claimed that the black schools and white schools were equal or promised to immediately bring the black schools up to a state of equality. In all five cases, U.S. district courts continued to rely upon the separate-but-equal doctrine; all five were appealed to the Supreme Court.

The Supreme Court heard arguments in the school segregation cases in December 1952. After a six-month silence, the Court set the cases for reargument in the fall of 1953 and asked both sides to prepare answers to a set of historical and practical questions. Among other things, the Court was interested in hearing evidence about the original intention of the Fourteenth Amendment's framers and ratifiers. Did the Congress which drafted and the state legislatures which ratified the Fourteenth Amendment "understand that it would abolish segregation in public schools"? If not, did they nevertheless understand that either future Congresses or the judiciary would "construe the amendment as abolishing such segregation"?

Answers to these questions were presented to the Supreme Court in December 1953. After six months of discussion, deliberation, and even coalition-building, the recently appointed Chief Justice Earl Warren announced the Court's unanimous opinion on May 17, 1954. In the case of *Brown* v. *Board of Education of Topeka,* the Court declared segregated public schools to be a violation of the Constitution. Chief Justice Warren's opinion was brief, a mere thirteen paragraphs. And after all the arguments presented concerning the intention of those who framed and ratified the Fourteenth Amendment, Warren decided that the historical arguments were inconclusive: "[What] Congress and the state legislatures had in mind cannot be determined with any degree of certainty." The Court had actually declared the historical question to be irrelevant. Warren wrote:

> We cannot turn the clock back to 1868 when the [Fourteenth] Amendment was adopted, or even to 1896 when *Plessy* v. *Ferguson* was written. We must consider public education in the light of its full development and its present place in American life throughout the Nation.

The Court ultimately made its decision about the basic inequality of segregated schools based upon the sociological and psychological evidence. Warren agreed with the NAACP position that to separate blacks "from others of similar age and qualifications solely because of their race generates a feeling of inferiority as to their status in the community that may affect their hearts and minds in a way unlikely ever to be undone." Citing the lower court's finding in the *Topeka* case, Warren stated:

Segregation of white and colored children in public schools has a detrimental effect upon the colored children. The impact is greater when it has the sanction of the law; for the policy of separating the races is usually interpreted as denoting the inferiority of the negro group. A sense of inferiority affects the motivation of a child to learn. Segregation with the sanction of law, therefore, has a tendency to [retard] the educational and mental development of negro children and to deprive them of some of the benefits they would receive in a racial[ly] integrated school system.

The Court concluded that "in the field of public education the doctrine of 'separate but equal' has no place. Separate educational facilities are inherently unequal." With this short stroke of its collective pen, the Supreme Court had voided fifty-eight years of constitutional precedent and over one hundred years of educational practice. And in *Bolling* v. *Sharpe,* the companion case arising out of the District of Columbia, the Court made a similar conclusion regarding the incompatibility of segregation and the Fifth Amendment. Warren wrote that the liberty protected by the Due Process Clause

extends to the full range of conduct which the individual is free to pursue and it cannot be restricted except for a proper governmental objective. Segregation in public education is not reasonably related to any proper governmental objective, and thus it imposes on Negro children of the District of Columbia a burden that constitutes an arbitrary deprivation of their liberty in violation of the Due Process Clause.

The court determined that racial segregation in education was unconstitutional; however, it postponed ruling upon the question of how to implement school desegregation. After hearing arguments from a number of different parties the next year,[16] the Court in what is called *Brown II* outlined its plan of action. Chief Justice Warren announced that the Court would send each case back to the district courts where it had originated, leaving it up to them to fashion decrees enforcing the Court's desegregation ruling. These lower courts would be guided by "constitutional principles" (the black children's right to be admitted to public schools on a nondiscriminatory basis), but they would be allowed to consider the local school's problems and situations in deciding how rapidly and in what manner desegregation would proceed. The justices of the Supreme Court recognized that some flexibility might be required to ensure that school desegregation took place in an effective and peaceful manner. But they wanted the lower courts to oversee the implementation of the *Brown* decision to make sure that black children were being admitted "to public schools on a nondiscriminatory basis *with all deliberate speed* [Emphasis added]." The justices hoped that their delicate blend of principle and practicality in *Brown II* would solve the problems they expected their desegregation decision would create.

Enforcing and Implementing the *Brown* Decision

The Court's decision in *Brown II* initiated the nationwide process of school desegregation. The process has been arduous in many instances, in large part because of resistance to the Court's ruling. Having no real enforcement mechanisms of its own, the Supreme Court had to rely upon its own prestige and help from other branches of government to enforce its desegregation decision. No such aid came from the other branches of the federal government. In fact, as Chapter 6 mentioned, 96 Congressmen from the eleven former Confederate states signed a southern manifesto, which called the *Brown* decision "a clear abuse of judicial power" and "commend[ed] . . . those States which have declared the intention to resist forced integration by any lawful means." In addition, President Dwight Eisenhower seemed reticent to organize executive branch support for the desegregation ruling. While he eventually sent federal troops to Little Rock, Arkansas, to ensure the peaceful carrying out of the court-ordered desegregation of Central High School, he maintained that "it is difficult through law and through force to change a man's heart." [17] The Supreme Court itself held off from ruling on the implementation of *Brown* for a number of years.

A campaign of massive resistance to the *Brown* decision was launched throughout the South. Eight state legislatures (Alabama, Arkansas, Florida, Georgia, Louisiana, Mississippi, South Carolina, and Virginia) passed resolutions that formally nullified the *Brown* decision and adopted laws that frustrated efforts to achieve integration. School districts either dragged their feet or drew up plans that did little to effect dramatic changes in the racial composition of the schools. Many federal district judges were unsympathetic to the *Brown* decision and delayed the process even further. Where school districts were unwilling to desegregate voluntarily, local citizens would have to incur the financial and even physical risks of bringing a lawsuit to have the schools desegregated. And where legal attempts to resist integration failed, white resisters resorted to violence in places like Clinton, Tennessee, Little Rock, and New Orleans.

The case of Little Rock is particularly instructive, as it drives home the point that the Supreme Court cannot enforce its own decisions, especially when, as in school desegregation, it takes the lead on an issue rather than responding to majority opinion. The Little Rock School Board, in its effort to comply with the *Brown* ruling, devised a plan in 1955 to completely desegregate the city's schools by 1963. As the first stage of this plan, nine black students were admitted to previously all-white Central High School for the fall of 1957. On the day before the black students were to attend their first class, Arkansas Governor Orval Faubus dispatched national guard units to Central High to prevent the black students from attending. This and other obstructive action by the state government energized local citizen opposition to integration. The combined citizen and state resistance made it impossible to carry out the first stage of the school board's plan until President Eisenhower sent federal troops on September 23.

In light of all the disruption caused at Central High, the Little Rock School Board petitioned the federal courts for a 2½-year suspension of their desegregation program to allow things to calm down. The Supreme Court, in *Cooper* v. *Aaron* (1958), rejected the school board's application and blamed hostile conditions in Little Rock on the failure of state officials to do their duty in enforcing the law. Quoting Chief Justice John Marshall's opinion in *United States* v. *Peters* (1809), the Court's *per curiam* opinion declared:

> If the legislatures of the several states may, at will, annul the judgments of the courts of the United States, and destroy the rights acquired under those judgments, the Constitution itself becomes a solemn mockery.

Although the justices admitted that they were powerless to enforce their judgments, they warned government officials about the serious implications of noncompliance: "No state legislator or executive or judicial officer can war against the Constitution without violating his undertaking to support it."

The Supreme Court's opinion in *Cooper* v. *Aaron,* however forceful, did not stop the regionwide fight against desegregation. So much legal and extralegal resistance occurred that by 1965, ten years after the *Brown* rulings, only 2 percent of black students in the eleven former Confederate states were enrolled in previously all-white schools.

The Supreme Court decided to step back into the legal fray more forcefully in 1964. The big legal question it now had to answer was this: did the *Brown* ruling merely mean that school districts would have to stop using discriminatory practices in administering the schools, or did *Brown* impose upon them a positive duty to achieve racial integration? During the 1960s the Court answered this question in a series of cases involving southern attempts to avoid true compliance with *Brown.*

Virginia had led the fight against school desegregation. In its brief submitted to the Court prior to *Brown II,* Virginia had declared that it was "unalterably opposed to the operation of nonsegregated public schools in the Commonwealth of Virginia," and that it would use "its power, authority and efforts to insure a continuation of a segregated school system." Prince Edward County, one of the five original *Brown* defendants, closed the public schools rather than comply with the Court's ruling. The county reasoned that it had no constitutional obligation to operate a public school system. Instead, it substituted a tax-credit plan combined with a state tuition-grant program that gave whites segregated private education and deprived blacks of education altogether. In *Griffin* v. *County School Board of Prince Edward County* (1964), the Supreme Court ruled that the county had acted with a discriminatory intent, in effect ordering the public schools reopened on an integrated basis that fall.

A more commonplace response to the *Brown* decision was for school districts to employ "freedom-of-choice" plans. Freedom-of-choice plans allowed children in a school district to attend the school of their choice. The district would no longer discriminate on the basis of race and would exert no pressure on children's choices. However, as a method of achieving desegregation, freedom-of-choice plans were inadequate because they depended upon blacks and whites to voluntarily integrate. Freedom-of-choice plans were widely adopted by school districts wishing to remain eligible for federal aid (the federal government had stipulated that school districts practicing racial discrimination could not receive federal funds) and yet retain basically segregated school systems. In *Green* v. *County School Board of New Kent County* (1968), the Court invalidated freedom-of-choice plans.

The *Green* case concerned a small school district in Virginia. After three years under a freedom-of-choice plan, no white child had chosen to attend former black schools, while 85 percent of the black children remained in all-black schools. Though no intent to discriminate on the part of the school district could be found, the Court decided that freedom-of-choice plans were inadequate methods of compliance with the *Brown* decision. Justice William Brennan's opinion stated that the goal of *Brown* was the achievement of "a unitary, nonracial system of public education . . . in which racial discrimination would be eliminated root and branch." Since freedom-of-choice plans effectively failed to achieve this goal, school districts would have to do more. The time for "all deliberate speed" had ended. One year later in *Alexander* v. *Holmes County Board of Education* (1969), the Court made this clear, announcing that "allowing 'all deliberate speed' for desegregation is no longer constitutionally permissible . . . every school district is to terminate dual school systems at once and to operate now and hereafter only unitary schools."

Combined with federal funding pressures, the Court's rulings against attempts to get around the *Brown* decision had a dramatic effect. In rural and small town school districts integration proceeded quickly. By 1970, 30 percent of black children attended at least somewhat integrated schools. Remaining problems existed in large metropolitan areas with a substantial amount of residential segregation, where nonracial attendance zoning of a unitary school system was not enough to break racial segregation. The Court began to tackle this problem in 1971.

The Positive Duty to Desegregate and Court-Ordered Busing

In a series of decisions in the 1960s, then, the Court ruled that school districts had a positive duty to integrate their previously segregated schools.[18] And in the *Green* case the Court suggested that it would look at the *effects* of desegregation plans to see if the "transition to unitary schools" was proceeding adequately. The justices would apply this logic to a large southern metropolitan school district in *Swann* v. *Charlotte-Mecklenburg Board of Education* (1971).

The Charlotte, North Carolina, metropolitan area (whose black student population was approximately 30 percent) had been operating for several years under court-approved desegregation plans that brought about half the black students into formerly white schools. The rest remained in all-black schools. After the *Green* decision, the district court judge overseeing desegregation in Charlotte ordered a new plan that would achieve more complete racial integration. Because of extensive residential segregation, the new plan called for the "pairing" of outlying white schools with inner-city black schools, with busing in both directions as the means to accomplish school integration. The Supreme Court was asked to rule upon the constitutional appropriateness of this new plan.

Chief Justice Warren Burger began his decision for a unanimous Court by stressing the breadth of the federal courts' authority "to remedy past wrongs" in light of the *Brown* decision. But Burger admitted that such judicial authority can only extend to cases where there has been a "constitutional violation." Given the state-action and purposeful-discrimination requirements to trigger the Equal Protection Clause, Burger contended that federal courts could only act upon a showing of *de jure* segregation, that is, segregation that is positively sanctioned by the state. But what beyond intentionally discriminatory school district policies could be considered by federal judges in reaching a verdict about the presence of *de jure* segregation? Burger announced that among other methods, judges could point to the presence of predominantly one-race schools in a system with a history of racial segregation (as in the Charlotte school district) as evidence of a constitutional violation that would need to be remedied. In such an instance, Burger wrote, "The burden upon the school authorities will be to satisfy the court that their racial composition is not the result of present or past discriminatory action on their part."

Once a constitutional violation is found, courts can order plans like the one in Charlotte that grouped noncontiguous school zones to achieve better integration. The concept of the neighborhood school would have to be sacrificed to the demands of racial equality:

> All things being equal, with no history of discrimination, it might well be desirable to assign pupils to schools nearest their homes. But all things are not equal in a system that has been deliberately constructed and maintained to enforce racial segregation.

For Burger and the Court, this meant that busing, as ordered in this case, was certainly an appropriate means to achieve racial integration. "Desegregation plans cannot be limited to the walk-in school," asserted the Court. Busing had previously been used by authorities to maintain racially separate schools; now the bus could be part of a plan to desegregate them.

The only limitation the Court imposed upon court-ordered remedies for segregated schools was that there be a finding of *de jure* segregation. This limitation had resulted in a distinction between *de jure* segregation, which had to be remedied, and *de facto* segregation (resulting not from legally imposed segregation, but usually from a combination of residential segregation and neighborhood schools), which did not require court-imposed remedies. After *Swann*, the *de jure/de facto* distinction meant that most southern school systems would have the affirmative duty to achieve complete integration, given past policies of school segregation, while most northern and western school systems, which were just as segregated, would be left alone. By the 1970s it was the large northern and western metropolitan areas that had the biggest problem with segregated public schools. According to a 1971 estimate by the Department of Health, Education, and Welfare (HEW), 44 percent of blacks in the South attended majority white schools as opposed to only 28 percent in the North and West; 57 percent of all black students in the North and West attended primarily minority schools, as opposed to only 32 percent who did so in the South. Beginning two years after the *Swann* decision, the Court was confronted with *de facto* segregation in northern and western city school districts.

In 1973, the Court agreed to hear a case from Denver, where segregated schools existed, but not as a result of past or present laws. In *Keyes* v. *School District No. 1, Denver, Colorado* (1973), the Court dodged the question of whether *de facto* segregation was also unconstitutional and should be remedied. The Court found that Denver school authorities had supported *de facto* segregation in their official policies, which amounted to *de jure* segregation even in the absence of school segregation laws. By showing that such school district policies involved a "purpose or intent to segregate," the Court was able to uphold the same kinds of remedial actions, including massive intra-district busing, that had been approved in Charlotte.

In *Milliken* v. *Bradley* (1974), the Court was not able to sidestep the question of the constitutionality of *de facto* segregation. At issue was a desegregation plan ordered for the Detroit metropolitan area. The area comprised the city school district (75 percent black) and a number of separate school districts for the suburban communities (predominantly white) surrounding Detroit. After finding that the Detroit school system had been guilty of official actions that constituted *de jure* segregation, a federal judge decided that a Detroit-only plan would be ineffective in achieving desegregation. He combined the Detroit school district with fifty-three surrounding suburban school districts to create a "desegregation area" and ordered "an effective desegregation plan" for the entire area.

By a slim majority, the Supreme Court reversed the lower court order, ruling that the scope of the remedy was not required by the extent of constitutional violations. The Court could find no evidence of *de jure* segregation on the part of the outlying suburban school districts. The suburban districts did not discriminate in their enrollment practices, and there were no claims that district lines had been drawn to foster segregation. The situation was a matter of *de facto* segregation. For the district court to order such an intervention into the policies of the various school districts, the Court argued, violated deeply rooted traditions of local control over education. Chief Justice Burger's majority opinion concluded that such judicial intervention is unwarranted without evidence of *de jure* segregation: "Without an inter-district violation and inter-district effect, there is no constitutional wrong calling for an inter-district remedy."

In a bitter dissent, Justice Thurgood Marshall called the *Milliken* decision "a giant step backwards" in the process of guaranteeing minority children an equal educational opportunity. Marshall concluded that the Court's ruling "is more a reflection of a perceived public mood that we have gone far enough in enforcing the Constitution's guarantee of equal justice than it is the product of neutral principles of law." Justice White also dissented, claiming that the state had "successfully insulated itself from its duty to provide effective desegregation remedies" because of the Court's "arbitrary rule that remedies for constitutional violations occurring in a single Michigan school district must stop at the school district line."

With the *Milliken* case, then, the Supreme Court continued to distinguish between *de jure* and *de facto* segregation. The justices maintained the distinction between purposeful discrimination in the arrangement of school systems, which is constitutionally wrong, and mere "adventitious" or "accidental" segregation, which is constitutionally permissible. This judicial requirement of deliberate discrimination has had the effect of leaving most schools in the nation's metropolitan areas racially segregated, even after massive court-ordered busing plans.

Justice Lewis Powell launched the most thoroughgoing attack on the *de jure/de facto* distinction. In his concurring opinion in the Denver case, Powell argued that the Court should abandon what had come to be a somewhat arbitrary and harmful *legal distinction*. He contended that the situation in Denver was typical of a nationwide pattern of segregated schools in large metropolitan areas. The pattern was the same in northern cities as well as in southern ones, regardless of whether past segregation laws existed or not. The tragedy, Powell argued, was that the Court's *de jure/de facto* distinction prevented any progress from being made in desegregating non-southern city schools. If the concern in *Brown* rested largely upon the impact of segregated schools upon minority children, then all segregated school systems ought to be remedied. And Powell rightly acknowledged that after the *Swann* and *Keyes* decisions, the distinction between *de jure* and *de facto,* between purpose and effect, had been rendered largely artificial. Powell concluded, "If our national concern is for those who attend such [segregated] schools, rather than for perpetuating a legalism rooted in history rather than in present reality, we must recognize that the evil of operating separate schools is no less in Denver [or as in *Milliken,* Detroit] than in Atlanta."

Powell's remedy was to abandon the *de jure/de facto* distinction in favor of a uniform national rule that would require all local school boards to "operate *integrated school systems* within their respective districts." In Powell's mind, this did not mean that every school across the country would be integrated according to a rigid racial ratio—in fact, in *Keyes* he stated that "an integrated school system does not mean . . . that *every school* must in fact be an integrated unit." What Powell argued for was an approach to equal protection that would balance the constitutional demands for desegregation against the equally legitimate concerns of local communities over "disruptive compulsory transportation." School districts could thus be given some flexibility in fashioning integrated systems responding to local demographics and concerns, rather than being forced to accept one method—busing—in response to a finding of *de jure* segregation.

But Powell's remedy has not been taken up by the Supreme Court as a whole. Court-ordered desegregation and busing continue to pose constitutional as well as political problems (see Brief 9.3). The *de jure/de facto* distinction remains in place today. This distinction raises a number of questions. For instance, going back to the *Brown* decision, if the Court's purpose in 1954 was to grant equal educational opportunities that it felt were lost as a result of school segregation, then doesn't *de facto* segregation cause the same constitutional problems as *de jure* segregation? In making this distinction, has the Court abandoned the original purposes announced in *Brown?* Can meaningful judicial distinctions be made between discriminatory intent and impact? And if there is no real distinction between *de jure* and *de facto* segregation, does that force the Court to make results-oriented rulings as opposed to procedural ones? Perhaps most important, can the Supreme Court truly address a problem—school segregation—that is more deep-seated than legal decrees can change? If, as has been argued, persistent segregation is more the result of socioeconomic factors and residual racism than it is the result of current legally sanctioned discrimination, then can the courts constitutionally mandate the desired outcome? These are difficult questions, ones that will be raised again in the discussion of affirmative action in the next chapter.

Racial Discrimination in Public Accommodations: The *Brown* Principle Extended

Following the *Brown* decision, the Supreme Court has extended the logic of equal protection to areas besides education and housing, including public accommodations. For example, the Court used the Fourteenth Amendment to outlaw racial segregation in public parks and recreation facilities, on municipal golf courses, on city buses, in public auditoriums, and in libraries and courtrooms.[25] In *Loving* v. *Virginia* (1967), the Court even declared unconstitutional a Virginia law forbidding whites and blacks to marry. Since anti-miscegenation laws were thought to be the last outpost of racial discrimination, the Court's ruling that such racial classifications were "directly subversive of the principle of equality" is significant.

In the area of public accommodations, however, the Court was still operating under the state-action concept as announced in the Civil Rights Cases. In order for the Court to invalidate racial discrimination under the Fourteenth Amendment, there had to be some link between the state's action and the discrimination in question. While the Court has never wavered from

☐ *Brief 9.3   School Desegregation in the 1980s: Advance or Retreat?*

Since *Milliken,* school desegregation and busing questions have continued to baffle the Supreme Court. While still adhering to the *de jure/de facto* segregation distinction, the Court has moved back and forth in specific desegregation cases.

For a short time following *Milliken,* the Court seemed to move away from mandating busing and other remedial programs. In cases coming from Pasadena, California, and Austin, Texas,[19] the Court ruled that once a desegregation plan had achieved a unitary school system, no further remedial action was required to end continued *de facto* segregation. In *Milliken II,* the district court substituted remedial and compensatory educational programs for an interdistrict transportation plan.

But beginning in 1979, the Court went back to a more expansive view of the authority of the federal courts in school desegregation decisions. In companion cases, *Columbus Board of Education* v. *Penick* (1979) and *Dayton Board of Education* v. *Brinkman (Dayton II)* (1979), the Court approved extensive desegregation remedies based upon the segregative impact of past school board "actions and omissions." Though badly split, the majority of the Supreme Court thought a loosened requirement of "segregative intent" was enough to mandate districtwide integration plans. District courts could infer discriminatory intent from present "effects," including the presence of predominantly one-race schools, the Court said. And in 1980, over the vociferous objections of Justice William Rehnquist, the Court let stand a decision to order an interdistrict school-busing plan for the Wilmington, Delaware, area.[20] More recently, the Court refused review of an updated remedial desegregation order for Nashville that the Reagan Justice Department had hoped would test the use of mandatory busing itself as a court-imposed desegregation remedy.[21]

Meanwhile, opposition to court-ordered busing from certain local communities and the federal legislative and executive branches was mounting. Court-ordered busing in Boston produced a violent reaction in white ethnic neighborhoods. A similar mandate in Los Angeles caused white parents to opt out of the public school system in large numbers. In a few instances, local referenda and state laws have sought to restrict mandatory busing plans.[22]

Congress in recent years has sought to reduce court-ordered desegregation, proposing laws that would restrict the jurisdiction of the federal courts to order transportation plans to achieve racial desegregation. And the Civil Rights Division of the Justice Department has been active in seeking an end to remedial desegregation efforts. With Assistant Attorney General William Bradford Reynolds in charge, the Reagan administration limited the conditions under which a federal judge can order desegregation remedies. It sought an end to all mandatory busing to achieve school integration, and instead proposed various voluntary plans that avoid busing. Reynolds stated, "[C]ourt supervision of our public schools under aged court decrees must come to an end . . . We are not going to compel children who don't choose to have an integrated education to have one."[23]

Outside the federal government, however, signs of progress appear. In a number of school districts in the 1980s, negotiated settlements have been reached to deal with the problem of educational segregation. From San Francisco to St. Louis to Cincinnati, school districts have instituted creative solutions to problems involving educational deprivation. These negotiated desegregation plans have not been limited to intradistrict busing, but have included "magnet" and alternative schools, faculty and staff training, and remedial reading and communication programs for deprived children. These voluntarily adopted comprehensive school programs that reach beyond mandatory busing or pupil assignment by race may be the wave of the future, for as Professor Alexander Bickel observed in 1970, "No [transportation] policy that a court can order, and a school board, a city or even the state has the capacity to put into effect, will in fact result in the forseeable future in racially balanced public schools. Only a reordering of the environment . . . might have an appreciable effect."[24]

---

this state-action doctrine, it has changed its interpretation of this requirement. A good example of this appears in the case of *Burton* v. *Wilmington Parking Authority* (1961). The case involved the Eagle Coffee Shop's refusal to serve a black man. Though privately run, the coffee shop was located in a facility owned and operated by an agency of the state of Delaware. The Supreme Court held that the restaurant's action was not purely "private," insofar as it was located in a publicly owned building operating under the state's authority. By allowing the restaurant to discriminate in its building, the state had become a party to such discrimination in violation of the Fourteenth Amendment.

In addition to the Supreme Court's broader interpretation of state action in public accommodations, Congress passed the Civil Rights Act of 1964. The Civil Rights Act assumed much of the Court's role in deciding what types of public accommodations are covered by the demands of racial equality. Originally introduced by President John F. Kennedy, Title II of the act guarantees "full and equal enjoyment" of most public accommodations and their facilities: inns, hotels, motels, restaurants, theaters, cinemas, concert halls, and sports arenas. It prohibits "discrimination or segregation" in any of these facilities on the basis of "race, color, religion, or national origin." All establishments "affecting commerce" or discriminating "under color of law" (i.e., with state support) would be covered; the only exceptions would be small boardinghouses (five rooms to rent or less) and private establishments not generally open to the public. Although the Supreme Court had previously struck down a similar law (the Civil Rights Act of 1875), in *Heart of Atlanta Motel Inc.* v. *United States* (1964) and *Katzenbach* v. *McClung* (1964), it upheld Title II of the Civil Rights Act of 1964 on Commerce Clause grounds (see Chapter 7 for a more extensive discussion of these cases).

Congress was also able to make effective civil rights strides through Title VI of the Civil Rights Act of 1964. In Title VI, Congress guaranteed that "no person in the United States shall, on the ground of race, color, or national origin, be excluded from participation in, be denied the benefits of, or be subjected to discrimination under any program or activity receiving Federal financial assistance." As Chapter 7 indicated, Congress has used its spending power to accomplish a number of regulatory ends, especially in the area of civil rights. Title VI provisions are significant because, like Title II, they prevent racial discrimination in private institutions (i.e., those receiving federal funds) that would not otherwise come under the Court's equal protection analysis, given the state-action doctrine. Although the Supreme Court moved to narrow Title VI applicability in 1984,[26] ruling that an institution need only abide by civil rights guarantees in the specific area that receives the federal money, Congress has since passed legislation, the Civil Rights Restoration Act, which once again broadens the coverage of antidiscrimination provisions. With few exceptions, as a result of this recent legislation, an institution receiving federal dollars cannot practice discrimination in *any* of its programs or parts.

Nevertheless, in the absence of clear congressional intent in the area of private discrimination, the Court has continued to make a private/state-action distinction. In *Moose Lodge No. 107* v. *Irvis* (1972), the Court allowed a private club to deny service to a black even though it received a liquor license from the state. A six-justice majority concluded that minimal state regulation in the form of a liquor license to a purely private club did "not sufficiently implicate the state in the discriminatory policies of Moose Lodge so as to make [the licensing] 'state action' " in violation of the Fourteenth Amendment. The *Moose Lodge* ruling, however, should be seen as the exception, although an important one, to the general line of recent Court reasoning about what constitutes impermissible state action. Generally, the Court has deemed any state action encouraging discrimination as violating the demands of the Equal Protection Clause.

Discrimination in Employment:
The Purposeful-Discrimination Test Examined

In Title VII of the Civil Rights Act of 1964, Congress prohibited employers from depriving individuals of employment opportunities "because of such individuals' race, color, sex, or national origin." Along with the Fifth and Fourteenth Amendments, which presumably make racial discrimination in employment unconstitutional if conducted "under color of law" or exhibited by the government itself, fairly strong federal protections against overt employment discrimination exist. But the Supreme Court has had to decide what constitutes illegitimate racial discrimination in employment. The main question has centered around the distinction between discriminatory "intent" on the part of the employer and discriminatory "impact" of employment policies.

The Court's early answers, primarily in discrimination claims under Title VII, suggested that discriminatory effect or impact would be just as illegitimate as discriminatory intent. In *Griggs* v. *Duke Power Co.* (1971), a unanimous Court ruled that Title VII of the Civil Rights Act of 1964 "proscribes not only overt discrimination but also practices that are fair in form, but discriminatory in operation. The touchstone is business necessity. If an employment practice which operates to exclude Negroes cannot be shown to be related to job performance, the practice is prohibited." The Court decided that an employer's requirement that employees have a high school diploma and pass a general intelligence test before being eligible for jobs was unrelated to successful job performance and had the effect of disadvantaging black applicants in violation of Title VII. Chief Justice Burger concluded for the Court that

> [good] intent or absence of discriminatory intent does not redeem employment procedures or testing mechanisms that operate as "built-in headwinds" for minority groups and are unrelated to measuring job capability. Congress directed the thrust of the Act to the *consequences* of employment practices, not simply their motivation. More than that, Congress has placed on the employer the burden of showing that any given requirement must have a manifest relationship to the employment in question.

The Court has continued to use "disparate-impact" analysis in examining Title VII discrimination claims. And in *Watson* v. *Fort Worth Bank and Trust* (1988), it extended this analysis to *subjective* as well as objective employment practices. But the *Watson* case indicates the difficulty the Court faces in including discriminatory impact as well as intent in its Title VII coverage. In a divided ruling, the justices in *Watson* sent a Title VII case back to the district court and set down somewhat confusing standards for future disparate-impact analysis of employment discrimination under Title VII.

However, the Court has employed the purposeful-discrimination test to judge constitutional (as opposed to statutory) claims about denial of equality in employment. As with the school desegregation rulings of the 1970s discussed earlier, minorities challenging employment classifications or criteria have had to show not only a discriminatory impact or effect, but also a discriminatory purpose or intent on the part of the employer. The Court's decision in *Washington* v. *Davis* (1976) illustrates this principle.

Washington v. *Davis* involved a suit brought by blacks challenging the constitutionality of hiring practices in the District of Columbia's police department. The D.C. police department required that a candidate seeking acceptance into the police training program receive a passing grade on a federal civil service test (one which gauged verbal ability, vocabulary, reading, and comprehension). Black applicants failed this test at a rate four times that of their white counterparts, which was the basis for the litigants' constitutional claim. Black plaintiffs asked the courts to invalidate the use of the test because it excluded a disproportionately high number of blacks and was unrelated to job performance.

The Supreme Court upheld the use of the employment test. Justice White's opinion for the majority stressed that a practice is not unconstitutional "solely because it has a racially disproportionate impact" unless it can be proven that it "reflects a racially discriminatory purpose." White said that while purposeful discrimination can be inferred in part from the effects of a law or practice, an action

> neutral on its face and serving ends otherwise within the power of government to pursue, is [not] invalid under the Equal Protection Clause simply because it may affect a greater proportion of one race than of another. Disproportionate impact is not irrelevant, but it is not the sole touchstone of an invidious racial discrimination forbidden by the Constitution.

A year later the Court clarified its position, stating that while disproportionate impact may "provide an important starting point . . . racially discriminatory intent or purpose is required to show a violation of the Equal Protection Clause." [27] Decisions regarding employment indicate that while Congress may have the power to employ an "effect" criterion in employment discrimination cases, the Court sticks to a purposeful-discrimination test wherever equal protection claims under the Constitution are involved. This means that the constitutional burden of proof as a rule lies initially with the individuals claiming that racial discrimination in employment has taken place.

Racial Discrimination and the Franchise

Black males were first made eligible to vote by Congress in 1867. The former Confederate states were ordered to form new constitutions that would guarantee black suffrage, and Congress tried to protect the black man's right to vote both in the Fourteenth Amendment and in a series of federal laws passed during Reconstruction. When it appeared that all of this still might not be enough, the Fifteenth Amendment to the Constitution was adopted in 1870, specifically stating that "the right of citizens of the United States to vote shall not be denied or abridged by the United States or by any State on account of race, color, or previous condition of servitude." Southern whites reacted swiftly to black voting rights, practicing violence and intimidation to prevent blacks from voting. But the mixture of federal guarantees protected black suffrage for almost thirty years. Throughout the Reconstruction period, blacks voted and were elected to public office (one black senator and ten representatives were elected in this period). But at the turn of the century, southern blacks were suddenly and effectively disenfranchised and remained so for over sixty years. For instance, in Louisiana in 1896, 130,334 blacks were registered to vote; eight years later only 1,342 remained on the registrar's rolls!

Methods of Disenfranchisement

How was this disenfranchisement of blacks effected? In addition to "private" practices of violence and intimidation, southern states used "legal" methods to keep blacks from voting. It must be noted at the outset that while the Constitution and federal law determine the broad parameters of citizen voting rights, the states can set specific qualifications for voting. As early as 1875, the Supreme Court announced that "the Fifteenth Amendment does not confer the right of suffrage upon anyone" and that states have the power to regulate elections and determine voting qualifications.[28] Beginning around 1890, southern states used this power to construct barriers to black suffrage. A discussion of some of the methods used by the states and the Supreme Court's response to them follows.

Literacy Tests.   By 1900, almost all the former Confederate states had enacted literacy and other tests designed to prevent blacks from being eligible to vote. State laws required potential voters to be able to read and write, and in many cases to be capable of understanding or interpreting provisions of the state or federal constitutions. These laws were based upon the fact that in the South at the turn of the century more than two-thirds of black adults were illiterate while less than one-fourth of white adults could not read or write. These voting tests were thus effective means of removing most blacks from the voter rolls. And they were administered in such a way as to keep illiterate whites eligible. Evidence indicates that voter registrars administered these tests differently to whites and blacks, giving whites easier versions and providing aid in answering questions, while blacks were asked difficult questions and often disqualified for inconsequential errors, like mispronouncing words. Nevertheless, the Supreme Court allowed the use of literacy and other such tests as requirements for voting. In *Lassiter* v. *Northampton County Board of Elections* (1959), a unanimous Court emphasized the broad discretion states had in setting voting qualifications:

> Residence requirements, age, previous criminal record [are] obvious examples indicating factors which a state may take into consideration in determining the qualifications of voters. The ability to read and write likewise has some relation to standards designed to promote intelligent use of the ballot. Literacy and illiteracy are neutral on race, creed, color and sex. Illiterate people may be intelligent voters, yet in our society where newspapers, periodicals, books, and other printed matter canvass and debate campaign issues, a state might conclude that only those who are literate should exercise the franchise.

The Court *did* declare invalid an attempt by Oklahoma to deny blacks the right to vote while keeping whites eligible. Shortly after being admitted to the Union, Oklahoma, in 1908, amended its constitution by imposing a literacy test for voting. However, all men lineally descended from ancestors entitled to vote in 1866 were exempt from taking the test. The purpose of this "grandfather clause" was clear, since no black man had been entitled to vote prior to 1867. In *Guinn* v. *United States* (1915), the Supreme Court unanimously decided that the Fifteenth Amendment prevented this discriminatory practice. However, black victory was short-lived, as Oklahoma passed a new election law bestowing permanent voting rights on all who voted in 1914 under the grandfather-clause law and requiring all others (namely blacks) to register within twelve days or be disenfranchised for life. This obvious discrimination in black voting rights was not ruled invalid by the Court until 1939.[29]

White Primary Laws.   In their attempt to disenfranchise blacks, southern states also used the power of the dominant political party to regulate the primary election process. Texas is exemplary in this regard. The Texas legislature in 1923 passed a statute declaring that "in no event shall a negro be eligible to participate in a Democratic primary election in the State of Texas." Using the Fourteenth Amendment's grant of equal protection, the Supreme Court ruled against this blatantly discriminatory action. Texas Democrats thought the Court's opinion meant that only direct state action disqualifying blacks from primary voting was prohibited. The Texas legislature passed a law giving the power to set primary voting qualifications to the state executive committee of each political party. The Democratic party responded by limiting primary voting to "all white Democrats." The Court held this practice to be unconstitutional as well, since the law in effect made the party's executive committee an agent of the state.

Undaunted by these setbacks, the Texas Democratic party, without any state authorizing legislation, adopted a resolution confining party membership to whites. At first, because political parties were considered voluntary private organizations, the Court allowed this racial exclusion.[30] But in *Smith* v. *Allwright* (1944), the Court decided that the party's practice was unconstitutional. The Court reasoned that political primaries are not merely private matters but an integral part of the electoral process. Since the state of Texas regulated many aspects of political parties and primary elections, a political party operating in the state became in effect "an agency of the state," and the party's discrimination constituted a form of state action in violation of the Constitution. The Court concluded that if a state that regulates the election process allows a political party to decide, on the basis of race, who may vote in its primary, the state "endorses, adopts and enforces the discrimination against Negroes." The decision in *Smith* v. *Allwright* was an important victory for blacks not only in the struggle to win equal voting rights. It also provided a precedent for later Court rulings in housing and other areas, broadening the concept of state action to include a number of implicit as well as explicit discriminatory practices.

Smith v. *Allwright* aside, by the 1960s, through the use of these legal and extralegal methods, the southern states had effectively prevented blacks from exercising their right to vote. In a 1961 report, the Civil Rights Commission found that less than one-fourth of all voting-age blacks were registered to vote in the southern states: more specifically, the commission selected seventeen "black belt" counties where blacks constituted a majority of the population and found only 3 percent to be registered in these counties.

Congressional Action: The Voting Rights Act of 1965

Congress passed civil rights laws in 1957 and 1960 to secure black voting rights, but these were modest measures that did little to change the voting situations in the South. Spurred by civil rights marches and demonstrations throughout the South, Congress followed up the Civil Rights Act of 1964 with a much stronger voting rights act the next year. The Voting Rights Act of 1965 focused upon eliminating the use of voting tests for purposes of discrimination. In any state or political subdivision where less than 50 percent of the persons of voting age had been registered to vote in the November 1964 election, the act specified that the following legal devices would be suspended: literacy and/or constitutional understanding tests; requirements of educational achievement or knowledge in a particular subject; and "good moral character" requirements. Congress believed that the 50-percent test would be a rough index of voting discrimination. A state could challenge the suspensions of these tests, but only if it could prove that they had not been used for purposes of racial discrimination. In addition, the Voting Rights Act of 1965 gave the attorney general of the United States the power to appoint federal "voting examiners" to oversee the process of voter registration in counties with a particularly bad record of discrimination. Moreover, the law shifted the burden of proof onto southern registrars to show why a person ought not to vote, where before it had been on the individual black to prove why he or she should be allowed to vote.

The Supreme Court ruled the Voting Rights Act of 1965 constitutional in *South Carolina* v. *Katzenbach* (1966). The affected states (see Table 9.1) contended that the law invaded their power to set voter qualifications and that it disregarded "local conditions which have nothing to do with racial discrimination." But the court cited earlier unsuccessful attempts by Congress to guarantee blacks voting rights and concluded that the formula employed in the 1965 law was "rational in both practice and theory." Chief Justice Warren premised his opinion for the Court upon the following principle: "As against the reserved powers of the States, Congress may use any rational means to effectuate the constitutional prohibition of racial discrimination in voting."

The impact of the Voting Rights Act was dramatic. By 1976, drastic increases in black voter registration in the southern states automatically covered by the act occurred, closing the gap between white and black registration (see Table 9.1). And perhaps most important, in these states 1,100 blacks had been elected to public office by 1974, whereas only a handful had been elected prior to 1965. Jesse Jackson's success as a presidential candidate in southern primaries in 1984 and 1988 would have been inconceivable without the Voting Rights Act.

When the Voting Rights Act came up for renewal in 1970, Congress suspended literacy tests nationwide, and in subsequent years Congress has extended and toughened the act's requirements even further, most notably requiring that bilingual voting information be provided to citizens (see Brief 9.4).

Electoral System Discrimination

In addition to denial of their right to vote, blacks have challenged various electoral schemes that have the effect of diluting minority voting strength. Unfair district-boundary drawing, two-stage primary processes, majority versus plurality vote rules, and at-large elections all tend to deny representation in public offices to black candidates, even though blacks may constitute a sizable proportion of the community. But the Supreme Court has consistently ruled that in instances involving such election laws, only a showing of purposeful intent to discriminate renders them unconstitutional.

Mobile v. *Bolden* (1980) offers a prime example. In Mobile, Alabama, the three-member city commission was elected at large. No black had ever been elected to the commission, even though blacks made up 40 percent of

☐ *Brief 9.4 The Voting Rights Act of 1982*

Certain provisions of the Voting Rights Act of 1965, which had been extended in 1970 and 1975, came up for renewal in 1982. Two provisions in particular raised controversies between Congress, which was attempting to strengthen the Voting Rights Act, and the Reagan administration, which was seeking to limit its application. Section 5 of the statute required certain states to obtain "preclearance" from the federal government of any changes in their election procedures. Congress in 1982 wanted to extend this requirement for twenty-five years, but finally accepted a compromise that contained a "bailout" mechanism. A state or subdivision that could show it had not discriminated and had made positive steps in aiding minority participation in its electoral policies for ten years would be free from this preclearance requirement.

The renewal of Section 2, prohibiting discriminatory election and voting practices, provoked the greatest conflict, however. Congress, largely in response to the Court's ruling in *Mobile* v. *Bolden,* wanted to provide for a "results" test to prove electoral violations of the law—if an official electoral procedure *resulted* in denial of voting rights in terms of its *effect,* minorities could bring suit against such a procedure. But after strong objections from the Reagan administration, a compromise bill was adopted that retained the results test but allowed the courts to examine the "totality of circumstances" surrounding a case to determine if illegal discrimination existed. In addition, as amended, the Voting Rights Act of 1982 would *not* allow minorities to call for proportional representation in election results.

Overall, the Reagan administration sought to limit the interpretation and application of the Voting Rights Act of 1982. For example, in 1985 the Justice Department went before the Supreme Court to claim that Congress did not intend for the courts to use any "results" or "effects" tests in enforcing the Voting Rights Act.[31]

the city's population. A district court judge ruled that the at-large election provision discriminated against blacks, but upon appeal the Supreme Court reversed this judgment. The Court held that an electoral system violates the Constitution "only if there is purposeful discrimination" or if the system devised is "motivated by a racially discriminatory purpose." According to the Court, "To prove such a purpose it is not enough to show that the group allegedly discriminated against has not elected representatives in proportion to its numbers." The Equal Protection Clause does not require proportional representation of all identifiable groups, and, since black citizens voted freely, no Fifteenth Amendment violation was present.

Table 9.1 Black Voter Registration, 1964–1976

	1964	1976
Alabama	23.0*	58.1
Georgia	44.0	56.3
Louisiana	32.0	63.9
Mississippi	6.7	67.4
South Carolina	38.8	60.6
Virginia	45.7	60.7

*Percent of black voting-age population registered to vote

Conclusion

Although the beginning of this chapter suggested that equality is cherished by both individualists and communitarians, the issue of racial equality has magnified the tension between the individualist's protection of minority rights and the communitarian's support of majority rule. Blacks in particular have borne the brunt of unbridled majoritarianism owing to the historical institution of slavery. Constitutionally, the post-Civil War amendments were designed to put an end to that unequal legal treatment of blacks by the white majority. But as the historical record shows, neither the Supreme Court nor the various state governments originally had a very generous vision of black legal and constitutional equality. In the Supreme Court's case, the triple requirement of state action, purposeful discrimination, and unreasonableness discussed in this chapter had the effect of severely narrowing the Fourteenth Amendment's application.

Beginning in the 1930s, however, the Supreme Court seemingly abandoned its narrow nineteenth-century understanding of equal protection. In many of the school segregation cases, including the landmark *Brown* decision, and in employment discrimination rulings like *Griggs* v. *Duke Power Co.*, the Court looked to the effect or impact of a practice rather than its underlying motivation to rule upon the demands of equal protection (thus seemingly discarding the purposeful-discrimination requirement). And justices had so expanded the concept of state action in the *Smith* v. *Allwright, Shelley* v. *Kraemer,* and *Burton* v. *Wilmington Parking Authority* rulings that almost any discriminatory practice associated with or encouraged by the government would qualify for protection under the Fourteenth Amendment. Additionally, congressional protection of civil rights for racial minorities beginning in the late 1950s provided yet another source of Supreme Court antidiscrimination rulings.

But recent events may suggest a shift back toward nineteenth-century understandings. The Reagan administration has been characterized by some as reversing the past half-century of gains for racial and other minorities (see Brief 9.5). Recent busing, employment, and election-procedure rulings have once again invoked a strict purposeful-discrimination standard, placing a heavy burden upon minorities to prove discriminatory intent on the part of public officials. And more recent state-action rulings suggest that the expansive days of *Shelley* have come to an end. In fact, the only component of nineteenth-century equal protection interpretation that has been and remains drastically revised in this century is the rational-scrutiny standard. The Court, beginning in the 1930s, has established a new criterion for certain types of equal protection claims, one which automatically requires justices to give "strict scrutiny" (as opposed to "rational scrutiny") to state laws and classifications. The following chapter will focus upon the "new equal protection" and what it entails.

☐ Brief 9.5   A Note on Civil Rights Under the Reagan Administration

During his two terms in office, President Ronald Reagan directed a major shift in federal civil rights policy. The Reagan administration based this shift on the belief that the Constitution is "color-blind" (to use Justice Harlan's term), and thus cannot allow beneficial treatment of minority group members to the detriment of the white majority. Using this rationale, the federal government under Reagan retreated from a twenty-year history of leadership in promoting civil rights for minorities.

The Reagan forces fought Congress on civil rights legislation, most notably the extension of the Voting Rights Act in 1982 (see Brief 9.4) and the Civil Rights Restoration Act. In the bureaucracy, the administration sought to reduce the funding and the role of major civil rights ombudsmen, such as the Civil Rights Commission. And most notably, Reagan policy toward the courts and civil rights litigation shifted.

The Department of Justice enacted a complete shift of emphasis from previous administrations in the civil rights field. The Reagan Justice Department refused to pursue class-action suits on behalf of groups who had suffered from discrimination. It opposed the use of mandatory, court-ordered busing to achieve school integration. It sought to reverse Internal Revenue Service (IRS) policy and grant tax-exempt status to a private college that discriminated on the basis of race (see Brief 13.4). It wrote **amicus curiae** briefs arguing for a narrow, intent-based interpretation of the Fourteenth Amendment and various acts of Congress, specifically opposing any "effects" tests in judging whether racial discrimination had occurred. Attorney General Edwin Meese consistently fought affirmative action plans that tried to compensate minorities in the face of past discrimination (see Chapter 10 for a further discussion).

President Reagan's appointments of women and minorities to the federal courts were considerably fewer than those of President Jimmy Carter (see Chapter 4). His selection for chief justice of the Supreme Court, William H. Rehnquist, was condemned by a number of civil rights groups during Senate confirmation hearings. And his attempted nomination of Robert Bork in 1987, a man who had once condemned the Civil Rights Act of 1964 and the Court's decision in *Shelley* v. *Kraemer*, was considered an affront by civil rights advocates, who successfully lobbied against Senate confirmation (see Brief 4.3). With these actions, the Reagan administration raised concern within the civil rights community that a reversal of federal policy toward and commitment to civil rights had taken place.

Questions

1. The *Brown* decision raises a number of questions. As the discussion in this chapter and in Chapter 4 indicates, the Court did not base its decision about school desegregation upon constitutional principles nor upon a historical examination of the intention of the framers of the Fourteenth Amendment, but rather, upon contemporary sociological findings about the effects of segregation upon black children. In retrospect, is this a legitimate basis for constitutional interpretation and decision making? Would implementation of the *Brown* decision have been easier had the Court articulated "neutral principles" as the reasoning behind the decision? Does the *Brown* decision say anything about the relationship between the Supreme Court and American public opinion; that is, can the Court succeed when it is clearly ahead of public opinion? (See next chapter's discussion of *Bowers* v. *Hardwick* for a more recent example and a different Court decision.)

2. Does the *de jure/de facto* distinction continue to hold weight as an approach to school desegregation? Or, as Justice Powell argued in 1973, has it lost all relevance to the reality of American public schooling? How does a person interested in racial equality in education address the current problem of school segregation? Is busing still an effective answer?

3. As presented in this chapter, both Congress and the Court have acted in various ways to ensure racial equality under the Constitution. Which seems the more appropriate body to govern in this area? Can Congress, owing to its representative nature

and its broad grant of authority under the post-Civil War amendments, better ensure equal protection of the laws for racial minorities (witness, for example, the Civil Rights Act of 1964 and the Voting Rights Act of 1965)? Or is the Court, being more insulated from majoritarian influences, better able to protect and advance minority rights (as evidenced in the *Brown* and *Shelley* decisions, for example)?

4. How do you evaluate the Supreme Court's nineteenth-century decisions under the Fourteenth Amendment? Did the Court have good reasons for its judgments in the Civil Rights Cases and in *Plessy?* Do the three major criteria the Court set down in these early protection decisions—state action, purposeful discrimination, rationality scrutiny—follow from the language or the original intent of the Fourteenth Amendment?

5. The state-action requirement has been the source of ongoing controversy over the Equal Protection Clause. What is the state-action requirement? How has the Supreme Court changed its view about the kind of state action prohibited by the Constitution? In your opinion, has the court adequately resolved the problems inherent in deciding whether or not state action is involved in a particular instance?

Endnotes

1. See Paul Brest, "The Supreme Court, 1975 Term—Foreword: In Defense of the Antidiscrimination Principle," *Harvard Law Review* 90 (1976): 1–54.

2. See Owen M. Fiss, "Groups and the Equal Protection Clause," *Philosophy and Public Affairs* 5 (1976): 107–77.

3. Don E. Fehrenbacher, *Slavery, Law, and Politics: The Dred Scott Case in Historical Perspective* (New York: Oxford University Press, 1981), 12.

4. Quoted in Staughton Lynd, *Class Conflict, Slavery, and the United States Constitution* (Westport, Conn.: Greenwood Press, 1980), 154.

5. Ibid., 159.

6. Herbert J. Storing, "Slavery and the Moral Foundations of the American Republic," in Robert Horwitz, ed., *The Moral Foundations of the American Republic* (Charlottesville, Va.: University Press of Virginia, 1977), 225.

7. Richard Kluger, *Simple Justice* (New York: Vintage Books, 1975), 626.

8. *Strauder* v. *West Virginia*, 100 U.S. 303 (1880).

9. Walter F. Murphy, James E. Fleming, and William F. Harris II, *American Constitutional Interpretation* (Mineola, N.Y.: Foundation Press, 1986), 744.

10. C. Vann Woodward, *The Strange Career of Jim Crow* (New York: Oxford University Press, 1966). In fact, Supreme Court Justice Bradley had been the deciding vote on the special commission which resolved the Hayes-Tilden deadlock.

11. *Pace* v. *Alabama*, 106 U.S. 583 (1883). For a general understanding of the Court's interpretation of the Equal Protection Clause, see Joseph Tussman and Jacobus TenBroek, "The Equal Protection of the Laws," *California Law Review* 37 (1949): 341.

12. Ironically, the Court had allowed the use of the Fourteenth Amendment to protect business corporations from state government regulation.

13. See the Court's ruling in *Corrigan* v. *Buckley,* 271 U.S. 323 (1926).

14. In addition to *Runyon* v. *McCrary,* see *Sullivan* v. *Little Hunting Park, Inc.,* 396 U.S. 229 (1969). The two recent cases involving Arabs and Jews are, respectively, *St. Francis College*

v. *Majid Ghaidan Al-Khazraji*, 107 S.Ct. 2022 (1987) and *Shaare Tefila Congregation* v. *Cobb*, 107 S.Ct. 2019 (1987). In 1988, the Supreme Court agreed to reconsider its ruling in the *Runyon* case.

15. The most important of these early victories were *Missouri ex rel. Gaines* v. *Canada*, 305 U.S. 337 (1938), where the Court decided that the state of Missouri had to furnish Lloyd Gaines, a black applicant to the state university law school, substantially equal legal education within the state's borders and could not offer to pay his tuition at an out-of-state law school that accepted blacks; and *McLaurin* v. *Oklahoma State Regents for Higher Education*, 339 U.S. 637 (1950), where the Court decided that to separate a black graduate student from his fellows within a state university was to violate his rights to equal protection.

16. The Court had invited parties besides the original litigants to file arguments in *Brown II*. Six states that were practicing school segregation filed separate briefs: Arkansas, Florida, Maryland, North Carolina, Oklahoma, and Texas. In addition, the federal government filed a separate brief that included its findings and recommendations about implementation of desegregation.

17. Quoted in Kluger, *Simple Justice*, 753. Chief Justice Warren, in his memoirs, lamented the fact that "no word of support for the [school desegregation] decision emanated from the White House." See Earl Warren, *The Memoirs of Earl Warren* (Garden City, N.Y.: Doubleday, 1977), 289–91.

18. In addition to the *Griffin, Green*, and *Alexander* cases cited in the text, the Court's rulings in *Goss* v. *Board of Education*, 373 U.S. 683 (1963), and *Monroe* v. *Board of Commissions*, 391 U.S. 450 (1968), all make this point clear.

19. *Pasadena City Board of Education* v. *Spangler*, 427 U.S. 424 (1976); *Austin Independent School District* v. *United States*, 429 U.S. 990 (1976).

20. *Delaware State Board* v. *Evans*, 446 U.S. 923 (1980).

21. *Metropolitan County Board of Education* v. *Kelley* (1983).

22. In Los Angeles and the state of Washington, respectively.

23. Quoted in "Civil Rights Note," *Minnesota Law Review* 69 (1985): 735.

24. Alexander M. Bickel, *The Supreme Court and the Idea of Progress* (New York: Harper & Row, 1970), 132.

25. Public parks: *New Orleans City Park Improvement Association* v. *Detiege* (1958); public recreation: *Mayor of Baltimore* v. *Dawson* (1955); municipal golf courses: *Holmes* v. *City of Atlanta* (1955); city buses: *Gayle* v. *Browder* (1956); public auditoriums: *Schiro* v. *Bynum* (1963); courtroom seating: *Johnson* v. *Virginia* (1963).

26. *Grove City College* v. *Bell*, 465 U.S. 555 (1984).

27. *Village of Arlington Heights* v. *Metropolitan Housing Development Corporation* (1977).

28. *Minor* v. *Happersett*, 21 Wall. 162 (1875).

29. *Lane* v. *Wilson*, 307 U.S. 268 (1939).

30. *Grovey* v. *Townsend*, 295 U.S. 45 (1935).

31. The case was *Thornburg* v. *Gingles*, 106 S.Ct. 2752 (1986), a North Carolina voting rights case. In response to the Justice Department's brief, ten leading members of Congress filed an *amicus curiae* brief refuting the Reagan administration's position. The Supreme Court upheld a lower court ruling in favor of the black plaintiffs, largely dispelling the administration's victim-specific, conscious-intent standard under the Voting Rights Act.

Suggested Readings

Bickel, Alexander M. "The Original Understanding and the Segregation Decision." *Harvard Law Review* 69 (1955): 1–65.

Devins, Neal. "School Desegregation Law in the 1980's: The Courts' Abandonment of *Brown* v. *Board of Education*." *William and Mary Law Review* 26 (1984): 7.

Fehrenbacher, Don E. *Slavery, Law, and Politics: The Dred Scott Case in Historical Perspective*. New York: Oxford University Press, 1981.

Graglia, Lino A. *Disaster by Decree: The Supreme Court Decisions on Race and the Schools*. Ithaca, N.Y.: Cornell University Press, 1976.

Greenberg, Jack. *Race Relations and American Law*. New York: Columbia University Press, 1959.

Harris, Robert J. *The Quest for Equality*. Baton Rouge, La.: Louisiana State University Press, 1960.

Kluger, Richard. *Simple Justice*. New York: Vintage Books, 1975.

Peltason, Jack. *Fifty-eight Lonely Men: Southern Federal Judges and School Desegregation*. New York: Harcourt, Brace & World, 1961.

TenBroek, Jacobus. *Equal Under Law*. Berkeley, Calif.: University of California Press, 1965.

Woodward, C. Vann. *The Strange Career of Jim Crow*. New York: Oxford University Press, 1966.

The New Equal Protection

Syllabus

Over the past few years, the nation's capital has been the site of numerous civil rights battles. At the beginning of 1987, the National Organization for Women kicked off a campaign to renew efforts at adopting an amendment to the Constitution guaranteeing equal rights for women. In October 1987, five hundred thousand people came to Washington for the National March for Lesbian and Gay Rights. The Campaign to End Hunger and Homelessness lobbied Congress throughout the fall of 1987 for a housing bill to address the needs of poor and homeless citizens, finally succeeding in December. In January 1988, pro-choice and right-to-life groups held competing rallies to commemorate the fifteenth anniversary of the Supreme Court's landmark abortion decision. In March 1988, deaf students at Gallaudet University marched to the Capitol to protest the selection of a nondeaf president and to symbolize the concerns of the handicapped across the country. And in May 1988, lobbyists representing illegal aliens went to Congress seeking an extension on the amnesty provisions of the federal immigration law. These actions represent some of the most hotly contested issues in contemporary American society. They also exemplify what is termed the "new equal protection," insofar as these citizens pressed their case for equal rights on a basis other than race, which was the traditional basis for equal protection claims. The question these challenges raise for the courts is, Does the Constitution speak to these citizens and their concerns for equality? Should the document be expanded to apply to claims made by those it wasn't originally intended to cover?

This Chapter Examines the Following Matters

☐ Over the past generation, the Fourteenth Amendment has been used to address social problems beyond those of racial minorities.

☐ The Supreme Court has adopted a multiple-tier approach to equal protection questions, exercising varying degrees of scrutiny depending upon the challenge made against a particular government classification scheme. The origins of and justifications for such an approach demonstrate the controversies involved in the new equal protection.

☐ The Supreme Court uses strict judicial scrutiny in cases involving suspect classifications. The characteristics that make a classification suspect are considered, as well as the Court's judgment about whether affirmative action programs and classifications based upon gender, age, alienage, illegitimacy, and handicap should be considered suspect.

☐ The Supreme Court also uses strict judicial scrutiny in cases where the government threatens fundamental rights. The characteristics that make a right

fundamental are examined, as well as the Court's consideration of claims that certain rights be regarded as fundamental.

☐ The Court's interpretation of the Equal Protection Clause as it relates to questions of poverty and the poor has been somewhat ambiguous. After initial indications during the 1960s that the Court would subject discrimination against the poor to strict scrutiny, the justices in more recent years have refused to consider wealth as a suspect classification or certain subsistence rights as fundamental.

☐ An overall assessment of the new equal protection finds the Court resolving difficult problems in the ongoing conflict between majority rule and minority rights. The new equal protection brings the Court into substantial criticism, and a number of constitutional scholars have suggested alternatives to the current multiple-tier approach to equal protection interpretation.

Photo: Constitutional issues falling under the rubric of "the new equal protection" have created significant conflict between citizens and their government. Supreme Court rulings on the controversial right to privacy and abortion have drawn constant fire from anti-abortion advocates like this individual who pickets the Supreme Court building regularly.

Equal Protection Old and New

As Justice Samuel Miller declared in the Slaughterhouse Cases (1873), the "pervading purpose" of the Fourteenth Amendment was to protect blacks against state-sponsored discrimination: "We doubt very much whether any action of a State not directed by way of discrimination against the negroes as a class, or on account of their race, will ever be held to come within the purview of this provision." With this understanding in mind, the Supreme Court narrowly construed the amendment's provisions and applied minimal standards when reviewing any governmental actions under the Equal Protection Clause. As discussed in Chapter 9, "rationality scrutiny" (also called the "rational-basis test") was the standard the Court adopted. Under this standard, justices acted deferentially toward governments seeking to embody the majority's sentiments in law. Individuals challenging the government on equal protection grounds were required to demonstrate the irrationality of the majority's actions, normally presumed reasonable. In fact, the Court was hostile to most equal protection claims prior to the 1930s: Justice Oliver Wendell Holmes once described them as "the usual last resort of constitutional arguments." [1]

The Fourteenth Amendment's language, however, offers hope of a more expansive, egalitarian constitutional vision. It guarantees equality and due process to "any person." And it announces the goal of federal protection to individuals who may be left out of the processes of representative democracy. In this sense the Fourteenth Amendment brings together in an often uneasy balance the individualist values of protection against majority tyranny with the communitarian values of democratic self-governance. In the beginning decades of this century, the balance was tipped on the side of legislative majorities. By the 1930s, however, the Supreme Court had set its task at tipping the balance in the other direction. The justices began to assert their power of judicial review against popular governments who were unjustly trampling upon the rights of individuals and minority groups. In specific areas, the Court has substituted **strict scrutiny** for the more self-restrained rationality scrutiny. In cases where the court exercises strict scrutiny, the burden of proof is shifted to the government attempting to deny equal rights to individuals to justify its actions.

Rather than being the "last resort of constitutional arguments," equal protection claims have outranked just about every other basis of constitutional argument and have been used to rule out countless governmental practices in many substantive areas. In addition to racial minorities, white males, women, the elderly, aliens, handicapped persons, homosexuals, and the poor, among others, have brought serious claims under the Fourteenth Amendment. The Supreme Court's consideration of these challenges to government programs based upon other than traditional racial discrimination grounds has been termed the **new equal protection.** This chapter will discuss the nature of this new equal protection, its expansion beyond racial discrimination, and the ongoing problems and issues such an expansion creates.

Origins of the New Equal Protection

Tracing the origins of a constitutional idea is never easy, but this discussion of the new equal protection begins with Justice Harlan Stone's famous footnote in *United States* v. *Carolene Products Co.* (1938). In an otherwise inconsequential decision, Justice Stone, in Footnote 4 of his majority opinion, laid out three possible exceptions to the rule that judges ought to presume government actions constitutional. He stated that normal deference toward government should be curbed in favor of a "more exacting judicial scrutiny" in cases (1) "when legislation appears on its face to be within a specific prohibition of the Constitution, such as those of the first ten amendments"; (2) when legislation "restricts those political processes which can ordinarily be expected to [prevent] undesirable legislation" (restrictions on the right to vote and other aspects of the democratic political process); and (3) where "prejudice against discrete and insular minorities . . . tends seriously to curtail the operation of those political processes ordinarily to be relied upon to protect minorities." Stone's footnote invited the Court to exert its authority against the government in these instances and to use the Fifth and Fourteenth Amendments as the basis for such judicial activism.

Four years later, in *Skinner* v. *Oklahoma* (1942), Justice William O. Douglas used the term "strict scrutiny" (in place of Stone's "more exacting judicial scrutiny") to describe the judicial standard the Court would apply to legislation depriving individuals of their civil rights. Under Oklahoma's Habitual Criminal Sterilization Act, persons convicted two or more times for felonies "involving moral turpitude" would be sterilized. Writing for the Court that voted to invalidate the Oklahoma law, Justice Douglas invoked the Equal Protection Clause to speak out against deprivation of an individual's fundamental rights. Ordinarily, Douglas wrote, the Court would defer to state criminal classifications and punishments, but "we are dealing here with legislation which involves one of the basic civil rights of man. Marriage and procreation are fundamental to the very existence and survival of the race." An individual falling under this law "is forever deprived of a basic liberty." Douglas concluded that in areas like this involving fundamental civil rights, "strict scrutiny of the classification which a state makes . . . is essential, lest unwittingly, or otherwise, invidious discriminations are made against groups or types of individuals in violation of the constitutional guaranty [in the Equal Protection Clause] of just and equal laws."

Over the next two years, the Court further clarified its new standard of scrutiny under the Fourteenth Amendment. This was done in cases involving restrictions on Japanese-Americans during World War II. In sustaining a curfew order against the Japanese in *Hirabayashi* v. *United States* (1943), Justice Stone stated:

> Distinctions between citizens solely because of their ancestry are by their very nature odious to a free people whose institutions are founded upon the doctrine of equality. For that reason, legislative classification or discrimination based on race alone has often been held to be a denial of equal protection.

A year later, in sustaining the infamous exclusion order against Japanese-Americans in *Korematsu* v. *United States* (1944) (see Chapter 5), Justice Hugo Black began the Court's opinion by setting out a standard of "rigid scrutiny" for all racially based classifications:

> It should be noted to begin with, that all legal restrictions which curtail the civil rights of a single racial group are immediately suspect. This is not to say that all such restrictions are unconstitutional. It is to say that courts must subject them to more rigid scrutiny.

With these two cases, although it upheld gross intrusions on personal freedom by the government in both instances, the Court had announced a new jurisprudence of active scrutiny of all governmental classifications upon the basis of race. It was only because of what they felt were overriding national security interests that the justices allowed racial classifications to stand in these instances. With the invalidation of racial classification schemes in the segregation cases preceding and including *Brown,* the Court definitely signaled an end to judicial deference to government under the Equal Protection Clause.

The Two-Tier Approach

From these rather modest beginnings, the Supreme Court came to adopt what has been called a two-tier approach to Fourteenth Amendment questions. Under it, the justices initially place governmental actions and classifications under one of two tiers of judicial review. The lower tier represents judicial review of classifications under the previously discussed "rationality scrutiny" (sometimes called "deferential scrutiny" or "rational-basis standard"). Most government classifications fall under this lenient standard, with the Court usually deferring to the judgment of the people's representatives in the legislative or executive branches of government. All the Court requires is that some reasonable relationship exist between the law under review and a valid governmental goal. In practice, this has meant that a statute placed on the lower tier of rationality scrutiny is almost always upheld.

The upper tier of the two-tier approach is reserved for those few instances where a government's laws or actions are held up to a rigorous standard of judicial review. Laws placed on the upper tier draw "strict scrutiny" from the Supreme Court. Currently the Court applies strict scrutiny to two kinds of laws: (1) laws that threaten "fundamental rights" (following Justice Douglas's analysis in *Skinner*); and (2) laws that use "suspect classifications" to make legal distinctions between people (following Black's statement in *Korematsu*). Only if the government can show a compelling interest for its actions, a close fit between the challenged law and the compelling interest, and evidence that no less drastic means were available, will the Court allow such a law to stand.

The Court's application of the strict-scrutiny standard has been, according to Professor Gerald Gunther, " 'strict' in theory and fatal in fact."[2] Professor Gunther's description is apt, because the Court has almost always invalidated legislation it felt used "suspect" classifications or interfered with what it felt were fundamental rights. Moreover, in the past fifty years, the Court has used both the Equal Protection and the Due Process Clauses of the Fourteenth Amendment to rule on behalf of those closed out by overbearing majorities in the democratic process (see Brief 10.1).

The Supreme Court developed this two-tier approach to aid it in making determinations about the legitimacy of particular classifications under the Equal Protection Clause. But over the years, the seemingly rigid, all-or-nothing character of two-tier judicial review has drawn criticism from judges and legal scholars, and the Court itself has abandoned the approach in certain instances. Some critics have argued that only the name remains to the Court's two-tier approach to the Fourteenth Amendment. In fact, they contend that the Court has actually used a multiple-tier, or "sliding-scale," approach as the basis for reviewing legislation under the Equal Protection Clause. In addition to covering the Court's two-tier approach as applied in particular cases, this chapter will

❏ *Brief 10.1   The Tie That Binds: The Equal Protection and Due Process Clauses*

This chapter may appear to fuse two distinct constitutional provisions—equal protection of the laws and due process of law—without any clear reason. While it is true that the Court often invokes the two clauses for different purposes, they are linked by the general concept of equality. Law professor Ronald Dworkin speaks of equality as the right to equal treatment and to treatment as an equal.[3] Equal treatment implies equal protection of the laws, while treatment as an equal suggests an equal respect for each person's life, liberty, and property rights (as required by the Due Process Clause).

The analysis of the new equal protection, from its origins to the present, also tends to join the two clauses together. Justice Stone's *Carolene Products* footnote (discussed earlier in this chapter) calls for strict scrutiny of laws threatening both the equal rights of "discrete and insular minorities" and fundamental constitutional rights (implied by the Due Process Clause).

In *Bolling* v. *Sharpe* (1954), the Washington, D.C., companion to the *Brown* decision, a unanimous Court ruled that the same demands presented to the states by the Equal Protection Clause would be placed on the federal government by the Fifth Amendment's Due Process Clause (some critics have even called this "reverse incorporation"—see Chapter 8). And in more recent years, Justice William Brennan endorsed the linkage of the two provisions in his opinion in *Plyler* v. *Doe* (1982):

> We have never suggested that the class of persons who might avail themselves of the equal protection guarantee is less than coextensive with that entitled to due process. To the contrary, we have recognized that both provisions . . . protect an identical class of persons, and to reach every exercise of state authority.

So, while the Due Process and Equal Protection Clauses are distinct, a tie does bind them together, a tie often articulated in the Court's analysis of the new equal protection.

examine the various criticisms justices have faced concerning this new equal protection.

Suspect Classifications and the Equal Protection Clause

The Court has subjected governmental actions to rigorous inspections when such actions are based upon a scheme of **suspect classification.** The question the Court has had to address is, What classifications ought to be considered serious threats to the ideal of equality and, as a result, considered constitutionally illegitimate on their face? True to the intentions of those who framed the Fourteenth Amendment, the Court moved quickly to put race and national origin in this category. Discrimination against racial or ethnic minorities continues to be considered "inherently suspect," and the Court subjects such classifications to strict scrutiny. The following passage from Chief Justice Earl Warren's opinion in *Loving* v. *Virginia* (1967) makes this clear:

> At the very least, the Equal Protection Clause demands that racial classifications, especially suspect in criminal statutes, be subjected to the "most rigid scrutiny," and if they are ever to be upheld, they must be shown to be necessary to the accomplishment of some permissible state objective, independent of the racial discrimination which it was the object of the 14th Amendment to eliminate.

In the last twenty years, however, other groups have brought equal protection claims against classifications they would like the Court to certify as "suspect" (see Brief 10.2). White males have argued that governmental affirmative action plans that benefit minorities in education and the workplace classify on the basis of race and therefore ought to be considered automatically invalid. Feminists contend that laws differentiating on the basis of gender should be considered constitutionally suspect. Aging persons, aliens, illegitimate children, the poor, and the handicapped have all asked the Court to elevate classifications against them to "suspect" status. A look at each of these claims and the Court's response follow.

Affirmative Action: Denial of Equal Protection to Whites?

Affirmative action, whereby racial minorities are given preference in admissions, hiring, and promotional practices, has been and continues to be a prominent part of government and business policy. Affirmative action plans reflect the group-based, equality-of-results approach discussed in Chapter 9. They rest upon an assumption that it is not enough to merely eliminate legal barriers and other governmental obstacles to a minority group's progress. A history of past discrimination against a disadvantaged group may require that in order to achieve true equality of opportunity, positive action must be taken by government and society to bring minority group members to an equal starting

---

☐ Brief 10.2   What Makes a Classification Suspect?

The raging controversy over classification schemes and equality under the Constitution raises questions about why a classification is considered suspect. The general guidelines applied in Supreme Court opinions have been broad and subject to a great deal of interpretation. Justice Stone's *Carolene Products* footnote spoke of classifications reflecting "prejudice against discrete and insular minorities," an open-ended invitation to include all sorts of groups, not just *racial* minorities.[4] Justice Lewis Powell only added confusion to the controversy in his opinion in *San Antonio School District* v. *Rodriguez* (1973). He stated that a suspect class is one that has been

saddled with such disabilities, or subjected to such a history of purposeful unequal treatment, or relegated to such a position of political powerlessness as to command extraordinary protection from the majoritarian political process.

But Powell and others have found this to be insufficient justification for making women, the poor, or handicapped persons suspect classes. In recent years, a few justices have tried to make the reasoning underlying suspect classifications clearer. Justice Brennan, in *Plyler* v. *Doe* (1982), deemed suspect "legislation imposing special disabilities upon groups disfavored by virtue of circumstances beyond their control [which] suggests the kind of 'class or caste' treatment that the Fourteenth Amendment was designed to abolish." And Justice Thurgood Marshall, the only Supreme Court justice coming from an acknowledged suspect class, defined a number of characteristics contributing to suspectness in *Cleburne* v. *Cleburne Living Center* (1985):

No single talisman can define those groups likely to be the target of classifications offensive to the Fourteenth Amendment and therefore warranting heightened or strict scrutiny; experience, not abstract knowledge, must be the primary guide. The "political powerlessness" of a group may be relevant . . . but that factor is neither necessary, as the gender cases demonstrate, nor sufficient, as the example of minors illustrates . . . Similarly, immutability of a trait at issue may be relevant, but many immutable characteristics, such as height or blindness, are valid bases of governmental action and classifications under a variety of circumstances.

The political powerlessness of a group and the immutability of its defining trait are relevant insofar as they point to a social and cultural isolation that gives the majority little reason to respect or be concerned with that group's interests and needs.

The discreteness and insularity warranting a "more searching judicial inquiry" must therefore be viewed from a social and cultural perspective as well as a political one. To this task judges are well suited, for the lessons of history and experience are surely the best guide as to when, and with respect to what interests, society is likely to stigmatize individuals as members of an inferior caste or view them as not belonging to the community. Because prejudice spawns prejudice, and sterotypes produce limitations that confirm the stereotype on which they are based, a history of unequal treatment requires sensitivity to the prospect that its vestiges endure . . . Where classifications based on a particular characteristic have [offended the principles of equality] in the past, and the threat that they may do so remains, heightened scrutiny is appropriate.

Do these more recent attempts to define the characteristics of suspect classes clarify the Court's criteria? Has the Court applied these general standards consistently in the specific claims documented in this chapter?

place in the competitive social race. As such, affirmative action programs are temporary, color-conscious actions designed to ensure true equality of opportunity.

The Supreme Court itself called for affirmative action in some of its school desegregation decisions, arguing that merely eliminating discrimination was not enough to end racial segregation in education (see Chapter 9). In the *Swann* case, for example, the Court unanimously concluded that "just as the race of students must be considered in determining whether a constitutional violation has occurred, so also race must be considered in formulating a remedy."

The federal government adopted affirmative action policies beginning in the Johnson administration. President Lyndon Johnson himself laid the groundwork for affirmative action. In announcing an executive order mandating affirmative action in the federal bureaucracy, Johnson stated that eliminating overt racial discrimination was not enough:

> You do not take a person who, for years, has been hobbled by chains and liberate him, bring him up to the starting line of a race and then say you are free to compete with all the others, and still just believe that you have been completely fair.[5]

The Department of Health, Education, and Welfare (HEW) followed suit in 1967. Using its authority under Title VI of the Civil Rights Act of 1964 (see Chapter 9 for a discussion of Title VI), HEW promulgated regulations ordering all agencies or institutions receiving federal funds to "take affirmative action to overcome the effects of conditions which resulted in limiting participation by persons of a particular race, color, or national origin even in the absence of . . . prior discrimination" by the institution. In line with these regulations, colleges and universities, employers, and state agencies all began consciously to design programs that would increase the number of minority participants.

By the 1970s, whites began challenging these affirmative action programs as an affront to their right to equality under the Fourteenth Amendment. The Court has subsequently been asked to decide whether government and private efforts to alleviate racism can be color-conscious to the detriment of whites. Should the use of racial classifications that burden whites be considered suspect under the two-tier approach? If, as Justice John Harlan announced in his *Plessy* dissent, the Constitution is color-blind, then doesn't affirmative action cause the same violation of constitutional equality as the racial discrimination/segregation ruled unconstitutional by the Court beginning in the 1950s? The Court has been deeply divided on these questions concerning affirmative action.

The Court's First Answer: The *Bakke* Decision

Having dodged an affirmative action case in 1974,[6] the Court was presented with a controversy four years later that it could not avoid. As part of its affirmative action plan in line with HEW's guidelines, the University of California at Davis established a special admissions program in its medical school for economically and/or educationally disadvantaged persons, specifically defined as members of minority groups. Davis reserved sixteen of the one hundred seats available in the medical school each year for special admissions applicants. The special admissions program would consider for admission minority group members with lower grades and Medical College Admission Test (MCAT) scores than the regular admissions program.

Allan Bakke, a white male, was denied admission to the Davis Medical School in 1973 and 1974, even though his grades and MCAT scores were higher than those admitted under the special program. After his second application was rejected, Bakke filed suit in the state courts, claiming primarily that the university's admissions program violated the Equal Protection Clause, as well as Title VI of the Civil Rights Act of 1964. The California Supreme Court, hearing the case on appeal, ruled in Bakke's favor. Because the Davis program classified according to race, the state supreme court applied the strict-scrutiny standard in coming to a decision. The state supreme court felt that though "the goals of integrating the medical profession and increasing the number of physicians willing to serve members of minority groups were compelling state interests," the means the university had adopted were illegitimate. The California Supreme Court concluded that the Equal Protection Clause required that "no applicant may be rejected because of his race, in favor of another who is less qualified, as measured by standards applied without regard to race" and ordered Bakke's admission to the medical school. The university sought and obtained review from the U.S. Supreme Court in *Regents of the University of California* v. *Bakke* (1978).

The justices strongly disagreed among themselves on the validity of the Davis program and on the issue of affirmative action in general. Four justices (Brennan, White, Marshall, and Blackmun) approved of the use of affirmative action and believed the Davis Medical School program to be constitutional and legal under Title VI. They voted to deny Bakke's claims. Four justices (Burger, Stewart, Rehnquist, and Stevens) believed that Title VI of the Civil Rights Act of 1964 was sufficient in itself to outlaw the kind of program Davis had established (remember Chapter 4 and Justice Louis Brandeis's admonition in *Ashwander* that courts dispose of cases on statutory rather than on constitutional grounds). They agreed with the California Supreme Court that Bakke was discriminated against because of his race and voted to affirm the court's order to admit him. That left Justice Powell to cast the deciding vote.

Justice Powell's opinion, which became the judgment of the Court, is a mixed bag. On the one hand, he agreed with the lower court that strict judicial scrutiny be applied to government programs that classify on the basis of race and ethnic status.

> [The] guarantee of equal protection cannot mean one thing when applied to one individual and something else when applied to a person of another color. If both are not accorded the same protection, then it is not equal . . . Racial and ethnic distinctions of any sort are inherently suspect and thus call for the most exacting judicial examination.

For Powell, then, state educational affirmative action plans disadvantaging whites would be subjected to the same degree of judicial scrutiny as a plan disadvantaging racial minorities. And applying this strict scrutiny, he felt the Davis program could not be justified, as it set a specific racial quota without compelling state interests to justify it.

On the other hand, Powell was unwilling to say that the state could never take race into account in its educational programs. Powell recognized that "the State has a substantial interest that legitimately may be served by a properly devised admissions program involving the competitive consideration of race and ethnic origin." An admissions program that makes race a plus in a candidate's favor without "insulat[ing] the individual from comparison with all other candidates for the available seats" would meet constitutional muster, according to Powell.

Powell's opinion for the Court agreed that the affirmative action plan at Davis too rigidly drew lines on the basis of race and ethnicity. The program's "principal evil" was its denial to Bakke of his "right to individualized consideration without regard to race." But Powell also affirmed the consideration of race in a "properly devised admissions program" to meet the state's legitimate goals of diversity and countering the effect of past societal discrimination.

Justices Brennan, Marshall, and Blackmun all wrote separate opinions defending the affirmative action program at Davis. Brennan rejected the idea that racial classifications that burden whites are "inherently suspect." Because the classification used in the Davis plan did not disfavor a traditionally mistreated "class" nor "stigmatize" any class with a brand of inferiority, Brennan would apply a "heightened-" but not "strict-"scrutiny standard under the Equal Protection Clause. Using the test applied to gender-discrimination cases (see the discussion of *Craig* v. *Boren* in "The Court's Turnaround"), Brennan concluded that "racial classification designed to further remedial purposes 'must serve important governmental objectives and must be substantially related to achievement of those objectives.' " He felt the Davis program met this test.

Marshall looked at the question historically:

[The] position of the Negro today in America is the tragic but inevitable consequence of centuries of unequal treatment. Measured by any benchmark of comfort or achievement, meaningful equality remains a distant dream for the Negro . . . In light of the sorry history of discrimination and its devastating impact on the lives of Negroes, bringing the Negro into the mainstream of American life should be a state interest of the highest order . . . [While] I applaud the judgment of the Court that a university may consider race in its admissions process, it is more than a little ironic that, after several hundred years of class-based discrimination against Negroes, the Court is unwilling to hold that a class-based remedy for that discrimination is permissible.

Justice Harry Blackmun's opinion put the pro-affirmative action position most succinctly. After expressing the "hope that the time will come when an affirmative action program is unnecessary," Blackmun admitted that at the present time "that hope is a slim one." He concluded his support of the Davis program by pointing out a profound paradox of constitutional equality in America:

In order to get beyond racism, we must first take account of race. There is no other way. And in order to treat some persons equally, we must treat them differently.

The Supreme Court decided little beyond the invalidity of the particular affirmative action program challenged in the *Bakke* case. *Bakke* was merely the first word on affirmative action. Since then, the Court has tried to clarify its position.

Affirmative Action Revisited: The Court in the 1980s

One year after the *Bakke* decision the Court voted to approve an employer's voluntary affirmative action program. In *United Steelworkers of America* v.

Weber (1979), a 5–2 majority held that it was permissible for a company, as part of a collective bargaining agreement, to reserve half of its openings in a skilled-craft job training program for black employees in order to increase the overall percentage of skilled black laborers. Brian Weber, a white male, claimed that this affirmative action plan discriminated against him in violation of Title VII of the Civil Rights Act of 1964, which prohibits employers from depriving individuals of employment opportunities on the basis of race, color, sex, or national origin (see Chapter 9). But the Court upheld the plan, with Justice Brennan denying that Title VII prohibited employer programs giving preference to racial minorities. Echoing Marshall's opinion in *Bakke,* Brennan insisted:

> It would be ironic indeed if a law triggered by a Nation's concern over centuries of racial injustice and intended to improve the lot of those who had "been excluded from the American dream for so long" constituted the first legislative prohibition of all voluntary, private, race-conscious efforts to abolish traditional patterns of racial segregation and hierarchy.

But Justice William Rehnquist, in a bitter dissent, proclaimed that "*no* racial discrimination in employment is permissible under Title VII, not even preferential treatment of minorities to correct racial imbalance." Accusing the majority of neglecting clear congressional intent to bar "all racial discrimination in employment," Rehnquist concluded:

> By a tour de force reminiscent not of jurists such as Hale, Holmes, and Hughes, but of escape artists such as Houdini, the Court eludes clear statutory language, "uncontradicted" legislative history, and uniform precedent in concluding that employers, are, after all, permitted to consider race in making employment decisions.

Fullilove v. *Klutznick* (1980) offered the Court a further opportunity to tackle the hard issue of affirmative action. But unlike the *Weber* case, which involved a voluntary affirmative action plan in the private sector, the *Fullilove* case dealt with a government-imposed affirmative action quota. Congress passed the Public Works Employment Act in 1977 to stimulate the economy by providing federal grants to states and localities for public works projects. The law provided that states and localities receiving federal funds under this program use at least 10 percent of those funds to purchase services or supplies from "minority business enterprises" (MBEs)—contracting firms owned by minority group members. Nonminority contractors filed suit against this "minority set-aside" program, saying that it violated their right to equality under the Due Process Clause of the Fifth Amendment.

The Supreme Court, by a 6–3 margin, upheld the act. Speaking for the majority, Chief Justice Warren Burger stated that Congress had the power to remedy the effects of past racial discrimination in this area through the use of temporary, race-conscious policies. And Justice Powell, in a concurring opinion, felt the program even met the demands of strict scrutiny he had announced in *Bakke.* The limited set-aside program, Powell said, "is consistent with fundamental fairness." Again reflecting the Court's deep divisions on this issue, Justice Potter Stewart vehemently dissented, opening with Harlan's words from his *Plessy* dissent: "Our Constitution is color-blind." Affirmative action, he stated, promotes the very opposite of color blindness and is therefore "inherently suspect and presumptively invalid."

Since *Fullilove* the Court has continued to be divided on the question of affirmative action. The Court ruled in *Firefighters Local Union No. 1784* v. *Stotts* (1984) that a seniority system that interfered with the goals of a court-ordered affirmative action plan for the Memphis Fire Department was nevertheless valid. Blacks thus lost their challenge to a last-hired, first-fired layoff plan that undermined the gains they had made in employment as firefighters in Memphis. The Reagan administration used this decision to bolster its opposition to affirmative action in general, maintaining that all group-based remedies for blacks and other minorities must cease consistent with the Constitution's demand for color blindness. The Reagan administration contended that affirmative action could only be upheld if particular individuals could demonstrate that they were victims of past discrimination.

But the Court has rejected this extreme stance. In 1986, the Court ruled that while preferential treatment against layoffs to minority employees violated the equal protection rights of white employees with greater seniority, governments and employers can use group-based affirmative action remedies for minorities in hiring and promotion policies.[7] The Court even approved the use of percentages and goals as legitimate means of achieving the end of greater minority hiring and promotions. And in *United States* v. *Paradise* (1987), the Court narrowly approved a court-ordered affirmative action plan for Alabama Department of Public Safety troopers which required that 50 percent of state trooper promotions go to blacks for a specified period of time. Justice Brennan concluded for the majority that even using a strict-scrutiny standard, the race-conscious promotion policy was justified by a "compelling government interest" in eradicating the vestiges of years of pervasive discrimination against blacks. Furthermore, the majority decided that the temporary remedy of the one-for-one promotion quota was "narrowly tailored" in a way that did not permanently burden "innocent white troopers."

Also in 1987, in its first gender-based affirmative action ruling, the Court upheld a government-sponsored affirmative action plan for women in the case of *Johnson* v. *Transportation Agency, Santa Clara County*. In 1978, the Santa Clara Transportation Agency adopted an affirmative action plan aimed at achieving a "statistically measurable yearly improvement in hiring, training, and promotion of minorities and women throughout the Agency." The goal was to attain a work force whose racial and gender composition reflected the area in general. Paul Johnson, Diane Joyce, and ten other county employees applied for a promotion to road dispatcher, a job which was classified in the "Skilled Worker" category. Both Johnson and Joyce were rated "Well Qualified" for the position, given their experience and interview test results. Johnson had scored a few points higher on the test than Joyce, but given the fact that none of the 238 positions in this skilled worker category were held by women, the county selected Joyce for the promotion in line with its affirmative action plans. Johnson then brought suit under Title VII and the Equal Protection Clause, claiming that he was more qualified for promotion and was denied the position as a result of reverse sex discrimination. The Supreme Court, however, ruled in favor of the affirmative action plan, in effect saying that a woman's gender could be taken into account in the county's promotion plan, especially given that both candidates were well qualified and that there appeared to be a history of past discrimination against women in this particular job classification.

To this day, then, the Supreme Court remains divided over the question of affirmative action (see Table 10.1). Affirmative action presents several dilemmas for justices wishing to be true to the Constitution's promise of "equal protection of the laws." Does the Constitution require color blindness? Or can government and the private sector alleviate racism by applying color-conscious remedies that discriminate against white males? Professor Laurence Tribe has argued that counting race in a minority group member's favor may actually be less discriminatory than "race-neutral" criteria, which often reflect bias or a prior experience of racism that still exists in current facially neutral procedures. Tribe notes, for example, that facially neutral university admissions policies may mask social, cultural, or economic realities that continue to be biased against minorities. To count an individual's minority status as a plus, then, may serve to counteract the built-in systemic and historical biases against minorities.[8] Do programs that classify on the basis of race to the detriment of

Table 10.1   The Supreme Court and Affirmative Action

DEGREE OF JUDICIAL SCRUTINY APPLIED

Strict Color Blindness	Strict Scrutiny, But Program Which Serves Compelling Gov't Interest and Is Narrowly Tailored to Purpose Permissible	Heightened Scrutiny: Program Must Serve Important Gov't Objective and Be Substantially Related to Achievement of Objective	Impartiality
Rehnquist	Powell (until 1987)		Stevens
O'Connor	White		
Scalia	Burger (until 1986)	Brennan	
Stewart (until 1981)		Marshall	
		Blackmun	

INDIVIDUAL CASES, 1978–1987

Case	Decision	Justices in Favor of AA	Justices Against AA
Bakke (1978)	against aa (5–4)	M, Bren, Blmn, Wh	**P,** Bur, Reh, Stw, Stv
Weber (1979)	upheld volunteer aa plan (5–2)	**Bren,** Wh, M, Blmn, Stw	Bur, Reh
Fullilove (1980)	upheld congressional aa provision (6–3)	**Bur,** Wh, P, M, Bren, Blmn	Stw, Reh, Stv
Stotts (1984)	against aa which interfered w/seniority system (6–3)	Blmn, Bren, M	**Wh,** Bur, Reh, P, O'C Stv
Wygant (1986)	against collective bargaining agreement giving minorities protection from layoffs (5–4)	M, Bren, Blmn, Stv	P, Bur, Reh, O'C, Wh
Sheet Metal Workers v. *EEOC* (1986)	for court-ordered aa hiring quota in union apprentice program (5–4)	**Bren,** M, Blmn, P, Stv	O'C, Wh, Reh, Bur
Firefighters v. *Cleve* (1986)	upheld court-ordered aa in firefighter promotions (6–3)	**Bren,** M, Blmn, P, Stv, O'C	Wh, Reh, Bur
Paradise (1987)	upheld aa promotion plan in Alabama (5–4)	**M,** Bren, Blmn, P, Stv	O'C, Wh, Reh, Scal

Code: Bren = Brennan; Stw = Stewart; Wh = White; M = Marshall; Bur = Burger; Blmn = Blackmun; Reh = Rehnquist; P = Powell; Stv = Stevens; O'C = O'Connor; Scal = Scalia. Boldface indicates the justice who wrote the majority opinion.

whites (or gender-based affirmative action that classifies to the detriment of men) draw the same degree of constitutional scrutiny as those that disfavor "discrete and insular minorities"? Or can the Court invoke a less rigorous test for such remedial racial preferences? Finally, affirmative action raises questions about whether the Equal Protection Clause applies to individuals as individuals or as members of racial and/or ethnic groups. As mentioned, proponents of affirmative action reflect the group-based approach to equal protection, as they contend that the purpose behind the Fourteenth Amendment was to aid a particular group of people (i.e., newly freed blacks). Thus, it is consistent with contemporary group-based remedies for past societal discrimination. But critics of affirmative action have argued that the word "person" refers to the individual, thereby ruling out race-conscious remedial programs unless individuals can show that past discrimination harmed them personally.

Gender-Based Discrimination and the Constitution

Next to those based upon race and national origin, classifications based upon gender have raised the most questions in this century. Sex-based classifications surely share with race and national origin many of the characteristics that caused the Court to consider them suspect. Gender is an essentially unalterable trait that has been the basis of legal and social stereotypes that discriminate against women. For much of this nation's history, women have been relegated to "a position of political powerlessness" (the formula Justice Powell used in determining suspect classifications; see Brief 10.2).

However, women are distinguished from blacks and other ethnic groups in certain ways. Women do not constitute a "discrete and insular minority" group; in fact, they are the political majority. Women are found in every class in every neighborhood; they live and work in close physical contact with men. They share economic profits with men, but the same men also have advantages and control over them. Moreover, some generalizations about the differences between the sexes used to make distinctions in law are either benign or "protecting" of women, and a very few are based upon factually valid biological distinctions between the sexes. As a result, the Supreme Court was slow in recognizing sex discrimination as a constitutional problem. A brief history follows.

Although Jefferson's Declaration proclaimed all men to be created equal, few of the founding generation believed this generic "men" to include women. At the time, culture and religion required women to marry, and marriage laws denied women their property, their power, and even their identity. A married woman could not bind herself by contract and could not sue or be sued in court. Her husband gained complete control over all her real and personal property. He had the right to any wages she earned, and she was even required by law to assume his name upon marriage. In his commentary on the English common law, eighteenth-century British jurist William Blackstone summed up the situation:

> By marriage, the husband and wife are one person in law; that is, the very being or legal existence of the woman is suspended during the marriage, or at least is incorporated into that of the husband.[9]

While the married woman's property acts in the late 1800s brought women legal recognition, they did not confer equal legal status. Justice Black commented in 1966 that up to that point in time the laws regarding married persons "have worked out in reality to mean that though the husband and wife are one, the one is the husband." [10]

With its birth at Seneca Falls, New York, in 1848, a women's rights movement began to redress the subjugation of American women. This nascent feminist movement held out the hope that the Fourteenth Amendment, passed in 1868, was broad enough to cover women as well as newly freed blacks (insofar as it referred to "persons"). But congressional deliberations over the amendment reveal that even its supporters denied that it applied to women. In response to a question on the House floor asking whether the Fourteenth Amendment would put married women on the same footing as men, Thaddeus Stevens replied that as long as all married women were treated equally and all unmarried women treated equally, the demands of the Equal Protection Clause would be satisfied. Senator Poland of Vermont even commented that women would not need political or legal equality since "the fathers, husbands, brothers and sons to whom the right of suffrage is given will in its exercise be as watchful of the rights and interests of their wives, sisters, and children who do not vote as of their own." [11]

The Supreme Court moved quickly to confirm this opinion. In *Minor* v. *Happersett* (1875), the justices unanimously decided that the Fourteenth Amendment did not guarantee women the right to vote. And in *Bradwell* v. *Illinois* (1873), the Court upheld the Illinois Supreme Court's denial to Myra Bradwell of a license to practice law on the grounds that she was a woman. In a concurring opinion, Justice Joseph Bradley gave this now infamous reasoning for his affirmation of the state's sex discrimination:

> The civil law, as well as nature herself, has always recognized a wide difference in the respective spheres and destinies of man and woman. Man is, or should be, womans' protector and defender. The natural and proper timidity and delicacy which belongs to the female sex evidently unfits it for many of the occupations of civil life. The constitution of the family organization, which is founded in the divine ordinance, as well as in the nature of things, indicates the domestic sphere as that which properly belongs to the domain and functions of womanhood . . . It is true that many women are unmarried and not affected by any of the duties, complications, and incapacities arising out of the married state, but these are the exceptions to the general rule. The paramount destiny and mission of women are to fulfill the noble and benign offices of wife and mother. This is the law of the Creator. And the rules of civil society must be adapted to the general constitution of things, and cannot be based upon exceptional cases.

Again in *Muller* v. *Oregon* (1908), the Court used "the woman's physical structure and the performance of maternal functions" as the primary justification for upholding a state maximum-hour law for women only (see Chapter 7). With the passage of the Nineteenth Amendment in 1920 women won the right to vote, but it would take fifty-one more years for the Supreme Court to extend the principle of equality to other areas of social and political life. In the interim, the Court sustained a Michigan law prohibiting all women except the wives and daughters of bar owners from bartending. Justice Felix Frankfurter's majority opinion in *Goesaert* v. *Cleary* (1948) reasoned:

> The Constitution does not require situations "which are different in fact or opinion to be treated in law as though they were the same." Since bartending by women

> may, in the allowable legislative judgment, give rise to moral and social problems against which it may devise preventive measures, the legislature need not go to the full length of prohibition if it believes that as to a defined group of females other factors are operating which either eliminate or reduce the moral and social problems otherwise calling for prohibition.

Michigan did not have a similar prohibition on women serving as barmaids.

Even the otherwise progressive Warren Court unanimously held constitutional a jury selection scheme that excluded women. Speaking for the Court in *Hoyt* v. *Florida* (1961), Justice John Harlan concluded that since

> woman is still regarded as the center of home and family life, [w]e cannot say that it is constitutionally impermissible for a State, acting in pursuit of the general welfare, to conclude that a woman should be relieved from the civil duty of jury service unless she herself determines that such service is consistent with her own special responsibilities.

By the time the Supreme Court changed its position, Congress had already acted to rectify women's position of inequality. An Equal Rights Amendment guaranteeing that "men and women shall have equal rights throughout the United States and in every place subject to its jurisdiction" was first introduced in Congress in 1923 and, though continuously defeated after that, created some debate on the principle of women's equality. In the 1960s Congress passed legislation to grant equality to women in specific job-related areas. The Equal Pay Act of 1963 amended the Fair Labor Standards Act to require equal pay for equal work regardless of sex. And Title VII of the Civil Rights Act of 1964 prohibited sex discrimination in employment.

The Court's Turnaround: *Reed* v. *Reed* (1971) and Progeny

The year 1971 marked the turning point in the Supreme Court's extension of equality to women. In *Reed* v. *Reed* (1971), the Court for the first time used the Equal Protection Clause to strike down a law that classified on the basis of sex. In question was an Idaho law that gave men an absolute preference over women as administrators of estates. When Richard Reed, a minor, died intestate in Ada County, Idaho, his separated parents, Cecil and Sally Reed, filed competing petitions in probate court to be declared administrator of their son's estate. In accord with the Idaho law, the probate court gave preference to Cecil Reed because he was male.

The Supreme Court invalidated the Idaho law. Chief Justice Burger, for the Court, stated:

> To give mandatory preference to members of either sex over members of the other, merely to accomplish the elimination of hearings on the merits, is to make the very kind of arbitrary legislative choice forbidden by the Equal Protection Clause of the Fourteenth Amendment.

Although the Court decided the question presented in *Reed* based upon a rationality-scrutiny standard, the justices' decision implied a stricter constitutional scrutiny toward sex discrimination. Of course, Congress had begun its hearings on the revived and reintroduced Equal Rights Amendment (ERA) in 1970, and presented the amendment to the states in 1972, so the push for women's equality was all around the Court.

Two years later, in *Frontiero* v. *Richardson* (1973), the Court (or at least four justices) moved toward adopting a strict-scrutiny position on sex discrimination that would parallel its stance on race. The Court ruled against a federal law that automatically provided benefits to the wives of male members of the armed services but not to the husbands of female military personnel. Justice Brennan, writing on behalf of three other justices, began his opinion by stating:

> There can be no doubt that our Nation has had a long and unfortunate history of sex discrimination. Traditionally, such discrimination was rationalized by an attitude of "romantic paternalism" which, in practical effect, put women, not on a pedestal, but in a cage.

After chronicling the history of women's legal inequality, Justice Brennan reached the conclusion that sex discrimination ought to be regarded as suspect, along with race and national origin:

> With these considerations in mind, we can only conclude that classifications based upon sex, like classifications based upon race, alienage, or national origin, are inherently suspect, and must therefore be subjected to strict judicial scrutiny. Applying the analysis mandated by that stricter standard of review, it is clear that the statutory scheme now before us is constitutionally invalid.

The conclusions Brennan reached in *Frontiero* brought the Court a long way in a short period of time. He did not represent the majority, however. Only four justices concluded that sex ought to be regarded as a suspect classification. For the other four justices who made up the eight-member majority that declared the law invalid, the rationality standard announced in *Reed* provided ample justification. In fact, Justice Powell's concurring opinion indicated that for the Court to declare sex a suspect classification was premature, given the ratification debate over the ERA:

> There is [a] compelling reason for deferring a general categorizing of sex classifications as invoking the strictest test of judicial scrutiny. The Equal Rights Amendment, which if adopted will resolve the substance of this precise question, has been approved by the Congress and submitted for ratification by the States. If this Amendment is duly adopted, it will represent the will of the people accomplished in the manner prescribed by the Constitution. By acting prematurely and unnecessarily, as I view it, the Court has assumed a decisional responsibility at the very time when state legislatures, functioning within the traditional democratic process, are debating the proposed Amendment. It seems to me that this reaching to pre-empt by judicial action a major political decision which is currently in process of resolution does not reflect appropriate respect for duly prescribed legislative processes.

The majority of justices, then, did not place gender classifications in the higher tier or the two-tier approach, to be given strict scrutiny. In 1976, a majority of the Court did accept a new standard of scrutiny for sex-based classifications, somewhere in between rationality and strict scrutiny. In *Craig* v. *Boren,* the Court invalidated sections of an Oklahoma law that allowed females to purchase 3.2 percent beer at age eighteen but prohibited males from doing so until they reached age twenty-one. For the majority, Justice Brennan declared that sex-based classifications would receive what has been termed a "heightened" or an "intermediate" level of scrutiny, governed by the following standards:

> To withstand constitutional challenge, previous cases establish that classifications by gender must serve important governmental objectives and must be substantially related to achievement of those objectives.

In *Mississippi University for Women* v. *Hogan* (1982), the Court gave greater specificity to this "intermediate level of scrutiny" established in *Craig*. Justice Sandra Day O'Connor wrote an opinion for a five-justice majority that denied the right to an all women's university to discriminate against a male applicant to its nursing school. Justice O'Connor, in laying out the framework for determining whether the state could prove that it had "important governmental objectives" and its means of achieving them were "substantially related to . . . those objectives," declared:

> Although the test for determining the validity of gender-based classifications is straightforward, it must be applied free of fixed notions concerning the roles and abilities of males and females. Care must be taken in ascertaining whether the statutory objective itself reflects archaic and stereotypic notions. Thus, if the statutory objective is to exclude or "protect" members of one gender because they are presumed to suffer from an inherent handicap or to be innately inferior, the objective itself is illegitimate.
>
> If the State's objective is legitimate and important, we next determine where the requisite direct, substantial relationship between objective and means is present. The purpose of requiring that close relationship is to assure that the validity of a classification is determined through reasoned analysis rather than through the mechanical application of traditional, often inaccurate, assumptions about the proper roles of men and women. The need for the requirement is amply revealed by reference to the broad range of statutes already invalidated by this Court, statutes that relied upon the simplistic, outdated assumption that gender could be used as a "proxy for other, more germane bases of classification."

In a series of cases beginning with *Reed*, then, the Supreme Court established that the Equal Protection Clause of the Fourteenth Amendment guaranteed women's equality. With these rulings, sex-based classifications would be treated as "somewhat suspect" and be given greater scrutiny by the Court than they had been given in the past. In addition, the justices had added a "third tier" to their equal protection analysis, that of intermediate scrutiny (in between rational and strict scrutiny).

Limitations on Equal Protection for Women

At the same time, however, the Supreme Court has upheld numerous classifications that either explicitly or implicitly differentiate on the basis of gender. These decisions upholding gender-based classifications came in three types of cases: (1) where the Court felt a government policy of "benign discrimination" was justified in order to help women overcome the effects of past disadvantages; (2) where the Court believed the classification was related to "real" biological or other differences between the sexes; and (3) where the government made a classification that was gender-neutral on its face but was claimed to have a discriminatory impact upon women. A brief look at these cases will show the ambivalence with which the Court regards gender-discrimination cases.

In the area of "benign discrimination," the Court has allowed governments to use gender-based policies to compensate women for past inequalities. In a series of cases beginning in 1974, the Court allowed

- a property-tax exemption to be granted to widows but not to widowers (*Kahn* v. *Shevin* [1974]),
- a promotion policy in the navy that gave female officers more time than their male counterparts to attain promotion (*Schlesinger* v. *Ballard* [1975]),

□ a Social Security retirement benefit policy that permitted women to drop more low-earning years than men (*Califano* v. *Webster* [1977]), and

□ a Social Security plan that treated nondependent wives more preferentially than nondependent husbands (*Heckler* v. *Mathews* [1984]).

The *Johnson* case discussed under affirmative action has also been classified by some as an example of benign discrimination.

The Court has also upheld laws or government programs that it felt classified according to gender schemes reflecting real biological differences between the sexes and therefore did not require the same degree of equal protection scrutiny. For instance, in *Geduldig* v. *Aiello* (1974), the Court majority rejected a claim that a California disability insurance scheme violated the Equal Protection Clause because it excluded normal pregnancy from the list of disabilities that were covered. The Court's reasoning, in this case, was that an exclusion based upon pregnancy was not a sex-based classification per se, since the distinction was between pregnant and nonpregnant *persons* (which would include men and women!). Given this conclusion, the Court only had to decide if the state's exclusion of pregnancy from its disability scheme was reasonable, which Justice Stewart did on the grounds of cost-effectiveness and governmental policy choice.

The *Geduldig* decision was extended to similar challenges of employer disability schemes under Title VII of the Civil Rights Act in *General Electric Company* v. *Gilbert* (1976). Again, the majority, led by Justice Rehnquist, ruled that discrimination on the basis of pregnancy was not gender discrimination "as such" and could be shown to be "neutral" with no discriminatory effect under Title VII. Though Title VII arguably offers stronger protection for women's equality than the Equal Protection Clause, Congress also proved feeble, in the Court's analysis, to rectify discrimination based upon this "real biological difference" between the sexes. Congress specifically responded to the *Gilbert* decision, however, passing the Pregnancy Discrimination Act (PDA) as an amendment to Title VII. The PDA provides that "women affected by pregnancy, childbirth, or related medical conditions shall be treated the same for all employment-related purposes, including receipt of benefits under fringe benefit programs, as other persons not so affected but similar in their ability or inability to work." The Court recently decided a case questioning the special treatment of pregnancy (see Brief 10.3).

The Court has also upheld sex classifications on the grounds of biological difference in cases involving unmarried fathers. In *Parham* v. *Hughes* (1979), and in *Lehr* v. *Robertson* (1983), the Court upheld state laws that treated unmarried mothers more favorably than unmarried fathers. The justices composing the majority in these cases concluded that women and men were not similarly situated with respect to the law's classification scheme; therefore, the state would only have to satisfy rationality scrutiny: "Unlike the mother of an illegitimate child whose identity will rarely be in doubt, the identity of the father will frequently be unknown." A majority of the justices believed that in both cases, the state could show a reasonable relation between the classification in question and a legitimate governmental purpose, given the woman's "unshakable responsibility for the care of the child."

A final case where the Court upheld what it considered to be a biologically based sex classification involved a statutory rape law in California. The law

☐ Brief 10.3   Pregnancy and Equality Reconsidered: The Cal Fed Case

California Federal Savings and Loan Association v. *Guerra* (1987) highlights many of the current dilemmas over what the Equal Protection Clause requires in terms of sexual equality. California law requires employers to provide female employees with an unpaid pregnancy leave of up to four months. It gives female employees a right to be reinstated in a "substantially similar job" after their return from pregnancy disability leave. California Federal Savings and Loan Association (Cal Fed) had a leave policy that allowed employees who had completed three months on the job to take unpaid leaves of absence for a variety of reasons, including pregnancy, but the company reserved the right to fire an employee who had taken a leave of absence if no similar positions were available upon his or her return.

Lillian Garland, who had worked as a receptionist at Cal Fed for a number of years, took a pregnancy/childbirth disability leave under company policy, but was informed upon her desired return date that no similar positions were available. The state of California charged Cal Fed with violating the state pregnancy leave law. Cal Fed in turn charged that the California law was preempted by the federal Pregnancy Discrimination Act (PDA). Cal Fed claimed that the state was requiring that the company violate Title VII by treating pregnant women better than it treated other disabled employees. The state of California argued that the law in question was entirely consistent with the objectives of Title VII.

In January 1987, the Supreme Court ruled that the PDA did not preempt California from passing legislation that would give preferential treatment to pregnant women. Writing for the majority, Justice Marshall concluded that the PDA and the California law were consistent, in that both were aimed at providing equal employment opportunities to pregnant women. In passing the PDA, Congress only intended that pregnant women be treated at least as well as other employees, and not that states could not legislate more complete protection. Quoting from the Ninth Circuit Court of Appeals decision, Marshall stated:

> The PDA does not "demand that state law be blind to pregnancy's existence" . . . [I]n enacting the PDA Congress intended "to construct a floor beneath which pregnancy disability benefits may not drop—not a ceiling above which they may not rise."

Furthermore, Marshall contended that the two laws were compatible, since the California law

> does not compel California employers to treat pregnant workers *better* than other disabled employees; it merely establishes benefits that employers must, at a minimum, provide to pregnant workers. Employers are free to give comparable benefits to other disabled employees, thereby treating "women affected by pregnancy" no better than "other persons not so affected but similar in their ability or inability to work."

An interesting thing about the *Cal Fed* case is that feminist groups devoted to securing women's equality divided over the case and filed conflicting *amicus curiae* briefs with the Court.[12] The question of pregnancy and the Equal Protection Clause divides not only the Court, then, but also women's rights interest groups.

---

made it illegal for a man to engage in an act of sexual intercourse with a woman under the age of eighteen who was not his wife. In *Michael M.* v. *Superior Court of Sonoma County* (1981), the Supreme Court denied that the law violated the Equal Protection Clause. Justice Rehnquist, writing for four members of the five-judge majority, ruled that the law served the legitimate purpose of preventing teenage pregnancy, thus satisfying the demands of rationality scrutiny:

> We need not be medical doctors to discern that young men and young women are not similarly situated with respect to the problems and the risks of sexual intercourse. Only women may become pregnant and they suffer disproportionately the profound physical, emotional and psychological consequences of sexual activity. The statute at issue here protects women from sexual intercourse at an age when those consequences are particularly severe . . . [and thus] is sufficiently related to the State's objectives to pass constitutional muster.

Rehnquist went on to say that a gender-neutral law was not a desirable alternative to a law that punished the man but not the woman:

> Because virtually all of the significant harmful and inescapably identifiable consequences of teenage pregnancy fall on the young female, a legislature acts well within its authority when it elects to punish only the participant who, by nature, suffers few of the consequences of his conduct. It is hardly unreasonable for a legislature acting to protect minor females to exclude them from punishment. Moreover, the risk of pregnancy itself constitutes a substantial deterrence to young females. No similar natural sanctions deter males. A criminal sanction imposed solely on males thus serves to roughly "equalize" the deterrents on the sexes.

Justice Brennan, writing a dissenting opinion joined by Justices White and Marshall, chastised the majority for failing to apply the appropriate standard of review to the discriminatory statute. Brennan argued that since the statute was based upon "outmoded sexual stereotypes," California had failed to meet "its burden of proving that the statutory classification is substantially related to the achievement of its asserted goal" (using the intermediate level of judicial scrutiny announced in *Craig*). And Justice John Paul Stevens, in a separate dissent, reiterated his long-standing position that equal protection requires "evenhanded enforcement of the law." He said, "A rule that authorizes punishment of only one of two equally guilty wrongdoers violates the essence of the constitutional requirement that the sovereign must govern impartially."

A third area in which the Court has allowed statutory classifications which burden or "protect" women on the basis of their gender is that of **disparate-impact legislation,** laws which are neutral on their face but which have a disproportionate impact upon women. In *Personnel Administrator of Massachusetts* v. *Feeney* (1979), Helen Feeney claimed that a gender-neutral statute on its face actually discriminated against women in violation of the Fourteenth Amendment. Massachusetts law gave veterans an absolute preference for employment in state civil service jobs. In all of the state government positions she applied for, Feeney was ranked below male veterans even though she scored higher on competitive civil service examinations. She claimed that since over 98 percent of Massachusetts's veterans were male, the statute giving veterans absolute preference in state hiring violated her right to equal protection. Justice Stewart concluded for the Court majority, however, that the law served a legitimate gender-neutral purpose which the state had the power to enact:

> Nothing in the record demonstrates that this preference for veterans was originally devised or subsequently reenacted because it would accomplish the collateral goal of keeping women in a stereotypic and predefined place in the Massachusetts Civil Service. . . [T]he law remains what it purports to be: a preference for veterans of either sex over nonveterans of either sex, not for men over women.

Justice Marshall, writing for himself and Justice Brennan, dissented, stating that, although the Massachusetts law is

> neutral in form, the statute is anything but neutral in application. It inescapably reserves a major sector of public employment to "an already established class which, as a matter of historical fact, is 98% male." Where the foreseeable impact of a facially neutral policy is so disproportionate, the burden should rest on the State to establish that sex-based considerations played no part in the choice of that particular legislative scheme. Clearly, that burden was not sustained here. . . [The State's] statutory scheme both reflects and perpetuates precisely the kind of archaic assumptions about women's roles which we have previously held invalid.

In a final case, which defies classification, the Court in 1981 allowed a gender-based classification when it sustained the males-only draft registration ordered by Congress and the president in 1980. In *Rostker* v. *Goldberg,* the justices deferred to Congress's broad authority over the armed forces in upholding the gender-based classification. Because women were ineligible to be drafted into armed combat, the Court concluded that Congress could legitimately exclude them from draft registration. No justice, not even the dissenters, challenged the sex-based nature of combat restrictions on women.

What conclusions can be drawn from this discussion of cases involving sex discrimination? The Supreme Court has acted ambiguously in interpreting the Fourteenth Amendment's application to gender classifications. A majority of the justices usually has invalidated laws containing explicit sex-based classifications that they feel operate to the detriment of women, especially when these laws have treated "similarly situated" men and women differently. But the Court's decisions on what Professor Wendy Williams has described as "hard cases" (i.e., ones that challenge the parameters of what American culture is willing to accept as appropriate sex-role behavior) have been more deferential to statutes that make distinctions on the basis of gender.[13] The Court majority has been generally unwilling to use the Equal Protection Clause to outlaw government practices involving pregnancy, rape, or sex distinctions in the military.

Closer examination of individual justice's opinions in gender-discrimination cases (see Table 10.2) reveals a division on the Court. On one side sit justices, led by Brennan and Marshall, who are consistent proponents of the *Craig* intermediate-level-of-scrutiny criterion. These justices have required that if the government is going to make a classification on the basis of gender, that classification "must serve important governmental objectives and must be substantially related to achievement of those objectives." They have almost always voted to vacate gender-based legal distinctions. On the other side of the issue sit justices, led by Chief Justice Rehnquist, who apply a straight rationality-scrutiny standard to all gender-classification schemes. Rehnquist, for example, has stressed the importance of deferring to legislative judgments and therefore has usually voted to sustain government classifications on the basis of gender. His general position is that

> the Equal Protection Clause does not "demand that a statute necessarily apply equally to all persons" or require "things which are different in fact . . . to be treated in law as though they were the same. . ." [Because of this,] this Court has consistently upheld statutes where the gender classification is not invidious, but rather realistically reflects the fact that the sexes are not similarly situated in certain circumstances.

In the middle of these two opposing camps sit justices, most notably Justice Stevens, who exercise independent judgment on a case-by-case basis, and thus act as the "swing votes" in gender-discrimination cases.

In summary, the Court, though divided, has brought the demands of equality found in the Fourteenth Amendment to governments classifying on the basis of gender. The justices have brought most laws differentiating according to gender under a heightened judicial scrutiny. At the same time, however, the majority has yet to conclude that gender-based classifications are suspect and, therefore, uniformly subjected to strict judicial scrutiny.

Table 10.2   Justices' Decisions in Gender-Classification Cases

CASE	JUSTICES										
	Bren	Stw	Wh	M	Bur	Blmn	Reh	P	Stv	O'C	Scal
Reed v. Reed (1971)	S	S	S	S	S	S					
Frontiero (1973)	S	S	S	S	S	S	U	S			
Kahn v. Shevin (1974)	S	U	S	S	U	U	U	U			
Geduldig (1974)	S	U	U	S	U	U	U	U			
Schles. v. Ballard (1975)	S	U	S	S	U	U	U	U			
Weinberger v. Wiesenfeld (1975)	S	S	S	S	S	S	S	S			
Stanton v. Stntn (1975)	S	S	S	S	S	S	U	S			
Craig. v. Boren (1976)	S	S	S	S	U	S	U	S	S		
Gilbert (1976)	S	U	U	S	U	U	U	U	S		
Califano v. Webster (1977)	U	U	U	U	U	U	U	U	U		
Parham v. Hughes (1979)	S	U	S	S	U	S	U	U	U		
Feeney (1979)	S	U	U	S	U	U	U	U	U		
Michael M. (1981)	S	U	S	S	U	U	U	U	S		
Rostker (1981)	S	U	S	S	U	U	U	U	U		
Hogan (1982)	S		S	S	U	S	U	U	S	S	
Lehr v. Robtsn (1983)	U		S	S	U	U	S	U	U	U	
Heckler (1984)	U		U	U	U	U	S	U	U	U	
Cal Fed v. Guerra (1987)	U		S	U		U	U	S	U	U	U
Johnson v. Sta Clara (1987)	U		S	U		U	U	U	U	U	S
Totals (Struck-Upheld)	14–5	5–9	14–5	15–4	4–13	7–12	3–15	6–12	4–8	1–4	1–1

Code: "S" refers to when a judge voted to strike down (rule invalid) a law which differentiated on the basis of gender or pregnancy.
"U" refers to a judge voting to uphold laws which differentiated according to gender or pregnancy.
Code: Bren = Brennan; Stw = Stewart; Wh = White; M = Marshall; Bur = Burger; Blmn = Blackmun; Reh = Rehnquist; P = Powell;
Stv = Stevens; O'C = O'Connor; Scal = Scalia. Boldface indicates the justice who wrote the majority opinion.

The Equal Rights Amendment and Constitutional Equality for Women

The Equal Rights Amendment reads as follows:

1. Equality of rights under the law shall not be denied or abridged by the United States or by any State on account of sex.
2. The Congress shall have the power to enforce, by appropriate legislation, the provisions of this article.
3. This amendment shall take effect two years after the date of ratification.

After a fifty-year struggle to win congressional approval for an equal rights amendment, the House of Representatives (by a vote of 354–23) and the Senate (by a vote of 84–8) passed the ERA in 1972 and sent it on to the states for ratification. Congress gave the states seven years to ratify the amendment. Within the first year of passage, thirty of the required thirty-eight states had ratified the amendment. But there the process broke down. Over the next five years only five additional states ratified the amendment, and three states sought to rescind their original enthusiastic approval of the ERA. Congress extended the original 1979 deadline by thirty-nine months, but, even at that, no additional states ratified the ERA by June 1982, and the amendment died.[14]
    What caused such a simple statement of egalitarian principles to fail? One argument holds that the Supreme Court's interpretation of the demands of the Fourteenth Amendment with respect to sex discrimination made an ERA unnecessary and redundant. Others contend that a very vocal minority succeeded in changing the discourse surrounding the ERA, making it into a women's military draft, unisex bathroom, abortion-enhancing, family-wrecking provision. Others partially fault the amendment's supporters, who often made radical claims for what the ERA would do, causing a decline in popular and state legislative support. Attempts have been and are being made to reintroduce the ERA in Congress, but for the present time, it lies dormant.[15] The Equal Rights Amendment, if ever passed, would probably clarify the question of how to regard gender consistent with the ideal of equality. But even an Equal Rights Amendment would require judicial interpretation and, given the current divisions on the Court, would still leave judges with the difficult task of deciding the "hard issues" of pregnancy, affirmative action for women, the military, and disparate-impact legislation.

Age Discrimination and Equality

The Court has never considered age-based classifications inherently suspect under the two-tier approach. Two Burger Court decisions exemplify the Court's approach to legislation that classifies by age. In *Massachusetts Board of Retirement* v. *Murgia* (1976), the Court upheld a state law requiring state police officers to retire at age fifty. Robert Murgia, an officer forced to retire even though he had just passed a rigorous physical and mental examination, challenged the law on equal protection grounds. But the Court, in a *per curiam* opinion, upheld the law using a lower-tier rationality standard:

> While the treatment of the aged in this Nation has not been wholly free of discrimination, such persons, unlike, say, those who have been discriminated against on the basis of race or national origin, have not experienced a "history

of purposeful unequal treatment" or been subjected to unique disabilities on the basis of stereotyped characteristics not truly indicative of their abilities. The class subject to the . . . statute consists of uniformed state police officers over the age of 50. It cannot be said to discriminate only against the elderly. Rather, it draws the line at a certain age in middle life. But even old age does not define a "discrete and insular" group in need of "extraordinary protection from the majoritarian political process." Instead it marks a stage that each of us will reach if we live out our normal life span. Even if the statute could be said to impose a penalty upon a class defined as the aged, it would not impose a distinction sufficiently akin to those classifications that we have found suspect to call for strict judicial scrutiny.

Using the lower-tier approach the Court decided that the state's announced purpose of protecting public safety "by assuring physical preparedness of its uniformed police" was a reasonable justification for the mandatory retirement scheme.

Three years later the Court reiterated its position that age was not a suspect classification. In *Vance* v. *Bradley* (1979), the Court sustained a federal law forcing Foreign Service personnel to retire at age sixty. It was reasonable for Congress to conclude, Justice Byron White said, "that age involved increased risks of less than superior performance in overseas assignments."

In lone dissenting opinions in each case, Justice Marshall took the opportunity to attack the rigid application of a two-tier analysis to equal protection. He claimed that the Court's adherence to this approach has meant that the Court almost always strikes down that limited class of laws subjected to strict scrutiny while almost always upholding all the rest under a rationality test. "The approach presents the danger that," Marshall stated in his *Murgia* dissent, "relevant factors will be misapplied or ignored. All interests not 'fundamental' and all classes not 'suspect' are not the same; and it is time for the Court to drop the pretense that, for the purposes of the Equal Protection Clause, they are." Instead of "suspectness" and "nonsuspectness," Marshall would have the Court focus upon "the character of the classification in question, the relative importance to individuals in the class discriminated against of the governmental benefits that they do not receive, and the state interests asserted in support of the classification." Using this more flexible approach, Marshall would have voided automatic retirement for individuals based upon their age alone.

While the Court has continued to disregard the aged as a suspect class,[16] Congress has acted to prohibit age discrimination. The Age Discrimination in Employment Act of 1967 forbids employers from discriminating against employees because of age, and the Age Discrimination Act of 1975 prevents age discrimination in any program receiving federal funds.

Aliens and the Equal Protection Clause

In the early 1970s, the Supreme Court elevated government classifications based upon alienage to the highest tier of scrutiny under the Equal Protection Clause. For example, in *Graham* v. *Richardson* (1971), the Court ruled that states could not deny welfare benefits to aliens. Justice Blackmun announced the Court's rationale in making alienage a suspect classification:

Classifications based on alienage, like those based on nationality or race, are inherently suspect and subject to close judicial scrutiny. Aliens as a class are a prime example of a "discrete and insular" minority for whom such heightened judicial solicitude is appropriate.

Blackmun then applied strict scrutiny to examine whether the states had a compelling interest in excluding aliens from receiving welfare benefits:

> We conclude that a State's desire to preserve limited welfare benefits for its own citizens is inadequate to justify [the denial of welfare benefits to aliens]. An alien as well as a citizen is a "person" for equal protection purposes; [a]liens like citizens pay taxes and may be called into the armed forces. There can be no "special public interest" in tax revenues to which aliens have contributed on an equal basis with the residents of the state.

Subsequent to the *Graham* decision, the Court struck down a Connecticut law excluding aliens from practicing law,[17] state and federal laws restricting state civil service jobs to American citizens,[18] and a New York law preventing aliens from receiving financial aid for higher education.[19] And in *Plyler* v. *Doe* (1982), a case referred to earlier, the Court decided that Texas could not deny free public education to the children of illegal aliens.

However, the Court does not always consider alienage to be a suspect classification. In *Plyler* v. *Doe*, for example, Justice Brennan's majority opinion relied upon intermediate scrutiny to invalidate Texas's denial of public education to aliens. And in numerous other cases, the Court using the lower-tier rationality standard has deferred to legislative restrictions on illegal aliens. In 1978, the Court allowed a New York law barring aliens from employment as state troopers.[20] And in *Ambach* v. *Norwick* (1979), the justices sustained a New York statute forbidding state certification as a public school teacher to noncitizens, unless they have "manifested an intention to apply for citizenship." In *Ambach* v. *Norwick,* the Court announced "the general principle that some state functions are so bound up with the operation of the State as governmental entity as to permit the exclusion from those functions of all persons who have not become part of the process of self-government."

Justice Marshall in a recent decision best characterized the Court's position on aliens and the Equal Protection Clause:

> As a general matter, a State law that discriminates on the basis of alienage can be sustained only if it can withstand strict judicial scrutiny. . . We have, however, developed a narrow exception to the rule that discrimination based on alienage triggers strict scrutiny. This exception has been labelled the "political function" exception and applies to laws that exclude aliens from positions intimately related to the process of democratic self-government.[21]

The Court's rulings on the constitutional status of aliens have drawn criticism from a number of sources. Some have questioned whether aliens as a class deserve the same kind of strict scrutiny that racial and ethnic minorities have been granted. After all, alienage is not an unalterable trait; noncitizens voluntarily change their status and, as a result, gain equal rights. Moreover, aliens have been totally excluded by both the courts and the Constitution itself from voting and from attaining elected public offices. Justice Rehnquist has stated his objections succinctly: "There is no language [or] any historical evidence as to the intent of the Framers [of the Fourteenth Amendment], which would suggest in the slightest degree that it was intended to render alienage a 'suspect' classification. . . The Constitution itself recognizes a basic difference between citizens and aliens."[22]

Others have suggested that the Court would be on more solid ground if it dealt with alienage issues from the standpoint of federal-state relations. That is, the Court could rule that federal power over immigration preempts state laws regarding aliens, thus rendering state restrictions on aliens "suspect," but for different reasons.[23]

Illegitimacy and the Equal Protection Clause

The unequal treatment of illegitimate children has come under the constitutional scrutiny of the Fourteenth Amendment. But as Gerald Gunther aptly observes, the Supreme Court's rulings on illegitimacy classifications have been inconsistent:

> The Court's course in reviewing classifications based on illegitimacy has been a wavering one. In no area of classifications triggering occasional heightened scrutiny have the Court's actions been more unpredictable—and more inarticulate in explaining what degree of heightened scrutiny is warranted.[24]

The Court first suggested heightened scrutiny of laws disfavoring non-marital children in *Levy* v. *Louisiana* (1968). There the justices found unconstitutional a law that denied illegitimate children the right to recover damages for the wrongful death of their mother. Though couched in the language of rationality scrutiny, Justice Douglas's majority opinion suggested stricter judicial scrutiny of illegitimacy classifications:

> [The] test [is] whether the line drawn is a rational one, [but] we have been extremely sensitive when it comes to basic civil rights and have not hesitated to strike down an invidious classification even though it had history and tradition on its side. The rights asserted here involve the intimate, familial relationship between a child and his own mother. . . [W]hy should the illegitimate child . . . be denied correlative rights which other citizens enjoy? [Illegitimacy] has no relation to the nature of the wrong inflicted on the mother. [It] is invidious to discriminate against [illegitimate children] when no action, conduct, or demeanor of theirs is possibly relevant to the harm that was done the mother.

In a similar ruling four years later, the Court struck down as a denial of equal protection a state workmen's compensation law depriving dependent illegitimate children of equal recovery rights in the event of their parent's death. In *Weber* v. *Aetna Casualty & Surety Co.* (1972), the Court reasoned that since illegitimacy involved "sensitive and fundamental personal rights," as well as classification schemes "relating to status of birth," any law based upon this category would be subjected to "strict scrutiny." Justice Powell concluded that bringing down legal condemnation of "irresponsible liaisons beyond the bonds of marriage . . . on the head of an infant is illogical and unjust."

However, the Court's rulings in the late 1970s blurred the issue of whether illegitimacy should be regarded as a constitutionally suspect classification. In a series of cases highlighted by *Lalli* v. *Lalli* (1978), the Court sustained laws that denied equal rights to illegitimate children. In *Lalli*, Justice Powell conceded that a law which denied unacknowledged illegitimates access to their father's estate "appears to operate unfairly." "But," he continued, "few statutory classifications are entirely free from the criticism that they sometimes produce inequitable results. Our inquiry under the Equal Protection Clause does not focus on the abstract 'fairness' of a state law, but on whether the statute's relation to the state interests it is intended to promote is so tenuous that it lacks the rationality contemplated by the 14th Amendment." The same Justice Powell who had announced strict scrutiny as the judicial criterion for illegitimacy classifications in *Weber* moved back to rationality scrutiny six years later in *Lalli*.

The Court's fluctuations have left the question about the constitutional status of discrimination against illegitimate children unresolved. Its inconsistencies in this area also suggest some of the inherent problems with the two- (or three-) tier approach itself, problems that will be discussed at the end of this chapter.

Handicapped Persons and the Equal Protection Clause

Physically and mentally disabled persons have begun to press claims for equal protection of the laws. Many commentators believe that state actions discriminating against the handicapped ought to be subjected to strict judicial scrutiny. After all, a handicap is usually unalterable, often subjects its bearer to "invidious discrimination," and usually condemns him or her to a position of economic, social, and political powerlessness. Professor Judith Baer even argues that "the disabled are as powerless and isolated a minority as any group in American society." [25]

But the Supreme Court has not yet seen fit to include the handicapped on the list of suspect classificaitons requiring its strict scrutiny. The Court has come far in recognizing the problem of discrimination against the handicapped. Only sixty years ago the justices enthusiastically approved a court order authorizing the sterilization of a "feeble-minded" woman, proclaiming that "three generations of imbeciles are enough." [26] Today the Court has shown a willingness to invalidate unreasonable actions taken against disabled persons. However, the Court has not been willing to subject differential treatment of the handicapped to any "more exacting standard of judicial review than is normally accorded economic and social legislation" (*Cleburne* v. *Cleburne Living Center* [1985]).

Justice White's opinion in *Cleburne* v. *Cleburne Living Center*, a decision dealing with mentally retarded persons, exemplifies the Court's rationale for lower-tier analysis of classifications applying to the handicapped:

> It is undeniable in that those who are mentally retarded have a reduced ability to cope and function in the everyday world. . . . They are thus different, immutably so, in relevant respects, and the states' interest in dealing with and providing for them is plainly a legitimate one.

The *Cleburne* case is significant because the Court of Appeals for the Fifth Circuit had invalidated a city ordinance discriminating against the mentally retarded using an intermediate level of judicial scrutiny. The Supreme Court rejected the judgment that mental retardation was a "quasi-suspect classification," using *Murgia* as its guide:

> The lesson of *Murgia* is that where individuals in the group affected by a law have distinguishing characteristics relevant to interests the state has the authority to implement, the courts have been very reluctant . . . to closely scrutinize legislative choices as to whether, how and to what extent those interests should be

pursued. In such cases, the Equal Protection Clause requires only a rational means to serve a legitimate end.

A majority of the Supreme Court, then, has concluded that because of real differences between disabled and nondisabled persons, the Equal Protection Clause only requires that judges exercise rationality scrutiny when ruling on legislation affecting the handicapped.

Congress has acted forcefully in the last two decades to protect the handicapped from discrimination and to provide them with access to various institutions essential to their goal of equal opportunity. For example, in the Rehabilitation Act of 1973, Congress provided that "no otherwise qualified handicapped individual . . . shall, solely by reason of his handicap, be excluded from participation, be denied the benefits of, or be subjected to discrimination under any program or activity receiving federal financial assistance." And in 1975, Congress passed the Education of All Handicapped Children Act, which establishes for "all handicapped children the right to a free appropriate public education" and provides federal funds to ensure that end. Although the Supreme Court has narrowly construed these two federal laws, their passage has brought progress in the struggle of handicapped people toward full equal opportunity.

Fundamental Rights and the Equal Protection Clause

In addition to legislation that invokes suspect classifications, laws that threaten fundamental rights have also come under strict scrutiny under the two-tier approach. The Supreme Court has used the Fourteenth Amendment to hold that "any classification which serves to penalize the exercise of a fundamental right, unless shown to be necessary to promote a compelling governmental interest, is unconstitutional." [27] Here again, the Court seems to combine aspects of the Equal Protection and Due Process Clauses of the Fourteenth Amendment. Using a fundamental rights analysis, the Court has not only ruled against laws which deter or penalize the exercise of a fundamental right, but also has invalidated government policies which create inequalities in access to or levels of a fundamental right. Thus, the Court says that the Constitution disallows relative deprivations that usurp the power of individuals to exercise rights and make choices in areas that ought to be beyond the majority's control.

But the interpretation of fundamental rights under the Fourteenth Amendment is even more controversial than the determination of suspect classifications. It involves the judiciary in making determinations about what constitutes a fundamental right, often absent any clear constitutional statement. Beyond the question of what makes a right fundamental (see Brief 10.4), judges have had to decide how far the protection of such rights goes. Are fundamental rights absolutely protected, absent a compelling governmental interest? Or can government regulate the exercise of these rights? If so, to what extent can government restrict the individual's fundamental rights?

The Supreme Court's answers to these questions about the nature and scope of fundamental rights have understandably brought it under constitutional criticism. Critics like Chief Justice Rehnquist and Professor John Hart

Ely argue that elected officials representing the people's will and not judges should make determinations about what rights beyond those explicitly listed in the Constitution itself are fundamental.[28] Others have contended that the scope of protection offered to fundamental rights under the Fourteenth Amendment suggests the Court's earlier substantive-due-process decisions, where property rights were given more or less absolute protection against any government interference. Arguments that the Court has recreated the despised substantive-due-process doctrine found in cases like *Lochner* v. *New York* (see Chapter 7) abound in the critical literature.

But whatever the problems with the open-endedness of the search for fundamental rights, with the overextension of judicial authority involved in such a search, and with the usurpation of the power of the people's tribunals

---

🖳 *Brief 10.4   What Makes a Right Fundamental?*

In the process of "discovering" fundamental rights, judges have attempted to answer the question of what makes a right fundamental, and what the source of such rights ought to be. For the strict interpretivist, of course, the only fundamental rights the Supreme Court can protect are those found explicitly in the text of the Constitution itself. All other rights are determined by popularly elected officials. For most judges and constitutional scholars, however, this strict interpretivism too narrowly defines the area free from governmental intrusion. And the Constitution itself, specifically the Ninth Amendment, tells judges to look beyond the document for "the enumeration . . . of [other rights] . . . retained by the people." Most constitutional commentators, therefore, would grant fundamental status to rights beyond those listed in the Constitution. But where is the line drawn between rights that are fundamental and ones that are not? A brief look at judicial reasoning may be instructive.

Justice Benjamin Cardozo, in seeking justification for incorporating specific provisions of rights into the Fourteenth Amendment (see *Palko* v. *Connecticut* in Chapter 8), said that rights "so rooted in the traditions and collective conscience of our people as to be ranked as fundamental" deserved constitutional protection. Cardozo also spoke of the fundamental nature of rights "implicit in the concept of ordered liberty." In more recent years justices have sought other lines of reasoning to find sources of fundamental rights. Justice William O. Douglas in *Griswold* v. *Connecticut* (1965) (to be discussed in a later section of this chapter) found substantive rights emanating from the Bill of Rights, which created "penumbras" of protection for rights implied by its specific provisions. In the same decision, Justice Arthur Goldberg saw the source of fundamental rights as the "entire fabric of the Constitution and the

purposes that underlthe its specific guarantees," and Justice John Harlan pointed to "history and tradition" as his source for fundamental rights. Chief Justice Earl Warren found the source of fundamental rights in "the evolving standards of decency that mark the progress of a maturing society."[29]

Justice Thurgood Marshall's dissent in *San Antonio* v. *Rodriguez* (1973) may offer the most comprehensive look at the sources of fundamental rights. Wishing to avoid "an unprincipled, subjective, 'picking-and-choosing' between various interests" to determine which rights were fundamental, Marshall came up with the following guidelines:

> Although not all fundamental interests are constitutionally guaranteed, the determination of which interests are fundamental should be firmly rooted in the text of the Constitution. The task in every case should be to determine the extent to which constitutionally guaranteed rights are dependent on interests not mentioned in the Constitution. As the nexus between the specific constitutional guarantee and the nonconstitutional interest draws closer, the nonconstitutional interest becomes more fundamental and the degree of judicial scrutiny applied when the interest is infringed on a discriminatory basis must be adjusted accordingly.

All of these different standards for determining what rights (beyond those explicitly listed in the Constitution) are fundamental may be more confusing than clarifying. And it is hard to escape the conclusion of Justice Byron White, who commented: "What the deeply rooted traditions of the country are is arguable; which of them deserve the protection of the Due Process Clause is even more debatable." Indeed, what makes a right fundamental may ultimately be rooted more in "judges' . . . personal and private notions" than in their disinterested interpretation of the Constitution.[30]

(the legislatures) to make policy on such matters, the Court has continued to use fundamental rights reasoning to place certain interests beyond the scope of majority control. The rest of this chapter will examine the issues surrounding the fundamental rights strand of the two-tier approach. What rights have (or have not) been deemed fundamental, their scope of protection by the Court, and the controversies raised by them will all be discussed in the case history that follows.

The Right to Vote

One of the first rights to be recognized as fundamental under the Court's newer equal protection analysis is the right to vote. Moreover, in the past twenty-five years, the Court has declared that inequalities in the franchise threaten the fundamental right to vote, and it has been willing to use the Equal Protection Clause to invalidate a wide range of governmental practices with respect to the franchise. Chapter 9 discussed the dismantling by both the courts and Congress of racial barriers to equal voting rights. In addition, the Supreme Court has used the Fourteenth Amendment to rule against: (1) legislative apportionment plans which give voters unequal representation; (2) state laws which deny equal access to the franchise; and (3) statutes which restrict candidate and party access to the ballot.

Legislative Apportionment

Chapter 4 examined the Supreme Court's landmark apportionment decisions beginning with *Baker* v. *Carr* (1962). As that discussion revealed, legislative apportionment raised few constitutional questions before the 1960s. States were generally free from any federal controls over how they set up districts for purposes of electing representatives to the state legislatures. Left to their own devices, many states deviated from a strict population standard in their legislative apportionment schemes. Voters began to realize that, though they had an equal right to vote, districting schemes which diluted their representation in the state legislature in effect made the impact of their vote unequal. In a series of cases culminating in *Reynolds* v. *Sims* (1964), the Supreme Court decided the Fourteenth Amendment meant that each vote must count equally in a state's legislative apportionment plan.

Reynolds v. *Sims* challenged the constitutionality of Alabama's legislative apportionment scheme. Alabama's constitution mandated that the legislature reapportion its electoral districts every ten years. It qualified this reapportionment, however, by providing that each county be provided at least one representative in the state's lower house and that each county be allocated only one senator in the upper house. No reapportionment had taken place in Alabama since 1901, resulting in highly skewed representation. Lower house districts ranged in population from 6,700 to 104,000 while state senatorial districts ranged from 15,000 to 634,000 population. Under this apportionment scheme, it was possible for 25 percent of the state's population to elect a majority in the state senate. A group of citizens challenged the apportionment plan on the grounds that it violated the Equal Protection Clause. The Supreme Court was eventually asked to decide the question after a district court invalidated several reapportionment plans.

The Supreme Court, in an 8–1 decision, decided that all state legislative apportionment plans would have to accord with the standard that each person's vote count equally with another's. Chief Justice Warren's majority opinion begins with a statement about the fundamental nature of the right to vote:

> Undoubtedly, the right of suffrage is a fundamental matter in a free and democratic society. Especially since the right to exercise the franchise in a free and unimpaired manner is preservative of other basic civil and political rights, any alleged infringement of the right of citizens to vote must be carefully and meticulously examined.

Applying this strict-scrutiny standard, Chief Justice Warren ruled that both houses of a state legislature must be apportioned according to population so as to preserve the standard of "one-person, one-vote":

> We hold that, as a basic constitutional standard, the Equal Protection Clause requires that the seats in both houses of a bicameral state legislature must be apportioned on a population basis. Simply stated, an individual's right to vote for state legislators is unconstitutionally impaired when its weight is in a substantial fashion diluted when compared with votes of citizens living in other parts of the State.

The Court conceded that it would be impossible as well as undesirable to require strict, mathematical equality in apportioning legislative districts. The chief justice said, "Mathematical exactness or precision is hardly a workable constitutional requirement." Nevertheless, the Court has made it a "constitutional requirement" that state legislatures make an honest and good-faith effort to construct their districts as equally as possible, not only to give voters their equal rights, but also to satisfy basic principles of democracy and majority rule.[31]

Equal Access to the Franchise

A second principle necessary to equality in the right to vote is that the franchise must be made available to all citizens on an equal basis. The Court has invoked strict scrutiny whenever a statute attempts to impede equal access to the voting booth. In a number of decisions the Court has struck down state laws restricting citizen access to the franchise.

For example, in 1966 the Court finally invalidated the poll tax as a requirement for voting in state elections. Poll taxes were yet another method some states adopted at the turn of the century to keep blacks and poor whites from voting. Although poll taxes had fallen into general disuse, the Court had upheld their use in *Breedlove* v. *Suttles* (1937). In 1965, a handful of states still required payment of a small tax to vote in state elections (the Twenty-fourth Amendment to the Constitution, ratified in 1964, had outlawed the poll tax in federal elections). But in *Harper* v. *Virginia State Board of Elections* (1966), the Supreme Court held that the poll tax violated the Equal Protection Clause. Justice Douglas, writing for the six-justice majority, contended that "the right to vote is too precious, too fundamental to be burdened or conditioned" by the payment of a fee, however small (Virginia's annual poll tax was $1.50). His reasoning for invalidating the poll tax continued:

> The interest of the state, when it comes to voting, is limited to the power to fix qualifications. Wealth, like creed, or color, is not germane to one's ability to participate intelligently in the electoral process. . . To introduce wealth or payment of a fee as a measure of a voter's qualifications is to introduce a capricious or irrelevant factor.

A few years later the Court extended the principle established in *Harper* and rejected New York's attempt to restrict school board elections to property owners and the parents of public school children. In *Kramer* v. *Union Free School District No. 15* (1969), the Court ruled that "statutes granting the franchise to residents on a selective basis always pose the danger of denying some citizens any effective voice in the governmental affairs which substantially affect their lives." The Court indicated that any restriction on the franchise would be subjected to strict scrutiny.

Another area where the Court has demonstrated hostility to state restrictions on the right to vote is durational residency requirements. *Dunn* v. *Blumstein* (1972), the seminal case here, involved the Court's invalidation of a Tennessee law requiring one year's residence in the state and three months in the county as a condition of voting. The Supreme Court subjected the statute to strict scrutiny, both because it limited the right to vote and because it burdened interstate travel (to be discussed in a later section of this chapter). After examining the state's claim of compelling interest to restrict the franchise, the Court struck down the residency requirements as a deprivation of the fundamental right to vote in violation of the Equal Protection Clause. The Court (and Congress) has basically limited state residency requirements for voting to thirty days.[32]

Equal Access to the Ballot: *Williams* v. *Rhodes* (1968)

The third principle the Court has enunciated in voting rights equality questions is that citizens be able to vote "meaningfully" and "effectively." What this has meant is that the Court has strictly scrutinized laws which restrict candidate and political party access to elections. The Court first addressed the issue of ballot access in *Williams* v. *Rhodes* (1968). In question were Ohio election laws that severely burdened the ability of third-party candidates to win a place on the presidential ballot, while automatically including the two major party candidates. The Court decided that the election laws impaired "the right of qualified voters, regardless of their political persuasion, to cast their votes effectively." Without a showing of a compelling state interest, the Court declared that Ohio could not—consistent with the Equal Protection Clause—establish such burdensome obstacles to third-party candidacy. The Court's logic in *Williams* has been applied consistently to outlaw a number of restrictive electoral practices in the past two decades.[33]

In short, then, the Court has declared the right to vote to be fundamental, something that must be provided on an equal basis. Moreover, in applying higher-tier analysis to voting rights questions, the Court has operated to the detriment of states attempting to carry out policies that were once within their sole authority. The Court has subjected a wide range of state electoral practices to strict scrutiny under the Fourteenth Amendment. The Court's general position is found in a statement by Chief Justice Warren: "Once the franchise is granted to the electorate, lines may not be drawn which are inconsistent with the Equal Protection Clause."[34]

The Right to Interstate Travel: *Shapiro* v. *Thompson* (1969)

Along with the right to vote, the Court has recognized as fundamental the right to travel and migrate from state to state. The Court had long ago established the citizen's right to travel. In the Passenger Cases (1849), Chief Justice Roger Taney announced that all "citizens of the United States . . . must have the right to pass and repass through every part of [the country] without interruption, as freely as in our own States." This position was echoed by the Court in *United States* v. *Guest* (1966):

> The constitutional right to travel from one State to another . . . occupies a position fundamental to the concept of our Federal Union. It is a right that has been firmly established and repeatedly recognized.

In *Shapiro* v. *Thompson* (1969), the Court's protection of the right to travel from state to state took on a broader significance. The justices began to use the Equal Protection Clause to prevent the states from enacting regulations having the effect of impairing interstate mobility. *Shapiro* concerned the validity of state laws denying welfare benefits to people who had not resided in the state for at least one year. Vivian Thompson, a pregnant, nineteen-year-old unwed mother, moved to Connecticut from Massachusetts, and subsequently applied for state aid under the Aid to Families with Dependent Children (AFDC) program. Upon being told that she did not meet Connecticut's one-year residency requirement, Thompson sued the state welfare commissioner, claiming a violation of her right to equal protection.

In a 6–3 decision, the Supreme Court invalidated the state's residency requirement. Justice Brennan delivered the opinion of the Court:

> There is no dispute that the effect of the waiting period requirement . . . is to create two classes of needy resident families indistinguishable from each other except that one is composed of residents who have resided a year or more, and the second of residents who have resided less than a year, in the jurisdiction. On the basis of this sole difference the first class is granted and the second class is denied welfare aid upon which may depend the ability of the families to obtain the very means to subsist—food, shelter, and other necessities of life—[We agree] that the statutory prohibition of benefits to residents of less than a year creates a classification which constitutes an invidious discrimination denying them equal protection of the laws.

Justice Brennan based his conclusions upon the statute's interference with a constitutional right to interstate travel. Although he acknowledged that the "right finds no explicit mention in the Constitution," he nevertheless felt that it was fundamental, and that the state would have to show a compelling interest to restrict the right to interstate travel. So, using the fundamental-rights strand of the two-tier approach, the Court protected individuals against state interference with their right to interstate mobility and migration.

Justice Harlan's dissent took issue with the Court's expansion of the Equal Protection Clause to protect fundamental rights. Harlan wrote that the "compelling state interest [test] is sound when applied to racial classifications," but unwise when applied under "the more recent extensions" to other classification schemes and to fundamental rights. Contending that "virtually every state statute affects important rights," Justice Harlan objected that

> to extend the "compelling interest" rule to all cases in which such rights are affected would go far toward making this Court a "superlegislature" . . . I know of nothing which entitles this Court to pick out particular human activities, characterize them as "fundamental" and give them added protection under an unusually stringent equal protection test.

The Court's decision in *Shapiro* banned the use of residency requirements to penalize a citizen's exercise of the right to travel interstate. Since *Shapiro*, the Court has protected this fundamental right in certain situations involving durational residency requirements for voting (see the *Dunn* v. *Blumstein* discussion) and for receiving medical and other welfare benefits.[35] But the Court has allowed the states to maintain residency restrictions for persons wishing to obtain a divorce, to gain admission to the state bar, to attend free public schools, or to be elected to the legislature. And the Court has refused to grant the same stringent protections to citizens against government interference with their right to travel outside the United States.[36]

The Right to Privacy

In a series of decisions, the Supreme Court has also enshrined the right to privacy as a fundamental right deserving stringent protection under the Fourteenth Amendment. Although not always covered in conjunction with the "newer" equal protection, the right to privacy is unarguably the most discussed and debated of the fundamental rights the Court has singled out for constitutional protection against governmental interference. Moreover, the justices have used the strict-scrutiny language of the two-tier approach in assessing the validity of government actions allegedly interfering with this fundamental right. And the Court's recognition and elaboration of the right to privacy epitomize the problems critics point to when attacking the entire judicial enterprise of the new equal protection. Thus, this chapter is the logical place for a discussion of privacy rights.

The Court's establishment of a constitutional right to privacy and its strict scrutiny of laws invading that right raise a number of controversies. The first concerns its constitutional locus. Since an expressly protected right to privacy cannot be found in the Constitution's text, where does it originate? A second controversy lies in the extent to which privacy rights are protected. What does the right to privacy protect, and how far does it extend? Finally, the Court's finding of a fundamental right to privacy has generated conflict about judicial authority within the constitutional system. Do the courts have the authority to give substance to certain rights (e.g., privacy), protecting them against almost any interference by government? This final question involves a more specific criticism that the Court, in giving near-absolute protection to the right to privacy, is actually engaging in the same kind of faulty analysis it used earlier this century under the substantive-due-process doctrine. The following analysis attempts to take up these larger questions involving the right to privacy.

Right to Privacy: Origins and Foundations

Louis Brandeis, a future justice on the Supreme Court, was the first to lobby for constitutional protections of the right to privacy. In a seminal 1890 law review article,[37] and later in a stinging Supreme Court dissenting opinion in *Olmstead* v. *United States* (1928), Brandeis argued that an individual's privacy was a right of significant constitutional concern:

> The makers of our Constitution undertook to secure conditions favorable to the
> pursuit of happiness. . . . They sought to protect Americans in their beliefs, their

thoughts, their emotions and their sensations. They conferred, as against the government, the right to be let alone—the most comprehensive of rights and the right most valued by civilized men. To protect that right, every unjustified intrusion of the government upon the privacy of the individual, whatever the means employed, must be deemed a [constitutional] violation.

Thirty-seven years later, Justice Brandeis's opinion was vindicated by the Court majority in *Griswold* v. *Connecticut* (1965). The *Griswold* case concerned a Connecticut law that made it a crime to use or advise as to the use of "any drug, medicinal article or instrument for the purpose of preventing conception."[38] Estelle Griswold, executive director of the Planned Parenthood League of Connecticut, was found guilty under this law of dispensing contraceptive "information, instruction and medical advice" to married persons throughout the state. She appealed, claiming that the law in question violated the Fourteenth Amendment. In a 7–2 decision, the Court ruled the law unconstitutional. Writing for the Court, Justice Douglas announced that the Constitution protected an individual's right to privacy. Although he acknowledged that this right was not explicitly mentioned in the document, Douglas argued that the "right to privacy [is] older than the Bill of Rights—older than our political parties, older than our school system." Looking to specific provisions in the First, Third, Fourth, Fifth, and Ninth Amendments, Douglas indicated that "specific guarantees in the Bill of Rights have penumbras, formed by emanations from those guarantees that help give them life and substance. . . Various guarantees create zones of privacy." Having enunciated this "penumbral" right to privacy, Justice Douglas went on to apply his reasoning to Griswold's case:

> The present case, then, concerns a relationship lying within the zone of privacy created by several fundamental constitutional guarantees. And it concerns a law which, in forbidding the *use* of contraceptives rather than regulating their manufacture or sale, seeks to achieve its goals by means having a maximum detrimental impact on that relationship. . . Would we allow the police to search the sacred precincts of marital bedrooms for telltale signs of the use of contraceptives? The very idea is repulsive to the notions of privacy surrounding the marriage relationship.

Justice Douglas, relying upon the penumbral shadow cast by other constitutional provisions, established the individual's vested right to privacy, free from governmental invasion. But not all justices would go along with Douglas's "astronomical" ("penumbras") reasoning. Justice Goldberg, joined by Chief Justice Warren, relied largely upon the Ninth Amendment (see Brief 10.5) as the constitutional source for a fundamental right to privacy. And Justices Harlan and White, in concurring opinions, lodged the right to privacy in the Due Process Clause of the Fourteenth Amendment.

In dissent, Justice Black wrote an opinion that would be echoed by other critics in more recent privacy cases. Though he found the Connecticut law "offensive," Black refused to vacate it without a direct conflict with "some specific constitutional provision." Justice Black questioned the majority's use of "natural-law" reasoning reminiscent of *Lochner* and other substantive-due-process-cases at the turn of the century. Black's main concern, then, was that the Court was using a vague "fundamental rights" reasoning to

> claim [the] power to invalidate any legislative act which the judges find irrational, unreasonable, or offensive. . . If these formulas based on "natural justice," or

☐ *Brief 10.5   What Does the Ninth Amendment Mean?*

The attempt to locate a right to privacy in the Ninth Amendment raises questions about the uses to which this amendment can be put. In his Senate confirmation hearings in 1987, Judge Robert Bork argued that the Ninth Amendment was originally designed to protect rights found in the various state constitutions in 1791. He disputed the contention that a judge could use the Ninth Amendment to give substance to "newly found" rights and to protect them from government interference.

But research into the intentions of the framers of the Bill of Rights suggests that Judge Bork's narrow interpretation of the Ninth Amendment may be misguided. When James Madison began to draft the Bill of Rights in 1789, one of his main fears, echoed in the words of other political leaders, was that by listing the rights protected against government interference, the implication might be that government could abridge equally important liberties not enumerated in the Bill of Rights. Some of Madison's colleagues held the idea that any such enumeration of certain rights might result in the violation of other basic human rights that were not specifically identified:

> The conclusion will be that [the framers of the Bill of Rights] have established all which they esteem valuable and sacred. On every principle, then, the people having begun, ought to go through enumerating, and establish particularly all the rights of individuals, which can by any possibility come in question in making and executing federal laws.[39]

To avoid an extensive, maybe even incessant enumeration of rights in amending the Constitution, Madison fastened on the Ninth Amendment. Madison's own words offer proof of his intent:

> It has been objected against a bill of rights, that, by enumerating particular exceptions to the grant of power, it would disparage those rights which were not placed in that enumeration; and it might follow by implication, that those rights which were not singled out, were intended to be assigned into the hands of the General Government, and were consequently insecure. This is one of the most plausible arguments I have ever heard urged against the admission of a bill of rights into this system; but I conceive, that it may be guarded against. I have attempted it, as gentlemen may see by turning to the last clause of the fourth resolution [the Ninth Amendment].[40]

It is clear from this examination of Madison's intent, then, that the Ninth Amendment potentially goes beyond any enumerated rights in either the federal or the various state constitutions of the time. The problem, however, is that to use the Ninth Amendment to create "new fundamental rights," a judge may be opening a Pandora's box of constitutional rights. As such, Supreme Court justices have been reticent to ground fundamental rights arguments in the Ninth Amendment, preferring the language of the Due Process Clause or even the "penumbras" argument of Justice Douglas in *Griswold*.

---

others which mean the same thing are to prevail, they require judges to determine what is or is not constitutional on the basis of their own opinion of what laws are unwise or unnecessary. . . The use by federal courts of such a formula or doctrine or whatnot to veto federal or state laws simply takes away from Congress and States the power to make laws based on their own judgment of fairness and wisdom and transfers that power to this Court for ultimate determination—a power which was specifically denied to federal courts by the convention that framed the Constitution.

The Court failed to heed Justice Black's fears, and seven years later expanded the protections of the right of privacy. In *Eisenstadt* v. *Baird* (1972), the Court ruled unconstitutional a Massachusetts law that prohibited the distribution of contraceptives to unmarried persons. Justice Brennan, writing for the majority, acknowledged that a law making it a crime to distribute contraceptives to unmarried persons differed from the law in *Griswold*, which penalized their *use* among married couples. Nevertheless, Brennan reached the conclusion that the fundamental right to privacy could not be impaired in accordance with the Equal Protection Clause:

If under *Griswold* the distribution of contraceptives to married persons cannot be prohibited, a ban on distribution to unmarried persons would be equally impermissible. It is true that in *Griswold* the right of privacy in question inhered in the marital relationship. Yet the marital couple is not an independent entity with a mind and heart of its own, but an association of two individuals each with a separate intellectual and emotional make-up. If the right of privacy means anything, it is the right of the individual, married or single, to be free from unwarranted governmental intrusion into matters so fundamentally affecting a person as the decision whether to bear or beget a child.

The *Eisenstadt* decision is important for a number of reasons. First, in contradistinction to *Griswold*, the Court recognized that the right to privacy inheres in the person rather than in a place ("the sacred precincts of marital bedrooms") or in a protected "relationship" (marriage). Second, Justice Brennan employed a broad concept of privacy to outlaw legislation, a practice that has continued since 1972, and which has brought the Court under substantial constitutional criticism for using the repudiated substantive-due-process reasoning. And finally, by attaching the right to privacy to the Equal Protection Clause, the Court seemed to be placing privacy questions under the strict scrutiny of the two-tier approach.

The Court was not finished extending the right to privacy. One year after *Eisenstadt,* the Court ruled that the right to privacy would protect women against restrictive abortion statutes, setting off a controversy that continues today. The discussion turns now to the famous case of *Roe v. Wade.*

The Right to Privacy and Abortion

In 1972, most states severely limited a woman's access to legal abortion. Only four states (Alaska, Hawaii, New York, Washington) allowed abortion with few legal restrictions, and the rest continued to operate under restrictive nineteenth-century statutes. Although a number of states liberalized their abortion laws beginning in 1967, in 1972 twenty-five states allowed abortion only to save the mother's life. *Roe* v. *Wade* (1973) challenged one of the most restrictive abortion statutes. The Texas law in question, first enacted in 1854, made it a crime to "procure an abortion" except "by medical advice for the purpose of saving the life of the mother." Jane Roe (the pseudonym of an unmarried woman who wished to terminate her pregnancy) filed suit "on behalf of herself and all other women" similarly situated against Henry Wade, district attorney for Dallas County, Texas, asking the courts to rule the Texas criminal abortion laws unconstitutional. She claimed that the abortion statute "abridged her right of personal privacy." The Supreme Court was asked to review Roe's case along with a challenge to a more liberal Georgia abortion statute.

By a 7–2 margin, the Supreme Court ruled that state criminal abortion laws like that of Texas violated a woman's right to privacy.[41] Justice Blackmun, writing for the court, began his opinion by surveying the history of abortion "for such insight as that history may afford" (Blackmun's prior membership on the board of directors of the Mayo Clinic may explain his intense interest in the medical and legal history behind abortion). After a lengthy historical survey, Blackmun determined that "at common law, at the time of the adoption of our Constitution, and throughout the major portion of the 19th century, abortion was viewed with less disfavor than under most American statutes [in effect in 1973]."

Justice Blackmun went on to state that the right of privacy, which he found in the "concept of personal liberty" in the Due Process Clause of the Fourteenth Amendment, "is broad enough to encompass a woman's decision whether or not to terminate her pregnancy." The fundamental right to privacy was involved in a woman's abortion decision, and, though her right was not absolute, it could only be abridged by the state if it could show a "compelling interest" (consistent with the strict-scrutiny approach to laws threatening fundamental rights).

The state of Texas contended that it had two compelling interests for enacting abortion restrictions: (1) to safeguard the mother's health; and (2) to protect the right to life of the fetus (also guaranteed, the state argued, under the Fourteenth Amendment). Blackmun denied both claims, at least in the early stages of pregnancy. With respect to the right of prenatal life, Blackmun uttered these provocative words:

> The word "person," as used in the Fourteenth Amendment, does not include the unborn. The unborn have never been recognized in the law as persons in the whole sense. . . We need not resolve the difficult question of when life begins. When those trained in the respective disciplines of medicine, philosophy, and theology are unable to arrive at any consensus, the judiciary, at this point in the development of man's knowledge, is not in a position to speculate as to the answer. . . We do not agree that, by adopting one theory of life, Texas may override the rights of the pregnant women that are at stake.

Still, the Court conceded that Texas had important and legitimate interests in protecting maternal health and the "potentiality of human life" represented in the fetus. Justice Blackmun noted that each of these state interests "grows in substantiality as the woman approaches term and, at a point during pregnancy, each becomes 'compelling.' " He then focused upon the sequence of a woman's pregnancy as the basis for balancing the woman's right to privacy with the state's compelling interests. For the majority, Blackmun reached certain conclusions which are summarized as follows:

1. During the first trimester of pregnancy, during which maternal mortality in abortion is actually less than maternal mortality in normal childbirth, the state's interests are minimal. In this period the abortion decision is a private matter left up to the woman in consultation with her physician, free from state interference.

2. "For the stage subsequent to approximately the end of the first trimester, the State, in promoting its interest in the health of the mother, may, if it chooses, regulate the abortion procedure in ways that are reasonably related to maternal health" (e.g., regulating the facilities in which the abortion operation is performed and the persons performing the procedure). Still, during the second trimester, the decision itself whether or not to have an abortion must remain unfettered, consistent with the pregnant woman's right to privacy.

3. After the second trimester, the state's two interests become compelling. At this stage the fetus is viable, and "the State in promoting its interest in the potentiality of life may, if it chooses, regulate, and even proscribe, abortion except where it is necessary, in appropriate medical judgment, for the preservation of the life or health of the mother."

Blackmun concluded by striking down both the Texas and Georgia laws as too restrictive of the pregnant woman's right to privacy guaranteed by the Fourteenth Amendment.

The Court's opinion in *Roe* v. *Wade* unleashed a barrage of moral and legal criticism. Of course, there are those who, on moral grounds, chastise the Court for denying the rights of prenatal life. And some feminists have faulted the Court for lodging abortion rights under the right to privacy, as opposed to granting abortion rights as a part of a woman's right to equality under the Fourteenth Amendment. But Justice Blackmun's opinion also draws fire from those concerned about the Court's unjustified exercise of judicial authority. Justice White's and Justice Rehnquist's dissenting opinions sum up this legal criticism best. Justice White said:

> The Court simply fashions and announces a new constitutional right for pregnant women and, with scarcely any reason or authority for its action, invests that right with sufficient substance to override most existing state abortion statutes. The upshot is that the people and the legislatures of the 50 States are constitutionally disentitled to weigh the relative importance of the continued existence and development of the fetus, on the one hand, against a spectrum of possible impacts on the mother, on the other hand. As an exercise of raw judicial power, the Court perhaps has authority to do what it does today; but in my view its judgment is an improvident and extravagant exercise of the power of judicial review that the Constitution extends to this Court.

And Justice Rehnquist raised the question of the Court's violation of the separation of powers, stepping into policy areas normally reserved to legislatures:

> The decision here to break pregnancy into three distinct terms and to outline the permissible restrictions the State may impose in each one, for example, partakes more of judicial legislation than it does of a determination of the intent of the drafters of the Fourteenth Amendment.

Though widely criticized, the Court's opinion on abortion remains basically intact. Various proposals for right-to-life constitutional amendments have failed to win congressional approval. The Supreme Court has continued to strike down state laws attempting to restrict abortions. For example, in *Planned Parenthood of Central Missouri* v. *Danforth* (1976), the Court ruled that states could not require a married woman to obtain her husband's consent before obtaining an abortion, nor could they require parental consent as a requirement for unmarried minors seeking an abortion. On the former question of spousal consent, Justice Blackmun's majority opinion argued that "since the State cannot [prohibit] abortion during the first stage [of pregnancy], the State cannot delegate authority to any particular person, even the spouse, to prevent abortion during that same period." Despite the husband's "deep and proper concern and interest in his wife's pregnancy. . . [the woman] is the more directly and immediately affected by the pregnancy [and], as between the two, the balance weighs in her favor." On the more sensitive issue of parental consent for a minor's abortion, Blackmun stated that "any independent interest the parent may have in the termination of the minor daughter's pregnancy is no more weighty than the right of privacy of the competent minor mature enough to have become pregnant."

Subsequent Court decisions have remained faithful to the *Roe* precedent, although by a lessening majority. In 1983, the Court reaffirmed the right to privacy asserted in *Roe,* striking down a number of state and local laws restricting abortions. The most notable of five cases arose out of an Akron, Ohio, ordinance. It required the following: hospital performance of all abortions after the first trimester; the consent of parents for abortions performed on pregnant minors under the age of fifteen; a twenty-four-hour "cooling-off period" between the time a woman signed the abortion consent form and the time the abortion could be performed; and the recitation of statements by physicians to patients that abortion "could result in severe emotional disturbances" and that "the unborn child is a human life from the moment of conception." In *Akron* v. *Akron Center for Reproductive Health* (1983), the Court, by a 6–3 margin, ruled the Akron ordinance unconstitutional on the grounds that it was an attempt to deny the woman's right to choose abortion under the guise of "legislative regulations." Justice Powell said for the majority that state "regulations . . . may not interfere with physician-patient consultation or with the woman's choice between abortion and childbirth."

Justice O'Connor's dissent in *Akron* v. *Akron Center for Reproductive Health* is noteworthy for two reasons. First, in signaling her displeasure with *Roe* she alleviated the earlier fears of some conservatives that she would vote a pro-choice position. Second, her opinion itself suggests a problem with the kind of "judicial legislation" the Court employed in *Roe.* Justice O'Connor questioned the Court's judgment going all the way back to *Roe* on the grounds that

> neither sound constitutional theory nor our need to decide cases based on the application of neutral principles can accommodate an analytical framework that varies according to the "stages" of pregnancy, where those stages, and their concomitant standards of review, differ according to the level of medical technology available when a particular challenge to state regulation occurs.

Her belief that judges must always attempt to articulate more or less universal neutral principles in deciding constitutional questions led her to conclude that "the trimester or 'three-stage' approach adopted by the Court in *Roe* . . . cannot be supported as a legitimate or useful framework for accommodating the woman's right and the State's interests." Moreover, her opinion contends that the progress in medical technology relating to abortion, pregnancy, and fetal viability has already made the Court's trimester-based approach to abortion obsolete:

> The *Roe* framework . . . is clearly on a collision course with itself. As the medical risks of various abortion procedures decrease, the point at which the State may regulate for reasons of maternal health is moved further forward to actual childbirth. As medical science becomes better able to provide for the separate existence of the fetus, the point of viability is moved further back toward conception. Moreover, it is clear that the trimester approach violates the fundamental aspiration of judicial decision making through the application of neutral principles "sufficiently absolute to give them roots throughout the community and continuity over significant periods of time. . ." The *Roe* framework is inherently tied to the state of medical technology that exists whenever particular litigation ensues. Although legislatures are better suited to make the necessary factual judgments in this area, the Court's framework forces legislatures, as a matter of constitutional

law, to speculate about what constitutes "acceptable medical practice" at any given time. Without the necessary expertise or ability, courts must then pretend to act as science review boards and examine those legislative judgments.

The Justice Department used Justice O'Connor's reasoning in its *amicus curiae* brief filed in a more recent case, *Thornburgh* v. *American College of Obstetricians and Gynecologists* (1986). But by a 5–4 vote the Court reaffirmed *Roe*, striking down the Pennsylvania Abortion Control Act of 1982, which contained a number of restrictions on the performing of abortions similar to the Akron ordinances.

Limitations on Abortion Rights: State and Federal Funding

The one area where antiabortion activists have won success lies in restricting state and federal abortion funding. In three cases decided in 1977, the Supreme Court held that neither the Constitution nor federal law requires states to pay for nontherapeutic (not medically necessary) abortions for poor women even though the same states pay for indigent childbirth costs. In one of those cases, *Maher* v. *Roe*, lawyers challenging state abortion funding restrictions contended that states "must accord equal treatment to both abortion and childbirth, and may not evidence a policy preference by funding only the medical expenses incident to childbirth." To deny payment to impoverished women for abortions was to disadvantage them solely on the basis of their indigency (thus operating to the disadvantage of the poor as a suspect class), as well as to interfere with their fundamental right to privacy inherent in the choice to terminate pregnancy.

But Justice Powell dismissed these equal protection claims made on behalf of indigent pregnant women. He found that the law did not operate to the disadvantage of any suspect class warranting strict judicial scrutiny (see a later section of this chapter for a further discussion of indigency and the Fourteenth Amendment). Justice Powell also denied that abortion funding restrictions operated to burden any fundamental right. The right established in *Roe* v. *Wade*, he claimed

> [only] protects the woman from unduly burdensome interference with her freedom to decide whether to terminate her pregnancy. It implies no limitation on the authority of a State to make a value judgment favoring childbirth over abortion, and to implement that judgment by the allocation of public funds . . . the Connecticut regulation [restricting abortion funding] places no obstacles—absolute or otherwise—in the pregnant woman's path to an abortion. An indigent woman who desires an abortion suffers no disadvantage as a consequence of Connecticut's decision to fund childbirth; she continues as before to be dependent on private sources for the services she desires. The State may have made childbirth a more attractive alternative, thereby influencing the woman's decision, but it has imposed no restriction on access to abortions that was not already there. The indigency that may make it difficult—and in some cases, perhaps, impossible—for some women to have abortions is neither created nor in any way affected by the Connecticut regulation.

Powell concluded that since no suspect class or fundamental right was burdened by laws prohibiting abortion funding to the poor, rationality scrutiny was the appropriate judicial standard. The state's "strong and legitimate interest in encouraging normal childbirth" rationalized such legislation. Exhibiting the kind of deference associated with rationality scrutiny, Powell concluded by saying that

> when an issue involves policy choices as sensitive as those implicated by public funding of nontherapeutic abortions, the appropriate forum for their resolution in a democracy is the legislature . . . Connecticut is free—through normal democratic processes—to decide that such benefits should be provided. We hold only that the Constitution does not require a judicially imposed resolution of these difficult issues.

Justice Brennan, writing for Justices Marshall and Blackmun, dissented. He accused the Court majority of "a distressing insensitivity to the plight of impoverished pregnant women." The Court's decision not to apply strict scrutiny to abortion funding restrictions did not make sense to Brennan, given previous rulings: "The Connecticut scheme cannot be distinguished from other grants and withholdings of financial benefits that we have held unconstitutionally burdened a fundamental right." Using a strict-scrutiny standard, Brennan concluded that the state's financial support of childbirth but not abortion "clearly operates to coerce indigent pregnant women to bear children they would not otherwise choose to have, and just as clearly, this coercion can only operate upon the poor." As such, the state regulation "constitutes an unconstitutional infringement of the fundamental right of pregnant women to be free to decide whether to have an abortion [by placing] financial pressures on indigent women that force them to bear children they would not otherwise have."

Despite Justice Brennan's criticisms, the Court has continued to uphold laws that prohibit funding for abortions to indigent women, even including medically necessary abortions. *Harris* v. *McRae* (1980) held that the Hyde Amendment, a series of congressional actions prohibiting the payment of federal Medicaid funds for even abortions deemed medically necessary, was constitutional. Justice Stewart, in his majority opinion, relied upon the *Maher* precedent to support his arguments:

> Although the liberty protected by the Due Process Clause affords protection against unwarranted governmental interference with freedom of choice in the context of certain personal decisions, it does not confer an entitlement to such funds as may be necessary to realize all the advantages of that freedom. To hold otherwise would make a drastic change in our understanding of the Constitution . . . Whether freedom of choice that is constitutionally protected warrants federal subsidization is a question for Congress to answer, not a matter of constitutional entitlement.

Justice Marshall continued the dissenter's line of reasoning in *Maher* to argue against the majority's opinion upholding the Hyde Amendment:

> The denial of Medicaid benefits to individuals who meet all the statutory criteria for eligibility, solely because the treatment that is medically necessary involves the exercise of the fundamental right to choose abortion, is a form of discrimination repugnant to [equality]. The Court's decision today marks a retreat from *Roe* v. *Wade* and represents a cruel blow to the most powerless members of our society.

In addition to Marshall, Brennan, and Blackmun, Justice Stevens joined in dissent in *Harris* v. *McRae*. His dissent illustrates his basic position that the Equal Protection Clause requires impartiality in government programs (see Table 10.1):

This case involves a special exclusion of women who, by definition, are confronted with a choice between two serious harms: serious health damage to themselves on the one hand and abortion on the other. The competing interests are the interest in maternal health and the interest in protecting potential human life. It is now part of our law that the pregnant woman's decision as to which of these conflicting interests shall prevail is entitled to constitutional protection. . . . Having decided to alleviate some of the hardships of poverty by providing necessary medical care, the Government must use neutral criteria in distributing benefits. It may not deny benefits to a financially and medically needy person simply because he is a Republican, a Catholic, or an Oriental—or because he has spoken against a program the Government has a legitimate interest in furthering. In sum, it may not create exceptions for the sole purpose of furthering a governmental interest that is constitutionally subordinate to the individual interest that the entire program was designed to protect. [The Hyde Amendment constitutes] an unjustifiable, and indeed blatant, violation of the sovereign's duty to govern impartially.

While the Supreme Court has not required abortion funding for indigent women, fifteen states and the District of Columbia currently choose to provide funding for at least some abortions.

The Future of Abortion Rights

The question of abortion has increasingly divided the Court in the last ten years. The majority of justices refuse to extend abortion rights to require government funding for the poor pregnant woman. And the most recent abortion cases indicate that the Court is just one vote away from having a majority willing to reconsider the entire question of privacy rights and abortion. By 1986, after the *Thornburgh* decision, the seven-justice majority supportive of the *Roe* ruling had been reduced to five, with Justice Powell casting a deciding swing vote. More recently, in *Hartigan* v. *Zbaraz* (1987), an equally divided Court (4–4) affirmed a court of appeals decision striking down part of an Illinois state law requiring parental notification and a twenty-four-hour waiting period for minors seeking an abortion. With Justice Powell's resignation and his replacement by Justice Anthony Kennedy, the *Roe* precedent may be in jeopardy. Many Court observers see Justice O'Connor as the potential future swing vote on abortion questions. There is still some dispute as to where O'Connor stands on abortion in general. Although she did question the Court's reasoning in the *Roe* decision, she also indicated that the "indisputably implicated" right to privacy at least "protects the woman from unduly burdensome interference with her freedom to decide whether to terminate her pregnancy." Just how she would balance the woman's right with the also "indisputably implicated" compelling state interests involved in abortion regulation in a case challenging the *Roe* precedent itself remains to be seen.

The Right to Sexual Privacy: *Bowers* v. *Hardwick* (1986)

While the Court has established a fundamental right to privacy and has extended that right to apply to a wide range of personal practices or decisions, it has also placed qualifications on the right to privacy (see Brief 10.6). No case better illustrates the Court's reluctance to further extend privacy protections under the Constitution than *Bowers* v. *Hardwick* (1986).[42] In question here was a claim by homosexuals that state sodomy laws impaired their fundamental right to privacy. Georgia law makes it a crime to engage in sodomy, punishable by imprisonment for one to twenty years. Michael Hardwick, an

---

☐ Brief 10.6   Qualifications on the Right to Privacy: Two Further Cases

Two cases decided in 1976 indicate the limitations the Court places on the constitutional right to privacy. In *Kelly* v. *Johnson* (1976), a policeman sought to overturn on the basis of his right to privacy a county regulation limiting the length of his hair. The Court majority denied that hair-length requirements for police officers invaded any zones of privacy established by the Constitution. Protections of the right to privacy, the Court explained, were linked to "a substantial claim of infringements on the individual's freedom of choice with respect to certain basic matters of procreation, marriage, and family life." In *Paul* v. *Davis* (1976), Edward Davis was named in a police flier listing "active shoplifters," even though he had never been convicted of the crime. Davis filed suit claiming that the injury to his reputation interfered with his constitutional right to privacy. The Court disagreed, finding the plaintiff's pri-

vacy claims "far afield" from the Court's previous "line of decisions" beginning with *Griswold:*

> [Davis] claims constitutional protection against the disclosure of the fact of his arrest on a shoplifting charge. His claim is based not upon any challenge to the State's ability to restrict his freedom of action in a sphere contended to be "private," but instead on a claim that the State may not publicize a record of an official act such as an arrest. None of our substantive privacy decisions hold this or anything like this, and we decline to enlarge them in this manner.

Of course, it is significant that these two decisions limiting the application of privacy rights were both written by Justice Rehnquist. The dissenters, led by Justices Marshall and Brennan, would have extended the individual's fundamental right to privacy to include protection from government intervention in both matters.

---

avowed homosexual, was charged with violating the law after being caught committing sodomy with another male in his bedroom. Although the charges were ultimately dropped, Hardwick challenged the constitutionality of the Georgia statute. He claimed that Georgia violated the individual's constitutional right to privacy as established in *Griswold,* since state law made criminal a private sexual act between consenting adults. The Court of Appeals for the Eleventh Circuit ruled in Hardwick's favor, holding that "his homosexual activity is a private and intimate association that is beyond the reach of state regulation by reason of the Ninth Amendment and the Due Process Clause of the Fourteenth Amendment."

The Supreme Court, however, by a 5–4 vote, refused to extend the right to privacy to homosexual conduct. Speaking for the Court, Justice White proclaimed that the Constitution does not confer any fundamental right upon homosexuals to engage in sodomy. Observing that "proscriptions against [sodomy] have ancient roots," White ruled that it was completely within the legislative authority of the state to prohibit such sexual acts, even when done in the privacy of one's home. White denied that precedents existed to support Hardwick's claims, pointing out that previous privacy cases involved "family, marriage, or procreation," none of which could be linked to "homosexual activity." Furthermore, the Court's conferral of fundamental rights had previously been based upon values "deeply rooted in this Nation's history and tradition," or "implicit in the concept of ordered liberty." In light of this principle, White found Hardwick's claim that homosexuals had "fundamental rights" to engage in sodomy "facetious." Justice White's opinion concludes with a general warning to judges against giving substantive content to the Fourteenth Amendment:

> The Court is most vulnerable and comes nearest to illegitimacy when it deals with judge-made constitutional law having little or no cognizable roots in the language

or design of the Constitution. . . There should be, therefore, great resistance to expand the substantive reach of [the Due Process Clause], particularly if it requires redefining the category of rights deemed to be fundamental. Otherwise, the Judiciary necessarily takes to itself further authority to govern the country without express constitutional authority. The claimed right pressed on us today falls short of overcoming this resistance.

In a vigorous dissent, Justice Blackmun, quoting Brandeis, criticized his judicial colleagues for failing to see that Hardwick's claim involved " 'the most comprehensive of rights and the right most valued by civilized men,' namely, 'the right to be let alone.' " Blackmun contended that the constitutionally protected right to privacy extended to two general areas: (1) the individual's interest in securing independence in making certain private decisions; and (2) "the privacy interest in protecting certain *places* without regard for the particular activities in which the individuals who occupy them are engaged." Hardwick's activity involved "both the decisional and the spatial aspects of the right to privacy." Using a strict-scrutiny standard, Blackmun could not agree that historical condemnation of personal conduct constituted a compelling enough interest for the state to ban that conduct in the present day. Accepting that giving individuals freedom to choose will mean that "different individuals will make different choices," Blackmun berated the majority for allowing Georgia to trample upon the individual's right to intimate association. He concluded his dissent with the hope that

> the Court soon will reconsider its analysis and conclude that depriving individuals of the right to choose for themselves how to conduct their intimate relationships poses a far greater threat to the values most deeply rooted in our Nation's history than tolerance of nonconformity could ever do.

The Court's decision in *Bowers* v. *Hardwick* indicates the inherent problems with a constitutional right to privacy. Without explicit textual support, the judiciary is forced to carve out this fundamental right based upon its own reading of the document. The justices' personal values also seep in here, complicating the constitutional issue. So does the court's long-term legitimacy in the public eye. While the Court has established a right to privacy and expanded its application (especially with respect to abortion), it has been unwilling to go further, undoubtedly feeling that it would "draw too heavily on its limited fund of public good will." [43] As a result, the Court's privacy decisions are confusing and contradictory. Comparing *Griswold* and *Hardwick*, an observer is forced to conclude that the "bedroom precincts" of certain citizens are not "sacred." Comparing *Roe* with the Court's earlier economic-due-process decisions, critics have asked why a woman's right to privacy gives her control over her body vis-a-vis an abortion, but not vis-a-vis a decision to sell her labor for less than a state-imposed minimum wage. And looking at the abortion funding decisions in conjunction with the poll tax and welfare residency requirement cases, an observer could rightly argue that the Court protects some fundamental rights against unequal economic burdens but not others. Right to privacy conflicts may best reflect the more general conflict between the individualist and communitarian perspectives on the proper role of government detailed in Chapter 2. The Court's resolution of right to privacy issues may be an attempt to reach a compromise between the private and public interests involved.

One final note is in order here. With all of the criticisms of the Court's use of judicial authority to create a right not explicitly granted in the Constitution, the case for a right to privacy has drawn support in circles outside the Supreme Court. Congress expressly acknowledged an individual's right to privacy in legislation passed in 1974, and seven state constitutions now contain right to privacy provisions as part of their bills of rights (Alaska, Arizona, California, Illinois, Montana, Ohio, and Washington). And in 1987, the American people as a whole seemed to assert, through their elected representatives in the Senate, their belief in an individual's right to privacy. This was seen, first, in Judge Robert Bork's failed confirmation hearings and, subsequently, in the tough questioning of Judge Anthony Kennedy on right to privacy issues in his confirmation hearings (see Brief 4.3).

The Equal Protection Clause and the Poor: Wealth Classifications, Poverty, and the Fundamental Necessities of Life

Impoverished citizens have sought refuge from governmental policies imposing an unequal burden upon them. Buoyed by the Court's new equal protection analysis, the poor have tried to redress economic inequalities. To this end, lawyers representing the poor have brought constitutional claims to the courts using both strands of the new equal protection: they have argued that wealth should be regarded as a suspect classification and that certain "necessities of life" are fundamental rights to be provided to all regardless of ability to pay. As this section will indicate, the Court has been reluctant to extend strict-scrutiny status under either strand of the two-tier approach to legislative programs that may burden indigent persons. For most purposes, discrimination against the poor on the basis of their wealth alone draws only minimal scrutiny under the Equal Protection Clause.

From one perspective, the Court's refusal to make economic inequality a constitutional issue seems justified. After all, a capitalist society based upon a relatively free market assumes that persons pay the full market price for the goods they receive. Inequalities in the distribution of wealth and other economic goods are seen as perfectly legitimate. Moreover, looking at the constitutional question of poverty, the framers of the Equal Protection Clause never intended it to touch the unequal distribution of income. Indeed, as Federal Judge Ralph K. Winter commented:

> The Fourteenth Amendment was enacted at a point in American history when notions of laissez-faire and Social Darwinism were about to peak. . . The Amendment was not designed to reduce inequality in the society generally or to serve as a device by which government might be compelled to take steps to bring about economic equality. Neither the men involved nor the spirit of the times favored social or economic equality, much less the notion that government had responsibilities to rework society along egalitarian lines.[44]

Even under the newer equal protection guidelines of today, wealth-based classifications would not seem to be suspect. Poverty is not an inalterable trait, and economic inequalities in society may indeed act as incentives to increase productivity and economic progress among all classes, including the poor.

Unlike race, poverty has not been the basis of laws that systematically discriminate, nor have the poor been "saddled with such disabilities" as to relegate them to "a position of political powerlessness" (see Brief 10.2).

From another perspective, however, a case can be made for heightened judicial scrutiny of wealth-based classifications. An individual's poverty can hamper access to the legal and political processes of American society. Furthermore, certain fundamental rights may be effectively denied if wealth is a criterion for their enjoyment. Frank Michelman, a consistent advocate of "minimum protection" for the poor, put it this way:

> To be hungry, afflicted, ill-educated, enervated, and demoralized by one's material circumstances of life is not only to be personally disadvantaged in competitive politics, but also, quite possibly, to be identified as a member of a group—call it "the poor"—that has both some characteristic political aims and values and some vulnerability to having its natural force of numbers systematically subordinated in the processes of political influence and majoritarian coalition-building.[45]

With this preliminary discussion in mind, the contemporary judicial history concerning poverty and the Fourteenth Amendment will be examined.

Poverty as a Potentially Suspect Class: The Warren Court

The first suggestion that the Court might regard wealth as a suspect classification occurred in a concurring opinion by Justice Robert H. Jackson in *Edwards* v. *California* (1941). Jackson argued that a California law that made it a crime to bring a nonresident indigent into the state illegitimately discriminated against the poor:

> We should say now, and in no uncertain terms that a man's mere property status, without more, cannot be used by a state to test, qualify, or limit his rights as a citizen of the United States. . . The mere state of being without funds is a neutral fact—constitutionally an irrelevance, like race, creed, or color.

The Warren Court built upon Justice Jackson's words in a series of cases dealing with wealth-based legislative schemes. *Griffin* v. *Illinois* (1956) held that states must provide indigent defendants with a free copy of trial transcripts necessary for filing a criminal appeal. Justice Black said, "In criminal trials a state can no more discriminate on account of poverty than on account of religion, race, or color." In *Douglas* v. *California* (1963), the Court ruled that indigent defendants had a right to court-appointed lawyers on their first criminal appeal. Reiterating its position in *Griffin,* the majority said, "There can be no equal justice where the kind of an appeal a man enjoys 'depends on the amount of money he has.' "

Justice Douglas's opinion in *Harper* v. *Virginia State Board of Elections* (1966) (discussed in an earlier section of this chapter) suggested that the Warren Court was willing to elevate all wealth-based classifications to the higher tier of scrutiny under the new equal protection analysis. In an oft-quoted passage, Douglas stated, "Lines drawn on the basis of wealth, like those of race, are traditionally disfavored." Three years later Chief Justice Warren echoed these sentiments, stating that "a careful examination on our part is especially warranted where lines are drawn on the basis of wealth or race, two factors which independently render a classification highly suspect and thereby demand a more exacting judicial scrutiny."[46] Finally, Justice Brennan's opinion in *Shap-*

iro v. *Thompson*, which talked of "food, shelter and other necessities of life" gave support to those who would use the fundamental rights strand of the new equal protection analysis to guarantee "minimum protection" for the poor. And in *Goldberg* v. *Kelly* (1970), whose due process implications were discussed briefly in Chapter 8, Brennan's opinion placed the same fundamental rights imprimatur on welfare assistance in general:

> Welfare, by meeting the basic demands of subsistence, can help bring within the reach of the poor the same opportunities that are available to others to participate meaningfully in the life of the community. . . Public assistance, then, is not mere charity, but a means to "promote the general welfare, and secure the Blessings of Liberty to ourselves and our posterity."

In retrospect, however, the Warren Court's rhetoric never reflected a majority consensus on the suspect status of wealth classifications. Those seeking equal justice for the poor could only point to possibilities implicit in certain justices' words. In fact, the Court had only applied strict scrutiny to indigency-based classification schemes when such schemes threatened either the right to vote or access to the state's criminal justice system (both declared fundamental interests under the Warren Court). The Warren Court never invalidated a law solely because it had a differential impact upon the poor. Still, the possibilities existed for heightened judicial scrutiny of economic inequalities during the Warren era. These possibilities were immediately dashed under the Burger Court.

The Return to Rationality Scrutiny: The Burger Court

Chief Justice Burger's arrival on the Supreme Court marked the narrowing of equal-protection doctrine with regard to the poor. In both its rhetoric and its rulings, the Burger Court denied the claims of equal protection for the poor as a class. This judicial restraint in dealing with statutes differentiating on the basis of wealth can be seen in cases as early as *Dandridge* v. *Williams* (1970).

The *Dandridge* case involved Maryland's provision under a joint federal-state AFDC program that no matter how large the family seeking aid, the maximum welfare payment could not exceed $250 a month. Linda Williams sued in federal court, contending that the maximum grant regulations denied members of large families both equal protection and the fundamental necessities of life. The Supreme Court upheld Maryland's welfare provision. Justice Stewart, writing for the majority, ruled that since this law "deal[t] with state regulation in the social and economic field, not affecting freedoms guaranteed by the Bill of Rights," rationality scrutiny was all that the Court need employ in making its judgment. Using this standard, Stewart found Maryland's welfare regulations rationally related to legitimate state interests (the Court mentioned the state's interests "in encouraging gainful employment, in maintaining an equitable balance in economic status between welfare families and those supported by a wage earner, in providing incentives for family planning, and in allocating available public funds in such a way as fully to meet the needs of the largest possible number of families"). Justice Stewart concluded by stating that the Court should not use the Equal Protection Clause to second-guess state legislatures on what constitutes wise economic and welfare policy: "The Equal Protection Clause does not require that a State must choose between attacking every aspect of a problem or not attacking the problem at all."

One year later, the Court sustained an explicit wealth-based classification without resorting to any heightened judicial scrutiny. In *James* v. *Valtierra* (1971), the Court rejected an equal protection claim against an amendment to California's constitution that denied poor people access to low-income housing. The amendment provided that no low-rent housing could be "developed, constructed, or acquired in any manner by a state public body until approved by a majority of voters at a community election." Low-income citizens brought suit claiming that this was an explicit wealth-based classification that in effect allowed a majority of people to band together and exclude the poor from their communities. But Justice Black's majority opinion denied the claim, explaining that "a law making procedure that 'disadvantages' a particular group does not always deny equal protection." For the Court to rule so in this case, he said, it would have to extend the principles involving racial discrimination to wealth-based classifications, "and this we decline to do." Justice Marshall, in a dissenting opinion, warned that it was "far too late in the day to contend that the Fourteenth Amendment prohibits only racial discrimination; and to me singling out the poor to bear a burden not placed on any other class of citizens tramples the values the Fourteenth Amendment was designed to protect."

In *Lindsey* v. *Normet* (1972), the Court denied an equal protection claim based upon a fundamental right to housing. Impoverished tenants challenged Oregon's Forcible Entry and Wrongful Detainer law, which established judicial procedures for eviction of tenants who failed to pay their rent. The indigent tenants argued that "the need for decent shelter and the right to retain peaceful possession of one's home are fundamental interests which are particularly important to the poor and which may be trenched upon only after the State demonstrates some superior interest." But Justice White's majority opinion rejected this claim, sustaining the statute in question:

> We do not denigrate the importance of decent, safe and sanitary housing. But the Constitution does not provide judicial remedies for every social and economic ill. We are unable to perceive in that document any constitutional guarantee of access to dwellings of a particular quality or any recognition of the right of a tenant to occupy the real property of his landlord beyond the term of his lease, without the payment of [rent]. Absent constitutional mandate, the assurance of adequate housing and the definition of landlord-tenant relationships is a legislative not a judicial function.

As these preceding opinions show, the Burger Court moved quickly to head off any claims by the poor calling for strict scrutiny of state programs that disproportionately burdened them. Probably no case better illustrates the Burger Court's position on wealth-based classifications than *San Antonio School District* v. *Rodriguez* (1973). A detailed analysis of this case follows.

Rationality Scrutiny Confirmed: *San Antonio School District* v. *Rodriguez* (1973)

With the exception of Hawaii and New Jersey, public schools in all the states are financed primarily through local property taxes. This results in differentials in public school funding, with richer districts spending more money on public education and poorer districts spending less. The Rodriguez family lived in the Edgewood district of San Antonio, Texas, a poor, predominately Hispanic, neighborhood. The per-pupil expenditures in Edgewood schools were barely half those spent on students in another part of town, the Alamo Heights district. Demetrio Rodriguez filed a class action suit on behalf of his children and other children across the state who were being deprived of equal education opportunities by Texas's property-tax system of school finance. Rodriguez claimed that the Texas system of financing public education violated the Equal Protection Clause, for two reasons: (1) it discriminated on the basis of wealth, by providing children in wealthy districts with a higher-quality education than those in poorer districts; and (2) since public education was acknowledged to be a fundamental interest that the state should provide to all its citizens without regard to their ability to pay for it, inequalities in school finance violated the equal protection rights of poor schoolchildren across Texas. In essence, Rodriguez was using both the suspect classification and the fundamental rights strands of the new equal protection to assert his claims for equal education.

The Supreme Court, however, rejected the claim that "the Texas system of financing public education operates to the disadvantage of some suspect class or impinges upon a fundamental right explicitly or implicitly protected by the Constitution, thereby requiring strict judicial scrutiny." Justice Powell's majority opinion first disposed of the claim that wealth was a suspect classification. Powell denied that the Texas public school finance system operated to the disadvantage of any suspect class of poor persons. The poor, he said, are not always congregated in the poorest property districts; they may live around major industrial or commercial centers which do contribute substantial property-tax income to the public schools. Moreover, the alleged discrimination against the poor was relative. No claim was made that children in poorer school districts were denied public education altogether; the only charge made was that "they are receiving a poorer quality education than that available to children in districts having more assessable wealth." In response to the relative deprivation contention, Powell explained that "at least where wealth is involved, the Equal Protection Clause does not require absolute equality or precise equal advantages." He concluded that "the Texas system does not operate to the peculiar disadvantage of any suspect class," leaving a general standard of suspectness against which future justices could measure equal protection claims:

> The system of alleged discrimination and the class it defines have none of the traditional indicia of suspectness: the class is not saddled with such disabilities, or subjected to such a history of purposeful unequal treatment, or relegated to such a position of political powerlessness as to command extraordinary protection from the majoritarian political process.

Of course, there still remained the question of whether education was a fundamental right, which would also cause the Court to exercise strict scrutiny. For this claim the Rodriguez lawyers drew upon numerous Supreme Court rulings, most prominently this passage from the original *Brown* decision:

> Education is perhaps the most important function of state and local governments. Compulsory school attendance laws and the great expenditures for education both demonstrate our recognition of the importance to our democratic society. It is required in the performance of our most basic public responsibilities, even service in the armed forces. It is the very foundation of good citizenship. Today it is a principal instrument in awakening the child to cultural values, in preparing

him for later professional training, and in helping him to adjust normally to his environment. In these days, it is doubtful that any child may reasonably be expected to succeed in life if he is denied the opportunity of an education. Such an opportunity, where the state has undertaken to provide it, is a right which must be made available to all on equal terms.

Justice Powell acknowledged these earlier Court statements about the importance of education, but he denied that they established education as a fundamental constitutional right: "The importance of a service performed by the state does not determine whether it must be regarded as fundamental for purposes of examination under the Equal Protection Clause." Powell then proceeded to put a damper on the Court's use of fundamental rights reasoning under the Fourteenth Amendment:

It is not the province of this Court to create substantive constitutional rights in the name of guaranteeing equal protection of the laws. Thus, the key to discovering whether education is "fundamental" . . . lies in assessing whether there is a right to education explicitly or implicitly guaranteed by the Constitution.

Powell concluded that there was not such a constitutional guarantee of education as a fundamental right.

Having dismissed the arguments for strict scrutiny, the Court's only question was whether the Texas system of school finance bore "some rational relationship to legitimate state purposes." Stressing "the traditional limitations of this Court's function," Powell upheld Texas's use of property-tax revenues to fund the public schools. Any educational inequities resulting from such a system, Powell said, would be a legislative, not a judicial problem; solutions to it "must come from the lawmakers and from the democratic pressures of those who elect them."

In a long and memorable dissent, Justice Marshall attacked the majority on all points of its opinion. Moreover, he offered an alternative to what he considered the "rigidified" two-tier approach to equal protection analysis, an alternative which has gained many adherents over the years. Using the *Brown* decision as his backdrop, Marshall began his dissent by saying that "the right of every American to an equal start in life, so far as the provision of a state service as important as education is concerned, is far too vital to permit state discrimination on grounds as tenuous as those presented by this record." Marshall continued by addressing the majority's denial of strict-scrutiny status to the Rodriguez claims. He asserted that Texas's program of public school finance clearly had a discriminatory impact upon an identifiable "class" of people. Moreover, he rejected the majority's conclusion that inequalities in education would not deny equal protection so long as children were not completely denied public education.

In addition, Marshall took offense at Powell's claim that only rights explicitly or implicitly guaranteed in the Constitution were fundamental. Where, he queried, does the Constitution "guarantee the right to procreate . . . or the right to vote in state elections . . . or the right to an appeal from a criminal conviction?"—all of which the Court had previously said to be fundamental rights. Marshall believed that equal educational opportunity certainly qualified for constitutional protection under the Fourteenth Amendment and was being denied by Texas in this instance.

As important as his specific arguments against the majority opinion in this particular case are, the legacy of Marshall's dissenting opinion lies in the alternative approach to equal protection analysis he offers. A "rigidified" two-tier approach, Marshall contended, simplistically drops all cases "into one of two neat categories which dictate the appropriate standard of review—strict scrutiny or mere rationality." He felt that this approach neglects the fact that different threats to equality may require different "degrees of care" from the Court. He would replace the two tiers of scrutiny with a "sliding-scale" approach. Marshall spelled out the elements of the sliding scale as follows: the Court's focus would be "placed upon the character of the classification in question, the relative importance to individuals in the class discriminated against of the governmental benefits they do not receive, and the asserted state interests in support of this classification." In fact, he contended that not only would this "spectrum" of standards allow the Court greater flexibility in assessing equal protection claims on a case-by-case basis, but also that it actually described the way the Court applied the Fourteenth Amendment. More will be said about Marshall's alternative approach in this chapter's conclusion.

As this analysis of cases concerning indigent claimants shows, the Court has generally refused to grant special status to equal protection claims brought by the poor. The Court only acts with strict scrutiny when individuals are denied fundamental rights on the basis of their lack of wealth. To use the justices' own words, "This Court has held repeatedly that poverty, standing alone, is not a suspect classification." [47] And recent attempts by the poor to make equal protection claims on the basis of fundamental rights (e.g., rights to welfare, housing, medical care, and education) have uniformly failed to win the Court's acceptance.

A recent example occurred when the Court turned aside a poor family's challenge of a North Dakota school district policy requiring parents to pay for their children's bus transportation to and from school. In *Kadrmas* v. *Dickinson Public Schools* (1988), the Supreme Court used the *Rodriguez* precedent to uphold the school district's policy. Justice O'Connor's opinion for a five-justice majority continued to deny that "statutes having different effects on the wealthy and the poor should on that account alone be subjected to strict equal protection scrutiny [and] that education is a 'fundamental right.' " O'Connor ruled that it was "manifestly rational" for North Dakota to allow local school boards to charge user fees for school bus service.

In a strong dissenting opinion, Justice Marshall reiterated his position (from the *Rodriguez* dissent) on the importance of equal educational opportunities for the poor:

> A statute that erects special obstacles to education in the path of the poor naturally tends to consign such persons to their current disadvantaged status. By denying equal opportunity to exactly those who need it most, the law not only militates against the ability of each poor child to advance herself, but also increases the likelihood of the creation of a discrete and permanent underclass . . . For the poor, education is often the only route by which to become full participants in our society. In allowing a State to burden the access of poor persons to an education, the Court denies equal opportunity and discourages hope. I do not believe the Equal Protection Clause countenances such a result.

The Supreme Court's continued reluctance to include the poor among those especially protected by the Equal Protection Clause has puzzled many constitutional scholars. Laurence Tribe has characterized the current Court's position on the poor as "minimal protection of the laws, with some of us very much more equal than others." [48]

Conclusion

A reading of recent Supreme Court opinions interpreting the Equal Protection Clause reveals much confusion. Originally intended to grant equality to newly freed blacks after the Civil War, the Fourteenth Amendment has been used by those alleging discrimination on the basis of gender, age, wealth, alienage, illegitimacy, and sexual preference. Moreover, citizens contending that they have been denied equal access to fundamental rights such as the right to vote and to travel interstate, and the right to privacy, to welfare, to education, and to housing have all used the Fourteenth Amendment to make their claims.

From an original understanding that applied a rationality-scrutiny standard to all equal protection claims, the Court has evolved a two-tier approach, with strict scrutiny being reserved for those governmental actions based upon "suspect classifications" or those denying "fundamental rights." The justices have even added a middle tier of intermediate scrutiny for gender classifications and, in some instances, affirmative action plans and cases involving alienage and illegitimacy. In addition, the justices have seemingly brought substantive due process back into the Fourteenth Amendment. By giving substance to certain unenumerated rights and offering individuals near-absolute protection from government interference with these rights, the Court has been criticized for overstepping the bounds of constitutional interpretation, much as it had been attacked for its economic decisions at the beginning of this century. The Court's divisions over how to interpret and apply the demands of equality remain confusing. The ongoing conflicts over this "newer" equal protection often reflect the tension between individualist concerns over minority rights and communitarian interests in majority rule.

The main problem, as Justice Stevens once put it, is that "there is only one Equal Protection Clause," [49] which implies a single standard for all cases. Answers to the question of what that one standard should be abound. Justice Marshall's sliding scale, discussed in conjunction with the *Rodriguez* case, is only one solution to the problem. Justice Rehnquist has fought for a quite different solution, based upon reading of the Fourteenth Amendment's original intent. To Rehnquist, modern-day problems with the Fourteenth Amendment come "not so much from the Equal Protection Clause but from the Court's insistence on reading so much into it." Rehnquist's solution is to go back to the original, deferential standard of rationality scrutiny to solve all equal protection claims, "except in the area of the law in which the Framers obviously meant it to apply—classifications based on race or national origin, the first cousin of race." [50]

Somewhere in between Marshall and Rehnquist lies the approach offered by Professor Gerald Gunther. Gunther, who was one of the first to coin the term "newer equal protection," has suggested a model he calls "rationality review with bite," which

> would have the Court take seriously a constitutional requirement that has never been formally abandoned: that legislative means must substantially further legislative ends . . . Putting consistent new bite into the old equal protection would mean that the Court . . . gauge the question of reasonableness of questionable means on the basis of materials that are offered to the Court, rather than resorting to rationalizations created by perfunctory judicial hypothesizing.[51]

In essence, Gunther calls for a rigorous case-by-case approach to equal protection, examining the evidence and arguments in each particular instance to determine if a constitutional claim to equality is justified. A major problem with Gunther's model, however, is that it only allows the Court to examine the means the government employs to achieve its purposes, not the purposes themselves.

Regardless of what standard the Court adopts, the new equal protection is probably here to stay. As Justice Marshall aptly explained in his *Valtierra* dissent, "It is far too late in the day to contend that the Fourteenth Amendment prohibits only racial discrimination." It is far too late because, to use an often-cited phrase from Archibald Cox, "once loosed, the idea of Equality is not easily cabined."[52] The expansive language of the Equal Protection Clause has set loose and given sustenance to those who perpetually find themselves dominated by majoritarian democracy. But the Court has delivered seemingly contradictory messages about the scope and application of the Fourteenth Amendment. The Court's future problem lies in devising consistent and reasonable standards by which to interpret the "loose" idea of equality.

Questions   1.   The Supreme Court's rulings on privacy have been controversial. Is the Court correct in asserting that, even without explicit mention, the Constitution creates a "zone of privacy" surrounding an individual into which the government may not intrude? How far does it extend? Does the right to privacy involve both a "decisional" and a "spatial" dimension, as Justice Blackmun argued in *Bowers* v. *Hardwick?* If so, where do you draw the line between what kinds of "private" matters are protected and which are not? Has the Court done an adequate job here?

2.   Do the words of the Fourteenth Amendment lend themselves to the particular interpretation the Court has devised? Is a multiple-tier approach to equal protection an appropriate method of applying the constitutional demands of equality? If so, what factors ought to be most relevant in the Court's determination of what constitutes a "suspect classification" or a "fundamental right"? Can courts adequately make those determinations?

3.   The Court's rulings on affirmative action seem to suggest that the strict scrutiny the justices normally apply to racial classifications is relaxed when race is used to *benefit* minorities who as a group have been discriminated against in the past. Is it appropriate for the government and other institutions to be color-conscious in the interest of compensating for past injustices? Or does the Constitution require strict color-blindness in all instances?

4.   One of the ongoing themes of American constitutional history is the conflict between majority rule and minority rights. The issues covered under the new equal protection often involve minorities making requests for recognition from the federal

courts. In a democracy based upon majority rule, is there any other recourse than the courts for those individuals who feel left out of the promises and protections of the constitutional system? Does the Supreme Court's taking up the claims of these "permanent" minorities on constitutional grounds de-legitimize it in the eyes of the public?

5.   What is the history of constitutional interpretation with regard to women's rights? How has the Supreme Court regarded gender discrimination under the Equal Protection Clause in more recent years? What would the proposed Equal Rights Amendment mean for constitutional interpretation in the area of women's rights?

Endnotes

1.   *Buck* v. *Bell,* 274 U.S. 200 (1927).

2.   Gerald Gunther, "The Supreme Court, 1971 Term—Foreword: In Search of Evolving Doctrine on a Changing Court: A Model for a Newer Equal Protection," *Harvard Law Review* 86 (1972): 1.

3.   Ronald Dworkin, *Taking Rights Seriously* (Cambridge, Mass.: Harvard University Press, 1978).

4.   Justice Rehnquist, in his dissenting opinion in *Sugarman* v. *Dougall,* 413 U.S. 634 (1973), stated that "it would hardly take extraordinary ingenuity for a lawyer to find 'insular and discrete' minorities at every turn of the road."

5.   Quoted in *Affirmative Action to Open the Doors to Job Opportunity* (Washington, D.C.: Citizen's Commission on Civil Rights, 1984), 27.

6.   In *De Funis* v. *Odegaard,* 416 U.S. 312 (1974), the Court ruled moot a claim by Marcus De Funis that an affirmative action program at the University of Washington discriminated against him (see further discussion in conjunction with the mootness doctrine in Chapter 4).

7.   See the Court's 1986 rulings in *Wygant* v. *Jackson Board of Education; Local 28 of Sheet Metal Workers International Ass'n.* v. *EEOC;* and *Local 93, International Ass'n. of Firefighters* v. *Cleveland.*

8.   Laurence Tribe, *American Constitutional Law* (Mineola, N.Y.: Foundation Press, 1978), 1043–52.

9.   William Blackstone, *Commentaries on the Laws of England,* quoted in Sylvia A. Law, "Rethinking Sex and the Constitution," *University of Pennsylvania Law Review* 132 (1984): 955, 957.

10.   *United States* v. *Yazell,* 382 U.S. 341 (1966), Black, J., dissenting opinion.

11.   Quoted in Judith Baer, *Equality Under the Constitution: Reclaiming the Fourteenth Amendment* (Ithaca, N.Y.: Cornell University Press, 1983), 91.

12.   The National Organization for Women (NOW), joined by a number of other groups and individuals, filed an *amicus curiae* brief asking the Court to void the California law on the grounds that it resembled "protective employment legislation" of the early 1900s. NOW argued for an equal treatment approach to women's equality, maintaining that women should get no better treatment for pregnancy than other similar work-related disabilities. On the other side, Equal Rights Advocates, Inc., filed an *amicus curiae* brief arguing in favor of the California law. The brief claimed that special treatment accorded to a woman during pregnancy and childbirth actually grants her equality, given the disadvantages women face in the workplace because of their reproductive biology.

13.   Wendy Williams, "The Equality Crisis: Some Reflections on Culture, Courts, and Feminism," *Women's Rights Law Reporter* 7 (1982): 175.

14.   The issues of how much control Congress has over the amending process and whether a state can re-

scind its original ratification of an amendment were both raised as a result of the Equal Rights Amendment battle. Although a federal district judge declared the congressional attempt to extend the period for ratification unconstitutional and the state of Idaho's rescission valid (*Idaho* v. *Freeman,* 507 F. Supp. 706 [1981]), the Supreme Court vacated this ruling in *National Organization for Women* v. *Idaho,* 459 U.S. 809 (1982). The case challenging the ERA extension legislation came to the Supreme Court on appeal after the extension deadline had passed, and so the Court declared the entire controversy moot.

15. For a comprehensive account of the struggle for and the final defeat of the ERA, see Jane Mansbridge, *Why We Lost the ERA* (Chicago: University of Chicago Press, 1986).

16. Judith Baer extends this analysis to include age-based discrimination against the young; see *Equality Under the Constitution,* 153–189.

17. *In re Griffiths,* 413 U.S. 717 (1973).

18. *Sugarman* v. *Dougall* (1973).

19. *Nyquist* v. *Mauclet,* 432 U.S. 1 (1977).

20. *Foley* v. *Connelie,* 435 U.S. 291 (1978).

21. *Bernal* v. *Fainter* (1984).

22. *Sugarman* v. *Dougall* (1973), dissenting opinion.

23. See note, "The Equal Treatment of Aliens: Pre-emption or Equal Protection?" *Stanford Law Review* 31 (1979): 1069.

24. Gerald Gunther, *Cases and Materials on Constitutional Law* (Mineola, N.Y.: Foundation Press, 1980), 898.

25. Judith Baer, "The Burger Court and the Rights of the Handicapped," *Western Political Quarterly* 35 (1982): 357.

26. *Buck* v. *Bell* (1927).

27. *Shapiro* v. *Thompson* (1969).

28. See John Hart Ely, *Democracy and Distrust* (Cambridge, Mass.: Harvard University Press, 1980).

29. *Trop* v. *Dulles,* 356 U.S. 86 (1958).

30. See Justice White's dissenting opinion in *Moore* v. *East Cleveland,* 431 U.S. 494 (1977).

31. The Court has had to deal with a number of apportionment and districting questions since 1964. See, for example, *Kirkpatrick* v. *Preisler* (1969); *Abate* v. *Mundt* (1971); *Mahan* v. *Howell* (1973).

32. However, the Court did allow fifty-day residency requirements in *Marston* v. *Lewis,* 410 U.S. 679 (1973), on the grounds that such a period served the state's important interest in accurate voter lists.

33. See *Lubin* v. *Panish,* 415 U.S. 709 (1974), and *Anderson* v. *Celebrezze* (1983) for two examples.

34. *Kramer* v. *Union Free School District No. 15* (1969).

35. See *Memorial Hospital* v. *Maricopa County,* 415 U.S. 250 (1974).

36. See *Sosna* v. *Iowa,* 419 U.S. 393 (1975), residency requirement for divorce; *Martinez* v. *Bynum,* 461 U.S. 321 (1983), residency restrictions on attending public schools; *Vlandis* v. *Kline,* 412 U.S. 441 (1973), residency requirement for receipt of in-state tuition benefits at state colleges. On the subject of restrictions of foreign travel, see *Haig* v. *Agee* (1981) and *Regan* v. *Wald* (1984).

37. Louis D. Brandeis and Samuel D. Warren, "The Right to Privacy," *Harvard Law Review* 4 (1980): 193.

38. The same Connecticut statute had been challenged in two previous instances, in *Tileston* v. *Ullman,* 318 U.S. 44 (1943), and *Poe* v. *Ullman,* 367 U.S. 497 (1961). In *Poe* v. *Ullman,* the Court invoked the ripeness doctrine (see Chapter 4) and refused to review the law upon a challenge

by doctors and their patients on the grounds that it had not been enforced for nearly a century.

39. "Federal Farmer No. 16, January 20, 1788," in Philip B. Kurland and Ralph Lerner, eds., *The Founders' Constitution,* vol. 5 (Chicago: University of Chicago Press, 1987), 399.

40. James Madison, "Speech Before the House of Representatives, June 8, 1789," in Kurland and Lerner, *The Founders' Constitution,* 399.

41. The state of Texas asked the Court to declare the case moot, on the grounds that Roe's claim for access to an abortion was moot by the time the Court heard the case four years later. But the Court agreed to hear the case, largely on the grounds that this was a condition (pregnancy) that could recur and present Roe with the same dilemma.

42. Prior to the *Hardwick* case, the Court had occasion to hear two privacy rights cases of a similar nature. In *Doe v. Commonwealth's Attorney for the City of Richmond,* 425 U.S. 901 (1976), the Court summarily affirmed a lower federal court's upholding of a Virginia sodomy law challenged by homosexuals. And in *Hollenbaugh v. Carnegie Free Library,* 439 U.S. 1052 (1978), the Court refused to review a decision allowing the discharge of two public library employees for "living together in a state of 'open adultery.'" Justice Marshall, who dissented from the Court's denial of review, stated,

"I believe that individuals' choices concerning their private lives deserve more than token protection from this Court, regardless of whether we approve of those choices."

43. Ralph A. Rossum and G. Alan Tarr, *American Constitutional Law: Cases and Interpretation,* 2d ed. (New York: St. Martin's Press, 1987), 629.

44. Ralph K. Winter, "Poverty, Economic Equality, and the Equal Protection Clause," in *Contemporary Debates on Civil Liberties,* eds. Glenn A. Phelps and Robert A. Poirier (Lexington, Mass.: Heath, 1985), 221.

45. Frank Michelman, "Welfare Rights in a Constitutional Democracy," ibid., 219.

46. *McDonald v. Board of Election,* 394 U.S. 802 (1969).

47. *San Antonio School District v. Rodriguez* (1973).

48. Tribe, *American Constitutional Law,* 1136.

49. *Craig v. Boren* (1976), Stevens, J., concurring opinion.

50. *Trimble v. Gordon* (1977), Rehnquist, J., dissenting opinion.

51. Gunther, "In Search of Evolving Doctrine on a Changing Court."

52. Archibald Cox, "The Supreme Court, 1965 Term—Foreword: Constitutional Adjudication and the Promotion of Human Rights," *Harvard Law Review* 82 (1966): 91.

Suggested Readings

Baer, Judith A. *Equality Under the Constitution: Reclaiming the Fourteenth Amendment.* Ithaca, N.Y.: Cornell University Press, 1983.

Brest, Paul. "The Fundamental Rights Controversy." *Yale Law Journal* 90 (1981): 1063–1109.

Dionisopoulos, P. Alan, and Craig R. Ducat. *The Right to Privacy: Essays and Cases.* St. Paul, Minn.: West Publishing, 1976.

Ely, John Hart. *Democracy and Distrust: A Theory of Judicial Review.* Cambridge, Mass.: Harvard University Press, 1980.

Gunther, Gerald. "The Supreme Court, 1971 Term—Foreword: In Search of Evolving Doctrine on a Changing Court: A Model for a Newer Equal Protection." *Harvard Law Review* 86 (1972): 1–48.

Law, Sylvia, A. "Rethinking Sex and the Constitution." *University of Pennsylvania Law Review* 132 (1984): 955–1040.

Michelman, Frank I. "On Protecting the Poor Through the Fourteenth Amendment." *Harvard Law Review* 83 (1969): 7–59.

Smith, Rogers M. "The Constitution and Autonomy." *Texas Law Review* 60 (1982): 175–205.

Tribe, Laurence H. *American Constitutional Law*. Mineola, N.Y.: Foundation Press, 1978. Chapters 11, 14, 16.

11

The First Amendment: Freedom of Speech and Assembly

Syllabus

A large percentage of communities in the world today do not enjoy political speech and assembly rights under a national constitution that adequately protects such freedoms. A glimpse at the evening news or daily newspapers on any given day will confirm this. Whether the setting is Gdansk, Poland; Seoul, South Korea; Belfast, Northern Ireland; the Gaza Strip and West Bank in Israel; Johannesburg, South Africa; or Santiago, Chile, many persons demonstrating against repressive governmental policies do so at great personal risk to life and limb. These international instances of governmental repression against political speech and assembly seem very foreign to an American setting. Americans assume that their government would never use such tactics. And yet, this country has had its own history of individuals attempting to express themselves and the government intervening to regulate that expression. In many instances, as the following pages will indicate, government has held the upper hand, notwithstanding a First Amendment that is the ideal of free people everywhere.

This Chapter Examines the Following Matters

☐ When compared with other societies now experiencing great turmoil and dissent over the ends of government and the legitimate means for achieving those ends, the United States seems like a paragon of tranquility. But this country has had several historical moments when the individual's constitutional rights to speak out and assemble peaceably have had to bow to government.

☐ Even though the First Amendment states that government "shall make no law . . . abridging the freedom of speech . . . or the right of the people peaceably to assemble," a large body of academic writing has generally conceded that the First Amendment cannot be taken literally. Some governmental regulation of those precious rights is essential in order to preserve stability in a community. The problem lies in discerning when the individual's right to speak out and the community's right to search for truth must yield to necessary constraints upon those rights.

☐ Federal courts have generally upheld some regulation of First Amendment speech and assembly rights. For most of the period between World War I and II, the Supreme Court gave little protection to the right of the people to experiment with leftist

or radical political ideas. Generally speaking, political ideas considered to have a "bad tendency" toward advocating the overthrow of the American system of government were quickly punished and repressed.

☐ Except for a brief period just prior to World War II, the Court deferred to legislative and executive authorities who acted to suppress speech considered antithetical to national security and vaguely defined national interests.

☐ The 1960s revealed a Supreme Court much more protective of free expression than its predecessors. However, there has been continued support for time, place, and manner regulations that set allowable limits to free speech and assembly.

☐ The Supreme Court has recognized that conduct, as well as pure speech, can promote First Amendment ends; therefore, symbolic speech has for some time been accorded First Amendment protection. Silent protest, demonstrations, and picketing can frequently be more effective than pure speech. But the Court has usually balanced the claims of free expression (individualism) against the pursuit of the public interest (communitarianism).

Photo: The freedom of citizens to speak and to peaceably assemble has been a check on the abuse of governmental power and a major source of change in American public policy. Left, one million citizens from across the country marched in New York City in June 1982 to protest the buildup of nuclear weapons between the United States and the Soviet Union.

The Scope and Theory of First Amendment Freedoms

Of all the liberties guaranteed by the Bill of Rights, none are more widely cherished than those of the First Amendment—the freedoms of speech, press, assembly, religion, and petition. For decades, these guarantees have been considered essential to individual freedom and dignity and the practice of self-government. The ability of individuals to express themselves freely on a wide array of subjects reflects the widespread belief that only through an open and public forum—where all are encouraged to air different ideas, preferences, and values—can democratic self-government be realized. As Justice Louis Brandeis observed long ago, "The freedom to think as you will and to speak as you think are means indispensable to the discovery and spread of political truth." [1]

As discussed in Chapter 8, the guarantees of the first eight amendments of the Constitution originally applied only to the federal government. Not until 1925 and several decades thereafter did the long and selective process of incorporation finally begin to compel all governments to honor Bill of Rights guarantees. But as this chapter will indicate, a formal Bill of Rights does not guarantee tolerance in the United States. American history has been filled with numerous examples of intolerance toward and discrimination against various political, racial, and religious minorities. Throughout the past two hundred years, the Bill of Rights has stood as a written reminder that the American system is founded upon the belief in the dignity of each individual and upon the ideal that people, if given the chance to govern themselves, can act to achieve the public good. Part of this noble goal is based upon the reality that the system must tolerate both ideas that are cherished and ideas that are hated.

The American people have historically supported in *principle* civil liberties and civil rights of the people. [2] But a statement of abstract support for civil liberties does not necessarily translate into mass support in specific cases (see Brief 11.1). For a disturbingly large majority of Americans, extending free expression to homosexuals, atheists, Nazis, Ku Klux Klansmen, and other unpopular minorities is asking too much. This ambivalence about basic provisions of the Bill of Rights has existed for a long time and reflects the continuing difficulty of applying abstract principles to concrete cases. It also reflects the difficulties implicit in the dual philosophical traditions of individualistic and communitarian political cultures.

Freedom of Expression in Historical Perspective

Because First Amendment freedoms occupy so prominent a position in American constitutional law, it might be assumed that these "preferred freedoms" have always had central importance in American history. This is definitely not the case. Actually, most litigation relating to First Amendment rights, especially free expression, has occurred during the twentieth century. It is virtually impossible to find any major cases on First Amendment freedoms emerging from the Supreme Court prior to World War I.

Although freedom of expression can be traced to classical times, as some recent surveys have documented, [3] in both the Greek and Roman empires, it

☐ *Brief 11.1 How Tolerant Are Americans?*

Fortunately, Americans seem to be more tolerant in the 1980s than they were three decades ago. When asked in 1954 if someone who is against religion should be allowed to speak, only 40 percent of the respondents said yes, and only 16 percent would have allowed the same individual to teach at a college or university in the United States. By 1985, 66 percent would have allowed that person to speak, and 46 percent would have allowed the person to teach at a university. In 1954, in the midst of the Red Scare in this country, 68 percent of the respondents to the poll would not have allowed a Communist to speak, and 89 percent would not have allowed a Communist to teach at a college or university. By 1985, the precentages had dropped to 41 percent and 53 percent, respectively. Thirty years seem to have had some positive impact.

With respect to variables affecting the tolerance of a person, it appears that age and level of education have a significant impact upon professed levels of tolerance. The more formal education a person has, the more likely he or she is to give a "tolerant" response, with college graduates exhibiting the most tolerance for diverse opinions. When asked if they would allow a racist to speak, 56 percent of persons without a high school diploma said no, thus denying that racist freedom of speech. But when college graduates were asked the same question, only 23 percent said that they would

deny a racist the right to speak. The younger an individual is, the more likely that person is to give a tolerant response. In a recent poll, 53 percent of the respondents over fifty-five years of age said that they would deny a racist the right to speak, whereas only 30 percent of people between the ages of thirty and thirty-nine said that they would not allow such a person to speak.

Finally, a poll conducted by the National Opinion Research Center in the spring of 1978 indicated overwhelming popular support for civil liberties in the abstract, but greatly reduced support for civil liberties in concrete situations. In the survey, 97 percent of the respondents agreed that "no matter what a person's political beliefs are, he is entitled to the same legal rights and protections as anyone else." And 92 percent said that "I believe in free speech for all no matter what their views might be." At the same time, 35 percent agreed that "when the country is in great danger we may have to force people to testify against themselves even if it violates their rights." And 43 percent agreed with the statement that anyone who advocates abolishing popular elections and letting the military run the country should not be allowed to make a speech in their community.

Source: "Opinion Roundup," *Public Opinion* 10 (July/August 1987): 29–39.

was severely limited by restrictions upon the speaker, content, and place of communication. Such restrictions allowed only a small minority of the population to express itself openly. And yet, even with these restrictions, there was a surprising amount of free expression in a system proud of its "pure democracy" based upon an assembly open to all citizens. The Roman Republic emphasized individual liberty, civic responsibility, and public order. As a result, freedom of speech was a *communal* right and responsibility rather than an *individual* civil liberty. The emphasis was on the "communitarian" aspects of public discourse, rather than on the "individualistic" entitlement to free expression, which might be stressed today. From these classical times and until the Middle Ages, no Western nation extended to its citizens freedom of speech in any modern sense. But in the early thirteenth century, an event of momentous importance for the development of liberty in the Anglo-American world occurred.

The signing of the Magna Carta in 1215 by King John was an early recognition of the principle of limited government, which took root in Great Britain and the United States (see Chapter 2). Even though freedom of speech was not specifically mentioned in the Magna Carta, the document did declare that justice was not to be sold, denied, or delayed, and that no free man could be deprived of his life or property except by judgment of his peers and in accordance with the law of the land. The word "liberty" appeared several times in the document, and subsequent reaffirmation of the Magna Carta strengthened the concept of personal liberty, including the ideal of free speech.

In the centuries following the Magna Carta, freedom of speech extended gradually from monarch, to members of Parliament, to commoners in an evolutionary process that was not completed until nearly 1900.[4] On one level, the adoption of the writ of *habeas corpus* protected persons with unpopular ideas or views from arbitrary arrest and imprisonment. On a second level, freedom of speech was gradually expanded in three distinct phases: initially, only monarchs and high clergymen could speak without restraint. Then, with the passage of the English Bill of Rights in 1689, members of Parliament in their official capacity could speak freely (see Brief 2.3). Finally, with the passage of Fox's Libel Act in 1792, and the Reform Bill in 1832 and the full implementation of those laws by the mid-1800s, most efforts to control the written and spoken word had faded. Freedom of speech for English citizens was slowly becoming a reality.

As stated earlier, freedom of speech in the United States, in many respects, is a relatively recent phenomenon. In his study of free speech in America, Leonard Levy noted:

> The persistent image of colonial America as a society in which freedom of expression was cherished is an hallucination of sentiment that ignores history . . . The American people simply did not understand that freedom of thought and expression means equal freedom for the other fellow, especially the one with hated ideas.[5]

Intolerance in colonial America was transplanted from England and flourished long after independence from Great Britain. Like the English experience, early American practice saw only high government officials and the clergy able to express themselves freely. Repression of political and religious dissent was very common prior to the adoption of the Bill of Rights in 1791. Members of the colonial assemblies who enjoyed considerable freedom made certain that the masses did not have the same privilege. Colonial authorities vigorously suppressed opinions that criticized the organized church or the government. In some of the colonies—most notably Massachusetts, New York, Pennsylvania, and Virginia—the press was limited in what it could print by a colonial licensing system that lasted until the 1720s.

By the early 1780s, the United States was struggling to construct a government that provided order and stability against domestic and foreign enemies, and also protection for individual liberties. But civil liberties still led a precarious existence in some respects. The original Constitution, as stated in earlier chapters, included no formal bill of rights, in part because the framers felt that to enumerate specific liberties and rights would risk omitting some important ones. How could any such document be inclusive enough? However, by the time the Constitution had been adopted in June 1788, as Chapter 3 indicated, Thomas Jefferson was urging the inclusion of a bill of rights.

For the next 150 years, both the states and the federal government passed laws designed to regulate liberties and punish individuals suspected of sedition, blasphemy, defamation of character, and obscenity. In addition to these purposes, the laws also resulted in: the denial of women's rights throughout the eighteenth and nineteenth centuries; the Black Codes passed during the Civil War and Jim Crow laws thereafter, which effectively denied most rights to blacks; and the Espionage Acts of 1917–18, which limited political criticism of governmental officials. The Supreme Court in 1897 approved of these and other restrictive actions on free expression with its decision in *Davis* v. *Massachusetts,* which will be discussed later in this chapter.

In summary, Anglo-American experience finds minimal support before 1900 for what Americans today take for granted as a constitutional right of free expression. But developments in theory and practice in the twentieth century would see freedom of expression finally gain much wider support.

Contrasting Views of Freedom of Expression

Recognizing that nearly all Americans place a high value on freedom of expression, at least in the abstract, does not mean that perfect consensus now reigns regarding the extent of this basic right or the obligation of government to safeguard it at all costs. The Supreme Court has never held that First Amendment freedoms prohibit *all* regulations of free speech (or other freedoms in the amendment). Some forms of speech are not protected, such as obscene, libelous, lewd, or "fighting words" remarks, as will be discussed in this and the following chapters. Throughout the twentieth century, the justices on the Court have disagreed greatly on the standards to apply to First Amendment claims and what actions by government are legitimate. Much of this disagreement merely reflects the long-standing diversity of opinion on the subject through many centuries.

Philosophical Writings on Free Expression

Defenders of free speech today, as might be expected, owe a debt of gratitude to a few champions of independent thought and the right of free expression. Such notables as John Milton, Thomas Jefferson, and John Stuart Mill had an important impact upon building this tradition of free discourse in both the written and spoken word. In his *Areopagitica,* written in 1644, Milton argued that restrictions upon an open press were foolish for four reasons:

1. they were used by tyrants not deserving allegiance or respect;
2. they inhibited the development of individual character and potential;
3. they were ultimately ineffective because suppressed ideas will eventually become known; and
4. they discouraged learning and the search for truth.[6]

In the late eighteenth and early nineteenth centuries, Thomas Jefferson emphasized the importance of free speech and free press. And in his 1859 essay *On Liberty,* John Stuart Mill authored what many consider to be one of the most eloquent defenses of free speech ever drafted. Mill insisted that several reasons justify why society ought to encourage the airing of dissent. First, censored ideas may be true and the majority opinion may be in error. Human beings are fallible and may be operating under a false sense of "truth." Second, even though the censored opinion may be wrong in certain respects, it may contain some elements of truth. The prevailing view is seldom the *whole* truth, which can only be achieved by the healthy exchange of differing views. Third, even if it constitutes the entire truth, prevailing opinion must be tested periodically and defended on rational grounds in order to avoid prejudice and deceit. Because of these several reasons, Mill believed that speech could only be restricted when it directly infringed upon the personal rights of others. In addition, he explained why free expression is so important to a society dependent upon an enlightened and inquiring public committed to public discourse and the search for moral truth.

After World War I, the federal courts began to struggle more with controversies involving freedom of expression. In this struggle, several different views of free speech began to take shape. These viewpoints influenced how judges resolved disputes between governmental authority and the exercise of personal freedoms. One of the first attempts to document the history of freedom of expression in the United States was authored by Zechariah Chafee, Jr. Chafee, a Harvard law professor, published an important work in 1942 entitled *Free Speech in the United States*. He distinguished between types of expression: that which serves a *personal* interest (opinions considered vital to individual development) and that which serves a more general *social* interest ("the attainment of truth, so that the country may . . . adopt the wisest course of action"). Chafee's distinction also reflects the individualist-communitarian dichotomy. In attempting to determine when, if ever, government can intervene to protect free speech, Chafee proposed the maximum protection for "worthwhile" speech that serves the social interest, while permitting constraints if speech endangered the community or the nation. Speech that is not worthwhile to a community (i.e., profanity, defamation) can be restricted since it contributes in no meaningful way to public dialogue and decision making. Chafee's work was very useful to what would soon become known as a two-tier system of speech—"worthwhile" and "worthless." However, as subsequent cases and discussion revealed, attempting to distinguish speech on the basis of social utility can be both limited and controversial. One person's useful speech may be another's threat to order and stability.

Another academic whose discussion of freedom of speech closely resembled that of Chafee was Alexander Meiklejohn. In his work entitled *Free Speech and Its Relation to Self-Government,* first published in 1948, Meiklejohn, like Chafee, developed a theory that provided for two types of freedom of speech— one *absolute* and entitled to complete protection, and the other *conditional* and subject to regulation by government. Meiklejohn distinguished between public speech, which discusses political issues, and private communications, which deal with personal matters. **Political speech** is protected absolutely under the First Amendment. All other speech is protected by the Fifth Amendment (from national encroachment) and the Fourteenth (from state regulation), but it can be regulated if due process standards are satisfied. According to Meiklejohn:

> Individuals have . . . a private right of speech which may on occasion be denied or limited, though such limitations may not be imposed unnecessarily or unequally. So says the Fifth Amendment. But this limited guarantee of the freedom of a man's wish to speak is radically different in interest from the unlimited guarantee of the freedom of public discussion, which is given by the First Amendment. The latter, correlating the freedom of speech in which it is interested with the freedom of religion, of press, of assembly, of petition for redress of grievances, places all these alike beyond the reach of legislative limitations, beyond even the due process of law. With regard to them, Congress has no negative powers whatever.[7]

Meiklejohn's **absolutist theory** of free speech has been very controversial. It was instrumental in the thinking and writing of Justice Hugo Black, but it was also soundly criticized by Chafee (a former student of Meiklejohn) and by a succession of writers and legal scholars who support government regulation of such public speech. The main criticism has been that this absolutist theory, though simple and convenient, does not accurately reflect the thinking and writings of the framers of the Constitution. Furthermore, it is impractical as a workable device by which to distinguish between *public* and *private* speech. As Chafee once noted, "There are public aspects to practically every subject." [8]

One other student of the First Amendment who was prominent in the mid-twentieth century is Thomas I. Emerson. A former Yale law professor, Emerson's theory of free speech first appeared in 1966 and was republished in 1970 under the title *The System of Freedom of Expression*. Emerson maintained that freedom of expression is essential to preserving "the precarious balance between healthy changes and necessary consensus." By the late 1960s, when freedom of expression was being tested extensively in the context of public protests against the Vietnam War, he sought to fill a void with his **expression-action theory** of First Amendment rights.

Emerson argued that freedom of expression includes the right to form and maintain beliefs on any subject and to communicate those beliefs by whatever medium the individual desires, such as speech, press, music, art, literature, poetry, and film. Furthermore, freedom of expression includes the right to hear the opinions of others and the similar rights to inquire, gain access to information, and assemble and associate with others. In a manner strongly reminiscent of John Milton centuries earlier, Emerson maintained that freedom of association is important to a flourishing democratic society. It is a necessary means of personal self-fulfillment, discovering truth, democratic decision making, and achieving a more adaptable, stable community by balancing between "a healthy cleavage and necessary consensus."

Referring to what he saw as the "chaotic state of First Amendment theory" in the United States, Emerson attributed much of the confusion to the failure of the Supreme Court to maintain any single theory of free expression. According to Emerson, the Court had not compiled any clear and consistent rule of law useful for resolving specific cases. He recommended that a new standard be devised:

> The central idea of a system of freedom of expression is that a fundamental distinction must be drawn between conduct which consists of "expression" and conduct which consists of "action." "Expression" must be freely allowed and encouraged. "Action" can be controlled, subject to other constitutional requirements, but not by controlling expressions.

The distinction between free expression and regulatable action is still unclear, although Emerson's working through hypothetical and real cases places him clearly in the civil libertarian (minimal restriction) camp of constitutional scholars. Free expression is the rule, and governmental restraint the exception. However, specific cases before the Supreme Court reveal that instances involving alleged sedition, defamation, obscenity, and incitement to riot sometimes require very fine distinctions between *expression* (protected in all instances) and *action* (regulated in some situations). Emerson's attempt during the turbulent 1960s to present a more practical theory of free expression that seeks to balance diversity and consensus has been important for both public officials and private citizens to consider.

Important Distinctions on Freedom of Expression by Two Court Giants

The struggle to develop a more workable theory of free expression found contrasting views on the Supreme Court as well during the twentieth century. Although both Justices Hugo Black and Felix Frankfurter were chosen by President Franklin Roosevelt to serve on the federal bench, and each compiled a distinguished career on the Supreme Court (Black 1937–71; Frankfurter 1939–62), each held a very different view of First Amendment rights, especially freedom of expression. Both men saw very different mandates regarding free speech in the First Amendment, which partially reflected the turmoil on the Court and in American society during the mid-twentieth century. Always the judicial activist on preferred freedoms, Justice Black read the guarantee of free speech as an absolutist. Frankfurter, a proponent of judicial self-restraint, was increasingly persuaded to balance the rights of society against those of the individual, and, frequently, the individual lost.

Meiklejohn's absolutist defense of the First Amendment was very attractive to Justice Black, who became a dominant supporter of First Amendment rights throughout his career. Though more cautious and supportive of some regulation of speech in the 1940s, he became increasingly critical of government's trampling upon these essential guarantees. Black's attraction to absolutism was a function of his literalism when it came to First Amendment issues. In 1959, Black revealed his support for literalism, when he stated that the First Amendment "provides in simple words that Congress shall make no law . . . abridging freedom of speech or of the press. I read 'no law abridging' to mean no law." [9] He further elaborated upon this view in a 1961 dissenting opinion:

> I believe that the First Amendment's unequivocal command that there shall be no abridgment of the rights of free speech and assembly shows that the men who drafted our Bill of Rights did all the "balancing" that was to be done in the field . . . the very object of adopting the First Amendment, as well as the other provisions of the Bill of Rights, was to put the freedoms protected there completely out of the area of any congressional control that may be attempted through the exercise of precisely those powers that are now being used to "balance" the Bill of Rights out of existence. [10]

Black also articulated the same impatience with the Court's balancing test in *Barenblatt* two years earlier (see Chapter 5). In his dissent in that decision, Black stated that balancing the defendant's refusal to answer questions before a congressional committee

> completely leaves out the real interest in Barenblatt's silence, the interest of the people as a whole in being able to join organizations, advocate causes and make political "mistakes" without later being subjected to governmental penalties for having dared to think for themselves. It is this right, the right to err politically, which keeps us strong as a Nation.

His defense of this position, synonymous with that of Meiklejohn, was that for whatever reasons, the national government could not under any circumstances control free speech. And the Fourteenth Amendment also prohibited the states from regulating free expression. As a result, Justice Black never tolerated the law of libel, antiobscenity laws, or censorship of political, religious, scientific, or artistic expression (see Chapter 12).

But Black's literal reading of Bill of Rights guarantees sometimes found him supporting restrictions on free speech, primarily because of how he interpreted "speech." Although he firmly supported individual expression, he also paid very close attention to time, place, and manner considerations. According to Black, an individual can express all thoughts in the context where he or she has a protected right to do so, but individual intrusions upon the rights of others are not a protected form of free speech. This paradoxical stance appeared in several cases during Black's career on the Court, such as *Brown* v. *Louisiana* (1966) and *Adderley* v. *Florida* (1966).[11] Black's dissents in two other cases, *Tinker* v. *Des Moines Independent Community School District* (1969) and *Katz* v. *United States* (1967), likewise allowed governmental restraints, primarily because the expressions in question (student armbands and private telephone conversations, respectively) did not conform to his literal reading of the First and Fourth Amendments. With his retirement in 1971, and that of his colleague, Justice William O. Douglas, in 1975, there were no new additions to the Court that even approached their strong support of the First Amendment in an absolutist sense.

Black's intellectual rival on the New Deal and Warren Courts was Felix Frankfurter. Frankfurter felt that an absolutist stance on free speech oversimplified very complex issues involving order and stability. His answer to those attracted to the simplicity of absolutism was that judges must frequently balance one provision of the Constitution against another, and, in doing so, they must pay particular attention to the preferences of popularly elected majorities which enact the laws of society. Frankfurter's deference to legislatures also oversimplified the lawmaking process, but that never seemed to worry this persistent supporter of statutory law, even when those laws conflicted with vital First Amendment freedoms. In his opinions, Frankfurter frequently reflected upon this need to balance social and individual interests.[12] Throughout his career on the Court, he cautioned against judges overturning the actions of legislatures and advocated balancing several different provisions of the Constitution. Although Frankfurter frequently justified his pleas on restraint grounds, they were often attempts to salvage questionable laws.

Freedom of Speech in the Twentieth Century

Governmental efforts to limit freedom of speech have existed throughout the history of the American Republic. Usually, they have occurred during periods of real or perceived national emergency when the political or economic system seemed more vulnerable. The states and the federal government have made substantial efforts to curtail and punish dissenters during four specific periods of American history:

1. in the 1790s, when Congress passed the Alien and Sedition Acts;
2. several years prior to, during, and after the Civil War, when both Union and Confederate authorities suppressed free speech and press in many instances;
3. during World War I, with the passage of federal laws severely limiting free expression; and

4. after World War II, when Sen. Joseph McCarthy (R-Wis.) and the House Un-American Activities Committee (see Chapter 5) directed the anti-Communist "witch-hunts."

Although the first two periods generated several trials and convictions of persons considered to have violated certain federal laws, none of the incidents ever found the Supreme Court ruling on the constitutionality of these government actions. But the two periods during the twentieth century that did reflect increased governmental surveillance presented several opportunities for the Court to rule on governmental actions. In deciding these several cases, the Court created a few critical tests for determining how to answer the perennial question, How much criticism of government should a society permit?

Shortly after the United States declared war against Germany in 1917, Congress passed the Espionage Act. This act made it a crime to publish or make false statements with the intent to interfere in any way with the armed forces; to cause insubordination, disloyalty, or mutiny in the armed forces; or to obstruct recruiting and enlistment efforts. One year later, passage of the Sedition Act of 1918 made it a federal crime to obstruct the sale of government war bonds; to say, print, write, or publish anything intended to cause contempt or scorn for the federal government, the Constitution, the flag, or the uniform of the armed forces; or to say or write anything that interfered with defense production. Although some states had already enacted sedition laws, the patriotic climate then sweeping the country, plus the public hysteria about the recent Russian Revolution, accelerated passage of similar laws in other states. By 1925, nearly two-thirds of the American states had passed criminal anarchy and **syndicalism** laws similar to the federal statutes. The Court decisions emerging from challenges to these laws initiated some significant developments in First Amendment doctrine.

The Crisis of War and the Advent of Clear and Present Danger

Under the Espionage Act of 1917 and the Sedition Act of 1918, more than two thousand Americans were prosecuted for various violations of federal law. Several cases emerged from this litigation, four of which will be discussed in this section. A key question arising in these cases was whether the right of free speech, as granted by the First Amendment, was absolute or susceptible to legislative restraint. If it could be limited, under what circumstances and to what extent? The Supreme Court had never dealt with these questions before. The answers provided by the Court proved momentous, both to the parties involved and to American society at large. It should be noted that none of the cases was handled by the Supreme Court during World War I, but only after hostilities had ceased in November 1918.

"A Question of Proximity and Degree"

In the first of the Espionage Act Cases, *Schenck* v. *United States* (1919), Justice Oliver Wendell Holmes spoke for a unanimous Court and upheld the conviction of Charles T. Schenck for violation of the Espionage Act. As the general secretary of the Socialist party, Schenck had been tried and convicted on three counts of conspiring to obstruct the draft by circulating leaflets urging civil resistance to the draft and using the mail to circulate that material. In upholding

Schenck's conviction, Justice Holmes qualified First Amendment protection of free speech by stating that it was not an *absolute* right:

> We admit that in many places and in ordinary times the defendants, in saying all that was said in the circular, would have been within their constitutional rights. But the character of every act depends upon the circumstances in which it is done. . . The most stringent protection of free speech would not protect a man in falsely shouting fire in a theatre, and causing a panic.

He then crafted a rule that would later be used as an important protection for free speech. According to Holmes, the Court must make a difficult judgment:

> The question in every case is whether the words used are used in such circumstances and are of such a nature as to create a clear and present danger that they will bring about the substantive evils that Congress has a right to prevent.

To Holmes, it was "a question of proximity and degree." The defendant's words, printed during wartime and with the intent to persuade men not to enlist in the armed forces, presented an obvious and immediate danger to the successful prosecution of the war. It made no difference that Schenck and others had failed in their effort to obstruct the draft, since the statute punished *conspiracy* to obstruct as well as the actual obstruction. The irony of the *Schenck* case is that the Court would soon discard this **clear-and-present-danger test** for judging acceptable government restraints on free expression for a more conservative and intrusive device.

The Aftermath of *Schenck:* A New Standard Emerges

One week after deciding the *Schenck* case, the Court announced its decision in a very similar case, *Debs* v. *United States* (1919). The case involved the well-known Socialist leader, Eugene V. Debs, a frequent candidate of the Socialist party for president of the United States. On June 16, 1918, at a park in Canton, Ohio, Debs made a speech that the government argued was intended to obstruct military recruitment and incite insubordination in the armed forces. He was later convicted by a trial court for having violated the 1917 Espionage Act and sentenced to ten years in federal prison. Based upon his reading of Debs's statements in the Canton park that day, Holmes's opinion for the Court said that a jury could reasonably conclude that Debs was opposed "not only [to] war in general but this war, and that the opposition was so expressed that its natural and intended effect would be to obstruct recruiting." Although the opinion did not specifically refer to any new rule, it did emphasize the *tendency* of Debs's remarks and his intention to convince draftees not to enlist.

The *Debs* case has never attracted much attention in American constitutional law, but it closely resembles the *Schenck* case and the two cases should be read together. But *Debs* presented a set of facts that today seem nothing like clear and present danger. Debs had expressed sharp criticism of war in general, and World War I in particular. He was sharply critical of the federal government and governmental policy. At the time, he was a national political figure and, running for the presidency in 1920, attracted 900,000 votes that year while serving time in federal prison. As law professor Harry Kalven, Jr., said when comparing the *Debs* case to antiwar activities in the United States in the 1970s, "It is somewhat as though George McGovern had been sent to prison for his criticism of the war."[13]

Approximately eight months after *Debs* was decided, the Supreme Court reviewed several convictions under an amended Espionage Act, and the consequence was a new test for determining when government could intervene to limit free speech. The case involved also was significant as the first of several in which Justices Holmes and Brandeis dissented from the majority. Rather than using the less restrictive test of clear and present danger for free speech cases, the majority said that even actions which *might* lead to a detrimental effect violated the law.

Abrams v. *United States* (1919) involved five Russian citizens living in the United States. They had been convicted for writing, publishing, and distributing two allegedly seditious pamphlets criticizing the federal government for deploying American military personnel to Russia in 1918. One of the pamphlets described President Woodrow Wilson as a coward and a hypocrite and implied that the real reason for sending the troops was to aid anti-Communist forces then trying to overthrow the Communist regime. The pamphlet also described capitalism as an "enemy of the workers." The original indictments were for having violated an amendment to the Espionage Act, that prohibited conspiracy to unlawfully "alter, print, write, and publish" seditious messages during wartime or advocate the "curtailment of . . . products . . . necessary and essential to the prosecution of the war." The trial court had sentenced the five defendants to twenty-year terms in prison.

In a 7–2 majority opinion, with Justices Holmes and Brandeis dissenting, Justice John H. Clarke upheld the Russians' convictions on the basis of the evidence contained in the two pamphlets. According to Clarke:

> The plain purpose of their propaganda was to excite, at the supreme crisis of the war, disaffection, sedition, riots, and, as they hoped, revolution in this country for the purpose of embarrassing and if possible defeating the military plans of the [U.S.] government in Europe.

Clarke then stated what was an early rationale for the **bad-tendency doctrine:**

> It will not do to say, as is now argued, that the only intent of these defendants was to prevent injury to the Russian cause. Men must be held to have intended, and to be accountable for, the effects which their acts were likely to produce. Even if their primary purpose and intent was to aid the cause of the Russian Revolution, the plan of action which they adopted necessarily involved, before it could be realized, defeat of the war program of the United States.

This reasoning was unpersuasive to Holmes and Brandeis, who thought that the majority had departed from a free speech standard that more properly protected First Amendment rights. Basing his judgment upon the *Schenck* and *Debs* precedents, Holmes maintained that the government could constitutionally punish speech "that produces or is intended to produce a clear and imminent danger that it will bring about forthwith certain substantive evils that the United States constitutionally may seek to prevent." Only the present danger of *immediate* evil or an intent to bring it about warrant governmental efforts to limit individual expression. To Holmes, the *Abrams* case did not present this imminent threat:

> Congress certainly cannot forbid all effort to change the mind of the country. Now nobody can suppose that the surreptitious publishing of a silly leaflet by an unknown man, without more, would present any immediate danger that its

opinions would hinder the success of the government aims or have any appreciable tendency to do so.

In addition to insisting that the wrong standard was used to judge individual rights versus societal interest, Holmes also criticized the excessive punishment given the defendants. In the closing passages of his dissent, Holmes provided an eloquent defense of free speech that would have a strong impact upon future Supreme Court deliberations:

> When men have realized that time has upset many fighting faiths they may come to believe even more than they believe the very foundations of their own conduct that the ultimate goal desired is better reached by free trade in ideas—that the best test of truth is the power of the thought to get itself accepted in the competition of the market, and that truth is the only ground upon which their wishes safely can be carried out. That at any rate is the theory of our Constitution. It is an experiment, as all life is an experiment. Every year if not every day we have to wager our salvation upon some prophecy based upon imperfect knowledge. While that experiment is part of our system I think that we should be eternally vigilant against attempts to check the expression of opinions that we loathe and believe to be fraught with death, unless they so imminently threaten immediate interference with the lawful and pressing purposes of the law that an immediate check is required to save the country.

As moving as Holmes's dissent was, it did not attract a majority of justices until the late 1930s, when the Court reverted to clear and present danger as a substitute for the more conservative and restrictive bad-tendency doctrine.

The final case prosecuted under the Espionage Act following World War I centered on an antiwar, anticonscription pamphlet entitled "The Price We Pay." It had been written by a prominent Episcopal clergyman and published by the Socialist Party of the United States. A judge and jury in Albany, New York, had convicted four defendants of the charge that the pamphlet was a deliberate attempt to cause insubordination in the armed forces and thus interfere with the war effort. The defendants appealed to the Supreme Court on the grounds that the government had failed to demonstrate intent to cause insubordination. Furthermore, the government had not proven that distribution of the pamphlet created any clear and present danger that insubordination would result. In the case of *Pierce* v. *United States* (1920), seven justices, with Holmes and Brandeis again dissenting, upheld the convictions on the grounds that a jury could logically conclude that many of the statements in the pamphlet were false, or that the pamphlet was distributed by the defendants without any regard for its truth or falsity. The majority opinion clearly applied the bad-tendency test, for as Justice Mahlon Pitney noted in the majority opinion, a jury might reasonably conclude that the pamphlet "would have a tendency to cause insubordination, disloyalty and refusal of duty in the military and naval forces."

Justice Brandeis disagreed with the majority's upholding the conviction of these defendants based upon their comment and interpretation of public issues, which, by definition, were personal conclusions and opinions:

> To hold that a jury may make punishable statements of conclusion or of opinion, like those here involved, by declaring them to be statements of fact and to be false would practically deny members of small political parties freedom of criticism.

Brandeis also criticized the Court's failure to demonstrate that even if some of the statements were false, no such proof had been presented at the trial, nor had there been any proof of intent to dampen military morale. Finally, he did not think that the pamphlet presented any clear and present danger of causing military insubordination.

As mentioned, the *Pierce* case was the last of the major seditious libel cases prosecuted under the Espionage and Sedition Acts of 1917–18. Although the *Schenck* precedent had generated the clear-and-present-danger standard to judge the limits of individual speech, it was quickly discarded in the *Debs, Abrams,* and *Pierce* cases for a more conservative and restrictive bad-tendency doctrine that enabled government to intervene earlier in the speech process. Not until *De Jonge* v. *Oregon* (1937) and after did the Hughes Court revert to the standard first devised by Holmes in *Schenck* and begin supporting civil liberties more aggressively in the New Deal era. In doing this, it added both new stature to the Court and new security to individual liberties protected by the Bill of Rights. But before leaving the post-World War I era, one other precedent must be examined because of its impact upon civil liberties and the development of American constitutional law.

Gitlow v. *New York* (1925): The Defendant Loses as Nationalization Begins

The facts of *Gitlow* v. *New York* (1925) reflect the internal problems and factionalism experienced by the Socialist party following World War I. Some members had tired of the inability of their party to realize any substantial gains following the Russian Revolution in 1917, and they argued for more radical political and economic change. At the same time, thirty-three states had enacted peacetime criminal syndicalism laws that made it illegal to advocate, teach, or assist in the violent overthrow of the political or economic system.

The model for many of these laws was a 1902 New York law that defined criminal anarchy as "the doctrine that organized government should be overthrown by force or violence, or by assassination of the executive head or any of the executive officials of government, or by an unlawful means." The New York law also prohibited advocacy of criminal anarchy by speech and the printing and distribution of any materials advocating or teaching criminal anarchy.

Benjamin Gitlow, a radical Socialist and a member of the Left Wing Section of the Socialist Party of the United States, had been convicted in New York courts for violating the 1902 state criminal anarchy law. Gitlow had allegedly participated in the printing and distribution of sixteen thousand copies of "The Left Wing Manifesto," a pamphlet which criticized moderate socialism for working through the democratic parliamentary process. Instead, the manifesto urged accomplishing the "Communist Revolution" by radical socialism based upon "the class struggle," and urged the staging of mass political strikes and destruction of the parliamentary state. It exhorted the proletariat to "organize its own state for the coercion and suppression of the bourgeoisie." This was too much for New York officials, and Gitlow was convicted in state court. Gitlow appealed his conviction to the U.S. Supreme Court, arguing that the state law unconstitutionally restricted his right of free speech. Implicit in Gitlow's appeal was an important assertion—that certain rights guaranteed by the First Amendment against infringement by Congress are also applicable to the states by virtue of the Fourteenth Amendment Due Process Clause.

Writing for a seven-member majority, Justice Edward Sanford upheld Gitlow's conviction for having violated the state criminal anarchy law. The majority opinion stated that "The Left Wing Manifesto" was neither abstract doctrine nor mere prediction of an eventual Socialist revolutionary order. Rather, the pamphlet urged the staging of mass strikes in order to foment industrial strife and revolutionary action aimed at the overthrow of organized government. According to Sanford:

> That utterances inciting to the overthrow of organized government by unlawful means, present a sufficient danger of substantive evil to bring their punishment within the range of legislative discretion, is clear. Such utterances, by their very nature, involve danger to the public peace and to the security of the State. They threaten breaches of the peace and ultimate revolution.

Sanford condemned the manifesto's message as being within proscribed conduct, regardless of how remote the likelihood of disruption and revolution. Government need not wait before prohibiting such conduct or sit idly by as revolution occurs:

> The State cannot reasonably be required to measure the danger from every utterance in the nice balance of a jeweler's scale. A single revolutionary spark may kindle a fire that, smoldering for a time, may burst into a sweeping and destructive conflagration. . . It cannot reasonably be required to defer the adoption of measures for its own peace and safety until the revolutionary utterances lead to actual disturbances of the public peace or imminent and immediate danger of its own destruction; but it may, in the exercise of its judgment, suppress the threatened changes in its incipiency.

But the most important aspect of *Gitlow* was its application of the Due Process Clause of the Fourteenth Amendment to the states regarding First Amendment freedoms (see Chapter 8 on selective incorporation). Constitutional scholars have never completely explained why and how the Supreme Court made this momentous alteration in constitutional law, which circumvented *Barron* v. *Baltimore* a century earlier. For whatever reason, after *Gitlow* in 1925, any citizen of any state could claim protection of the First Amendment against state laws that sought to constrain freedom of expression.

The final point about *Gitlow* concerns the dissenting opinion of Justice Holmes. As might be expected, he disagreed with the Court majority (along with Brandeis) primarily because he thought Gitlow had been convicted by a more restrictive standard judging freedom of expression:

> If what I think the correct test is applied, it is manifest that there was no present danger of an attempt to overthrow the government by force on the part of an admittedly small minority who shared the defendant's view.

Holmes then disparaged the wording of the majority opinion:

> It is said that this manifesto was more than a theory, that it was an incitement. Every idea is an incitement. It offers itself for belief and if believed it is acted on unless some other belief outweighs it or some failure of energy stifles the move-

ment at birth. The only difference between the expression of an opinion and an incitement in the narrower sense is the speaker's enthusiasm for the result. Eloquence may set fire to reason. But whatever may be thought of the redundant discourse before us it had no chance of starting a present conflagration.

Holmes concluded that had there been an attempt to induce violent revolution immediately, the law might have been applied, but Gitlow's indictment and conviction had resulted from mere *publication* of these ideas. That was too much for Holmes to condone.

The *Gitlow* decision symbolized much of the Court's activity in the 1920s, when Americans were anxious to flee the problems of the European continent and remain isolated at home. The citizenry turned inward and distrusted all voices of political dissent (see Brief 11.2). And the majority on the Supreme Court supported this conservative isolation and distrust of dissenting opinion, as the discussion of *Whitney* v. *California* (1927) later in this chapter will indicate.

Increasingly, in the next decade, the Court viewed itself primarily as an economic policymaker, rather than as a watchdog of civil liberties. Not until the Court Revolution of 1937 did the Court more consistently support freedom of expression. But even then, its civil libertarian stance, announced first in the Holmes-Brandeis dissents of the 1920s and strengthened by "preferred-freedoms" developments, would be abandoned temporarily through the early post-World War II era, as American society entered a fourth period of doubt and fear about seditious speech.

The Preferred Position of Free Speech in Times of Crisis

During the twentieth century, the idea of constitutional rights grew to include elements besides simply property in an economic sense. As a result of this development, a distinction emerged between property, or tangible, rights and human, or more intangible, guarantees. This trend was aided by several Supreme Court justices who argued that some rights are so basic, that when they

---

❑ Brief 11.2   The Trial and Execution of Sacco and Vanzetti

The famous murder trial of two Italian immigrants reflected the political, economic, and social forces affecting American society in the 1920s. Nicola Sacco and Bartolomeo Vanzetti were arrested on May 5, 1920, for the murder of two persons in South Braintree, Massachusetts. Known for their leftist political views and prominent in Socialist politics at the time, Sacco and Vanzetti were convicted on July 14, 1921, in a judicial proceeding that by most accounts was badly conducted and politically biased. In addition to prejudicial statements made privately by the presiding judge, no procedural concessions were made to the defense, and the climate of the entire trial reflected anti-immigration feelings and hostility toward political agitators. From the time of their conviction in 1921 until August 23, 1927, when they were both executed, Sacco and Vanzetti became symbols of oppressed immigrants denied fairness in the American criminal justice system. To the present day, the case represents an ugly incident in American history and shows how individuals with minority political views can be convicted because of those views as much as on any evidence presented in the courtroom.

are restricted, they drastically inhibit the political process and prevent the repeal of undesirable legislation.

The Beginning of a Two-Tier Approach to Civil Liberties

According to Justice Harlan Stone's famous footnote in *United States* v. *Carolene Products Co.* (1938), judges should normally practice restraint and defer to popularly elected assemblies. But in matters dealing with civil liberties as outlined in the first ten amendments of the Constitution, popular assemblies frequently restrict personal freedoms by passing restrictive legislation. When this happens, courts must intervene to protect these guarantees as outlined in the Bill of Rights (see Chapter 10).

There has been much debate over the legitimacy of Stone's assertion that some constitutional rights are more important than others. But it did not take long for most of the Supreme Court justices to endorse the underlying premise in the *Carolene Products* footnote. According to Justice James McReynolds in *Schneider* v. *State of New Jersey, Town of Irvington* in 1939:

> Mere legislative preferences or beliefs respecting matters of public convenience may be insufficient to justify such as diminishes the exercise of rights so vital to the maintenance of democratic institutions.

The preferred-position concept (see Chapter 8) had some problems after 1939, primarily because of increased public concern about national security in wartime, although the war against Germany and Japan may have actually strengthened the idea of preferred freedoms. Justice Stone himself first used the term in his dissenting opinion in *Jones* v. *Opelika* (1942), and, when the Court overruled that decision in 1943 in *Murdock* v. *Pennsylvania*, the majority opinion also referred to "preferred freedoms." In 1943, Justice James Byrnes was replaced by Wiley Rutledge, a liberal Democrat and former federal appellate judge. Within two years of his appointment, Rutledge authored what has become known as one of the strongest defenses of the preferred-freedoms doctrine (see Chapter 8):

> Any attempt to restrict [First Amendment] liberties must be justified by clear public interest threatened not doubtfully or remotely, but by clear and present danger. The national connection between the remedy provided and the evil to be curbed . . . will not suffice. These rights rest on firmer foundation. Accordingly, whatever occasion would restrain orderly discussion and persuasion, at appropriate time and place, must have clear support in public danger, actual or impending. Only the gravest abuses, endangering paramount interests give occasion for permissible limitation.[14]

As discussed in Chapter 10, the Court has created a two-tier approach to examining cases involving basic constitutional rights. A lower level or rational-basis standard allows government to legislate for a valid purpose or goal, whereas an upper level or strict-scrutiny standard protects fundamental rights and prevents the development of suspect classifications based upon race, alienage, ethnicity, handicapped status, or the like. For more than a decade following World War II, the term "preferred freedoms" was used in more than two dozen cases by seven different justices. Although the specific phrase eventually declined, the Court never formally abandoned the concept. To this day, the Supreme Court maintains that statutes which limit First Amendment freedoms are suspect, requiring close judicial scrutiny and compelling justification for their existence.

Following World War II, the United States entered a period in which civil liberties were curtailed. Judicial behavior on the Supreme Court followed the Frankfurter call for judicial restraint, and, until a more liberal Warren Court in the 1960s began once again to protect freedom of expression, the early cold war period saw First Amendment freedoms severely restricted in the name of national security. The Red Scare of the post-World War II era had arrived.

Freedom of Speech and the Cold War

Judicial recognition of the freedom to espouse any political belief and to associate with others sharing that belief is exclusively a development of the twentieth century. As a corollary to free thought and expression, political association also began in the series of post-World War I rulings discussed in the previous section. As the Court made clear in announcing the clear-and-present-danger and the bad-tendency tests, the right of political association, like freedom of speech, is not absolute. It, too, can be curtailed in time of national peril. Following World War II, the Court tried to strike a balance between individual freedom and national security. In a span of nearly two decades, it considered several cases involving federal and state laws restricting political association. By the early 1960s, its precedents had established an important point—that individuals have a constitutional right not to be prosecuted for belonging to a particular political group.

Before considering the case law that emerged in this period, the internal security laws that were the focus of Court activity on political association and free speech should be examined. World War II had extracted a terrible toll in personnel, materiel, and national energy, but the effort finally won a clear victory for the Allies. No sooner had that victory been won than a new threat emerged—global communism—which posed both a military and ideological challenge to democratic government. Militarily, the spread of communism in Europe in the late 1940s—across territory that the Allies had just recently lifted from the scourge of national socialism—posed a serious threat to freedom and self-determination.

The Legislative Response

Congress passed four major federal laws to deal with the threat of subversion by Communist organizations in the United States. These were the Alien Registration Act of 1940 (known as the Smith Act), the Taft-Hartley Amendments to the National Labor Relations Act (passed in 1947), the Internal Security Act (known as the McCarran Act) of 1950, and the Communist Control Act of 1954.

Under the Smith Act, it was illegal to advocate the violent overthrow of government or to organize or to belong to any group advocating such revolutionary activity. It also forbade the publication or distribution of any materials advocating or teaching the overthrow of government by force. Also, in language directly limiting freedom of political association, the Smith Act made it unlawful to organize any group committed to teaching, advocating, or encouraging the overthrow or destruction of government by force or to become knowingly a member of any organization or group dedicated to the violent overthrow of any government in the United States.

Growing concern in Congress over Communist infiltration of the American labor movement and the fear of "political strikes" against key elements of American industry spurred passage of the Labor Management Relations Act of 1947 as part of the Taft-Hartley Act. A key component of the act was a provision requiring officers of all labor organizations in the United States to sign sworn statements (affidavits) attesting to the fact that they were not members of or affiliated with the Communist party in any way, and that they did not believe in or hold membership in any organization that advocated violent overthrow of the federal government. Any union official refusing to sign such an oath was denied all protections afforded under the National Labor Relations Act, which was the primary collective bargaining statute affecting organized labor.

In 1950, fearing that the Smith Act did not provide enough protection against the domestic Communist movement, Congress passed the McCarran Act over President Harry Truman's veto. This particular statute required all Communist-action or Communist-front organizations to register with the Justice Department and to disclose their membership lists. It further penalized members of such groups by prohibiting them from holding any government- or defense-related position of employment. The obvious purpose of the act was to expose Communist party leaders and members of any front organizations. Somewhat naively, sponsors of the statute assumed that mere exposure would control the activities of such organizations. Title I of the McCarran Act established a five-member, presidentially appointed Subversive Activities Control Board (SACB). The mission of the board was to determine, subject to judicial review, whether a particular organization was affiliated with the Communist party in any way. Once labeled as a subversive organization, the group had to turn over its membership lists, and any government-employed members would lose their jobs. The ineffectiveness of the law is demonstrated by the fact that never during the next fifteen years did the Communist party ever register with the SACB as a subversive organization. By the mid-1960s, the SACB and the law passed into obscurity.

The last major statute passed by Congress in the 1950s to limit speech and association of Communist party sympathizers was the Communist Control Act of 1954. This statute branded the Communist party as a treasonable conspiracy against the United States government. As such, the party had none of the rights and privileges of political parties in the United States. The act went farther than any of the preceding three in denying constitutional rights to certain political organizations. Although it prevented the party from participating in free and open elections, it generated the least activity before federal courts, primarily because the Warren Court would soon initiate a new era in civil liberties and grant more latitude to freedom of speech and political association. But until the late-1950s, as the following section will indicate, political dissent was limited in major respects by a conservative Supreme Court.

The Judicial Response

One of the first opportunities for the Supreme Court to examine these federal restrictions on speech and association came at the peak of the McCarthy era in the early 1950s. As mentioned in the discussion of Supreme Court cycles in Chapter 4, this period was marked by more conservative Court personnel and a noticeable deference to congressional authority, especially concerning matters of national security. In 1950, in the case of *American Communications*

Association v. *Douds,* the Supreme Court upheld Section 9(h)—the non-Communist affidavit provision—of the Labor Management Relations Act of 1947. The American Communications Association had long been one of the more radical elements of the American labor movement, and its officers specifically disapproved of Congress's attempt to regulate members' beliefs. Only six of the justices participated in hearing arguments in this case, and the majority (with Justice Black dissenting) avoided considering the constitutional issue of free speech. Instead, it ruled that the affidavit provision requiring disavowal of the Communist party was a legitimate exercise of Congress's power to regulate commerce among the states. According to Chief Justice Fred M. Vinson, writing for the majority:

> There can be no doubt that Congress may, under its constitutional power to regulate commerce among the several states, attempt to prevent political strikes and other kinds of direct action designed to burden and interrupt the free flow of commerce.

Vinson insisted that Congress was justified in treating the Communist party differently than other political parties. Its legislation could be used to prevent the party from influencing union members to call strikes for political purposes. To the charge that the affidavit requirement infringed upon personal freedoms, Vinson said that it

> is designed to protect the public not against what Communists and others identified therein advocate or believe, but against what Congress has concluded they have done or are likely to do again.

In a vigorous dissenting opinion, Justice Black chastised his colleagues on the Court for ignoring the vital First Amendment issues involved here and deciding the case upon weaker interstate commerce grounds. As Black noted:

> Freedom to think is inevitably abridged when beliefs are penalized by impositions of civil disabilities . . . But the postulate of the First Amendment is that our free institutions can be maintained without proscribing or penalizing political belief, speech, press, assembly, or party affiliation. This is a far bolder philosophy than despotic rulers can afford to follow. It is the heart of the system on which our freedom depends.

By the late 1950s, the affidavit requirement had failed miserably to ferret out Communist sympathizers among organized labor. As a result, Congress replaced it in 1959 with a provision in the Labor Management Reporting and Disclosure Act that prohibited members of the Communist party from holding any union office. Six years later, the Warren Court ruled that provision unconstitutional as an illegal bill of attainder prohibited by Article I, Section 9, Clause 3, of the Constitution.[15] The cases that follow came before the Supreme Court in the 1950s and had a significant impact upon civil liberties in the country. Although one case endangered free speech and political association substantially, some later deliberations actually restored much of the lost territory.

Dennis v. United States (1951)   In July 1948, with Congress and the American public growing increasingly alarmed about the threat of an international Communist conspiracy, the federal government indicted Eugene Dennis, secretary general of the Communist Party of the United States, and ten other top-level members of the central committee of the party. After a six-month trial, the defendants were convicted for violating Section 2 of the Smith Act, which punished speech advocating the overthrow of government by force, and Section 3, which prohibited any person from conspiring to organize any group advocating the forceful overthrow of government. Their conviction was upheld by the U.S. Court of Appeals for the Second Circuit, which asserted that sufficient evidence had been presented during the trial to demonstrate that the defendants had conspired to overthrow the government by force. In fact, the only pieces of evidence introduced in the trial were the writings of Karl Marx and Vladimir Lenin. In the appellate ruling, Chief Judge Learned Hand revised in a major way the clear-and-present-danger test, when he stated:

> In each case [courts] must ask whether the gravity of the "evil," discounted by its improbability, justifies such invasion of free speech as is necessary to avoid the danger.

Dennis and the others appealed their conviction to the Supreme Court on the grounds that the Smith Act violated the First and Fifth Amendments to the Constitution. In 1951, on a vote of 6–2, the Supreme Court in *Dennis v. United States* upheld the convictions. The members of the Court differed widely about their reasoning in reaching a decision, as evidenced by several concurring and dissenting opinions.

Most of the opinions reflected very different assessments of how serious a threat the Communist party posed to the nation. In writing for the majority, Chief Justice Vinson mentioned the clear-and-present-danger rule, but seemed to apply quite a different standard, one that has often been referred to as the sliding-scale rule. He argued that the Smith Act did not allow persons to be prosecuted for engaging in the academic discussion of revolution. As he observed, "Congress did not intend to eradicate the free discussion of political theories, to destroy the traditional rights of Americans to discuss and evaluate ideas without fear of governmental sanction." But government, he noted, must also be alert to long-term danger:

> Overthrow of the Government by force and violence is certainly a substantial enough interest for the Government to limit speech. Indeed, this is the ultimate value of any society, for if a society cannot protect its very structure from armed internal attack, it must follow that no subordinate value can be protected.

Given this paramount interest in preserving governmental order, the issue then became one of deciding what the words "clear and present danger" actually meant as guidelines for congressional action. Again, Vinson commented:

> Obviously, the words cannot mean that before the Government may act, it must wait until the putsch is about to be executed, the plans have been laid and the signal is awaited. If Government is aware that a group aiming at its overthrow is attempting to indoctrinate its members and to commit them to a course whereby they will strike when the leaders feel the circumstances permit, action by the Government is required. . . *Certainly an attempt to overthrow the Government by force, even though doomed from the outset because of inadequate numbers or power of the revolutionists is a sufficient evil for Congress to prevent.* [Emphasis added]

This last sentence indicates that the majority had drastically revised the clear-and-present-danger test. The Court was no longer concerned about the probable success of the group's objectives, but rather about the *seriousness* of the threat—and overthrow of the government by force was serious. To those arguing that conspiracy to organize revolutionary activity should be protected by the First Amendment, the chief justice remained unconvinced:

> The formation . . . of such a highly organized conspiracy with rigidly disciplined members subject to call when the leader . . . felt that the time had come for action, coupled with the inflammable nature of world conditions . . . convince us that their convictions were justified. . . It is the existence of the conspiracy which creates the danger . . . if the ingredients of the reaction are present we cannot bind the Government to wait until the catalyst is added.

Vinson noted that the *Dennis* case presented circumstances far different from those operating in the *Gitlow* case, where Holmes and Brandeis had shown concern for the wrong test being employed to judge Gitlow's actions. Vinson insisted that the Communist party was dedicated to the overthrow of the government; thus, a more stringent rule for protecting the government was necessary. His remedy was to adopt the device used by Judge Learned Hand and quoted earlier about the "gravity of the evil." The opinion thus gives symbolic support to clear and present danger but actually uses the bad-tendency test for judging the limits of free speech.

In a lengthy concurring opinion, Justice Frankfurter agreed with the majority's handling of the case, but he felt compelled to justify the Smith Act on judicial restraint grounds. The major point made by Frankfurter was that when the demand for free speech and the need for internal security collide, Congress is the best judge of which should take precedence:

> Full responsibility for the choice cannot be given to the courts. Courts are not representative bodies. They are not designed to be a good reflex of a democratic society. Their judgment is best informed . . . within narrow limits. Their essential quality is detachment, founded on independence. History teaches us that the independence of the judiciary is jeopardized when courts become embroiled in the passions of the day and assume primary responsibility in choosing between competing political, economic and social pressures.

Frankfurter, thus, was willing to defer to Congress in its regulation of the Communist party, which he thought differed greatly from other political parties in ideology and objectives.

Justice Robert H. Jackson's concurring opinion argued that the clear-and-present danger test was inadequate in the *Dennis* case, because a "well-organized, nationwide conspiracy" of the Communist party was vastly different from the political dissidents of World War I. He argued that the "subtlety and efficiency of modernized revolutionary techniques used by totalitarian parties" demanded more vigilance and application of a rule other than clear and present danger. In his mind, there was little doubt that conspiracy to overthrow the government existed and Congress was justified in its action under the Smith Act.

The two dissenting justices in *Dennis* were Black and Douglas, both of whom maintained that the defendants should never have been charged. They insisted that the government had no right to punish speech and association in this instance. After stating that the unregulated communication of ideas necessarily involves some risk, Justice Black wrote that the drafters of the First Amendment considered that the benefits of unregulated speech outweighed the risk. Said Black, "I have always believed that the First Amendment is the keystone of our Government, that the freedoms it guarantees provide the best insurance against destruction of all freedom." Black felt that allowing Congress to "water down" the First Amendment by regulating free speech and political association as it did here was wrong, and he stated why he thought the First Amendment was being ignored by the Court in this instance:

> Public opinion being what it now is, few will protest the conviction of these Communist petitioners. There is hope, however, that in calmer times, when present pressures, passions and fears subside, this or some later Court will restore the First Amendment liberties to the high preferred place where they belong in a free society.

Also in dissent, Justice Douglas insisted that the majority had strayed too far from the clear-and-present-danger test as he understood it:

> There comes a time when even speech loses its constitutional immunity. Speech innocuous one year may at another time fan such destructive flames that it must be halted in the interests of the safety of the Republic. That is the meaning of the clear and present danger test. When conditions are so critical that there will be no time to avoid the evil that the speech threatens, it is time to call a halt. Otherwise, free speech which is the strength of the Nation will be the cause of its destruction . . . we deal here with speech alone, not with speech plus acts of sabotage or unlawful conduct. Not a single seditious act is charged in the indictment. To make a lawful speech unlawful because two men conclude it, is to raise the law of conspiracy to appalling proportions.

Douglas emphasized that he thought the Communist party was weak and "crippled as a political force," mainly because free speech had destroyed it by exposing it as an unworkable and unacceptable ideology: "The country is not in despair; the people know Soviet Communism; the doctrine of Soviet revolution is exposed in all of its ugliness and the American people want none of it." According to Douglas, the meeting of a handful of Communist party leaders in the United States did not pose a clear and present danger to the American system; therefore, they should not have been prosecuted.

Yates v. *United States* (1957) Six years after *Dennis,* in the case of *Yates* v. *United States* (1957), the Court overturned the conviction of fourteen "second-string" members of the Communist party by distinguishing between abstract doctrine and action taken to overthrow the government. Oleta Yates and thirteen others, all members of the Communist party in California, had been convicted in federal court of conspiring to violate the Smith Act by advocating the forcible overthrow of the federal government. By a 6–1 vote, the Supreme Court overturned the conviction of the defendants for several reasons.

Although the *Dennis* precedent was left intact, that decision became the high-water mark of judicial tolerance of various state and federal actions designed to uncover and prosecute persons suspected of engaging in subversive activities against the government. The Court apparently was saying that the nation still may act to defend itself against threats to its security interests, but, in so doing, the government must take care that it not violate important First Amendment freedoms.

The majority opinion authored by Justice John Harlan marked a major shift in the Supreme Court's attitude toward the Smith Act. First, the opinion adopted a narrow view of the scope of the Smith Act provision that made it illegal to organize a group advocating the forcible overthrow of government. Harlan explained that "organization" of the Communist party actually occurred in 1945, rather than, as the government maintained, on a continual basis throughout the postwar period. Because Yates and others had not been indicted until 1951, the three-year statute of limitations had expired; therefore, the indictment was invalid.

Second, the trial judge had improperly instructed the jury prior to its deliberation on the evidence presented against the defendants. He had failed to distinguish properly between advocacy of an *abstract doctrine,* a protected activity under the First Amendment, and actual incitement of illegal *action,* a prosecutable offense under the Smith Act:

> The essential distinction is that those to whom the advocacy is addressed must be urged to *do* something, now or in the future, rather than merely to *believe* in something.
>
> We recognize that distinctions between advocacy and teaching of abstract doctrines with evil intent, and that which is directed to stirring people to action, are often subtle and difficult to grasp, for in a broad sense, as Mr. Justice Holmes said in his dissenting opinion in *Gitlow,* "Every idea is an incitement." But the very subtlety of these distinctions required the most clear and explicit instructions with reference to them.

Harlan's distinction here between abstract doctrine and action seemed to reflect a new majority moving away from much of the *Dennis* precedent and closer to the clear-and-present-danger test. Apparently, the Black and Douglas argument in *Dennis* that the defendants should never have been indicted and that the Communist party did not pose an obvious and immediate danger to the nation had now been accepted by a new majority on the Court. One factor that had accelerated this development was the addition of two Eisenhower appointees to the Court, Justices William Brennan and Charles Whittaker.

In separate concurring opinions, Black and Douglas urged that all of the charges against the defendants should have been dropped. According to Justice Black, the Smith Act provisions on which the charges had been based "abridge freedom of speech, press and assembly in violation of the First Amendment." He insisted that the First Amendment "forbids Congress to punish people for talking about public affairs, whether or not such discussions incite to action, legal or illegal." In dissent, Justice Thomas Clark felt that the defendants in *Yates* should have been handled in the same manner as those in *Dennis,* since they "served in the same army and were engaged in the same mission."

Although the Court in *Yates* v. *United States* did not declare the Smith Act unconstitutional, as Justices Black and Douglas had urged it to do, the majority's insistence that the government would, in the future, have to prove that the accused advocated illegal conduct was sufficiently tough to discourage future litigation against Community party members. No new Smith Act prosecutions were filed after *Yates,* although there was one final case that had to be heard. All together, 141 persons had been indicted under the Smith Act; of that number, 29 served prison terms, including 11 in *Dennis* and 17 in two other cases not reviewed by the Supreme Court.[16]

***Scales* v. *United States* (1961)**   In 1961, the Supreme Court reviewed the only conviction of an individual ever obtained under the membership provisions of

Section 2 of the Smith Act. In the case of *Scales* v. *United States* (1961), the Court upheld the conviction of Junius Scales, director of a Communist training school in Greensboro, North Carolina. In a 5–4 judgment—with Justices Black, Douglas, and Brennan, along with Chief Justice Earl Warren, dissenting—Justice Harlan wrote a majority opinion that distinguished between active, "knowing" membership and passive, nominal membership in a subversive organization. Harlan wrote that the membership claim in the Smith Act did not violate First Amendment protection of experience and free association. According to Harlan:

> The clause does not make criminal all association with an organization which has been shown to engage in illegal advocacy. There must be clear proof that a defendant "specifically intend[s] to accomplish [the aims of the organization] by resort to violence."

Harlan and the majority reasoned that *Scales* was sufficiently different from *Yates* to warrant the conviction of the defendant. Examination of the record indicated that Scales and others were continuously and systematically preaching the doctrine of violent revolution as a guide to future action. Therefore, unlike *Yates*, "advocacy of action" was present in this case. The dissenting justices insisted that the 1950 Internal Security Act preempted prosecution for membership in any political party. Perhaps indicating that the Court had decided wrongly in *Scales,* on Christmas Eve of 1962, Scales was released from federal prison after having been pardoned by President John Kennedy. The president had reacted to a petition presented to him by several prominent theologians and clergymen who believed that Scales had been improperly convicted under an illegal act of Congress.

Communist Party v. *Subversive Activities Control Board* (1961)

Before leaving the topic of seditious speech and federal legislation to regulate it, the Court's handling of the McCarran Act of 1950 should be discussed. As mentioned, the main purpose of that law was to identify Communist party leaders and members of Communist-front organizations by requiring them to register with the Justice Department. The act also created the Subversive Activities Control Board within that department to identify and monitor subversive organizations threatening the security of the United States.

Eventually abolished in the 1960s, the SACB was continually frustrated by the failure of suspected or known Communists to register with the Justice Department. The SACB twice ordered the Communist party to register, but the party refused to do so. Both orders were appealed to the federal courts. In the second order in 1961, the Supreme Court upheld the registration order in the case of *Communist Party* v. *Subversive Activities Control Board* (1961). On a vote of 5–4, the Court rejected the party's arguments that the registration provisions constituted an unlawful bill of attainder and violated the First Amendment's freedoms of speech and association.

In a majority opinion, Justice Frankfurter said that the McCarran Act's provisions required only the registration of an organization, not specifically named individuals; therefore, it was not a bill of attainder within the meaning of Article 1, Section 9, of the Constitution. He also maintained that the act did not violate the First Amendment because in requiring the registration, Congress was simply balancing private rights of free speech and association against the larger public interest in disclosure. Again, Frankfurter's view of the Communist party as a serious threat to American interests was obvious:

> When the mask of anonymity which an organization's members wears serves the double purpose of protecting them from popular prejudice and of enabling them to cover over a foreign-directed conspiracy, to infiltrate into other groups, and enlist the support of persons who would not, if the truth were revealed, lend their support . . . it would be a distortion of the First Amendment to hold that it prohibits Congress from removing the mask.

In separate dissenting opinions, Chief Justice Warren and Justices Black, Douglas, and Brennan offered different reasons for disagreeing with the majority, but the common thread in their dissents was that the Internal Security Act had violated both the First Amendment speech and association provisions and the Fifth Amendment protection against self-incrimination.

Within the next few years, the Supreme Court grew increasingly disenchanted with the McCarran Act. In 1964, it declared unconstitutional the act's passport denial provisions as an invalid limitation of the individual's freedom to travel.[17] In 1965, it finally struck down the act's registration requirements applying to individuals, as a violation of the Fifth Amendment prohibition against compelled self-incrimination, thus vindicating Justice Douglas and Brennan's point mentioned four years earlier in *Communist Party* v. *Subversive Activities Control Board*. As a result of these decisions, the registration provisions of the McCarran Act were finally repealed in 1968, and the Subversive Activities Control Board was never reauthorized by Congress.

The Executive Response

Not only Congress and the Supreme Court, but also the executive branch became preoccupied with the international Communist movement in the troubled decade following World War II. A major consequence of this national fervor was the protection of national security at the expense of individual liberties. A major device used by the executive branch toward this end was the federal loyalty program. To ensure that only "loyal" Americans held federal jobs, both Presidents Truman and Eisenhower took actions that provoked much controversy. A major criticism of the various plans was that they penalized persons for allegedly holding certain *opinions,* rather than for demonstrating *acts* of disloyalty. Additionally, the programs also led to many individuals losing their jobs and being dismissed from federal service on grounds of suspected disloyalty. Advocates of the loyalty programs maintained that there was no constitutional right to federal employment and that the steps taken were necessary to protect government security.

Bowing to political and public pressure to do something in the face of threatened Communist party activity, President Truman signed an executive order in 1947 creating the federal loyalty program for all civilian employees of the executive branch. The order established the Loyalty Review Board within the Civil Service Commission, required loyalty investigations on all current federal civilian employees, and allowed for the dismissal of any person whose loyalty was subject to "reasonable doubt." In the 1940s, this summary dismissal applied only to the Departments of Defense and State and the Atomic Energy Commission. In 1950, it was extended to Treasury, Commerce, and Justice; beginning in 1953, under President Eisenhower, a more stringent loy-

alty security program was extended to all executive agencies. Under the Eisenhower plan, an employee was guilty until proven innocent, which is a tragic
reversal of the customary due process procedures of the American judicial
system. Individuals suspected of being disloyal to the federal government had
to prove that their employment was clearly consistent with national security.
The loyalty program went beyond detecting and prosecuting disloyal activity
considered threatening to national security. It degenerated eventually into
dismissal for suspected drug or alcohol abuse, sexual misconduct, and physical
or mental disorders.

   The constitutional issues raised by the loyalty programs focused upon
three different provisions of the Constitution: First Amendment protection of
free speech and association; Fifth Amendment prohibition against denying a
person liberty or property without due process of law; and the Article I prohibition against a bill of attainder. Only the due process provision attracted
much attention in federal courts. At no time during the operation of the
program under Truman and Eisenhower did the Supreme Court address the
key constitutional issues. In the case of *Joint Anti-Fascist Refugee Committee
v. McGrath* (1951), the Court upheld the Justice Department's authority under
the Truman loyalty program to maintain and furnish the Loyalty Review Board
with a list of allegedly subversive organizations. And in *Peters v. Hobby* (1955),
the Court ruled that the dismissal of two federal employees was unjustified
because the defendants had been twice cleared of any suspicion of disloyalty.
The case of *Cole v. Young* (1956) found the Court overturning the dismissal
of an employee in a nonsensitive position that could not be justified on national
security grounds. Finally, in 1959, in *Greene v. McElroy,* the Supreme Court
seriously weakened the federal government's ability to continue its loyalty
program by casting doubts upon the methods used to revoke security clearances
and dismiss employees on the basis of anonymous informants.

Summary of Freedom of Speech and the Cold War

In reviewing the post-World War II era and governmental behavior in the face
of political dissent, a few major conclusions can be drawn. First, the international Communist movement following World War II changed the government's agenda noticeably from what had existed in the 1920s. Having defeated
totalitarianism in Germany and Japan, the United States was both confused
and intimidated by the intentions and behavior of the Soviet Union. As entire
countries in Eastern Europe slipped behind the iron curtain following World
War II, the United States reacted defensively to this perceived threat by passing
restrictive legislation that it hoped would stem the Communist tide. But the
fundamental question confronted by both the American people and the federal
courts was how much of a threat the Communist party posed to national
security. Justices Frankfurter and Jackson and Chief Justice Vinson considered
it to be a major threat, but Justices Black and Douglas thought that the country
was overreacting and that civil liberties were being violated in the process.

   A second point to consider is that all three branches of government
participated in the curtailment of important civil liberties during the 1940s
and 1950s. Under both a Democratic and a Republican president, the White
House initiated programs considered essential to preserving national security,
but in the process important civil liberties were curtailed. Congress passed

several laws considered important for restricting the dissemination of Communist propaganda, literature, and doctrine. The Supreme Court decided several cases that presented some vital constitutional questions concerning freedom of speech and political association, and the outcomes were often unpleasant to individuals attempting to express themselves openly in a free society.

The last point is that during this postwar era the Supreme Court eventually changed its view as to what the First Amendment meant in terms of speech and association. The fundamental question of how much criticism of government a society should permit found the Supreme Court modifying its answer under Earl Warren. In so doing, it moved away from the bad-tendency test of the late 1940s and early 1950s and toward one that more closely resembled clear and present danger.

In summary, the actions of the courts have most usually reflected the temper of the times and the climate of public opinion, as well as the external forces impacting upon the nation and the need to defend itself. This has been the case ever since the *Schenck* decision in the aftermath of World War I.

Other Free Expression Before the Supreme Court

Thus far, the concept of free speech has only dealt with political speech—oral statements that are intended to convey a particular political message (i.e., stop the war, resist the draft, overthrow the government). However, certain other forms of expression, also designed to convey a particular message or idea, present a different set of constitutional problems requiring the courts to intervene and to devise certain protections to preserve freedom of expression. These different, non-oral forms of expression include symbolic speech, campaign spending, picketing, and commercial speech.

Are Political Symbols Included in the Meaning of "Speech?"

Symbolic speech, the expression of ideas and beliefs through symbols rather than words, has generally been thought to be protected by the First Amendment. Because the variations on symbolic speech are limited only by the ingenuity of the "speaker" and the audience, any effort to develop a coherent and definitive philosophy reflecting a single constitutional standard is frustrating. But in spite of the problems in devising a satisfactory constitutional guide for protecting symbolic speech, many Supreme Court cases have emerged over several years that simplify this difficult task. The following discussion will examine six cases spanning five decades.

Early Symbolic Speech Cases

The Supreme Court first dealt with symbolic speech in 1931. In *Stromberg* v. *California,* the Court invalidated a state law that made it a crime to use certain symbols to demonstrate opposition to organized government. This case reflected the public hatred of socialism and communism that existed during the 1930s. Yetta Stromberg, a member of the Youth Communist League in California, had led a group of league members in saluting a Russian flag. Recognizing the communicative element of a flag as a symbol, the state law made it a felony to, among other things, "display a red flag and banner in a public place and in a meeting place as a sign, symbol and emblem of opposition to organized government."

In its first mention of the "vagueness" doctrine against legislation considered too restrictive because it tended to limit both protected and unprotected speech, the Supreme Court held that the California law unconstitutionally infringed upon free speech. The Court argued that displaying any banner or symbol that advocated a change in government through even peaceful means conceivably could be penalized under the California law. Writing for the majority, Chief Justice Charles Evans Hughes stated:

> The maintenance of the opportunity for free political discussion to the end that government may be responsive to the will of the people and that changes may be obtained by lawful means . . . is a fundamental principle of our constitutional system. A statute which upon its face . . . is so vague and indefinite as to permit the punishment of the fair use of this opportunity is repugnant to the guarantee of liberty contained in the Fourteenth Amendment.

Unlike the Pamphlet Cases following World War I and II, the *Stromberg* case dealt with symbolic speech advocating *peaceful* change.

Although usually discussed in the context of religious freedom, the Flag Salute Cases of the early 1940s (discussed more fully in Chapter 13) relate to political symbolism and free speech. The relevance of those cases to the present discussion lies in the majority opinion of Justice Jackson in *West Virginia State Board of Education* v. *Barnette* in 1943. In this case, the Court struck down mandatory flag salute laws. As Jackson noted, "Symbolism is a primitive but effective way of communicating ideas."

> There is no doubt that in connection with the pledges, the flag salute is a form of utterance. Symbolism is a primitive but effective way of communicating ideas. The use of an emblem or flag to symbolize some system, idea, institution, or personality, is a short cut from mind to mind . . . Symbols of State often convey political ideas just as religious symbols come to convey theological ones . . . A person gets from a symbol the meaning he puts into it, and what is one man's comfort and inspiration is another's jest and scorn.

According to Justice Jackson, the compulsory flag salute and pledge required an affirmation of a belief and an attitude of mind that did a great injustice to the First Amendment. He closed with an impassioned plea to recognize the negative consequences of the compulsory flag salute when he stated, "Those who begin coercive elimination of dissent soon find themselves exterminating dissenters. Compulsory unification of opinion achieves only the unanimity of the graveyard."

The *Barnette* case is remarkable because it reflects one of the few instances when the Supreme Court reversed itself within a short span of time and because it came during World War II, when public displays of nationalism were frequent and normally considered a strength. Finally, *Barnette* is a good example of symbolic speech and how the First Amendment can also protect the person's right to remain silent and not speak.

Symbolic Speech and the Vietnam War Era

In the 1940s, with few exceptions, Americans overwhelmingly supported the war effort. The situation was quite different for a later generation and a different war. As the following cases indicate, although the First Amendment protects some instances of symbolic speech, that protection is qualified. The period in question is the late 1960s, and the American public's growing disenchantment with the Vietnam War. This overseas conflict generated several cases concerning symbolic speech, especially among draft-age American citizens.

On the morning of March 31, 1966, David Paul O'Brien burned his Selective Service registration card on the steps of a Boston courthouse as a symbolic protest against the draft and the Vietnam War. A crowd witnessed the event (including several FBI agents). Following the protest, O'Brien was convicted in federal district court for his actions. The court found that O'Brien had violated a 1965 federal law making it unlawful to alter, forge, knowingly destroy, or mutilate a draft card. The Court of Appeals for the First Circuit reversed the conviction on First Amendment grounds, accepting O'Brien's claim that the Constitution protected such symbolic expression. The government appealed the case to the Supreme Court and in 1968, in a 7–1 opinion in *United States* v. *O'Brien,* the justices reversed the appellate ruling and upheld O'Brien's conviction.

The majority opinion authored by Chief Justice Warren reflected upon the speech and nonspeech elements of O'Brien's protest:

> We cannot accept the view that an apparently limitless variety of conduct can be labelled "speech" whenever the person engaging in the conduct intends thereby to express an idea. However, even on the assumption that the alleged communicative element in O'Brien's conduct is sufficient to bring into play the First Amendment, it does not necessarily follow that the destruction of a registration certificate is constitutionally protected activity. This court has held that when "speech" and "nonspeech" elements are combined in the same course of conduct, a sufficiently important governmental interest in regulating the nonspeech element can justify incidental limitations on First Amendment freedoms.

Warren maintained that a governmental regulation limiting speech was justified if four conditions existed: (1) if it were within the constitutional power of the government; (2) if it furthered an important or substantial governmental interest; (3) if that interest was unrelated to the suppression of free expression; and (4) if a minor restriction on a First Amendment freedom was necessary for furthering that governmental interest. The Court thought that the 1965 amendment to the Universal Military Training and Service Act met all these requirements; consequently, O'Brien could be constitutionally tried for violating it. Warren argued that the government needed certain important information about the registrant contained on the card; therefore, a substantial governmental interest existed to justify protection of the card. Since O'Brien had willfully destroyed the card, he could lawfully be prosecuted. Justice Douglas dissented in the case, avoiding the potential First Amendment question involved. He argued that the basic problem in the *O'Brien* case was the constitutionality of a draft "in the absence of a declaration of war," and he felt that the case should have been remanded to the trial court and reargued on this issue.

Tinker v. *Des Moines Independent Community School District* (1969) was another case in which symbolic speech was used to protest against the Vietnam War. In *Tinker,* the Supreme Court reviewed a suit brought by three high school students who had been suspended from public school in Iowa for violating a local school ban on wearing armbands as a symbol of protest against the Vietnam War. The suspended students argued in court that the First Amendment protected their symbolic protest against the war. In a 7–2 decision, with Justices Black and Harlan dissenting, the Supreme Court upheld the students' alleged right of symbolic expression as protected by the First Amendment.

The majority opinion in *Tinker* was authored by Justice Abe Fortas, who would soon resign from the Court over criticism of his role as an advisor to President Lyndon Johnson. In his opinion for the seven-member majority, Fortas stressed that for more than a half-century, First Amendment rights had been available to teachers and students in public schools. According to Fortas, "It can hardly be argued that either students or teachers shed their constitutional rights to freedom of speech or expression at the schoolhouse gate." The fact that the school officials had sought to suspend the students for their silent and passive expression of opinion was contrary to constitutional protections afforded by the First Amendment. Fortas also emphasized that school authorities had, in effect, discriminated against these particular students because they had not prevented other students from wearing forms of symbolic expression such as political campaign buttons and even a Nazi iron cross. For these reasons, the majority struck down the Des Moines school regulation and upheld students' rights in this important case of symbolic expression.

In dissent, Justice Black disagreed with the majority's finding that the armbands did not disrupt normal school operations. He believed that classroom and school disturbances had occurred as a result of the armband display, and he also believed that the Court should refrain from trying to resolve matters of local school administration. Justice Harlan also thought that school administrators should be given substantial authority in upholding discipline and good order in their institutions.

In these cases involving symbolic speech, several points should be emphasized. First, although some nonverbal communication is protected under the First Amendment, the Court has never said that symbolic speech is entitled to exactly the same degree of protection as verbal communication. Pure speech becomes more susceptible to regulation as it seeks to include particular actions. Second, in incidents involving what is sometimes referred to as "speech-plus"— incidents that involve verbal and nonverbal communication as a form of protest—"pure" speech has received *more* protection under the First Amendment than has "speech-plus" conduct, which is intended to dramatize the intensity of an individual's feelings and protest. The best example of this is *O'Brien*, where a liberal Warren Court maintained that the government had a sufficiently substantial interest in preventing the destruction of draft cards. Inasmuch as the Court has, since 1969, become more conservative in some respects and sympathetic to governmental authority confronting civil liberties, it might be assumed that individuals involved in similar instances of symbolic protest might have a more difficult time pressing their claim and winning before the Burger and Rehnquist Courts (see Brief 11.3).

Two other cases under symbolic speech should also be mentioned. One deals with desecration of the American flag and the other with a silent, provocative protest against the Vietnam War.

❑ *Brief 11.3   The Homeless Seek a Day in Court*

In the 1980s, the number of homeless people became more prominent, primarily because of the de-institutionalization of patients from state-local facilities for the mentally ill and the declining federal support for the disadvantaged. In 1982, the National Park Service issued a permit to the Community for Creative Non-Violence (CCNV) to conduct a daytime demonstration in Lafayette Park across from the White House. The group, however, decided to make more than a day of it by erecting two tent cities in the park and sleeping out overnight to dramatize to the public the constant plight of the homeless. Although the park service emphasized that regulations clearly prohibited camping and sleeping on federal park property, CCNV argued that sleeping was a fundamental component of the message that the group was trying to convey to both the administration and the larger American public. Two lower federal courts handed down different rulings, one siding with the government and the other with CCNV. The case was appealed to the Supreme Court, which finally granted certiorari.

In *Clark* v. *Community for Creative Non-Violence* (1984), a 7–2 majority, with Justice Byron White speak-

ing for the Court, ruled in favor of the National Park Service. White stated that expression, "whether oral or written or symbolized by conduct, is subject to reasonable time, place and manner restrictions," provided that they are neutral and not directed at regulating the content of the speech. The Court reasoned that the park service's "substantial interest in maintaining the parks in the heart of our capital in an attractive and intact condition" outweighed any alleged right to symbolic expression by the homeless. The majority was also sensitive to the implications of allowing CCNV to stage its symbolic sleep-out. As White noted, "Absent the prohibition on sleeping, there would be other groups who would demand permission to deliver an asserted message by camping in Lafayette Park," many of which would most likely have as credible a claim as did CCNV. In dissent, Justices Thurgood Marshall and William Brennan felt that the majority was too lenient in evaluating the purpose and effect of the park service's regulations and too strict in applying those standards. The consequence is a "diminution of First Amendment protection."

In one of the last cases heard by the Warren Court, a closely divided Court overturned a state conviction of an individual for burning an American flag and using disrespectful language against this important national symbol. In the summer of 1966, in the midst of considerable racial strife in several regions of the country, civil rights activist James Meredith, the first black to attend the University of Mississippi, was shot by a sniper in Mississippi. Upon hearing the news about Meredith, a young Brooklyn man named Sidney Street took an American flag from his drawer and proceeded to burn it in the street in front of a small crowd. A police officer testified that he had heard Street exclaim, "If they did that to Meredith, we don't need an American flag . . . We don't need no damn flag." Street was convicted under a New York law that made it illegal to publicly "mutilate, deface, defile, or defy, trample upon or cast contempt upon, either by words or act," the American flag.

Street appealed to the Supreme Court, claiming that the First Amendment protected symbolic expression. By a 5–4 opinion in *Street* v. *New York* (1969), without ever reaching the issue of flag burning, the Court overturned his conviction, saying that it had been obtained by virtue of a law that was "overly broad." Because the law made it illegal to display contempt for the flag by either pure speech or nonverbal speech (burning the flag) it was impossible to tell precisely the grounds upon which Street had been convicted. Was it his language or his actions? Writing for the majority, Justice Harlan said that the statute "was unconstitutionally applied in appellant's case because it permitted him to be punished merely for speaking defiant or contemptuous words about the American flag." The point made by the majority in *Street* v. *New York* was that the Constitution protected an individual's right to abuse the flag verbally, but it was unclear about whether an individual had a constitutional right to burn the flag as an expression of protest.

Four justices—three of whom were considered the most liberal on the Court—dissented. Chief Justice Warren and Justices Fortas, Black, and White argued that state and federal laws against flag desecration were constitutional. And later in 1982, the Burger Court refused to hear an appeal of a case in *Kime* v. *United States,* in which two individuals had been convicted of burning the American flag as a sign of political protest.

Another case cited here to demonstrate the limits of symbolic speech is also from the Vietnam War era. On April 26, 1968, Paul Cohen was arrested in the Los Angeles County Courthouse for wearing a jacket inscribed with the slogan "Fuck the Draft." He was tried and convicted under a state law that made it illegal to engage in "offensive conduct." Although he maintained that his silent protest was directed against the Vietnam War, and not against public peace or any particular individual, he was sentenced to one month in jail. On appeal, in the case of *Cohen* v. *California* (1971), the Supreme Court reversed Cohen's conviction and dealt at length with the important legal issue of whether government can punish "shocking words" as opposed to obscene or "fighting words" (see *Chaplinsky* v. *New Hampshire* [1942] in Chapter 12).

In the *Cohen* decision, Justice Harlan, writing for a five-member majority, narrowed the "fighting words" precedent of *Chaplinsky* v. *New Hampshire* by holding that the protest here by Cohen was neither obscene nor erotic:

> It cannot plausibly be maintained that this vulgar allusion to the Selective Service System would conjure up such psychic stimulation in anyone likely to be confronted with Cohen's crudely defaced jacket.

Nor was the message on the Cohen jacket synonymous with "fighting words" intended to provoke or abuse individuals personally:

> While the four letter word displayed by Cohen in relation to the draft is not uncommonly employed in a personally provocative fashion, in this instance it was clearly not "directed to the person of the bearer." No individual actually or likely to be present could reasonably have regarded the words on appellant's jacket as a direct personal insult.

Harlan thought that the constitutional right of free expression, which was intended to remove governmental restraints from public debate, occasionally yields distasteful language such as Cohen's. Fearing that regulation unlawfully suppressed both the prudent as well as the imprudent, Harlan insisted that the state law went too far. As he observed, "While the particular four letter word being litigated here is perhaps more distasteful than most others of its genre, it is nevertheless often true that one man's vulgarity is another's lyric." Chief Justice Burger, along with Justices Black, Blackmun, and White, dissented in the *Cohen* case and argued that Cohen's protest involved mainly *conduct* and little pure speech; thus, it fell within the "fighting words" prohibition of *Chaplinsky.*

Speech and the Electoral Process

In the wake of the Watergate scandal, concern grew about political corruption and the unfair advantage that money and wealth can provide for candidates in the electoral process. Changes in campaign expenditures under the Federal Election Campaign Act Amendments of 1974 raised several questions about freedom of expression under the First Amendment. The 1974 legislative amendments (1) limited the amount of money that candidates could spend in political campaigns, (2) restricted the size of individual and group contributions to federal candidates to $1,000 and $5,000, respectively, (3) required full disclosure of campaign contributions and expenditures, (4) provided for public financing of presidential campaigns, and (5) created the Federal Election Commission to administer the act.

Several of these provisions were challenged in federal court soon after the act went into effect and in the midst of the 1976 presidential election. *Buckley* v. *Valeo* (1976) dealt with challenges to the campaign-financing regulations. In an extensive *per curiam* decision that included over three hundred pages of concurring and dissenting opinions by the justices, the Court upheld the provisions of the act dealing with public financing of presidential campaigns, the president's power to appoint members to the Federal Election Commission, and limitations on campaign *contributions* by individuals and groups. But it struck down as unconstitutional the limitations on campaign *expenditures*. The Court initially reaffirmed that the act's contribution and expenditure limitations "operate in an area of the most fundamental First Amendment activities." In upholding the contribution ceilings under the act, the Court stated:

> The overall effect of the Act's contribution ceilings is merely to require candidates and political committees to raise funds from a greater number of persons and to compel people who would otherwise contribute amounts greater than the statutory limits to expend such funds on direct political expression.

But the Court then went on to claim that "the governmental interest in preventing corruption and the appearance of corruption is inadequate to justify [the] ceiling on independent expenditures." The limits imposed by the act on what candidates could spend of their own personal funds and from their cumulative campaign assets were unconstitutional. According to the Court:

> The First Amendment denies government the power to determine that spending to promote one's political views is wasteful, excessive, or unwise. In the free society ordained by our Constitution it is not the government, but the people . . . who must retain control over the quantity and range of debate on public issues in a political campaign.

Although *Buckley* had found the Court ruling that Congress could not constitutionally limit independent expenditures in presidential campaigns generally, it was still unclear whether Congress could limit independent expenditures when the candidate had accepted federal funding. This issue was later dealt with in *Federal Election Commission* v. *National Conservative Political Action Committee* (1985). In this ruling, the Court struck down an amendment to the Federal Election Campaign Act that limited political action committees (PACs) from making "independent" expenditures beyond $1,000 in support of presidential candidates that had accepted public funding.

Writing for a 7–2 majority, Justice William Rehnquist conceded that both the National Conservative Political Action Committee (NCPAC) and the Fund for a Conservative Majority (FCM), the latter of which was also party to the suit, were "self-described ideological organizations with a conservative political philosophy." But their expenditures in the 1980 Reagan campaign were independent in the sense that "they were not made at the request of or in coordination with the official Reagan election campaign committee or any of its agents." Rehnquist then wrote that the $1,000 limitation on PACs had the effect of denying legitimate groups access to the political process:

> For purposes of presenting political views in connection with a nationwide Presidential election, allowing the presentation of views while forbidding the expenditure of more than $1,000 to present them is much like allowing a speaker in a public hall to express his views while denying him the use of an amplifying system.

Rehnquist also wrote that the spending limitation raised important questions about freedom of association under the First Amendment and the ability of persons "of modest means" to join together and have some effect upon the political process.

These cases involving free speech and the electoral process—and the attempts by Congress since the early 1970s to reform certain aspects of presidential campaign spending—demonstrate how the entire area of money and elections still contains loopholes and pitfalls that can be exploited under the First Amendment. Future litigation will undoubtedly arise. An obvious omission in federal campaign spending is the entire area of *congressional* campaign expenditures and contributions. In the eyes of many observers of the contemporary political scene, the Will Rogers line about having "the best Congress that money can buy" necessitates some major reforms in how members of Congress fund their increasingly more expensive reelection campaigns.

Picketing and the First Amendment

Another form of symbolic speech that has long been entitled to First Amendment protection is picketing. In 1940, peaceful picketing was brought under the protection of free speech with the Court's decision in *Thornhill* v. *Alabama*. In this case, the Court struck down an Alabama law as overbroad because it prohibited *all* labor picketing in the area of a labor dispute. Writing for the Court majority, Justice Frank Murphy stated that abridging free speech in labor disputes was permissible "only where the clear danger of substantive evils arises under circumstances affording no opportunity to test the merits of ideas by competition for acceptance in the market of public opinion."

Since *Thornhill*, the Court has handled numerous picketing cases that have involved time-place-manner restrictions on picketing and free speech, and the rulings in these cases have left a meandering path of legal precedents. In *Marsh* v. *Alabama* (1946), the Court upheld the guarantees of the First Amendment against attempts by an Alabama deputy sheriff to limit picketing and literature distribution by a member of Jehovah's Witnesses in a section of town largely controlled by a shipbuilding company. Justice Black noted that despite the fact that a private company had legal title to the town, it was not authorized to impair "channels of communication" of its inhabitants or persons passing through the community. Black also observed that when owners, for their advantage, avail their property for public use in general, they are obligated to honor the statutory and constitutional rights of those using that property.

In *Amalgamated Food Employees Union* v. *Logan Valley Plaza* (1968), a 6–3 Court majority used the "company-owned town" analogy of *Marsh* to uphold the right of union members to picket a privately owned shopping center in Altoona, Pennsylvania, employing non-union workers. Justice Marshall said that the owners could not exclude "those members of the public wishing to exercise their First Amendment rights on the premises in a manner and for a purpose generally consonant with the use to which the property is actually put." One of the dissenters in *Logan Valley* was Justice Black, who insisted that the *Marsh* analogy was totally inappropriate. Not only did the shopping center bear little resemblance to a town, but also

> to hold that store owners [in *Logan Valley*] are compelled by law to supply picketing areas for pickets to drive store customers away is to create a court-made law wholly disregarding the constitutional basis on which private ownership of property rests in this country.

Logan Valley raised questions about whether picketing directed against larger political or social issues, rather than a particular store, would be protected. A qualified no was offered in *Lloyd Corporation* v. *Tanner* (1972), which saw a 5–4 Court uphold the banning of the distribution of anti-Vietnam War handbills inside an enclosed mall. And in *Hudgens* v. *National Labor Relations Board* (1976), which found the Court specifically overruling *Logan Valley*, the Court determined that a privately owned, self-contained shopping mall was *not* the functional equivalent of a municipality, as *Logan Valley* had held. Therefore, the owners did not have to abide by the same First Amendment guarantees barring discrimination in regulating the content of free expression.

But the rule of law governing shopping-mall settings and regulatable speech has subsequently been muddled again with the Court's ruling in *Pruneyard Shopping Center* v. *Robins* (1980). In that case, a unanimous Court upheld a state-created constitutional right of free speech at shopping centers over a property owner's claim that his property rights under the Fourteenth Amendment had been interfered with by the state action. A group of high school students in California had been told by the owners of the shopping center that they could not distribute leaflets or collect petition signatures on a public issue on the mall premises. The Court ruled in favor of the students and against the mall owners.

Over the past two decades, these decisions dealing with free speech in privately owned shopping centers have resulted in much confusion and instability in constitutional law. The twisted path of Court rulings exhibits the following signposts: although shopping-mall picketing is permitted (*Logan Valley*), the distribution of handbills on larger social issues can be prohibited (*Tanner*), and persons do not have an unqualified constitutional right to speak, demonstrate, picket, or distribute handbills on privately owned shopping-mall property without the permission of the owners (*Hudgens*). Finally, notwithstanding these rulings, states can guarantee this right to speak, demonstrate, picket, or distribute material on such property if they choose to do so (*Pruneyard Shopping Center*). Given the Court's changing composition over the next few years, as well as the unsettled status of the law in this area of free speech, confusion and recasting of prevailing law will most likely continue. Finally, **commercial speech,** or advertising, and the limits of the First Amendment (see Brief 11.4) will be an interesting area of law to observe in coming years.

☐ *Brief 11.4   The Evolving Area of Commercial Free Speech*

Since the early years of the twentieth century, American consumers have come to expect more fairness and integrity from businesses marketing their products and services. The passage by Congress of pure food and drug legislation in 1906, followed by the establishment of the Federal Trade Commission in 1914, reflected a more expectant public and a more responsive federal government in monitoring the American open market. Commercial speech is subject to much more governmental regulation than other kinds of speech, particularly political speech. Advertising the sale of anything illegal can be forbidden by government, as can false or misleading commercial advertising.

But it was not until the 1960s that the Supreme Court began to apply the First Amendment to commercial speech. When asked during World War II to consider the issue, the Court had responded by saying that there was no constitutional protection for "purely commercial speech" (*Valentine* v. *Chrestensen* [1942]).

But that precedent began to erode during the 1960s, especially with the Court's ruling in the important libel lawsuit of *New York Times* v. *Sullivan* (1964), wherein a paid political advertisement was given constitutional protection. Two of the most important commercial speech cases in recent years were handed down by the Burger Court. In *Bigelow* v. *Virginia* (1975), the Court extended First Amendment protection to an advertisement for an abortion referral service. And in *Virginia State Board of Pharmacy* v. *Virginia Citizens Consumer Council* (1976), the Court said that advertising of prescription drugs was also protected by the First Amendment. Developments in the area of commercial speech appear to be based upon the public's need for fair and accurate advertising in order to make wise consumer decisions, as well as the benefit that attends to the larger market by honest and accurate marketing of products and services.

Freedom of Assembly

Another First Amendment right closely related to freedom of expression is freedom of assembly. The amendment states, "Congress shall make no law . . . abridging . . . the right of the people peaceably to assemble." The key word here is "peaceably," for as this section will indicate, the courts have allowed government to impose certain regulations to maintain public peace. This right of assembly is so closely tied to freedom of expression that many of the cases discussed earlier in this chapter, such as *Schenck, Gitlow, Abrams, Douds,* and *Dennis*, might just as easily be discussed in the context of free assembly.

Speech, Dissent, and Civil Order in Public Places

The right to assemble peaceably was one of the first privileges recognized by the Supreme Court as far back as 1876, in the case of *United States* v. *Cruikshank*. In that case, the rights of speech, assembly, and petition were seen as interdependent.

> The right of the people peaceably to assemble for the purpose of petitioning Congress for a redress of grievances, or for anything else connected with the powers or the duties of the national government, is an attribute of national citizenship, and, as such, under the protection of and guaranteed by, the United States. The very idea of a government . . . implies a right on the part of its citizens to meet peaceably for consideration in respect to public affairs.

It should be noted that this endorsement of the citizen's right of assembly related to the federal government, not the states. The Fourteenth Amendment's Due Process Clause was not even a decade old at the time; thus, there had been no effort to apply this First Amendment guarantee to the states. As the following cases should demonstrate, most of the noteworthy case activity regarding the right of assembly has involved state, rather than federal, regulation of freedom of assembly.

The Boston Common Case: Early Regulation of a Public Forum

One case just prior to 1900 found the Supreme Court ruling on the right of the people to assemble peaceably. *Davis* v. *Massachusetts* (1897), frequently referred to as the Boston Common Case, concerned the limits to which government could go to restrict a "public forum" for speech and assembly. This case posed a fundamental question that would be addressed by the Court for the next several decades—What regulation of time, manner, and place of expression can government enforce without violating the First Amendment? In the Boston Common Case, a preacher by the name of Davis was convicted of violating a local Boston ordinance that prohibited "any public address" on publicly owned property without first obtaining a permit from the mayor of Boston. The message preached was neither obscene, blasphemous, defamatory, or seditious. But it was delivered in a "public forum," the Boston Common, and Davis had failed to obtain the required permit. The Supreme Court of Massachusetts, with Justice Holmes, writing the opinion, upheld Davis's conviction and the local ordinance. Holmes wrote:

> For the legislature absolutely or conditionally to forbid public speaking in a highway or public park is no more an infringement of rights of a member of the public than for the owner of a private house to forbid it in the house.

When the case was appealed, a unanimous Court on May 10, 1897, adopted the Holmes position, with Justice Edward D. White writing the Court's opinion:

> The right to absolutely exclude all right to use [public property] necessarily includes the authority to determine under what circumstances such use may be availed of.

This view survived for the next several decades, allowing government to restrict the time, place, and manner of speech and assembly in *public* places.

Whitney v. *California* (1927): No Constitutional Right to Assemble

A prominent case dealing with the right of assembly in the immediate post-World War I period illustrates how closely related are the guarantees of expression and assembly. *Whitney* v. *California* (1927) actually did not involve speech and assembly in a public forum regulated by government, but it did focus upon the right of assembly, and the opinions advanced in the case indicated the evolving thought of the justices soon after the important *Gitlow* precedent had emerged in 1925.

The case began with the indictment of Anita Whitney, a sixty-year-old member of the Communist Labor party, who had participated in a party convention and had argued for the adoption of a resolution urging that the party seek change through the ballot box rather than through violent revolution. Whitney failed in her attempt to persuade the party to follow a more peaceful route to change and, though remaining a member, she became much less active in the party. California indicted her for having violated the state's criminal syndicalism law. After being convicted in state court, she appealed to the Supreme Court on First Amendment grounds.

A unanimous Supreme Court upheld her conviction, saying that her case differed little from *Gitlow* two years earlier, even though Whitney argued that she had no intention of helping to assist an organization through illegal means to bring about political or economic change. The Court's opinion, authored by Justice Sanford who had written the *Gitlow* opinion, stressed her continued membership in the party and her association with those who advocated radical change:

> The essence of the offense denounced by the Act is the combining with others in an association for the accomplishment of the desired ends through the advocacy and use of criminal and unlawful methods. It partakes of the nature of a criminal conspiracy. That such united and joint action involves even greater danger to the public peace and security than the isolated utterances and acts of individuals is clear. *We cannot hold that . . . the Act is an unreasonable or arbitrary exercise of the police power of the state, unwarrantably infringing any right of free speech, assembly or association,* or that those persons are protected from punishment by the due process clause who abuse such rights by joining and furthering an organization thus menacing the peace and welfare of the state. [Emphasis added]

In a concurring opinion, Justice Brandeis elaborated upon the value of freedom of speech and assembly in a free society and how government can restrict these freedoms only when there is a clear and present danger resulting from an intended evil. He disagreed with the reasoning used by the majority, and regretted that Whitney had failed to argue, to his mind, the proper issue in this case:

> [Whitney] claimed below that the statute as applied to her violated the federal Constitution; but she did not claim that it was void because there was no clear and present danger of serious evil, nor did she request that the existence of these conditions of a valid measure thus restricting the rights of free speech and assembly be passed upon by the court or a jury.

A few months after the Court's ruling, the California governor pardoned Whitney. The Brandeis concurrence may well have played an important role in winning the pardon by the governor, who stated that the Communist Labor party posed no clear and present danger to the state.

De Jonge v. *Oregon* (1937): Right of Assembly Is Incorporated

A decade after *Whitney*, in the case of *De Jonge* v. *Oregon* (1937), the Supreme Court confronted another instance of alleged criminal syndicalism and a state regulation that attempted to punish members of certain organizations for both expression and assembly in defiance of a state ban on such activity. By the late 1930s, the arguments of Brandeis and Holmes on First Amendment issues resulted in the Court's departing from the type of standard used in *Whitney*. The *De Jonge* case involved a member of the Communist party who had been convicted under an Oregon law that forbade criminal syndicalism. It therefore resembled the New York and California laws involved in *Gitlow* and *Whitney*. Dirk De Jonge had been arrested after making a speech at a public meeting of union members. In his speech, he had criticized law enforcement officials of Portland, Oregon, and their treatment of striking longshoremen. In this case, it is important to note that De Jonge was not indicted for participating in or being a member of the Communist party, for soliciting members, for distributing literature, or for advocating syndicalism or any illegal acts of sabotage. The indictment and the charge on which he was convicted and sentenced to seven years in prison was that he had *participated* in a public meeting sponsored by the Communist party. The Oregon Supreme Court upheld his conviction, and he appealed to the U.S. Supreme Court, arguing that the First Amendment protection of peaceable assembly should apply to the states under the Fourteenth Amendment Due Process Clause.

A unanimous Supreme Court overturned De Jonge's conviction, and, in so doing, recognized that the right of free assembly was on an equal status with the rights of free speech and free press. Furthermore, that right was applicable to the states under the Due Process Clause of the Fourteenth Amendment. Writing for the majority, Chief Justice Hughes stated:

> Freedom of speech and of the press are fundamental rights which are safeguarded by the due process clause of the Fourteenth Amendment of the Federal Constitution . . . The right of peaceful assembly is a right cognate to those of free speech and free press and is equally as fundamental.

Hughes then cited the *United States* v. *Cruikshank* precedent of 1876 and the very excerpt quoted previously from that case to substantiate his point on this fundamental nature of peaceable assembly. He then later in the opinion stated:

> Consistently with the Federal Constitution peaceable assembly for lawful discussion cannot be made a crime. The holding of meetings for peaceable political action cannot be proscribed. Those who assist in the conduct of such meetings cannot be branded as criminals on that score.

The Court, therefore, struck down the Oregon statute as an unconstitutional invasion of freedom of assembly protected by the First and Fourteenth Amendments.

Hague v. *Committee of Industrial Organization* (1939): Right of Assembly Cannot Be Prohibited

Two years after it had incorporated freedom of assembly into the Due Process Clause, the Supreme Court implicitly overruled its holding in *Davis* v. *Massachusetts*—that government may prohibit assembly and speech in public places without infringing upon the First Amendment. The question of citizens using a public forum to express opinion was reopened in *Hague* v. *Committee of Industrial Organization* (1939), which involved a local ordinance in Jersey City, New Jersey, requiring that demonstrators first obtain a permit for all public meetings in public areas of the community. Jersey City Mayor Frank Hague was fervently opposed to any attempt by organized labor to encourage workers in "his" city to join labor unions. To discourage any and all organizing attempts, Hague intimidated members of the Committee of Industrial Organization (CIO) by searching them when they entered city limits and arresting them if they distributed any union materials. He also refused to grant any union members the necessary ordinance for speaking on public property. The CIO filed a suit to prevent the mayor from enforcing the statute, which it maintained was a violation of freedom of assembly under the First and Fourteenth Amendments.

In June 1939, a five-member majority on the Court, with recently appointed Justices Frankfurter and Douglas not participating in the decision, ruled in this landmark case that the First Amendment required public streets, parks, highways, and other public places to be accessible for public assembly and discussion of public issues. Although access to a public forum could be regulated with reference to time, place, and manner, it could not be *prohibited* by government. A plurality opinion representing three justices' reasoning and authored by Justice Owen J. Roberts contained an important principle regarding access to all public forums for speech and assembly:

> [Public places] have [long] been used for purposes of assembly, communicating thoughts between citizens, and discussing public questions. Such use of the streets and public places has, from ancient times, been a part of the privileges, community rights and liberties of citizens. [This privilege of a citizen] is not absolute but relative, and must be exercised in subordination to the general comfort and convenience, and in consonant with peace and good order; but it must not, in the guise of regulation, be abridged or denied.

The *Hague* decision also incorporated freedom of petition of the First Amendment into the Fourteenth Amendment Due Process Clause, thus making it applicable to states and local governments.

Later Extensions of *Hague*

A few months after the court announced the *Hague* ruling, it strengthened the precedent with a 8–1 judgment striking down ordinances in four different cities that prohibited the distribution of leaflets in public places. In *Schneider v. State of New Jersey, Town of Irvington* (1939), Justice Roberts again drafted the majority opinion and noted that "the streets are natural and proper places for the dissemination of information and opinion; and one is not to have the exercise of his liberty of expression in appropriate places abridged on the plea that it may be exercised in some other place."

Common to both the *Hague* and *Schneider* decisions was the right of states and localities to regulate certain aspects of public speaking, although they could not *prohibit* public assembly. This right to regulate was further elaborated upon a few years later in *Cox v. New Hampshire* (1941), which is the basic precedent for the Court's rulings on parades and demonstrations. In this case, the Court held that the time, manner, and place of public speeches or other forms of expression can be regulated if that regulation is applied in a neutral manner to all speakers and demonstrators. The controversy in *Cox* involved members of Jehovah's Witnesses who paraded without a permit in Manchester, New Hampshire. Sixty-eight paraders were tried and convicted in state court of violating a state law requiring a parade permit. They appealed to the U.S. Supreme Court which unanimously sustained the state law and its intent to regulate under strictly prescribed considerations. In the words of Chief Justice Hughes for the Court:

> If a municipality has authority to control the use of its public streets for parades and processions, as it undoubtedly has, it cannot be denied authority to give consideration, without unfair discrimination, to time, place and manner in relation to the other proper uses of the streets.

Two years after *Cox v. New Hampshire*, the Supreme Court took the final step toward renouncing the Boston Common Case of 1897. In the case of *Jamison v. Texas* (1943), a unanimous Court speaking through Justice Black explicitly overruled *Davis*, thereby confirming the open public forum policy it had initially announced in *Hague v. Committee of Industrial Organization* in 1939.

The several cases considered between 1939 and 1943—admittedly a difficult period for the Court to be developing coherent case law dealing with peaceful assembly—established the principle that public thoroughfares must be accessible to citizens for purposes of communication. The use of these public forums, however, could be regulated in a neutral fashion, without regard to speech content, for the purpose of public safety and convenience. Neither the *Hague, Schneider, Cox,* or *Jamison* decisions had dealt with political dissent. Since these rulings on time, place, and manner regulation of public forums, the Court has on many occasions considered many other instances of groups assembling for protest or communication, but the precedents established starting with *Hague* have been the ruling law on the issue.

The Modern Era and Peaceful Assembly

State laws dealing with criminal syndicalism were revived during the 1960s, as several states tried to limit both civil rights and antiwar protests within their borders. In a 1969 opinion that called into question any state criminal syndicalism act, the Court handed down an important decision dealing with free speech and assembly. The case of *Brandenburg* v. *Ohio* (1969) involved Clarence Brandenburg, a leader in the Ku Klux Klan in Ohio. Brandenburg had appeared at a public rally in the state, to which he had invited the media from a Cincinnati television station. With the cooperation of the rally organizers, a reporter and cameraman filmed certain events that were later televised over both the local station and a national network. A short speech by Brandenburg was also broadcast on television. In the speech, he stated that "if our President, our Congress, our Supreme Court, continues to suppress the white, Caucasian race, it's possible that there might have to be some revengence [sic] taken." For that statement, and on the basis of other evidence introduced at his trial, Brandenburg was tried and convicted of having violated Ohio's criminal syndicalism act, which made it illegal to advocate the use of violence or terrorism to accomplish industrial or political reform. (For a somewhat similar recent case dealing with political speech, see Brief 11.5.) Brandenburg appealed his conviction to the U.S. Supreme Court.

A unanimous Supreme Court overruled Brandenburg's conviction, and, in the process, overturned the *Whitney* ruling. A *per curiam* opinion said that the *Whitney* precedent had been "thoroughly discredited" in a long line of Court rulings. Furthermore,

> the constitutional guarantee of free speech and free press do not permit a State to forbid or proscribe advocacy of the use of force or of law violation except where such advocacy is directed to inciting or producing imminent lawless action and is likely to incite or product such action . . . Measured by this test, Ohio's Criminal Syndicalism Act cannot be sustained.

In a short, but strident concurring opinion, Justice Douglas took aim at the loyalty-security hearings before Congress in the late 1940s as invasions of privacy and "blatant violations" of the First Amendment. He also reviewed the Court's decisions in *Dennis* and *Barenblatt* during the 1950s and characterized them as "twisted and perverted" renditions of the "clear-and-present-danger" test.

With the *Brandenburg* ruling, the Court went beyond previous uses of clear and present danger and established an *incitement* standard. This new

❑ Brief 11.5   When a "Slip of the Tongue" Can Bring a "Pink Slip"

On March 30, 1981, Ardith McPherson, an employee of the Harris County constable's office in Houston, Texas, heard about the attempt to assassinate President Ronald Reagan. In a private comment to a fellow employee at work McPherson said that "if they go for him again, I hope they get him." The remark was overheard by another party, who reported it to the constable. McPherson, who was still serving a three-month trial period with her new employer, was fired from her position as deputy constable. She sued her former employer, claiming that her First Amendment rights to free expression had been violated.

In July 1987, just a few days before ending its 1986 term, the Supreme Court ruled 5–4 in *Rankin* v.

McPherson that the dismissed employee's constitutional rights had been violated by the action to fire her. Writing for the majority, Justice Marshall recognized the need to balance an individual's right of free speech with the state's interest in promoting efficient public services. The state legitimately could be concerned about how particular incidents among employees might interfere with work, personnel relationships, or job performance. But in this instance, the comment by the employee, although indiscreet, was a private comment made with the expectation of not being overheard. The dismissal was based solely upon the *content* of the remark, which the Court said was an infringement upon First Amendment rights.

principle meant that government had to prove that the danger presented in provocative speech was real, not imagined, and that it was directed to inciting or producing immediate illegal activity. The Court, thus, assumed the responsibility for judging intent and deciding if speakers were likely to incite immediate hostile action against the government, rather than simply trying to impress their audience. Obviously, in this case, the Court thought that Brandenburg did not pose the serious threat of imminent hostile action that the state sought to repress. The ruling, with its new incitement standard, signaled that the Court was entering a new decade with a more stringent standard by which to judge assembly and speech as possible threats to civil order.

The Right of Association

The U.S. Constitution guarantees freedom of speech, assembly, religion, and petition, but it nowhere explicitly guarantees the right of political association, or the right to associate freely with others who share the same beliefs and aspirations. But in the twentieth century, the Supreme Court eventually recognized this right of association so implied in the First Amendment's guarantee of free speech and free assembly and in the Fourteenth Amendment's concept of personal liberty. The right of association is implicit in several of the cases dealing with speech and assembly, such as *Whitney* and *De Jonge* and in many of the cases emerging in the cold war period after World War II. Although suggested by a few of the justices in their opinions, none of these cases was decided primarily upon the basis of political association.

In the civil rights era of the 1950s, the Supreme Court began to recognize this right of association as fundamental in a series of cases that dealt with membership in the National Association for the Advancement of Colored People (NAACP). These cases began when several southern states, deeply disturbed by that organization's pivotal role in organizing civil rights demonstrations in the South and in arguing desegregation cases before the Supreme Court, attempted to hamstring the NAACP's ability to continue operation within their state boundaries.

One of the first cases that produced Court recognition of a fundamental right of association began in Alabama, where the state attorney general tried to argue that the NAACP was a "business" rather than a nonprofit organization. If it were the former, the NAACP had to comply with a state law requiring all out-of-state corporations to register with the state and disclose their membership lists before doing business in the state. The NAACP refused to comply with the order to produce membership lists; it was found in contempt of court and ordered to pay a substantial penalty. The U.S. Supreme Court agreed to hear the case, and in the *National Association for the Advancement of Colored People* v. *Alabama ex rel Patterson* (1958), a unanimous Court found in favor of the NAACP and against the state law. In the opinion written by Justice Harlan, the Court emphasized:

> Effective advocacy of both public and private points of view . . . is undeniably enhanced by group association, as this Court has more than once recognized by remarking upon the close nexus between the freedom of speech and assembly. It is beyond debate that freedom to engage in association for the advancement of beliefs and ideas is an inseparable aspect of the "liberty" assured by the Due Process Clause of the Fourteenth Amendment, which embraces freedom of speech . . . [S]tate action which may have the effect of curtailing the freedom to associate is subject to the closest scrutiny.

Harlan stated that past disclosure of rank-and-file members of the NAACP had exposed members to various incidents of economic reprisals, physical intimidation and harm, loss of employment, and public hostility:

> Under these circumstances, we think it apparent that compelled disclosure . . . is likely to affect adversely the ability of [NAACP] and its members to pursue their collective effort to foster beliefs which they admittedly have a right to advocate.

Though it firmly established the fundamental right of political association, this ruling by the Court continued to be ignored by many southern states, which forbade the NAACP from operating in their jurisdictions. Later Court rulings forced the issue and were accompanied by changes in the public's receptivity to civil rights and more support for associational rights.

A Postscript on Freedom of Speech and Assembly

Free speech and assembly, like most of the other First Amendment freedoms, have historically found the Court resorting to certain devices for judging the constitutionality of laws regulating the claimed right. It should be remembered that these freedoms, like the other First Amendment guarantees, have never found a majority endorsing an absolute right of individual expression. Although a few commentators such as Alexander Meiklejohn, Thomas Emerson, and Justice Hugo Black have adhered to an absolutist position on political speech, this attitude has never attracted a majority on the Supreme Court. Ever since *Schenck* v. *United States,* the Court has endorsed some regulation of speech under certain circumstances. The problem for courts ever since then has been trying to determine when conditions demand free speech to end and governmental restrictions to begin.

One of the techniques used by the Supreme Court for many decades now to judge governmental restrictions on free speech has been a relaxed "presumption of constitutionality." As discussed in Chapter 4, courts should try to preserve a law that is challenged as unconstitutional. According to the doctrine of judicial restraint, courts should function as reviewing bodies and as courts of last resort, not as policy-making bodies that seize legislative authority of representative bodies. When federal courts review laws that may be interpreted in several ways, they should do everything to preserve the law. Beginning in the 1930s, the Supreme Court began to modify this tenet of restraint with respect to First Amendment rights and to treat laws regulating civil liberties as suspect. This trend was reflected in *Schneider* v. *State of New Jersey, Town of Irvington* (1939), *Thornhill* v. *Alabama* (1940), and *Thomas* v. *Collins* (1943). A key point to remember about this first device for judging the constitutionality of restrictive legislation is that it tilts the legal scales against the law and in favor of civil liberties.

A second technique for evaluating such restrictions is the "void-for-vagueness" doctrine. This standard requires that all laws, especially those regulating First Amendment freedoms, should be written precisely enough to warn people clearly about what actions are illegal. The *Stromberg* decision in 1931 found the Court, for the first time, striking down a state law on the basis of its being too vague in its restriction upon protected as well as unprotected speech. And as the Court wrote in 1975, "Where . . . First Amendment freedoms are at stake, we have repeatedly emphasized that precision of drafting and clarity of purpose are essential." [18]

The final standard often used to strike down laws restricting First Amendment freedoms is the "overbreadth" doctrine. This standard is used when laws are so broad that they sweep aside both speech and actions that are legal, as well as other actions that are illegal. The case of *Street* v. *New York* dealing with the disgruntled resident who ridiculed the American flag was decided on the basis of this overbreadth doctrine. The New York law in question was ruled unconstitutional on its face because it prohibited verbal criticism of the flag, which is protected speech. In addition, it was applied in an unconstitutional manner because it was unclear whether Street had been convicted because of his speech or his actions.

Prior to the existence of these techniques for reviewing restrictive legislation were two other tests that became very prominent during the early and mid-twentieth century, the clear-and-present-danger test and the bad-tendency test. The former, though created immediately following World War I, was not used much until the early years of World War II. And the justices really have not referred to it in many years. The bad-tendency test became very prominent during the post-World War II era, especially during the early 1950s. Since then, it, too, has been eclipsed by activist decision making on the Supreme Court that has reflected any one of the three techniques cited here.

The present status of free speech litigation before the Supreme Court, like all First Amendment rights, is complex, with great diversity and flexibility in the tools used by the justices to resolve complex First Amendment controversies. Each of the devices for judging the constitutionality of restrictive legislation was born in a particular historical period, and together they provide the Court with several instruments with which to resolve complicated and important First Amendment issues. Some might say that that makes for unsettled law and a tenuous position for crucial First Amendment rights. But it also reflects that the Court is always open to the environmental forces around it, as well as the belief that no one test for even "preferred freedoms" can resolve all controversies. Inasmuch as the American constitutional system has always been a search for acceptable solutions for complex problems, perhaps comfort can be found in this adaptable and pragmatic blend of principle and practice. This combination of principle and practice is equally important for the long-standing guarantee of a free press in American society, to which the discussion turns in the next chapter.

Conclusion

As Justice Benjamin Cardozo stated a half-century ago, free speech is "the matrix, the indispensable condition, of nearly every form of freedom." [19] As this and the remaining chapters indicate, First Amendment freedoms have found the Supreme Court placing considerable emphasis upon these sacred ideals of American constitutional law and political practice. In the present chapter, the emphasis has been upon freedom of speech and assembly. There is little doubt that the Court has been very vigilant about protecting political, or pure, speech in American society, although the degree of protection has varied greatly with the climate of the times and the magnitude of perceived threats to internal order and national security.

The period following World War I was an especially difficult time for individuals with minority political views to speak out without fear of discrimination or punishment. The Supreme Court had a mixed record during the interwar years, with such cases as *Abrams, Pierce, Debs,* and *Gitlow* representing the upholding of restrictive laws. And again following World War II, the federal government seemed very intent upon limiting the freedom of speech of individuals with leftist political ideas. Through several legislative, executive, and judicial decisions, the First Amendment seemed temporarily suspended for many years until the Warren Court began to restore it to its more preferred place in American constitutional law. By the 1960s, when American society was undergoing a severe test of its Bill of Rights guarantees, the Supreme Court consistently endorsed the high place that political speech occupied in the hierarchy of civil liberties. In a 1964 case dealing with the law of libel, Justice William Brennan stated that "speech concerning public affairs is more than self-expression; it is the essence of self-government." [20] And in 1966, Justice Hugo Black commented that, regardless of the differing interpretations of the First Amendment," there is practically universal agreement that a major purpose of the [First] Amendment was to protect the free discussion of governmental affairs." [21]

Symbolic speech, or individual expression conveyed through conduct, has not enjoyed quite the same degree of protection as pure speech, although many of the cases in this important area—such as *Tinker, Street,* and *Cohen* —demonstrate the Court's growing sympathy for persons expressing themselves through symbolic protest. Finally, although not covered in this chapter, commercial speech (see Brief 11.4) and sexually explicit speech (see Chapter 12) have not enjoyed the same degree of protection as political and symbolic speech. Sexually explicit speech, in particular, has often been seen by the justices as unworthy of constitutional protection, primarily because it is not considered of intrinsic social value.

Paralleling these developments in free speech law have been some important freedom of assembly cases before the Supreme Court. A key word in these assembly cases has been "peaceful" assembly. Balanced with the public's right to assemble to debate public affairs has been the right of government to regulate that activity for permissible time, place, and manner reasons. Key cases before the Court that have established this principle of free assembly have been *De Jonge* v. *Oregon, Hague* v. *Committee of Industrial Organization,* and *Brandenburg* v. *Ohio. De Jonge* finally incorporated the First Amendment right of assembly into the Fourteenth Amendment, thereby making it applicable to state and local governments. *Hague* found the Court saying that public streets, parks, and other public forums could be regulated, but not in a manner that prohibited peaceful assembly. The *Brandenburg* judgment overruled *Whitney* v. *California* (1927), and, in so doing, developed an important "incitement" standard that government must consider in the context of regulating the right of assembly.

Having examined a variety of Supreme Court decisions on freedom of speech and assembly, a few general observations are appropriate. First, over the past several decades, the Court has greatly expanded the range of expression protected by the First Amendment. In addition to the extended coverage occasioned by *Gitlow* v. *New York* in 1925, the Court has also extended protection to such previously excluded forms of expression as symbolic speech, commercial speech, and freedom of assembly.

Second, although these developments might suggest broader protections for self-expression, the Court has not developed a single, uniform standard for deciding First Amendment cases. Instead, it has avoided any broad, encompassing legal doctrine and resorted to a case-by-case approach with standards limited to the time, place, and manner regulations of free expression.

This gradual expansion and case-by-case approach have also been apparent when the Court has considered such topics as obscenity and the law of libel, which will be discussed in the next chapter in the broader context of freedom of the press.

Questions

1. Over several decades, statements by many Supreme Court justices indicate that the First Amendment may well be the cornerstone of a system that depends upon the free and unfettered interplay of ideas, preferences, and opinions. Do you think that any one set of constitutional freedoms is more basic and fundamental than another? If so, do First Amendment guarantees of free speech and assembly, along with a free press and petition, serve that indispensable function in American society? Is there some other liberty or freedom that is even more crucial?

2. The bad-tendency doctrine devised in 1919 was an important departure by the Court from the earlier clear-and-present-danger guideline for judging the constitutionality of restrictions on free expression. To what extent did bad tendency accurately reflect the serious threat to organized government in the 1920s? Or was it an unjustifiable tool by which legislatures and courts repressed dissent and debate by diverse elements in society attempting to find answers to social and political problems?

3. Although many people talk about the "preferred position" of First Amendment freedoms, it might be argued that recent Supreme Courts have departed noticeably from honoring this preferred status. What examples do you think best support the view that the First Amendment has lost much of its preferred status? What Supreme

Court justices presently have the best record for upholding this preferred status? What ones have the worst record?

4.   Do the close votes on several recent decisions by the Court indicate the preferred-position doctrine is in danger of being ignored? Or is it merely time that the Court move beyond what was only "judge-made" preference for First Amendment freedoms in the first place? What do you think is the likelihood that the Rehnquist Court, with a more identifiable conservative bloc, will effect some major changes in preferred-position cases? How do you expect Justice Anthony Kennedy to vote on free speech and assembly cases?

5.   Paradoxically, Justice Hugo Black's philosophy on free speech found him insisting upon no restrictions whatsoever on *pure* speech. But he regularly upheld many instances of government regulating *symbolic* speech, primarily because he thought that the framers did not intend to safeguard it when they drafted the First Amendment. How legitimate is his distinction between pure speech and symbolic speech? How responsible is his position that government can make no law limiting freedom of speech, under any conditions or circumstances? Is that position really consistent with his frequent voting to uphold government restrictions on symbolic speech or protest (i.e., picketing in segregated public libraries, armbands protesting the Vietnam War)?

Endnotes

1.   Quoted from *Whitney* v. *California*, 274 U.S. 357 (1927), at 375.

2.   John L. Sullivan et al., "The Sources of Political Tolerance: A Multivariate Analysis," *American Political Science Review* 75 (March 1981): 98.

3.   For a history of free expression in ancient Greece and Rome, see Herbert J. Muller, *Freedom in the Ancient World* (New York: Harper & Row, 1961); Max Radin, "Freedom of Speech in Ancient Athens," *American Journal of Philology* 48 (1927): 215–30; Robert J. Bonner, *Aspects of Athenian Democracy* (New York: Russell & Russell, 1967), reprint of the 1963 edition; and Charles Wirszubski, *"Libertas" as a Political Idea at Rome During the Late Republic and Early Principate* (Cambridge: Cambridge University Press, 1950).

4.   For a history of the evolving concept of liberty and free speech, see Leonard Levy, *Freedom of Speech and Press in Early American History: Legacy of Suppression* (New York: Harper & Row, 1963) and Frederick S. Siebert, *Freedom of the Press in England: 1476–1776* (Urbana, Ill.: University of Illinois Press, 1952).

5.   Levy, *Freedom of Speech and Press in Early American History,* 18.

6.   These justifications of free speech and a free press were reiterated by several Supreme Court justices in some famous espionage and sedition cases following World War I. Special note should be made of Justice Brandeis's concurring opinion in *Whitney* v. *California* (1927), which will be discussed under freedom of assembly.

7.   Alexander Meiklejohn, *Political Freedom: The Constitutional Powers of the People* (New York: Harper and Brothers, 1960), 37.

8.   From Chafee's review of *Free Speech and Its Relation to Self-Government* in *Harvard Law Review* 62 (1949): 891.

9.   From *Smith* v. *California*, 361 U.S. 147 (1959), at 157.

10.   *Konigsberg* v. *State Bar of California*, 366 U.S. 36 (1961), at 61.

11.   In both of these civil rights cases, Justice Black dissented; in *Brown* v. *Louisiana* and in *Adderley* v. *Florida,* he vigorously defended the right of the state to limit the use of public

facilities as long as that regulation was applied consistently toward all persons.

12. See especially Frankfurter's majority opinion in *Minersville School District* v.*Gobitis,* 310 U.S. 586 (1940), his dissent in *West Virginia State Board of Education* v. *Barnette,* 319 U.S. 624 (1943), and his concurring opinion in *Dennis* v. *United States,* 341 U.S. 494 (1951).

13. Harry Kalven, Jr., "Ernst Freund and the First Amendment Tradition," *University of Chicago Law Review* 40 (1973): 235–7.

14. From *Thomas* v. *Collins,* 323 U.S. 516 (1945), at 529–30.

15. The relevant case here is *United States* v. *Brown,* 381 U.S. 437 (1965). A bill of attainder is any legislative act that inflicts punishment or determines guilt without the benefit of a trial. In declaring the Labor Management Reporting and Disclosure Act of 1959 unconstitutional, Chief Justice Warren wrote: "The statute . . . designates in no uncertain terms the persons who possess the feared characteristics and therefore cannot hold union office without incurring criminal liability—members of the Communist Party."

16. Thomas Emerson, *The System of Freedom of Expression* (New York: Random House, 1970), 124.

17. *Aptheker* v. *Secretary of State,* 378 U.S. 500 (1964). See also *Communist Party* v. *Subversive Activities Control Board,* 382 U.S. 70 (1965).

18. *Erznoznik* v. *Jacksonville,* 422 U.S. 205 (1975).

19. Quoted in *Palko* v. *Connecticut,* 302 U.S. 319 (1937).

20. Quoted in *Garrison* v. *Louisiana,* 379 U.S. 64 (1964).

21. *Mills* v. *Alabama,* 384 U.S. 214 (1966).

Suggested Readings

Berns, Walter. *The First Amendment and the Future of American Democracy.* New York: Basic Books, 1976.

Brennan, William J. "The Supreme Court and the Meiklejohn Interpretation of the First Amendment." *Harvard Law Review* 79 (November 1965): 1–20.

Chafee, Zechariah, Jr. *Free Speech in the United States.* Cambridge, Mass.: Harvard University Press, 1942.

Denvir, John. "Justice Brennan, Justice Rehnquist and Free Speech." *Northwestern University Law Review* 80 (April 1985): 285–320.

Douglas, William O. *Points of Rebellion.* New York: Random House, 1970.

Emerson, Thomas I. *The System of Freedom of Expression.* New York: Random House, 1970.

Haiman, Franklyn S. *Speech and Law in a Free Society.* Chicago: University of Chicago Press, 1981.

McClosky, Herbert, and Alida Brill. *Dimensions of Tolerance: What Americans Believe About Civil Liberties.* New York: Sage, 1983.

O'Brien, David M. *The Public's Right to Know: The Supreme Court and the First Amendment.* New York: Praeger, 1981.

12

The First Amendment: Freedom of the Press, Obscenity, and the Law of Libel

Syllabus

In recent years, such people as Howard Morland, Earl Caldwell, Larry Flynt, and Cathy Kuhlmeier have all sought protection under the First Amendment's guarantee of a free press. Although their individual cases differed greatly in terms of the actual facts, the courts had to resolve the controversies by weighing different rights in American society.

As this chapter will emphasize, whether controversies involve national security interests, a defendant's right to a fair and public trial, the elusive search for an acceptable standard for judging obscenity, or the longtime protection of persons against libelous statements by newspaper publishers, the limits of a free press under the First Amendment, like those of free speech, have been the object of great inquiry and interpretation. The issues have usually involved particular cases where newspapers, magazines, radio, film, television, or other publications have insisted that the public's right to know is paramount and a prerequisite for enlightened self-government.

This Chapter Examines the Following Matters

☐ The doctrine of prior restraint upon publications has been prominent in twentieth-century American constitutional practice. This is partly a consequence of the long-standing repression of a working press that developed in early English-American history. This history prompted Thomas Jefferson to react at the time that "were it left to me to decide whether we should have a government without newspapers or newspapers without a government, I should not hesitate for a moment to prefer the latter."

☐ Although prior restraint may imply that government should not act as a self-proclaimed censor of the public's right to know, the Supreme Court has recognized the right of government to intervene in some rare instances and restrict the dissemination of certain types of information, particularly when it affects national security. The problem becomes one of determining whether national security is genuinely at risk or merely a cover to avoid embarrassment to or deception by government officials.

☐ Because of the tremendous power of modern mass media, the courts have been especially protective of the defendant's right to a fair trial under the Fifth and Sixth Amendments. As a consequence, they have sought to ensure that the media act responsibly in informing the public at several stages of the criminal justice process.

☐ While first seeming to offer more protection for allegedly obscene material, the Supreme Court since the early 1970s has allowed local communities much more latitude in restricting pornography. In recent years, with an increased emphasis upon deterring crime, violence, and the rising tide of child abuse, the courts have become less protective of free expression in this area, especially as it relates to child pornography.

☐ Since the mid-1960s, the federal courts have enforced a standard governing the national law of libel that requires individuals seeking libel damages to prove actual malice. This has proven to be a very rigorous standard protecting freedom of the press, and there has been mounting pressure to accord individuals more protection from the working press.

Photo: The tradition of a vigorous press free from government censorship, which predates even the First Amendment, continues in pressrooms across the country.

The Doctrine of Prior Restraint:
The Evil of Governmental Censorship

In a democratic society, people are vitally dependent upon an unhindered press in order to obtain information for making responsible judgments about public affairs and to disseminate enlightened ideas about those affairs. This reciprocal process must be open and free of censoring governmental activity. Government imposes **prior restraint** when it restrains or forbids expression before it is communicated. Obtaining governmental approval for expression *prior* to publication, dissemination, or broadcast has several negative implications for thought and communication in a free society. One problem is that prior restraint undermines the basic principle that the author is entitled to a trial before being deprived of his or her liberty. When government imposes prior restraint, it *presumes* that the material is "harmful" to society in some respect and thereby prevents it from being judged fairly under normal due process procedures. Imposing any prior restraint upon expression deprives the community of determining whether the expression will actually harm society in some way, since the communication has had no opportunity for a fair and open public hearing.

Another difficulty with imposing a prior restraint is that it violates the principle that the author is entitled to a fair trial by an impartial judge of one's peers. Unlike a normal criminal process where the prosecutor and the judge perform different functions, when prior restraint occurs, the government acts as *both* prosecutor and judge. It builds a *prima facie* ("on first appearance") case against the author and then declares the defendant guilty without the benefit of a fair and open trial, thereby violating safeguards of both the Fifth and Fourteenth Amendments.

Finally, prior restraint has a chilling effect upon *all* speech, protected and unprotected. As the Supreme Court has said, "The special vice of a prior restraint is that communication will be suppressed, either directly or by inducing excessive caution in the speaker, before an adequate determination that it is unprotected by the First Amendment." [1]

Early English and American Experience

Notwithstanding the admonition of William Blackstone, the English jurist and author, that the "liberty of the press consists in laying no previous restraints upon publication," [2] early Anglo-American practice exhibited many instances of prior restraints and relatively few successful protests against its imposition. The classical prior restraints upon publication were the English licensing laws that began in the early sixteenth century under King Henry VIII (1509–47), Edward VI (1547–53), and Queen Mary I (1553–58). The reign of Queen Elizabeth I (1558–1603) was memorable for many things, including a strengthened prior restraint system that had begun under Queen Mary with the passage in 1557 of England's first monopoly copyright law. The English Parliament eventually allowed the copyright law to expire in 1694. In 1710, it passed a law that granted the right to publish to the author, rather than to the publisher. But the history of censorship in England from 1538 to 1695, with its pervasive control of religious and political publications, was a deliberate attempt to censor what the English citizenry read and wrote.

With this legacy, it is not surprising that licensing of the press in the American colonies existed in some areas until the early eighteenth century, although it was never as pervasive as in England. Prior restraints upon printing existed in Virginia, until the late seventeenth century, and in Massachusetts, New York, and Pennsylvania until the 1720s. But by 1725, licensing of the press by colonial legislatures had been abolished as inconsistent with the rising tide of public pressure for self-government and autonomy from official constraints.

Two of Virginia's favorite sons occupy a special place in the movement for freedom of the press. With his unlimited faith in "the good sense of the people" and their capacity for self-correction, Thomas Jefferson was well aware of the critical role performed by a free press. In a letter to his friend Edward Carrington in 1787, Jefferson regretted the omission of any reference to a free press in the new Constitution and expressed why it was so vital to society:

> The way to prevent . . . irregular interpositions of the people is to give them full information of their affairs through the channel of the public papers, and to contrive that those papers should penetrate the whole mass of the people.[3]

When the First Congress began drafting a formal bill of rights in the summer of 1789, James Madison's original proposal to protect free communication read in part:

> The people shall not be deprived or abridged of their right to speak, to write, or to publish their sentiments, and the freedom of the press, as one of the great bulwarks of liberty, shall be inviolable.[4]

As it was modified by the new Congress and eventually included in the First Amendment, freedom of the press was widely assumed to mean freedom from *any* prior restraint upon the press. Throughout American history, relatively few prior restraints have been imposed by government upon the press, unlike the efforts by government discussed in Chapter 11 to regulate free speech, especially seditious speech. However, as this chapter will indicate, free press doctrine varies with the particular medium at issue, the circumstances surrounding an alleged claim, and the weighing of the different rights of individuals and society at large.

The Classic Case: *Near* v. *Minnesota* (1931)

In 1931, the U.S. Supreme Court reviewed for the first time a case dealing with prior restraint of the press and, in so doing, established a major precedent for American constitutional law. The controversy began in 1925, with the passage by the Minnesota legislature of the Public Nuisance Law, prohibiting any publication of "malicious, scandalous and defamatory" newspapers, magazines, or other periodicals. Two years later, a Minneapolis tabloid known as the *Saturday Press* began publishing articles charging that various Minneapolis public officials had failed to expose and punish gangsters responsible for the gambling, bootlegging, and racketeering prevalent in the city. The publisher of the newspaper was J. M. Near, who two recent commentators have portrayed as notoriously "anti-Catholic, anti-Semite, anti-black, and anti-labor."[5]

Acting upon the basis of the state law, a state court in 1927 issued a temporary injunction against Near because of the prejudicial nature of several articles appearing in the *Saturday Press*. The trial court convicted Near in spite of his objections that the law violated the First and Fourteenth Amendments. The Minnesota Supreme Court upheld the conviction, stating that "our Constitution was never intended to protect malice, scandal and defamation when untrue or published with bad motives or without justifiable ends." Near then appealed to the U.S. Supreme Court, which subsequently ruled 5–4 that the Minnesota Public Nuisance Law violated both the First and Fourteenth Amendments.

The majority opinion was drafted by Chief Justice Charles Evans Hughes, who had been appointed to the Court in 1910 by President William Howard Taft. In striking down the state law, Hughes's argument came in two waves— one constitutional and the other practical. First, Hughes argued that even though freedom of the press was not absolute, restraint was the rare exception:

> The fact that for approximately one hundred and fifty years there has been almost an entire absence of attempts to impose previous restraints upon publications relating to the malfeasance of public officers is significant of the deep-seated conviction that such restraints would violate constitutional right.

He stated that there were four circumstances wherein prior restraint might be justified under the First Amendment: the publication of critical wartime information such as the number and location of troops; obscene publications; publications inciting "acts of violence" or the violent overthrow of the government; or, finally, publications that invade "private rights." Since none of these special circumstances existed in *Near*, Hughes wrote that "liberty of the press . . . has meant, principally although not exclusively, immunity from prior restraints or censorship." According to the chief justice the public sometimes had to suffer with vile journalism that profited from such protection:

> The fact that the liberty of the press may be abused by miscreant purveyors of scandal does not make any the less necessary the immunity of the press from previous restraint in dealing with official misconduct.

Hughes also indicated that for practical reasons, the restraint law went too far in restricting Near. First, public officials who felt that they or their official conduct had been defamed could still seek redress through existing libel laws. Furthermore, the law did not in any way deal with the circulation of scandalous or defamatory statements about *private* individuals, but rather the alleged misconduct or criminal behavior of *public* officials. According to Chief Justice Hughes:

> Charges of reprehensible conduct, and in particular of official malfeasance, unquestionably create a public scandal, but the theory of the constitutional guaranty is that even a more serious public evil would be caused by authority to prevent publication.

With this, the majority seemed suspicious of the legislature's attempt to limit press criticism of only *public* officials; therefore, the motive for the law was suspect. This rationale would become important decades later in *New York Times* v. *Sullivan* (1964) dealing with libel law.

A third rationale for striking down the Minnesota law was that the law went too far in disciplining the errant publisher of the *Saturday Press*. The object of the statute, said Hughes, "is not punishment, in the ordinary sense, but suppression of the offending newspaper or periodical." And, finally, Hughes said that the Public Nuisance Law "not only operates to suppress the offending newspaper or periodical but to put the publisher under an effective censorship."

The views of the four dissenters in the *Near* case were represented in a dissent by Justice Pierce Butler who, like the majority, based his argument upon both legal and practical grounds. First, the state law was not technically a "prior" restraint, since it did not "authorize administrative control in advance." Butler also doubted the practical ability of existing libel law to ferret out shoddy journalism of the kind represented by the *Saturday Press,* since conspiring publishers "may have purpose and sufficient capacity to contrive to put into effect a scheme . . . for oppression, blackmail or extortion."

The major principle established in *Near* v. *Minnesota* is a vital one for freedom of the press. Because a prior restraint upon the press is an extreme measure which extracts a high price for preserving order, the First Amendment allows it only in very rare circumstances, as briefly catalogued by Chief Justice Hughes. Those conditions are important, for in future years, several cases would deal with alleged national security, threats to public decency from "obscene" publications, or public incitement, and the press would have to defend itself against governmental restraints prior to publication, dissemination, or broadcast. Furthermore, in the entire area of libel law, which will conclude this chapter, the Court has used some elements evident in *Near*. At the center of Hughes's argument is his firm belief that libel laws, not suppression of the press, afford society—and especially public officials—the best protection against false accusations and defamation of character.

In retrospect, *Near* stands as a vital safeguard of a free press, regardless of whether that press practices responsible or sensationalized journalism. (For a recent case of censorship of a student newspaper, see Brief 12.1.) Checks upon the latter are the Jeffersonian faith in the public's ability to reject faulty reasoning and libel laws that might serve to make journalism more accurate and courageous.

Prior Restraint Meets the Vietnam War:
New York Times v. *United States* (1971)

Before *New York Times* v. *United States,* also known as the Pentagon Papers Case, arrived at the Supreme Court in the summer of 1971, the federal government had never before used the federal courts as instruments to suppress publication of communications. (There had been reports during the early 1960s, however, that the Kennedy administration had persuaded both the *New York Times* and the *Washington Post* to delay or alter their coverage of the Bay of Pigs fiasco and the Cuban Missile Crisis.[6]) In June 1971, the publication by the *New York Times* and the *Washington Post* of a series of articles based upon a top-secret history of American involvement in the Vietnam War occasioned an unprecedented collision between the federal government's protection of national security and the press's freedom to publish. The focus of the court controversy, which arose and was settled by the courts in an uncharacteristically brief three-week period,[7] was a 47-volume, 7,000-page document entitled "History of U.S. Decision-Making Process on Viet Nam Policy." Initiated in the early 1960s by Secretary of Defense Robert S. McNamara, the lengthy report covered the nation's growing involvement during the Truman-

☐ *Brief 12.1 The Students' Right to Speak Can Be Regulated*

In May 1983, the principal of the high school in Hazelwood, Missouri, deleted two pages from the student newspaper entitled *Spectrum,* published as part of the school curriculum. He considered two articles that appeared in the paper to be inappropriate. One of the purged articles reported interviews with three anonymous, but possibly identifiable, students concerning their pregnancies and personal experiences with sex and birth control. Another article discussed divorce and included a student's complaints about her father, naming the student. Neither article contained graphic accounts of sexual activity, violence, or other highly questionable activities.

Student staff members of *Spectrum* filed a suit in federal court claiming that their right to free speech under the First Amendment had been violated. In 1988, the Supreme Court ruled 5–3 in the case of *Hazelwood School District* v. *Kuhlmeier* that public school officials do have extensive power to censor student newspapers and other "school-sponsored expressive activities." The ruling argued that those school activities which are part of the school curriculum carry the imprint of school

authority and legitimacy; therefore, officials have a right to regulate the dissemination of information relating to drugs, sexual activity, pregnancy, birth control, and other contentious political and social issues.

The majority opinion in this speech-press case was authored by Justice Byron White, who recognized the school authorities' right to intervene and limit publication of information inconsistent with the school's "basic educational mission." White reaffirmed the longtime principle that had emerged in *Tinker* v. *Des Moines Independent Community School District* (1969) (see Chapter 11) guaranteeing students the right of free expression on school grounds. But the justices also said that the *Tinker* principle did not apply in the *Hazelwood* case because the latter occurred as incident to the school curriculum and carried the "imprimatur of the school." Justice William Brennan dissented along with two other justices in the case. Brennan criticized the "blanket censorship authority" assumed by the school principal in the *Hazelwood* case and the rule that apparently jeopardized a large body of student expression channeled through the campus newspaper.

Eisenhower-Kennedy-Johnson administrations and indicated that the United States had been more deeply involved in the Vietnamese civil war during the 1950s and 1960s than American public officials had ever disclosed.

Copies of the classified study had been obtained by former Defense Department analysts Daniel Ellsberg and Anthony Russo, who had helped prepare the survey. Since their departure from government service, Ellsberg and Russo, increasingly disillusioned with the war effort, had become active in the antiwar movement gripping the country. They apparently gave the report to the *New York Times,* which began on June 13, 1971, to serialize excerpts from the study. The *Washington Post* began publishing its own account of the survey soon thereafter, and the government brought suit in federal court to stop publication of the Pentagon Papers. In an effort to resolve differing federal court rulings, the Supreme Court agreed to hear the case.

On a vote of 6–3 and in a brief, 202-word *per curiam* opinion, the Supreme Court decided on June 30 to deny the U.S. government's request for a permanent restraining order because it had failed to show sufficient justification why prior restraint was necessary to preserve national security. The precise ruling in this case is important because it established that government can impose prior restraint in instances where it can prove that publication will pose a serious threat to national security (in accordance with one of the circumstances established in *Near).* However, in the Pentagon Papers Case, the government did not meet the stringent standard. The divided Court in this case discussed several issues and rationales, as all nine justices authored separate opinions to explain their respective votes.

In their concurring opinions, Justices Hugo Black and William O. Douglas adopted an absolutist stance, arguing that under *no* circumstances could prior restraint be tolerated by the First Amendment. In what would be his last opinion of a long and distinguished Court career, Justice Black stated:

> For the first time in the 182 years since the founding of the Republic, the federal courts are asked to hold that the First Amendment does not mean what it says, but rather means that the Government can halt the publication of current news of vital importance to the people of this country.

Black insisted that both "the history and language of the First Amendment support the view that the press must be left to publish news, whatever the source, without censorship, injunctions or prior restraints." Justice Douglas also insisted that the First Amendment barred all governmental restraints upon the press.

Four other justices authored concurring opinions stating that under some circumstances, they would support restraining orders upon the two newspapers. For example, to Justice Brennan, the government could conceivably impose prior restraint in rare circumstances; but, in this instance, the government had not met the heavy burden of proof.

> Only governmental allegation and proof that publication must inevitably, directly and immediately cause the occurrence of an event kindred to imperiling the safety of a transport already at sea can support even the issuance of an interim restraining order. In no event may mere conclusions be sufficient.

To Brennan, since the materials presented nothing even remotely resembling the leaking of vital military secrets to an adversary, the federal government's request was unjustified.

Justices Potter Stewart and Byron White, in separate concurrences, distinguished between some of the documents and the type of damage that might result from publication. Both thought that some of the releases could result in "substantial damage to public interests," as Justice White stated, but neither felt that the government had justified imposing prior restraint. As Justice Stewart stated, "I cannot say that disclosure of any of them will surely result in direct, immediate, and irreparable damage to our Nation or its people."

More than any other justice, Justice Thurgood Marshall focused upon the separation-of-powers principle and Congress's past refusal to provide the president with broad authority to restrain the press. To him, the delineation of constitutional powers was clear and unequivocal:

> The Constitution provides that Congress shall make laws, the President execute laws, and courts interpret laws . . . It did not provide for government by injunction in which the courts and the Executive "make laws" without regard to the action of Congress.

Chief Justice Warren Burger and Justices John Harlan and Harry Blackmun each authored dissenting opinions in the Pentagon Papers Case. They emphasized the unusual haste with which the Court was being asked to consider such important issues as free press and national security. Chief Justice Burger referred specifically to the "unwarranted deadlines and frenetic pressures" in which the majority seemed compelled to function. Justice Harlan criticized the "irresponsibly feverish" manner in which the Court was being asked to deal with the case. Both Harlan and Blackmun indicated their support for the inherent-powers doctrine, which, as Blackmun stated, gave the president "primary power over the conduct of foreign affairs and . . . responsibility for the Nation's safety."

In summary, *New York Times* v. *United States* reinforced the principle, articulated in *Near,* that in times of national crisis, when the government can prove that publications will result in irreparable damage to national security or the national interest, prior restraint upon publication is justified. Given the fact that the absolutist position of Justices Black and Douglas has never been endorsed by any of the justices on the Burger or Rehnquist Courts, it would be interesting to note how they would handle a somewhat similar case.

Prior Restraint and Intelligence Gathering: The *Marchetti* and *Snepp* Cases

Both the press and the government learned from the Pentagon Papers Case that prior restraints upon the printed word are difficult to obtain. Only in extreme circumstances would prior restraint be tolerated by the Supreme Court. The Pentagon Papers Case also raised one of the toughest issues affecting the relationship between government and the press: national security and the limits of governmental secrecy. "National security" means different things to public officials, private citizens, and the working media. Generally speaking, the position of the federal government, especially within the executive branch, has been that if Congress has the constitutional power to declare war, and the chief executive has the power to wage war, then both must possess the power to keep certain military and intelligence information secret. Ironically, in a democratic society, which is vitally dependent upon a vigilant press to communicate important information to its citizenry, the very existence of the constitutional order may at times depend upon government keeping secrets from the people. Again, it should be remembered that the Court in *Near* ruled that prior restraint is justified in those instances where a grave national emergency exists. But what are those precise conditions, and who is to decide what secrets should be kept—the president, unelected bureaucrats, military commanders, members of Congress, or judges? This issue, like so many others, involves precious civil liberties on the one hand and governmental stability and order on the other. As Abraham Lincoln reflected in the midst of the Civil War, "Must a government be too strong for the liberties of its people or too weak to maintain its own existence?"

One of the institutional casualties of the Vietnam War era and the Watergate scandal was the American intelligence-gathering community. In particular, the Central Intelligence Agency (CIA) had its antennae clipped during the 1970s by an aroused Congress that sensed growing public concern about a CIA that was out of control. Some of the revelations that proved most embarrassing to the agency came from former employees who chose to publish personal accounts of their experiences inside the American intelligence community. Two federal court cases, in particular, raised some important questions about military secrets, national security, and the right of government to suppress information.

For several years, the CIA has required employees to sign a secrecy agreement as a condition of employment. The agreement commits the employee not to reveal classified information or publish any material obtained during the period of employment without obtaining the prior approval of the agency. During the Vietnam War era, the case of *United States* v. *Marchetti* (1972) presented the first major test of the constitutionality of these agreements. Victor

Marchetti, a former employee of the CIA, and John Marks, a former State Department employee, both signed one of these agreements upon joining their respective agencies. But in the early 1970s, they announced their intention to write a book entitled *The CIA and the Cult of Intelligence* and their unwillingness to abide by their signed pledge. They argued in federal court that the agreement constituted an unlawful prior restraint upon publication. The federal government sought an injunction against publication of the book until it had been cleared of all classified information. A federal district court denied Marchetti his request for the right to publish and held that a CIA employee can legally be subject to restrictions that would plainly be unconstitutional if applied to an average private citizen.

The Supreme Court denied certiorari in *Marchetti* v. *United States,* thereby allowing the government to delete sensitive, classified material from the book, which was eventually published by A. A. Knopf with several blank spaces. Initially, the CIA had ordered the deletion of 339 passages of varying length, but, after demands made to the agency by attorneys for the authors and the filing of a countersuit against the CIA, all but 168 of the initial deletions were reinstated. Throughout the Marchetti-CIA controversy, federal courts dealt with the issue as a contractual dispute involving a sensitive government agency and its employees; thus, the constitutional issue of a free press was never dealt with directly.

A similar case reached the Supreme Court in 1980. Frank W. Snepp had worked for the CIA since 1968 and had signed the same secrecy agreement that bound Marchetti. When he resigned from the agency in 1976, he also signed an agreement in which he reaffirmed his obligation never to divulge any classified information or any material without first obtaining prepublication clearance from the agency director. He, too, later wrote a book based upon his experiences, entitled *Decent Interval,* without submitting the manuscript to the CIA for clearance in accordance with the signed agreement.

The federal government sued Snepp for breach of contract and the district court found in favor of the government, ordering Snepp to refrain from publishing any further material without first obtaining agency clearance. The trial court also granted the government's request to establish a trust for the government's benefit into which all book royalties would go. The Fourth Circuit Court of Appeals agreed that Snepp had breached a valid contract, but disagreed with the trial court about the constructive trust. Because both the trial and appellate courts ruled that Snepp had indeed violated the terms of his contract with the CIA, rather than his having published classified material, the First Amendment issue of free press and prior restraint was never technically decided.

In a 6–3 *per curiam* opinion handed down in 1980, in the case of *Snepp* v. *United States,* the Supreme Court upheld the decision of the district court in all respects, including the breach of contract, the establishment of a constructive trust, and the obligation of Snepp not to publish anything in the future without agency clearance. In a thinly disguised slap at the appellate tribunal, the Court's opinion read in part:

> Undisputed evidence in this case shows that a CIA agent's violation of his obligation to submit writings about the Agency for prepublication review impairs the CIA's ability to perform its statutory duties . . . [The Fourth Circuit's decision]

> denies the Government the most appropriate remedy for Snepps' acknowledged wrong. Indeed, as a practical matter, the decision may well leave the Government with no reliable deterrent against similar breaches of security.

The three dissenting justices in this case—Justices Stevens, Marshall, and Brennan—felt that the critical element lacking in the conviction was the absence of any classified information in the publication. According to Justice John Paul Stevens:

> Snepp admittedly breached his duty [but] the Government has conceded that the book contains no classified nonpublic material. Thus, by definition, the interest in confidentiality that Snepp's contract was designed to protect has not been compromised. Nevertheless, the Court today grants the Government unprecedented and drastic relief.

Although the *Snepp* case did not raise directly the issue of prior restraint, it undoubtedly received negative reviews among the journalistic profession. Snepp was prohibited from ever publishing anything without CIA approval, which, in effect, constitutes a permanent prior restraint order. And, according to the Supreme Court decision, sworn-to-secrecy covenants with the federal government are legal under the First Amendment. The allowance for a constructive trust into which all book royalties will go in effect says that "you can only publish what we approve and we get all proceeds from the sale of the material." That has rather discomforting implications for a free press.

Throughout the presidency of Ronald Reagan, the administration doggedly pursued several suspected "leaks" of government information to the press and the public. Several of the suspected leaks allegedly dealt with sensitive government information, and the administration consistently tried to manage government offices in their relations with the press.[8] On March 11, 1983, President Reagan issued the National Security Decision Directive 84, which required 120,000 federal employees with access to classified information to submit for prepublication review everything they would write for the rest of their lives. The order would have further expanded the use of lie-detector tests within the government. Soon thereafter, congressional opposition in both Houses resulted in the administration's suspending its plan to implement the order. But reports circulated that agencies were requiring their personnel to take polygraph tests and submit writings for agency review, regardless of what Congress said they could do. As Congressman Jack Brooks (D-Tex.) noted, "They're doing most of [the screening] now under other directives."[9]

Prior Restraint and Nuclear Secrets: *United States* v. *Progressive* (1979)

A slight variation on the right of the press to publish and the government's obligation to protect occurred in the late 1970s and involved a public glimpse inside the American nuclear arsenal. In 1979, *The Progressive* magazine announced that it planned to publish in its April issue an article by one of its reporters, Howard Morland, entitled "The H-Bomb Secret—How We Got It, Why We're Telling It." The editors argued that publication of the article would inform the public about nuclear war and the pitfalls of a system of governmental secrecy. They insisted that the classification system mostly kept information from the general reading public, not the determined foreign intelligence-gathering community. When informed by the editors of their intent to publish, the government conceded that some of the material to be printed was already "in the public domain." But it also maintained that national security compelled it to censor material which, if released, might inflict "immediate, direct and irreparable harm to the interests of the United States." [10]

In 1979, a federal district judge granted a temporary injunction against the magazine in the case of *United States* v. *Progressive,* thereby preventing it from publishing or disclosing any information designated by the government as "restrictive data" within the meaning of the Atomic Energy Act of 1954. The judge's opinion read like a classic statement of balancing individual and societal interests:

> A mistake in ruling against *The Progressive* will seriously infringe cherished First Amendment rights. [A] mistake in ruling against the United States could pave the way for thermonuclear annihilation for us all. In that event, our right to life is extinguished and the right to publish becomes moot.

The Progressive appealed the judgment to the U.S. Court of Appeals for the Seventh Circuit, and a hearing was scheduled for September 1979, well past the intended publication date. In parallel proceedings, the author, the editors of the magazine, and supporters of the right to publish continued to argue that much of the information contained in the article had already appeared in several popularly circulated journals and newspapers. This argument seemed convincing since, by mid-September, the federal government had dropped its case against Howard Morland and *The Progressive*. The Morland article appeared in its original form in the November 1979 issue of the magazine. With probably some relief among free-press advocates and perhaps the justices themselves, the Supreme Court never ruled on the case. Given the composition of the Court and the increasing public concern about international terrorism and the threat of nuclear proliferation, the Court might well have ruled against the periodical and in favor of prior restraint.

What do these developments reveal about prior restraint in the twentieth century? First, although the Anglo-American legacy does contain some instances of substantial restraints upon a free press, by the mid-eighteenth century, prior restraints had been generally recognized as wrong and to be avoided at all possible costs. Impetus for freedom of the press was substantial by the late 1780s; at the urging of Jefferson and Madison especially, protecting the freedom to communicate ideas with a minimum of governmental censorship became a reality when the First Amendment was ratified in 1791.

Second, not until the twentieth century did any cases involving governmental attempts to impose prior restraints upon the press reach the Supreme Court. The landmark case of *Near* v. *Minnesota* (1931) finally established an important principle in American constitutional law: prior restraint is justified in only a few rare instances. Although the Supreme Court struck down a state prior restraint in *Near,* the possibility of future restraints being imposed became a strong possibility.

Finally, as the irreversible march of technology and instantaneous communications has made the world stage more congested with actors and more difficult to manage, public officials have frequently felt compelled to restrict what the public knows about its government and the secrets it keeps, all in the name of "national security." That particular term has been at the forefront of several cases considered by the Supreme Court during the past two decades. When debate over the First Amendment injunction concerning a free press subsides, observers might again ponder that important provision of the Bill of Rights: "Congress shall make no law . . . abridging the freedom of the press." Since the founding of the Republic two centuries ago, Congress has never passed any law specifically abridging a free press, although the states have occasionally attempted to do so. But in the modern era, especially in the 1970s, the executive branch has made several attempts to impose unilaterally prior restraints upon the press or upon public and private citizens—and always in the name of alleged threats to national security. And like it has in so many instances involving other constitutional issues, the Supreme Court has often found itself in the eye of the storm attempting to locate that delicate balance between private rights and public good, between liberty and social order. In some respects, viewing the conflict as merely a struggle between private rights and public order is too simplistic. Where the courts may uphold prior restraint in some qualified instances or authorize prepublication contracts between employee and employer, they rationalize their action as essential to the larger good—namely, the preservation of a governing system which occasionally must restrict individual freedoms in certain sensitive areas.

Free Press and Fair Trial: Special Problems When Rights Collide

Society is very dependent upon a complex communications network to keep citizens informed of a wide range of news stories. The United States has become a society that can receive hourly updates on news events occurring on the other side of the world.[11] But this technology also raises some very important problems for safeguarding the rights of individuals. What happens when an evening news program informs the public of fast-breaking news developments relating to a sordid murder scene where a suspect has been taken into custody? Or what about a much-publicized trial involving a defendant already considered to be guilty by a prejudiced or outraged public that is not interested in what the court has to say?

Much of this dilemma arises because the federal Constitution provides its citizens with competing rights—the First Amendment's guarantee of a free press and the Sixth Amendment's promise of a fair trial by an impartial jury of one's peers. The provision for a fair trial based solely upon the presentation of evidence fairly obtained can be difficult to guarantee, especially in an era when mass media can influence how viewers perceive events beyond their personal experience. In cases concerning famous people or sensationalized crimes, pretrial publicity can prejudice the jury selection, the actual trial proceedings, and, sometimes, even the punishment phase of the judicial process. When local newspaper or television coverage must compete for a lucrative market under the rush toward deadlines for evening editions or for the six o'clock broadcast, the potential for overreaction or abuse is always present. As a result, an important question to be discussed here is, What, if any, restrictions on a free press are permissible in order to ensure a defendant a fair trial?

Over the past few decades, the Supreme Court has frequently dealt with several aspects of pretrial and trial publicity. Many of the cases have paralleled the advent of television as the main vehicle for public information. Television, however, is not the only medium affecting the collision between free press and fair trial. In 1961, the case of *Irvin* v. *Dowd* marked the first time that the Supreme Court struck down a state court conviction solely on the grounds of prejudicial pretrial publicity. In that case, the defendant Leslie Irvin had been arrested, tried, and convicted of committing one of six murders in Evansville, Indiana, after newspapers and radio—as well as television—had given extensive coverage to the local investigation and Irvin's confession to the murder. Media coverage of the crimes and subsequent trial made it very difficult to select an impartial jury. A unanimous Supreme Court held that the trial court had not done enough to ensure the selection of an unbiased jury capable of rendering a decision based solely upon the evidence presented in the courtroom, instead of inflammatory pretrial publicity surrounding the crime.

Television in the Courtroom

Two other cases in the mid-1960s extended the analysis of pretrial publicity to media coverage of the trial itself. *Estes* v. *Texas* (1965) raised the issue of whether the presence of working journalists, specifically television commentators and technicians, in or near the courtroom adversely affects the trial proceedings and the rendering of a just verdict. The case involved the flamboyant Texas financier Billy Sol Estes and his conviction for fraud in a nationally publicized trial. Both the pretrial and trial phases of the proceeding involved extensive television and radio coverage. At the trial, the media equipment was encased in a booth to minimize any disruption in the proceeding, although film footage of the trial was regularly shown to local, state, and even national audiences. After the trial, Estes appealed his conviction to the U.S. Supreme Court on the grounds that the publicity before and during the trial effectively denied him a fair trial as guaranteed under the Sixth Amendment.

When the case reached the Supreme Court in 1965, the justices overturned the Estes conviction. In a 5–4 opinion authored by Justice Thomas C. Clark, the Court said that "the defendant is entitled to his day in court—not in a stadium or city or nationwide arena." Clark and three other members of the majority (Chief Justice Warren, Justices Douglas and Goldberg) considered the introduction of television into the courtroom to be inherently prejudicial to the trial; therefore, cameras should have been barred from the outset. But Justice Harlan, the fifth member of the majority, thought that the television ban should only pertain to "criminal trials of great publicity," and the Estes trial did not fall into that category.

The four dissenting justices (Stewart, Black, Brennan, and White) had reservations about televising courtroom proceedings, but they were more concerned about restricting communication to the public. Writing for the minority, Justice Stewart said that, notwithstanding his concern about introducing television into the courtroom, he could not recommend a general constitutional rule that banned television, primarily because of the precedent that would be established for future trials and the resultant chilling effect upon First Amendment freedoms. As he noted in his dissent:

> The idea of imposing upon any medium of communication the burden of justifying its presence is contrary to where I had always thought the presumption must lie

in the area of First Amendment freedoms. And the proposition that nonpartici-
pants in a trial might get the "wrong impression" from unfettered reporting and
commentary contains an invitation to censorship which I cannot accept.

The key point advanced by *Estes* v. *Texas* in 1965 was that there was no
definitive constitutional guarantee which justified banning television from
courtroom trials.

Following *Estes,* many states began experimenting with television in the
courtroom, and, inevitably, some defendants challenged the use of certain types
of media in their trials. Florida is one state where only the approval of the
presiding judge is necessary for televised proceedings in a court trial. In *Chandler* v. *Florida* in 1981, two former Miami police officers had been convicted
of conspiracy to commit burglary and grand larceny. Over the defendants'
objections, the trial court permitted television coverage of the proceedings. A
Florida appeals court upheld their conviction, the Florida Supreme Court
denied review, and the defendants appealed the ruling to the U.S. Supreme
Court on the grounds that their Sixth and Fourteenth Amendment rights had
been violated. In 1981, the Supreme Court upheld their convictions and ruled
7–2 that media coverage for public broadcast of a state criminal trial does
not inherently deprive defendants of their constitutional guarantees. The *Estes*
and *Chandler* precedents allowed states and localities to experiment with the
visual media so long as the media did not jeopardize the constitutional rights
of the litigants.

Pretrial Publicity by the Mass Media

Two prominent murder trials—one in a large metropolitan area in the 1950s
and the other in the rural Midwest in the 1970s—compelled the Supreme
Court to deal with the questions of pretrial publicity and "gag rules." In one
of the most famous "trial by newspapers" cases in the twentieth century, a
Cleveland doctor by the name of Samuel Sheppard was implicated in the brutal
murder of his pregnant wife in their suburban home in 1954. In some of the
most sensationalized news coverage ever to accompany a murder investigation,
reporters questioned witnesses and prosecutors before the trial ever began,
thus leaking important information on the state's case. During the trial, reporters were seated a few feet from the jury box; throughout the proceedings,
the defendant, jurors, defense counsel, and witnesses were accessible to reporters and photographers as they entered and left the courtroom. Considerable publicity generated by the media concerned information that was never
introduced into the trial, and the jury was never sequestered until it began its
final deliberations. Sheppard was convicted and sentenced to prison for the
crime.

More than a decade later, the U.S. Supreme Court reversed the Sheppard
conviction in *Sheppard* v. *Maxwell* (1966), comparing the atmosphere at the
original trial to that of a "Roman holiday" created by the news media. In an
8–1 opinion authored by Justice Clark, the Court noted that "bedlam reigned"
at the courthouse, and it placed much of the blame for the blundered trial
upon the court itself, especially the presiding judge. Had steps been taken to
obtain a change of venue to a more neutral setting, or to delay the trial or to
limit the number of reporters covering the trial, a prejudicial environment

might have been avoided. But the Court also indicated its reluctance to impose any direct limitations upon a free press, for "what transpires in the courtroom is public property." According to Clark, the press "does not simply publish information about trials but guards against the miscarriage of justice by subjecting the police, prosecutors, and judicial processes to extensive public scrutiny and criticism."

During the decade following the *Sheppard* ruling and the Court's insistence that state courts should try to minimize the chances of prejudicial media coverage of trials, local jurisdictions increasingly imposed protective orders that limited media coverage of investigations and trials in order to prevent adverse publicity that might jeopardize a fair trial. Sometimes referred to as **gag orders,** these restraints upon the press can limit or prohibit the publication of material about ongoing trials and investigations. Refusal by the press to comply with such orders can result in a contempt-of-court citation.

In 1976, the Supreme Court reviewed for the first time the constitutionality of a judge-imposed gag order, and the result was an incomplete victory for the press. The case involved the trial and conviction of Edwin Charles Simants, who had been apprehended, questioned, and indicted for the grisly murder of six family members in Sutherland, Nebraska, in October 1975. Because of the nature of the crimes and the isolated location of the trial, the trial court prohibited the release or publication of any information, testimony, or evidence introduced at the preliminary hearing and trial of Simants.[12] The initial gag order was modified somewhat by a state judge, but it still prohibited the press from reporting any confessions or incriminating statements by the defendant to law enforcement officials or to any third parties. The order was to remain in effect until a jury could be selected and sequestered. The Nebraska Press Association challenged the protective order; after losing in both the district court and the state supreme court, the press group appealed to the U.S. Supreme Court.

A unanimous Supreme Court in the case of *Nebraska Press Association* v. *Stuart* (1976) struck down the gag order as a violation of both the First and the Fourteenth Amendments. In an opinion drafted by Chief Justice Burger, the Court referred to both *Near* and the Pentagon Papers Case and insisted that the sanctity of a free press must be safeguarded:

> The thread running through [these cases], is that prior restraints on speech and publication are the most serious and the least tolerable infringement on First Amendment rights . . . [A] prior restraint [has] an immediate and irreversible sanction. If it can be said that a threat of criminal or civil sanctions after publication "chills" speech, prior restraint "freezes" it at least for the time.

In striking down the gag order, the Court cited several points. Such orders might be justified if a fair trial is deemed impossible without them. But before imposing them, courts should use less drastic means to preserve the integrity of the judicial process, such as changing venue, delaying the trial until public sentiment subsides, taking more care to select an impartial jury, and giving more detailed instructions to the jury on the need to preserve objectivity. The trial judge should also instruct the prosecutor, defense counsel, police, and witnesses about using discretion when talking with the media. In summation, Burger emphasized that even though "the guarantees of freedom of expression are not an absolute prohibition under all circumstances . . . the barriers to prior restraint remain high and the presumption against its use continues intact."

In a separate concurring opinion, Justice Brennan implied that he could envision virtually *no* circumstances that would justify prior restraints in barring reporters from a trial, except perhaps military necessity. According to Brennan, "there is . . . a clear and substantial damage to freedom of the press whenever even a temporary restraint is imposed on reporting of material concerning the operations of the criminal justice system." In another concurrence, Justice Lewis Powell commented upon the "unique burden" resting upon anyone trying to justify a prior restraint on publication. And somewhat surprisingly, given his more conservative stance on such issues, Justice White expressed "grave doubts" that protective orders "would ever be justifiable."

The *Stuart* ruling placed gag orders at a distinct disadvantage, and state courts have had little success since 1976 in imposing them. However, even though this holding was applauded by the media, some other Supreme Court rulings in the 1970s regarding media access to the judicial process and, conversely, the legal system's access to the media would not be welcome news for journalists.

When News Gathering Collides with the Judicial Process

What happens when the media's right of access to the courtroom conflicts with a defendant's right to a fair trial? Can the media make it more difficult for defendants to receive a truly objective determination of their guilt or innocence? Both of these rights are guaranteed by the Constitution, in the First and Sixth Amendments, respectively, and yet on occasion, they seem incompatible. In these instances, judges are usually called upon to settle the matter.

A Ban on Publicity at the Hearing Stage

Does the public have a constitutional right of access to a pretrial hearing, even though the defendant, the prosecutor, and the trial judge have all agreed to bar the media from the proceedings? In 1979, the Supreme Court said no to this question in the case of *Gannett Co.* v. *DePasquale*. In this case, a series of stories by two Rochester, New York, newspapers had implicated two individuals in the abduction, disappearance, and murder of a Rochester police officer. The defendants were charged with the crime, in part because of allegedly coerced confessions to police about the abduction and murder, all of which were reported diligently by the Gannett newspapers. The defendants later pleaded not guilty to the charges and tried to have their confessions suppressed in a pretrial hearing. At the suppression hearing, defense attorneys argued that the adverse publicity surrounding the case was jeopardizing their clients' chances of receiving a fair trial, and they requested that the public and the media should be barred from the hearing. Neither the prosecutor nor the judge objected to this request, and the proceedings were closed to the public and media. When one of its reporters was among those excluded from the proceedings, the newspaper argued that such action violated both the media's and the public's right of access to the judicial process. The newspaper based its argument upon the First Amendment's guarantee of a free press and the Sixth Amendment's provision for public trials. When the New York Court of Appeals upheld the closure order on the grounds of threatened prejudicial publicity, the newspaper appealed to the U.S. Supreme Court.

In a divided 5–4 ruling, the Supreme Court held that the closure order was justified in this instance, grounding its judgment solely upon the Sixth Amendment. In a majority opinion authored by Justice Stewart, the justices reasoned that the Sixth Amendment's guarantee of a right to a public trial applied only to the *defendant,* and not to the general public or to the press. That guarantee is to be personal and directed toward the benefit of the accused. Since both defendants in this case had requested the closed hearing and the judge had acted upon that request, Stewart maintained that the trial court here had properly recognized that even though the press had a constitutional right of access, under the circumstances of this case, that right was outweighed by the defendant's right under the Sixth Amendment to a fair trial. Noting that any denial of access to the proceedings was temporary until the published transcript of the hearing could be obtained by the interested media, fairness of the proceedings could still be ensured. By turning on its head the argument that secrecy promotes possible injustice, Stewart observed that the closing of pretrial proceedings is often one of the most effective ways for the court to minimize the chance of prejudicial information being released prior to the trial. Although he voted with the majority in the *Gannett* judgment, Justice William Rehnquist recommended even more judicial restraint and deference to local judicial authorities who ought to be allowed to close pretrial hearings for reasons besides merely the avoidance of prejudicial disclosures. The four dissenting justices in *Gannett* (Justices Blackmun, Brennan, White, and Marshall) insisted that the trial judge had not properly weighed society's interest in gaining immediate access to the hearing process.

A Media Ban at the Trial Stage

The *Gannett* decision proved to be rather disastrous for the media, for its ambiguities encouraged many local and state courts to close their proceedings in order to avoid public scrutiny. Recognizing its complicity in this mischievous decision, the Supreme Court moved quickly to correct it. Whereas *Gannett* dealt with public access to pretrial *hearings,* the Court considered another case in 1980 involving the right of public access to criminal *trials.* The case of *Richmond Newspapers, Inc.* v. *Virginia* (1980) involved a defendant whose attorney, without objections from either the prosecutor or two reporters that were present, requested to have the trial closed to the public. The trial judge granted the motion, in accordance with the discretion allowed him by state law designed to ensure the defendant a fair, nonprejudicial trial. The trial eventually resulted in the acquittal of the defendant. Richmond Newspapers, Inc., which had objected to being barred from the trial, appealed to the Supreme Court for a definitive ruling on the right of access to criminal trials.

In July 1980, the Supreme Court ruled 7–1 that the Sixth Amendment required that trials must be open to the public. In distinguishing for the first time between pretrial proceedings and actual trials with respect to accessibility, the majority opinion drafted by Chief Justice Burger stressed the openness of the judicial process. He insisted that "the administration of justice cannot function in the dark," and it can best be protected "by allowing people to observe it." In noting the long history of trials being open to the public, he stressed that "the explicit, guaranteed rights to speak and to publish concerning what takes place at a trial" would be meaningless if public access were foreclosed arbitrarily. As a consequence,

> we hold that the right to attend criminal trials is implicit in the guarantees of the First Amendment; without the freedom to attend such trials, which people have exercised for centuries, important aspects of freedom of speech and of the press could be eviscerated.

Five separate concurring opinions in *Richmond Newspapers* indicated disagreements among the justices about why they voted as they did. Justice Brennan insisted that the First and Fourteenth Amendments, *on their own,* secure for the public a right of access to formal trial proceedings, and the Court should have earlier been more specific in recognizing this right. Justice Stewart also agreed that these amendments "clearly give the press and the public a right of access to trials themselves," although a legislature may impose reasonable time, place, and manner restrictions upon this freedom. In their concurring opinions, Justices White and Blackmun were troubled that *Gannett* found the Court reading the Sixth Amendment as not requiring public access to *all* criminal proceedings, including pretrial hearings. And in his concurrence, Justice Stevens referred to the *Richmond Newspapers* ruling as a "watershed" case, in that for the first time, the Court was recognizing that arbitrary interference with the public's access to important information in a trial violates First Amendment freedoms. The lone dissenting voice in the decision belonged to Justice Rehnquist, who objected to the majority's reading into either the First or the Sixth Amendments an implicit right of public access to the legal process. Echoing his sentiments in *Gannett,* Rehnquist felt that state and local courts should be able to conduct their legal proceedings without unnecessary interference from the federal government.

Three points should be mentioned about these last two cases. First, unfortunately, the Supreme Court did not clarify the rather ambiguous *Gannett* decision, which permits closure of pretrial hearings if judges feel that undue publicity might contaminate the fair trial process. That ruling might have been strengthened had the Court reiterated some of the points suggested by Burger in *Stuart* concerning how local authorities should act to ensure an objective public atmosphere in which to conduct a trial. The same safeguard should hold for pretrial hearings, but so should the desire to preserve openness. On this point, the *Gannett* and the *Richmond Newspapers* rulings are inconsistent.

A second point about *Richmond Newspapers* is that the Burger opinion did not assert any *absolute* right of public access to criminal trials, let alone pretrial hearings. Burger's closing words are that "absent an overriding interest," a criminal trial must be open to the public, which means that under some undefined circumstances, the public can be barred from a state criminal trial. This is a loophole that Justice Brennan did not condone, for he read the First Amendment as mandating public access in *all* instances.

One final point about *Gannett* and *Richmond Newspapers* concerns the media's reaction to the decisions, and how two justices on the Burger Court characterized the First Amendment mandate for a free press. Comments by Justices Brennan and Stevens were published during the brief period between the two rulings.[13] Justice Brennan maintained that society should consider two different models for a free press: one is the "speech" model that sees the primary purpose of the First Amendment as "more or less absolutely to prohibit any interference with freedom of expression." But this absolutist view clashes with another "structural," or societal, model that sees the interests of the press competing with other societal interests. This second model protects the "structure" of communications, which includes the several tasks necessary for the media to gather and disseminate the news. The Court on numerous occasions must weigh the effects of imposing restraints upon the press against societal interests that are sometimes served by the imposition. This balancing of interests is quite different from the first model that preserves a free press and free expression at *all* costs.

After the *Gannett* decision, which was soundly criticized by the media, Brennan, a strong defender of a free press, said that the press tended to treat many cases involving freedom of the press as if they involved only the absolutist model:

> [It] matters a great deal whether the press is abridged because restrictions are imposed on what it might say, or whether the press is abridged because its ability to gather the news or otherwise perform communicative functions necessary for a democracy is impaired . . . The tendency of the press to confuse these two models has . . . been at the root of much of the recent acrimony in press-Court relations.

He noted that the press had occasionally acted as if its role as a public spokesman had been restricted and, as a result, it had overreacted.

In another post-*Gannett* comment, Justice Stevens also distinguished between "the dissemination of information or ideas," which composes the core of First Amendment press freedom, and the "acquisition of newsworthy matter," which still must await further legal clarification by the courts. Both of these analyses by Supreme Court members emphasize the need to be more specific in the legal and practical analysis of First Amendment freedom of the press. The justices implied that the media would do their cause more good if their criticisms of some court decisions restraining the press dealt more with the "structural" aspects of news gathering and information dissemination. The media often treat all "anti-press" decisions under the "absolutist" banner. They claim that the courts are being too restrictive in monitoring what the media can say and print. As the justices observed, some of the recent cases that have been criticized by the media have dealt with restrictions upon the news-gathering process, rather than upon ideas expressed. The fact that this comment came from two of the most "pro-press" justices on the Court holds important implications for those who are hoping for major change in the thrust of precedents like *Gannett* and *Richmond Newspapers*.

The Issues of Source Confidentiality and Access to Newsrooms

To conclude this discussion of the frequent clash between a free press and the guarantee of a fair trial, two other topics warrant some examination—the media's right to protect the confidentiality of their sources, and governmental access to the newsroom. In the 1970s, the Burger Court dealt with both issues in ways that many journalists found disturbing. For a long time, many reporters have maintained that the First Amendment entitles them to preserve the confidentiality of their news sources, a privilege they say is essential to encouraging in-depth reporting. Furthermore, they argue that the public will eventually be deprived of the more complete body of newsworthy information if these sources cannot be guaranteed anonymity. This interpretation of the First Amendment and the relationship between journalist and source resembles that of "doctor-patient" or "lawyer-client," and it even extends to protecting information that may be relevant to a criminal investigation. By the early 1970s, several states had testified to the credibility of this interpretation by passing **shield laws** that protected journalists' sources from judicial scrutiny.

In 1972, the Supreme Court consolidated three different cases relating to shield laws and ruled that journalists have no constitutional right to refuse to testify before a grand jury investigating possible criminal activity (see Brief 12.2). The justices first elaborated upon the many virtues and the sanctity of a free press, and the virtually unlimited ability to pursue the news via any source "by means within the law." But the majority opinion authored by Justice White, in *Branzburg* v. *Hayes,* narrowly confined the issue addressed to the press's obligation to respond to a grand jury's **subpoena** (an order to appear in court) relating to an ongoing criminal investigation. White emphasized that the Constitution did not protect journalists from performing the same duty incumbent upon normal citizens—namely, appearing before and providing information in a grand jury proceeding. He insisted that if possible criminal activity were involved, it would be absurd to

> seriously entertain the notion that the First Amendment protects a newsman's agreement to conceal the criminal conduct of his source . . . on the theory that it is better to write about crime than to do something about it.

Justices Brennan and Marshall joined in a dissenting opinion authored by Justice Stewart (Justice Douglas authored a separate dissent), wherein the latter criticized the Court's "crabbed view of the First Amendment [which] reflects a disturbing insensitivity to the critical role of an independent press in our society. . ." Stewart insisted that the majority ruling would eventually impair the performance of the media's constitutionally protected functions, as well as the administration of justice. He reasoned that journalists need sources to gather the news, and confidentiality is essential to much of the news-gathering process. Additionally, he argued that an unlimited subpoena power would deter some sources from divulging information and discourage many reporters from aggressively pursuing and publishing certain information. However, although Stewart insisted that a free press occupied a "preferred position" to the administration of justice, he did not grant journalists absolute immunity from the subpoena process.[15] This opening for government to compel journalists to respond to court subpoenas under rare circumstances, coupled with the majority ruling that they can be compelled on demand to testify, has made the media much more leery of subpoena power in confidentiality cases.

One final issue in the area of press freedom to be dealt with here concerns the constitutionality of police searches of newsrooms. The Supreme Court in 1978 ruled that the First Amendment does not protect newspaper offices from

☐ *Brief 12.2   Can a Reporter Repress Knowledge of a Crime?*

Several cases in the past two decades have involved the alleged right of reporters to refuse to disclose their sources and the countervailing demand of criminal prosecutors to obtain evidence needed in a criminal investigation. Three celebrated cases were decided by the Supreme Court on the same day in 1972, during the heat of civil rights demonstrations, drug trafficking, and antiwar protests in the United States.

Branzburg v. *Hayes* involved a reporter for the *Louisville Courier-Journal* who had written several articles, based upon personal observations, about the processing of hashish. Branzburg was subpoened to testify before a grand jury but refused to appear on First Amendment freedom-of-the-press grounds, which the state, in turn, refused to concede. The second case, *In re Pappas,* involved a Massachusetts television reporter who had visited a Black Panther headquarters after promising not to reveal its location or activities. Like the *Branzburg* case, the state court refused to honor Pappas's refusal to testify before a grand jury. Finally, in the case of *United States* v. *Caldwell,* Earl Caldwell, a *New York Times* journalist, also refused to reveal the sources for his information on the Black Panthers organization.[14] On appeal to the U.S. Supreme Court, the Court in all three instances said that re-

porters do not have an unqualified right to shield information and evidence needed in a criminal investigation. This point became very important in the White House Tapes Case two years later.

One other case that followed these rulings by several years, *In re Farber* (1978), involved the same issue of journalists' having to divulge their sources in particular circumstances. An investigative reporter for the *New York Times,* Myron Farber, had written a series of stories claiming that an unidentified physician, "Doctor X," had caused the death of several patients at a New Jersey hospital. A doctor by the name of Jascalevich was tried for murder but eventually acquitted. During the course of the trial, at the defendant's request, the trial court ordered Farber to turn over all his interview notes and any other information. Farber relied upon a state shield law and refused to comply with the court order, whereupon he was held in contempt, sentenced to jail, and ordered to pay a fine along with his employer, the *New York Times.* The New Jersey Supreme Court upheld the conviction, and, on two separate occasions, the U.S. Supreme Court refused to grant a stay. In 1982, Governor Brendan Byrne pardoned Farber, and both his fine and that paid by the *New York Times* were remitted.

police searching for evidence needed in a criminal investigation. The case of *Zurcher* v. *Stanford Daily* (1978) concerned a police search of the offices of the campus newspaper at Stanford University in the early 1970s. The police were searching for photographs of a campus demonstration in which several people had been injured. The newspaper sued the Palo Alto police chief and others on the grounds that the search violated the First and Fourth Amendments. A federal district court struck down the search on Fourth Amendment grounds, and the court of appeals upheld that decision. On appeal, the U.S. Supreme Court, in a 5–3 judgment, reversed the ruling and said that the police action did not constitute an "unreasonable search and seizure." Since the search was based upon probable cause that the photographs were located in the newspaper office, the search was warranted. Justice Stewart wrote a strong dissent in which he recommended resorting to the subpoena power rather than to a search warrant, since the latter "allows police officers to ransack the files of a newspaper, reading each and every document until they have found the one named in the warrant." In addition to preferring the specificity of a subpoena, Stewart also regretted the search in the first place, since it jeopardizes the disclosure of confidential information and diminishes the "flow of potentially important information to the public."

The *Zurcher* ruling was immediately criticized by the press, which felt threatened by the possibility of newsrooms nationwide being exposed to the probing eyes of government armed with an easily obtained search warrant. This fear of Big Brother watching was eventually countered in 1980, when

Congress passed and President Jimmy Carter signed the Privacy Protection Act. The act prohibited police searches of newsrooms except for the purpose of preventing personal injury or death or destruction of materials. Police searches were also justified if a subpoena had failed to obtain the requested information or for the protection of a journalist believed to be a party to a crime.[16]

Obscenity and the First Amendment

Perhaps no area of the First Amendment and free press law contains as many ambiguities as that dealing with obscenity. Since the 1950s, the Supreme Court has struggled with numerous controversies involving allegedly obscene materials in search of constitutional protection, and the result has usually been a divided Court and a confusing line of precedents. This section highlights the major cases responsible for paving this troubled path of judicial policy-making. It will also discuss some of the key questions raised when government at any level tries to define what people should read, listen to, or view in both public and private accommodations.

Early Attempts to Define Obscenity

One of the earliest attempts in Anglo-American history to define obscenity occurred before a British court in 1868, in the case of *Queen* v. *Hicklin,* and involved an anti-Catholic pamphlet entitled "The Confessional Unmasked." In ruling that the publication was not legally obscene, a British judge said that the test of obscenity should be whether the material tends to "deprave and corrupt those whose minds are open to such immoral influences."[17] Although there was no attempt to define "immoral influences," the "*Hicklin* rule" would have a substantial impact upon the future regulation of obscenity. As Professor Thomas Emerson noted, the rule allowed government to ban any publication containing even isolated passages that courts felt might exert "immoral influences on susceptible persons."[18] And even though it was never specifically endorsed by the U.S. Supreme Court, as Harry Clor noted, the vague guideline became "the predominant test of obscenity in American courts."[19]

By 1873, Congress joined the antiobscenity bandwagon by passing the Obscene Literature and Articles Act, known as the Comstock Act, which made it illegal to import or mail

> any obscene book, pamphlet, paper, writing, advertisement, circular, print, picture, drawing or other representation, figure, or image on or of paper or other material, or any cast, instrument, or other article of an immoral nature, or any drug or medicine, or any article whatever, for the prevention of conception, or for causing unlawful abortion.[20]

Nowhere did the act define "obscenity" or "immoral nature," and some of its provisions, such as those relating to the distribution of birth control information, were later ruled unconstitutional. The Comstock Act would be the focus in a famous obscenity case before the Supreme Court in the 1950s, and it still remains in effect to this day.

By the early twentieth century, the *Hicklin* rule came under increasing scrutiny by those advocating less regulation of the press. Although Judge

Learned Hand felt obliged to follow the principle in a 1913 case, by the 1930s he was expressing doubt about its continued utility, in light of "the morality of the present time":

> If there be no abstract definition . . . should not the word "obscene" be allowed to indicate the present critical point in the compromise between candor and shame at which the community may have arrived. . . To put thought in leash to the average conscience of the time is perhaps tolerable, but to fetter it by the necessities of the lowest and least capable seems a fatal policy.[21]

By the mid-1930s, an appellate court judge found that James Joyce's book *Ulysses* was not obscene and, in the process, mentioned that the proper test of whether a book is obscene is its "dominant effect":

> In applying this test, relevancy of the objectionable parts to the theme, the established reputation of the work in the estimation of approved critics, if the book is modern, and the verdict of the past, if it is ancient, are persuasive pieces of evidence, for works of art are not likely to sustain a high position with no better warrant for their existence than their obscene content.[22]

The appellate court noted that the real problem with the *Hicklin* rule was that it weighed too heavily in favor of moral considerations, and tended to ignore or underestimate scientific or literary values of the work. For the next two decades, the prevailing standard would be the dominant effect of the objectionable material, rather than mere isolated passages as inherited from the *Hicklin* rule.

A Supreme Court decision handed down during World War II also had some important implications for the struggle over obscenity in the late twentieth century. *Chaplinsky* v. *New Hampshire* (1942) was not really an obscenity case, but rather a case dealing with the limits of free speech in provoking a public disturbance. Justice Frank Murphy referred in the majority opinion of *Chaplinsky* to certain "limited classes of speech," such as the "lewd and obscene" which were not entitled to constitutional protection:

> Such utterances are no essential part of any exposition of ideas, and are of such slight social value as a step to truth that any benefit that may be derived from them is clearly outweighed by the social interest in order and morality.

This stance by the Supreme Court in 1942 honored many of the state laws regulating obscenity then in existence; but, like preceding legal attempts to define obscenity, the problem continued to be how to interpret "lewd and obscene" and "slight social value." In the twentieth century, the recognized law had moved away from a Victorian-like aversion toward many materials with even isolated passages of obscene material to a more generalized and tolerant view that focused upon the dominant effect of the work in question.

Search for a National Standard: The *Roth* Test

Fifteen years after *Chaplinsky,* the Supreme Court began to stumble toward another definition of obscenity. In companion cases involving individuals who had been convicted of using the mails to distribute allegedly obscene materials, the Supreme Court reiterated that "obscenity is not within the area of constitutionally protected speech or press." Speaking for a six-member majority in *Roth* v. *United States* and *Alberts* v. *California* (1957), Justice Brennan stated that the First Amendment was intended to protect *ideas* and their "un-fettered interchange," but obscenity did not contain expressions worthy of protection, since it was "utterly without redeeming social importance." Brennan then fashioned a new standard that drew heavily upon historical antecedents, which considered obscene material as

> whether to the average person, applying contemporary community standards, the dominant theme of the material taken as a whole appeals to prurient interest.

Because the *Hicklin* rule focused upon isolated passages and the susceptibility of particular persons, it was too restrictive in its treatment of obscenity; therefore, a new standard was needed. Of the three justices who dissented in the *Roth* decision, Justice Douglas stated that this new test for determining what is obscene "gives the censor free range over a vast domain." As a result of this subjective judgment of what is obscene, "the test that suppresses a cheap tract today can suppress a literary gem tomorrow." Like Thomas Jefferson, John Stuart Mill, and Alexander Meiklejohn, Douglas was more comfortable with the innate ability of people to reject worthless literature in the same way that they might discount false theology, politics, economics, or other fields of thought.

Over the next several years, the Supreme Court struggled in numerous cases with this *Roth* test, which placed major emphasis upon "redeeming social importance," the "average person," "contemporary community standards" (which came to be interpreted as "national" standards), and the "dominant theme" of the material in question. The ambiguity of these terms prevented any consistent majority from adopting any one standard. It also meant that the Court had to look at the materials on a case-by-case basis. In 1973, the Court would adopt a new standard, but until then, the 1957 precedent would generate what one author has referred to as "the Grapes of Roth." [23]

The Aftermath of *Roth*

In the early 1960s, the *Roth* standard was modified slightly. In *Manual Enterprises* v. *Day* (1962), the Supreme Court overturned the lower court conviction of a firm engaged in the publication of magazines deliberately designed to appeal to homosexuals. In a majority opinion drafted by Justice Harlan, the Court added a new element to the previous appeal to "prurient interest in sex" guideline from *Roth* for regulating obscenity. The Court spoke of "patent offensiveness," which meant materials "so offensive on their face as to affront current community standards of decency." In overturning the conviction of the defendant, Harlan wrote that the photographs of male nude models in the magazines were no more objectionable than many portrayals of female models, which society tolerates. And since the magazines were presumably read almost entirely by male homosexuals, they would not appeal to the average adult, which was a major element of *Roth*.

In 1964, the ruling in another obscenity case added to the growing baggage surrounding this topic. In *Jacobellis* v. *Ohio* (1964), an Ohio court had convicted a theatre manager for showing an allegedly obscene film in violation of a state antiobscenity law. Dividing 6 to 3, the Supreme Court overturned the conviction, although the six-member majority could not agree upon a single majority opinion that summarized its rationale. Two justices (Goldberg and Brennan) tried to argue that the phrase "contemporary community standards" meant "national" standards. And Justice Brennan reiterated the *Roth* element defining obscenity as those materials "utterly without redeeming social importance." He then stated that "material dealing with sex in a manner that advocates ideas . . . or has literary or scientific or artistic value or any other form of social importance" is entitled to constitutional protection. One other excerpt from *Jacobellis,* perhaps the most memorable, was from Justice Stewart, who stated that although he could not specifically define obscenity, "I know it when I see it."

In 1966, the Supreme Court consolidated three obscenity cases for resolution, each of which added a new twist to evolving obscenity law. In the first case entitled *Memoirs of a Woman of Pleasure* v.*Massachusetts* (1966), the Court overturned a lower court judgment against distribution of the eighteenth-century novel *Fanny Hill* as an obscene book. Sharp disagreements among the justices emerged in this case, and the majority was unable to agree upon one opinion. But Justice Brennan, authoring a concurring opinion in which he was joined by two other justices, said that for material to be obscene, three elements must be present: (1) the dominant theme appeals to a prurient interest in sex; (2) it is patently offensive to contemporary community standards; and (3) it is without redeeming social value. The Supreme Court ruled that since the trial court had found the novel to have "some minimal literary value," it was not obscene under the new test.

Announced the same day as *Memoirs* was *Ginzburg* v. *United States* (1966). In this case, a New York publisher had been convicted in a federal district court for mailing obscene publications in violation of the Comstock Act. On appeal, the Supreme Court upheld the conviction, not because the material was obscene, but because the publisher was guilty of "pandering," which is "purveying textual or graphic matter openly advertised to appeal to the erotic interests" of consumers. The publisher had initially attempted to have some of his materials mailed from Intercourse and Blue Ball, Pennsylvania, in order to have their postmarks appear on the front. When these efforts failed, he succeeded in having them mailed from Middlesex, New Jersey. These actions led the Court majority, speaking through Justice Brennan, to conclude that the advertising was distinguished by "the leer of the sensualist." The *Ginzburg* ruling established the precedent that publishers and vendors are responsible for the manner in which they market particular materials. In a strong dissent in which he criticized the Court of suspending First Amendment protection for individuals simply because it disapproves of their business, Justice Stewart said that the Court was forsaking "a government of law" and replacing it with "government by Big Brother."

Also announced on the same day as *Memoirs* and *Ginzberg* was a third judgment in response to a rather novel rationale for selling obscene publications (see Brief 12.3). In reviewing these several decisions, a confusing line of precedent emerges. *Memoirs* found the Court adding "patent offensiveness" and "without redeeming social value" to the ambiguous *Roth* test; *Ginzburg* adopted "pandering," which deals more with the context in which materials are marketed, rather than the materials themselves; and *Mishkin* focused rather narrowly upon the sexual interests of a decidedly small group of individuals. In the years following these three cases, the Court overturned several lower court convictions unless they dealt with the distribution of obscene materials to

❏ Brief 12.3   What Actually Appeals to the "Average Person"?

One other decision handed down by the Supreme Court on March 21, 1966, was the case of *Mishkin* v. *New York*. This case involved a New York publisher who had been convicted of distributing such works as *Screaming Flesh, Mistress of Leather, Stud Broad, Queen Bee, Swish Bottom,* and *The Whipping Chorus Girls.* The books described unorthodox sexual behavior; as a consequence, the defendant contended that they would not appeal to an "average person" within the meaning of the *Roth* test.

The trial court did not agree with this rationale, nor did the Supreme Court on appeal. In a majority opinion upholding the conviction on a 6–3 vote, Justice Brennan reasoned that the *Roth* test still applied in this instance, since the prurient appeal requirement must be assessed "in terms of the sexual interests of its in-

tended and probable recipient group." But this focus upon an "intended and probable recipient group" was a definite addition to the distant *Roth* test, and the justices in the minority did not like the change effected by the majority. Among the three dissenters, Justice Black regretted the Court's performance as a "national board of censors." He also reiterated his insistence that the First Amendment should be interpreted in an absolutist manner:

> I think the Founders of our Nation in adopting the First Amendment meant precisely that the Federal Government should pass "no law" regulating speech and press but should confine its legislation to the regulation of conduct... the First Amendment ... leaves the States vast power to regulate conduct but no power at all, in my judgment, to make the expression of views a crime.

juveniles, nonconsenting adults, or consumers who had been attracted by pandering.[24]

In one of its rare displays of unity in an obscenity case, the Court delivered in 1969 a decision that was applauded by most courtwatchers. In the case of *Stanley* v. *Georgia,* a defendant had been convicted after police, armed with a search warrant for gambling materials, found movie film in his possession that was later judged to be obscene. The Georgia law under which he was convicted made *private possession* of such materials illegal. But a unanimous Supreme Court overturned the conviction. In a strongly worded majority opinion, Justice Marshall insisted that government "has no business telling a man, sitting alone in his own house, what books he may read or what films he may watch." Georgia insisted that it was obligated to protect the individual's mind from the effects of obscenity, but Marshall maintained that such action was neither constitutionally permissible nor empirically sound. According to Marshall:

> The State may no more prohibit mere possession of obscenity on the ground that it may lead to antisocial conduct than it may prohibit possession of chemistry books on the ground that they may lead to the manufacture of homemade spirits.

Summary of the National Standard

By the late 1960s, the Supreme Court had constructed a rather confused and imprecise *national* standard dealing with obscenity, sometimes referred to as "*Roth*-plus." To be judged obscene, materials had to be utterly without redeeming social value (*Jacobellis*) and sexually lewd to the average person (*Roth*) or the intended and probable recipient group (*Mishkin*); applying contemporary community standards (*Roth*), the dominant theme of the material as a whole had to appeal to a prurient sexual interest (*Roth*) or be advertised to appeal to prurient interests (*Ginzburg*). However, government could not punish a citizen for mere private possession of obscene materials intended for personal use (*Stanley*).

In addition to this cumbersome and confusing standard for judging obscenity, some political developments forecast continuing controversy and possible change. Richard Nixon was elected president in 1968 on a strong law-and-order platform that promised to restore the tranquility of an earlier decade—although by 1970, public protests over the expanding Vietnam War, civil rights, women's liberation, and other social issues were disrupting the social order. In 1969, President Nixon appointed Warren Burger, a law-and-order judge from the D.C. Court of Appeals, to replace the activist-libertarian Earl Warren as chief justice. By 1971, three more Nixon appointees joined Burger in fashioning what was expected to be a more conservative Court. The expectation was that the Burger Court would cut back on decisions supporting a strong free-speech/free-press agenda.

One other development occurred in the fall of 1970. On September 30, the President's Commission on Obscenity and Pornography, which had been appointed by former President Lyndon Johnson in 1967, released its final report. Among other things, the report recommended that the five federal laws, forty-eight state laws, and numerous local ordinances prohibiting the distribution of sexually explicit materials to consenting adults be repealed. Contrary to what President Nixon wanted to hear, the report alleged that the regulations had been "extremely unsatisfactory in their practical application," and their frequent misuse "constitutes a continuing threat to the free communication of ideas among Americans." [25]

Criticism of the report was immediate and broad-based. The U.S. Senate voted soon after the release of the report, with only five dissenting votes, to condemn it, and President Nixon's reaction to the report was very predictable. In a written statement released on October 24, he referred to its conclusions and recommendations as "morally bankrupt." He maintained that as president, there would be "no relaxation of the national effort to control and eliminate smut from our national life." In recognizing the constitutional issues at stake in the controversy, Nixon made a somewhat irrelevant comparison to individual freedom:

> I am well aware of the importance of protecting freedom of expression. But pornography is to freedom of expression what anarchy is to liberty; as free men willingly restrain a measure of their freedom to prevent anarchy, so must we draw the line against pornography to protect freedom of expression. [26]

Less than one year after this report, Nixon completed his appointment of the Burger Court. Within days of each other, Justices Hugo Black (who had served continually on the Court since 1937) and John Harlan announced their retirements. They were replaced by Justices William H. Rehnquist and Lewis F. Powell after a protracted struggle over two earlier nominees by President Nixon. With these important personnel changes and the publicity being given to law and order and "family values," a challenge to the *Roth*-plus standard was probably inevitable. As became clear within a few years, the Supreme Court tried to resolve the confusion by adopting a new, more restrictive guideline for evaluating obscenity.

A Change in Direction: Advent of a Local Standard

As the 1970s began, it was clear that the Supreme Court was still struggling with the problem of defining obscenity. Not since the *Roth* decision in 1957, had a majority been able to agree on a single definition of pornography. But that would change soon. The case that finally stirred a major change in obscenity law involved an individual in California who had been convicted under a state antiobscenity law for distributing obscene materials to recipients who apparently had not requested them. The trial judge instructed the jury hearing the case to evaluate the prurient nature of the materials based upon the *state* rather than a national standard for obscenity. The conviction was upheld by the state appellate court, and the defendant appealed to the U.S. Supreme Court.

A thin 5–4 majority in *Miller* v. *California* (1973) adopted a new standard to judge obscenity. For the materials to be judged obscene required the presence of any *one* of three elements:

> a) whether the "average person, applying contemporary community standards" would find that the work, taken as a whole, appeals to the prurient interest, b) whether the work depicts or describes, in a patently offensive way, sexual conduct specifically defined by the applicable state law, and c) whether the work, taken as a whole, lacks serious literary, artistic, political, or scientific value.

This new standard meant that the new majority was rejecting the "utterly without redeeming social value" element of *Jacobellis* and *Memoirs* and, more importantly, the prevailing *national* standard by which to evaluate what is obscene. A *local* standard was now being permitted in obscenity cases. In drafting the majority opinion, Chief Justice Burger explicitly stated that the First Amendment did not require any "hypothetical and unascertainable 'national standards' " for judging what is obscene. As he noted:

> It is neither realistic nor constitutionally sound to read the First Amendment as requiring that the people of Maine or Mississippi accept public depiction of conduct found tolerable in Las Vegas, or New York City . . . People in different States vary in their tastes and attitudes, and this diversity is not to be strangled by the absolutism of imposed uniformity.

In addition to the latitude for local obscenity standards, another important new direction stated by the Court in *Miller* was that the outlawed sexual conduct had to be "specifically defined by the applicable state law." In other words, if states or local communities were going to impose their own standards for defining obscenity, they had to get very specific in stating what kinds of sexual conduct would be unlawful. According to Burger, such examples of what the state or locality could define for regulation included

> patently offensive representations or descriptions of ultimate sexual acts, normal or perverted, actual or simulated . . . [or] of masturbation, excretory functions, and lewd exhibition of the genitals.

Of the four dissenters in the decision, Justice Douglas insisted that the decision would effect censorship at the state and local levels. "To send men to jail for violating standards they cannot understand, construe, and apply," said Douglas, "is a monstrous thing to do in a Nation dedicated to fair trials and due process." To Douglas, it was immaterial whether the guideline for evaluating what is "obscene" was national, state, or local. Expecting the courts at *any* level to rule on materials that some find "offensive" while others consider them to be "staid" was asking the impossible. For, as Justice Harlan noted in *Cohen* v. *California* (1971), "One man's vulgarity is another's lyric" (see Chapter 11).

Another case decided the same day as *Miller, Paris Adult Theatre* v. *Slaton* (1973), raised some other important questions. Many issues arose in this case: the rights of consenting adults; the burden of proof in defining what is obscene; the relationship between exposure to pornography and antisocial behavior; and, finally, the degree to which state-local regulators may depart from elements of the new standard announced in *Miller*. In upholding the conviction of an Atlanta theatre owner for showing obscene films to consenting adults, a Burger majority dismissed the assumption that simply because adults freely choose to view such matter does not cloak it with constitutional protection. Burger also insisted that rather than the state having to prove that the questionable material was in fact obscene, it actually fell to the defendant (theatre owner) to prove that it was *not* obscene. In other words, if an individual runs afoul of a local regulation on obscenity, he or she is assumed to be guilty until proven innocent. Concerning the question of causality, Burger observed that "[although] there is no conclusive proof of a connection between antisocial behavior and obscene material, the legislature of Georgia could quite reasonably determine that such a connection does or might exist." And, finally, the chief justice said that states can regulate the sale and display of obscene materials in public accommodations, including adult theatres from which minors are excluded by law.

The major dissenting opinion in *Paris Adult Theatre*, authored by Justice Brennan, reveals the increasing frustration of some with the Court's efforts to define and regulate pornography. After noting the inability to define obscenity, the continuing problems that would follow from *Miller*, and the unacceptability of the several alternatives for dealing with the material, Brennan concluded, like the president's commission a few years earlier, that regulation should not be practiced except in situations involving juveniles or "obtrusive exposure to unconsenting adults." On the same day as *Miller* and *Paris Adult Theatre*, the Court also released three other decisions that held that (1) a book consisting only of narrative was obscene under the new *Miller* standard; and (2) material destined for private use could be denied entry into the United States as obscene material.[27]

Continued Areas for Adjudication of Obscenity Law

In spite of the limitations imposed by resort to a *local* community standard under *Miller*, it should not be assumed that the Court has abdicated *all* responsibility for interpreting and applying First Amendment protection. Since 1973, the Supreme Court on several occasions has disposed of obscenity cases brought by parties insisting that state-local restrictions were too limiting. Most of the cases have dealt with three areas: (1) debate over content and whether it is obscene; (2) the "reasonableness" of several time, place, and manner restrictions on obscenity; and (3) child pornography.

In the case of *Jenkins* v. *Georgia* (1974), the Court expanded upon what it had meant by the phrase "patently offensive sexual conduct," used in *Miller*

v. *California*. A Georgia trial court and the state supreme court had found the popular film *Carnal Knowledge* to be obscene; but, in 1974, a unanimous Supreme Court overturned the lower court finding and said that the film did not depict or describe hard-core sexual conduct as described in *Miller*. Notwithstanding some nudity in the film, the Court held that "nudity alone is not enough to make material legally obscene" under the *Miller* standard. The major implication to be drawn from *Jenkins* v. *Georgia* is that local authorities do not have unbridled authority to define obscenity on the basis of local sensitivities and preferences.

A second area of continuing activity by the Court concerns the constitutionality of certain types of regulation dealing with obscenity. Several Supreme Court cases have involved local jurisdictions imposing "anti-Skid Row" zoning restrictions in order to disperse the location of "adults only" bookstores, theatres, and bars. A very divided Supreme Court ruled in *Young* v. *American Mini Theatres* (1976) that a local zoning ordinance in Detroit restricting such facilities within 1,000 feet of each other or within 500 feet of a residential area did not violate either the First Amendment or the Equal Protection Clause of the Fourteenth Amendment. The majority held that the city could regulate the place where such activities could occur, and its interest "in the present and future character of its neighborhood adequately supports its classification of motion pictures." In a dissenting opinion joined by Justices Brennan, Marshall, and Blackmun, Justice Stewart criticized the majority for riding "roughshod over cardinal principles of First Amendment law."

Finally, when the issue deals with child pornography, the Court has been quick to impose stern restrictions. As with several issues concerning children in American society, child pornography has leaped onto the public agenda in recent years in ways that have made it virtually impossible for policymakers to avoid. During the 1970s and early 1980s, such issues as child abuse, sexual molestation, and kidnapping became a *cause célèbre* that galvanized a wide spectrum of political, economic, and social forces behind an effort to eradicate sexual exploitation of adolescents in American society. In July 1982, the Supreme Court upheld a New York law that made it illegal for persons to knowingly promote a sexual performance by a child under sixteen years of age by distributing any material which depicts a real or simulated act. In the case of *New York* v. *Ferber* (1982), a unanimous Court, with Justice White writing the majority opinion, noted that child pornography had become a "serious national problem" and Congress and forty-seven states had enacted laws that restricted it. Twenty states, including New York, had prohibited the distribution of material depicting children engaged in sexual acts without requiring that the material itself was legally obscene. In upholding the New York law and the conviction of an individual prosecuted under that law, Justice White said that states had greater leeway in regulating child pornography than they did other obscene materials because of a "compelling" state interest, the need to curb materials that encourage continued sexual abuse of minors, and the fact that, in the balance of competing interests, "the evil to be restricted so overwhelmingly outweighs the expressive interests . . . at stake."

The preceding discussion has covered several aspects of obscenity case law: nineteenth-century struggles over how to define obscenity, early twentieth-century modifications of those definitions, the *Roth* and *Miller* precedents, and several decisions following each of these critical redirections. Several major questions about this critical area of legal interpretation suggest certain moral, definitional, constitutional, and psychological dimensions of the entire issue of obscenity:

1. Does government have a right or obligation to censor the moral messages and images that adult citizens receive, or should it be entirely left to the discretion of citizens to choose what they read, view, or listen to?

2. Given the difficulty that American courts and legislatures have experienced during the past century, is it possible to define *clearly* what "obscenity" is? If so, who is best suited to define it and for what duration?

3. Given what has been established thus far in this text regarding the First Amendment freedoms of speech and press, which, if any, of the major definitions of obscenity is more firmly rooted in the Constitution?

4. Should the First Amendment protect legally obscene materials which speakers/publishers see as the only available means by which to communicate their message or persuade their audience to accept certain unorthodox forms of sexual activity?

5. Finally, what does past experience of this muddled area of constitutional law suggest about either the individualistic or the communitarian models for describing the prevailing political culture of American society?

These questions are not easily answered, which is precisely why they have troubled policymakers for decades. The moral, semantic, legal, and psychological nature of these questions continues to pose a wide spectrum of views for debate in the twentieth century. The student of freedom of expression confronts them nearly every time he or she examines recent developments in obscenity law. There is no complete and infallible answer to what Justice Harlan referred to many years ago as "the intractable obscenity problem." [28] Because of the major definitional problems surrounding obscenity, the potential damage done to free expression by most attempts to prohibit sexually explicit materials, and the immense burden placed upon policymakers in struggling with obscenity disputes, there is merit to Justice Brennan's attempt in *Paris Adult Theatre* to forge a new path on the subject. Brennan suggested that the First and Fourteenth Amendments should be interpreted as prohibiting *all* restrictions on obscene materials, except those being distributed to juveniles or thrust upon unconsenting adults. This standard would still require courts to hear controversies regarding obscenity, but the list of cases would be much shorter, and the competing interests more easily reconciled. In this respect, differing views of individual expression could more legitimately be aired in a free society, and perhaps the "intractable obscenity problem" might become more manageable.

The Law of Libel and the First Amendment

Question: In the 1980s, what did actress-comedienne Carol Burnett, General William Westmoreland, and former Israeli Defense Minister Ariel Sharon have in common? *Answer:* According to them, "bad press" as a result of stories fabricated by the media about their public lives and behavior. [29] These three individuals all sued for libel damages against particular elements of the American mass media because of stories they believed erroneously defamed them as public figures.

As many of the cases discussed in this chapter indicate, the courts have held that, except for very rare instances, the press may not be restrained in advance. But it must take responsibility for what it says and, on occasion, it can be punished for what it says. **Libel** can be defined as the written defamation of a person's reputation or character. Like obscenity, during the 1960s libel underwent a major change in the manner in which it was interpreted under the First Amendment.

Background to Libel Law in the United States

Laws that punish individuals for defamation of character by either the spoken or written word (slander and libel, respectively) have ancient origins. Ancient Greece and Rome prohibited accusations against the dead or criticism of public officials or private citizens in any manner which tended to damage the personal reputation of the individual. Fifteenth- and sixteenth-century England also had laws that punished those who criticized seditiously the policies of political and religious leaders. Although there is disagreement about whether the First Amendment's guarantee of a free press was supposed to prevent Congress from passing seditious libel laws that prohibited criticism of government policy, some of the most controversial legislation ever passed in the United States were the Alien and Sedition Acts by the Federalist-controlled Congress in 1798 (see Chapter 6). They were immediately criticized by the Democratic-Republican party of Jefferson and Madison and never really enforced by President John Adams, who considered them unconstitutional. They eventually expired in 1800. Their constitutionality was never examined by the Supreme Court, and later justices on the Court also considered them to be unconstitutional, including the Court in *New York Times* v. *Sullivan*.[30]

The law of libel underwent great change in the twentieth century until eventually by the 1960s, general criticism of governmental policy and public officials by the media was seen as protected by the First Amendment. However, as discussed in Chapter 11 on free speech, criticism of government may be considered at times to be seditious speech or press which threatens to interfere with national policy (i.e., the Sedition Act of 1918 and the Smith Act of 1940). As these earlier discussions indicated, expressions tolerable in peacetime can be repressed in time of war or perceived national crisis.

A few important statements by the Supreme Court prior to the 1960s are relevant to this discussion of the evolving law of libel. In addition to *Near*, the Court in *Chaplinsky* v. *New Hampshire* (1942) found libelous statements, obscenity, profanity, "fighting words," and statements threatening national security to be outside the bounds of First Amendment protection, since they were not an "essential part of any exposition of ideas." A decade later, in the case of *Beauharnais* v. *Illinois* (1952), a 5–4 Supreme Court majority upheld the conviction of a private citizen who had been convicted under a state libel law prohibiting any publication that made defamatory or derogatory remarks about "a class of citizens of any race, color, creed or religion." Writing for the majority, Justice Felix Frankfurter reiterated that libelous statements did not constitute protected speech. Four justices in dissent each criticized the state law as too restrictive and violative of free expression.

But in another closely divided decision in 1959, *Barr* v. *Matteo*, the Court held that federal officials, even if acting "within the outer perimeter" of their official duties, have an absolute immunity from libel suits for statements made by them against other individuals. Of course, if they are found to be acting beyond their official duties, they can be prosecuted as private citizens for having violated the laws. The important distinction in these last two cases is that *Beauharnais* involved a *private* citizen making libelous statements against a particular racial group, whereas the latter case concerned statements made by *public* officials. The assumption made by the majority in *Barr* v. *Matteo* was that public officials should enjoy the widest possible latitude while performing their public duties.

Historically, the truth of a particular statement by a publisher was an adequate defense in a libel suit brought by an individual claiming to have been libeled. But the truth is sometimes hard to prove in certain instances. Demanding that a publisher "prove" the truth of political opinion or judgment could result in self-censorship and a constraint upon the airing of ideas and issues in a newspaper. As a result, several states passed laws during the twentieth century that protected publishers from libel suits. If a defamatory statement were false but made in "good faith" that it was true, it was known as **simple malice**. If it were deliberately false or displayed a reckless disregard for the truth, it was known as **actual malice**. This particular rule, which was eventually adopted by the U.S. Supreme Court nearly a half-century later, was stated by the Kansas Supreme Court in 1908, in a libel suit brought by a political candidate against a newspaper publisher (*Coleman* v. *McLennan,* 98 P 281 [1908]). Political criticism of public officials was virtually outside the realm of libel law, except in those instances where deliberate, malicious falsehoods could be proven. But for the first half of the twentieth century, libel law had been almost entirely a matter for *state* courts to decide, and there was great variability in how the states discharged their libel law responsibilities. A major unanswered question regarding the law of libel into the 1960s was whether public officials could sue for libel against those who criticized them for their performance of official duties.

Public Officials and the Actual-Malice Doctrine

Prior to the early 1960s, public officials could sue for libel damages if they could prove that statements made about them were false, and courts generally awarded damages to officials who were falsely accused or depicted in news stories. This trend changed noticeably after the landmark decision of *New York Times* v. *Sullivan* in 1964. The case involved a city commissioner in Montgomery, Alabama, L. B. Sullivan, who had responsibilities for managing the municipal police department. Sullivan had sued the *New York Times* and four black clergymen for allegedly libelous statements made in a March 1960 issue of the newspaper. The *Times* had carried a paid advertisement which stated that "truckloads of police armed with shotguns and tear-gas ringed Alabama State College Campus" in the city and that "the Southern violators [had] bombed [Dr. Martin Luther King, Jr.'s] home, assaulted his person [and] arrested him seven times." Some of the statements in the advertisement were later found to have been false, and Sullivan was able to prove in state court that he had not participated in the incidents attributed to him or his department. Under Alabama libel law, an official had only to prove that the statements were false. Upon such a finding in this case, the court awarded Sullivan $500,000 in damages. The Alabama Supreme Court upheld the verdict against the newspaper and the award. The newspaper objected to these findings and to the implication that the First Amendment did not protect the media from libel suits brought by public officials against criticisms of their official conduct if those statements were proven to be false.

In 1964, the U.S. Supreme Court delivered a unanimous decision which said that the First Amendment *does* protect publishers from those seeking libel damages, although that protection is not unlimited. Writing for six of the nine justices, Brennan emphasized both the then-raging civil rights debate in the country (which had occasioned the original advertisement) and the crucial role and function of the press in a free society:

> We consider this case against the background of a profound national commitment to the principle that debate on public issues should be uninhibited, robust, and wide-open, and that it may well include vehement, caustic, and sometimes unpleasantly sharp attacks on government and public officials. . . The present advertisement, as an expression of grievance and protest on one of the major public issues of our time, would seem clearly to qualify for the constitutional protection. The question is whether it forfeits that protection by the falsity of some of its factual statements and by its alleged defamation of [Sullivan].

Brennan maintained that a rule compelling a publisher to prove the absolute truth of all statements made in print would be comparable to "self-censorship," and thereby "[dampen] the vigor and [limit] the variety of public debate." Relying heavily upon a restated *McLennan* rule from the 1908 decision, Brennan stated what has become known as the actual-malice or *Times-Sullivan* doctrine. Before public officials can be awarded libel damages for any statement made about their official conduct, they must first prove that the statement was made with "actual-malice—that is, with knowledge that it was false or with reckless disregard of whether it was false or not."

Applying this rule to the *Sullivan* case, the Court was unable to find grounds for actual malice. Although the newspaper's staff might have verified the truthfulness of some of the statements with considerable effort, and some evidence did suggest "negligence in failing to discover the misstatements," there was no proof of actual malice. Three concurring justices—Black, Douglas, and Goldberg—agreed with the holding but chose not to join the majority opinion, arguing that the First Amendment granted *absolute* immunity to newspapers being sued for libel. Justice Black held that state libel laws "threaten the very existence of an American press virile enough to publish unpopular views on public affairs" and bold enough to criticize conduct of those officials. And, in a separate concurring opinion, Justice Arthur Goldberg anticipated a future issue surrounding what is meant by actual malice: can "freedom of speech . . . be effectively safeguarded by a rule allowing the imposition of liability upon a jury's evaluation of the speaker's state of mind?" This point would be raised fifteen years later in the case of *Herbert* v. *Lando*.

As with many landmark decisions, the *Times-Sullivan* case immediately raised new legal questions. The case involved *civil* libel, meaning that it was initiated by Sullivan for pecuniary damages. Had the newspaper been found guilty of libel, it would have had to pay a fine and a financial award to Sullivan, but no jail term could have been imposed. Thus, it left unanswered the question of whether actual malice must be proven in *criminal* libel suits.

The Supreme Court addressed this important question soon thereafter in the case of *Garrison* v. *Louisiana* (1964). The role of the press was indirect in this case in that the newspapers were reporting charges levied by Jim Garrison, the controversial district attorney of New Orleans, against state judges he accused of being inefficient, lazy, and hindering his investigation of crime in the city. As a consequence of his charges, he was convicted under a state criminal libel law that prohibited statements made with actual malice or false statements made with ill will or a reasonable belief that they were inaccurate. In reviewing this case, the U.S. Supreme Court ruled unanimously that Garrison's conviction was illegal under the actual-malice doctrine, and the Louisiana law was declared unconstitutional. As a result of this decision, the *Times-Sullivan* doctrine was applied to both civil and criminal libel suits. The Brennan opinion for the Court said that public debate on important issues would be inhibited "if the speaker must run the risk that it will be proved in court that he spoke out of hatred." Claiming that the libel doctrine would not unleash rampant criticism or accusation, Brennan said that "speech concerning public affairs . . . is the essence of self-government."

Public Figures and Actual Malice

By implication, *New York Times* v. *Sullivan* also raised the issue of whether the actual-malice doctrine applied only to public officials, or whether it also applied to what might be termed "public figures." Justice Brennan defined "public official" in a 1966 case as including "those among the hierarchy of government employees who have, or appear to the public to have, substantial responsibility for or control over the conduct of government affairs." [31] Since 1971, the Court has also considered candidates for public office to be "public officials." [32] Defining "public figure" is much more problematic, as several cases during the past two decades indicate.

Soon after the *Times-Sullivan* case, the Court was asked to apply the actual-malice test to libel suits brought by individuals who were not public "officials" as defined by previous precedents, but were allegedly "public figures" by virtue of publicity or notoriety in their profession or industry. Two cases in 1967 addressed themselves to this question. *Curtis Publishing Co.* v. *Butts* involved a suit brought by the athletic director at the University of Georgia, Wallace Butts, against the publisher of the *Saturday Evening Post.* The magazine had printed a story in which it had accused Butts of "fixing" a football game by revealing significant portions of his team's strategy to Coach Paul "Bear" Bryant of the University of Alabama. The original trial was conducted prior to the *Times-Sullivan* decision being announced; Butts convinced the trial court of the magazine's careless investigation and preparation of the story, and he was awarded $480,000 in damages. In a related case, *Associated Press* v. *Walker* (1967), a trial court had awarded libel damages to a retired army general, Edwin A. Walker, the commander of federal troops policing the integration of the University of Mississippi in 1958. The Associated Press had alleged in a copyrighted story that Walker had contributed to a riot at the school as a consequence of his official conduct. The Supreme Court accepted both cases on appeal, unanimously reversing the award given in the *Walker* case, but dividing 5–4 and upholding the libel award to Butts.

In handling these two cases, the justices all agreed that defamatory publications concerning "public figures" were entitled to some First Amendment protection, but they differed over how much protection. Four of the justices (Harlan, Stewart, Clark, and Fortas) favored applying a less rigorous standard for proving libel, three of the majority (Warren, Brennan, and White) would have applied the actual-malice test, and two (Black and Douglas) believed that the First Amendment accorded *absolute* immunity to the press from libel suits. In the formal opinion for the Court, Justice Harlan said that a public figure could recover damages for a defamatory falsehood

> whose substance makes substantial danger to reputation apparent, on a showing of highly unreasonable conduct constituting an extreme departure from the standards of investigation and reporting ordinarily adhered to by reasonable publishers.

In applying a less stringent standard of an individual's proving "substantial damage to reputation," Harlan said that the magazine had failed to take the necessary journalistic precautions before printing the story about Butts. However, the libel award to Walker had to be overturned because there was no "departure from accepted journalistic standards." The major difference in these two cases, from Harlan's perspective, was that the *Post*, being a magazine, was not under the same press deadlines as a wire service was, and it should have verified the facts before printing the story.

Another libel case many years later dealt with this issue of public figures, and a new issue concerning the sanctity of the editorial process. *Herbert* v. *Lando* (1979) raised the important question, How far must a public figure seeking libel damages go in proving actual malice? Following his retirement from the U.S. Army, Lt. Colonel Anthony Herbert publicly accused military personnel of committing atrocities in Vietnam, most notably in the infamous My Lai Massacre for which Lt. William Calley was eventually court-martialed. Herbert's accusations were aired in a February 1973 segment of the CBS weekly news magazine program *60 Minutes*. The CBS producer of the program, Barry Lando, also authored an article that appeared in the *Atlantic Monthly* which raised serious questions about the accusations and service activities of the retired officer. Herbert ultimately sued CBS, Lando, and reporter Mike Wallace for defamation of character. In order to prove that the defendants were guilty of actual malice, Herbert's attorneys tried to question the defendants about several matters, including their prebroadcast assumptions and beliefs surrounding the reports of military wrongdoing. Lando refused to answer any questions concerning his thoughts, attitudes, or conclusions about the broadcast, claiming that the First Amendment protected the editorial process from inquiry. The district court found in favor of Herbert and directed Lando to answer all inquiries, the appellate court reversed that judgment, and the case was then accepted for review by the Supreme Court.

In 1979, the high court ruled 6–3 that the First Amendment does *not* protect the editorial process. Contrary to the network's argument regarding freedom of the press, Lando was informed that he had to answer relevant questions concerning his prebroadcast/prepublication thoughts, conclusions, and general state of mind about the subject. The majority opinion written by Justice White mentioned that plaintiffs in libel cases must be allowed to prove their case by resorting to "direct as well as indirect evidence" in order to discourage the publication of "erroneous information known to be false or probably false." The justices in the majority did not think that frank discussion among reporters and editors would be endangered by requiring them to answer occasional inquiries in libel suits directed toward proving actual malice. Three dissenters in this case (Justices Brennan, Stewart, and Marshall), for different reasons, felt that the editorial process should be shielded from such inquiries.

Private Individuals and the Law of Libel

The distinction between public officials, public figures, and private citizens initiating libel suits has been refined somewhat in many cases over several years. To conclude this discussion of libel law and freedom of the press, three recent cases warrant some attention. In 1974, the Supreme Court argued that individuals who act only temporarily as public figures by thrusting themselves into some public activity or speaking out on some public issue of the time need not adhere to the same standard as public officials or public figures who occupy positions of "persuasive power and influence." The case of *Gertz* v. *Welch* in 1974 found the Court modifying somewhat the ground rules by which states can determine liability in libel cases. In an inflammatory article appearing in the April 1969 issue of *American Opinion*, published by the John Birch Society, the author had referred to Chicago attorney Elmer Gertz as a "Leninist" with a criminal record, an "architect" in a "communist frameup" of a policeman accused of shooting a teenager, and a "communist fronter" seeking to discredit local law enforcement. Gertz sued the magazine for libel. During the trial, the judge informed the jury that since Gertz was neither a public official nor a public figure, actual malice need not be proven. The jury found in favor of Gertz and against the magazine, but the presiding judge dismissed the judgment in light of a case then pending before the U.S. Supreme Court. This case ruled that the actual-malice doctrine extended to *subjects* of general public interest, even when the person seeking damages was a *private citizen*.

In accepting *Gertz* v. *Welch* (1974) for review, the Supreme Court had to deal with the issue of whether a newspaper, magazine, or broadcaster that proclaims a **defamatory falsehood** about a private citizen is immune from liability in libel suits. A five-member majority in the decision ruled that the actual-malice doctrine did not apply in libel cases brought by private citizens. In this instance, *American Opinion* was liable for its statements under a less rigorous standard. In a majority opinion, Justice Powell stated that many private citizens have not *voluntarily* thrust themselves into the spotlight, nor sought greater public scrutiny for their actions. A private person, said Powell,

> has not accepted public office nor assumed an "influential role in ordering society" . . . He has relinquished no part of his interest in the protection of his own good name, and consequently he has a more compelling call on the courts for redress of injury inflicted by defamatory falsehood.

As a result, states should have more latitude in defining for their citizens the appropriate liability standard in libel suits brought by private citizens against the media.

Gertz v. *Welch* clarified some important matters regarding libel suits brought by private citizens. First, because private individuals are entitled to more protection from media statements than public officials or public figures who voluntarily thrust themselves before the public eye through their profession (e.g., entertainers, professional athletes, television personalities), actual malice need not be proven to award damages in a libel suit. Defamatory falsehood is sufficient to prove libel. Second, since media defendants must be protected under the First Amendment, each state can establish its own minimum standard of fault, as long as that standard can demonstrate "negligence" by the media. Finally, in order to limit liability of the media in such suits, only actual damages to an individual's reputation can be awarded, rather than presumed or punitive damages. Hypothetical or possible damage to reputation is immaterial; demonstration of actual damage is necessary.

Another case in the late 1970s cast further light upon the distinction between public figure and private citizen. *Hutchinson* v. *Proxmire* (1979) involved an otherwise obscure research scientist, Ronald Hutchinson, who had attracted considerable publicity by virtue of his having received one of Sen. William Proxmire's (D-Wis.) infamous Golden Fleece awards. Proxmire had accused Hutchinson on the Senate floor of receiving federal money from two different sources for work on aggression in monkeys. Hutchinson sued the senator for libel on the grounds that he had suffered both professional disrepute and mental anguish as a consequence of the accusations. On appeal, the Supreme Court held that Hutchinson was not a public figure by virtue of his having received a federal grant; therefore, he did not have to prove the same actual malice demanded of public figures. A less rigorous standard was acceptable for awarding libel damages, and the Court ruled that Senator Proxmire could be sued for libel damages.

In early 1986, the Supreme Court decided a case that was applauded by most media news organizations. In the case of *Philadelphia Newspapers, Inc.* v. *Hepps* (1986), the Court ruled 5–4 that a private individual suing a newspaper for libel must prove that damaging statements are false, at least on "matters of public concern." The case involved a Philadelphia businessman who had been accused in a series of articles appearing in the *Philadelphia Inquirer* in 1975–76 of having links to organized crime and using those connections to influence the political process. Under Pennsylvania libel law, which was similar to that in eight other states, the defendant in a libel suit must prove that the allegedly defamatory statements are true. The trial court ruled that the state law was unconstitutional and that the plaintiff had to prove the falsity of the charges. The state supreme court reversed that decision and the newspaper appealed to the U.S. Supreme Court, which declared the state law unconstitutional and ruled in favor of the newspaper.

According to Justice Sandra Day O'Connor who crafted the majority opinion, the key points were that the case was brought by a private individual and that the speech being examined involved "matters of public concern." In citing several of the precedents discussed earlier (*Sullivan, Gertz, Garrison,* and *Herbert*), O'Connor favored great latitude for the press:

> To ensure that true speech on matters of public concern is not deterred, we hold that the common-law presumption that defamatory speech is false cannot stand.

She also recognized that, in some instances, falsehoods would be punished but cited *Gertz* to reinforce the principle that "the First Amendment requires that we protect some falsehood in order to protect speech that matters." In dissent, Justice Stevens likened the majority ruling to an "obvious blueprint for character assassination" and trading "on the good names of private individuals with little First Amendment coin to show for it."

In the 1990s, the *Times-Sullivan* doctrine may well undergo some modification, pending personnel changes on the Supreme Court and a changing public mood about the news media. The elevation of William Rehnquist to the chief justiceship and the appointment of Antonin Scalia have brought to the high court judicial temperaments much less inclined to grant the mass media such wide discretion as has been enjoyed under the formidable actual-malice test. In two of the recent libel suits mentioned earlier, even though that doctrine was preserved, the press did not emerge unscathed. The suit by Israeli General Ariel Sharon against Time, Inc., which had accused him of complicity in the 1984 massacre of Palestinian refugees, resulted in no finding of actual malice in some errors by *Time*'s reporters. But a trial court reprimanded the magazine for its preventable errors in news gathering and reporting of Sharon's role in the incident. And in the case brought by General William Westmoreland against CBS for its documentary "The Uncounted Enemy: A Vietnam Deception," the retired general withdrew his suit when it became increasingly clear that actual malice would be nearly impossible to prove. But few who followed the trial believed, as CBS had intimated, that Westmoreland had *deliberately* conspired to deceive President Johnson about war casualties. In the libel case involving comedienne Carol Burnett, a California trial court did find actual malice and thus ruled in favor of Burnett and against the *National Enquirer*. The court ordered the tabloid to pay $300,000 in libel damages for a recklessly inaccurate story about the actress.

As the mass media have become more pervasive in their ability to influence what the viewer thinks and thinks about, so have the intuitive misgivings about the behavior of some media practitioners and the status of libel law (see Brief 12.4). Here, as in so many areas of constitutional law, it will be interesting to see if the Court will reflect that public view in its interpretation of the law and how it will secure its decisions within the U.S. Constitution.

Conclusion

Most students of press rights would agree that the United States probably has the most open and diverse communications and media industry in the world. To a significant degree, that openness and diversity are a direct consequence of the manner in which this nation has been able to avoid prior restraints being imposed by government. The constitutional landscape has been surprisingly free of government censorship of the media in the United States, much more so than has the record of government regulation of political speech. Like other First Amendment freedoms, the courts have never interpreted press rights as absolutes in and by themselves, for on rare occasions, prior restraints are tolerated, as some of the cases in this chapter have indicated.

The contemporary student of a free press should remember that unlike other First Amendment freedoms of speech, assembly, and religion, freedom of the press by definition employs an intermediary to transmit the message from the sender to the receiver. This dependence upon a medium—be it newspaper, film, photograph, or broadcast—can complicate protection of this important constitutional right. While the medium can either enhance or detract from the message, depending upon the context, purpose, and professional competence of the messenger, reliance upon that intermediary can also make

☐ *Brief 12.4   Flynt and the Preacher: The* Hustler *Magazine Parody of Jerry Falwell*

In 1983, *Hustler* magazine ran an ad parody on the Reverend Jerry Falwell. The ad portrayed the prominent Baptist minister as having had a drunken and incestuous rendezvous with his mother in an outhouse. The fictionalized interview with Falwell quoted the former head of Moral Majority as saying, "I always get sloshed before I go out to the pulpit." Falwell sued the magazine and its controversial publisher, Larry Flynt, for libel damages. A Virginia court ruled in his favor, awarding him $200,000 in damages for what the jury considered to be "emotional distress." Later, a divided federal appellate court in Richmond upheld the damage award to Falwell. Even though the interview parody was not libelous under the actual-malice doctrine of *Times-Sullivan,* inasmuch as it was not intended to be interpreted as factually correct, the appellate court said that it was "sufficiently outrageous" to justify damages on grounds of "intentional infliction of emotional distress."

In February 1988, in a ruling that surprised many courtwatchers and bouyed civil libertarians, the U.S. Supreme Court unanimously overturned the lower court judgment. In *Hustler Magazine* v. *Falwell* (1988), the Court ruled 8–0 (Justice Kennedy had not joined the Court in time to hear oral argument) that the First Amendment protects even "vehement, caustic and sometimes unpleasantly sharp attacks." Chief Justice Rehnquist, who often has adopted a rather constricted view of the First Amendment's protection of speech and press rights, stated that "we must decide whether a public figure may recover damages for emotional harm caused by the publication of an ad parody offensive to him, and doubtless gross and repugnant in the eyes of most." In citing and quoting liberally from the long line of decisions since *Roth* in 1957, Rehnquist thus cut off any chance that the actual-malice test would be modified when publications involved obviously fictitious caricatures of social or political events or persons. As might be expected, Reverend Falwell expressed dismay at the Court ruling, saying that "no sleaze merchant like Larry Flynt should be able to use the First Amendment as an excuse for maliciously and dishonestly attacking public figures as he has so often done."[33]

it more difficult to devise any one standard that will adequately protect the audience.

Of the several moral, definitional, constitutional, and technological problems that surround the free press issue, it is probably the *technological* dimension that in future years will compel the courts to modify their approaches to interpreting and applying press law. For example, the destructive capacity of modern weaponry, and therefore the stakes of potential global confrontation, compel governments, even democratic ones, to keep a large body of information from their people. Many of the Supreme Court judgments noted in earlier sections of this chapter find the American government seeking prior restraints in order to protect national security.

With respect to a free press and a defendant's right to a fair trial, broadcast media have pressured the courts to consider certain changes in the law. As is so often the case when adjudicating disputes involving the Bill of Rights, the main reason that press-trial cases present such difficult controversies to resolve is that they involve not one, but two, rights—the defendant's right to be treated fairly and justly under the law and the public's corresponding right to be informed. Without an enterprising and investigative media operating to counter government's monopoly on coercion, a people would rapidly lose their precious freedoms as the state moved to consolidate its power over the citizenry.

And even though obscenity law seems at first glance to be preoccupied with the definitional and moral questions surrounding what people see, hear, and view, and what the role of governments should be in regulating this activity, technological developments in cable networks, satellite dishes, home videos and fiber optics raise several questions about privacy, ownership, copyright, and access to the airwaves that jurists must ponder. Finally, libel law has undergone great change in the late twentieth century with the advent of television and potentially ruinous character assassination for personal, political, or economic gain. But the courts have insisted that particularly with public officials, the public is entitled to a full debate on and criticism of their leaders, without which an important check upon irresponsible power would eventually disappear.

In summary, the guarantee of a free press in the twentieth century is continually changing, in part because of the different media by which people communicate with each other. Print, film, and broadcast media are changing so rapidly that they will constantly challenge the courts to stay abreast of those changes in order to safeguard this crucial First Amendment freedom. Every innovation in this vast communications network will compel judges to reconsider existing case law and judicial policy. The only alternative will be for the law to become an irrelevant vestige of an earlier and simpler era. The courts must remain current or else be swept aside by the rush of a citizenry experimenting with novel forms of expression, communication, and creativity.

Questions

1. Like other First Amendment freedoms, freedom of the press has never attracted a majority of the Supreme Court arguing that press rights should be interpreted in an absolutist manner. Since the *Near* case in 1931, the Court has condoned prior restraints upon the press's right to publish under certain rare and unique circumstances. Do you think that the few exceptions cited in *Near* are equally legitimate? Are some more legitimate than others?

2. In recent years, some states have begun to experiment with allowing cameras in the courtroom, which results in certain constitutional problems in protecting the public's right to know and the defendant's right to a fair trial. What kinds of fair trial accommodations should a judge be attentive to when allowing cameras and reporters in the courtroom during a prominent trial? Under what circumstances is a gag order justified? Do you think that a protective order limiting media coverage is more likely to protect the defendant's right to a fair trial or disguise the government's ability to dominate the trial proceedings?

3. The area of obscenity law has confounded the legal system for decades. Do you think that the *Miller* standard reflects this frustration of the federal courts to derive a clear and pragmatic definition of what is "obscene"? Or is the new standard merely the recognition that personal tastes and tolerance levels are so varied that no one standard is practical? Does this local standard mean that there is unequal treatment of individuals and their right to express themselves based upon regional disparities of obscenity standards? What aspects of obscene material do you find most offensive and legitimate for regulation?

4. The law of libel since the *Times-Sullivan* doctrine has allowed for great protection and encouragement of free press rights. To what extent has this actual-malice doctrine been a license for the media to range far and wide for material that seriously damages the status and reputations of public officials and public figures? Do you think that public officials should expect much of their privacy to be reduced when they assume public office? Does this considerable sacrifice deter many potential leaders from pursuing the prize of high electoral office? Do you think the actual-malice doctrine needs to be revised in some ways?

5. A reporter's assertion that to be forced to divulge his or her sources will very quickly result in fewer reliable sources has major implications for news gathering and dissemination of the public's business. Given the fact that several states have both before and since *Branzburg* passed state shield laws, to what extent do you think that this is a matter that should be left entirely to the states? Should courts be allowed to intervene and occasionally override state shield laws in order to assist in the apprehension of criminals? Should a clear distinction be made between *criminal* and *civil* proceedings and the power of government to compel disclosure?

Endnotes

1. *Pittsburgh Press Co.* v. *Pittsburgh Commission on Human Rights,* 413 U.S. 376 (1973), at 390.

2. Quoted in *Near* v. *Minnesota,* 283 U.S. 697 (1931), at 713.

3. Quoted in Julian Boyd, ed., *The Papers of Thomas Jefferson,* vol. 2 (Princeton, N.J.: Princeton University Press, 1950), 49.

4. Quoted in Thomas L. Tedford, *Freedom of Speech in the United States* (New York: Random House, 1985), 38.

5. Fred W. Friendly and Martha J. H. Elliott, *The Constitution: That Delicate Balance* (New York: Random House, 1984), 32.

6. Ibid., 51–63.

7. Seldom has the federal court system operated as quickly as it did in the Pentagon Papers Case. Because of the gravity of the issue, the Court moved very quickly in this case once the government invoked national security as justification for imposing prior restraint. On June 12–14, 1971, the *New York Times*—and on June 18, the *Washington Post*—began publishing excerpts from this top-secret Pentagon study of the Vietnam War and American involvement therein. Government attempts to obtain temporary restraining orders and permanent injunctions to stop further publication progressed through two district courts and two courts of appeal between June 15–23, with the appellate tribunals allowing publication in one case (*Washington Post*) and suspending publication in the other (*New York Times*). The Supreme Court consented to hear arguments in the *Times* case, scheduled for June 26, and four days later, a divided Court handed down its decision in a judgment that included one *per curiam* opinion, six concurring opinions, and three dissenting opinions. All this transpired barely three weeks after the initial publication of the excerpts in the *New York Times*.

8. See *Congressional Quarterly Weekly Report,* January 21, 1984, 83–84; February 18, 1984, 336–7; and April 21, 1984, 931–3.

9. Ibid., September 22, 1984, 2336.

10. *United States* v. *Progressive,* 467 F. Supp. 990 (W.D. Wis., 1979), at 991.

11. For an interesting account of some of the different ways by which the three major commercial television networks in the United States have covered selected crises in the late 1970s and early 1980s, see Dan Nimmo and James E. Combs, *Nightly Horrors: Crisis Coverage in Television Network News* (Knoxville, Tenn.: University of Tennessee Press, 1985).

12. One of the incriminating statements reported prior to the gag order being imposed was a purported statement by the defendant—a retarded neighbor of the murdered family—to his father the morning after the murders that he had in fact killed the six family members.

13. See William J. Brennan, Jr., "Address," *Rutgers Law Review* 32 (1979): 173–83; and John Paul Ste-

vens, "Some Thoughts About a General Rule," *Arizona Law Review* 21 (1979): 599–605.

14. Unlike the first two cases, Caldwell's earlier conviction was reversed by a federal court of appeals, which held that the First Amendment protected the journalist from having to testify or appear before the grand jury. The Department of Justice appealed the *Caldwell* case to the U.S. Supreme Court.

15. Stewart observed that reporters could be required to appear before a grand jury and be compelled to testify if newsmen had information that was clearly relevant to a crime, if government could prove that the information sought was available from no other source, or if it could demonstrate a "compelling and overriding interest in the information."

16. For more information on the legislative action surrounding eventual passage of the Privacy Protection Act in 1980, see *Congressional Quarterly Almanac*, 96th Congress, 2nd sess., 1980, vol. 36, 387–8.

17. Quoted in Harry M. Clor, *Obscenity and Public Morality: Censorship in a Liberal Society* (Chicago: University of Chicago Press, 1969), 15.

18. Thomas Emerson, *The System of Freedom of Expression* (New York: Random House, 1970), 469.

19. Clor, *Obscenity and Public Morality,* 17.

20. 18 U.S. Code, Section 1461.

21. *United States* v. *Kennerley,* 209 F. 119 (1913).

22. *United States* v. *One Book Entitled "Ulysses,"* 72 F. 2d 705 (2d circ., 1934).

23. See C. Peter Magrath, "The Obscenity Cases: Grapes of Roth," in Phillip Kurland, ed., *The Supreme Court Reporter* (Chicago: University of Chicago Press, 1966), 7–77.

24. See *Redrup* v. *New York,* 386 U.S. 767 (1967) and *Ginsberg* v. *New York,* 390 U.S. 629 (1968).

25. Quoted in the *New York Times,* October 1, 1970, A-20.

26. Ibid., October 25, 1970, 71.

27. *Kaplan* v. *United States,* 413 U.S. 115 (1973); *United States* v. *12,200-Foot Reels of Super 8mm Film,* 413 U.S. 123 (1973); and *United States* v. *Orito,* 413 U.S. 139 (1973).

28. *Interstate Circuit, Inc.* v. *Dallas,* 390 U.S. 676 (1968), at 704.

29. *Burnett* v. *National Enquirer,* 9 Med. L. Rptr. 1921 (1983); *Westmoreland* v. *CBS, Inc.,* DCNY 596 F. Supp. 66 (1987); *Sharon* v. *Time, Inc.,* DCNY 609 F. Supp. 1291 (1987).

30. See the Holmes dissent in *Abrams* v. *United States,* 250 U.S. 616 (1919), at 630; Black and Douglas opinions in *Beauharnais* v. *Illinois,* 343 U.S. 250 (1952), at 272.

31. *Rosenblatt* v. *Baer,* 383 U.S. 75 (1966), at 85–86.

32. *Monitor Patriot Co.* v. *Roy,* 401 U.S. 265 (1971) and *Ocala Star-Banner Co.* v. *Dameron,* 401 U.S. 295 (1971).

33. Quoted in the *New York Times,* February 25, 1988, 14.

Suggested Readings

Bollinger, Lee J., Jr. "Freedom of the Press and Public Access: Toward a Theory of Partial Regulation of the Mass Media." *Michigan Law Review* 75 (1976): 1–42.

Clor, Harry M. *Obscenity and Public Morality: Censorship in a Liberal Society.* Chicago: University of Chicago Press, 1969.

Friendly, Fred W. *Minnesota Rag: The Dramatic Story of the Landmark Supreme Court Case That Gave New Meaning to Freedom of the Press.* New York: Random House, 1981.

de Grazia, Edward, and Robert K. Newman. *Movies, Censors and the First Amendment.* New York: Bowker, 1983.

Hoffman, Daniel N. *Governmental Secrecy and the Founding Fathers: A Study in Constitutional Controls*. Westwood, Conn.: Greenwood Press, 1981.

Linz, Daniel, et al. "Issues Bearing on the Legal Regulation of Violent and Sexually Violent Media." *Journal of Social Issues* 42 (Fall, 1986): 171–93.

Morland, Howard. *The Secret That Exploded*. New York: Random House, 1981.

O'Brien, David M. *The Public's Right to Know: The Supreme Court and the First Amendment*. New York: Praeger, 1981.

Schauer, Frederick F. *The Law of Obscenity*. Washington, D.C.: Bureau of National Affairs, 1976.

Shapiro, Andrew O. *Media Access*. Boston: Little, Brown, 1976.

Smith, Jeffrey. "Prior Restraint: Original Intentions and Modern Interpretations." *William and Mary Law Review* 28 (Spring 1987): 439–72.

13

The First Amendment: Freedom of Religion

Syllabus

The three most recent presidential elections have all had strong religious over-tones. In each campaign, several candidates vying for the Oval Office appealed to a religious tradition in American society. Perhaps the only thing that kept the 1988 presidential campaign from being an encore of the 1980 and 1984 campaigns was the negative press that TV evangelism received in 1988, fol-lowing the sex scandals of Jim Bakker and Jimmy Swaggart. With these em-barrassing episodes, even Rev. Pat Robertson soon labored to persuade voters that he was actually an accomplished businessman capable of sound executive decisions, rather than a TV evangelist. But recent presidential campaigns aside, these glimpses at preachers in public life tend to distort the long-standing relationship that has existed between church and state in the United States. There has always been an important connection between religion and politics in American culture, and provisions in the American Constitution have per-petuated that relationship.

This Chapter Examines the Following Matters

☐ The cultural, historical, and constitutional context of religious freedom in the United States predates the Constitutional Convention and the ratification of the First Amendment. The religious roots of American civilization are deep, and they confirm what Justice William O. Douglas said nearly four decades ago, that Americans are a "religious peo-ple whose institutions presuppose a Supreme Being."

☐ Working in partnership, the Establishment and Free Exercise Clauses of the First Amendment reflect the two major perspectives treated throughout this book—the *individualistic* and the *communitarian.* These clauses were intended to safeguard freedom of conscience and promote the public good in a religiously diverse land. The two clauses were to ensure the widest possible latitude for religious expression, and yet protect against the possibility of any one church or denomination becoming the official state church.

☐ In trying to reconcile these two clauses, the Su-preme Court has established a somewhat confus-ing line of precedents in some areas. During the past two decades many citizens have stressed the need for more governmental *accommodation* of religion, and the justices have tried to deal with this issue discreetly.

☐ Such subjects as aid to parochial schools, tuition tax credits, silent prayer in public schools, Nativity displays on public property at public expense, and creationism have prompted the Court to grapple with the meaning of "establishment" within the First Amendment. There have been several asser-tions, some by Court justices, that Thomas Jeffer-son's metaphor about a "wall of separation be-tween church and state" has actually distorted the law today and undermined the religious tradition that defines American culture.

☐ The same metaphor has led the justices over many decades to debate the height and strength of that wall. Several theories have developed that allow for varying degrees of insulation between church and state. As the constitutional debate over this topic continues, so will the line of controversies awaiting review by the Supreme Court.

Photo: Freedom to worship according to the dictates of individual conscience was a primary motivation for many to emigrate to America's shores and is a key provision in the Bill of Rights. St. Olaf's Lutheran Church in Cranfills Gap, Texas, founded in 1886 by Norwegian settlers, is testimony to the spirit of religious freedom held so deeply by Americans.

The Constitution, Religious Freedom, and American Culture

Over 150 years ago, Alexis de Tocqueville described religion in America as "a political institution which powerfully contributes to the maintenance of a democratic republic among the Americans" by supplying a strong moral consensus amid incremental change.[1] Several religious historians have noted the unique place that religion occupies in American public life.[2] Robert Bellah has noted how American presidents since George Washington have consistently referred to images of God, a "chosen" people, thanksgiving, redemption, and rebirth to establish their own legitimacy and inspire the American people. To Bellah, religion in America has always had both a private and a public face— a *publicly* expressed belief in God (which may mean many different things to many people) and *personal* belief in the liberty of conscience and the right to worship. It has been a virtual prerequisite for American political leaders to articulate this belief in God. According to Bellah:

> Although matters of personal religious belief, worship, and association are considered to be strictly private affairs, there are, at the same time, certain common elements of religious orientation that the great majority of Americans share. These have played a crucial role in the development of American institutions and still provide a religious dimension for the whole fabric of American life, including the political sphere.[3]

Bellah calls this set of symbols, beliefs, and rituals the American "civil religion," which allows secular American politics to exhibit an important religious dimension. This dichotomy between private and public religion in the United States during the past half-century partially explains the existence of several theories advanced to explain church-state separation. These theories will be discussed later in this chapter.

Early English and American Colonial Experience

The dualistic approach to religion in the United States has both historical and constitutional antecedents. In many respects, contemporary religious controversies in the United States derive from Anglo-American culture and experience. One of the reasons that English settlers emigrated to the New World in the early seventeenth century was to escape religious persecution. When the British Parliament adopted the Book of Common Prayer in 1548–49, it fueled great debate about the inability of individuals to worship freely. The Church of England was the established church, and those wishing to deviate from official teachings did so at considerable risk.

Ever since the settlement of the Jamestown Colony in Virginia in 1607 and the arrival of the Pilgrims at Plymouth Colony on the rugged coast of Cape Cod in 1620, a succession of religious groups sought to worship in a free and undisturbed manner. One irony of this settlement pattern and the variety of groups espousing particular religious ideas was the frequent intolerance toward and sometimes punishment of religious minorities that refused to conform to the tenets of the prevailing majority. Early American colonial history is filled with portrayals of the Puritans' impatience with religious dissenters, especially in Massachusetts Bay Colony founded in 1630, that eventually led to later settlements in Rhode Island and the Connecticut River valley. Subsequent colonizations in New York, Pennsylvania, and Maryland established religious pluralism as an early characteristic in the American colonies.[4]

American Experience During and After the Founding

Religious intolerance was not unique to the Puritans. Prior to the American Revolution, only three American colonies (Pennsylvania, Rhode Island, and Delaware) had no established church. In Connecticut, Massachusetts, and New Hampshire, the Congregational church was the officially recognized order, with some provision for Anglicans and others to form their own churches. In New York, New Jersey, Georgia, North and South Carolina, Maryland, and Virginia, the officially established church was the Anglican church. Not until the early 1800s did the states finally abolish officially sanctioned churches or religions, with New Hampshire and Massachusetts being the last to do so in 1819 and 1833, respectively.

Virginia was the first American colony that acted to protect religious freedom in the United States. Through the efforts of individuals like George Mason, Thomas Jefferson, and James Madison during the 1770s and 1780s, religious toleration became a prominent objective of the fledgling American Republic. When a state constitutional convention convened in Williamsburg in 1776, George Mason, a liberal Anglican, proposed a bill of rights with a provision granting "the fullest Toleration in the Exercise of Religion." A young James Madison also offered a substitute amendment stating that "all men are equally entitled to the full and free exercise of religion." The Virginia Declaration of Rights adopted that same year held that "all men are equally entitled to the free exercise of religion according to the dictates of conscience; and . . . it is the mutual duty of all to practice Christian forebearance, love and charity toward the other."[5] Probably more than anything else, the efforts of Madison and Jefferson to defeat state support for established religion in Virginia were crucial to contemporary religious freedom in the United States (see Brief 13.1).

Although Madison and Jefferson played the most prominent role in the defense of religious liberty, other political leaders of the era also warrant brief comment. Varying greatly in their degree of personal piety, such people as Benjamin Franklin, George Washington, Alexander Hamilton, and John Adams all recognized the need for religion as an important foundation for cohesive, republican government. They generally agreed that government served to check the natural tendency in human nature toward self-interest, but they also thought that government itself was to be distrusted (see Chapter 3). Finally, in recognizing the practical utility of religion for constructing a more moral policy, they were convinced that government should be kept largely secular, in part because no single religious group composed the majority in American society during the late 1700s.[7] The dilemma then became how to balance the need for a largely secular state with the reality of a society that had, even then, been strongly shaped by religion. This task was eventually addressed in the First Amendment of the Bill of Rights.

Brief 13.1   Two Sons of Virginia Labor for Religious Freedom

Of the multitude of writings by Thomas Jefferson and James Madison that had a crucial impact upon the drafting of the First Amendment and the place of religious freedom, three are of special note. In 1784, the state of Virginia was considering a bill to reinstate direct state financial support for the Christian religion. As an outspoken opponent of this plan, James Madison, in 1785, authored his famous *Memorial and Remonstrance Against Religious Assessments*. He contended that "the Religion . . . of every man must be left to the conviction and conscience of every man; and it is the right of every man to exercise it as these may dictate." Madison argued that a tax to support organized religion should be defeated because "the same authority which can establish Christianity, in exclusion of all other Religions, may establish with the same ease any particular sect of Christians, in exclusion of all other Sects." He also reflected tolerance for nonbelievers, when stating, "Whilst we assert for ourselves a freedom to embrace, to profess and to observe the Religion which we believe to be of divine origin, we cannot deny an equal freedom to those whose minds have not yet yielded to the evidence which has convinced us." Madison's broadside attack on religious assessments was vehemently criticized by many Baptists, Presbyterians, Quakers, Catholics, and Methodists, but it was directly responsible for defeat of the assessments bill, which died in committee in December 1785.

A second document, which reflected the combined efforts of Madison and Jefferson, was the Virginia *Bill for Establishing Religious Freedom*. The bill was originally introduced into the Virginia General Assembly in 1779 and soon thereafter defeated. But it attracted renewed attention following the defeat of the assessments bill in 1785. Commonly referred to as the "Virginia Statute of Religious Freedom," this important plea for liberty of conscience reaffirmed that "Almighty God hath created the mind free." A key provision of the bill was found in Clause 2:

> Be it enacted by the General Assembly, That no man shall be compelled to frequent or support any religious worship, place or ministry whatsoever, nor shall be enforced, restrained, molested, or burthened in his body or goods, nor shall otherwise suffer on account of his religious opinions or belief; but that all men shall be free to profess, and by argument to maintain, their opinions in matters of religion, and that the same shall in no wise diminish, enlarge, or affect their civil capacities.

The Virginia Statute was passed by the state assembly in January 1786. Along with Madison's *Memorial and Remonstrance*, it was vitally important to the drafting of the religion clauses of the First Amendment.

A final document that has frequently been referred to by authorities, including Supreme Court justices, for defining the meaning and intent of the First Amendment religion clauses is Jefferson's letter to the Danbury Baptist Association of Connecticut. The letter, written in 1802 when Jefferson was serving as president, said that "religion is a matter which lies solely between man and his God, that he owes account to none other for his faith or his worship, [and] that the legitimate powers of government reach actions only, and not opinions." But the most memorable passage in the letter is Jefferson's statement that the religion clauses of the First Amendment were intended to erect "a wall of separation between Church & State."[6] That brief passage has generated an immense amount of both conjecture and constitutional law during the past two centuries.

The Bill of Rights and the Religion Clauses

The Constitution of 1787 did not mention religion anywhere, except for a short reference in Article VI, Section 3. This passage states that "no religious Test shall ever be required as a Qualification to any Office or public Trust under the United States." As noted in Chapter 3, one of the key arguments of those opposing ratification of the new Constitution in 1787 was that it lacked a formal bill of rights protecting the liberties of the people; consequently, the states were promised such amendments after the ratification battle. When the First Congress convened in 1789, the legislators sought to make good on their promise; by September, Congress had completed work on what would soon become the first ten amendments to the Constitution. In conference committee, Madison won agreement on the opening passage of the crucial First Amendment: "Congress shall make no law respecting an establishment of religion, or prohibiting the free exercise thereof."

Not until the early twentieth century did there arise much question over precisely what the two religion clauses—Free Exercise and Establishment—actually meant. One thing is certain—they applied only to the *federal* government in 1791. Thomas Jefferson's reference to a "wall of separation between church and state" has generated great debate among scholars who maintain that there is little evidence to support the contention that the framers insisted upon a *strict,* complete separation.[8] Given their insistence that religion both informed and ordered representative government, the question was not whether there should be some relation between the two, but rather, what the nature of that relationship should be. As happened with so many aspects of the new Constitution, precise definition was allowed to drift as the new nation set out to consolidate government under a document that contained many hidden meanings. It fell to the Supreme Court to search for these meanings within the words and phrases used to structure this noble experiment in responsible government.

The Free Exercise Clause and Religious Freedom

As noted in Chapter 8, the Bill of Rights, including the First Amendment and its two religion clauses, originally applied only to the national government. The Free Exercise Clause involves cases challenging governmental interference with the practice of a citizen's faith. The Establishment Clause involves cases challenging alleged governmental support for or hostility toward religion. For 150 years, the Supreme Court had few occasions to interpret the meaning of the Free Exercise or the Establishment Clauses, since so few controversies emerged requiring the Court to render an opinion. Given the variety of denominations in twentieth-century American society, it could be argued that religious liberty has flourished in this country. Because no one denomination has emerged as dominant, which has happened in several other countries, overt government discrimination toward any one religion has seldom posed any serious problem. In several free exercise cases, the Supreme Court has tried to reconcile secular governmental regulations with the demands of persons claiming sincere religious beliefs.

Conflict with State-Federal Regulations: "Free to Believe, But Not to Act"

The first freedom of religion case heard by the Supreme Court dealt with the Free Exercise Clause, and the Court's handling of the issue in question held great significance for future government regulation of religious behavior. The case was *Reynolds* v. *United States* (1879) and involved the right of Mormons to practice polygamy, then an accepted tenet of the Mormon faith. George Reynolds, convicted of violating a federal law prohibiting polygamy, appealed to the Supreme Court claiming a violation of the Free Exercise Clause. A unanimous Supreme Court upheld his conviction. In the majority opinion,

Chief Justice Morrison Waite stated that monogamous marriage was a practice of Western moral tradition and a foundation upon which "society may be said to be built." As a result, Congress had acted properly in outlawing polygamy. In upholding the lower court ruling, Waite made an important distinction that had great significance for future free exercise cases. Under the First Amendment, "Congress was deprived of all legislative power over mere opinion, but was left free to reach actions which were in violation of social duties or subversive of good order." This reference was important because it implied that the federal government could not legislate regarding opinions. But it also sanctioned the government's right to inhibit particular religious actions or behavior considered harmful to public health, morality, or order. In other words, people are free to believe, but they may not be allowed to act upon those beliefs in all instances. This became more evident in several civil liberty cases in the twentieth century and indicated that religious rights, like all others, are not absolute, but must be balanced against other competing societal rights.

Following the *Reynolds* decision, very few controversies emerged until the early 1900s. In 1905, the same general principle regarding the state's power to regulate certain actions arose in a Massachusetts case. The incident involved a state law which mandated that persons be vaccinated for smallpox despite their opposition to such a practice on religious conviction grounds. In *Jacobson* v. *Massachusetts* (1905), the Supreme Court again distinguished between religious beliefs and actions and found that the state law had a valid secular purpose under its police power to protect its citizens. Two decades later, although the Court did not rule on free exercise grounds, an Oregon case established an important principle allowing parental discretion in the education of their children. In *Pierce* v. *Society of Sisters* (1925), the Supreme Court declared invalid an Oregon law compelling attendance in a public school for all children from ages eight to sixteen on the grounds that the statute interfered with the "liberty" protected by the Fourteenth Amendment. The Court reasoned that this liberty included the right of parents to supervise the education of their children, including having them enrolled in church-related schools. In the larger scope of civil liberties cases before the Court, this decision became one of many in which the Court became more suspicious of state regulation of personal liberties. Because *Pierce* emerged shortly after the famous *Gitlow* v. *New York* decision (discussed more fully in Chapters 8 and 11), it indicated growing concern about important civil liberties during the twentieth century.

The Recognition of Religious Freedom as Fundamental

Concern on the Supreme Court for protecting civil liberties intensified with the advent of the more liberal New Deal Court, although some decisions during World War II sacrificed individual liberties for public order and "military necessity." But even in the heat of battle, some decisions advanced religious freedom in the country. In 1940, the U.S. Supreme Court incorporated the Free Exercise Clause into the Fourteenth Amendment Due Process Clause, thereby making it applicable to the American states. The incident leading to this important development involved Newton Cantwell, a member of Jehovah's Witnesses, who had been convicted of disturbing the peace in New Haven, Connecticut. Cantwell had been charged with playing a record that attacked the Roman Catholic religion. He had played the record on a public street in a predominantly Catholic neighborhood. He had also failed to obtain a license to solicit, required under state law, from the secretary of the Public Welfare Council in Connecticut.

In *Cantwell* v. *Connecticut* (1940), the Supreme Court unanimously overturned the defendant's conviction on the grounds that his First and Fourteenth Amendment rights under the Free Exercise Clause had been violated. Regardless of how disturbing Cantwell's utterances against Catholics might have been, the Court insisted that he still had the constitutional right to say whatever he pleased about other religious faiths. Furthermore, the state had no right to judge what constituted a valid religion; to do so would result in the possible censorship of religion, and this was not allowed under the First Amendment.

The main significance of *Cantwell* was that the Court held for the first time that the Free Exercise Clause applied to the states. As Justice Owen Roberts stated in the opinion for the Court:

> The [Constitution] forestalls compulsion by law of the acceptance of any creed or the practice of any form of worship. Freedom of conscience and freedom to adhere to such religious organization or form of worship as the individual may choose cannot be restricted by law.

But beyond that, the Court also reiterated the distinction between beliefs and actions mentioned first in *Reynolds:*

> [Free exercise] embraces two concepts—freedom to believe and freedom to act. The first is absolute but, in the nature of things, the second cannot be. [The] freedom to act must have appropriate definition to preserve the enforcement of that protection [although] the power to regulate must be so exercised as not . . . unduly to infringe the protected freedom.

Cantwell became the first of several important cases in the 1940s involving Jehovah's Witnesses challenging state regulations that allegedly infringed upon their religious beliefs. Although the Court consistently invalidated state regulations that limited door-to-door solicitation for religious purposes, it was less sympathetic to this particular religious group in another situation involving minority rights and a perceived national crisis.

Religious Freedom at Risk: Is National Unity Always the Basis of National Security?

In the same year as *Cantwell*—and as Adolf Hitler continued to conquer several European countries—the Supreme Court considered a state law compelling public school students to salute the American flag. A Pennsylvania law requiring a daily flag salute had been challenged by the parents of a child who had been expelled for refusing to do so on religious grounds. The parents, members of Jehovah's Witnesses, challenged the state law on First Amendment grounds. The district court upheld the law, while the federal court of appeals struck it down as a violation of the First Amendment. When the case was appealed to the Supreme Court, an 8–1 majority ruled in *Minersville School District* v. *Gobitis* (1940) that the statute did not violate the First Amendment. Writing for the majority, Justice Felix Frankfurter emphasized the "conflicting claims of liberty and authority" and the need to balance the "conscience of individuals" with the "felt necessities of society." He insisted that in this particular case, the state was justified in its attempt to promote national cohesion. "We are dealing," noted Frankfurter, "with an interest inferior to none in the hierarchy of legal values. National unity is the basis of national security." Justice Harlan Stone was the only dissenting voice in the decision. He saw a small, defenseless minority being coerced by the majority. The Constitution, said Stone, does not indicate that "compulsory expressions of loyalty play any such part in our scheme of government as to override the constitutional protection of freedom of speech and religion."

During the next three years, two developments resulted in an unusually quick reversal of a Supreme Court decision. First, Justices Black, Douglas, and Murphy, who had ruled with the eight-member majority in the *Minersville* judgment, changed their minds about their earlier vote. In a three-member dissent in *Jones* v. *Opelika* (1942), the three justices stated that both the *Minersville* and *Opelika* decisions were, in their minds, wrongly decided, and that the First Amendment required greater protection for religious minorities than those two decisions reflected. The other factor affecting the *Minersville* precedent was the appointment of two new members to the Court, Robert Jackson in 1941 and Wiley Rutledge in 1943. This change in attitude by three justices and the appointment of two new justices meant that, if given an opportunity to reconsider the *Minersville* decision, the Court might handle the issue differently.

The Court did not have to wait very long. Following the *Minersville* decision, several other states, including West Virginia, passed similar flag salute and Pledge of Allegiance laws. In 1943, in *West Virginia State Board of Education* v. *Barnette*, the Supreme Court overruled the flag salute precedent of three years earlier. The facts of the *Barnette* case were virtually identical to the 1940 case, with the parents of children claiming that the compulsory flag salute law violated their religious beliefs under the Free Exercise Clause. In a 6–3 decision, Justice Jackson wrote a majority opinion that is often quoted to exemplify the new attitude emerging on the New Deal Court. According to Jackson, First Amendment freedoms are not absolute, but they are to be safeguarded by a very high standard:

> To sustain the compulsory flag salute we are required to say that a Bill of Rights which guards the individual's right to speak his own mind, left it open to public authorities to compel him to utter what is not in his mind . . . [F]reedoms of speech and of press, of assembly, and of worship may not be infringed on . . . slender grounds. They are susceptible of restriction only to prevent grave and immediate danger to interests which the state may lawfully protect . . . *If there is any fixed star in our constitutional constellation, it is that no official, high or petty, can prescribe what shall be orthodox in politics, nationalism, religion, or other matters of opinion or force citizens to confess by word or act their faith therein.* [Emphasis added]

The *Barnette* case established a significant civil liberties principle. Rather than narrowly interpreting the status of Jehovah's Witnesses before the law and exempting that religious minority from the law on religious grounds, the Court actually said that *no one* should be required to salute the flag or, more broadly, be forced to utter any belief or opinion against his or her will. Therefore, this case won rights for all citizens and upheld the view that government cannot compel personal beliefs.

Laws That Burden Free Exercise: A New Emphasis on Religious Behavior

Another type of conflict under the Free Exercise Clause involves Sunday closing laws aimed at providing a uniform day of rest for businesses and citizens. The problem with these laws has usually been that some religions, such as Judaism and Seventh-Day Adventist, do not consider Sunday their sabbath. Therefore, state laws that mandate business closings on Sunday discriminate against proprietors who recognize their sabbath on another day and have to close their businesses two days a week. In 1961, the Supreme Court upheld Pennsylvania's Sunday Closing Law in the case of *Braunfeld* v. *Brown*. Writing for a six-member Court, Chief Justice Earl Warren argued that

> if the State regulates conduct by enacting a general law within its power, the purpose and effect of which is to advance the State's secular goals, the statute is valid despite its indirect burden on religious observance unless the State may accomplish its purpose by means which do not impose a burden.

In dissent, Justice William Brennan was troubled by the "compelling state interest" justified by the majority which honored the "mere convenience of having everyone rest on the same day." And Justice Potter Stewart, like Brennan, was disturbed by the Court's ruling which compelled citizens to make a "cruel choice" between practicing their religion or their trade, all "in the interest of enforced Sunday togetherness." In these Sunday Closing Laws Cases the Court was comfortable with resolving the controversies on statutory, rather than on constitutional, grounds; as a result, no precise standard was devised for defining acceptable and unacceptable secular purpose.

Soon after these cases, an opportunity arose for the Court to clarify state regulations that placed an unlawful, though indirect, burden upon religious denominations. Adell Sherbert, a resident of South Carolina, belonged to the Seventh-Day Adventist church, but was fired by her employer when she refused to work on Saturday, her sabbath. Unable to find work that allowed her to worship on Saturday, she applied for state unemployment benefits. Her claim was denied, primarily because she refused to accept jobs requiring her to work on Saturdays. Losing in state courts, she appealed to the Supreme Court, which ruled that this denial of state benefits violated the First and Fourteenth Amendments. Writing for the majority in *Sherbert* v. *Verner* (1963), Justice Brennan said, "To condition the availability of benefits upon [Sherbert's] willingness to violate a cardinal principle of her religious faith effectively penalizes the free exercise of her constitutional liberties." In dissent, Justice John Harlan felt that the *Sherbert* ruling, in effect, overruled *Braunfeld* and compelled a state, attempting to condition unemployment benefits on an applicant's availability for work, to "carve out an exception" and make benefits available to those refusing to work on religious grounds.

Both the *Braunfeld* and the *Sherbert* cases marked a major shift in the Supreme Court's interpretation of the Free Exercise Clause. Until *Braunfeld* and its companion cases, the Court relied upon the **secular-legislation rule** in evaluating free exercise cases. Under this rule, state legislation had to serve some legitimate secular purpose and could not discriminate against particular religious groups. If those stipulations were met, though, the fact that the legislation might conflict with some person's perceived religious obligations did not necessarily invalidate it. According to this pre-1960 interpretation, the First Amendment did not require government to give special recognition to religious beliefs or religiously motivated behavior.

Beginning with the *Braunfeld* decision, and continuing in *Sherbert,* the Court seemed to create a new standard for evaluating state legislation being challenged on First Amendment grounds. Laws that adversely affected religious practices and behavior were upheld only if they served an important state purpose and if that purpose could not be achieved by a tactic less burdensome to religious minorities. According to Warren, the closing laws did serve a legitimate secular purpose, and the Court felt that no other alternative would be less adverse for religious groups. In the case of South Carolina's administration of unemployment benefits, the Brennan opinion reflected the view that the state had not sufficiently considered alternative means for ensuring financial integrity and preventing fraud in dismissing Sherbert's claim before the state board.

Special Treatment for Some Religions: A "Pandora's Box" for the Court?

By the early 1960s, the Supreme Court apparently was willing to grant certain exemptions to religious groups based upon their claim of free exercise rights under the First Amendment. This raises the fundamental question concerning the Free Exercise Clause as it has appeared before the Court in recent decades. To what extent can individuals claim exemption to universally applicable laws on religious freedom grounds? Can government compel behavior that is contrary to people's sincere religious beliefs or, conversely, prohibit behavior that is claimed to be an integral part of their religion?

One of the most difficult examples of this periodic conflict between universal laws and religious groups demanding exemption from those laws on free exercise grounds concerns compulsory school attendance laws. An important case came to the Burger Court in 1972, requiring the Court to answer this fundamental question about compelled behavior and religious beliefs. *Wisconsin* v. *Yoder* (1972) involved several persons, including Jonas Yoder, belonging to the Old Amish faith. They had defied an Wisconsin law requiring children to attend either private or public school until age sixteen. The Amish have traditionally been very industrious, self-sufficient, law-abiding citizens who have usually considered themselves far removed from contemporary society. According to Amish doctrine, members must withdraw from most worldly aspects of modern society and commit themselves to a life of hard work, a simple lifestyle, and a deep commitment to religious values. Although committed to educating their children, they have historically supplemented the first few years of public schooling with in-home education that reinforces their religious values. Specifically, they have shunned a high school education in the belief that the environment debased their culture and religion.

Because of this withdrawal from public school, in defiance of Wisconsin's compulsory school attendance law, Yoder and other Amish believers were prosecuted by the state. The law required that students attend school until the age of sixteen, and the state argued that it had a compelling duty to educate children within its jurisdiction. The Wisconsin Supreme Court found in favor of Yoder, and the state appealed the decision to the U.S. Supreme Court.

In a 6–1 opinion that became a landmark case concerning the Free Exercise Clause, the Supreme Court also found in favor of the Amish respondents in this case. In writing for the majority, Chief Justice Warren Burger first considered whether the Amish claim for an exemption from the law was motivated by a deep religious belief, or merely a personal preference. The Court was comfortable with the conclusion that the Amish lifestyle was not merely personal preference, but a sincere religious conviction reflected in the biblical injunction to "be not conformed to this world." To comply with the compulsory attendance policy, the Court reasoned, would compel the Amish to "perform acts undeniably at odds with fundamental tenets of their religious beliefs."

The Court then weighed the state's perceived goal of educating its citizens against Yoder's religious beliefs. On this point, the justices found that if education is vital to self-sufficiency and self-reliance, then the Amish display an exemplary record, inasmuch as they have been industrious, have refused to accept public welfare, and have already been exempted from Social Security taxation. On the point that education is essential to developing job skills, the Court felt that, here too, the Amish system of "learning by doing" was "ideal" for preparing Amish children to live as adults in their religious community. Finally, Wisconsin argued that its compulsory school attendance law recognized the substantive right of all children to a secondary education. But the law did not say that parents must consult with their children about whether they want to attend public school. After noting that the state cannot hold Amish parents to a stricter standard than they hold non-Amish parents (who have not been proven to have consulted their children), Burger invoked the *Pierce* precedent of 1925 to emphasize the discretion of parents:

> *Pierce* stands as a charter of the rights of parents to direct the religious upbringing of their children. And, when the interests of parenthood are combined with a free exercise claim of the nature revealed by this record, more than merely a "reasonable relation to some purpose within the competency of the state" is required to sustain the validity of the State's requirement under the First Amendment.

The lone dissenter in this case was Justice Douglas, who disagreed with the majority's opinion on several points. Douglas felt that too much emphasis was placed upon the law-and-order record of the Amish, which he considered irrelevant to the case. If mainline religions were held up to the same law-abiding standard that the Court here implied the Amish had met, many of those denominations might be found wanting. He also disagreed with the Court's contrasting Amish beliefs with those of Henry David Thoreau, whose views were largely "philosophical and personal rather than religious" and therefore not within the framework of the Free Exercise Clause. Not only was Thoreau a hero to Douglas, but also the justice wanted to ensure that the Court focus more on the true *religious* nature of the claim at issue in the case.

Wisconsin v. *Yoder* is significant for two reasons. Ever since the *Reynolds* case in 1878, the Court had recognized the distinction between religious beliefs and actions based upon those beliefs. The former were inviolable, but the latter could be regulated by government in order to protect society. *Cantwell* v. *Connecticut* recognized the same latitude for the state, even though the state law requiring a solicitation license was struck down. In *Yoder,* the Court rejected this pattern and held that, without totally ignoring a state's compelling interest in some instances, "there are areas of conduct protected by the Free Exercise Clause . . . and thus beyond the power of the State to control."

The second novelty introduced by the *Yoder* case was that, for the first time, by granting certain privileges to persons under the Free Exercise Clause, the Court was obligating itself to consider for future claims that government might be violating the Establishment Clause. By exempting the Amish from compulsory school attendance laws, was Wisconsin granting special support for that religious group in violation of the other religion clause? This issue would arise in many future cases (see Brief 13.2).

The Meaning of "Religion" and Conscientious Objectors

Whereas the *Yoder* case found the Court dealing with the sincerity of Amish religious beliefs, a larger issue troubling the Supreme Court for several years has been defining what constitutes "religion" in the context of the First Amendment. How the justices answered this question had major implications for several conscientious objection cases in the 1960s and 1970s. The Supreme Court first confronted this problem in 1944, in *United States* v. *Ballard*, when it ruled that a jury was not able to define the legitimacy of "religious beliefs" for another individual. Speaking for the Court, Justice Douglas stated:

> Religious experiences which are as real as life to some may be incomprehensible to others. [The] miracles of the New Testament, the Divinity of Christ, life after death, the power of prayer are deep in the religious convictions of many. If one

---

☐ *Brief 13.2   Public School Textbooks and Secular Humanism*

In recent years, parents in public school districts in the South have taken issue with materials that their children have been required to read. In 1983, parents in Church Hill, Tennessee, organized a group called Citizens Organized for Better Schools and began lobbying for removal of some textbooks that the state had adopted for use during the 1983–84 school year. The parents maintained that the books promoted a "secular humanist" value system that conflicted with their children's religious beliefs. They filed suit in federal court against the local school board. After a protracted set of proceedings involving dismissal for a lack of standing and an appellate court order to reconsider the merits of the case, the case was finally treated to full argument and decision in 1986. In the case of *Mozert* v. *Hawkins County Public Schools,* Judge Thomas G. Hull ruled in favor of the fundamentalist families on two grounds. First, the rights of the parents and their children were violated because the children were forced to read books that presented material considered contrary to their religious beliefs. Furthermore, Hull found that the children had a constitutional right to an education and that the school district had to accommodate them by

allowing them to study at home. This decision was ultimately overruled by the U.S. Court of Appeals for the Sixth Circuit.

A similar case also occurred in Alabama. *Smith* v. *Board of School Commissioners, Mobile County, Alabama* concerned alleged teaching of secular humanism in Mobile schools. After a lengthy district court trial involving fundamentalist and separationist groups, Judge Brevard Hand delivered a 169-page decision in March 1987. In his decision, the judge ordered over forty textbooks in history, social studies, and various other subjects to be removed because they supported secular humanism. Judge Hand wrote that the challenged books made no reference to religion, instructed the children to make up their own minds concerning right and wrong, and discriminated against theistic religion. As a result, he claimed that secular humanism was, in fact, a religion being taught in the public schools. This was the first time that a federal court had ever made this assertion, but it had limited impact because it was ultimately overruled in August 1987 by the U.S. Court of Appeals for the Eleventh Circuit.

could be sent to jail because a jury in a hostile environment found those teachings false, little indeed would be left of religious freedom.

Although the Court upheld the conviction of the defendant for fraud and misuse of the mails, the *Ballard* case found the justices saying that religion was a personal matter, not one susceptible to definition by an outside group. Nearly two decades later, in *Torcaso* v. *Watkins* (1961), the Court unanimously ruled that a Maryland law requiring a religious test for public office was unconstitutional. It also stated that a personal belief in God was not an essential component of all religions.

But the real conflicts over the definition of religion developed during the late 1960s, when social, political, and economic norms were under seige in American society. During the Vietnam War, the issue of conscientious objection forced the Supreme Court to deal with several cases involving persons opposed to the selective service system and American participation in an "immoral" war. Prior to 1965, the Court had required that in order to claim "CO" status and exemption from military service, the person had to prove sustained "religious training and belief" in a particular pacifist sect, such as the Quakers or the Mennonites. Under the Universal Military Training and Service Act passed by Congress in 1948, persons had to prove that they were "conscientiously opposed to participation in war in any form." Furthermore, this religious training and belief had to involve a person's "belief in a relation to a Supreme Being involving duties superior to those arising from any human relation."

In 1965, this provision of the Universal Military Training and Service Act was challenged on the grounds that it discriminated against nonreligious conscientious objectors and certain kinds of religious expression. In *United States* v. *Seeger* (1965), the Supreme Court ruled that three individuals, none of whom claimed a personal belief in God, were entitled to be exempted from compulsory military service on religious grounds. In ruling this way, the Court concluded that when Congress referred in the federal law to a Supreme Being, rather than to God, it was only trying to clarify the meaning of religious training and beliefs so as to include all religions and exclude mere philosophical, political, or sociological views. In writing for the majority, Justice Thomas Clark said that the test of an individual's beliefs was based upon whether those beliefs are "sincere and meaningful, and occupy a place in the life of its possessor parallel to that filled by the orthodox belief in God."

Seeger was significant because it created the **parallel-place doctrine** for evaluating the sincerity of religious beliefs. Although the Court retained the demand for "religious motivation" in order to be exempt from the draft, the new standard eliminated formal religious *instruction* as a requirement. This tactical definition avoided the criticism that by exempting pacifist sects, the Court was discriminating against other religious beliefs that also might lead some individuals to morally oppose war. After *Seeger*, there was no longer an exclusive exemption for Quakers and Mennonites, but for others as well who could claim a parallel religious motivation, regardless of their belief in God or formal religious training.

In the early 1970s, with public opposition to the Vietnam War continuing under the Nixon administration, three other cases before the Supreme Court required the justices to clarify further conscientious objection status and how it qualified under the Free Exercise Clause. In *Welsh* v. *United States* (1970), the Court allowed CO status to an individual even though he denied that religion had anything to do with his opposition to military service. But two cases in 1971 indicated some limits to how far the Court would go in granting these exemptions. In *Gillette* v. *United States* (1971), the Court refused to grant a draft exemption to a person who selectively opposed American involvement in the Vietnam War. Although they gave wide berth to the definition of religious beliefs, the justices refused to allow individuals to make personal distinctions between the *types* of war in which they would participate. Finally, in *Clay* v. *United States* (1971), involving the famous heavyweight boxing champion Cassius Clay (his name had already been changed to the more recognizable Muhammed Ali), the Court awarded CO status to Clay after stating that three conditions had to be satisfied: individuals must show that they are conscientiously opposed to all wars; that the opposition is based upon genuine religious training and belief; and that the objection is sincere.

The Supreme Court's handling of the Free Exercise Clause over many decades brought about many changes in this portion of the First Amendment. First, the Court eventually made the clause applicable to the states in 1940, at a time when selective incorporation was slowly applying Bill of Rights guarantees to all persons living under the U.S. Constitution. Second, ever since the Court encountered the Free Exercise Clause in the late nineteenth century in *Reynolds* v. *United States,* it has insisted that people are entitled to religious beliefs, but not necessarily to the right to act upon those beliefs—a dichotomy that persists to the present day. Third, since the early 1960s, the Court has become more deeply involved in judging the sincerity of a person's religious beliefs and in defining what constitutes "religion" under the First Amendment. This has been necessary in order to decide whether persons are entitled to certain beliefs under the law. Even if personal beliefs are sincerely held, they still must be considered "religious" in the eyes of the Court. This prolonged process of line-drawing has continued to the current day and will, most likely, persist in the future. The irony here is that as the Supreme Court has worked to protect religious beliefs from the burden of government regulations, it has become ever more deeply involved in protecting the religious freedom of American citizens. This is the cost of a system that places such responsibility upon the "marble temple" known as the United States Supreme Court. As the discussion turns now to a consideration of the Establishment Clause, the difficulty surrounding constitutional and statutory interpretation can be seen.

The Establishment of Religion

Although the Free Exercise Clause has caused the courts some difficulties in trying to define "religion" and in determining whether certain individuals should be exempt from universal rules, the Establishment Clause has been even more difficult for the courts to decipher in the twentieth century. The First Amendment begins with a deceptively simple prohibition that "Congress shall make no law respecting an establishment of religion." For a long time, a key question has been, What does "establishment" mean? Some have argued that the phrase should be interpreted in the context of the times in which it was drafted, and that it was intended to ensure that the new national government would not allow an official, established church supported at public expense. This view would still allow the states to support religious institutions as long as that support did not prefer any one religion or church over another.

Another interpretation leads in a quite different direction and is based upon Jefferson's allusion to a "wall of separation between church and state." This phrase might be understood as prohibiting not only an established church, but also various forms of state support for religious activities, institutions, ideas, and practices. In the latter half of the twentieth century, as the following discussion will indicate, the "wall" that separates the "church" from the government has been rather permeable. For four decades, several cases concerning the Establishment Clause have focused upon two primary areas—public financial *assistance* to parochial institutions and religious *practices* in the public schools. Public aid to parochial institutions will be discussed first, since that topic prompted the application of the Establishment Clause to the states.

Public Assistance to Parochial Schools:
The Child-Benefit Rationale

Few cases concerning the Establishment Clause came before the Supreme Court prior to 1947. In 1930, the Supreme Court upheld a Louisiana law that authorized public funding for nonsectarian textbooks to be used by students in parochial schools.[9] A major feature of this decision was the **child-benefit rationale,** which held that a law allowing textbooks to be purchased with public money did not violate the Establishment Clause because it was the child, and not the religious institution, that benefited from the book purchases.

An important case after World War II finally applied the Establishment Clause to the states. *Everson* v. *Board of Education* (1947) involved a taxpayer in New Jersey who challenged the constitutionality of a state law that allowed local school districts to reimburse parents for expenses incurred in using public transportation to send their children to parochial schools. A significant aspect of the *Everson* case is the reference by Justice Hugo Black to the minimal meaning of the Establishment Clause. In a frequently quoted passage from the majority opinion, Black dealt with what that clause means:

> The "establishment of religion" clause of the First Amendment means at least this: Neither a state nor the Federal Government can set up a church. Neither can pass laws which aid one religion, aid all religions, or prefer one religion over another. Neither can force nor influence a person to go to or to remain away from church against his will or force him to profess a belief or disbelief in any religion. No person can be punished for entertaining or professing religious beliefs or disbeliefs, for church attendance or non-attendance. No tax in any amount . . . can be levied to support any religious activities or institutions, whatever they may be called, or whatever form they may adopt to teach or practice religion. Neither a state nor the Federal Government can, openly or secretly, participate in the affairs of any religious organizations or groups and vice versa. In the words of Jefferson, the clause against establishment of religion by law was intended to erect "a wall of separation between Church and State."

After delineating what in his view the Establishment Clause required, Black then added that it "requires the state to be a neutral in its relations with groups of religious believers and non-believers; it does not require the state to be their adversary."

This was all prelude to Black's opinion for a five-member majority upholding the constitutionality of the New Jersey law. According to the justices, New Jersey contributed no money to parochial schools, but instead provided a general program to allow parents to get their children safely to and from accredited schools. Although the Establishment Clause was intended to build a wall between church and state, which could not allow the "slightest breach," the New Jersey law was constitutional. Undoubtedly, a major rationale of the *Everson* majority opinion was, once again, the child-benefit explanation. The state was providing an important service to the parents and the children, not to any religious denomination.

Justice Rutledge, who cast one of four dissenting votes in the *Everson* case, was troubled by the precedent established in this decision. Arguing that providing aid to some would leave the door open to expand that assistance in the future, Rutledge stated that this was "the very thing Jefferson and Madison experienced and sought to guard against, whether in its blunt or in its more screened form."

Everson is an interesting case with respect to the Establishment Clause. In it the Supreme Court applied the same anti-establishment restrictions on state activity that had been imposed on the national government since ratification of the Bill of Rights in 1791. Furthermore, although it would be relaxed several years later, the Black standard implied that government could not provide *any* aid to religion. The state was compelled to be completely neutral in its stance toward religion and nonreligion. Finally, in spite of the specific prohibitions cited in the Black opinion, the divisions on the Court and future controversies over the precise meaning of "wall of separation" would create many problems for later justices trying to understand the meaning of the Establishment Clause. Public pressures would soon arise for a more "accommodating" attitude by government toward religion.

With the *Everson* case, the Supreme Court for the first time confronted the difficult issue of what constitutes government aid to religion. At the time, some considered the public transportation subsidies to parents as clearly encouraging and facilitating attendance at parochial schools, which Black's "no-aid" reference would seem to preclude. In fact, Justice Jackson noted this effect in a dissenting opinion to the case, when he noted that "the case which irresistibly comes to mind as the most fitting precedent is that of Julia who, according to Byron's report, 'whispering "I will ne'er consent,"—consented.' " Those who supported state aid to church schools argued that for New Jersey to deny transportation to students attending parochial schools would have reflected governmental hostility, not neutrality, toward religion. During the next two decades, the question of state aid to church schools and its questionable status under the Establishment Clause subsided and was overshadowed by the issue of religious activities in public schools. When state aid returned to prominence in the 1970s, the Supreme Court was not prepared to follow a clear line of reasoning.

When Aid to Religion Is Not Really Aid: Emergence of the Three-Prong Test

As parochial schools found it increasingly more difficult to meet their financial obligations in the 1960s and 1970s, parents and church authorities became more vocal in pressing state legislatures to authorize subsidies for church-school operations. In 1968, the Supreme Court ruled that a New York law requiring local school districts to lend textbooks on secular subjects to parochial school students at no cost was not a violation of the Establishment Clause. In *Board of Education* v. *Allen* (1968), the Court ruled 5–4 that the law had both "a secular legislative purpose and a primary effect that neither advances nor inhibits religion." This two-prong guideline had been created five years earlier in the Bible Reading Cases of 1963 (to be discussed as the "*Schempp* test"). Writing for the majority, Justice Byron White invoked the familiar child-benefit theory, stating that the financial benefit provided by New York State was to the parents and the children, not to the religious schools. Within three years, in the early years of the new Burger Court, the issue of aid to parochial schools would receive more extensive review; in the meantime, one additional case, which had nothing to do directly with such "parochiaid," occurred and affected future Establishment Clause cases.

Walz v. *Tax Commission of New York City* in 1970 concerned tax exemptions for property owned by religious organizations and used for religious purposes. This particular controversy had been festering for some time. The argument put forth by strict separationists was twofold. First, granting tax-exempt status to churches and other religious organizations violated the Establishment Clause by providing yet another benefit to religion. Furthermore, it also denied an important source of tax revenue to governments, inasmuch as the exempted property was often located in valuable urban and suburban settings. Chief Justice Burger wrote in *Walz* that, under the First Amendment, the Court would tolerate neither state-established religion nor governmental interference with religion. Short of these prohibited governmental acts, said Burger, "There is room for play in the joints productive of a *benevolent neutrality* which will permit religious exercise to exist without sponsorship [or] interference [Emphasis added]." He argued that the tax exemptions neither advanced nor inhibited religion and were granted in the same manner that many other nonprofit properties, such as libraries, hospitals, and a host of community organizations, enjoyed. Finally, given the particular demands of the Establishment Clause, Burger emphasized that these tax exemptions had to be provided in a way that did not result in "an excessive government entanglement with religion." This last requirement and the two earlier elements noted in *Allen*—secular purpose and primary effect—soon became important criteria by which to judge future Establishment Clause cases before the Supreme Court.

The 1970s were especially active years regarding aid to parochial schools and court challenges to those programs. In several decisions concerning the parochiaid issue, the Burger Court gradually moved away from the earlier emphasis upon benefits being provided to the *students* involved and toward the nature of the relationship between government and religion. The most prominent case, *Lemon* v. *Kurtzman* (1971), involved two separate state-aid-to-schools programs. Under a 1968 Pennsylvania law, the state directly reimbursed parochial schools for expenditures incurred for teacher salaries and for the purchase of textbooks and various instructional materials in selected secular subjects. Under a similar law passed by the Rhode Island legislature in 1969, that state contributed up to 15 percent of the salaries for teachers in parochial schools who were engaged in teaching only secular subjects offered in the public schools.

In this case, again with Chief Justice Burger delivering the majority opinion, the two state laws were declared unconstitutional. After reviewing the background of the two state laws, Burger observed that this "extraordinarily sensitive area of constitutional law" had to pass three important elements:

> First, the statute must have a secular legislative purpose; second, its principal or primary effect must be one that neither advances nor inhibits religion, *Allen;* finally, the statute must not foster "an excessive government entanglement with religion" *Walz.*

The third element—excessive entanglement—is what condemned both of the state-aid programs in Pennsylvania and Rhode Island. The Court said that both programs involved too close a relationship between government and religion. In the Rhode Island example, the Court thought that some teachers involved might find it virtually impossible "to make a total separation between secular teaching and religious doctrine." In addition, because the state education board had to inspect and evaluate the religious content of the curriculum in order to ensure secularism, the program was "fraught with the sort of entanglement that the Constitution forbids." The Pennsylvania program was burdened by basically the same aspects as the plan in Rhode Island, with the additional problem of providing direct financial aid to the parochial schools. Although drawn from earlier precedents, the **Lemon test**—secular purpose, primary effect, and excessive entanglement—would be very important to future aid-to-parochial-schools controversies.

Decided on the same day as *Lemon,* another case dealt with the constitutionality of federal aid to higher education. Under Title I of the Higher Education Facilities Act of 1963, private colleges could receive federal construction grants for buildings and facilities, if they guaranteed that the monies would not be used for religious education. The act was challenged as a violation of the Establishment Clause. In a 6–3 decision, in *Tilton v. Richardson* (1971), the Burger Court upheld the constitutionality of the law. According to the majority opinion, significant differences distinguished the two cases. College students were "less impressionable and less susceptible to religious indoctrination" than were primary and secondary students. There was also a more secure climate of academic freedom at the four private colleges involved, and the federal grant in question was a one-time, single-purpose grant not requiring any continuing audits or administration. These distinctions did not convince the dissenters in the *Tilton* case. They found the majority's handling of the two cases unacceptable. As Justice Brennan, himself a Roman Catholic, said in a separate dissent, "A sectarian university is the equivalent in the realm of higher education of the Catholic elementary schools in Rhode Island; it is an educational institution in which the propagation and advancement of a particular religion is a primary function of the institution." He saw the same purposes present in both sets of institutions—secular education *and* religious instruction.

As might be expected, controversies continued to arrive at the Supreme Court throughout the early 1970s, especially from New York and Pennsylvania, which have substantial Roman Catholic populations. In 1973, the Supreme Court again divided 6–3 in striking down three separate programs in New York State for subsidizing parochial schools. In the case of *Committee for Public Education* v. *Nyquist* (1973), the Court declared unconstitutional plans for funding facility maintenance grants to schools serving several students from low-income families, tuition reimbursements to low-income families, and tax benefits to parents with children in parochial schools. The three dissenting justices—Burger, Rehnquist, and White—voted with the majority to invalidate the first program, which provided maintenance and repair grants to the schools involved, but they argued that the reimbursements and benefits plans did not violate the Establishment Clause.

Two years after *Nyquist,* Pennsylvania's recently revised aid program was examined by the Court. *Meek* v. *Pittenger* (1975) dealt with three plans for subsidizing parochial schools within the state. The first provided assorted instructional materials and equipment to private schools, 75 percent of which were church related, and a second program authorized auxiliary services— such as counseling, testing, and speech and hearing therapy—for both disadvantaged and exceptional students. A third plan authorized lending textbooks to children in the nonpublic schools. Justice Stewart wrote a majority opinion for another 6–3 decision in which the Court set aside all but the textbook plan. The Court majority ruled that the other two plans had a primary *effect* of advancing religion.

Two final cases dealing with parochiaid in the 1970s indicate that the Supreme Court would uphold aid to parochial schools, even if the programs failed the *Lemon* test. Both cases, however, reflect the Court's subjectivity in considering the "safe" features of such plans. The Court in 1976 upheld a Maryland plan that provided financial aid to church-related colleges. So divided was the Court in its 5–4 decision in *Roemer* v. *Board of Public Works* (1976) that there emerged no majority opinion, but instead a series of separate opinions stressing different reasoning. Many of the opinions reiterated the same points cited in *Tilton* v. *Richardson,* concerning the ability of the colleges to separate the secular and religious functions, the less impressionable nature of the students, and the less likelihood of indoctrination of the students. Noting the historic emphasis placed upon separation of church and state, Justice Harry Blackmun observed that a "hermetic separation of the two is an impossibility." Regarding the third prong of the *Lemon* test, he also stated that "there is no exact science in gauging the entanglement of church and state." Finally, in *Wolman* v. *Walter* in 1977, another very divided Supreme Court found certain Ohio programs for aiding parochial schools constitutional (those providing textbooks; speech, hearing, and psychological diagnostic services; and standardized testing and scoring plans), while striking down other programs (an assortment of instructional materials and equipment).

These cases in the 1970s dealing with assorted state plans to aid sectarian schools left a rather tangled path constructed by a very divided Burger Court. The general trend was for the Court to deny most forms of *direct* state aid to primary and secondary schools on any one of the *Lemon* test guidelines, the one most frequently invoked being "excessive entanglement." The justices in the 1970s were much more prone to allow direct government aid programs to sectarian colleges and universities and directly to students (e.g., *Tilton* and *Roemer*) than they were to allow states to indirectly aid parochial primary and secondary schools (*Lemon, Nyquist,* and *Pittenger*). Grants and tax benefits paid to parents of parochial students, facility maintenance grants for parochial institutions (*Nyquist),* and the payment of teacher salaries in parochial schools (*Lemon*) were unconstitutional under the Establishment Clause. However, programs involving the lending of secular textbook materials to parochial institutions (*Allen, Pittenger,* and *Wolman*) were usually allowed during the 1970s.

When the issue of religious aid continued into the 1980s, the Supreme Court departed from many of its earlier rulings. None of the preceding judgments has been overruled, but the Court has resorted at times to tortuous reasoning to distinguish prior judgments from a case under consideration. The result by the mid-1980s was a maze of Establishment Clause decisions. Before focusing upon recent Establishment Clause cases, and a possible change from a Court grown weary of the many problems inherent in the two religion clauses, attention must be given to the other major aspect of Establishment Clause controversy—religious activities in public schools. Instead of concentrating upon what programs affecting *parochial* schools may violate the First Amendment, the focus will be what religious activities in the *public* classroom are violative of that amendment.

Religious Activities in Public Schools

As soon as the Supreme Court applied the Establishment Clause to the states in *Everson,* an issue arose in Illinois requiring the Court to determine what sort of activities in the public school classroom involved possible violations of the First Amendment. *McCollum* v. *Board of Education* (1948) dealt with the validity of the Champaign, Illinois, released-time program for religious instruction for public school students. In 1940, an interfaith group of religious leaders in Champaign petitioned the municipal school board to offer classes in religious instruction to public school students in grades four through nine. Privately employed religious teachers were invited into the public schools to offer weekly classes to children of parents who had signed a permission slip authorizing the inclusion of their children in the weekly exercises. Nonparticipating students studied various secular subjects elsewhere in the school building.

Scarcely one year after applying the Establishment Clause to the states, the Court overturned the Champaign released-time program as a violation of the First Amendment. Justice Black rested most of the Court's decision upon the fact that the Champaign program utilized the state's tax-supported facilities for disseminating religious teachings and the state's compulsory school attendance law to ensure a readily available audience. In a concurring opinion in which he was joined by Justices Jackson, Rutledge, and Burton, Justice Frankfurter disapproved of the Champaign plan because "the momentum of the whole school atmosphere and school planning is presumably put behind religious instruction." The lone dissenting vote in this case was that of Justice Stanley Reed, who felt that the Court had grossly misinterpreted the intent of the framers to ban only establishment of a state church or religion:

> Never until today . . . has this Court widened its interpretation to . . . such degree as holding that recognition of the interest of our nation in religion, through the granting, to qualified representatives of the principal faiths, of opportunity to present religion as an optional, extracurricular subject during released school time in public school buildings, was equivalent to an establishment of religion.

This major disagreement over what the Establishment Clause actually means has been at the core of many of the disagreements among the justices for forty years as the Supreme Court has struggled with Establishment Clause cases.

Given the conservative climate of postwar United States and the American public's perception of a serious threat from international communism, *McCollum* was not a popular decision. Whether influenced by the heat of public opinion or the circumstances of the case, four years later, the Supreme Court upheld a released-time program in New York City in *Zorach v. Clauson* (1952). The main differences between the Champaign plan and the New York City program were that the latter was held in church buildings, rather than in the public schools, and there was no visible expenditure of public funds. Curiously, the *Zorach* decision found Justice Douglas, one of the most liberal justices on the Court, authoring the majority opinion for a 6–3 decision. In his opinion, Douglas listed several examples of how the Establishment Clause did not require a complete separation of church and state. His examples included tax exemptions, police and fire protection for churches, prayers in legislative assemblies, and courtroom oaths that include the reference "so help me God." He maintained that the released-time program in New York demonstrated respect for the "religious nature of our people and accommodates the public service to their spiritual needs." In a passage often cited to counter criticisms that the Supreme Court was antireligious and working to "banish God from the classroom," Justice Douglas stated:

> We are a religious people whose institutions presuppose a Supreme Being . . . When the state encourages religious instruction or cooperates with religious authorities by adjusting the schedule of public events to sectarian needs, it follows the best of our traditions.

Justices Black and Jackson dissented in the *Zorach* case—Black because he found no meaningful differences between *McCollum* and *Zorach,* and Jackson because he thought that the wall being erected between church and state was "even more warped and twisted than I expected." The latter felt that *Zorach* would be more valuable to "students of psychology and the judicial processes than to students of constitutional law."

The Delicate Issue of School Prayer

Following World War II, *Everson, McCollum,* and *Zorach* were the main freedom of religion cases decided by the Supreme Court. During the 1950s, the Court did not have many occasions to elaborate upon its emerging Establishment Clause doctrine, although the *Everson* and *Zorach* decisions indicate that the justices were willing to allow some cooperation between government and religion. By the 1960s, the public debate over the role of religion in public schools became more heated, as the Court tackled one of its most controversial subjects—prayer in public schools. In many respects, the impact of three decisions on this topic has persisted to the present day and has embroiled the Court in a major wave of public hostility that accuses it of becoming a "super-legislature" unaccountable to the American people.

The furor began with the Court's decision in *Engel v. Vitale* in 1962 that state-sponsored prayer in public schools was a violation of the Establishment Clause. At issue in this landmark decision was a nondenominational prayer of twenty-two words that had been recommended by the New York

State Board of Regents in 1951, for recitation at the beginning of each school day in New York public schools.[10] Although not required by the state, in 1958 the New Hyde Park school district on Long Island decided to make the prayer mandatory and have it read or recited each day in the presence of a teacher. Those children whose parents did not want them to participate in the prayer exercise could be excused from the classroom.

A group of parents in the district, led by Steven Engel, brought suit in federal court, claiming that the prayer exercise violated the First and Fourteenth Amendments of the Constitution. Writing for a six-member majority, Justice Black, whose opinion in *Everson* first defined what was prohibited by the Establishment Clause, wrote that in spite of the ambiguity of the clause, it did have substantive meaning:

> The constitutional prohibition against laws respecting an establishment of religion must at least mean that in this country it is no part of the business of government to compose official prayers for any group of the American people to recite as part of a religious program carried on by government . . . It is neither sacreligious nor antireligious to say that each separate government in this country should stay out of the business of writing or sanctioning official prayers and leave that purely religious function to the people themselves and to those [to whom] the people choose to look for religious guidance.

According to Black, the prayer had definite religious content, and the fact that it was nondenominational and voluntary did not save it from limitations imposed by the First Amendment. "When the power, prestige, and financial support of government," said Black, "is placed behind a particular religious belief, the indirect coercive pressure upon religious minorities to conform to the prevailing officially approved religion is plain." The only dissenting vote in *Engel* was that of Justice Stewart, who regretted the Court's denying the school children the opportunity to share "in the spiritual heritage of our Nation."

This particular decision was immediately condemned by citizens, church leaders, and many members of Congress. Clearly, if oral prayer in public schools were unconstitutional, other religious activities would most likely be scrutinized soon. Within one year, the Court had before it two more cases that required further curtailment of mandatory practices in the public schools. In *Abington School District* v. *Schempp* (1963), the practice in question was a Pennsylvania law requiring that at least ten verses from the Bible be read without comment at the beginning of each school day in all public schools of the state. Any child could be excused from the exercise with parental permission. The parents of two students belonging to the Unitarian church contended that the law violated the religious rights of their children under the First Amendment. A three-judge federal district court held the law unconstitutional, and the school district appealed to the Supreme Court.

Another case from the state of Maryland decided on the same day, entitled *Murray* v. *Curlett,* involved the Baltimore Board of School Commissioners and its policy, based upon a state law, which required reading at least one chapter from the Bible or reciting the Lord's Prayer at the beginning of each school day. The law and its local implementation were challenged by Madelyn Murray and her son William, both professed atheists, as an unconstitutional infringement upon their First Amendment rights. The Murrays lost their case in state courts and appealed to the Supreme Court.

In an 8–1 ruling, the Court struck down the state requirements for daily Bible readings and the recitation of the Lord's Prayer as violations of the Establishment Clause. In drafting the majority opinion, Justice Clark articulated two of the three requirements that would several years later compose the *Lemon* test used to judge alleged Establishment Clause violations:

> The test may be stated as follows: what are the *purposes* and the *primary effect* of the enactment? If either is the advancement or inhibition of religion then the enactment exceeds the scope of legislative power... That is to say that to withstand the strictures of the Establishment Clause there must be a secular legislative purpose and a primary effect that neither advances nor inhibits religion.

When the activities prescribed by these state laws were compared to previous exercises in public schools, the differences were marked. Pennsylvania and Maryland were here requiring religious exercises as part of the curricular activities of students having to attend public school, and the activities were held in public facilities and supervised by government employees. To those who argued that a few minutes for prayer at the beginning of each school day were beneficial for moral inspiration, Clark stated that "the breach of neutrality that is today a trickling stream may all too soon become a raging torrent." Noting that an individual's education is not complete without a study of comparative religions and that reading the Bible has both historical and literary value, Clark, as Douglas had in 1952, reaffirmed the importance of religion to Americans:

> The place of religion in our society is an exalted one, achieved through a long tradition of reliance on the home, the church and the inviolable citadel of the individual heart and mind. We have come to recognize through bitter experience that it is not within the power of government to invade that citadel, whether its purpose or effect be to aid or oppose, to advance or retard. In the relationship between man and religion, the State is firmly committed to a position of neutrality.

In a separate concurring opinion, Justice Brennan emphasized that the Establishment Clause was intended to prevent more than simply the creation of an official state church or religion. He was convinced that the founding generation, which included Jefferson and Madison, was committed to preventing "interdependence between religion and state." The task of judges who authoritatively interpret the Constitution is to apply the "majestic generalities of the Bill of Rights" to the problems of the twentieth century. Again, the only dissenter in the cases was Justice Stewart, who regretted the "insensitive definition" and the "fallacious oversimplification" of the Establishment Clause into a single standard of separation. He felt that banishing these religious exercises from the public classroom placed religion at an "artificial and state-created disadvantage" and violated the students' religious rights.

The Status of School Prayer Today

In the twenty-five years since these three decisions, there has been a firestorm of public criticism of the Court for "expelling God from American classrooms." With the possible exception of the period following *Brown* v. *Board of Education* in 1954–55, and the massive civil resistance accompanying desegregation decisions, perhaps no other Supreme Court decisions of the twentieth century have met with as much noncompliance as have the *Engel, Schempp,* and *Murray* decisions. Dozens of school districts throughout the United States have simply ignored the rulings in these three cases. Deliberate violations of the rulings have, in fact, been encouraged by public officials at all levels of government. Henry Abraham has noted that by 1986 over 380 proposed constitutional amendments designed to reverse the Court's prayer and Bible reading decisions had been introduced in Congress, some of which nearly passed.[11] Public opinion polls in the 1980s have consistently shown that 70–75 percent of the American public favors the return of "voluntary" prayer to the classroom, however that word might be interpreted. President Ronald Reagan consistently pushed voluntary prayer as a major "social-agenda" item, invoking it frequently in State of the Union addresses, in speeches to religious organizations, and on the campaign trail (see Brief 13.3).

One point ought to be kept in mind regarding this much-debated topic of prayer in public schools. The Supreme Court has never said that school children may not pray in school. Rather, it has consistently reaffirmed its decisions in *Engel* and *Schempp*—that government must ensure that *prescribed, oral* prayer not be mandated in the classroom. To do so could expose impressionable elementary and secondary students to the heavy hand of the state and coerce what ought to be a deeply personal matter. What many Supreme Court critics over the past few decades seem to have forgotten is that the Bill of Rights was not drafted in order to safeguard *majority* rights, opinions, or prerogatives, but rather to protect the rights of vulnerable *minorities.* So many of those who have railed against the activist Supreme Court during the past several years on this issue of school prayer seem to have forgotten that simple lesson of American history.

❑ *Brief 13.3   The Move to Get School Prayer "Out of the Closet"*

Oral prayer enthusiasts rejoiced in 1980 over the election of Ronald Reagan, who arrived in Washington prepared to install a new moral order in America. Among the issues that prayer supporters pushed for was a major policy change in the *Engel* and *Schempp* precedents. After numerous speeches extolling the virtue of prayer in public schools, the president finally took action. In 1982, Reagan sent to Congress a proposed constitutional amendment allowing oral prayer in the public school classroom. The amendment sent to Capitol Hill read: "Nothing in this Constitution shall be construed to prohibit individual or group prayer in public schools or other public institutions. No person shall be required by the United States or by any state to participate in prayer. Neither the United States nor any state shall compose the words of any prayer to be used in public schools."

The suggested amendment garnered little support at first, but by early 1984, in the midst of a pres-

idential campaign with the president and a host of Democratic presidential contenders vying for public approval, the proposal gathered momentum. On March 20, 1984, the Senate voted to approve the proposed amendment by a vote of 56–44, which was still eleven votes short of the necessary two-thirds vote required to send it to the respective states.

By July 1984, school prayer strategists had shifted their sights to "moment-of-silence" laws. On July 26, the Democratic-controlled House of Representatives voted overwhelmingly to allow moments of individual silent prayer in public classrooms, after narrowly defeating a much stronger Republican-sponsored proposal that would have condoned spoken prayer in public schools. Lawmakers on both sides of the issue said that the silent prayer proposal was little more than an expression of support for the status quo.

The Establishment Clause in the 1980s

If school prayer and Bible reading decisions were topics of the chaotic 1960s, and parochiaid cases troubled the Court in the 1970s, the 1980s generated a mixed batch of church-state decisions, both in terms of issue and content. The Burger Court seemed to veer in one direction and then another, approving some state legislation affecting religion and striking down other practices. The result has been a confusing line of judicial precedents that please some, but trouble others. For example, one decision in 1980 struck many Court critics as being too rigid in its interpretation of the Establishment Clause. Although the vote was very close, the Burger Court in *Stone* v. *Graham* (1980) said that a Kentucky law requiring the posting of the Ten Commandments in public classrooms was unconstitutional because it violated the secular purpose of the *Lemon* test. But several other decisions of the Court, with the exception of an important free exercise case in 1983 having prominent racial overtones (see Brief 13.4), saw the Supreme Court ruling in favor of practices that it said did not violate the Establishment Clause. This section will attempt to follow the Establishment Clause trail by referring to several cases of the Burger Court in the 1980s that have built a porous "wall of separation."

☐ *Brief 13.4   Tolerance, Taxes, and the Old Testament*

The Reagan administration encountered a dilemma in early 1982 that had important implications for both civil rights and church-state separation. Like so many legal issues, this particular one started many years earlier. Until 1970, the Internal Revenue Service (IRS) had granted tax-exempt status to all private schools, regardless of their racial admissions policy, under Section 501 (c) of the IRS Code. In July 1970, the IRS said it could no longer legally justify allowing such status to private schools practicing racial discrimination. By November, the agency had notified all private schools of its new policy.

Bob Jones University in Greenville, South Carolina—a nonprofit private school with a student body of about 5,000 students—was forced to change its admissions policy as a result of the IRS ruling. Maintaining that the Bible forbids interracial marriage and dating, the school had denied all blacks admission to the college until 1971. Between 1971 and 1975, the institution accepted only qualified married black applicants.

Finding that Bob Jones University was still discriminating, the IRS, in April 1975, notified the school that its tax-exempt status would be revoked. Bob Jones University sued in federal court, claiming a violation of its rights under the Free Exercise Clause. The district court found in favor of the school, and the court of appeals reversed that decision. By July 1981, Bob Jones

University and another institution (Goldsboro Christian Schools in Goldsboro, North Carolina) appealed the adverse ruling to the U.S. Supreme Court. The Reagan administration initially filed a brief with the Court supporting denial of the tax-exempt status for the schools, but in January 1982, the White House reversed itself and argued that the IRS had no authority to take such drastic action. Then, not wanting to endure further criticisms that his administration was insensitive to civil rights issues, President Reagan quickly issued a statement saying that Congress should pass legislation authorizing the IRS to take the action that it did.

In May 1983, the Supreme Court ruled 8–1 that racially discriminatory private schools are not eligible for federal tax-exempt status. In the case of *Bob Jones University* v. *United States* (1983), the majority said that the IRS's antidiscrimination policy was a proper interpretation of federal tax law, that the agency had proper congressional authority to carry out its policy, and that the policy did not violate any constitutional rights of the schools or their students.

Not everyone was pleased with the decision. The Reverend Bob Jones, president of the university, observed in a sermon to the student body in school chapel that "we're in a bad fix when eight evil old men and one vain and foolish woman can speak a verdict on American liberties." [12]

The Movement Toward Governmental Accommodation of Religion

The new tolerance for religion in public schools began with a Missouri case in 1981 entitled *Widmar* v. *Vincent*. In an effort to encourage on-campus activities, the University of Missouri at Kansas City (UMKC) had for many years recognized over one hundred student organizations, providing them with meeting facilities on the UMKC campus. Between 1973 and 1977, a registered religious group on the UMKC campus named Cornerstone had regularly sought and received university permission to conduct its meetings on the campus. But in 1977, the administration told the group that it could no longer use campus facilities. Campus authorities explained that the denial was based upon a 1972 regulation. The regulation, which had not been properly enforced, prohibited the use of school buildings "for purposes of religious worship or teaching." Eleven student members of Cornerstone, including Clark Vincent, sued the university, challenging the regulation as a violation of their constitutional rights under the First Amendment entitlement to free exercise of religion and freedom of speech and on Fourteenth Amendment equal protection grounds. The federal district court trying the case ruled in favor of the university's policy, the court of appeals reversed the judgment, and UMKC appealed the adverse ruling to the Supreme Court.

In an 8–1 decision, the Court said that public universities which made their facilities generally available for the activities of registered student organizations cannot exclude religious groups from such facilities because of the content of their speech. In striking down the university's policy, the majority reasoned that by providing the campus organizations with facilities in which to meet, the school had created a "forum generally open" for use by student groups. Having done that, it then had to justify why it had discriminated against Cornerstone. The university claimed that it had a compelling interest in maintaining strict separation of church and state, which it based upon both the state constitution and the federal Constitution.

The Court's decision in *Widmar* turned upon the primary-effect element of *Lemon,* since the university's policy clearly met the secular-purpose and no-excessive-entanglement prongs of the 1971 ruling. The university insisted that to grant religious groups access to public facilities would advance religion. But the Court did not agree with this contention, insisting that, as past rulings indicated, a religious organization's enjoying "incidental" benefits did not necessarily constitute advancement of religion. Using the facilities did not indicate any specific state approval of religious groups or their practices, since the facilities were available to a broad class of groups, nonreligious and religious. Justice White dissented in *Widmar,* stating that the majority ruling would "inevitably lead to . . . contradictions and tensions between the Establishment and Free Exercise Clauses." White also thought that the Court was being inconsistent in ignoring the religious content of the speech involved here in *Widmar*. In numerous other cases, it had struck down such practices as the posting of the Ten Commandments (*Stone* v. *Graham*), school prayer and Bible readings (*Engel* and *Schempp*), and the declaration of belief in God as a condition of state employment (*Torcaso* v. *Watkins*) because of religious *content*. Therefore, it seemed like the Court was now contradicting previous rulings on similar content-based practices.

This ruling had an important effect in building momentum for the issue that has come to be known as **equal access** of religious groups to public facilities. Substantial majorities in both houses of Congress passed the Equal Access Act by late July 1984, which President Reagan signed into law on August 11, 1984. This legislation allowed primary and secondary public school groups, religious and nonreligious, the same right to meet in public facilities, thus extending the principle established in *Widmar* to public schools.

Two other decisions in 1983 found the Burger Court going in a very different direction on church-state matters and encouraging those who had bristled for years with a Supreme Court that had produced the *Engel* and *Schempp* precedents. But these two decisions—one authorizing tuition tax credits to parents with children in parochial schools and another dealing with prayers by a state-sponsored chaplain—are difficult to reconcile with past activity in federal courts.

The Supreme Court first tackled the issue of the ability of states to offer residents tuition tax credits for expenses incurred in sending their children to parochial schools. It should be recalled that a decade earlier, in *Committee for Public Education* v. *Nyquist,* the Court had declared invalid a New York law that had allowed both tuition grants and tuition tax credits for parents whose children attended church-related institutions. In that decision, Justice Lewis Powell insisted for a five-member majority that the grants-credits plans were not merely rendering economic assistance to parents sending their children to sectarian schools, but their "purpose and inevitable effect are to aid and advance those religious institutions."

For many years, Minnesota had authorized its taxpayers to deduct from their gross income up to $700 for expenses they incurred for school tuition, textbooks, transportation, and other supplies for dependents who attended elementary and secondary schools within the state. Although the state law specifically extended this benefit to all parents, regardless of whether the children attended public or private institutions, the court record indicated that over 95 percent of the parents taking advantage of the tax credit had children enrolled in religious schools. Some Minnesota taxpayers contested the law, arguing in federal court that it violated the Establishment Clause. Both the trial and the appellate courts upheld the constitutionality of the law, and the judgment was appealed to the Supreme Court.

A 5–4 majority in *Mueller* v. *Allen* (1983) affirmed the lower court decisions and found the Minnesota law constitutional. In writing the majority opinion, Justice William Rehnquist's main task was to distinguish this case from several other parochiaid controversies of the preceding two decades. In examining the three elements of *Lemon*, Rehnquist considered the secular-purpose element to have been satisfied:

> An educated populace is essential to the political and economic health of any community, and a state's efforts to assist parents in meeting the rising cost of education expenses plainly serves this secular purpose . . . Similarly, Minnesota . . . could conclude that there is a strong public interest in assuring the continued financial health of private schools, both sectarian and non-sectarian. By educating a substantial number of students such schools relieve public schools of a correspondingly great burden—to the benefit of all taxpayers.

The second element of the tripartite *Lemon* test, primary effect, was the most difficult to justify because the Court here was upholding a program that so closely resembled similar programs struck down in previous cases. Rehnquist said *Mueller* was "vitally different" from *Nyquist* because the New York law in 1973 had allowed tuition deductions only for parents with children in *nonpublic* schools, whereas the Minnesota law was designed to benefit both public and private school parents. In response to critics claiming only a "facial neutrality" in the law, Rehnquist said that the Court would not establish a rule requiring annual reports attesting to how many parents took advantage of the law. Finally, the excessive-entanglement element of *Lemon* was not violated, since Minnesota was not involved in any extensive monitoring program to screen instructional materials used in parochial schools.

In dissent, where he was joined by Justices Brennan, Blackmun, and Stevens, Justice Thurgood Marshall was astounded to see the Court ignoring the *Nyquist* precedent:

> [*Nyquist*] . . . established that a State may not support religious education either through direct grants to parochial schools or through financial aid to parents of parochial school students . . . [F]inancial aid to parents of students attending parochial schools is no more permissible if it is provided in the form of a tax credit than if provided in the form of cash payments.

Marshall found no appreciable difference between the defective New York law struck down in 1973 and the Minnesota law upheld in *Mueller*. To him, both had "a direct and immediate effect of advancing religion." Finally, he noted that just because the Minnesota law made "some small benefit available to all parents" this did not alter the fact that of all parents eligible for the tuition deduction, 96 percent of them sent their children to religious schools.

Soon after handing down the *Mueller* decision, the Court addressed the long-standing practice in many legislative assemblies in the United States, including the U.S. Congress, of employing legislative chaplains. The case of *Marsh* v. *Chambers* (1983) concerned the sixteen-year practice of Nebraska of having a state-employed chaplain pray before each day of legislative business. A 6–3 Court majority upheld this procedure as constitutional under the Establishment Clause. Chief Justice Burger characterized the practice as "part of the fabric of our society." According to the chief justice, "To involve Divine guidance on a public body entrusted with making the laws is not . . . an 'establishment' of religion or a step towards establishment; it is simply a tolerable acknowledgement of beliefs widely held among people of this country." He further insisted that the framers of the First Amendment clearly did not intend to exclude this custom, since the same practice had been followed by the national government ever since the first Congress in 1789. Justice Brennan, who dissented in the *Marsh* decision, thought that official prayers in state legislatures were unconstitutional and contrary to "the underlying purpose of the Establishment Clause."

Coming at the end of the 1982 term, these two decisions revealed a Supreme Court that was both deeply divided in its interpretation of the Establishment Clause and willing to ignore many of its earlier precedents. During the next two terms, the Court also handed down some very important decisions in which the justices tacked in one direction and then in another.

One case involved a city-sponsored Nativity scene in Pawtucket, Rhode Island. For four decades, the city had cooperated with downtown merchants in erecting a Nativity scene as part of its Christmas holiday season observance. The display included both secular and religious figures—including Santa's sleigh and reindeer, a Christmas tree, carolers, and a crèche consisting of the traditional Nativity figures of the Christ child, Mary, and Joseph. All the components of the display were owned by the city of Pawtucket and erected at public expense in a privately owned park. A group in the city challenged the display as a violation of the Establishment Clause, and both the federal district and appellate courts said that it violated the Establishment Clause.

The case was appealed to the Supreme Court, and, in *Lynch* v. *Donnelly* (1984), the Court upheld the Nativity display. In a 5–4 judgment, Chief Justice Burger began by stating that Establishment Clause cases involved an "inescapable tension" between church and state and a realization that "total separation of the two is not possible." In Burger's mind, the Constitution "affirmatively mandates *accommodation,* not merely tolerance, of all religions, and forbids hostility toward any [Emphasis added]." He characterized the display as a "passive" symbol only remotely benefiting any religion and insisted that it served as a useful reminder of a national holiday's roots. Toward the latter portion of his opinion, in response to the criticisms of his dissenting colleagues, Burger viewed the display in largely secular terms:

> [It] engenders a friendly community spirit of good will in keeping with the season. . . That the display brings people into the central city, and serves commercial interests and benefits merchants and their employees, does not . . . determine the character of the display.

He also indicated that those who argue that this sort of holiday display offends some religious sensitivities and violates the Establishment Clause are overreacting. In a passage dripping with sarcasm, the chief justice observed:

> We are unable to perceive the Archbishop of Canterbury, the Vicar of Rome, or other powerful religious leaders behind every public acknowledgement of the religious heritage long officially recognized by the three constitutional branches of government. Any notion that these symbols pose a real danger of establishment of a state church is farfetched indeed.

In a dissenting opinion, Justice Brennan faulted the majority for its distorted application of the *Lemon* test. He thought that the Nativity display violated both the secular-purpose and the primary-effects elements of that standard. If the city were only interested in celebrating the holiday and attracting the public to the downtown retail area, it could have done that without including the crèche in the holiday display. Its inclusion of a "distinctly religious element like the crèche . . . demonstrates that a narrower sectarian purpose lay behind the decision to include a nativity scene." Furthermore, the inclusion of that scene in the display has the effect, according to Brennan, of placing "the government's imprimatur of approval on the particular religious beliefs exemplified by the crèche." Although he recognized the tensions imposed by First Amendment guarantees of religious freedom, Brennan wrote that in order to remain "scrupulously neutral in matters of religious conscience," government must avoid overly broad acknowledgements of religious beliefs and practices. On this score, the Pawtucket crèche fell short. Finally, Brennan was troubled by the majority's attempt to "explain away the clear religious import" of the Nativity scene. He differed with the majority's attempt to trivialize this important symbol of Christianity:

> To suggest, as the Court does, that [the crèche] is merely "traditional" and therefore no different from Santa's house or reindeer is not only offensive to

those for whom the crèche has profound significance, but insulting to those who insist for religious or personal reasons that the story of Christ is in no sense a part of "history" nor an unavoidable element of our national "heritage."

A short accompanying dissent by Justice Blackmun echoed Brennan's sentiments, saying that the majority "does an injustice to the crèche and the message it manifests."

Lynch v. *Donnelly* marked the fourth decision, beginning with *Widmar* in 1981, that demonstrated the Supreme Court's increased acceptance of the accommodationist relationship between church and state in the United States. Ever since *Zorach* v. *Clauson* in 1952, the Court has frequently acknowledged the role of religion in American life. But the *Lynch* decision, even more than *Widmar, Mueller,* and *Marsh,* found the Court majority adroitly reclassifying as secular those activities that reflect America's religious heritage. In reaching the conclusions that it did, the Court radically diluted the first two elements of *Lemon* and expanded the range of activities that may survive judicial scrutiny. As Justice Brennan noted in dissent, the Pawtucket citizens sought not mere accommodation of their religious beliefs, but rather the active participation of the city in celebrating Christmas in accordance with their particular view of that holiday's Christian content. But the decision also indicated a disturbing tendency to explain away the peculiarly Christian nature of the crèche. In its rush to approve what the Pawtucket officials had done, the Court seemed anxious to purge an important symbol of Christianity and personal faith of most of its religious significance. Ironically, evangelicals who might normally applaud this decision should pay close attention to the reasoning of the Court. The Nativity scene now seems to carry more secular and commercial significance than it does religious meaning. In the eyes of many, Christmas after *Lynch* has been thoroughly "Santa-tized and sanitized"!

The Court Veers Back Toward Separation

Three more decisions in 1985 had very important implications for the two church-state issues that had preoccupied the Court for over two decades—school prayer and aid to parochial schools. To the dismay of those who were encouraged by many of the decisions of the previous few terms, the Supreme Court seemed to veer back toward a more pronounced separationist stance on church-state issues.

A Setback for School Prayer

By the mid-1980s, roughly one-half of the states had passed what are usually referred to as "moment-of-silence" laws that allow public schools to set aside a brief period at the beginning of each school day for meditation or reflection. Alabama had passed such a law in 1981, under which "a period of silence not to exceed one minute in duration shall be observed for *meditation or voluntary prayer* [Emphasis added]." Ishmael Jaffree, the father of three children enrolled in the Mobile public school system, had failed on several occasions to have vocal prayer sessions in the public schools discontinued. Finally, he sued in federal court, claiming that the prayers violated his First and Fourteenth Amendment rights. The lower courts had no trouble finding that the Mobile practice of oral prayer, as *Engel* v. *Vitale* had established in 1962, was a violation of the Establishment Clause. But the moment-of-silence issue was more difficult. Federal Judge Brevard Hand, an opponent of strict separation of church-state relations, upheld the Alabama law. The decision was reversed by the court of appeals, and the state appealed the judgment to the Supreme Court.

In June 1985, by a vote of 6–3 in the case of *Wallace* v. *Jaffree,* the Supreme Court ruled the law unconstitutional, saying that it constituted an official establishment of religion by fostering religious activity in the classroom. Writing for the majority, Justice John Paul Stevens said that the Alabama law had failed the purely secular-purpose prong of *Lemon.* In introducing the Alabama law in 1981, the key sponsor of the bill in the Alabama legislature had indicated that the legislation was an "effort to return voluntary prayer" to the public classroom, and the state presented no other purpose in justifying the law. Arguing that the bill clearly sought to change existing Alabama law, Justice Stevens noted that the legislature had passed the bill "for the sole purpose of expressing that state's endorsement of prayer activities at the beginning of each school day." He said that since the law specifically allowed for "meditation or voluntary prayer," the state fully intended to characterize prayer as a favored practice. According to Stevens, "Such an endorsement is not consistent with the established principle that the government must pursue a course of complete neutrality toward religion."

In separate concurring opinions, Justices Lewis Powell and Sandra Day O'Connor each noted that the Alabama law did not display a clear secular purpose because of its specific reference to "voluntary prayer." Justice O'Connor emphasized that the Establishment Clause does not prohibit the states from allowing schoolchildren to voluntarily pray silently during a moment of silence, but the Alabama law had crossed the line between an allowable period of silence and the state's endorsement of a religious practice. As O'Connor noted, "This line may be a fine one, but our precedents and the principles of religious liberty require that we draw it."

In separate dissenting opinions, Chief Justice Burger and Justices Rehnquist and White criticized the majority ruling. Emphasizing that both the U.S. Congress and the Supreme Court commence their daily proceedings with oral prayer, the chief justice said that treating prayer as "a step toward creating a [state] church borders on, if it does not trespass into, the ridiculous." Justice Rehnquist regretted the "mistaken understanding of constitutional history" and Jefferson's "misleading metaphor" about a "wall of separation" between church and state. He insisted that the Establishment Clause does not require government "to be strictly neutral between religion and irreligion," nor does it prevent the states from pursuing secular ends through "nondiscriminatory sectarian means." More will be said about this view of the Establishment Clause in the conclusion of this chapter.

A Bad Day in Court for Parochial School Aid

One day before concluding its 1984 term, the Supreme Court handed down two decisions in school-aid cases that had been expected for months. The decisions, *Grand Rapids School District* v. *Ball* and *Aguilar* v. *Felton* (1985), reinforced the trend evidenced by the *Wallace* v. *Jaffree* decision: the Court seemed more comfortable with the separationist philosophy instead of the accommodation of religion by government. In both cases, the Supreme Court decided that public funds may not be used to pay for public school teachers providing remedial or enrichment instruction in parochial schools. These 1985 decisions are important because the programs in question resemble similar parochaid plans in hundreds of schools throughout the United States.

Ever since the mid-1970s, the Grand Rapids, Michigan, school district had operated two programs—shared time and community education—that provided instruction for private school students in private facilities at state expense. The shared-time program offered classes during the regular school day to supplement the normal core curriculum required by the state. The program included various enrichment and remedial classes in mathematics, reading, music, art, and physical education. The community education program offered classes at the end of the regular school day in such subjects as modern languages, arts and crafts, home economics, nature appreciation, and drama for both school-aged children and adults. The teachers in this program were part-time public school employees, and all but one of the forty-one area schools involved in the community education program were parochial schools.

The New York City program, the largest in the United States at the time, had an annual budget of $20 million, which was funded by the federal government under Title I of the Elementary and Secondary Education Act of 1965. The program was designed to aid about 300,000 educationally deprived students from low-income families, only 25,000 of whom were enrolled in parochial schools. The program paid public school teachers to teach in the parochial schools, and an extensive monitoring program by field personnel was designed to avoid all involvement with religious activities at the religious schools and to bar the use of religious materials in the classroom. Both the Grand Rapids and the New York City programs were challenged by taxpayers claiming violations of the Establishment Clause.

Near the end of its term in 1985, a 5–4 Supreme Court majority struck down all three programs as unconstitutional. After reviewing the precedents governing parochaid programs, Justice Brennan wrote that the two Grand Rapids programs were invalid because they violated the primary-effects guideline in three ways. First, the public teachers might be influenced by the sectarian schools and inadvertently or overtly indoctrinate the students in various religious tenets. Second, the "symbolic union" of the government and the church might convey a message of state endorsement of a particular religion and thereby influence the children. Finally, both state-aid programs had the effect of directly subsidizing the religious functions of the parochial schools by assuming much of the teaching responsibilities of those institutions.

In examining the New York City program, the Court ruled that it passed the secular-purpose and primary-effects elements of *Lemon,* but it violated the excessive-entanglements standard because of the supervisory system devised to prevent religious indoctrination by the teachers. Brennan again found this program wanting in its implications for both Establishment Clause guarantees and religion:

> When the state becomes enmeshed with a given denomination in matters of religious significance, the freedom of religious belief of those who are not adherents of that denomination suffers, even when the governmental purpose underlying the involvement is largely secular. In addition, the freedom of even the adherents of the denomination is limited by the governmental intrusion into sacred matters.

Brennan found the same elements that entangled government with religion in both the *Lemon* and the *Pittenger* cases to be present in *Aguilar* v. *Felton,* namely, a pervasively sectarian climate and required inspections to ensure the absence of a religious message. Because of these conditions, "the scope and duration of New York's Title I program would require a permanent and pervasive State presence in the sectarian schools receiving aid."

The four justices dissenting in these two decisions criticized the majority's refusal to inquire into the *actual* effects of the three parochiaid plans. Justices White and Rehnquist supported the constitutionality of all three programs. Chief Justice Burger and Justice O'Connor voted to uphold the constitutionality of the Grand Rapids shared-time plan and the New York program, but not the community education program. All four of the dissenting justices were disturbed by the Court's refusal to inquire into whether public school teachers actually proselytized their students within the religious school environment. The chief justice regretted the impact that these decisions would have upon low-income schoolchildren in need of educational assistance. Noted Burger, "Federal programs designed to prevent a generation of children from growing up without being able to read effectively are not remotely steps in [establishing a state religion]."

Tale of Two Theories: Evolution Versus Creationism

In the 1986 term, the Supreme Court tackled an issue that had been dormant for decades—the teaching of evolution in public schools. With the arrival of the Reagan administration in 1981—and its sympathies for such "social-agenda" topics as oral prayer, antiabortion laws, equal access to the public classroom, tuition tax credits, and legislative chaplains—the climate seemed ripe for the reconsideration of an issue long popular with fundamentalist Christians in the United States. Nearly twenty years earlier, the Court had struck down as unconstitutional an Arkansas law patterned somewhat after the Tennessee law at issue in *Scopes* v. *State of Tennessee* in 1925 (see Brief 13.5). By 1968, Arkansas had made it a crime to teach that humans were descended from a lower order of animals or to use any textbook that taught that theory. A unanimous Supreme Court in *Epperson* v. *Arkansas* (1968) said that the Arkansas law violated the Establishment Clause by embodying a specific religious belief and prohibiting all others. The state's power to determine the public school curriculum did not include the right to ban the teaching of established scientific theory simply because it conflicted with biblical teachings or a particular religious doctrine.

After the Epperson decision, fundamentalists resorted to another strategy to inject their views into the public classroom. One tactic was to ask for equal time—if evolutionary theory (and they emphasized the *theory*) were taught, so must what they termed "creation science." This theory argues that Genesis accurately details the origins of mankind as occurring with a single spontaneous event between 6,000 and 10,000 years ago, and it deserves to be covered in the classroom along with evolution. One of several states that passed laws after *Epperson* to allow for the teaching of creation science in public schools was Arkansas. In 1982, a federal district court in Little Rock struck down that state law as a violation of the Establishment Clause.

☐ *Brief 13.5   The Scopes "Monkey Trial": In the Image of Man or a Monkey?*

The battle among different religious and scientific groups over the teaching of the evolution of living species began with the first printing of Charles Darwin's *The Origin of Species* in 1859, but it was not until the 1920s that the matter received much publicity in the United States. During the 1920s, John T. Scopes, a biology teacher in Tennessee, was indicted for violating a state law that forbade teaching in public schools of the state "any theory which denies the story of the divine creation of man as taught in the Bible" which holds instead that "man is descended from a lower order of animals." The state of Tennessee retained the three-time Democratic presidential nominee and famous orator William Jennings Bryan to prosecute Scopes and to proclaim his own personal and the state's belief in the literal truth of the Book of Genesis. Defending Scopes

was the equally celebrated lawyer, Clarence Darrow, who argued valiantly that the then-cumulative body of evidence established that humans were, indeed, descended from a long line of primates.

Despite the efforts of Darrow and national publicity that portrayed Tennessee as an intellectual backwater, Scopes was convicted of violating the state law and fined $100. A subsequent state appellate court reversed that conviction because of a technical procedural error in sentencing; as a result, the case was never appealed to the U.S. Supreme Court. The primary effect of the trial was the widespread ridicule of religious opponents of evolutionary theory and the ultimate vindication of Scopes, scientific theory, and academic freedom.

In an effort to prevent a succession of challenges to state laws and the possibility of courts handing down conflicting decisions, the Supreme Court accepted for review a Louisiana case, *Edwards* v. *Aguillard* (1987), involving a state law that two lower federal courts had said conflicted with the Establishment Clause because it sponsored a religious belief. At issue in the case was the Louisiana Balanced Treatment for Creation-Science and Evolution-Science in Public School Instruction Act, the so-called "Creationism Act," passed in 1981, but never put into effect because of a succession of court challenges. The law did not require the teaching of creationism, but instead mandated that if either evolution or creationism were taught in the public schools, *both* had to be taught. The case became the *cause célèbre* for a large assortment of parents, civil libertarians, scientists, religious leaders, and school teachers and administrators on both sides of the evolution-creationism debate. It also was important because it provided a clear opportunity to assess the first term of the Rehnquist Court in 1986–87 on church-state issues.

In June 1987, the Supreme Court, with only two justices dissenting, declared the law to be a violation of the Establishment Clause. After reviewing the well-worn path of *Lemon* v. *Kurtzman*, Justice Brennan for the majority said that parents with children in the public schools expect both a quality education and the "understanding that the classroom will not purposely be used to advance religious views that may conflict with the private beliefs of the student and his or her family." [13] Notwithstanding the state's insistence that the purpose of the creationism law was secular, namely, to protect academic freedom, Justice Brennan felt that after examining the legislative record of the 1981 bill, the main purpose of the law was to narrow the science curriculum in schools. Furthermore, it limited academic freedom because it had "the distinctly different purpose of discrediting 'evolution by counterbalancing its teaching at every turn with the teaching of creation science.' " To Brennan, "The pre-eminent purpose of the Louisiana Legislature was clearly to advance the religious viewpoint that a supernatural being created human-kind."

The two dissenting votes were those of the new chief justice, William Rehnquist, and his new ideological colleague, Antonin Scalia, only the latter of whom wrote a separate opinion. Scalia's main points were that the legislative purpose of the law was secular, not religious; it in no way advanced religion; and the Court was too activist in ascribing false motives to the Louisiana legislators. With regard to the purpose of the statute, Scalia said the Court majority ignored a detailed reading of the state legislative debates:

> Although the record contains abundant evidence of the sincerity of [secular] purpose . . . the Court today holds, essentially on the basis of "its visceral knowledge regarding what must have motivated the legislators," that the members of Louisiana Legislature knowingly violated their oaths and then lied about it.

Scalia also regretted the activism of the Court. As he observed in his dissent:

> My views (and the views of this Court) about creation science and evolution are (or should be) beside the point. Our task is not to judge the debate about teaching the origins of life, but to ascertain what the members of the Louisiana Legislature believed. The vast majority of them voted to approve a bill which explicitly stated a secular purpose; what is crucial is not their wisdom in believing that purpose would be achieved . . . but their sincerity in believing it would be.

The *Edwards* v. *Aguillard* decision would seem to put to rest, for the time being, any push for a creationist agenda. The high school principal in Lafayette, Louisiana, who originally brought the suit challenging the law said that he was pleased with the Court's decision. Said Donald Aguillard, "We just don't have the money now to spend on bad science." The executive director of the Louisiana Interchurch Conference, Rev. James L. Stovall, who had also argued against the law, said that he was glad that there would not be another Scopes trial. But the original sponsor of the legislation, former state senator Bill Keith, showed dismay at the decision. Said Keith, "Evolution is no more than a fairy tale about a frog that turns into a prince, but this is what we are teaching our schoolchildren today." [14]

The Supreme Court's Mixed Message

In the 1980s, the Supreme Court dealt with five major cases regarding the Establishment Clause—four by the Burger Court and one by the new Rehnquist Court. The main question that arises is, How can the *Lynch* decision be reconciled with the other four? The majority in *Lynch* v. *Donnelly* went to great lengths to save the Pawtucket Nativity scene and, in the process, transformed a sacred religious holiday season for Christians into little more than a secular retail shopping holiday for the public. In an effort to save the Nativity scene, the majority opinion stripped it of its religious content. The other four cases dealing with moment-of-silence, parochiaid, and creationism, however, reached for a much more neutral ground on church-state relations. How can this quite different application of the Establishment Clause coexist with *Lynch?*

One study of these church-state decisions says that a key role was played in all the decisions by Justice Lewis Powell, who voted with the majority in all instances. [15] A noticeable turnaround in the Court's view of what the Establishment Clause permits came after *Lynch,* which is a departure from a more neutral view of the Establishment Clause. Justice Powell—who voted to uphold the crèche in Pawtucket, but also voted to strike down the moment-of-silence law in Alabama, the public aid to schools in Grand Rapids and New York City, and the balanced-treatment law in Louisiana—was the swing vote in the first four cases. A major reason for his vote is hinted at in his concurring opinion to strike down the Title I aid plan of New York City in *Aguilar* v. *Felton:*

> There remains a considerable risk of continuing political strife over the propriety of direct aid to religious schools and the proper allocation of limited governmental resources. As this Court has repeatedly recognized, there is a likelihood whenever direct governmental aid is extended to some groups that there will be competition and strife among them and others to gain, maintain, or increase the financial support of government.

Powell recognized the political and religious diversity of many states like New York, and he felt that allowing government to aid one sectarian group might sow the seeds of an increasingly more divisive and less stable social order.

Although it is risky to predict long-term directions for the Rehnquist Court in church-state relations, this much is evident for the foreseeable future. The Court seems more protective of the "wall of separation," however fragile, in cases involving more impressionable primary and secondary school students. But it has also been closely divided on many of these cases, and a single vote or a personnel change on the Court could have major consequences for the future. Four of the most recent Establishment Clause cases—*Wallace* v. *Jaffree, Grand Rapids* v. *Ball/Aguilar* v. *Felton,* and *Edwards* v. *Aguillard*—all dealt with potentially more vulnerable young schoolchildren. The Court in the past few years has adhered to a narrower view of the Establishment Clause that makes it more difficult for oral prayer, aid to parochial schools, and suspect religious doctrine to survive judicial scrutiny.

The Continuing Search for the Meaning of "Establishment"

For the past four decades, the Supreme Court has been struggling with the meaning of the Establishment Clause. Constitutional scholars have differed greatly over what the clause compels in contemporary society.[16] Several authorities have noted at least three constitutional theories to explain the large majority of Establishment Clause cases.[17]

The "strict-separation" or "no-aid" theory incorporates Jefferson's reference to a "wall of separation" and reflects a rigid division between secular and religious authorities and structures. This first theory was implicit in *Everson* v. *Board of Education* in 1947, but more explicitly stated by Justice Black in *McCollum* in 1948 and *Engel* v. *Vitale* in 1962. The no-aid theory has also been displayed in decisions that have prohibited fifty-foot lighted crosses from being displayed on public property[18] and military service academies from requiring that cadets attend chapel religious services.[19]

A second theory used to explain how the Court has applied the Establishment Clause is known as the "government-neutrality" theory. It requires that government be neutral in various matters involving religion in the public order. It maintains that government must do nothing either to aid or hamper religion. Perhaps the first articulation of this theory came in 1963 with the *Abington* v. *Schempp/Murray* v. *Curlett* cases. As Justice Clark then wrote for the majority, "In the relationship between man and religion, the state is firmly committed to a position of neutrality." It has also been displayed in numerous decisions since 1963, most notably, *Walz* v. *Tax Commission, Lemon* v. *Kurtzman, Grand Rapids* v. *Ball/Aguilar* v. *Felton,* and *Edwards* v. *Aguillard.* A large problem with this test is determining what actually is meant by "religion" and what particular governmental actions benefit or burden religion. As several decisions detailed in this chapter indicate, particularly those dealing with state aid to parochial schools, there has been much dissension over what the Establishment Clause allows and disallows. Since the neutrality test asks whether the state is placing religion at a distinct advantage or disadvantage by its policy actions, several prescriptions have emerged. Justice O'Connor's concurrence in *Lynch* v. *Donnelly* reflects the turmoil in present neutrality theory and the quest for a new standard to define the role of the state vis-a-vis religion in the United States. Unhappy with the secular-purpose and primary-effects component of the *Lemon* decision, Justice O'Connor now seeks re-definition of that murky standard. As she noted in *Lynch:*

> The purpose prong of the *Lemon* test asks whether government's actual purpose is to endorse or disapprove of religion. The effect prong asks whether, irrespective of government's actual purpose, the practice under review in fact conveys a message of endorsement or disapproval. An affirmative answer to either question should render the challenged practice invalid.

As several recent commentaries on church-state issues have pointed out, this attempt by O'Connor to recast the *Lemon* test to determine whether government actions constitute "endorsement or disapproval" may be, with certain personnel changes on the Court, a trend for the future.[20]

A third test that has been very prominent in recent years is the "government-accommodation" theory. This view of the church-state relationship was prominent in Justice Douglas's majority opinion in *Zorach* v. *Clauson* in 1952, wherein he referred to Americans as "a religious people." It was also hinted at in Brennan's concurring opinion in *Abington* v. *Schempp*. In that decision, he noted that only by some form of secular accommodation of religion can Americans reconcile the inherent clash between the two religion clauses of the First Amendment. Several of the matters sustained by the Court over the past few decades—such as the reference to God on U.S. coinage, in the Pledge of Allegiance, and in prayers at commencements exercises—and many of the topics covered in this chapter—such as tuition tax credits, legislative chaplains, Nativity displays, and tax exemptions for religious organizations—are all embedded in the accommodationist school.

These three theories attest to the fact that the Supreme Court has left a rather confused path to follow through the church-state maze. One author recently referred to the body of constitutional law concerning permissible state aid to parochial schools as being "clearly in a shambles."[21] Part of the confusion about the precise meaning of the Establishment Clause derives from the historically loaded area of religion and public life in American politics, as well as the uncertain constitutional prescription embodied in the clause. The inevitable tension between America's "civil" religion and the ever-present "wall of separation" between church and state has meant that the American public has looked to the Supreme Court for "final" answers, but in that pursuit the Court itself has often generated new disagreements over the preferable interpretation of the law.

Conclusion

This chapter has discussed two provisions of the First Amendment that have made the United States the most religiously diverse society in the world. Several points should be apparent from this chapter. First, the Establishment and Free Exercise Clauses reflect the concern in late eighteenth-century America for preserving liberty of conscience in the young republic. A history of religious persecution in England and colonial America, as well as the spectre of established religions in most of the American states, convinced framers such as Madison that they had to devise certain "auxiliary precautions" to protect religious freedom in the United States from the power and influence of the state. If religious liberty were to flourish, guarantees protecting the people from an encroaching state were essential. That is why the two religion clauses were inserted into the First Amendment in the late 1780s.

It took 150 years to apply the two clauses to the American states; but, since that process began in the 1940s, the Supreme Court has been besieged with numerous cases dealing with church-state issues. The Free Exercise Clause has generally been interpreted as affording absolute protection for religious *beliefs* and qualified protection for religious *actions* based upon those beliefs. Beginning in the 1960s, with a more liberal Warren Court, and later affirmed by the Burger Court in the 1970s, the justices granted some individuals and groups exemptions from universal laws, mainly on the grounds of religious conscience and tradition. As the United States has become a more religiously diverse nation in the past half-century, the Supreme Court has been at the center of having to define "religion" and what actions justified on religious principle qualify for protection.

Since applying the Establishment Clause to the states in 1947, the Supreme Court has contended with two main areas of debate—What constitutes acceptable *aid* to parochial schools and what religious *activities* are prohibited by the clause? Although decisions by the Court in the activities area have probably generated the most public hostility and noncompliance, the Court has had the greatest difficulty constructing a consistent legal and judicial philosophy for the aid-to-schools controversy. The Supreme Court has gradually retreated from a strict-separationist stance that emerged in *Everson* in 1947 and has continued to allow some governmental assistance to parochial schools. Its justification for doing so has usually been based upon how selected justices interpret "establishment" in the First Amendment, and whether the state aid in question violates the shifting consensus on the meaning of that term. Several of the Court's decisions in the 1980s have highlighted this debate about the meaning of the clause. The Court has continued to limit how far the state may go to accommodate religion. During the past five decades, many of the Court's decisions have been sharply criticized, and legislation has been introduced in Congress on numerous occasions to counter the actions of the Court in applying decisions flowing from its interpretation of the Establishment Clause.

How the Supreme Court has interpreted and applied the religion clauses raises the question of where the particular decisions reside on the individualistic-communitarian continuum. It might be argued that being able to have "voluntary" prayer or a daily Bible reading in public school is in the best tradition of individuals practicing religious freedom. Or that tuition tax credits, a Nativity display at Christmas, and religious clubs meeting in public facilities reflect harmless accommodations of popular religious preferences. All of these examples might be justified as legitimate exercises of religious faith of various persons or concessions to spiritual traditions in the United States, and thus they lie within the individualistic tradition.

But it could also be argued that all these examples contain the potential for divisiveness and discord in society; and, as such, they are counterproductive to building a sense of community. They also have the serious potential for enabling government at various levels to tell people how they can pray, what they should read for spiritual enlightenment, and what religious beliefs and traditions are better than all others. Eventually, as a people strive to act upon their religious beliefs, they discover that the state has expropriated their freedom to believe or not believe. That is why the framers were so vigilant about protecting religious freedom. They knew that unless there were specific limits upon what the state could do vis-a-vis an individual's freedom of conscience, that freedom would be jeopardized. Religious freedom was best ensured by keeping government largely out of the realm of religion. The real strength of an enduring democratic system lies in nurturing diversity and open debate, not in coercion and conformity. Nowhere is that more important than in protecting religious freedom for all Americans.

As the justices have noted in numerous opinions over several decades, there is inevitable tension between the Establishment and the Free Exercise Clauses. One compels government, at a minimum, to neither favor nor disfavor religion, and the other insists that government allow individuals to act upon the basis of their religious beliefs with a minimum of governmental constraints. Many argue that to protect the latter violates the former, and others insist that the justices have too narrowly interpreted and applied one or the other of the two religion clauses. The criticisms of the Court's actions will most likely continue to reflect the disagreements that have existed ever since the Bill of Rights was drafted in 1789.

Questions

1.   Without a doubt, the United States is a much more religiously diverse society today than it was in the late eighteenth century. As the country has been a beacon to different elements seeking opportunity and a new beginning, it has attracted a global population that exhibits very different traditions with respect to religion. How do you regard the relative worth of religious diversity in American society? Do you see it as a potentially divisive element that complicates achieving consensus over public policy? Have decisions by the Supreme Court during the past few decades been responsible for this "strength in diversity" with respect to religion, or has the Court instead cultivated a disrespect for and alienation from religious traditions?

2.   In addition to the nineteenth-century practice of polygamy among Mormons, other more recent religious practices—such as the opposition to inoculations, the handling of dangerous snakes, and the smoking of marijuana—have all been alleged to be sincere practices of various individual's religious faith. On what grounds should the state be allowed to prevent such religious practices? Does state intervention indicate that free-

dom of religion is not really a "preferred freedom," as a half-century of constitutional law might suggest? What sort of test might be devised to determine if certain practices fall outside true "religion" and thus can be banned by government?

3.   Ever since the *Engel* decision in 1962, which banned prescribed prayer in the public school classroom, those opposed to the decision have lobbied for a constitutional amendment reinserting this practice in public schools. If added to the Constitution, this prayer clause would add to the present confusion implicit in the Establishment and Free Exercise Clauses. How might a new prayer clause be worded to avoid this dilemma? Which clause should take precedence? Would such a new prayer amendment be the next step down the road to government-imposed religious instruction? Would it be the final remedy to the present situation of noncompliance with *Engel?*

4.   The *Grand Rapids* v. *Ball* and *Aguilar* v. *Felton* decisions found "liberal" justices saying no to federal aid to poor children in parochial schools, and "conservative" justices lamenting the inability of the federal government to use federal funds to aid the indigent and educate the underprivileged. Given this curious switch of justices' ideologies and their application, can it be said that judicial philosophies frequently have little to do with policy outcomes?

5.   The Supreme Court's decisions in *Mueller* v. *Allen, Marsh* v. *Chambers,* and *Lynch* v. *Donnelly* are difficult to reconcile with its rulings in *Wallace* v. *Jaffree, Grand Rapids* v. *Ball/Aguilar* v. *Felton,* and *Edwards* v. *Aguillard.* The earlier decisions support accommodation, whereas the latter reflect strong support for strict separation. How consistent and plausible do you think the Court's rationale has been in resolving these controversies? To what extent do you think the Court should simply do what it has done in the area of obscenity law, that is, allow local communities to set their own standards?

Endnotes

1.   Alexis de Tocqueville, *Democracy in America,* vol. 1 (New York: Vintage Books, 1945), 310.

2.   See Edwin S. Gaustad, "Church, State, and Education in Historical Perspective," *Journal of Church and State* 26 (Winter 1984): 17–29; and for a more elaborate analysis, see Martin E. Marty, *A Nation of Behavers* (Chicago: University of Chicago Press, 1976).

3.   Robert Bellah, "Civil Religion in America," *Daedalus* 96 (1967): 3–4.

4.   For a thorough discussion of some distinctions between the Puritans, Pilgrims, Anabaptists, and a succession of other religious colonizers in early America, see A. James Reichley, *Religion in American Public Life* (Washington, D.C.: Brookings Institution, 1985), chap. 3.

5.   Ibid., 86.

6.   Quoted in *Basic Documents Relating to the First Amendment* (Washington, D.C.: Americans United for the Separation of Church and State, 1965).

7.   Reichley notes that Congregationalists and Presbyterians comprised the largest followings, though neither was a majority, followed by Baptists, Episcopalians, Dutch and German Calvinist Reformed, Lutherans, Roman Catholics, and a smattering of Jews. There were also smaller groups of Quakers and Methodists, the latter of which would become the most prominent denomination during the early nineteenth century.

8.   See Walter Berns, *The First Amendment and the Future of American Democracy* (New York: Basic Books, 1970); Paul Weber, "James Madison and Religious Equality: The Per-

fect Separation," *Review of Politics* 44 (April 1982): 179–83; and A. James Reichley, *Religion in American Public Life* (Washington, D.C.: Brookings Institution, 1985).

9. *Cochran v. Louisiana State Board of Education,* 281 U.S. 370 (1930). Decades later, the Supreme Court would disallow the same sort of textbook aid law for parochial students. One possible explanation for this apparent disparity is that the *Cochran* case came before the Establishment Clause had been applied to the states.

10. Devised by the New York State Board of Regents, the prayer read: "Almighty God, we acknowledge our dependence upon Thee, and we beg Thy blessings upon us, our parents, our teachers, and our country."

11. Henry J. Abraham, *The Judiciary: The Supreme Court in the Governmental Process,* 7th ed. (Boston: Allyn and Bacon, 1987), 148.

12. Quoted in the *New York Times,* May 25, 1983, A-23.

13. Ibid., June 20, 1987, 6.

14. Ibid., 7.

15. Daan Braveman, "The Establishment Clause and the Course of Religious Neutrality," *Maryland Law Review* 45 (1986): 352–86. This particular study does not include the *Edwards* v. *Aguillard* decision, although here, too, Justice Powell voted with the majority, so the explanation noted in the text still applies.

16. For one view of this debate over the meaning of the Establishment Clause, see Leonard Levy, *The Establishment Clause: Religion and the First Amendment* (New York: Macmillan, 1986). Levy believes that the clause prohibits not only an established church or religion, but also any aid, benefit, exercise, or law which tends to favor one religion over another, or religion over irreligion.

He also argues that the Court was correct in applying the Establishment Clause to the states in 1947, regardless of the intentions of the framers. For a very different view that the Establishment Clause should only prohibit an established church, and not a broad array of state actions that may accommodate religion without favoring one particular denomination, see A. James Reichley, *Religion in American Public Life* (Washington, D.C.: Brookings Institution, 1985). Reichley also maintains that the Establishment Clause should not have been applied to the states as of 1947, but only to the federal government, as the framers intended in 1791.

17. These theories, along with several others, are discussed extensively in Paul Kauper, *Religion and the Constitution* (Baton Rouge, La.: Louisiana State University Press, 1964), chap. 3; Richard E. Morgan, *The Supreme Court and Religion* (New York: Free Press, 1972), chap. 3; Jesse C. Choper, "The Religion Clauses of the First Amendment: Reconciling the Conflict," *University of Pittsburgh Law Review* 41 (Summer 1980): 673–701; and Henry J. Abraham, *Freedom and the Court,* 4th ed. (New York: Oxford University Press, 1982), chap. 6.

18. *Eugene Sand and Gravel* v. *Lowe,* 397 U.S. 591 (1970).

19. *Laird* v. *Anderson,* 409 U.S. 1071 (1972).

20. Three sources that comment upon the somewhat disjointed area of Establishment Clause law are Arnold H. Loewy, "Rethinking Government Neutrality Towards Religion Under the Establishment Clause: The Untapped Potential of Justice O'Connor's Insight," *North Carolina Law Review* 64 (1986): 1050–70; Mark P. Gibney, "State Aid to Religious-Affiliated Schools: A Political Analysis," *William and Mary*

Law Review 28 (Fall 1986): 119–53; and Donald L. Beschle, "The Conservative as Liberal: The Religion Clauses, Liberal Neutrality, and the Approach of Justice O'Connor,"

Notre Dame Law Review 62 (1987): 151–91.

21. Gibney, "State Aid to Religious-Affiliated Schools," 153.

Suggested Readings

Beschle, Donald L. "The Conservative as Liberal: The Religion Clauses, Liberal Neutrality and Justice O'Connor." *Notre Dame Law Review* 62 (1987): 151–91.

Braveman, Daan. "The Establishment Clause and the Course of Religious Neutrality." *Maryland Law Review* 45 (1986): 352–86.

Choper, Jesse C. "The Religion Clauses of the First Amendment: Reconciling the Conflict." *University of Pittsburgh Law Review* 41 (1980): 673–701.

Cord, Robert L. *Separation of Church and State: Historical Fact and Current Fiction.* New York: Lambeth Press, 1982.

Malbin, Michael J. *Religion and Politics.* Washington, D.C.: American Enterprise Institute, 1978.

Miller, Robert T., and Ronald Flowers. *Toward Benevolent Neutrality: Church, State, and the Supreme Court.* 3d ed. Waco, Tex.: Baylor University Press, 1987.

Pfeffer, Leo. *Religion, State and the Burger Court.* Buffalo, N.Y.: Prometheus Books, 1984.

Sorauf, Frank J. *The Wall of Separation: The Constitutional Politics of Church and State.* Princeton, N.J.: Princeton University Press, 1970.

14

American Constitutionalism: Continuing Conflict over Its Meaning and Perfectibility

Syllabus

On September 17, 1987, the American public paused to pay tribute to those who had drafted the American Constitution two hundred years earlier. Probably most of those who joined in the joyous celebration and commemorative bell ringing felt some surge of national pride at having the oldest surviving national constitution in existence. To be able to enter a third century of constitutional government with basically the same instrument governing a people is no small accomplishment. And yet, some others in the celebration may have been questioning whether that same instrument might not need a facelift and overhaul for meeting the challenges of the twenty-first century.

Can the same document deal effectively with the continuing conflicts over the meaning of constitutionalism, the role of federal courts and judges, and the powers and responsibilities of the national and state governments in a federal system? Furthermore, what trade-offs are tolerable in a system that demands the preservation of law and order, as well as equal justice under the law? To what extent can this society tolerate the social costs of protecting the rights of crime victims while safeguarding the rights of criminals? What is implied in the concept of "equality," and how should the system operate to achieve those implications? And finally, assuming that the Bill of Rights contains no absolutes, under what conditions should an individual's right to dissent take precedence over the government's responsibility to impose order and to coerce conformity?

This Chapter Examines the Following Matters

☐ American constitutionalism has demanded a healthy tension between controlled power in governing institutions and assured protections for personal rights. An adjunct of this conflict has been very different visions of how best to achieve the public good—what has been described here as the individualistic and the communitarian perspectives.

☐ A system of "mixed government" that divides power among branches and levels of government has also sought to protect the individual freedoms and constitutional rights of its citizens. One of the main instruments for accomplishing this end has been the judicial system, which allows its courts to review the constitutionality of the actions of the legislature and the executive.

☐ Contemporary constitutional government finds the American public significantly divided over the consequences of separate institutions sharing power, the social costs of protecting the rights of criminal defendants, the meaning of such terms as "equality" and "justice," and the limits of First Amendment freedoms.

☐ Given the significant problems confronting a free people trying to govern themselves, the question becomes, Under what circumstances and to what extent can or should the present constitutional system undergo significant structural, electoral, or political change?

Photo: Even as Americans celebrated the bicentennial of the Constitution's drafting in 1987, some critics called for constitutional reforms which would make the document more applicable to the political circumstances of the late twentieth century.

A Continuing Experiment in Self-Government

The preceding chapters have attempted to focus upon some of the distinct features and contributions of American constitutional government. Some major themes of that constitutional experience should have emerged—the long-standing distrust of concentrated political power; a preoccupation with the principles of liberty and equality amid the countervailing traditions of individualistic and communitarian political cultures; the tendency of the American people to resolve societal conflicts in legal terms; and the struggle between the need for stability and social order for the majority versus the rights of minorities. Finally, the gradual elaboration of the constitutional text by courts has applied most of the Bill of Rights to states and their local governments, which has greatly advanced freedom and equality in the United States. This concluding chapter summarizes the rich legacy of American constitutional government, assesses some constitutional issues that still divide the American public, and questions whether the American constitutional system requires minor or major constitutional reform in order to cope with the increasing complexity of an interdependent world.

The Context of American Constitutionalism

Part I of this book emphasized both the substantial debt that the framers of the American constitutional system owed preceding generations and the unique aspects of their handiwork in Philadelphia in 1787. Although the idea of constitutional government did not originate with the American colonies, it certainly found fertile ground here in which to take root. The belief that governmental power should be limited to protect individual liberties can be traced to the Magna Carta in 1215. The concept was expanded during the next several centuries so that power by one, a few, or the many would not trample upon the natural rights of the people.

When the founders of the American system gathered in Philadelphia in 1787, they were concerned with many problems then troubling the young United States. Although rather pessimistic about human nature's ability to act beyond self-interest and greed, they were optimistic about their own ability to fashion a new governing order that could control these popular passions. Two primary concerns dominated their efforts—increasing national authority and protecting individual rights.

With regard to *increased order and stability,* there simply was no true national authority then operating directly upon the citizens of the United States. The system of government constructed under the Articles of Confederation in 1777 was a loose league of states with no one in charge. There was no authority to raise revenue for national purposes, no power to regulate commerce among the states or with foreign nations, and no tribunal to arbitrate disputes between the states. By the 1780s, it was increasingly apparent to both commercial and agrarian interests that the national government had neither form nor substance. People were doubting the staying power of the United States.

Regarding the second concern of the framers—*protection of individual rights*—the founding generation was deeply concerned about how best to protect citizens' rights, especially economic rights. Having struggled openly since the 1770s against King George III and the English Parliament, the drafters of the Constitution were in no mood to replace one form of minority tyranny with another. Had they opted for a very centralized form of government, it never would have been accepted by the states. Concerns about individual rights were paramount in the minds of both those gathered in Philadelphia and the American people at large.

The product of these dual concerns was *American constitutionalism.* What did the phrase mean to those drafting this new constitutional order? At a minimum, it meant that governmental power was limited, that government must act within the confines of the law, and that public officials derive their authority from either specific federal laws or the Constitution. It also assumed that no person, public or private, was above the law. The devices used at the Philadelphia convention to control governmental power included the separation of powers, a federal structure that divides power between the national government and the states, a bicameral legislature, numerous checks and balances among the three branches, and eventually a formal Bill of Rights added in 1791.

But American constitutional government also embodies certain assumptions about politics and political life that influence societal views of human nature and the relationship between people and their government. As Chapter 2 argued, two very different theories of politics and the proper relationship between people and government have persisted throughout most of American constitutional history. The individualistic perspective presumes that people take precedence over government and have certain inalienable rights that government should preserve and promote. It insists that people are entitled to free choice without government coercion. Government should provide the structure, institutions, and processes that allow people to exercise their rights and pursue their own self-interest. The main purpose of government is to protect those rights and moderate conflict between diverse interests.

To the individualist, justice achieved through this government action is purely *procedural.* As long as government applies fair rules and procedures equally to all persons, that is all that government is required to do. This view insists upon equal opportunity, but not equal results. A guaranteed right to vote, admission to college, or advancement in a company should be based upon merit and proficiency standards, and nothing more. According to the individualistic perspective, no intrinsic value is fulfilled by the political community beyond this protection of individual rights, and government must minimize its intrusion upon personal freedoms.

The communitarian perspective stresses a more positive view of government and the political arena. It asserts that individuals are not completely independent entities, but instead have an inherent need to associate with others in the political community. Whereas the individualistic perspective assumes that persons can choose and develop on their own, the communitarian view maintains that people need each other and the political community in order to nurture their own development and to make proper choices. Government must do more than simply protect individual rights—it must facilitate popular participation in a political community in order to assure the larger public interest. Politics is not a necessary evil that should always be limited in scope, but a positive exercise that raises the condition of everyone. Communitarians are concerned not merely with personal ends, but also with the common good of the larger community.

Communitarians take a more *substantive* view of justice in the political order. The inequalities that exist among persons can be reduced if government uses its power to achieve greater substantive justice in the community through more equitable social and economic programs. Even though these actions may sometimes discriminate against persons who enjoy a particular social or economic benefit, obtaining just results for all elements in society justifies government intervention.

Some Unique Aspects of American Structures and Processes

Although the drafters of the American constitutional system owed much to earlier experiments with limited government, Part II of this book concentrated upon three major ideas—judicial review, the separation-of-powers principle, and the doctrine of federalism—which have had some unique consequences for American constitutional government. As noted in Chapter 4, the proper role of judges and the legitimate exercise of judicial power have been a contentious matter throughout the past two centuries. Even before Chief Justice John Marshall proclaimed in *Marbury* v. *Madison* that it was the unique function of courts to interpret the Constitution and the law, there were serious debates about inserting judicial authority into matters deemed beyond the business of judges. The Eleventh Amendment in 1798, overruling the Court's decision in *Chisholm* v. *Georgia* five years earlier, implies that the Supreme Court does not necessarily have the final word. Controversy over the role of the Supreme Court in interpreting and applying provisions of the Constitution has continued to the present day, as the debate over the nomination of Robert Bork to the Supreme Court in 1987 indicated.

Likewise, conflict over the proper balance of power between Congress and the president has existed throughout much of American political experience. Among the founding generation, there existed an abiding distrust of executive and administrative power and an insistence that a too vigorous executive contradicted republican government. As a result, the Constitution firmly established Congress as the primary institution in American politics. However, there was also a consensus in Philadelphia that the president, as well as the federal courts, should provide necessary checks upon popular preferences enacted by the legislature. Since both the president and the federal judiciary were further removed from local passions and preferences, they were better equipped to balance the excesses of popular rule. Beginning in the twentieth century, with several social and economic reforms under such labels as the New Nationalism, the New Deal, and the Fair Deal, the American people have increasingly relied upon the national government generally as the predominant guarantor of economic security. To protect the nation from both foreign and domestic enemies, successive American presidents have been called upon to initiate major public programs in a vast arena of accepted government activity.

This increasing reliance upon the executive branch has also had major implications for the third major structural trait of the American constitutional system, federalism. As discussed briefly in Chapter 3, and elaborated upon extensively in Chapters 6 and 7, American federalism has been a major contribution of the framers to constitutional democracy. Nothing quite like it existed before 1787, and it was most likely accepted as a prerequisite for ratification of the Constitution, rather than as any deliberate design for efficient government. Given the early emphasis upon economic liberties of the people, property rights enjoyed considerable protection under successive Supreme Courts throughout the nineteenth century and well into the twentieth century. Under such banners as dual federalism, vested-rights doctrine, substantive due process, and freedom of contract as covered in Chapter 7, both state and federal attempts to regulate certain economic and social practices normally met with judicial veto prior to 1937. But even before then, the pendulum of political power had begun to shift in favor of the national government and against state and local governments. What began as a trickle of national regulation during the late nineteenth century accelerated after successive cries for Congress and the executive branch to undertake extensive government programs designed to reduce social and economic uncertainty. Legislators and presidents were all too happy to answer these calls for an increased federal presence. More often than not, federal courts in the twentieth century have upheld this growing federal role. In so doing, they have revised fundamentally the meaning of "rights" protected by the Constitution. This does not mean, however, that American federalism is an empty shell from an earlier era. On the contrary, in the current climate of mounting federal debts and demands for continuing the service-state economy, there is an urgent need to revitalize state and local governments as policy innovators. It is important to remember that those governments still remain at the heart of American democracy and representative government.

The Movement Toward More Liberty and Equality

A major message emerging from Part III of this survey is that the American people now enjoy far more liberty and equality as they begin their third century of constitutional government than they did in 1787. This development has not always been one of uninterrupted progress. On some occasions, both the masses and political elites have interpreted certain provisions of the Constitution in ways that have severely limited personal freedoms. But throughout the past two centuries, the Constitution that began as an instrument to structure and limit political power has become much more protective of individual rights through the addition of the Fourteenth Amendment in 1868 and the application of the Bill of Rights to the American states after 1925.

As the chapters in Part III indicated, the Due Process Clause and the Equal Protection Clause of the Fourteenth Amendment became very important instruments in the hands of the Supreme Court during the middle of the twentieth century to protect fundamental constitutional rights. Not only would the Bill of Rights be given new life and meaning after 1925, but also the Court would later begin finding new freedoms and guarantees emanating from the Fourteenth Amendment's Equal Protection Clause. Undoubtedly, the nation's individualistic political culture, along with its deeply imbedded preference for a government with dispersed power and a federal structure, complicated this movement toward a more just society. But eventually, the process of selectively applying the Bill of Rights to the states with respect to preferred First Amendment freedoms, along with most of the rest of the first eight amendments to the Constitution, reflected the Court's evolving recognition of these basic constitutional guarantees as crucial to limited government.

Continuing Conflict over the Meaning of Constitutional Government

The debate continues today over the meaning of the Constitution and the proper relationship between the citizens and their government. In at least four major areas relating to constitutional government—the locus of power and leadership, protection against crime, equal protection, and First Amendment guarantees—continuing debate can be found over what the Constitution says about the relationship between government and the people.

Is Anyone Prepared to Make a Decision Here?

In their attempt to ensure limited government and responsible political power, the framers of the Constitution dispersed political power. Only by ensuring that power could be used to check power would individual liberty be truly protected under the new constitutional order beginning in 1787. So the framers divided power between the central government and the states; among Congress, the president, and the courts; within the legislative branch itself; and between the people and the formal government. But what happens when problems arise in both domestic and foreign policy that require immediate attention? Who is entitled to decide certain issues? Who takes charge of the situation and acts to resolve the problem or preserve national security? Who has the right to determine whether a nuclear power plant or a hazardous waste dump will be located in one community or another? Who decides where to dump a barge full of garbage that no citizens want in their town? Who has the last word on whether a halfway house for drug addicts or AIDS patients can be located in one town or another? Who is responsible for an annual federal budget deficit of $175 billion? Who must act forcefully to win the return of American citizens held captive in a foreign country by a group of terrorists accountable to no one? Who decides whether rebellious troops in a foreign country are truly "freedom fighters" acting in the best tradition of America's founders, or merely militaristic thugs who will bring little or no improvement in the ruling government in a Socialist country? The Constitution does not provide specific answers to these difficult questions of modern society. As a political community living under that written Constitution, Americans are left with having to apply a document that is two hundred years old and incapable of providing the simple, neat answers that most people crave in their quest for solutions.

"To Preserve Domestic Tranquility"

One of the basic tasks of government is to preserve stability and protect the property and lives of its citizens. Rules are necessary in a community in order to prevent chaos and violence from becoming the norm. People have a right to expect law enforcement to be able to provide a measure of domestic peace and safety. But accomplishing this official duty can require sharpening a double-edged sword. To ensure public order, government is given certain powers that can potentially intrude upon constitutional rights under the Fourth Amendment and its promise of freedom from "unreasonable search and seizure." The Fifth Amendment protection against self-incrimination means that government must prove a person's guilt without resorting to coerced confessions. And if accused of a crime, a person is guaranteed the right to be represented by an attorney, regardless of whether or not he or she can afford legal assistance. In recent years, some people have questioned whether government can effectively control crime without violating the rights of innocent people. To control crime by violating procedural rights of private citizens is a high price to pay for preserving law and order.

Recent cries for random drug testing of American citizens—whether they be police officers, firefighters, transportation workers, or private citizens—raise important questions about Fourth Amendment freedoms. Public fears about the increase in crime and violence have compelled law enforcement to produce more results in getting the criminal element off the streets and behind bars. In this charged atmosphere, it is important to remember that constitutional rights are the only safeguards that protect individuals from the unlimited power of the state. Increasing public support for imposing the death penalty on capital offenders may unfortunately reflect both the fear of the public about hardened criminals and the failure of society to nurture, educate, and employ the alienated. American constitutional history is full of occasions when some have demanded that government "solve the problem" by taking short cuts to achieve "justice." That is a detour down a very dangerous path toward more injustice.

How Equal Do Americans Want to Be?

Americans have been struggling with the concept of equality ever since the Declaration of Independence. In the Preamble to the Constitution, the words "We the People" meant something quite different in 1787 than they do today. At that time, blacks were generally regarded as the property of the white race, and women were not even mentioned in the Constitution. The country has made great progress in the last three decades toward reducing racial discrimination in American society, through the actions of courts, Congress, and state legislatures, and in a series of executive actions by several American presidents. But recent incidents in several American communities are a reminder of the bitter legacy of racial bigotry in this country. Continued strides toward extending constitutional guarantes to women, the handicapped, the elderly, and aliens are important gains in which Americans should take pride.

But the American people continue to be deeply divided over what the term "equality" really means—equal *opportunity* or a condition of *sameness* (see Chapter 9). Discrimination continues to occur in the workplace, in education, and in public and private housing. Affirmative action offends many people who claim that the Constitution does not allow the government to extend preferential treatment to individuals from groups discriminated against in the past. Is applying racial quotas appropriate in the workplace, the classroom, the promotion list, or in awarding government contracts? Recent court cases in all these areas have found federal judges advancing a qualified yes. The continuing deliberations raise the question, How much diversity can the American republic tolerate?

First Amendment Freedoms

Another area of continuing conflict concerns First Amendment freedoms, particularly those of freedom of expression, freedom of the press, and freedom of religion. Ever since 1791, these freedoms have been fundamental to the American concept of limited government. Under the Constitution, citizens have a guaranteed right to express themselves freely and without fear of retribution by government officials. They even have the right to criticize government actions and not be imprisoned without due process of law. *Political speech* has been relatively diverse in American society, certainly in comparison with many other countries in recent memory. The governmental structures and political leadership of the American system have generally allowed the American people to voice differing views of politics and public policy. However, as Chapter 11 indicated, this right has been frequently restricted in times of perceived threats to national security. Popular dissent in American society during the 1960s and the 1970s over the Vietnam War was tolerated generally, especially when the overwhelming tide of dissent made it virtually impossible for the government to avoid a policy change. Peaceful demonstrations over such issues as abortion, American policy in South Africa, and labor-management disputes indicate how relatively open American society is in its tolerance of free expression.

The ever-present conflict in society about the meaning and intent of the *religion clauses* continues. Issues such as organized prayer in public schools, the meaning of "secular humanism" and "establishment" of religion, the right of parents to deny their children urgent medical attention on religious grounds, and the tax-exempt status of TV evangelists all involve alleged church-state separation questions. Several issues in recent years have called into question whether the courts can interpret and apply both religion clauses in the First Amendment without inevitably giving short shrift to one or the other.

Finally, the debate continues over the role of a *free press* in American society and what privileges that "fourth branch" of government should enjoy. The case from Missouri decided by the Supreme Court in 1988, contrasting the right of students to distribute a student newspaper and a principal's right to censor certain portions, raises some troubling questions for those who value the importance of teaching by example. It makes little sense to teach students about press rights in a democratic system and then deny those very rights to students trying to exercise them. The rash of libel suits by individuals claiming that the press has published false or misleading stories indicates the public's frequent distrust of the mass media. Public opinion polls indicating that the public questions the "liberal" press's handling of political news also reflect suspicion of the "fourth estate."

In view of these issues consuming much of the current political debate in the United States, it is apparent that the American public is still very divided about what American constitutionalism actually means. Beyond such abstractions as limited government, the accountability of political power, and the preeminence of the written law, Americans' continuing differences of opinion about basic political concepts are striking. What is the real impact and effect of constitutional guarantees, especially those in the First Amendment? What is meant by the terms *equality* and *justice*? To what extent can government be expected to preserve order in society without violating other basic constitutional guarantees of each citizen? These questions about the limits of American constitutional government reflect the ambiguity that this nation has always exhibited concerning politics, political power, and the proper relationship between people and their government. Several factors might explain these honest differences of opinion, at least some of which, it has been suggested here, are a consequence of the individualistic and communitarian preferences that pull American citizens in different directions. These differences over the meaning and application of the Constitution have also been responsible in recent years for speculation about whether aspects of a system devised two hundred years ago are able to cope with many contemporary problems that defy easy solution. The discussion now considers some suggestions for reform in American constitutional government.

The Ghost of Constitutional Reform: Problems, Solutions, and Prospects for Change

Concerns about the ability of American government to govern effectively have been voiced for many years. Ever since the early 1950s, when the American Political Science Association issued a report expressing concern about deadlock among the several branches of government, a disintegrating party system, and excessive power in executive hands, calls for reassessment and reform have been frequently heard.[1] Such national political calamities as the Vietnam War, the Watergate scandal, and the recent Iran-contra debacle occasioned renewed claims that the American system needs major reform. But to many national political observers, these failures in policy and administration signal a larger problem in American politics: the inability of political institutions to resolve in a unified manner growing public concern about a long list of domestic and international problems—rising crime rates, declining educational achievement, increased environmental pollution, an insecure energy picture, escalating health-care costs, a permanent social and economic underclass in a relatively affluent society, a mounting federal budget deficit, growing trade imbalances with foreign nations, declining productivity and competitiveness in relation to other national economies, and a nuclear arms race that seems to defy rationality.

One group of critics of the American constitutional system in the late twentieth century indicts the frequency of "divided government," whereby Congress and the White House have been increasingly controlled by different political parties. According to Lloyd Cutler, a former presidential advisor under President Jimmy Carter, Congress and the presidency during the nineteenth century were usually controlled by the same party, which simplified legislative-executive relations and increased the chances of public programs being passed with a minimum of alteration in Congress. But since World War II, only nine of twenty Congresses have seen the legislature and the presidency in the hands of the same political party. Since 1968, "unified government" has existed only once, and that was during the Carter years.

"Change the System!"

Several calls for surgery on the American constitutional system have been heard in recent years. The diagnosis of the precise problem and the prescription for dealing with it vary in terms of consequences for the overall system. Some say that minor changes within the present institutions of government will not be enough to break the "deadlock of democracy,"[2] and that major constitutional reform is necessary to accommodate the present constitutional system to contemporary conditions that the framers could in no way foresee. This group of constitutional reformers, reflected in a recent publication by the Committee on the Constitutional System,[3] insists that the role of the federal government today has become so extensive and public expectations so great that government must be made to work more efficiently and effectively. Some of the major proposals for reforming the American constitutional system, all of which would require amending the Constitution, include:

1. *coordinated terms of office* for members of the House of Representatives and the Senate, with representatives serving a four-year term and senators an eight-year term, half of the latter being elected every four years.

2. creation of a *federal team ticket,* whereby the president, vice-president, senators, and representatives would run on a political party slate, and voters would have an opportunity to vote for a party slate in its entirety.

3. *concurrent service in government,* whereby members of Congress could serve in the executive branch without relinquishing their congressional seat, and, conversely, allowing the president's cabinet secretaries to serve an appointed term in Congress.

4. *repeal of the Twenty-second Amendment,* thereby abolishing the two-term limit on incumbent presidents (another proposal would create a single six- or eight-year term for president).

5. allowance for the president and Congress to dissolve each other through a *no confidence vote* and call a new election; an affirmative vote by both houses would be necessary to approve a resolution of no confidence.

6. creation of a *line-item veto* for the president, whereby the president can approve individual items of an appropriations bill, without approving the entire bill.

7. creation of a *legislative veto* for Congress, whereby that branch may disapprove specific actions of executive agencies and the White House; either one- or two-house resolutions would be necessary to disallow the executive action.

Although proponents of these constitutional amendments argue that the proposals would reduce the chance of policy deadlock between Congress and the White House, several critics of the reforms insist that they would also undermine the framers' success at controlling the irresponsible use of political power. Major objections to the coordinated-terms-of-office plan are that it would unwisely shift the major focus of legislators from their local constituencies to the party leader in the White House, and that it might allow the national government to be dominated by one party. The team-ticket idea is criticized for reducing voter discretion to vote for the *person* rather than the party and for being biased against minor-party candidates. Allowing dual officeholding is criticized for being biased in favor of the president who would most likely dominate any such arrangement. The no-limit presidency plan, which would require repealing the Twenty-second Amendment, is seen as returning to the days of Franklin Roosevelt when one person dominated national politics like few others in American history. Arguments for preserving the two-term limit are that lame-duck presidents can lobby for particular programs without having to weigh the political consequences for reelection. Furthermore, critics of this idea argue that available evidence does not support the charge that lame ducks are hopelessly ineffective.

The dissolution-of-government proposal might encourage more instability in government, similar to some parliamentary systems of Europe, although defenders of the idea find great stability in such systems as Great Britain, West Germany, and France. Critics charge that the two veto proposals—a president's ability to veto specific items in appropriations bills and Congress's capacity to negate executive rules by simple majority vote—would give the respective institutions too much unilateral power to defeat legitimate actions taken by the other branch.

"Change the Electoral Linkage System"

Another group of critics of the current system of American government argue that necessary changes can be made without resorting to formal constitutional amendment.[4] A major focus of those calling for certain structural changes is the electoral process itself, which includes voters, political parties, interest groups, and politicians. Their argument is that representative government demands popular elections that are competitive, open, and accessible to all eligible voters and candidates, conducive to popular participation, and likely to produce an effective program that resolves the public's problems. One indictment of recent federal elections, particularly congressional elections, is that they are noncompetitive, inaccessible to all but a few affluent candidates, unlikely to encourage any more than 30–40 percent of the eligible electorate in nonpresidential election years, and unlikely to produce a workable program that both wins a broad popular consensus and effectively deals with the cause of many problems. Declining voter turnouts, endless presidential campaigns that drain the candidates and bore the voters, increasing campaign costs, superficial coverage by television (which is now the primary source of political news of most Americans), a disintegrated political party system that fails to link properly the voters with candidates, and a proliferating interest-group system that frequently misrepresents popular preferences all contribute to apathy and distortion in the American electoral process.

Several recommendations have been advanced by those finding flaws in the present electoral system. Reforms requiring changes in party or congressional rules, or new federal laws include:

1. establishing a *bicameral nominating convention* for presidential nominations, consisting of a *popular* chamber composed of delegates chosen by primaries and party caucuses, and a *congressional* chamber, consisting of selected members of Congress and candidates for a congressional post.

2. holding *presidential elections several weeks before congressional elections,* thus decreasing the likelihood of voters splitting their vote on congressional-presidential elections.

3. creating a *shadow cabinet* within Congress that duplicates the president's appointed cabinet and encourages members of Congress to provide a more visible and focused party leadership outside the White House.

4. encouraging state political parties to have a *straight-ticket voting* lever for all federal candidates.

5. creating a *congressional campaign broadcast fund* supported by public financing and intended to provide the political party more control of campaign strategy and finance.

6. establishing federal *campaign-financing limits* on the total amount of money that candidates can receive from political action committees.

These proposals for structural changes in the electoral system are aimed at strengthening the political party system in the United States, particularly at the national level. By doing so, the parties would be better able to select qualified candidates for more competitive contests and thereby give voters the opportunity for more informed participation.

But the recommendations are not without their critics. A reformed national nominating convention that gives a larger role to party activists is often seen as a threat to input from the democratic masses who now have more say in presidential selection through the direct primary system. Holding congressional elections after the presidential race strikes some as actually encouraging the voters to vote for the other party as a check on the new president's power, thus perpetuating divided government. It might also result in the same sort of apathy and voter dropout that now distinguishes off-year elections. Critics claim that voters will stay home just the same as before, whether the congressional elections are two weeks or two years after a presidential election. The party-slate recommendation is also criticized as potentially discouraging local candidates from running for office in an election dominated by national candidates. This might have a very negative effect upon participation in local contests and local participatory democracy. The suggestions for reforming campaign financing to favor limits on amounts and strengthening party management of funds are criticized for favoring major over minor political parties, encouraging parties to spend money on mediocre candidates rather than jeopardize losing to the opposition party, and, finally, running afoul of freedom of expression guarantees under the First Amendment.

"Change the Leadership!"

Until Ronald Reagan broke the trend in 1984, no American president since Dwight Eisenhower had concluded his presidency under anything resembling "normal" circumstances. As assassination, a discredited war policy in Southeast Asia, the Watergate scandal, and the public's quest for a change in 1976 and 1980 left the impression that no president in recent memory could live up to public expectations. In many respects, the increasing fragmentation and policy disarray in Congress since the 1960s found an American public searching for an effective leader in the White House, but the incumbents always seemed to come up short.

However, a feverish search for the "right stuff" in the Oval Office or major tampering with the institutional presidency must be careful to avoid inflicting serious damage to the office and its ability to function responsibly. A recent article by political scientist Bert Rockman cautions against reforming the presidency in the post-Iran-contra atmosphere and argues that "yesterday's reform often is today's problem."[5] Rockman maintains that good leadership is a scarce commodity in both private and public life, so citizens must refrain from changing the presidential selection process merely to attract qualified leaders. Some observers say that a decline in ethical standards has equally afflicted the corporate and professional realms, just as it has public service. Rockman also says that democratic accountability can take different forms. Errant presidents ultimately get what is coming to them, whether that punishment is meted out by the legal system or by the judgment of history. Recent claims that the American presidency is either too powerful or not powerful enough miss a larger point. As many authors have argued for the past few decades, most notably, Richard Neustadt, presidential power is ultimately determined by environmental conditions, political coalition-building, and the personal skills of the incumbent.[6]

Rockman's major suggestion for reform of the presidency is as old as the Constitution itself—finding a healthy balance between the practice of governing and the art of political compromise. To resolve some of the problems of modern-day governance, presidents should pay closer attention to prudent advice from experienced and enlightened advisors who have served previous administrations, rather than engaging in public relations campaigns to put the best face on poor tactics and strategy and playing to public expectations. Herein lies an important lesson to all who seek to address some of the problems uncovered by the probes into the Iran-contra affair. In the rush to prevent future breaks in established procedures, the nation should be careful not to pass a series of laws that constrain future presidents by severely limiting their ability to take decisive action or exercising important leadership in time of crisis.

"Let the Public Change the Status Quo!"

One other indication of public dissatisfaction with some aspects of the contemporary constitutional scene is the abundance of public opinion polls. Such polls have sampled the public mood on a wide range of issues. Care must be taken in interpreting certain poll results. Depending upon sample size, degree of randomness, phrasing of the questions, mood of the respondent, expectations by the respondent of what the pollster is looking for, and several other factors, poll results can be contradictory. But public opinion polling has become such a major part of modern American politics that dismissing it entirely because of a fear of political bias is to deny the existence of an important technique for sensing public moods.

Policies that have attracted supportive majorities of the American public during the past several years are the Equal Rights Amendment, a balanced federal budget, and organized prayer in public school. Constitutional amendments on these three issues would drastically reverse current public policy in the United States. The abortion issue has also generated much heated debate and dissension in American society, although a slim majority of the public seems to support a woman's right to choose whether or not to have an abortion during the first six months of pregnancy.

Some proposals for policy change have been aimed at democratizing the American political process and allowing the masses to participate more directly in the selection of leaders and policies. Proposals along this line include efforts to abolish the electoral college and directly elect the president and to eliminate the proliferating presidential primaries and adopt either a smaller number of regional primaries or one national primary wherein the voters select the presidential nominees of the major political parties. One other proposal that indicates support for more direct voter involvement is to allow national legislation by popular initiative, comparable to the systems that currently exist in several states.

Finally, the American public has shown varying degrees of support for some of the proposals discussed earlier to correct the problem of divided government, such as allowing the president an item-veto over appropriations, altering the terms of office for Congress and the presidency, and letting cabinet members serve simultaneously in Congress. However, the incidence of split-ticket voting at the national and state levels may indicate that a large percentage of American voters are comfortable with the reins of government being controlled by candidates from different parties. Evidently, the American public is not nearly as troubled by divided control of Congress and the White House as are academic and political elites.

Conclusion: Prospects for Constitutional Change

Amending the U.S. Constitution has never been an easy task in this country. As mentioned in Chapter 10, the experience during the 1970s with the Equal Rights Amendment testifies to the difficulty of changing the constitutional status quo through the formal amending process. Since 1791, with the adoption of the Bill of Rights, only sixteen amendments have been added to the original document. And the Constitution has been amended only five times since World War II. Moreover, these amendments (Twenty-two through Twenty-six) deal with noncontroversial changes in the American electoral system: limiting the president to two terms in office; allowing residents of Washington, D.C., to vote in presidential elections; outlawing the poll tax in national elections; regulating presidential succession in times of disability or death; and giving eighteen-year-olds the right to vote. None of these amendments ever engendered any committed opposition to ratification, unlike the case of the Equal Rights Amendment.

The founding generation was very confident about the virtues of the new system of government that they had created in 1787, and they did not want it changed easily. Article V of the Constitution describes the procedure for amending the document. Figure 14.1, which details the formal amending process, indicates that the "normal" procedure for changing the Constitution is for an amendment to be approved by two-thirds of both houses of Congress and then ratified by three-fourths of the state legislatures. Stated another way, an amendment to the Constitution can be blocked by 34 percent of the voting members of one house of Congress. It can also be defeated by either a negative vote or simple inaction in thirteen of the ninety-nine state legislative houses. The United States is virtually unique among nations in requiring such a high degree of national consensus before changing the text of the Constitution through formal amendment. And when compared with the states, which through the mid-1980s had adopted over five thousand amendments to their individual constitutions, the U.S. Constitution stands alone as a beacon of stability in

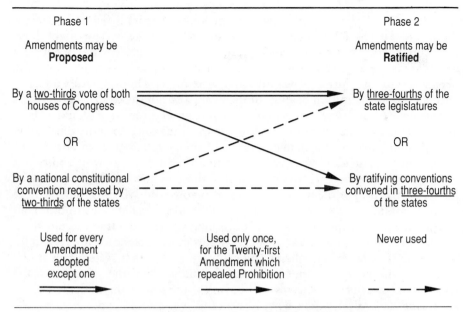

Figure 14.1
How the U.S. Constitution can be Amended

Source: From Robert L., Lineberry, *Government in America: People, Politics and Policy*, Third Edition, p. 95, ©1986 by Robert L. Lineberry. Reprinted by permission of Scott, Foresman and Company.

the formal text! Of course, it should be mentioned that some states trivialize the amending process by using it primarily as a common legislative device to change substantive policy, rather than to define the broad outlines of governmental structure.

As much of this concluding chapter indicates, deciding precisely what route to follow for changing the American constitutional system ultimately depends upon whether the American people see major problems detracting from the performance and effectiveness of the current system. If they are convinced that elements of the basic structure are in serious disarray, as some reformers have argued, then change might be effected through formal constitutional amendment. But major change through the amending process would be difficult to realize, primarily because of the innate difficulty of that process. Furthermore, those arguing for major structural reform face a difficult task, since major institutional change is not something for which popular enthusiasm can be easily aroused. Only five of the twenty-six amendments to the Constitution deal with structural change (the Eleventh—dealing with states not being sued in federal courts; the Twelfth—providing for a separate ballot for president and vice-president; the Twentieth—changing the dates for presidential inauguration and convening Congress; the Twenty-second—limiting presidents to two terms; and the Twenty-fifth—dealing with presidential disability and succession).

But if the people are persuaded that change *outside* the formal amending process is both necessary and adequate, such as rescheduling elections, reforming political campaign financing, and altering nominating convention procedures, then change can be made through congressional or party rule changes or through federal laws. The suggestions cited earlier concerning amendments to balance the budget or reinstitute organized school prayer may suffer from the same parochialism that ultimately plagued Prohibition and therefore might be unwise to pursue.

Continued pleas that the nation suffers merely from deficient leadership do not adequately address many shortcomings that have been written about for many years. To assume that the system devised in 1787 will work if only the right people are chosen to administer it misses a major point of the ongoing debate about the current constitutional system. As Thomas Jefferson once wrote, "The Constitution belongs to the living and not the dead." The framers never intended to devise a system in the eighteenth century that would answer all problems for time immemorial. It is a living, breathing document that must be accommodated to the changing needs of the people with each new generation. They devised an imperfect system that depends for its workability not only upon the competence and good will of those in power, but also upon the ability of the people themselves to remain involved in self-government. Benjamin Franklin's legendary response to a bystander outside Constitution Hall in Philadelphia in September 1787, concerning whether the framers had given the people a monarchy or a republic, contains much insight for today. Franklin's response was "a republic, if you can keep it." [7] If that system fails in the future, it will most likely not be exclusively the fault of the structure or the leaders, but because the masses will have lost interest in the difficult task of governing *themselves* wisely. That is what this two-century experiment in self-government has been all about. And the American public must remember that it is an experiment that is still evolving as it enters its third century.

Questions

1. Foreign observers are frequently struck by the lack of cooperation between the president and Congress over major matters of policy, both foreign and domestic. What aspects of structural reform in the congressional-presidential relationship do you think would be the best to adopt? Which ones do you think have the most potential for being accepted? Do you think that governmental performance will have to deteriorate much more before the American people recognize the need for major structural change?

2. What do you think are the chances of a second constitutional convention being convened within the next few years? What issues would most likely precipitate such a convention? Should Congress pass legislation that places strict limitations upon precisely what such a gathering could consider? Would that sort of limitation be constitutional?

3. The procedures outlined in Article V detailing the amending process require a "super majority" for amending the Constitution—two-thirds in Congress and three-fourths of the states. Do you think that this required majority has been a strength or liability in the American system? Has it saved the system from countless amendments that would have debilitated the political system and led to a trivialized system for addressing public concerns and needs? Or, conversely, has the difficulty of achieving this super majority led to the deadlock of democracy discussed in some of the professional literature?

Endnotes

1. Committee on Political Parties, American Political Science Association, *Toward a More Responsible Two-Party System* (New York: Rinehart, 1950).

2. This particular term was coined by James MacGregor Burns, *The Deadlock of Democracy* (Englewood Cliffs, N.J.: Prentice-Hall, 1963).

3. Committee on the Constitutional System, *Reforming American Government*, Donald L. Robinson, ed. (Boulder, Colo.: Westview Press, 1985).

5. Bert A. Rockman, "Reforming the Presidency: Nonproblems and Problems," *PS* 20 (Summer 1987): 643–9.

6. Richard E. Neustadt, *Presidential Power* (New York: Wiley, 1960).

7. Cited in Earl Warren, *A Republic, If You Can Keep It* (New York: Quadrangle Books, 1972).

4. Compare David S. Broder, *The Party's Over* (New York: Harper & Row, 1971); Gerald S. Pomper, ed., *Party Renewal in America* (New York: Praeger, 1980); and David E. Prince, *Bringing Back the Parties* (Washington, D.C.: Congressional Quarterly, Inc., 1984).

Suggested Readings

Burns, James MacGregor. *The Power to Lead: The Crisis of the American Presidency.* New York: Simon & Schuster, 1984.

Castro, David. "A Constitutional Convention: Scouting Article Five's Undiscovered Country." *University of Pennsylvania Law Review* 134 (April 1986).

Committee on the Constitutional System. *Reforming American Government.* Ed. Donald L. Robinson. Boulder, Colo.: Westview Press, 1985.

Peltason, J. W. *Corwin and Peltason's Understanding the Constitution.* 11th ed. New York: Holt, Rinehart & Winston, 1988.

Sundquist, James L. *Constitutional Reform and Effective Government.* Washington, D.C.: Brookings Institution, 1986.

A

Constitution of the United States of America*

We the People of the United States, in Order to form a more perfect Union, establish Justice, insure domestic Tranquility, provide for the common defence, promote the general Welfare, and secure the Blessings of Liberty to ourselves and our Posterity, do ordain and establish this Constitution for the United States of America.

Article I.

SECTION 1. All legislative Powers herein granted shall be vested in a Congress of the United States, which shall consist of a Senate and House of Representatives.

SECTION 2. The House of Representatives shall be composed of Members chosen every second Year by the People of the several States, and the Electors in each State shall have the Qualifications requisite for Electors of the most numerous Branch of the State Legislature.

No Person shall be a Representative who shall not have attained to the Age of twenty five Years, and been seven Years a Citizen of the United States, and who shall not, when elected, be an Inhabitant of that State in which he shall be chosen.

Representatives and direct [Taxes][1] shall be apportioned among the several States which may be included within this Union, according to their respective Numbers [which shall be determined by adding to the whole Number of free Persons, including those bound to Service for a Term of Years, and excluding Indians not taxed, three fifths of all other Persons].[2] The actual Enumeration shall be made within three Years after the first Meeting of the Congress of the United States, and within every subsequent Term of ten Years, in such Manner as they shall by Law direct. The Number of Representatives shall not exceed one for every thirty Thousand, but each State shall have at Least one Repre-

---

*The spelling, capitalization, and punctuation of the original have been retained here. Brackets indicate passages that have been altered by amendments to the Constitution.
[1]Modified by the Sixteenth Amendment.
[2]Modified by the Fourteenth Amendment.

sentative; and until such enumeration shall be made, the State of New Hampshire shall be entitled to chuse three, Massachusetts eight, Rhode Island and Providence Plantations one, Connecticut five, New York six, New Jersey four, Pennsylvania eight, Delaware one, Maryland six, Virginia ten, North Carolina five, South Carolina five, and Georgia three.

When vacancies happen in the Representation from any State, the Executive Authority thereof shall issue Writs of Election to fill such Vacancies.

The House of Representatives shall chuse their Speaker and other Officers; and shall have the sole Power of Impeachment.

SECTION 3.   The Senate of the United States shall be composed of two Senators from each State [chosen by the Legislature thereof],[3] for six Years; and each Senator shall have one Vote.

Immediately after they shall be assembled in Consequence of the first Election, they shall be divided as equally as may be into three Classes. The Seats of the Senators of the first Class shall be vacated at the Expiration of the second Year, of the second Class at the Expiration of the fourth Year, and of the third Class at the Expiration of the sixth Year, so that one third may be chosen every second Year [and if Vacancies happen by Resignation, or otherwise, during the Recess of the Legislature of any State, the Executive thereof may make temporary Appointments until the next Meeting of the Legislature, which shall then fill such Vacancies].[4]

No Person shall be a Senator who shall not have attained to the Age of thirty Years, and been nine Years a Citizen of the United States, and who shall not, when elected, be an Inhabitant of that State for which he shall be chosen.

The Vice President of the United States shall be President of the Senate, but shall have no Vote, unless they be equally divided.

The Senate shall chuse their other Officers, and also a President pro tempore, in the Absence of the Vice President, or when he shall exercise the Office of President of the United States.

The Senate shall have the sole Power to try all Impeachments. When sitting for that Purpose, they shall be on Oath or Affirmation. When the President of the United States is tried, the Chief Justice shall preside: And no Person shall be convicted without the Concurrence of two thirds of the Members present.

Judgment in Cases of Impeachment shall not extend further than to removal from Office, and disqualification to hold and enjoy any Office of honor, Trust, or Profit under the United States: but the Party convicted shall nevertheless be liable and subject to Indictment, Trial, Judgment, and Punishment, according to Law.

SECTION 4.   The Times, Places and Manner of holding Elections for Senators and Representatives, shall be prescribed in each State by the Legislature thereof; but the Congress may at any time by Law make or alter such Regulations, except as to the Places of chusing Senators.

[The Congress shall assemble at least once in every Year, and such Meeting shall be on the first Monday in December, unless they shall by Law appoint a different Day.][5]

---

[3]Repealed by the Seventeenth Amendment.
[4]Modified by the Seventeenth Amendment.
[5]Changed by the Twentieth Amendment.

SECTION 5.   Each House shall be the Judge of the Elections, Returns, and Qualifications of its own Members, and a Majority of each shall constitute a Quorum to do Business; but a smaller Number may adjourn from day to day, and may be authorized to compel the Attendance of absent Members, in such Manner, and under such Penalties as each House may provide.

Each House may determine the Rules of its Proceedings, punish its Members for disorderly Behaviour, and, with the Concurrence of two thirds, expel a Member.

Each House shall keep a Journal of its Proceedings, and from time to time publish the same, excepting such Parts as may in their Judgment require Secrecy; and the Yeas and Nays of the Members of either House on any question shall, at the Desire of one fifth of those Present, be entered on the Journal.

Neither House, during the Session of Congress, shall, without the Consent of the other, adjourn for more than three days, nor to any other Place than that in which the two Houses shall be sitting.

SECTION 6.   The Senators and Representatives shall receive a Compensation for their Services, to be ascertained by Law, and paid out of the Treasury of the United States. They shall in all Cases, except Treason, Felony and Breach of the Peace, be privileged from Arrest during their Attendance at the Session of their respective Houses, and in going to and returning from the same; and for any Speech or Debate in either House, they shall not be questioned in any other Place.

No Senator or Representative shall, during the Time for which he was elected, be appointed to any civil Office under the Authority of the United States, which shall have been created, or the Emoluments whereof shall have been encreased during such time; and no Person holding any Office under the United States, shall be a Member of either House during his Continuance in Office.

SECTION 7.   All Bills for raising Revenue shall originate in the House of Representatives; but the Senate may propose or concur with Amendments as on other Bills.

Every Bill which shall have passed the House of Representatives and the Senate, shall, before it become a Law, be presented to the President of the United States; If he approve he shall sign it, but if not he shall return it, with his Objections to the House in which it shall have originated, who shall enter the Objections at large on their Journal, and proceed to reconsider it. If after such Reconsideration two thirds of that House shall agree to pass the Bill, it shall be sent together with the Objections, to the other House, by which it shall likewise be reconsidered, and if approved by two thirds of that House, it shall become a Law. But in all such Cases the Votes of both Houses shall be determined by Yeas and Nays, and the Names of the Persons voting for and against the Bill shall be entered on the Journal of each House respectively. If any Bill shall not be returned by the President within ten Days (Sundays excepted) after it shall have been presented to him, the Same shall be a Law, in like Manner as if he had signed it, unless the Congress by their Adjournment prevent its Return in which Case it shall not be a Law.

Every Order, Resolution, or Vote to which the Concurrence of the Senate and House of Representatives may be necessary (except on a question of Adjournment) shall be presented to the President of the United States; and before the Same shall take Effect, shall be approved by him, or being disapproved by him, shall be repassed by two thirds of the Senate and House of Representatives, according to the Rules and Limitations prescribed in the Case of a Bill.

SECTION 8. The Congress shall have Power To lay and collect Taxes, Duties, Imposts and Excises, to pay the Debts and provide for the common Defence and general Welfare of the United States; but all Duties, Imposts and Excises shall be uniform throughout the United States;

To borrow Money on the credit of the United States;

To regulate Commerce with foreign Nations, and among the several States, and with the Indian Tribes;

To establish a uniform Rule of Naturalization, and uniform Laws on the subject of Bankruptcies throughout the United States;

To coin Money, regulate the Value thereof, and of foreign Coin, and fix the Standard of Weights and Measures;

To provide for the Punishment of counterfeiting the Securities and current Coin of the United States;

To establish Post Offices and post Roads;

To promote the Progress of Science and useful Arts, by securing for limited Times to Authors and Inventors the exclusive Right to their respective Writings and Discoveries;

To constitute Tribunals inferior to the supreme Court;

To define and punish Piracies and Felonies committed on the high Seas, and Offences against the Law of Nations;

To declare War, grant Letters of Marque and Reprisal, and make Rules concerning Captures on Land and Water;

To raise and support Armies, but no Appropriation of Money to that Use shall be for a longer Term than two Years;

To provide and maintain a Navy;

To make Rules for the Government and Regulation of the land and naval Forces;

To provide for calling forth the Militia to execute the Laws of the Union, suppress Insurrections and repel Invasions;

To provide for organizing, arming, and disciplining the Militia, and for governing such Part of them as may be employed in the Service of the United States, reserving to the States respectively, the Appointment of the Officers, and the Authority of training the Militia according to the discipline prescribed by Congress;

To exercise exclusive Legislation in all Cases whatsoever, over such District (not exceeding ten Miles square) as may, by Cession of particular States, and the Acceptance of Congress, become the Seat of the Government of the United States, and to exercise like Authority over all Places purchased by the Consent of the Legislature of the State in which the Same shall be, for the Erection of Forts, Magazines, Arsenals, dock-Yards, and other needful Buildings;—And

To make all Laws which shall be necessary and proper for carrying into Execution the foregoing Powers, and all other Powers vested by this Constitution in the Government of the United States, or in any Department or Officer thereof.

SECTION 9. The Migration or Importation of such Persons as any of the States now existing shall think proper to admit, shall not be prohibited by the

Congress prior to the Year one thousand eight hundred and eight, but a Tax or duty may be imposed on such Importation, not exceeding ten dollars for each Person.

The privilege of the Writ of Habeas Corpus shall not be suspended, unless when in Cases of Rebellion or Invasion the public Safety may require it.

No Bill of Attainder or ex post facto Law shall be passed.

[No Capitation, or other direct, Tax shall be laid, unless in Proportion to the Census or Enumeration herein before directed to be taken.][6]

No Tax or Duty shall be laid on Articles exported from any State.

No Preference shall be given by any Regulation of Commerce or Revenue to the Ports of one State over those of another: nor shall Vessels bound to, or from, one State, be obliged to enter, clear, or pay Duties in another.

No Money shall be drawn from the Treasury, but in Consequence of Appropriations made by Law; and a regular Statement and Account of the Receipts and Expenditures of all public Money shall be published from time to time.

No Title of Nobility shall be granted by the United States: And no Person holding any Office of Profit or Trust under them, shall, without the Consent of the Congress, accept of any present, Emolument, Office, or Title, of any kind whatever, from any King, Prince, or foreign State.

SECTION 10.   No State shall enter into any Treaty, Alliance, or Confederation; grant Letters of Marque and Reprisal; coin Money; emit Bills of Credit; make any Thing but gold and silver Coin a Tender in Payment of Debts; pass any Bill of Attainder, ex post facto Law, or Law impairing the Obligation of Contracts, or grant any Title of Nobility.

No State shall, without the Consent of the Congress, lay any Imposts or Duties on Imports or Exports, except what may be absolutely necessary for executing its inspection Laws; and the net Produce of all Duties and Imposts, laid by any State on Imports or Exports, shall be for the Use of the Treasury of the United States; and all such Laws shall be subject to the Revision and Controul of the Congress.

No State shall, without the Consent of Congress, lay any Duty of Tonnage, keep Troops, or Ships of War in time of Peace, enter into any Agreement or Compact with another State, or with a foreign Power or engage in War, unless actually invaded, or in such imminent Danger as will not admit of delay.

Article II.

SECTION 1.   The executive Power shall be vested in a President of the United States of America. He shall hold his Office during the Term of four Years, and, together with the Vice President, chosen for the same Term, be elected, as follows.

Each State shall appoint, in such Manner as the Legislature thereof may direct, a Number of Electors, equal to the whole Number of Senators and Representatives to which the State may be entitled in the Congress; but no

[6]Modified by the Sixteenth Amendment.

Senator or Representative, or Person holding an Office of Trust or Profit under the United States, shall be appointed an Elector.

[The Electors shall meet in their respective States, and vote by Ballot for two Persons, of whom one at least shall not be an Inhabitant of the same State with themselves. And they shall make a List of all the Persons voted for, and of the Number of Votes for each; which List they shall sign and certify, and transmit sealed to the Seat of the Government of the United States, directed to the President of the Senate. The President of the Senate shall, in the Presence of the Senate and House of Representatives, open all the Certificates, and the Votes shall then be counted. The Person having the greatest Number of Votes shall be the President, if such Number be a Majority of the whole Number of Electors appointed; and if there be more than one who have such Majority, and have an equal Number of Votes, then the House of Representatives shall immediately chuse by Ballot one of them for President; and if no Person have a Majority, then from the five highest on the List the said House shall in like Manner chuse the President. But in chusing the President, the Votes shall be taken by States, the Representation from each State having one Vote; A quorum for this Purpose shall consist of a Member or Members from two thirds of the States, and a Majority of all the States shall be necessary to a Choice. In every Case, after the Choice of the President, the Person having the greater Number of Votes of the Electors shall be the Vice President. But if there should remain two or more who have equal Votes, the Senate shall chuse from them by Ballot the Vice President.][7]

The Congress may determine the Time of chusing the Electors, and the Day on which they shall give their Votes; which Day shall be the same throughout the United States.

No person except a natural born Citizen, or a Citizen of the United States, at the time of the Adoption of this Constitution, shall be eligible to the Office of President; neither shall any Person be eligible to that Office who shall not have attained to the Age of thirty five Years, and been fourteen Years a Resident within the United States.

[In Case of the Removal of the President from Office, or of his Death, Resignation or Inability to discharge the Powers and Duties of the said Office, the same shall devolve on the Vice President, and the Congress may by Law provide for the Case of Removal, Death, Resignation or Inability, both of the President and Vice President, declaring what Officer shall then act as President, and such Officer shall act accordingly, until the Disability be removed, or a President shall be elected.][8]

The President shall, at stated Times, receive for his Services, a Compensation, which shall neither be increased nor diminished during the Period for which he shall have been elected, and he shall not receive within that Period any other Emolument from the United States, or any of them.

Before he enter on the Execution of his Office, he shall take the following Oath or Affirmation: "I do solemnly swear (or affirm) that I will faithfully execute the Office of President of the United States, and will to the best of my Ability, preserve, protect and defend the Constitution of the United States."

---

[7]Changed by the Twelfth Amendment.
[8]Modified by the Twenty-fifth Amendment.

SECTION 2.   The President shall be Commander in Chief of the Army and Navy of the United States, and of the Militia of the several States, when called into the actual Service of the United States; he may require the Opinion, in writing, of the principal Officer in each of the executive Departments, upon any Subject relating to the Duties of their respective Offices, and he shall have Power to grant Reprieves and Pardons for Offences against the United States, except in Cases of Impeachment.

He shall have Power, by and with the Advice and Consent of the Senate, to make Treaties, provided two thirds of the Senators present concur; and he shall nominate, and by and with the Advice and Consent of the Senate, shall appoint Ambassadors, other public Ministers and Consuls, Judges of the supreme Court, and all other Officers of the United States, whose Appointments are not herein otherwise provided for, and which shall be established by Law; but the Congress may by Law vest the Appointment of such inferior Officers, as they think proper, in the President alone, in the Courts of Law, or in the Heads of Departments.

The President shall have Power to fill up all Vacancies that may happen during the Recess of the Senate, by granting Commissions which shall expire at the end of their next Session.

SECTION 3.   He shall from time to time give to the Congress Information of the State of the Union, and recommend to their Consideration such Measures as he shall judge necessary and expedient; he may, on extraordinary Occasions, convene both Houses, or either of them, and in Case of Disagreement between them, with Respect to the Time of Adjournment, he may adjourn them to such Time as he shall think proper; he shall receive Ambassadors and other public Ministers; he shall take Care that the Laws be faithfully executed, and shall Commission all the Officers of the United States.

SECTION 4.   The President, Vice President and all civil Officers of the United States, shall be removed from Office on Impeachment for, and Conviction of, Treason, Bribery, or other high Crimes and Misdemeanors.

Article III.

SECTION 1.   The judicial Power of the United States, shall be vested in one supreme Court, and in such inferior Courts as the Congress may from time to time ordain and establish. The Judges, both of the supreme and inferior Courts, shall hold their Offices during good Behaviour, and shall, at stated Times, receive for their Services a Compensation, which shall not be diminished during their Continuance in Office.

SECTION 2.   The judicial Power shall extend to all Cases, in Law and Equity, arising under this Constitution, the Laws of the United States, and Treaties made, or which shall be made, under their Authority;—to all Cases affecting Ambassadors, other public Ministers and Consuls;—to all Cases of admiralty and maritime Jurisdiction;—to Controversies to which the United States shall be a Party;—to Controversies between two or more States;[—between a State and Citizens of another State;—]⁹ between Citizens of different States;— between Citizens of the same State claiming Lands under Grants of different States, [and between a State, or the Citizens thereof, and foreign States, Citizens or Subjects.]¹⁰

In all Cases affecting Ambassadors, other public Ministers and Consuls, and those in which a State shall be a Party, the supreme Court shall have original Jurisdiction. In all the other Cases before mentioned, the supreme Court shall have appellate Jurisdiction, both as to Law and Fact, with such Exceptions, and under such Regulations as the Congress shall make.

The Trial of all Crimes, except in Cases of Impeachment, shall be by Jury; and such Trial shall be held in the State where the said Crimes shall have been committed; but when not committed within any State, the Trial shall be at such Place or Places as the Congress may by Law have directed.

SECTION 3.   Treason against the United States, shall consist only in levying War against them, or, in adhering to their Enemies, giving them Aid and Comfort. No Person shall be convicted of Treason unless on the Testimony of two Witnesses to the same overt Act, or on Confession in open Court.

The Congress shall have Power to declare the Punishment of Treason, but no Attainder of Treason shall work Corruption of Blood, or Forfeiture except during the Life of the Person attainted.

Article IV.

SECTION 1.   Full Faith and Credit shall be given in each State to the public Acts, Records, and judicial Proceedings of every other State. And the Congress may by general Laws prescribe the Manner in which such Acts, Records and Proceedings shall be proved, and the Effect thereof.

SECTION 2.   The Citizens of each State shall be entitled to all Privileges and Immunities of Citizens in the several States.

A Person charged in any State with Treason, Felony, or other Crime, who shall flee from Justice, and be found in another State, shall on Demand of the executive Authority of the State from which he fled, be delivered up, to be removed to the State having Jurisdiction of the Crime.

[No Person held to Service or Labour in one State, under the Laws thereof, escaping into another, shall, in Consequence of any Law or Regulation therein, be discharged from such Service or Labour, but shall be delivered up on Claim of the Party to whom such Service or Labour may be due.]¹¹

SECTION 3.   New States may be admitted by the Congress into this Union; but no new State shall be formed or erected within the Jurisdiction of any other State; nor any State be formed by the Junction of two or more States, or Parts of States, without the Consent of the Legislatures of the States concerned as well as of the Congress.

---

⁹Modified by the Eleventh Amendment.
¹⁰Modified by the Eleventh Amendment.
¹¹Repealed by the Thirteenth Amendment.

The Congress shall have Power to dispose of and make all needful Rules and Regulations respecting the Territory or other Property belonging to the United States; and nothing in this Constitution shall be so construed as to Prejudice any Claims of the United States, or of any particular State.

SECTION 4.   The United States shall guarantee to every State in this Union a Republican Form of Government, and shall protect each of them against Invasion; and on Application of the Legislature, or of the Executive (when the Legislature cannot be convened) against domestic Violence.

Article V.

The Congress, whenever two thirds of both Houses shall deem it necessary, shall propose Amendments to this Constitution, or on the Application of the Legislatures of two thirds of the several States, shall call a Convention for proposing Amendments, which, in either Case, shall be valid to all Intents and Purposes, as part of this Constitution, when ratified by the Legislatures of three fourths of the several States, or by Conventions in three fourths thereof, as the one or the other Mode of Ratification may be proposed by the Congress; Provided that no Amendment which may be made prior to the Year One thousand eight hundred and eight shall in any Manner affect the first and fourth Clauses in the Ninth Section of the first Article; and that no State, without its Consent, shall be deprived of its equal Suffrage in the Senate.

Article VI.

All Debts contracted and Engagements entered into, before the Adoption of this Constitution shall be as valid against the United States under this Constitution, as under the Confederation.

This Constitution, and the Laws of the United States which shall be made in Pursuance thereof; and all Treaties made, or which shall be made, under the Authority of the United States, shall be the supreme Law of the Land; and the Judges in every State shall be bound thereby, any Thing in the Constitution or Laws of any State to the Contrary notwithstanding.

The Senators and Representatives before mentioned, and the Members of the several State Legislatures, and all executive and judicial Officers, both of the United States and of the several States, shall be bound by Oath or Affirmation, to support this Constitution; but no religious Test shall ever be required as a Qualification to any Office or public Trust under the United States.

Article VII.

The Ratification of the Conventions of nine States shall, be sufficient for the Establishment of this Constitution between the States so ratifying the Same.

Done in Convention by the Unanimous Consent of the States present the Seventeenth Day of September in the Year of our Lord one thousand seven hundred and Eighty seven and of the Independence of the United States of America the Twelfth. IN WITNESS whereof we have hereunto subscribed our Names,

Go. WASHINGTON
Presid't. and deputy from Virginia

Attest
WILLIAM JACKSON
Secretary

DELAWARE
Geo. Read
Gunning Bedfordjun
John Dickinson
Richard Basset
Jaco. Broom

MASSACHUSETTS
Nathaniel Gorham
Rufus King

CONNECTICUT
Wm. Saml. Johnson
Roger Sherman

NEW YORK
Alexander Hamilton

NEW JERSEY
Wh. Livingston
David Brearley.
Wm. Paterson.
Jona. Dayton

PENNSYLVANIA
B. Franklin
Thomas Mifflin
Robt. Morris
Geo. Clymer
Thos. FitzSimons
Jared Ingersoll
James Wilson.
Gouv. Morris

NEW HAMPSHIRE
John Langdon
Nicholas Gilman

MARYLAND
James McHenry
Dan of St. Thos. Jenifer
Danl. Carroll.

VIRGINIA
John Blair
James Madison Jr.

NORTH CAROLINA
Wm. Blount
Richd. Dobbs Spaight.
Hu. Williamson

SOUTH CAROLINA
J. Rutledge
Charles Cotesworth
  Pinckney
Charles Pinckney
Pierce Butler.

GEORGIA
William Few
Abr. Baldwin

Articles in addition to, and amendment of the Constitution of the United States of America, proposed by Congress and ratified by the Legislatures of the several states, pursuant to the Fifth Article of the original Constitution.

Amendment I [12]

Congress shall make no law respecting an establishment of religion, or prohibiting the free exercise thereof; or abridging the freedom of speech, or of the press; or the right of the people peaceably to assemble, and to petition the Government for a redress of grievances.

---

[12]The first ten amendments were passed by Congress on September 25, 1789, and were ratified on December 15, 1791.

Amendment II

A well regulated militia, being necessary to the security of a free State, the right of the people to keep and bear arms, shall not be infringed.

Amendment III

No Soldier shall, in time of peace be quartered in any house, without the consent of the owner, nor in time of war, but in a manner to be prescribed by law.

Amendment IV

The right of the people to be secure in their persons, houses, papers, and effects, against unreasonable searches and seizures, shall not be violated, and no warrants shall issue, but upon probable cause, supported by oath or affirmation, and particularly describing the place to be searched, and the persons or things to be seized.

Amendment V

No person shall be held to answer for a capital, or otherwise infamous crime, unless on a presentment or indictment of a Grand Jury, except in cases arising in the land or naval forces, or in the militia, when in actual service in time of war or public danger; nor shall any person be subject for the same offence to be twice put in jeopardy of life or limb; nor shall be compelled in any criminal case to be a witness against himself, nor be deprived of life, liberty, or property, without due process of law; nor shall private property be taken for public use, without just compensation.

Amendment VI

In all criminal prosecutions, the accused shall enjoy the right to a speedy and public trial, by an impartial jury of the State and district wherein the crime shall have been committed, which district shall have been previously ascertained by law, and to be informed of the nature and cause of the accusation; to be confronted with the witnesses against him; to have compulsory process for obtaining witnesses in his favor, and to have the assistance of counsel for his defence.

Amendment VII

In Suits at common law, where the value in controversy shall exceed twenty dollars, the right of trial by jury shall be preserved, and no fact tried by jury, shall be otherwise re-examined in any Court of the United States, than according to the rules of the common law.

Amendment VIII

Excessive bail shall not be required, nor excessive fines imposed, nor cruel and unusual punishments inflicted.

Amendment IX

The enumeration in the Constitution, of certain rights, shall not be construed to deny or disparage others retained by the people.

Amendment X

The powers not delegated to the United States by the Constitution, nor prohibited by it to the States, are reserved to the States respectively, or to the people.

Amendment XI—(Ratified on February 7, 1795)

The Judicial power of the United States shall not be construed to extend to any suit in law or equity, commenced or prosecuted against one of the United States by Citizens of another State, or by Citizens or Subjects of any Foreign State.

Amendment XII—(Ratified on June 15, 1804)

The Electors shall meet in their respective states, and vote by ballot for President and Vice-President, one of whom, at least, shall not be an inhabitant of the same state with themselves; they shall name in their ballots the person voted for as President, and in distinct ballots the person voted for as Vice-President, and they shall make distinct lists of all persons voted for as President, and of all persons voted for as Vice-President, and of the number of votes for each, which lists they shall sign and certify, and transmit sealed to the seat of the government of the United States, directed to the President of the Senate;—The President of the Senate shall, in the presence of the Senate and House of Representatives, open all the certificates and the votes shall then be counted;—The person having the greatest number of votes for President, shall be the President, if such number be a majority of the whole number of Electors appointed; and if no person have such majority, then from the persons having the highest numbers not exceeding three on the list of those voted for as President, the House of Representatives shall choose immediately, by ballot, the President. But in choosing the President, the votes shall be taken by states, the representation from each state having one vote; a quorum for this purpose shall consist of a member or members from two-thirds of the states, and a majority of all states shall be necessary to a choice. [And if the House of Representatives shall not choose a President whenever the right of choice shall devolve upon them, before the fourth day of March next following, then the Vice-President shall act as President, as in the case of the death or other constitutional disability of the President.][13]—The person having the greatest number of votes as Vice-President, shall be the Vice-President, if such number be a majority of the whole number of Electors appointed, and if no person have a majority, then from the two highest numbers on the list, the Senate shall choose the Vice-President; a quorum for the purpose shall consist of two-thirds of the whole number of Senators, and a majority of the whole number shall be necessary to a choice. But no person constitutionally ineligible to the

---

[13]Changed by the Twentieth Amendment.

office of President shall be eligible to that of Vice-President of the United States.

Amendment XIII—(Ratified on December 6, 1865)

SECTION 1. Neither slavery nor involuntary servitude, except as a punishment for crime whereof the party shall have been duly convicted, shall exist within the United States, or any place subject to their jurisdiction.

SECTION 2. Congress shall have power to enforce this article by appropriate legislation.

Amendment XIV—(Ratified on July 9, 1868)

SECTION 1. All persons born or naturalized in the United States, and subject to the jurisdiction thereof, are citizens of the United States and of the State wherein they reside. No State shall make or enforce any law which shall abridge the privileges or immunities of citizens of the United States; nor shall any State deprive any person of life, liberty, or property, without due process of law; nor deny to any person within its jurisdiction the equal protection of the laws.

SECTION 2. Representatives shall be apportioned among the several States according to their respective numbers, counting the whole number of persons in each State, excluding Indians not taxed. But when the right to vote at any election for the choice of electors for President and Vice President of the United States, Representatives in Congress, the Executive and Judicial officers of a State, or the members of the Legislature thereof, is denied to any of the male inhabitants of such State, being [twenty-one][14] years of age, and citizens of the United States, or in any way abridged, except for participation in rebellion, or other crime, the basis of representation therein shall be reduced in the proportion which the number of such male citizens shall bear to the whole number of male citizens twenty-one years of age in such State.

SECTION 3. No person shall be a Senator or Representative in Congress, or elector of President and Vice President, or hold any office, civil or military, under the United States, or under any State, who having previously taken an oath, as a member of Congress, or as an officer of the United States, or as a member of any State legislature, or as an executive or judicial officer of any State, to support the Constitution of the United States, shall have engaged in insurrection or rebellion against the same, or given aid or comfort to the enemies thereof. But Congress may by a vote of two-thirds of each House, remove such disability.

SECTION 4. The validity of the public debt of the United States, authorized by law, including debts incurred for payment of pensions and bounties for services in suppressing insurrection or rebellion, shall not be questioned. But neither the United States nor any State shall assume or pay any debt or obligation incurred in aid of insurrection or rebellion against the United States, or any claim for the loss or emancipation of any slave, but all such debts, obligations and claims shall be held illegal and void.

---

[14]Changed by the Twenty-sixth Amendment.

SECTION 5. The Congress shall have power to enforce, by appropriate legislation, the provisions of this article.

Amendment XV—(Ratified on February 3, 1870)

SECTION 1. The right of citizens of the United States to vote shall not be denied or abridged by the United States or by any State on account of race, color, or previous condition of servitude.

SECTION 2. The Congress shall have power to enforce this article by appropriate legislation.

Amendment XVI—(Ratified on February 3, 1913)

The Congress shall have power to lay and collect taxes on incomes, from whatever source derived, without apportionment among the several States, and without regard to any census or enumeration.

Amendment XVII—(Ratified on April 8, 1913)

The Senate of the United States shall be composed of two Senators from each State, elected by the people thereof, for six years; and each Senator shall have one vote. The electors in each State shall have the qualifications requisite for electors of the most numerous branch of the State legislatures.

When vacancies happen in the representation of any State in the Senate, the executive authority of such State shall issue writs of election to fill such vacancies: *Provided*, That the legislature of any State may empower the executive thereof to make temporary appointments until the people fill the vacancies by election as the legislature may direct.

This amendment shall not be so construed as to affect the election or term of any Senator chosen before it becomes valid as part of the Constitution.

Amendment XVIII—(Ratified on January 16, 1919)

SECTION 1. After one year from the ratification of this article the manufacture, sale, or transportation of intoxicating liquors within, the importation thereof into, or the exportation thereof from the United States and all territory subject to the jurisdiction thereof for beverage purposes is hereby prohibited.

SECTION 2. The Congress and the several States shall have concurrent power to enforce this article by appropriate legislation.

SECTION 3. This article shall be inoperative unless it shall have been ratified as an amendment to the Constitution by the legislatures of the several States, as provided in the Constitution, within seven years from the date of the submission hereof to the States by the Congress.[15]

Amendment XIX—(Ratified on August 18, 1920)

The right of citizens of the United States to vote shall not be denied or abridged by the United States or by any State on account of sex.

Congress shall have power to enforce this article by appropriate legislation.

---

[15]The Eighteenth Amendment was repealed by the Twenty-first Amendment.

Amendment XX—(Ratified on January 23, 1933)

SECTION 1.   The terms of the President and Vice President shall end at noon on the 20th day of January, and the terms of Senators and Representatives at noon on the 3d day of January, of the years in which such terms would have ended if this article had not been ratified; and the terms of their successors shall then begin.

SECTION 2.   The Congress shall assemble at least once in every year, and such meeting shall begin at noon on the 3d day of January, unless they shall by law appoint a different day.

SECTION 3.   If, at the time fixed for the beginning of the term of the President, the President elect shall have died, the Vice President elect shall become President. If a President shall not have been chosen before the time fixed for the beginning of his term, or if the President elect shall have failed to qualify, then the Vice President elect shall act as President until a President shall have qualified; and the Congress may by law provide for the case wherein neither a President elect nor a Vice President elect shall have qualified, declaring who shall then act as President, or the manner in which one who is to act shall be selected, and such person shall act accordingly until a President or Vice President shall have qualified.

SECTION 4.   The Congress may by law provide for the case of the death of any of the persons from whom the House of Representatives may choose a President whenever the rights of choice shall have devolved upon them, and for the case of the death of any of the persons from whom the Senate may choose a Vice President whenever the right of choice shall have devolved upon them.

SECTION 5.   Sections 1 and 2 shall take effect on the 15th day of October following the ratification of this article.

SECTION 6.   This article shall be inoperative unless it shall have been ratified as an amendment to the Constitution by the legislatures of three-fourths of the several States within seven years from the date of its submission.

Amendment XXI—(Ratified on December 5, 1933)

SECTION 1.   The eighteenth article of amendment to the Constitution of the United States is hereby repealed.

SECTION 2.   The transportation or importation into any State, Territory, or possession of the United States for delivery or use therein of intoxicating liquors, in violation of the laws thereof, is hereby prohibited.

SECTION 3.   This article shall be inoperative unless it shall have been ratified as an amendment to the Constitution by conventions in the several States, as provided in the Constitution, within seven years from the date of the submission hereof to the States by the Congress.

Amendment XXII—(Ratified on February 27, 1951)

No person shall be elected to the office of the President more than twice, and no person who has held the office of President, or acted as President, for more than two years of a term to which some other person was elected President shall be elected to the office of President more than once. But this Article shall not apply to any person holding the office of President when this Article was proposed by the Congress, and shall not prevent any person who may be holding the office of President, or acting as President, during the term within which this Article becomes operative from holding the office of President or acting as President during the remainder of such term.

Amendment XXIII—(Ratified on March 29, 1961)

SECTION 1.   The District constituting the seat of Government of the United States shall appoint in such manner as the Congress may direct:

A number of electors of President and Vice President equal to the whole number of Senators and Representatives in Congress to which the District would be entitled if it were a State, but in no event more than the least populous State; they shall be in addition to those appointed by the States, but they shall be considered, for the purposes of the election of President and Vice President, to be electors appointed by a State; and they shall meet in the District and perform such duties as provided by the twelfth article of amendment.

SECTION 2.   The Congress shall have power to enforce this article by appropriate legislation.

Amendment XXIV—(Ratified on January 23, 1964)

SECTION 1.   The right of citizens of the United States to vote in any primary or other election for President or Vice President, for electors for President or Vice President, or for Senator or Representative in Congress, shall not be denied or abridged by the United States, or any State by reason of failure to pay any poll tax or other tax.

SECTION 2.   The Congress shall have power to enforce this article by appropriate legislation.

Amendment XXV—(Ratified on February 10, 1967)

SECTION 1.   In case of the removal of the President from office or of his death or resignation, the Vice President shall become President.

SECTION 2.   Whenever there is a vacancy in the office of the Vice President, the President shall nominate a Vice President who shall take office upon confirmation by a majority vote of both Houses of Congress.

SECTION 3.   Whenever the President transmits to the President pro tempore of the Senate and the Speaker of the House of Representatives his written declaration that he is unable to discharge the powers and duties of his office, and until he transmits to them a written declaration to the contrary, such powers and duties shall be discharged by the Vice President as Acting President.

SECTION 4.   Whenever the Vice President and a majority of either the principal officers of the executive departments or of such other body as Congress may by law provide, transmit to the President pro tempore of the Senate and the Speaker of the House of Representatives their written declaration that the President is unable to discharge the powers and duties of his office, the Vice

President shall immediately assume the powers and duties of the office as Acting President.

Thereafter, when the President transmits to the President pro tempore of the Senate and the Speaker of the House of Representatives his written declaration that no inability exists, he shall resume the powers and duties of his office unless the Vice President and a majority of either the principal officers of the executive department or of such other body as Congress may by law provide, transmit within four days to the President pro tempore of the Senate and the Speaker of the House of Representatives their written declaration that the President is unable to discharge the powers and duties of his office. Thereupon Congress shall decide the issue, assembling within forty-eight hours for that purpose if not in session. If the Congress, within twenty-one days after receipt of the latter written declaration, or, if Congress is not in session, within twenty-one days after Congress is required to assemble, determines by two-thirds vote of both Houses that the President is unable to discharge the powers and duties of his office, the Vice President shall continue to discharge the same as Acting President; otherwise, the President shall resume the powers and duties of his office.

Amendment XXVI [Ratified on July 1, 1971]

SECTION 1. The right of citizens of the United States, who are eighteen years of age or older, to vote shall not be denied or abridged by the United States or by any State on account of age.

SECTION 2. The Congress shall have power to enforce this article by appropriate legislation.

B Chronology of Supreme Court Justices

Name of Justice	Justice's Nominal Party	Appointing President	Presidents' Party	Dates of Service on Supreme Court
THE PRE-MARSHALL ERA (1789–1801)				
Jay, John	**Federalist**	**Washington**	**Federalist**	**1789–1795**
Rutledge, John	Federalist	Washington	Federalist	1789–1791
Cushing, William	Federalist	Washington	Federalist	1789–1810
Wilson, James	Federalist	Washington	Federalist	1789–1798
Blair, John	Federalist	Washington	Federalist	1789–1796
Iredell, James	Federalist	Washington	Federalist	1790–1799
Johnson, Thomas	Federalist	Washington	Federalist	1791–1793
Paterson, William	Federalist	Washington	Federalist	1793–1806
Rutledge, John[1]	**Federalist**	**Washington**	**Federalist**	**1795**
Chase, Samuel	Federalist	Washington	Federalist	1796–1811
Ellsworth, Oliver	**Federalist**	**Washington**	**Federalist**	**1796–1800**
Washington, Bushrod	Federalist	Adams	Federalist	1798–1829
Moore, Alfred	Federalist	Adams	Federalist	1799–1804
THE MARSHALL COURT (1801–1835)				
Marshall, John	**Federalist**	**Adams**	**Federalist**	**1801–1835**
Johnson, William	Dem-Repub	Jefferson	Dem-Repub	1804–1834
Livingston, Henry	Dem-Repub	Jefferson	Dem-Repub	1806–1823
Todd, Thomas	Dem-Repub	Jefferson	Dem-Repub	1807–1826
Duval, Gabriel	Dem-Repub	Madison	Dem-Repub	1811–1835
Story, Joseph	Dem-Repub	Madison	Dem-Repub	1811-1845
Thompson, Smith	Dem-Repub	Monroe	Dem-Repub	1823–1843
Trimble, Robert	Dem-Repub	Adams, John Q.	Dem-Repub	1826–1828
McLean, John	Democrat	Jackson	Democrat	1829–1861
Baldwin, Henry	Democrat	Jackson	Democrat	1830–1844
THE TANEY COURT ERA (1835–1864)				
Wayne, James M.	Democrat	Jackson	Democrat	1835–1867
Taney, Roger B.	**Democrat**	**Jackson**	**Democrat**	**1836–1864**
Barbour, Philip P.	Democrat	Jackson	Democrat	1836–1841
Catron, John	Democrat	Jackson	Democrat	1837–1865
McKinley, John	Democrat	Van Buren	Democrat	1837–1852
Daniel, Peter V.	Democrat	Van Buren	Democrat	1841–1860

Name of Justice	Justice's Nominal Party	Appointing President	President's Party	Dates of Service on Supreme Court
Nelson, Samuel	Democrat	Tyler	Whig	1845–1872
Woodbury, Levi	Democrat	Polk	Democrat	1846–1851
Grier, Robert C.	Democrat	Polk	Democrat	1846–1870
Curtis, Benjamin R.	Whig	Fillmore	Whig	1851–1857
Campbell, John A.	Democrat	Pierce	Democrat	1853–1861
Clifford, Nathan	Democrat	Buchanan	Democrat	1858–1881
Swayne, Noah H.	Republican	Lincoln	Republican	1862–1881
Miller, Samuel F.	Republican	Lincoln	Republican	1862–1890
Davis, David	Republican	Lincoln	Republican	1862–1877
Field, Stephen J.	Democrat	Lincoln	Republican	1863–1897

THE REVIVAL OF JUDICIAL POWER (1864–1890)

Name of Justice	Justice's Nominal Party	Appointing President	President's Party	Dates of Service on Supreme Court
Chase, Salmon P.	**Republican**	**Lincoln**	**Republican**	**1864–1873**
Strong, William	Republican	Grant	Republican	1870–1880
Bradley, Joseph P.	Republican	Grant	Republican	1870–1892
Hunt, Ward	Republican	Grant	Republican	1872–1882
Waite, Morrison	**Republican**	**Grant**	**Republican**	**1874–1888**
Harlan, John M. I	Republican	Hayes	Republican	1877–1911
Woods, William B.	Republican	Hayes	Republican	1880–1887
Matthews, Stanley	Republican	Garfield	Republican	1881–1889
Gray, Horace	Republican	Arthur	Republican	1881–1902
Blatchford, Samuel	Republican	Arthur	Republican	1882–1893
Lamar, Lucius Q. C.	Democrat	Cleveland	Democrat	1888–1893
Fuller, Melville	**Democrat**	**Cleveland**	**Democrat**	**1888–1910**
Brewer, David J.	Republican	Harrison	Republican	1889–1910

THE ERA OF JUDICIAL SUPREMACY (1890–1937)

Name of Justice	Justice's Nominal Party	Appointing President	President's Party	Dates of Service on Supreme Court
Brown, Henry B.	Republican	Harrison	Republican	1890–1906
Shiras, George, Jr.	Republican	Harrison	Republican	1892–1903
Jackson, Howell E.	Democrat	Harrison	Republican	1893–1895
White, Edward D.	Democrat	Cleveland	Democrat	1894–1910
Peckham, Rufus W.	Democrat	Cleveland	Democrat	1896–1909
McKenna, Joseph	Republican	McKinley	Republican	1898–1925
Holmes, Oliver W., Jr.	Republican	Roosevelt	Republican	1902–1932
Day, William R.	Republican	Roosevelt	Republican	1903–1922
Moody, William H.	Republican	Roosevelt	Republican	1906–1910
Lurton, Horace	Democrat	Taft	Republican	1909–1914
Hughes, Charles E.	Republican	Taft	Republican	1910–1916
White, Edward D.[2]	**Democrat**	**Taft**	**Republican**	**1910–1921**
Van Devanter, Willis	Republican	Taft	Republican	1911–1937
Lamar, Joseph R.	Democrat	Taft	Republican	1911–1916
Pitney, Mahlon	Republican	Taft	Republican	1912–1922
McReynolds, Jas. C.	Democrat	Wilson	Democrat	1914–1941
Brandeis, Louis D.	Republican	Wilson	Democrat	1916–1939
Clarke, John H.	Democrat	Wilson	Democrat	1916–1922
Taft, Wm. Howard	**Republican**	**Harding**	**Republican**	**1921–1930**
Sutherland, George	Republican	Harding	Republican	1922–1938
Butler, Pierce	Democrat	Harding	Republican	1922–1939
Sanford, Edward T.	Republican	Harding	Republican	1923–1930

Name of Justice	Justice's Nominal Party	Appointing President	President's Party	Dates of Service on Supreme Court
Stone, Harlan F.	Republican	Coolidge	Republican	1925–1941
Hughes, Charles E.	**Republican**	**Hoover**	**Republican**	**1930–1941**
Roberts, Owen J.	Republican	Hoover	Republican	1930–1945
Cardozo, Benjamin	Democrat	Hoover	Republican	1932–1938

THE NEW DEAL COURT (1937–1953)

Name of Justice	Justice's Nominal Party	Appointing President	President's Party	Dates of Service on Supreme Court
Black, Hugo L.	Democrat	Roosevelt	Democrat	1937–1971
Reed, Stanley F.	Democrat	Roosevelt	Democrat	1938–1957
Frankfurter, Felix	Independent	Roosevelt	Democrat	1939–1962
Douglas, William O.	Democrat	Roosevelt	Democrat	1939–1975
Murphy, Frank	Democrat	Roosevelt	Democrat	1940–1949
Byrnes, James F.	Democrat	Roosevelt	Democrat	1941–1942
Stone, Harlan F.[2]	**Republican**	**Roosevelt**	**Democrat**	**1941–1946**
Jackson, Robert H.	Democrat	Roosevelt	Democrat	1941–1954
Rutledge, Wiley B.	Democrat	Roosevelt	Democrat	1943–1949
Burton, Harold H.	Republican	Truman	Democrat	1945–1958
Vinson, Fred M.	**Democrat**	**Truman**	**Democrat**	**1946–1953**
Clark, Tom C.	Democrat	Truman	Democrat	1949–1967
Minton, Sherman	Democrat	Truman	Democrat	1949–1956

THE WARREN COURT (1953–1969)

Name of Justice	Justice's Nominal Party	Appointing President	President's Party	Dates of Service on Supreme Court
Warren, Earl	**Republican**	**Eisenhower**	**Republican**	**1953–1969**
Harlan, John M. II	Republican	Eisenhower	Republican	1955–1971
Brennan, William J.	Democrat	Eisenhower	Democrat	1956–
Whittaker, Charles	Republican	Eisenhower	Republican	1957–1962
Stewart, Potter	Republican	Eisenhower	Republican	1958–1981
White, Byron R.	Democrat	Kennedy	Democrat	1962–
Goldberg, Arthur	Democrat	Kennedy	Democrat	1962–1965
Fortas, Abe	Democrat	Johnson	Democrat	1965–1969
Marshall, Thurgood	Democrat	Johnson	Democrat	1967–

THE BURGER COURT (1969–1986)

Name of Justice	Justice's Nominal Party	Appointing President	President's Party	Dates of Service on Supreme Court
Burger, Warren	**Republican**	**Nixon**	**Republican**	**1969–1986**
Blackmun, Harry A.	Republican	Nixon	Republican	1970–
Powell, Lewis F., Jr.	Democrat	Nixon	Republican	1972–1986
Rehnquist, Wm. H.	Republican	Nixon	Republican	1972–1986
Stevens, John Paul	Republican	Ford	Republican	1975–
O'Connor, Sandra D.	Republican	Reagan	Republican	1981–

THE REHNQUIST COURT (1986–present)

Name of Justice	Justice's Nominal Party	Appointing President	President's Party	Dates of Service on Supreme Court
Rehnquist, Wm. H.[2]	**Republican**	**Reagan**	**Republican**	**1986–**
Scalia, Antonin	Republican	Reagan	Republican	1986–
Kennedy, Anthony M.	Republican	Reagan	Republican	1988–

Notes: Bold type denotes Chief Justice
[1]Unconfirmed recess appointment, rejected by U.S. Senate
[2]Promoted from Associate Justice

Glossary

Absolutist theory of free speech   The view that certain forms of free expression are protected absolutely by the First Amendment from governmental encroachment, normally associated with such persons as Zechariah Chafee, Alexander Meiklejohn, and Justice Hugo Black.

Actual malice   The principle, derived from *New York Times* v. *Sullivan* (1964) wherein a person suing for libel damages must prove that statements either were made with the knowledge that they were false or demonstrated a reckless disregard for their truth or falsity.

Amicus curiae   "Friend of the Court"; an interested third party who presents a brief to the Supreme Court on behalf of one or the other parties in a case.

Appeal, writ of   A writ identifying the type of case brought to the Supreme Court as a matter of right, such as those coming from federal courts or highest state courts when state or federal laws are found to conflict with the Constitution or a treaty. Such cases are brought to the Court "on appeal."

Appellate jurisdiction   The power and authority of a higher court to review and, if necessary, to correct errors of law that may have occurred in the trial court. Most cases heard by the U.S. Supreme Court each year are reviewed under its appellate jurisdiction, which can be regulated by Congress according to Article III.

Bad-tendency doctrine   A test devised by the Supreme Court in *Pierce* v. *United States* (1920) to determine the permissible bounds of free speech; holds that First Amendment freedoms can be limited if there is a possibility that their exercise might lead to some harm or evil to government.

Bill of attainder   The direct infliction of punishment by a legislature upon a person without benefit of a trial or other due process of law guarantees.

Bill of rights   A list of guaranteed individual rights and liberties normally attached to a constitution. The first ten amendments to the U.S. Constitution constitute a bill of rights, protecting freedoms such as speech, press, religion, and jury trial.

Certification, writ of   A method of taking a case from an appellate court to the Supreme Court in which the lower court asks that some questions or interpretation of law be certified or clarified.

Certiorari, **writ of**   Literally, "to make sure"; a writ issued at the discretion of the Supreme Court which orders the lower court to send the record of a case to the Court for review. This route is the normal procedure for appealing a case to the Supreme Court.

Child-benefit rationale   The view that government aid to parochial schools is justified and no violation of the Establishment Clause occurs if the aid is judged to be beneficial to the child and not the religious denomination.

Clear-and-present-danger test   A test devised by Justice Holmes in *Schenck* v. *United States* (1919) to measure the permissible bounds of free speech; individual expression may be restrained only if it is likely to lead to imminent violence or serious, immediate harm to national security.

Collateral estoppel   A concept, first developed in civil litigation, which holds that when an issue of ultimate fact (such as guilt or innocence) has been determined by a valid and final judgment (such as a jury verdict), that issue cannot again be litigated between the same parties in any future lawsuit; see *Ashe* v. *Swenson* (1970).

Comity   A term from international law which refers to friendly and cooperative relations among independent states. This principle underlays the Articles of Confederation and accounted for the relatively calm dealings among the states.

Communitarian approach to government   One of the twin foundations of American constitutionalism; a theory which stresses the public interest and community values over those of the individual. Government is seen as a positive force in achieving the common good.

Concurrent jurisdiction   The type of jurisdiction which might find a case being heard in either a federal or state court, depending upon the nature of laws allegedly violated. Examples might include bank robbery or fraud cases.

Concurrent-sentence doctrine   The judicial doctrine which holds that persons serving concurrent sentences for different offenses should not be entitled to judicial review of one of the convictions, since even if they prevailed, they would still have to serve the sentences for the other charges; see *Benton* v. *Maryland* (1969).

Confederation   A loosely organized grouping of independent states or other units in which sovereignty is retained by the states. The result, as in the Articles of Confederation, is a weak central government.

Constitutional courts   Federal courts established under the authority of Article III, Section 1, of the Constitution; examples include the U.S. Supreme Court, the U.S. Courts of Appeal, and the U.S. District Courts.

Constitutionalism   The principle that government should be limited in its scope and functions, based upon the underlying idea that unlimited governmental power can become corrupt and tyrannical.

Creative federalism   The approach taken by the administration of President Lyndon B. Johnson in structuring national-state relations. In creative federalism, the role of the national government was expanded, and national grants-in-aid programs grew rapidly.

Current (stream) of commerce   A judicial doctrine first stated by Justice Holmes in the *Swift* case which holds that commerce is not a legal concept, but a concept drawn from the course of business. The doctrine played a large role in the expansion of the federal commerce power.

Defamatory falsehood   Statements made about a private citizen which, if untrue and injurious to one's reputation, can be grounds for the awarding of damages; in recent years, states have been given more latitude to award libel damages for defamatory falsehoods. See *Gertz* v. *Welch* (1974).

De jure   "Of right"; lawful. Applied to questions of race, *de jure* segregation refers to separation of the races resulting from some past or present government action; see *Swann* v. *Charlotte-Mecklenburg Board of Education* (1971).

Direct-indirect effects doctrine   The principle, first noted by the Court in the *E. C. Knight* case, holding that only those activities with a direct effect upon commerce can be reached by Congress. In *Knight*, manufacturing was held to be only indirectly related to commerce.

Disparate-impact legislation   Laws which on their face are fair but when applied have a disproportionate impact upon one group (e.g., racial minorities or women); see *Personnel Administrator of Massachusetts* v. *Feeney* (1979).

Diversity cases   Lawsuits involving citizens of different states; the Constitution (Art. III, Sec. 2) confers jurisdiction in such cases on the federal courts, which generally apply relevant state law in resolving the issue. If the controversy involves more than $10,000, federal courts customarily settle the dispute.

Double jeopardy   From the Fifth Amendment, the idea that a person may not be tried by the same jurisdiction twice for the same offense.

Dual federalism (dual sovereignty)   The theory of federalism associated originally with Chief Justice Taney which holds that the national and state governments are sovereign in the respective spheres of authority.

Eminent domain   The government's power to take property for public use by providing just compensation, as noted in the Fifth Amendment.

Equal access   A principle, endorsed by both the Supreme Court and Congress, which says that public schools granting access to nonreligious groups for the purpose of meetings and activities must also provide the same access to religious groups. Equal access cannot be denied on the basis of the content of a group's speech; see *Widmar* v. *Vincent* (1981).

Exclusionary rule   A Supreme Court-created rule in which illegally obtained materials may not be used as evidence to obtain a conviction at trial. The rule has been limited by numerous exceptions.

Exclusive jurisdiction   The type of jurisdiction in which only a particular court can hear a case or controversy that arises. Examples in which the Supreme Court has exclusive jurisdiction are cases involving ambassadors, U.S. consuls, or one of the fifty states.

Executive agreement   An agreement with foreign heads of state concluded by presidents under their power as commander in chief and their general authority in foreign affairs. An executive agreement does not need senatorial approval.

Executive privilege The right of executive officials to refuse to appear before or to withhold information from a legislative committee or a court on the grounds that certain communications between presidents and their advisors are protected from disclosure. Limited executive privilege was recognized in *United States* v. *Nixon* (1974).

Ex post facto laws Retroactive criminal laws that make a particular act committed before the law was passed a crime, or laws that retroactively reduce the proof necessary to convict an individual of a crime that occurred before the act's passage; see *Calder* v. *Bull* (1798).

Expression-action theory of First Amendment rights The concept sometimes associated with Professor Thomas Emerson which maintains that individual expression should not be limited by government and is completely protected by the First Amendment, whereas some actions that threaten national security might be regulated by government.

Extradition In international relations, the returning by one nation to another of a person who has fled from justice. Article IV of the Constitution establishes a general obligation for a state to return a fugitive to another state, although this practice, sometimes called interstate rendition, cannot be compelled.

Federalism The method of organizing government in which a constitution divides powers between different levels of government, usually national and state governments.

Freedom of contract A Supreme Court-created liberty holding that each person has the constitutional right to make his or her own economic arrangements, including wages, hours, and working conditions. Found in the "liberties" of the Due Process Clauses, this freedom owes a strong debt to laissez-faire economic theory.

Gag (protective) orders Governmental restrictions upon what the press may write about a case prior to a trial; see *Nebraska Press Association* v. *Stuart* (1976).

Habeas corpus, writ of An order to an official having custody of a person to produce the prisoner before a court to determine the legality of the prisoner's detention.

Horizontal federalism The relationship among state governments themselves. Article IV addresses state-to-state cooperation in matters of full faith and credit, privileges and immunities, and extradition.

Impeachment power The power derived from Article I of the Constitution, which gives Congress the power to remove, under certain conditions, various federal officials from office. More formally, impeachment is an accusation or indictment by the lower house of a legislative body which commits an accused civil official for trial in the upper house.

Implied powers Powers not specifically delegated to the national government but which can reasonably be inferred. Implied powers stem from the Necessary and Proper Clause and were first given official recognition in *McCulloch* v. *Maryland* (1819).

Impoundment The process whereby the president either defers spending or refuses to spend money appropriated by Congress; see *Train* v. *City of New York* (1975).

Indictment A formal charge by a grand jury which results in the person as being bound over for trial. The Fifth Amendment requires a grand jury indictment for all federal crimes.

Individualist approach to government One of the twin foundations of American constitutionalism; a theory based upon the assumption that individuals and their interests take precedence over the larger community. Government exists to preserve and protect individual rights.

Information An affidavit presented by a prosecutor to a judge in lieu of a grand jury indictment in some instances. An information affidavit cannot be used in the federal judicial process.

Interposition A states' rights concept which holds that states may exercise their sovereignty to block, or interpose themselves between, an unjust national law and their own citizens. Interposition was asserted in the Virginia and Kentucky Resolutions.

Judicial activism The view that judges must, on occasion, overrule the actions of popularly elected representatives if those actions are either "unwise" public policy or contrary to some specific provision of the Constitution.

Judicial nationalism The judicial philosophy associated with Chief Justice John Marshall; articulated in several decisions advancing such principles as popular sovereignty, supremacy of the national government, an authoritative role for the Supreme Court to interpret the Constitution, and the need for flexibility in interpreting that document.

Judicial restraint   The view that judges should defer to officials in the legislative and executive branches, because they are more politically responsible to the voters. This view also maintains that judges should not inject their own views of "good" or "wise" public policy into their decision making, but rather leave that determination to popularly elected representatives of the people.

Judicial review   The power of courts to determine the validity of governmental acts. Although not specifically mentioned in the Constitution, this principle was firmly established in *Marbury* v. *Madison* (1803), and it has given the Supreme Court, in particular, vast power to determine whether legislative or executive acts conform to the Constitution.

Jurisdiction   Literally, "to say the law"; authority vested in a court to hear and decide a case. The jurisdiction of federal courts is determined by the Constitution and Congress.

Legislative courts   Federal courts established under the authority of Article I, Section 8, Clause 9, of the Constitution which gives Congress the power to "constitute Tribunals inferior to the supreme Court." Examples include the U.S. Court of Claims and the U.S. Court of International Trade.

Legislative veto   The rejection of an executive action or that of an administrative agency by either one or two houses of the legislature without the consent of the chief executive. The legislative veto was declared unconstitutional in *Immigration and Naturalization Service* v. *Chadha* (1983).

Lemon test   A concept dealing with controversies involving separation of church and state, wherein governmental policies that allocate public aid to parochial schools must demonstrate three elements; a valid secular purpose; a primary effect that neither advances nor inhibits religion; and no excessive entanglement between government and religion.

Libel   The defamation of character or reputation by the written word. Libelous statements expose persons to hatred, contempt, ridicule, or injury to their character by imputing to them a criminal act, see *New York Times* v. *Sullivan* (1964).

Line-item veto   A power exercise by some state governors to veto portions of a bill and accept others. The president of the United States does not have the line-item veto authority.

Mixed constitution   A form of government dating back to ancient Greek and Roman times, whereby different institutions of government reflective of the different classes of society share governmental power; the form of government present in England at the time of the American Revolution.

Mootness   The situation that arises when an individual brings a case or controversy to a court after the issue presented has already been settled elsewhere, thus making the matter "moot."

Negative freedom   The absence of external restraint (e.g., law) on individual choice; associated with the individualist approach to government.

Neutral principles   The ideal where judges search for impartial and objective principles that transcend the immediate case under consideration and that might be useful for resolving future cases.

New equal protection   The use of the Equal Protection Clause of the Fourteenth Amendment to secure rights for persons other than the racial minorities for whom the clause was originally intended.

Notice   From the Sixth Amendment, the right of persons to be informed of charges and other legal matters for which they may be held accountable.

Nullification   John C. Calhoun's doctrine of extreme state sovereignty which holds that state governments can legally nullify unjust national laws. Tried by South Carolina in the early 1830s, nullification failed as a device for settling constitutional disputes.

Original jurisdiction   The jurisdiction of a court of first instance or a trial court; where the legal action begins. The U.S. Supreme Court has original jurisdiction under Article III of the Constitution, which cannot be regulated by Congress; see *Marbury* v. *Madison* (1803).

Parallel-place doctrine   A test for evaluating the sincerity of a person's religious beliefs with reference to a claim for CO (conscientious objector) status. The Supreme Court held in *United States* v. *Seeger* (1965) that persons without formal or traditional religious training or belief could qualify as conscientious objectors if their beliefs occupy "a place parallel to that filled by the God of those admittedly qualifying for the exemption."

Parliamentary system of government   A form of government in which executive and legislative powers are fused rather than separated. The British parliamentary system has served as a model for many other nations.

Pauper's petition   A request by an indigent or poor defendant that an appellate court review one's conviction; has accounted for much of the increased workload of the Supreme Court in recent years.

Per curiam   "By the Court"; an opinion of the Supreme Court which is authored collectively by the justices.

Police powers   The obligation and authority of a government to protect the health, safety, morals, and welfare of its people. The national government has generally relied upon its commerce and taxation powers to police these matters.

Political questions   Questions considered more appropriate for resolution by elected officials in the legislative or the executive branches. In recent years, federal courts have become more prone to intervene in controversies involving these matters, as the issue of legislative apportionment indicates; see *Baker* v. *Carr* (1962).

Political speech   Expression dealing with public affairs which is generally seen as worthy of a greater level of protection under the First Amendment because it allows citizens to deliberate openly in arriving at approximations of truth.

Positive freedom   Liberty devoted to achieving the public good and to carrying out the community's values; associated with the communitarian approach to government.

Preferred-position doctrine   A position taken by several Supreme Court justices, especially Wiley Rutledge and Frank Murphy in the 1940s, which holds that First Amendment freedoms deserve a "preferred" place among protected rights and liberties. The doctrine has largely remained a minority view on the Court.

Preventive (pretrial) detention   The practice of denying bail to a person in custody before trial on the grounds that the public safety would be endangered by the person's release. The practice was upheld by the Court in *United States* v. *Salerno* (1987).

Prior restraint   The power of the government to restrain or forbid individual expression prior to publication or broadcast; see *Near* v. *Minnesota* (1931).

Procedural due process   The view that due process guarantees are confined to specific procedural protections—such as notice, confrontation of witnesses, and counsel—rather than to substantive rights. In general, procedural due process refers to the idea that persons are entitled to their "day in court."

Procedural justice   A condition which exists when society's rules are fair and apply equally to all persons.

Rationality scrutiny   An approach applied by the Supreme Court to most equal protection challenges of legislative classifications. Justices ask if the distinc-

tion made by law or government is reasonable; the burden of proof falls upon the individual claiming unequal treatment.

Ripeness   The situation which occurs when a case is ready for adjudication and decision by a court. The issues presented must not be hypothetical, and the parties must have exhausted all other routes of appeal and resolution. The federal cases of *United Public Workers* v. *Mitchell* (1947) and *Poe* v. *Ullman* (1961) found the Supreme Court refusing to decide the cases because the issues presented were not "ripe" for judicial resolution.

Rule of law   A system of government in which the highest authority is the law, not one person or a group of persons; no one is above the law.

Rule of reason   The judicial doctrine appearing in the early twentieth century by which certain monopolies and trusts be held "reasonable" and thereby escape dissolution under the Sherman Antitrust Act.

Secession   The ultimate weapon of advocates of states' rights; the power of a state of leave the Union; see *Texas* v. *White* (1869).

Secular-legislation rule   State legislation which may conflict with one's perceived religious obligations, but which may not necessarily violate the Free Exercise Clause as long as it can be demonstrated as serving some legitimate secular purpose and not discriminate against particular religious groups. See *Braunfeld* v. *Brown* (1961).

Selective exclusiveness   The doctrine associated with Chief Justice Taney's opinion in the *Cooley* case holding that, while the congressional commerce power is exclusive, it is only exclusive in those areas in which Congress has selected to exercise it. As a result, states are free to regulate certain matters relating to interstate commerce when not in conflict with congressional authority.

Selective incorporation   The judicial doctrine, first enunciated in *Palko* v. *Connecticut* (1937), which provides for the expansion of certain guarantees in the Bill of Rights to the States via the Due Process Clause of the Fourteenth Amendment. Only those guarantees "implicit in the concept of ordered liberty" have been selected to be incorporated.

Senatorial courtesy   An unwritten agreement that requires the president to confer with certain senators before nominating an individual to fill a vacancy within the federal judiciary. The president seeks the approval of the senators from the prospective nominee's state; the senators must belong to the same political party as the president.

Separate-but-equal doctrine   An approach to the Equal Protection Clause, beginning with *Plessy* v. *Ferguson* (1896), that allowed states to segregate the races in schools and other public facilities as long as the separate facilities were "equal." The doctrine was overruled by the Court in *Brown* v. *Board of Education* (1954).

Separation of powers   The division of governmental powers among legislative, executive, and judicial branches on the premise that each has some unique characteristics and each keeps the others from becoming too powerful; reflected in the first three articles of the Constitution.

Shield laws   Laws passed by several states that protect journalists from having to disclose their news sources in certain instances. The journalist-source relationship has been compared with that of lawyer-client, doctor-patient, and priest-penitent; see *Branzburg* v. *Hayes* (1972).

Simple malice   Defamatory statements about a person which are false but made in "good faith" that they are true; insufficient for public officials or public figures to be awarded libel damages.

Social contract   A theory that bases the authority of a government upon the consent of the governed, who enter into a hypothetical covenant or contract with those who rule.

Sovereignty   The final and ultimate authority of the state to make binding decisions and resolve conflicts. Arguments over whether the national government or state governments sovereign have raged throughout significant portions of American constitutional history.

Standing   A person's right to bring a lawsuit because he or she is directly affected by the issues raised; having the appropriate characteristics to bring or participate in a case.

Stare decisis   Literally, "let the decision stand"; the principle of adherence to settled cases; the doctrine that principles of law established in earlier cases should be accepted as authoritative in subsequent cases that are similar.

Strict construction   The idea that the Constitution should be read narrowly so as to limit the expansion of national powers. Originally embraced by Jeffersonians and Anti-Federalists, this position was contrasted with the so-called "loose construction" of the Federalists.

Strict scrutiny   The approach taken by the Supreme Court in those few equal protection cases where the government uses a suspect classification scheme (e.g., one based upon race or national origin) or interferes with a fundamental right. The government bears the burden of showing a compelling state interest before the Court will allow the program to stand.

Subpoena   An order by a court to present oneself before a grand jury, court, or legislative hearing to present evidence in a case.

Substantive due process   The idea that clearly identifiable, concrete rights can be found among due process guarantees. This view holds that the due process of law goes beyond mere procedural fairness and includes specific rights and liberties. Examples of substantive due process have included freedom of contract and freedom to travel.

Substantive justice   A results-oriented approach which calls for governmental power to adjust inequalities among individuals in society.

Suspect classification   A condition which arises when government or the law distinguishes between persons on the basis of an illegitimate characteristic, such as race, national origin, or religion.

Symbolic speech   The expression of ideas and beliefs through symbols (i.e., armbands, sit-ins, signs) rather than spoken words; generally seen as protected by the First Amendment, although it can be regulated under time, place, and manner guidelines.

Total incorporation   A judicial doctrine, never accepted by a majority of the Supreme Court, which holds that the Due Process Clause of the Fourteenth Amendment incorporated the entire Bill of Rights and applied it to the states. Primary supporters of this view were the first Justice Harlan and Justice Black.

Total incorporation plus   The concept which holds that the Fourteenth Amendment's Due Process Clause contains liberties beyond those in the first eight amendments. Justices Goldberg and Douglas, for example, argued that the Ninth Amendment might contain a "right to privacy" which could be applied to the states.

Unitary system of government   A centralized governmental organization in which all power stems from central authorities. Although local governments usually exist, they do so at the pleasure of national authorities.

Vested rights   Rights which are held to be so fundamental as to be inseparable from the individual and therefore beyond the reach of any government.

Index